Computer Graphics
Software
Construction

PRENTICE HALL
ADVANCES IN COMPUTER SCIENCE SERIES
Editor: Richard P. Brent

Computer Graphics Software Construction

USING THE PASCAL LANGUAGE

John R. Rankin

Department of Computer Science
La Trobe University

with the assistance of
Anita Mackiewicz
for the diagrams

PRENTICE HALL

NEW YORK   LONDON   TORONTO   SYDNEY   TOKYO

Prentice Hall, Inc., *Englewood Cliffs, New Jersey*
Prentice Hall of Australia Pty Ltd, *Sydney*
Prentice Hall Canada, Inc., *Toronto*
Prentice Hall Hispanoamericana, SA, *Mexico*
Prentice Hall of India Private Ltd, *New Delhi*
Prentice Hall International, Inc., *London*
Prentice Hall of Japan, Inc., *Tokyo*
Prentice Hall of Southeast Asia Pty Ltd, *Singapore*
Editora Prentice Hall do Brasil Ltda, *Rio de Janeiro*

Printed and bound in Australia by
Globe Press Pty Ltd, Brunswick, Vic.

3 4 5 92 91 90 89
ISBN 0 7248 0194 9 (paperback)
ISBN 0-13-162793-7 (hardback)

National Library of Australia
Cataloguing-in-Publication Data

Rankin, John R.
  Computer graphics software construction.

  Bibliography.
  Includes index.
  ISBN 0 7248 0194 9.

  1. Computer graphics. 2. Computer graphics—Computer programs.
  3. Computer graphics—Equipment and supplies. I. Title.

006.6

Library of Congress
Cataloguing-in-Publication Data

Rankin, John R., 1950–
  Computer graphics software construction/by John R. Rankin.
    p.   cm.
  Bibliography: p.
  ISBN 0-13-162793-7
  1. Computer graphics. 2. Computer software—Development.
I. Title.
T385.R36 1987
006.6'6—dc19   87-16600
                                                      CIP

 PRENTICE HALL

A division of Simon & Schuster

Contents

Preface

1 Purpose of the book

This book grew out of computer graphics programming courses taught by the author at the Royal Melbourne Institute of Technology. The overall theme of the book is portable (vector) graphics software, and integrated portable graphics software package construction. It is aimed at competent programmers and software designers who wish to develop skills as graphics programmers or graphics systems programmers. The design decisions and alternatives in building graphics software systems are presented along the way.

The purpose of this book is not to explain how to control particular graphics hardware devices although it does explain some cases by way of illustrative examples. More detailed device control information can be found in the appropriate manuals. Likewise the book is not meant to be a survey of all types of available graphics equipment. The book's purpose is not to teach how to use a particular graphics standard (which might not be ubiquitous or the 'final' standard anyway). Nor is it meant as a vehicle for teaching elementary Pascal programming. Although there are simple Pascal programs in this book they are there for greater clarity in expressing algorithms and ideas. The programs and procedures in this book have been all tested and run but they are not meant to be highly efficient 'live' code. Simpler coding usually illustrates the ideas better. Finally, this book is not designed to instruct graphics programmers in the most sophisticated facilities and methods in computer graphics programming. On the contrary, the book shows what graphics software development can be done with the minimum of graphics primitives and device characteristics.

The book is introductory in scope in the sense that it is meant for mathematical programmers who have not had to do graphics programming before. It contains material for a one semester first course in computer graphics suitable for second or third year undergraduate students and also the material for an advanced computer graphics course. The book was not originally intended to go beyond the level of introductory two dimensional static graphics, but advanced topics of three dimensional graphics, computer graphics realism and standards were included to round out the book according to current needs. The required background for students is undergraduate mathematics and geometry coupled with programming skills. Students should be familiar with Pascal and structured modular programming. Ideally they should know the languages C and FORTRAN 77 as well.

The purpose of the book is to educate and train graphics programmers at the applications and systems level. At the systems level it shows how by ideas, methods and considerations of alternative design decisions, to create an easy-to-use graphics application program development environment. At the applications level it presents many interesting, novel and stimulating ideas for graphics applications and shows how programs can be designed for these applications.

A lot of the theory of computer graphics, its problems and types of algorithms can be demonstrated on any graphics output device that draws straight lines. Consequently this book mostly teaches the graphics programming skills associated with monochrome static graphics output. One chapter entitled 'Computer graphics realism' is included to ensure that the student becomes aware of the techniques for programming devices with more impressive graphics output capabilities such as color shading and animation.

The requirements on any graphics device to implement the programs taught in the book are simply:

two integer quantities:

ndh = the number of addressable dots horizontally, and
ndv = the number of addressable dots vertically,

two real quantities:

width = the width of the graphics output display in millimeters, and
height = the height of the graphics output display in millimeters,

two graphics output procedures:

procedure moveto(hp,vp)
    - moves the current graphics drawing position to the
    position (hp ,vp) where hp and vp are the horizontal and vertical
    integer dot position numbers:

    hp = 0 to ndh - 1
    vp = 0 to ndv - 1,

procedure drawto(hp,vp)
    - draws a line from the current graphics drawing
    position to the position specified in the parameters (hp ,vp),

and two other functions:

procedure clear
    - clears the graphics screen (for a VDU) or ejects the plot (for
    hardcopy) or moves the plotter carriage and pen to the home position,

and
procedure getpoint(ch,hp,vp)
- allows the user to move a cross hair cursor or
the plotter pen under keyboard control and return the 'hit code' *ch* and
final position of the current graphics drawing point.

These requirements on the graphics devices are chosen to be so minimal that the
graphics software described in the book should be applicable to virtually all graphics
output devices. These parameters and functions will be described within the book for
several graphics devices and it will be shown how to interface the software described in
the book to these devices. The hardware graphics primitives listed above are the *vector
graphics* primitives. Other equivalent sets and supersets (such as the *raster graphics*
primitives) of hardware primitives for graphics are discussed within the book. The vector
graphics primitives are the most basic and portable set for computer graphics and they can
provide ninety percent of all graphics software package features and most user graphics
requirements.

2 Language choice

Although Pascal is used extensively within the universities and tertiary teaching institutes
it is not a language that has been adopted by industry or government. It does not have
many of the language features required for graphics system programming. In practice
FORTRAN has been used to build graphics packages. Pascal can then be used to call the
routines in the FORTRAN graphics library by declaring them as external procedures. (The
concept of external procedures in Pascal is itself a non-standard extension to Pascal.) The
apparent direction of computer graphics programming is to use the C language which has
nearly all the desirable features for graphics system programming. The predecessor of the
C language is Ratfor which is a preprocessor for FORTRAN. However, throughout this
book algorithms will be described in an 'industry extended' version of the Pascal language.
Examples of programs will be given in Pascal both at the device control level, and at the
level of usage of a graphics package of routines that control the hardware. Where direct
graphics programming is required in real world applications C programs or functions
would probably be written. The implementations of both a two-dimensional and a three-
dimensional graphics package are described through the book. The reader could build such
graphics packages by piecing these procedures defined in various chapters, together. They
may be easily translated into whatever language (such as C) is convenient for the
implementor.

Some of the disadvantages of standard Pascal that are needed in a graphics language in
the author's view are:

• Pascal does not provide dynamic strings;
• Pascal does not allow 'external' files to be opened interactively by name;
• Pascal does not allow for direct access files;

- Pascal does not allow for separate compilation units;
- nesting of procedures is not particularly useful in industrial applications where reusable code is very important;
- Pascal does not allow data sharing between routines as for example in FORTRAN commons. All data must be passed even if intermediate routines in a chain of calls do not need the data. More significantly, it does not allow for data sharing amongst modules in a library with the data information hidden from the user of the library;
- Pascal has no simple direct bit manipulation capability;
- Pascal forces a code arrangement which is the opposite to top down design with the main routine being at the end. It does not allow the procedures to be in alphabetical order say for quick reference purposes;
- Pascal has no I/O or other error trapping capabilities;
- Pascal was originally designed for batch programming only;
- Pascal has no provision for making Operating System calls to provide functions such as deleting or renaming files or testing to see if a file exits on a secondary storage medium;
- Pascal cannot chain to other programs by call or run mechanisms, nor can it load in other programs or procedures during execution;
- Pascal does not allow for initialization of data structures. The data must be explicitly set by coding statements;
- Pascal does not have I/O specifiers such as tabbing in write statements;
- Pascal has no halt function or equivalent;
- the standard Pascal case statement has no otherwise clause;
- Pascal's main routines variables are global to all of its procedures which prevents true information hiding;
- Pascal programs do not accept a number of input arguments on the execution command string;
- Pascal cannot dynamically allocate (contiguous) arrays of arbitrary size;
- in Pascal, a procedure or function parameter cannot be used to pass arrays of different sizes.

While no language has all the ideal software engineering notions and features useful for graphics programming, Pascal has some useful advantages over other older languages such as:

- control structures for structured programming;
- user definable data types;
- allows for recursion;
- allows long names (however these do not carry across compilation units, and in the standard do not allow the underscore character);
- allows records without carriage return and line feeds or other end of line markers being forced into the output;
- does not have fixed format code layout.

Pascal was not designed to be a computer language for business, but rather as a teaching vehicle for the theoretical concepts of computer science. Some of the disadvantages of the original Pascal standard as a language for business in the list above can be lived with but most necessitate extending the language for real world applications. Many of these requirements have been incorporated into various industry extended versions of Pascal. The Pascal code used in this book is a free combination of extended Pascal as found in American National Standard Pascal, LisaPascal, MacPascal, Berkeley Pascal version 3.0 and SVS (Silicon Valley Software) Pascal. Again note that the Pascal procedures given in this book do not represent necessarily the most efficient programming style : they are aimed rather at presenting the algorithms as simply and clearly as possible.

3 Book overview

Chapter 1 introduces the reader to the subject of computer graphics by giving a brief survey of the sort of equipment and applications of computer graphics. Device dependent and device independent coordinate systems are introduced with routines to convert graphics point data between them. The problem of correcting for non-square display shapes is discussed. The next two chapters present details of typical graphics equipment and show how they are programmed at the hardware level. Chapter 4 concerns the first and most obvious use of computer graphics - obtaining data plots. The chapter presents more than just line graphs. It shows how to plot the general mathematical curve, and how to fit various curves to a given set of data points.

Chapters 5 through to 8 are concerned with more advanced graphics software systems, the graphics software packages that allow the user to easily place and manipulate complex two-dimensional graphics objects at desired positions in the output picture. They introduce the concepts of graphics object oriented programming. Chapter 5 starts by explaining what sort of elementary geometrical constructs would be needed for display purposes in computer graphics. Data structures for these individual graphics elements are discussed as well as data structures for collective groupings of graphics elements into individual graphics objects. The important concepts of hierarchical structuring of graphics pictures in terms of graphics objects and graphics objects in terms of graphics elements with the possibility of nesting of graphics objects are discussed. Chapter 6 is about the transformations that are often applied to the graphics object groupings, such as rotations and translations. More advanced two dimensional graphics algorithms are presented in Chapter 7. Chapter 8 discusses typical traditional two-dimensional graphics packages and shows some examples of what can be done with G2D, the two-dimensional graphics package developed through these chapters of the book.

Chapters 9 through to 12 generalize the concepts developed in chapters 5 to 8 from two-dimensional graphics to three-dimensional graphics software packages. The algorithms for three-dimensional geometry are significantly more complex than for two dimensions, and these differences are highlighted. These chapters explain the routines that go to make the three-dimensional graphics package G3D based on G2D. The final part of the book concerns more advanced and realisic computer graphics. Chapter 13 discusses color, animation, fractals, and other special topics.The concepts and examples of sorts of graphics languages are discussed in Chapter 14. This chapter also presents a nice way of creating a rapid user friendly environment for graphics application development. Chapter 15 is an important chapter on the currently used graphics standards. The graphics packages discussed in the book and the so called graphics standards can be viewed as parts of graphics languages as discussed in Chapter 14. The chapter finishes with a discussion on future trends in computer graphics. The Appendixes are a valuable collection of reference material which are needed in various places within the book.

4 Acknowledgements

The author wishes to thank the many people who have generously assisted in the production of this book. The book grew out of courses in computer graphics developed by the author at the Royal Melbourne Institute of Technology, and the author wishes to thank RMIT for allowing him the time and facilities needed to put the book together. In particular, there is Tony Montgommery, the head of the Division of Information Technology of the RMIT, to thank for his encouragement and support of the project and his enthusiasm for building up the departmental graphics laboratory. Anita Mackiewicz contributed her artistic skills and her knowledge of the introduction to computer graphics, and advanced computer graphics courses for the benefit of the book. Other students contributed through their ideas and questions. In particular, the work on the fish-eye lens (problem 10.9) came from Paul Larkin, and Angelina Wong contributed to the section on graphics language comparisons. Finally, I would like to thank Prentice-Hall for staying with this project to see it through.

John R. Rankin

1

Introduction to computer graphics

1.1 What is computer graphics

Computer graphics is a modern visual picture-style input-output technology for computers, involving the creation, manipulation, and display of pictures with the aid of a computer. As such, computer graphics represents the most recent development in improving the efficiency of communications between human beings and computers.

In the past, computer output was confined to the tabulation of results as printed characters: a batch processing job would produce printed output. The long turnaround time from input to output in those days was a significant factor in slowing the process of software development and problem solution. Interactive computing, which has almost universally supplanted these earlier batch processing methods, has been a very important improvement in the computer to human interface (the user interface): it allows us to get results quickly, almost instantaneously, from the computer. With the standard interactive processing method, the user types in commands at a keyboard and immediately receives the computer's response either on a visual display unit (VDU) screen or on a hard-copy printing device. The communication between computer and human in this technology is still however an exchange of alphanumeric text – letters and numbers are typed in by the user and the computer responds by printing other letters and numbers. Another revolution is now underway where computer graphics is regarded as the generalization of alphanumeric data; and the latest technologies use icons (graphic symbols displayed on a VDU) and the mouse to more rapidly and efficiently handle the man–computer communication interface.

We can assimilate far more information from a graphically displayed diagram or the perspective view of a three-dimensional model than we can from scanning a table of numbers or reading a textual message from the computer over the same length of time. Computer graphics output presents much more data in the same amount of screen space and communicates a message far more rapidly than alphanumeric output alone. This is one of the main reasons for the emphasis on computer graphics in modern computer systems – faster communication. A picture is worth a thousand words.

Modern graphics systems use a wide variety of devices and technologies for producing graphics. A graphics picture can be displayed on a cathode ray tube (CRT) for example or plotted on a digital plotter. The display or plot may be monochrome (two shades of the one color, for example, white on black, green on black, bright green on dark green etc.) or color. A color display may use a CRT, similar to a color TV, with three screen phosphors representing the primary colors of red, green, and blue which can be added to form most colors in the spectrum. A color plot, in contrast, is usually restricted to a choice of a small number of pen colors – say red, green, blue, and black. Another graphics output device (used for instance in education with the language LOGO) is the turtle, a computer-controlled robot that moves around on the floor. It can move in any direction and, by supporting a pen vertically, trace its path on a piece of paper lying on the floor.

Interactive computer graphics is now widely available to business for production of visually appealing bar charts, pie charts, and graphs to show trends in company profits, calendarized sales volumes, spending in various areas, and so forth. For fast graphics output, the output device is normally a graphics CRT. The user enters the commands and the data values into the computer and the screen picture responds almost immediately to produce the required sort of chart. Hard-copy graphics output, such as color prints or slides, generally takes longer to produce and therefore is used only for the final copies needed in reports.

While the main intention of computer graphics is for immediate interactive work, some output takes a long time to develop owing to the large amount of data involved (e.g. in weather satellite data, mining stratigraphic data, seismic data, and census mapping data), the large amount of computation involved (such as ray tracing realistic scenes for a movie), or perhaps just due to the particular kind of output device being used. In these cases interactive graphics may not be necessary and batched computer graphics output can be used. Nongraphic hardware, such as the host mainframe, can perform most of this sort of data processing, with the results stored on tape for later transfer to graphics output equipment.

In conjunction with the modern graphics output devices, there are a number of new analog-to-digital input devices, for example, light pens, paddles, joy sticks, touch tablets, the mouse, and the puck. The puck is a device that looks like a doughnut with a handle except that the hole has small cross hairs in it. By moving the puck along the outline of a drawing on a graphics tablet, the drawing appears on the screen of the computer. On the handle are two or more switches which may be used to tell the computer to record a single point or a stream of points.

1.2 Some current uses of computer graphics

Computer-aided design and computer-aided manufacturing, CAD/CAM, is a quickly growing computer graphics application area in the commercial environment. For instance, the circuit design of integrated circuit (IC) chips can be stored as a graphics picture in a file in a computer's secondary storage device. A typical integrated electronic circuit used in a computer is often so complex that it would take an engineer weeks to draw by hand and an equally long time to redraw in the case of a major or minor modification. Using an interactive graphics system the engineer can draw the circuit in a much shorter time. Then the computer can be used to help in checking the design, and quick modifications can easily be made. This is the CAD side of the use of graphics. The graphics designs can then be used to aid manufacture. For example, the computer plots the design; the plot is photographed, reduced (either photographically or by computer), and used as a mask for etching a printed circuit board. This is the CAM side of computer graphics. CAD/CAM is used in many areas of engineering manufacture from nuts and bolts to motor cars.

Low-cost CAD systems are available for the modern personal computer. For example, one system consisting of an Apple microcomputer with single disk drive, black-and-white monitor, and graphics tablet with associated software is available for not much more than a thousand dollars. The system displays a menu of electronics symbols that can be selected by pressing a small penlike attachment against the digitizing graphics tablet and then as the pen is moved along the surface of the tablet the logic gate element selected from the menu floats across the screen following the pen movements. When the pen is gently pressed against the graphics tablet again, the gate symbol is fixed in place on the screen. Other gates and connecting wires are similarly placed until the circuit on the screen looks complete. The circuit design can then be saved in a floppy-disk file for later reference or editing.

Interactive computer graphics is used to train airline pilots. The flight simulator is a mock-up of an aircraft flight deck, containing all the usual controls, surrounded by screens on which are projected panoramic computer-generated views of the simulated terrain during the flight from takeoff to landing. As the pilot maneuvers the 'aircraft', these views and the computer-graphics-generated cockpit dials change to maintain an accurate impression of the airplane's motion. (Sound effects and vibrations are also often included for further realism.) Flight simulators have many advantages over real aircraft for training purposes, such as safety, fuel savings, the capability of storing the flight information then rerunning it to show where mistakes were made by the flight crew, and the ability to familiarize the trainee with a large number of the world's airports and different airplanes. Cheap and compelling graphics flight simulation games (for airplanes and space shuttles) are also available on microcomputers such as the IBM PC, Apple Macintosh, and Commodore Amiga.

Designers at NASA have created computer simulations of the flight of experimental rockets and spacecraft. All aspects of the flight are programmed into the computer – everything a pilot would see out the window appears on the screens. NASA has used computer graphics to perfect the motions of the space shuttle so that it can easily maneuver in space, deploy satellites, use attached telescopes, and manipulate its robot arm. They have also produced a breathtaking animation of a Saturn flyby.

Video games represent the first major use by the general public of interactive computer graphics. The first game of this type was the Ping-pong game which used an ordinary black-and-white TV set for output and two paddles (turning knobs) for input from each player. Two thin white blocks, one on each side of the screen represented the players' ping-pong bats; and a square white block, representing the ping-pong ball, would continually move smoothly across the screen at various angles depending on how the last 'bat' hit it. Video games have become a lot more sophisticated both in color graphics and sound output since then. The first of the more sophisticated games was Space Invaders, closely followed by Pac-Man and Galaxians; and today there are many derivatives based on these popular games. These more sophisticated games were originally only available in arcade centers, but in many cases they have been converted to run on personal home computers. The home-computer versions are very similar to the arcade versions but usually the graphics are somewhat poorer. The fast high-resolution color-graphics effects of the modern arcade games are astonishing to the newcomer. The availability of simplified versions of these arcade games, as programs which will all run on the same home computer, has contributed to the boom in sales of home computers.

Computer graphics is used across virtually all professions. The following examples illustrate:

- Computer graphics is used to help architects design complex building structures on the screen. Using special graphics controls, the designer can maneuver the positions of the structures anywhere in the simulated three-dimensional space displayed on the CRT. Special graphics programs allow the designer to manipulate perspective, angle of view, and scale to show the buildings and gardens as if they were being viewed from a helicopter.
- Interior designers can use computer graphics to select the best arrangement for office furniture in a given floor space.
- Builders can use graphics to show prospective home buyers what their chosen design will look like from various points of view. The buyers may then ask to have changes made in the design.
- Cartographers use computer graphics extensively to put together maps. Government departments use huge and expensive computer equipment for converting aerial photographs of the state or country into computer graphics files that contain fine detail down to every building and fence post plus land contours. The equipment can readily plot out maps of any part of the country to any scale.
- Computer graphics have been used in medicine to show cross sections of the human body. The color graphics pictures are pieced together by the computer from an EMI body scanner which, while taking X-ray pictures, circles a person lying on a table. From the display console the researcher can rotate the image, change its color, and even appear to go inside and look outwards.

Modern science-fiction motion pictures depend heavily on computer graphics for effects. For instance, the Star Wars film had some displays of computer graphics in the scene in which the rebel pilots were briefed on how to attack the 'Death Star', and in a later film Tron there are long sequences of entirely computer-generated film. Longer and more realistic computer graphics film segments can be seen in the film The Last Starfighter. Computer graphics can simulate people in action, visually, and in voice –

people both past and present. Computer graphics is constantly being used in TV studios to generate logos and titles for TV shows. TV advertisements are becoming more dependent on computer-generated images for dramatic effects. In these cases, the graphics output can be recorded on film or sent directly to video recorders.

There are many further applications for computer graphics, in all spheres of life: in education, in industry, in art and advertising, and more. This book does not intend to explore the full scope of the applications of computer graphics, but rather to learn the general concepts of computer graphics programming that lie behind these applications. Additionally this book will show how to construct complete computer graphics packages for two-dimensional and three-dimensional graphics programming through the description of sample packages called G2D and G2/3D. In this way the reader will learn not only about using computer graphics packages in graphics applications, but also how to construct such a package to suit the reader's own area of interest.

1.3 Categories of computer graphics

A computer graphics hardware system consists essentially of special graphics input and output (I/O) devices (some of which were described above) linked to a computer. This can be depicted as shown in Figure 1-1. The set of graphics I/O devices allocated for use by one person at a time is generally called a *graphics workstation*. A multiuser graphics system may well have many graphics workstations so that more than one of several kinds of graphics I/O devices may be simultaneously online to and using the host computer.

As computer graphics often deal with very large amounts of data, the computer represented in Figure 1-1 should be equipped with suitable large-capacity secondary storage devices. Additionally, a high-speed communication link is needed to reduce unacceptable waiting periods. This is normally achieved by local communication over a parallel bus with data speeds of the order of a million bits per second. If the graphics equipment must be remote from the processor, then a serial link may have to be used. Asynchronous serial transmission can be used at speeds up to 19.2 kbps (19.2 thousand bits per second). Even this speed can be too slow for some purposes such as with detailed high-resolution graphics animation where each frame consists of about one megabyte of graphics data. An ideal linkup in this case is a Local Area Network (LAN), such as Ethernet.

The graphics hardware can be categorized by whether the peripherals are digital or analog in nature. Thus a mouse gives analog input signals, whereas the graphics bit pad,

Figure 1-1 A computer graphics system.

the touch tablet, and the light pen give digital input signals. A monochrome CRT and a six-pen recorder give analog graphics output, while a digital plotter gives digital graphics output.

The categories of analog and digital graphics output result in two areas of study in computer graphics called *vector graphics* (or stroke graphics), which draws pictures using short line segments (vectors), and *raster graphics* , which makes graphics pictures by filling in a matrix (or 'raster') of dots or pixels. These two areas are described in Chapters 2 and 3 respectively. Vector graphics is somewhat analogous to making pencil drawings by using only a pencil with a straight ruler. It is the simpler kind of graphics and is fundamental to the more general kind of graphics, raster graphics. Raster graphics generally offers more powerful graphics capabilities than vector graphics, such as colored areas and realistic animation. This book concentrates on graphics software design for two-dimensional vector graphics and three-dimensional vector graphics. The greater functionality of raster graphics will be mainly discussed towards the end of the book from Chapter 13 onwards.

Graphics output can be further categorized as hard copy or soft copy. Examples of hard-copy output are photographs or slides of the screen, digital plotters, and Tektronix hard-copier units. Soft-copy output, as exemplified by VDU screen graphics, can be further categorized into storage and refresh VDU tubes, and these are presented in more detail in Section 2.3 and Sections 2.2 and 3.2 respectively.

1.4 Typical graphics resolutions

Virtually all graphics devices use a rectangular grid of addressable locations for the graphics I/O. This rectangle is called the *graphics I/O rectangle* or the *display rectangle*. Graphics devices are rated according to their *graphics resolution*, the number of horizontal versus vertical positions that the device can distinguish. For some devices there is a difference between addressable resolution and viewable resolution with the latter being the smaller. In these cases the graphics output device stores the graphics picture data in its addressable resolution area, only portions of which can be displayed at any one time.

Resolution can vary enormously among graphics output devices. The list in Table 1-1 shows typical graphics VDU resolutions ranging from low-cost microcomputers, through to professional graphics terminals. The resolutions listed in the table are the viewable resolutions. For most devices in the list the viewable and addressable resolutions are the same; however for the Tektronix 4010 and NEC APC, the addressable resolution is 1024 x 1024.

Four parameters in this table define virtually all that we need to know about the visual impact of the graphics data for any graphics device. They are the *basic graphics characteristics* of any graphics device and are of more importance to us than the make, internal hardware architecture, and so forth. The four parameters are:

1. *ndh* – the number of addressable graphics locations horizontally;
2. *ndv* – the number of addressable graphics locations vertically;
3. *width* – the physical width of the output rectangle in millimeters;
4. *height* – the physical height of the output rectangle in millimeters.

From these four graphics characteristics, many quantities of interest in graphics can be computed. By using these quantities to make quantitative comparisons of graphics devices the user can select, from the range of devices, the one most suitable for a given application. The quantities of interest and their relationship to the basic graphics characteristics are as follows:

Table 1-1 Comparison of some graphics devices.

Name of device	Type	*ndh*	*ndv*	*width* (mm)	*height* (mm)	Nr of colors
Apple 2c	VDU	560	192	150.0	105.0	16
Apple IIe	VDU	280	192	185.5	134.0	8
Apple Lisa	VDU	720	364	221.0	162.5	2
Apple MacIntosh	VDU	512	342	170.0	127.0	2
Amiga	VDU	320	200	259.5	158.5	64
CDC-MPC	VDU	640	200	235.0	175.0	2
Commodore Amiga	VDU	320	200	259.0	158.0	32
DEC Rainbow 100	VDU	800	240	211.0	158.0	2
Digital VT240	VDU	640	480	211.0	158.0	2
Epson FX-100	Printer	816	512	343.0	235.0	2
Ericsson 3111	VDU	640	400	218.0	153.0	2
Hitachi MB1600	VDU	640	400	246.0	183.0	8
HP 150	VDU	512	390	160.0	120.0	2
IBM PC	VDU	640	200	245.0	186.0	2
IBM XT	VDU	320	200	254.4	190.8	4
Intergraph DSP025	VDU	1280	1024	360.0	252.0	8
Megatek 7000	VDU	4096	4096	346.8	346.8	2
NEC APC I	VDU	640	475	191.0	153.0	8
Roland CC-121	VDU	640	240	220.0	155.0	2
Roland DXY-800	Plotter	4200	2970	420.0	297.0	8
Roland MA-121	VDU	640	240	195.0	146.0	2
Roland MA-122	VDU	720	350	195.0	146.0	2
Sord M68	VDU	640	400	219.5	132.0	16
Sun 2-160	VDU	1152	900	337.0	269.0	256
Tandy 2000	VDU	640	400	284.8	213.6	8
Tektronix 4010	VDU	1024	781	188.5	138.5	2
Tektronix 4115B	VDU	1280	1024	346.0	274.0	256
Tektronix 4107	VDU	640	480	241.0	178.0	16
Tektronix 4662	Plotter	4096	2732	381.0	254.0	4

1. *horizontal resolution*:

   horiz_res := ndh / width

2. *horizontal dot size*:

   horiz_dot_size := width / ndh

3. *vertical resolution*:

   vert_res := ndv / height

4. *vertical dot size*:

   vert_dot_size := height / ndv

5. the total number of addressable dots in the output rectangle:

total_nr_dots := ndh * ndv

6. *area resolution* (i.e. the ratio of the total number of dots to the total area of the display rectangle):

area_res := total_nr_dots / (width * height)

The horizontal, vertical, and area resolutions defined above are *physical resolutions* in contrast to the graphics resolution (by which is understood the product $ndh \times ndv$) because they involve the physical measurement of distances: devices can have the same graphics resolution but quite different physical resolutions.

The *graphics aspect ratio* is the ratio of the height to the width of a single addressable dot cell:

aspect_ratio := vert_dot_size / horiz_dot_size

In contrast, the *physical aspect ratio* of the display area (e.g. the VDU screen) is defined as:

physical_aspect_ratio := height / width

(The *character aspect ratio* which is the height of each character cell divided by its width can also be considered, where the cell size includes the interline and intercharacter gaps.)

Ideally, graphics output devices should have 'square dots' (or 'square pixels'), that is, an aspect ratio as close to unity as possible. This would result in rectangles with equal numbers of dots along the horizontal and vertical axes appearing on the output rectangle as squares. For those devices where the aspect ratio is not equal to unity such a square arrangement of dots will not appear as a square but be distorted to a rectangle. This problem is considered in Section 1.6. The program to be written for problem 1.1 will compute these quantities of interest from the four input parameters defining the graphics capability of a graphics output device.

In the general graphics system installation, a variety of graphics input and output devices could be on-line to the host computer as shown in Figure 1-2. The characteristics of each of these devices will need to be known within the software so that the software can easily change the I/O direction to the devices currently selected by the user. For this to occur the following data structures are needed:

```
type
    device = record
        ndh, ndv : integer;
        width, height : real;
        end;
    device_names = (screen,plotter,digitizer);
var {global variables}
    output_device : array[device_names] of device;
    input_device : array[device_names] of device;
    curr_out_dev : device_names;
    curr_inp_dev : device_names;
```

In addition, the data in these global data structures will need to be initialized and the current I/O devices selected. Routines such as 'select output device' and

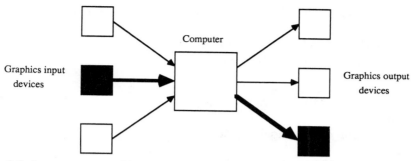

Figure 1-2 A computer graphics system incorporating several graphics workstations.

'select_input_device' shown in Box 1-1 will suffice for this purpose. Although the actual initialization values will vary according to the specific device, in these sample versions the data for two output devices – the screen and a digital plotter – and the data for two input devices – the screen again and a digitizer – are set up. These parameters and the names in the type 'device_names' would of course have to be changed for some other graphics installation. Only one input device and one output device can be selected at a time for the graphics data I/O by means of these two routines. Figure 1-2, illustrates a graphics system with three different graphics input devices and three different graphics output devices on-line. Currently the second input device and the third output device (shown by the highlighted parts of the figure) are selected for input to and output from the computer. There is no communication with the other graphics devices until they are explicitly selected by calls to 'select_input_device' and 'select_output_device' routines.

Box 1-1 Routines to select online I/O graphics devices.

```
procedure select_output_device(dev_name : device_names);
begin
    {Initialize the data for all output devices :}
    with output_device[screen] do
    begin
        ndh := 640; ndv := 400;
        width := 219.5; height := 132.0;
    end;
    with output_device[plotter] do
    begin
        ndh := 4200; ndv := 2970;
        width := 420.0; height := 297.0;
    end;
    {Set the current output device :}
    case dev_name of
        screen,plotter : curr_out_dev := dev_name
    otherwise
        writeln('** Device ',dev_name,' not available for output **')
    end;
end;
```

```
procedure select_input_device(dev_name : device_names);
begin
    {Initialize the data for all input devices :}
    with input_device[screen] do
    begin
        ndh := 640; ndv := 400;
        width := 219.5; height := 132.0;
    end;
    with input_device[digitizer] do
    begin
        ndh := 3800; ndv := 2600;
        width := 380.0; height := 260.0;
    end;
    {Set the current input device :}
    case dev_name of
        screen,digitizer  :  curr_inp_dev := dev_name
    otherwise
        writeln('** Device ',dev_name,' not available for input **')
    end;
end;
```

1.5 Coordinate systems

In computer graphics, large amounts of data are dealt with, and these data are largely quantified by various coordinate systems as are appropriate. As previously stated, all graphics output devices have a rectangular array of addressable graphics dots and any graphics pattern is produced by setting or clearing these dots. The dots are addressed by two integers, the horizontal dot number, dcx, and the vertical dot number, dcy , where:

$$0 \le dcx \le ndhm1 \equiv ndh - 1$$

and:

$$0 \le dcy \le ndvm1 \equiv ndv - 1$$

The value $dcx+1$ is the column number of the addressed dot, and $dcy+1$ is the row number of the addressed dot, in the matrix of graphics dots. The dot addressed as (0,0) is usually the lower left corner of the graphics display rectangle. The coordinates (dcx, dcy) are called the *hardware* or *device coordinates* . Note that device coordinates take integer values only.

Table 1-1 shows that device coordinate ranges vary considerably from device to device. For the purposes of a standard approach to all graphics equipment, the notion of *normalized device coordinates* has been invented. Normalized device coordinates, or NDCs, will be denoted by the parameters (*ndcx, ndcy*) throughout this book. NDCs (*ndcx, ndcy*) are real variables in contrast to device coordinates (*dcx, dcy*) which are integers. They are usually only defined to range from 0 to 1:

$$0 \le ndcx \le 1$$
$$0 \le ndcy \le 1$$

The NDC coordinate (0,0) could correspond to the device-coordinate origin (0,0), that is, the lower left addressable dot, and the NDC coordinate (1,1) refer to the upper right dot which is (*ndhm*1, *ndvm*1) in device coordinates. The advantage of NDCs is that graphics patterns can be discussed using a standard coordinate system independent of any particular graphics device. However, there will come a need to transform graphics data described in this device independent way onto a real graphics device. The mapping from NDCs (reals) to device coordinates (integers) is 'linear', for example:

```
dcx := round(ndcx * ndhm1);
dcy := round(ndcy * ndvm1);
```

and this can be implemented in a simple procedure 'ndc_to_out'. (See problem 1.2.)

Some systems prefer to use the range -1 to +1 or 0 to 100 (i.e. screen or display area percentages), instead of 0 to 1, for possible NDC coordinate values. The former are *centered normalized coordinates* (*cncx, cncy*). They are easily transformed to NDCs by adding one and then dividing by two. An advantage of the latter, called *screen percentages* (*spcx, spcy*), is that they are easy to visualize or enter on graph paper. Screen (or display area) percentage coordinates are readily converted to NDCs by dividing them by 100.

Two other coordinate systems are useful in computer graphics. The first is the *physical coordinate system* (*pcx, pcy*) where *pcx* is the physical distance along the *x* axis direction from the left, and *pcy* is the physical distance vertically from the bottom, of the display area. The units used here are either inches or millimeters. Throughout this book the metric system is used, so physical coordinates will be in millimeters. The transformation from physical coordinates to device coordinates is:

```
dcx := trunc(ndhm1 * pcx / width);
dcy := trunc(ndvm1 * pcy / height);
```

The second is the *user* or *world coordinate system* . These are cartesian coordinates (*x, y*) of any size selected by the user:

$$xmin \le x \le xmax$$
$$ymin \le y \le ymax$$

The parameters that define the range of *x* and *y* values, *xmin, ymin, xmax,* and *ymax,* define a rectangular area in abstract mathematical two-dimensional space. The user must first tell the graphics software what ranges are to be mapped onto the graphics output display. This range is called a *window* in the abstract two-dimensional space. A routine is needed to set these values. The following procedure will perform this function:

```
procedure set_window(xmin,ymin,xmax,ymax : real);
{Sets the valid ranges of the x and y coordinates that map onto the devices
   output rectangle.}
```

```
begin
    window.xmin := xmin;
    window.ymin := ymin;
    window.xmax := xmax;
    window.ymax := ymax;
    window.width := xmax - xmin;
    window.height := ymax - ymin;
end;
```

Note that an external data structure, a record 'window', is used by this routine to store the user-window limits in a global data area where other routines can access this information at a later time:

```
var
    window : record
        xmin, ymin, xmax, ymax, width, height : real;
    end;
```

The width and height components of the window are stored for computational convenience and, as shown in the next section, to bring out the analogy between user coordinates and I/O devices. The transformation from user coordinates (x, y) to NDCs ($ndcx$, $ndcy$) is accomplished by the following assignments:

```
ndcx := (x - xmin) / (xmax - xmin)
ndcy := (y - ymin) / (ymax - ymin)
```

This transformation is called the *normalization transformation.*

Routines that transform data in NDC, user, or physical coordinates to output-device coordinates need to be supplemented with corresponding routines for conversion of graphics input data. (Remember that the graphics coordinate data transmitted between the host processor and the graphics I/O device (screen, plotter, digitizer etc.) is by definition device coordinate data.) Therefore routines are needed to transform from input-device coordinates to NDCs, and from NDCs to user coordinates. This will give a complete set of data-transferring routines, allowing data to be transformed between any of the four representations shown in Figure 1-3. For example, to transform graphics data from user-coordinate representation to output-device coordinate form, two procedure calls can be made as in the following routine:

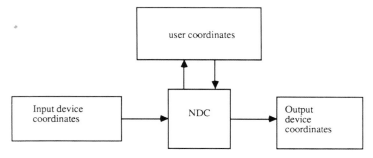

Figure 1-3 Coordinate systems used in graphics, and their transformations.

```
procedure user_to_out(x,y : real; var dcx,dcy : integer);
var
    ndcx,ndcy : real;
begin
    user_to_ndc(x,y,ndcx,ndcy);
    ndc_to_out(ndcx,ndcy,dcx,dcy);
end;
```

Notice that all these transformations are linear, one-to-one, and onto from source rectangle to destination rectangle. The entire source rectangle maps onto the entire destination rectangle regardless of their relative aspect ratios.

1.6 Aspect ratio correction

For most graphics output devices, the display rectangle (the total region where graphics output can occur on the device) is not a square, that is:

$$width \neq height$$

(See Table 1-1.) Similarly for graphics input devices, the physical aspect ratio of the input rectangle is very rarely equal to unity. Therefore a physical square, when input, will be squashed to rectangular form in NDCs and stretched again by the output transformations. If the output is directed to a different graphics output device then the proportions would again be changed.

Often in computer graphics it is desired that figures drawn in user coordinates should appear in the same proportions on the output device. For example, a unit square in the user coordinates should be transformed into a square shape, not a rectangular shape, on the VDU screen. And when a graphics pattern is transferred from a VDU screen to a hard-copy device usually it is not wanted squashed or stretched disproportionately in either the x or y directions: a true copy of the original is wanted including its proportions.

These examples illustrate the problem of aspect ratio correction: preserving faithfully the original proportions of a graphics picture when it is produced on various output graphics devices.

The simple case is where the user defines graphics patterns in a square area of user coordinates that map neatly into the NDC unit-square space. If a user defines a graphics shape such as a square in user coordinates then the routine 'user_to_ndc' will convert this nicely to a square in NDC coordinates. However if the output device does not have unit physical aspect ratio, then the routine 'ndc_to_out' will distort the square into a rectangle on the output display. For instance, if the whole NDC unit square is mapped onto a display rectangle which is not a square. How should this routine be modified to ensure that proportions are preserved in mapping from NDCs to output-device coordinates?

Three possible methods for preserving proportion during output transformations are given here. In the first, the NDC square maps onto the largest physical square inside the device's display rectangle. (See Figure 1-4.) This preserves proportions and no graphics are lost (by being mapped outside the display rectangle). However, full use of all the graphics area of the display rectangle is not made. In the second method, the NDC square

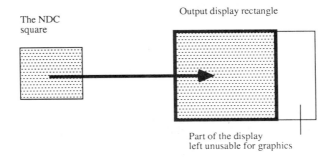

Figure 1-4 A transformation from NDCs to output device coordinates.

is mapped onto the smallest square containing the entire display rectangle. (See Figure 1-5.) Now the entire graphics area of the display rectangle is available for output, but some of the graphics in the NDC square could be lost because it is mapped outside the display rectangle. These two methods mean that 'ndc to out' should be replaced with one of two alternative routines 'proportional output1' or 'proportional output2'. (See problems 1.6 and 1.7.)

The third method takes quite a different approach: it extends the user coordinate window limits in the minimal way to correspond to the output device's physical aspect ratio. Thus the routines of the previous section are not replaced but supplemented with another routine which has the effect of fixing the output transformation so that aspect ratios are preserved. This new routine 'extend axes for output' will adjust the user window limits in a minimal way so that the rectangular window in the abstract mathematical two-dimensional space is geometrically similar to the output device's display rectangle:

procedure extend_axes_for_output;
{Adjust the ranges in the user coordinates so that the user window size
  matches the shape of the graphics devices output area.}

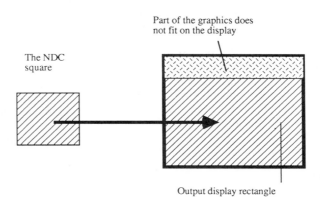

Figure 1-5 An alternative transformation from NDCs to output device coordinates.

```
var
    x_range, y_range, delta , xupmm, yupmm : real;
begin
    with output_device[curr_out_dev] do
    begin
        {compute the number of x units per mm :}
        xupmm := window.width/width;
        {compute the number of y units per mm :}
        yupmm := window.height/height;
        if xupmm > yupmm then
        begin
            delta := (yupmm - xupmm) * width;
            window.xmax := window.xmax + delta/2.0;
            window.xmin := window.xmin - delta/2.0;
        end;
        if xupmm < yupmm then
        begin
            delta := (xupmm - yupmm) * height;
            window.ymax := window.ymax + delta/2.0;
            window.ymin := window.ymin - delta/2.0;
        end;
        window.width := window.xmax - window.xmin;
        window.height := window.ymax - window.ymin;
    end;
end;
```

Now every time a new output device is selected, this routine must be called to readjust the user window. After many such changes the user window could grow too large; that is, the graphics appears too small on the output. Furthermore if after selecting a second output device the user reselects the first output device, the output graphics will in general have shrunk; that is, the output graphics will not have a constant size for the same output device. This nasty side effect could be avoided by having the user window limits copied to another global data area when the window is set, and have 'extend_axes_for_output' first restore the backed up window limits before extending them.

Consider now the other side of the aspect-ratio-correction problem in computer graphics: correcting for input devices with physical aspect ratios differing from unity. This problem can be solved with any of the three methods described above for correcting graphics output. That is, replace 'dc_to_ndc' with 'proportional_input1' or 'proportional_input2' or else call a routine 'extend_axes_for_input' after every selection of an input device. Note that this last method assumes that the graphics data is stored undistorted in user coordinates rather than in NDC form. The NDC values are just an intermediate step in receiving the input or sending the output data.

A further complication arises when the user coordinate data does not use equal scaling in its coordinates. User coordinate graphics data can enter the computer without the use of a graphics input device and thus without requiring the device coordinates to be transformed to user coordinates. A simpler graphics input method is to design the desired graphics on a sheet of graph paper, read off the coordinates of specific points, and type these values into the computer at the keyboard. When a person selects user coordinates and designs graphics data on a piece of graph paper for entry into a computer, the number of x units per millimeter is not necessarily equal to the number of y units per millimeter. For example, when plotting profits in thousands of dollars vertically against month number horizontally, there are obviously more *y* units per millimeter on the graph paper than *x* units per millimeter. A unit square in this set of user coordinates would look like a short horizontal line and this should not be transferred to a true square on the graphics output device. What is required is that physical distances between points on the graph paper and corresponding points on the screen remain in constant proportion.

If the graph paper used has width *w* and height *h* in millimeters, and that, as before, the user coordinates (x, y) with *x* ranging from *xmin* to *xmax* and *y* from *ymin* to *ymax*. And assuming that the *x* and *y* axes are not equally scaled; that is, the number of *x* units per millimeter (the *x* scaling):

$$xupmm = (xmax - xmin) / w \qquad (1.1)$$

is not necessarily equal to the number of *y* units per millimeter (the *y* scaling):

$$yupmm = (ymax - ymin) / h \qquad (1.2)$$

Then a simple way to derive appropriate transformations that will preserve graphic proportions is to first transform the user coordinates (x, y) to physical coordinates (px, py) on the graph paper, and then scale these to physical coordinates for the graphics device's output rectangle. The transformation from (x, y) to (px, py) simply amounts to a rescaling of the user coordinates using equations 1.1 and 1.2:

$$px = (x - xmin) / xupmm \qquad (1.3)$$
$$py = (y - ymin) / yupmm \qquad (1.4)$$

These coordinates must now be uniformly scaled, say by a constant *K*, to the physical coordinates on the graphics device:

$$pcx = K \ px \qquad (1.5)$$
$$pcy = K \ py \qquad (1.6)$$

The screen physical coordinates can then be transformed to device coordinates as discussed in Section 1.3:

$$dcx = \text{round}(pcx \ / \ width \ ndhml) \qquad (1.7)$$
$$dcy = \text{round}(pcy \ / \ height \ ndvml) \qquad (1.8)$$

The total aspect-ratio-preserving transformation is therefore:

$$dcx = \text{round}(K \ ndhml \ / \ width \ / \ xupmm \ x) \qquad (1.9)$$
$$dcy = \text{round}(K \ ndvml \ / \ height \ / \ yupmm \ y) \qquad (1.10)$$

One method of selecting *K* is to map the *x* values (*xmin* to *xmax*), so that they neatly fit across the graphics display rectangle. Then equation 1.10 gives:

$$\Delta dcx = ndhml$$
$$= \text{round}(K \ ndhml / width \ / xupmm \ (xmax - xmin))$$

which can be satisfied by:

$$K = width \, / \, w \tag{1.11}$$

With this choice of K the range in dcy that would correspond to the total range in the y coordinate would be from equation 1.10:

$$\Delta dcy = \text{round}(ndvm1 \, (h \, / \, w \,) \, / \, (width \, / \, height \,))$$
$$= \text{round}(ndvm1 \, (\alpha_{inp} \, / \, \alpha_{out} \,)) \tag{1.12}$$

where:

$$\alpha_{inp} = h \, / \, w$$
$$\alpha_{out} = height \, / \, width$$

are the physical aspect ratios of the graph paper and the graphics output device respectively. Therefore Δdcy will exceed the available range in vertical dot numbers if:

$$h \, / \, w = \alpha_{inp} > height \, / \, width = \alpha_{out} \tag{1.13}$$

That is, stretching the graph paper to fit the physical width of the graphics output rectangle will cause some of the picture to fall outside the display rectangle if the physical aspect ratio of the original graph paper is greater than the physical aspect ratio of the graphics output display rectangle.

Similarly it can easily be seen from equations 1.9 and 1.10 that the choice:

$$K = height \, / \, h \tag{1.14}$$

ensures that the entire range in y coordinates fits neatly into the vertical size of the display rectangle but will mean that the range of x values will be wider than the display screen if:

$$\alpha_{out} > \alpha_{inp} \tag{1.15}$$

that is, if the aspect ratio of the graphics output device rectangle exceeds the aspect ratio of the graph paper.

In order for the entire graph paper to be mapped proportionately onto the graphics device output rectangle, K should be chosen according to the algorithm:

$$\textbf{if } \alpha_{inp} < \alpha_{out} \textbf{ then } K = width \, / \, w \textbf{ else } K = height \, / \, h$$

This algorithm is implemented in the procedure in Box 1-2.

So far the methods discussed for overcoming the distortions introduced into the graphics data by the use of the algorithms of Section 1.5, allow the user to maintain graphics data in NDC form which has the desirable feature of device independence, that is, transportability of graphics data bases. However there is a different solution to the aspect ratio problem. This solution is to abandon the use of NDCs in favour of physical coordinates. Physical coordinates also provide device independence and therefore graphics data base compatibility between different systems. When graphics data is stored in physical units (millimeters say), there can be no physical distortion of the patterns when

Box 1-2 Preserving user coordinate aspect ratio on output.

```
procedure proportionate_transform(x,y : real; var dcx,dcy : integer);
{Transform user coordinates to a graphics device without unequal distortions
in the x or y directions.}
    const
        w = 280.0; { width of the graphics area on the graph paper }
        h = 178.0; { height of the graphics area on the graph paper }
        width = output_device[curr_out_dev].width;
        height = output_device[curr_out_dev].height;
    var
        phys_aspect_inp, phys_asp_out, K, xupmm, yupmm : real;
begin
    xupmm := (xmax-xmin)/w; yupmm := (ymax-ymin)/h;
    phys_aspect_inp := h/w; phys_aspect_out := height/width;
    K := height/h;
    if phys_aspect_inp > phys_aspect_out then K := width/w;
    dcx := round(K*ndh/width*x/xupmm);
    dcy := round(K*ndv/height*y/yupmm);
end;
```

the data is copied from device to device. Transformations will preserve proportions and sizes: the output to various devices would have identical appearances. Furthermore, user coordinates will be regarded as a conceptual graphics I/O device with (x, y) as its 'device coordinates' and width and height given by:

$$width = (xmax - xmin) / xunit$$
$$height = (ymax - ymin) / yunit$$

The quantities 'width' and 'height' are stored as components of the record 'window'. They are computed from 'xunit' and 'yunit' which are the number of x and y units per physical unit respectively. 'Xunit' and 'yunit' are more convenient than 'width' and 'height' for specifying the user coordinate area because the user may not have any particular dimensions in mind but rather wishes to specify how many y units there are relative to the size of an x unit. To implement this style of graphics data transfer, a routine 'select_user_coords' (an analogy with 'select_input_device' and 'select_output_device') is needed:

```
procedure select_user_coords(xmin,ymin,xmax,ymax,xunit,yunit : real);
{ Set up user coordinates to look like a graphics I/O device.}
begin
    window.xmin := xmin;
    window.ymin := ymin;
    window.xmax := xmax;
    window.ymax := ymax;
    window.width := (xmax - xmin) / xunit;
    window.height := (ymax - ymin) / yunit;
```

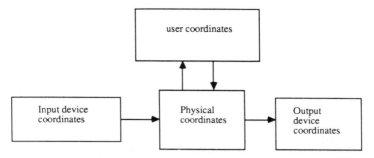

Figure 1-6 A system of graphics coordinate systems that preserves aspect ratios.

end;

The approach to graphics data representation depicted in Figure 1-6 provides a standard data format which can be used directly on any computer and any graphics device without picture distortion. An advantage of the NDC approach (Figure 1-3) on the other hand is that it will never develop device coordinates outside the valid range for any graphics output device. With physical coordinates (Figure 1-6), it is possible for a graphics picture to be physically larger than the output display rectangle and causing these transformation routines to develop invalid device coordinate addresses. It is the responsibility of the I/O software which takes the device coordinates and performs the appropriate hardware functions to detect such circumstances. These routines are presented in the following two chapters. Large graphics pictures are not really a problem though because the graphics patterns may be uniformly scaled down to fit the output rectangle if so desired by the user. Routines for scaling and manipulating graphics patterns will be presented further on in the book.

A set of routines which will allow the transformation of the various representations of graphics data, as shown in Figure 1-6, should be developed (see problem 1.2). These routines will be similar to the routines discussed in Section 1.5 in relation to Figure 1-3. Graphics software will be developed around this set of routines rather than the NDC approach.

Problems

1.1   Write a Pascal program 'resolutions' to ask for the characteristics of a graphics output device:

> Number of addressable locations horizontally = ?
> Number of addressable locations vertically = ?
> Width of the graphics output rectangle in mm = ?
> Height of the graphics output rectangle in mm = ?

and then compute and print out :

> Total number of addressable graphics dots = ...
> Area of the graphics output rectangle = ... square mm
> Graphics (i.e. pixel) aspect ratio = ...
> Physical (i.e. screen) aspect ratio = ...
> Horizontal resolution = ... dots per mm
> Horizontal dot size = ... mm
> Vertical resolution = ... dots per mm
> Vertical dot size = ... mm
> Area resolution = ... dots per square mm
> Area per graphics dot = ... square mm

as presented in Section 1.4. Use your program to derive the graphics characteristics of all the devices listed in the table in that section. Compare the devices against each other on the basis of area resolution, aspect ratio, and total number of addressable dots.

Run the program again for three different input devices and six different output devices of your choice.

1.2   Write the procedures, 'inp_to_ndc', 'ndc_to_user', 'user_to_ndc', and 'ndc_to_out' to transform data between the various coordinate systems in a graphics system as shown in Figure 1-3. Repeat this exercise with 'dpc' (display area percentages) replacing 'ndc', 'cnc' (centered normalized coordinates) replacing 'ndc', and 'phys' (physical coordinates in mm) replacing 'ndc'. The latter set of four procedures correspond to Figure 1-6. This set, rather than any of the three previous sets of coordinate transformation routines mentioned is the preferred set for the rest of this book.

1.3.   Prove the assertion in Section 1.6 that if the proportional scaling factor is $K = height / h$ then part of the graphics will be missing from the screen if $\alpha_{inp} < \alpha_{out}$ also. What fraction of the graphics pattern on graph paper would not fit onto the graphics display in this case?

1.4   What pixels are at the corners of a square of side 2 cm whose bottom left corner is at the center of the M68 screen and whose sides are horizontal and vertical? (Refer to Table 1-1.) Write a sequence of routine calls that will select the M68 screen for graphics input, convert these four points to NDCs, select the plotter for output, and convert the NDC values to plotter device coordinates.

1.5   The coordinates of points on the circumference of a circle with radius 10 cm are entered into the computer from a digitizer which has resolution 1000 x 800 and dimensions 40 cm by 30 cm. The output is to go to a graphics VDU which has resolution 640 x 200 and dimensions 245 mm by 186 mm. If the NDC values were plotted on graph paper by hand the result would be an ellipse rather than a true circle. Determine the eccentricity of this ellipse. What sizes are the semi-major and semi-minor axes of the output on the graphics screen measured in centimeters?

1.6   Write procedures, 'proportional_output1' and 'proportional_input1' to preserve aspect ratios of graphics data represented internally in normalized device coordinates by method 1 discussed in Section 1.6. Recall that in method 1, 'proportional_input1' is the aspect-ratio-preserving transformation from input device coordinates to NDCs achieved by mapping the input device's rectangle onto the largest similar rectangle inside the NDC square. Explain how these routines would be used.

1.7   Write Pascal code to implement the aspect-ratio-preserving transformation from input-device coordinates to NDCs by mapping the input device's rectangle onto the smallest similar rectangle containing the NDC square. Call this procedure 'proportional_input2'. Write the analogous procedure for outputing graphics 'proportional_output2'. Explain how these would be used. Compare their usage to that of the two routines of problem 1.6.

1.8   Write a Pascal routine 'extend_axes_for_input' that transforms input-device coordinates to NDCs and preserves proportions on graphic input by adjusting the user-coordinate window limits analogous to the routine 'extend_axes_for_output' as presented in Section 1.6. Discuss how these two routines would be used to preserve aspect ratios instead of methods 1 and 2 of problems 1.6 and 1.7.

1.9   The routines of Section 1.6 provide for adjusting graphics data due to the differences in *physical* aspect ratio of different graphics devices. Why is no adjustment required for differences in the *graphics* aspect ratios between graphics I/O devices?

1.10   Redesign the window record 'set_window' and rewrite the aspect ratio correcting routines 'extend_axes_for_output' and 'extend_axes_for _input' to store and restore the user coordinate limits so that the user window does not continue to grow larger, as discussed in the text.

1.11   An NEC APC graphics microcomputer (see Table 1-1 for its graphics characteristics) has a standard graphics package called GSX built into its operating system CPM/86. (See Chapter 15 and Appendix H for a discussion of GSX.) In GSX, the APC screen is addressed as a normalized device of coordinate ranges 0 to 32767 both horizontally and vertically. Determine the aspect ratio of the pixels and of the GSX normalized screen units. How would you adjust coordinates when using GSX normalized screen units to avoid aspect ratio distortions?

1.12   Suppose that the resolution of a graphics VDU is unknown except that it is known to be less than 1000 x 1000 with the device coordinate origin in the lower left corner. Assuming that two procedures 'DC_line(dcx1,dcy1,dcx2,dcy2)' and 'clear' are provided, which draw a line from ('dcx1','dcy1') to ('dcx2','dcy2') in device coordinates, and clear the screen respectively, devise a method for determining the four characteristic quantities, *ndhm*1, *ndvm*1, *width* and *height*. Could your method be used to find the viewable ranges of device coordinates if, due to a misalignment in the CRT, the device coordinate origin was off the screen?

2

Line oriented graphics equipment

2.1 Digital plotters

A digital plotter is a device that moves a pen over a sheet of paper to any of a finite number of possible grid points. The pen may be in the up or down condition during this motion and in this way any graphics pattern can be drawn on the paper. Because the pen cannot move to any position and can only move a multiple of a fixed unit of distance in the x or y directions, this is a digital rather than an analog output device. However it is still a vector graphics device since it draws by lines rather than by sequences of dots: the pen stays down until the line is completed. The digital plotter may also be able to select or change pens from a pen stock and in this way colored graphics hard copy can be obtained.

An example of a high-cost digital plotter is the Calcomp 1051 drum plotter. This plotter uses a continuous roll of paper to automatically output a sequence of plots. Completed plots are ejected and cut off, and the plotter winds the paper forward for the next plot. The y position of the pen is obtained by backward and forward motion along a fixed arm across the paper. To get the x position of the pen, the drum actually moves the paper underneath the pen to the required position. Figure 2-1 shows a typical drum plotter.

The HP7475A graphics plotter is a lower cost professional digital plotter. It produces quality plots with color-filled areas in up to six pen colors on A3 or A4 sized paper. The plotting range is 413.9 mm by 257.8 mm for A3 paper and 257.8 mm by 198.1 mm for

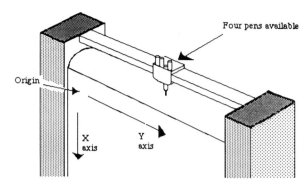

Figure 2-1 A typical drum plotter.

A4 paper. The plotting step size is 0.025 mm and the plotting speed is 381 mm/sec. The paper is rolled backwards and forwards creating the y coordinate values, and the pen moves back and forth across the page sliding along a fixed arm to plot the x coordinate. It has an extensive range of commands which form a language called HP-GL, which stands for Hewlett-Packard Graphics Language. This language is studied in some detail in Chapter 14.

An example of low-cost digital plotters is the Roland series of digital plotters. This sort of plotter has a flat bed in which the sheet of paper is placed by the operator. A sliding arm is moved left and right by a stepper motor controlling a pulley arrangement. This gives the x coordinate value to the plotter's pen. Another stepper motor and pulley under the cover of the sliding arm moves the pen holder along the sliding arm thus providing the y coordinate. The Roland plotter can select from any of eight different colored pens. The plotting area is 420 mm horizontally by 297 mm vertically and the pen can be moved in 0.1 mm steps. This means that the resolution is 4200 x 2970. (This is the plotter mentioned in Section 1.4.) The plotting speed is 180 mm/sec. It has simple commands to move to a given location on the page, to draw a line to another point, to draw circles and print text in various sizes, and so forth. Some of these commands are discussed in Sections 2.5 and 2.7.

All of the plotters mentioned in this section have device coordinates proportional to their corresponding physical coordinates. The physical-to-device-coordinate transformation 'phys_to_out' is very simple and this feature makes it easy to transport graphics patterns from one to the other without distortions of shape.

2.2 **Vector refresh display tubes**

In the early years of computer graphics the main video display device was not a TV-like monitor but an expensive CRT, like the kind used in oscilloscopes. Like the oscilloscope the display had x and y voltage inputs that directed the electron beam directly to the

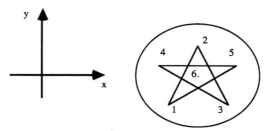

Here only five (x,y) points define the shape. This requires little memory.
The lines were drawn in the order 123451. Point 6 is the origin.

Figure 2-2 Vector graphics output of a pentagram.

specified point on the screen. This kind of display is called a vector graphics display because the display is sent voltage point pairs and the beam draws a line in one stroke or vector movement from the last point to the next point. (See Figure 2-2.)

The screen phosphors glow momentarily when hit by electrons in the electron beam. This glow usually lasts for only a few milliseconds and so the whole graphics picture consisting of any number of vectors must be continuously retraced in order for the graphics to remain on the screen. This process is called *refreshing* the picture and hence the name, *vector refresh tubes* . If the graphics picture being displayed consists of too many vectors then a significant delay from drawing the first vector to drawing the last vector in the picture exists, and during this delay some of the initial vectors may fade from view. The result is that the tube cannot refresh the picture fast enough to avoid a flickering effect becoming painfully apparent in the graphics picture.

The analog voltages sent as x and y inputs to the vector graphics display tube define the shape displayed. Therefore comparatively little memory is required to maintain a complex picture made of lines, because only the end-point and corner coordinates need to be stored. (This was important in the early days of computing, because memory was much more expensive then than it is today.) Once a computer has generated the points that define the shape to be sent to the display, an expensive digital-to-analog converter (DAC) is needed to convert these digital points to voltages for the CRT (see Figure 2-3).

The vector graphics display technology has tended to be expensive because the DAC contains complex analog circuits that must be trimmed periodically and because it also contains temperature dependent components. Another disadvantage of the vector refresh display, already mentioned, is the screen flicker that occurs when a sizable amount of graphics is output. Only limited memory in the 'display file' (the memory buffer that

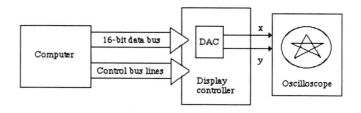

Figure 2-3 The use of digital to analog circuits for calligraphic output.

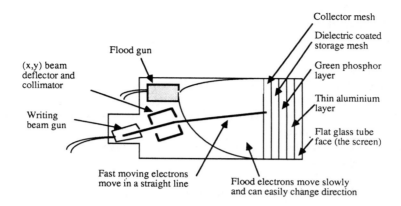

Figure 2-4 A schematic representation of a direct view storage tube.

holds the endpoint coordinates) is usually available, so that complex detail is not possible. However it is a high-resolution graphics device (i.e. at least 1000 x 1000) and fast in displaying simple line figures which makes it useful for animation. For the latter reason, vector refresh tubes are often used for quick trials of graphics output outlines. When the outline appears satisfactory on a vector refresh tube then the time can be taken to build up a complex colored pattern on a raster VDU. (Raster graphics are discussed in the next chapter.) An example of a vector refresh VDU is the Megatek. (See Table 1-1.)

2.3 **Direct view storage tubes**

The direct view storage tube (DVST) is a graphics display tube developed after the refresh tube but before the raster graphics CRTs. Figure 2-4 illustrates how the DVST works. The writing electron beam does not write directly on the phosphor of the screen but instead electrifies the dielectric coating on a fine wire mesh grid immediately before the phosphor coating on the screen. The electron beam knocks electrons out of the dielectric and all electrons are collected in the wire grid which is connected to a positive potential. This leaves a pattern of positive charges on the dielectric side of the collector. A flood gun emits low energy electrons that tend to spread evenly over the collector surface owing to the uniform low positive potential of the collector. Flood electrons pass through the collector at low velocity and are attracted to the positively charged areas of the storage mesh. Those flood electrons attracted to the mesh pass through it and strike the phosphor coating of the screen. In order to have a display of acceptable intensity, the screen is maintained at a high positive potential by means of a positive voltage applied to a thin aluminium coating between the tube face and the phosphor. Until they pass through the mesh, the flood electrons are still moving fairly slowly and therefore hardly affect the charge on the mesh - hence the storage nature of the storage mesh. Anything written there by the writing electron gun remains until erased by a positive voltage momentarily sent to the storage mesh. This removes the charge on the dielectric but also generates an unpleasant flash over the entire screen surface.

The DVST graphics system has a number of advantages:

1. High resolution (at least 1024 x 781) is available.
2. The display is flicker free as it does not require constant refreshing and the display is not granulated (as on raster graphics VDUs described in the next chapter).
3. Lines and curves are easily drawn and are of uniform density no matter at what angle they are drawn on the screen.
4. For the amount of graphics resolution given, DVSTs have been relatively cheaper than their competitors.

However the DVST system has some disadvantages too:

1. As already mentioned, screen erasure causes the screen to flash and this phenomenon is rather distracting.
2. No part of the screen can be modified - there is no 'selective erasure' - the whole screen must be erased and redrawn. The unchanged part must be remembered by the software and the changed part must be added. These two properties combined mean that animated graphics is not possible on DVST equipment.
3. As only green phosphor tubes are available, DVSTs are not suitable for color graphics.
4. Only a single level of intensity can be displayed and there is no capability for smooth shading of surfaces.
5. DVSTs have poor contrast compared with raster screens because the accelerating potential of the flood electrons must be low.
6. Gradual degradation of the picture quality occurs as the background glow accummulates due to the small amounts of charge deposited on the storage mesh by the repelled flood electrons.
7. The tubes wear out and need regular replacement.

Direct view storage tubes are an old technology now: they have been displaced to a large extent by the more flexible modern raster VDUs. Nevertheless, the DVSTs provide valuable vector-graphics software concepts which apply to all graphics equipment technologies.

2.4 Vector graphics software primitives

A software *primitive* is a routine or command in a language that achieves the simplest function in a given application: therefore a software primitive implements a single function. Primitives are a familiar concept from the discipline of Software Engineering (Jensen & Tonies 1979, pp. 103, 116). A large applications software system is ultimately constructed from calls to its primitives in a hierarchical way.

Vector graphics is the simplest kind of graphics output, and is analogous to making pencil drawings composed of straight line segments. Virtually all vector graphics output devices work on two very simple software primitives 'moveto(dcx, dcy)' and 'drawto(dcx, dcy)'.The first of these moves the current beam position (the CBP or more briefly the CP) in the case of a vector graphics VDU or the current pen position (also called the CP) in the case of a plotter to the specified device coordinates. The second primitive routine draws a straight line (also called a 'vector' and hence the name *vector graphics*) on the output rectangle from the current position (CP) to the position on the output rectangle specified by the device coordinates (*dcx, dcy*). After each of these are called the CP is updated to the position specified that is (*dcx, dcy*).

From a theoretical point of view, these are not the only possible software primitives for describing any vector graphics output, but they are the simplest. An alternative set of three functions is:

1. raise the pen off the paper or switch off the writing electron beam, 'pen_up';
2. lower the pen onto the paper or switch on the writing electron beam, 'pen_down';
3. locate the CP at a given point on the output rectangle, 'locate(dcx, dcy)'.

Any vector graphics output can be designed with these three functions.

To prove that these three primitive functions are equivalent (so far as vector graphics is concerned) to the set of two primitives stated earlier, it is sufficient to demonstrate that the former set can be coded using only the latter set and vice versa as follows:

1. The simulation of the 'moveto' and 'drawto' primitives on hardware providing only the 'pen_up', 'pen_down', and 'locate' primitives:

   ```
   procedure moveto(dcx, dcy : integer);
   { Move the CP to the location (dcx, dcy) in device coordinates on the
   display rectangle without drawing a line.}
   begin
       pen_up;                 { ensure that the 'pen' is in the 'up condition' }
       locate(dcx, dcy); {locate desired absolute device coordinate position}
   end;


   procedure drawto(dcx, dcy : integer);
   { Draw a line from the CP to the location (dcx, dcy) in device coordinates
   on the display rectangle.}
   begin
       pen_down;               {ensure that the 'pen' is in the 'down condition'}
       locate(dcx, dcy); {locate the desired absolute device coordinate position}
       pen_up; {return the 'pen' to the 'up condition' for consistency }
   end;
   ```

2. The simulation of the 'pen up', 'pen down', and 'locate' primitives on hardware providing only the 'moveto' and 'drawto' primitives:

```
type pen_conditions = (up, down);
var cp = record {Define the current position as a global data structure}
    x,y : integer;                          { device coordinates are integers}
    pen_status : pen_conditions;
    end;

procedure init_cp;
begin
    cp.x := 0;
    cp.y := 0;
    pen_status := up
end;

procedure locate(dcx, dcy : integer);
begin
    if cp.pen_status = down then
        drawto(dcx, dcy)
    else
        moveto(dcx, dcy);
    cp.x := dcx; cp.y := dcy   {update the CP}
end;

procedure pen_up;
begin
    moveto(cp.x, cp.y)
end;

procedure pen_down;
begin
    drawto(cp.x, cp.y)
end;
```

Notice that these routines depend upon shared data in the record 'cp' which needs to be initialized. In case 1, where the 'pen_up', 'pen_down', and 'locate' functions are actually done by the hardware, the shared data is kept in the hardware in register locations and their values are initialized by the hardware at start-up time. In case 2, these hardware pieces must be simulated in software by the record 'cp' and 'init_cp'.

For a general computer graphics system where there are several possible output devices on-line to the host computer, 'moveto' and 'drawto' will have to be implemented for each device. To have general purpose 'moveto' and 'drawto' routines means that these routines will contain case statements with alternative code segments for each device supported. The case selector is the value of the current output device global parameter (called 'curr_out_dev' in Chapter 1). Because device coordinate systems are different for most graphics devices, it is appropriate to address the general purpose 'moveto' and 'drawto' routines in a device independent way - either by NDCs or as preferred here in physical coordinates :

```
procedure move_to(px, py : real);
{ Move the CP on the current output device's display rectangle to the point
(px, py) in physical coordinates (millimeters).}
var
    dcx, dcy : integer;
begin
    phys_to_out(px, py, dcx, dcy); {convert to appropriate device coords}
    case curr_out_dev of
        tek4010 : tek4010_moveto(dcx, dcy)
        plotter : plotter_moveto(dcx, dcy)
    end;
end;


procedure draw_to(px, py : real);
{ Draw from the CP on the current output device's display rectangle to the
point (px, py) in physical coordinates (millimeters).}
var
    dcx, dcy : integer;
begin
    phys_to_out(px, py, dcx, dcy); {convert to appropriate device coords}
    case curr_out_dev of
        tek4010: tek4010_drawto(dcx, dcy)
        plotter: plotter_drawto(dcx, dcy)
    end;
end;
```

Actual implementations require the use of a procedure to output a specified byte to the specified device, 'send_output(device, byte)'. The parameter 'byte' is a var parameter (i.e. it is passed by its reference address). If the value returned in 'byte' after the call is made is negative then this indicates that the specified device was not ready or not available and therefore did not receive the byte value. Having this routine available to the programmer allows each device to be controlled at the machine-code level from within a high-level language such as Pascal. It also allows the programmer to avoid having software hang or crash simply because someone forgot to plug in the plotter, or because a device was not switched on or had the wrong communications settings. The routine 'send_output' will be different for different operating systems and different device communication hardware.

When I/O faults are not expected, the following output routine can be used to control the hardware devices:

```
procedure write_output(device : device_names; byte : integer);
const
    max_tries = 10; {any maximum number of retries will do here}
var
    status,try : integer;
```

```
begin
    try := 0; {initialize the counter of output tries}
    status : = byte;
    repeat
        send_output(device, byte_to_send); {try to send it}
        try := try + 1;
        byte_to_send := byte; {recover the byte value to send}
    until (status > 0) or (try > max_tries);
    if status < 0 then
        error('** Output device is unavailable **');
end;
```

This routine, in contrast to 'send_output', waits for a successful output operation to be completed. If after a certain number of tries the output device does not respond properly, the fault is logged by the 'error' routine. This 'error' routine in its simplest form is designed to send a message and possibly other information to the terminal or an error-log file and in this case consists essentially of a writeln-statement with another routine to set the default destination (terminal or file) for the messages. More generally the 'error' routine can be designed to respond to errors on a severity or priority basis - depending on the severity of the error detected it will abort or allow the execution to continue.

2.5 Programming a plotter

Most plotters work on a simple text command sequence. Two commands of interest from a typical plotter are:

M dcx,dcy

and:

D dcx,dcy

Thus if the plotter is sent the character sequence: 'M', space, then the character string representation of the device coordinate x component, comma, the device coordinate y component, and the return character; the CP (current pen position) will change (move) to the position (dcx, dcy). If, as in the second command, a 'D' is sent as the first character instead of an 'M', the plotter draws a line from the CP to the location specified (in device coordinates) and then updates the CP to that location.

For example, to draw a line from the device coordinate (10, 10) to (50, 40) the following bytes must be sent to this plotter:

'M' '' '1' '0' ',' '1' '0' cr 'D' '' '5' '0' ',' '4' '0' cr

where cr stands for the carriage-return control character. Using the ASCII character code (see Appendix A), the sequence of byte values required to draw this line is:

77, 32, 49, 48, 44, 49, 48, 13, 68, 32, 53, 48, 44, 52, 48, 13

Most plotters will ignore some characters such as the line-feed character (ASCII value = 10). Therefore each carriage-return character (ASCII value = 13) in the above stream can be followed by a line-feed character as is normally done in output statements.

The drawing of a line from (10, 10) to (50, 40) can be programmed by calling the procedure 'write_output(plotter, byte)' 16 times, with the parameter 'byte' set to the ASCII values listed above in turn. To assist, 'plotter_moveto' and 'plotter_drawto' code could be implemented for this plotter and in this case the calling sequence:

```
plotter_moveto(10, 10);
plotter_drawto(50, 40);
```

is made. However it is preferable for the general 'move_to' and 'draw_to' routines to be used. Since these routines require physical coordinates to work, using the plotter step size of the typical plotter (0.1 mm) the following calls would be made:

```
select_output_device(plotter);
move_to(1.0, 1.0);
draw_to(5.0, 4.0);
```

An implementation of the vector graphics primitive routines, 'plotter_moveto' and 'plotter_drawto', follows. Note the routine 'write_integer' which is needed to convert an integer value from its internal binary representation to a string of ASCII bytes that represent the digits of the integer in decimal form: these bytes are then transmitted to the specified output device.

```
procedure write_integer(device : device_names; value : integer);
var
    i, byte : integer;
    int_string : string[6];
begin
    int_string := integer_to_string(value);
    for i:= 1 to length(int_string) do
    begin
        byte := ord(int_string[i]); write_output(device, byte);
    end;
end;

procedure plotter_moveto(dcx, dcy : integer);
{Implement a 'moveto' on the plotter}
const
    lf = 10;
```

```
        cr = 13;
        space = 32;
        comma = 44;
begin
        write_output(plotter, ord('M'));
        write_output(plotter, space);
        write_integer(plotter, dcx);
        write_output(plotter, comma);
        write_integer(plotter, dcy);
        write_output(plotter, cr); write_output(plotter, lf);
end;

procedure plotter_drawto(dcx, dcy : integer);
{Implement a 'drawto' on the plotter}
const
        lf = 10;
        cr = 13;
        space = 32;
        comma = 44;
begin
        write_output(plotter, ord('D'));
        write_output(plotter, space);
        write_integer(plotter, dcx);
        write_output(plotter, comma);
        write_integer(plotter, dcy);
        write_output(plotter, cr); write_output(plotter, lf);
end;
```

The typical plotter, such as the Roland plotter, has a number of other single letter commands, and these form the language for all Roland plotters. For instance, there are commands to plot arcs, print text symbols, change pens, and so forth. There are graphics input commands as well and these are be discussed in Section 2.7. The Roland plotter command language and other similar graphics languages are discussed further in Chapter 14.

2.6 Programming a Tektronix DVST

Examples of DVSTs are the Tektronix 40xx range of display terminals, for instance, the Tektronix 4010. They are a 188.5 mm by 138.5 mm DVST coupled to an alphanumeric keyboard with extra control keys. The physical screen coordinate system is divided into 1024 positions horizontally and 781 positions vertically as shown in Figure 2-5.

From these figures the horizontal resolution is:

$$horiz\_res = 1024 / 188.5 = 5.43$$

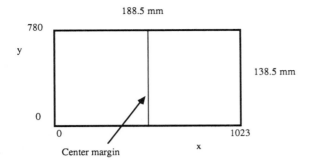

Figure 2-5 The Tektronix direct view storage tube screen arrangement.

and the vertical graphics resolution is:

$$vert\_res = 781 / 138.5 = 5.63$$

and so the aspect ratio is close to 1:

$$graphics\_aspect\_ratio = horiz\_res / ver\_res = 0.963$$

The Tektronix terminal connects to a host computer by means of a serial line protocol (RS-232-C or 20 milliamp current loop). The Tektronix device controller receives bytes from the host via this serial line and interprets these as instructions for displaying a single graphics element (dot, line, or alphanumeric character) of the picture at the specified device coordinates. The controller converts these coordinates into voltages that are applied to the deflection yoke to move the beam to the right position on the screen. The most significant bit of an eight-bit byte (bit 7) is a parity bit. The data bits (bits 0 to 6) give instructions to the device controller to change its mode or to operate within a mode. The Tektronix 4010 has the following functional modes and submodes:

1. Alpha mode
    (a) View submode
    (b) Hold submode
2 Graphics plot mode
    (a) Dark vector submode
    (b) Light vector submode
3. Graphics input modes
    (a) Get alpha cursor location mode
    (b) Get current beam position (CP) mode
    (c) Cross-hairs cursor positioning mode
4. Hard-copy mode

If the controller is in alpha mode (this is the default start-up condition), then all printable ASCII bytes received are displayed as the corresponding ASCII symbol at the current cursor location maintained by the controller. In this mode the 4010 behaves like an ordinary terminal with its own inbuilt character set. It displays 35 lines of 74 characters per line. However, the 4010 is unlike an ordinary terminal in four ways:

1. When the left-hand side of the screen fills up with alphanumeric text, that is, for the 36th line, the cursor goes to the top line at the center margin. This allows 70 lines of text to be visible on the screen. However if any of the first 35 lines are longer than 37 characters, they will interfere with characters on the right-hand side of the screen. Since the characters are written as graphics symbols on the storage tube, superimposed characters become almost impossible to decipher. Backspacing along a line does not delete characters; an additional cause of characters becoming superimposed.

2. The Tektronix screen does not scroll (since the text is held in the storage tube). When the last line of the screen is filled and the user types a carriage return, the screen remains fixed waiting for the user to type the screen-erase key. When the screen-erase key is pressed, the screen flashes and then clears: alphanumeric data can again be displayed starting from the cursor home position. (This feature can be optionally disabled and then output to the screen will overwrite itself after one screenfull and be difficult to read.)

3. After about 60 seconds the screen blanks out automatically until the next keypress from the user reactivates it. This is called the *hold submode* and it is designed to prolong the life of the storage tube. The hardware automatically switches off the flood gun after a set period of keyboard inactivity. The storage tube, however, retains its charge and when the flood gun is switched on again (by pressing any key, even the shift key which does not generate a character) the same text and graphics are restored to view.

4. On the Tektronix 4010 the alphanumeric characters can be placed at any graphic coordinates on the screen rather than only within character cells as on an ordinary terminal. This is again because the characters are basically generated as graphics symbols on the storage tube. A 14 x 14 matrix as illustrated in Figure 2-6 is used to make a character and the linefeed character introduces an interline gap of eight pixels.

The other three modes (graphics plot, graphics input, and hard copy) can be entered from alpha mode by means of control characters or escape sequences. Likewise to exit from any of these other modes, certain control characters or escape sequences must be issued and the default alpha mode returned to. For example, to enter the graphics plot

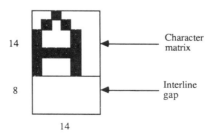

Figure 2-6 The Tektronix character format.

mode the control byte called GS in the ASCII code must be sent to the Tektronix 4010. The numerical code for the GS character is:

$$0011101 \quad \text{binary} = 1D \text{ hex} = 29 \text{ decimal.}$$

Thus the following procedure will put the Tektronix 4010 into graphics mode from alpha mode:

```
procedure tek4010_enter_graphics_mode;
const
    gmode = 29;
begin
    write_output(tek4010, gmode);
end;
```

Similarly to return to alpha mode a control character, US in the ASCII code, must be sent. The numerical code for US is:

$$0011111 \quad \text{binary} = 1F \text{ hex} = 31 \text{ decimal.}$$

The following procedure will cause the Tektronix 4010 to exit from graphics mode to alpha mode:

```
procedure tek4010_leave_graphics_mode;
const
    amode = 31;
begin
    write_output(tek4010, amode);
end;
```

Once in graphics plot mode, the Tektronix terminal interprets incoming bytes as coordinate data coded in binary as follows:

$$\text{first byte received after GS} = P \; 01yhi$$
$$\text{second byte received after GS} = P \; 11ylo$$
$$\text{third byte received after GS} = P \; 01xhi$$
$$\text{fourth byte received after GS} = P \; 10xlo$$

where P represents the parity bit (if there is one in the byte), yhi and ylo are the high and low binary parts of the y coordinate, and xhi and xlo are the high and low parts of the x coordinate. Physical screen coordinates are specified in ten bits with five bits supplied per byte. Thus yhi represents the high five bits of the y coordinate and ylo the low five bits. Similary xhi represents the high five bits of the x coordinate and xlo holds the low five bits.

The first four bytes after entering the graphics plot mode (i.e. following the GS control character) set the current beam position without drawing a vector. These first four bytes are called the 'dark (meaning invisible) vector submode'; that is, they implement a move-to operation. The next four bytes set the destination screen position to which a visible vector is drawn. The latter set of four bytes are called the 'light (meaning visible) vector submode'; they implement a draw-to operation. The Tektronix 4010 now remains in the light vector submode until an exit-graphics-mode control character is sent or another GS control character is sent to it. Therefore repeated consecutive groups of four bytes, like the above, will produce a *polyline*, that is, a sequence of connected straight-line segments.

The following two routines code the move-to and draw-to vector graphics primitives for the Tektronix 4010:

```
procedure tek4010_drawto(dcx, dcy : integer);
{Draw a vector from the CP to (dcx, dcy) in device coordinates and then
update the CP to (dcx, dcy).
NOTE: the Tektronix 4010 must be already in graphics plot mode for this
routine to function correctly.}
const
    tag_yhi = 1;
    tag_ylo = 3;
    tag_xhi = 1;
    tag_xlo = 2;
var
    x,xhi,xlo,y,yhi,ylo,byte : integer;
begin
    x := dcx mod 255; { ensure that x has only 10 bits }
    xlo := x mod 32; xhi := (x - xlo) div 32;
    y := dcy mod 255; { ensure that y has only 10 bits }
    ylo := y mod 32; yhi := (y - ylo) div 32;
    byte := yhi + 32*tag_yhi; write_output(tek4010, byte);
    byte := ylo + 32*tag_ylo; write_output(tek4010, byte);
    byte := xhi + 32*tag_xhi; write_output(tek4010, byte);
    byte := xlo + 32*tag_xlo; write_output(tek4010, byte);
end;


procedure tek4010_moveto(dcx, dcy : integer);
{Move to the point (dcx, dcy) in device coordinates without drawing a line, and
update the CP}
begin
    tek4010_enter_graphics_mode;
    tek4010_draw_to(dcx, dcy);
end;
```

It is possible to optimize the codes sent to the Tektronix terminal. If two successive end points have coordinates that differ only in their lower order five bits, it is unnecessary to transmit the higher order bits. To reposition the initial point for another vector, a 1D byte is sent again. (This is equivalent to sending 1F followed by 1D.)

A computer can use the Tektronix 4010 for graphics input as well as output by sending it commands to put it into one of its graphics input modes. These modes are dealt with in detail in Section 2.7. Finally there is the hard-copy mode which is entered by the host sending the escape sequence ESC, ETB to the Tektronix terminal. Of course the hard-copy unit must be connected and switched on. A hard copy can also be generated by the user pressing the COPY key on the keyboard. Use of the terminal is suspended until the screen has been copied to the hard-copy unit and then the terminal automatically returns to alpha mode. The following routine causes the Tektronix 4010 terminal with Tektronix hard-copy unit to generate a hard copy under program control:

```
procedure tek4010_make_hard_copy;
const
    esc = 27; etb = 23; {ASCII codes}
begin
    write_output(tek4010, esc); write_output(tek4010, etb);
end;
```

Although the Tektronix 4010 terminal is an old graphics terminal by todays standards (it was first released in 1964), it was so popular that today most educational institutions have several Tektronix terminals. Some of these may have the associated Tektronix hard copier which copies the screen to paper at the touch of the print button on the terminal or by software control as described above. The terminal also has a knob for adjusting the contrast in the printed output.

The popularity of the 4010 has resulted in it becoming almost a standard graphics device for all graphics software to address. Tektronix have produced many upgrades on the original 4010 graphics terminal but they have maintained compatibility with the original 4010 command set. In addition, many other manufacturers of graphics terminals decided that Tektronix 4010 compatibility was a desirable sales feature and ensured that at least machine-code programming compatibility was provided in their graphics VDU terminals. If hardware compatibility is not available on a terminal then Tektronix command compatibility can be achieved by a Tektronix 4010 emulation routine. (See problem 2.9, a programming exercise in building Tektronix 4010 emulators.)

2.7 Graphics input methods

Some digital plotters and vector graphics VDUs are capable of graphics input as well as their normal graphics output functions. In all the graphics output functions, the host computer sends byte streams to the graphics device. For a graphics input function on a graphics device, the reverse must occur; that is, the graphics device must send byte streams to the host computer.

To read bytes from any input device, a hardware-dependent software primitive (e.g. 'sample_input(device, byte)') is needed, which samples the specified device and returns an integer value in the var parameter 'byte'. Sampling input means that the status of the input device is first checked to see if there is a character byte coming from the device. If there is no character available from the input device at the time of sampling then a negative number is returned in 'byte'. Otherwise 'byte' returns with the ASCII value of the character available from the input device. It is useful for the programmer to have access to this routine so that I/O errors such as disconnected devices can be detected and suitably handled. It is analogous to the 'send_output' routine.

A related routine is the request-input or wait-for-input routine which samples the input device until a character is available and then returns its ASCII value. This can be implemented as follows:

```
procedure read_input(device : device_names; var byte : integer);
{Read a character from the specified input device. Processing is
suspended until a character is available from the device.}
const
    max_tries = 1000;
var
    try : integer;
begin
    try := 0; {Initialize the count of read tries }
    while byte < 0 do
    repeat
        sample_input(device, byte);
        try := try + 1; {Count the sample tries}
    until (byte >= 0) or (try > max_tries);
    if byte < 0 then
        error('** Input device not ready **');
end;
```

This routine is analogous to the 'write_output' routine which holds up program execution until a byte has been successfully received by the output device. In reading the graphics input data from a digital plotter, Tektronix DVST, or any other similar on-line device in graphics input mode, the routine 'read_input' may be used rather than 'sample_input' since it is known that the device will return a specific stream of bytes. Two worked examples of this follow: first, graphics input from a digital plotter, and then, graphics input from a Tektronix 4010 DVST.

To enable a plotter to send graphics (dcx, dcy) coordinate data to the host computer, the host computer must send the plotter a special byte stream which is a command to the plotter for it to enter the 'graphics input mode'. Once in graphics input mode, the operator must press any of four arrow control buttons on the front of the plotter. The up arrow moves the plot pen carriage up the page, the down button moves it down, and similarly for the left and right arrow buttons. Some plotters allow the use in the pen holder of a small magnifying lens in the shape of a pen so that by looking closely at the plot page precise locations can be obtained. Once the user has located the plotter 'pen' at the exact point wanted on the plot page, the pressing of the send button (also located on the front of the plotter) causes the digital plotter to transmit a special byte stream to the host computer. Often this byte stream consists of a key ASCII character followed by the dcx

and *dcy* decimal values in ASCII character form separated by a comma and terminated by a carriage-return character. The host computer should be programmed to interpret this byte stream and extract the device coordinates (*dcx*, *dcx*) as a pair of binary integers.

In the case of two low-cost plotters, the Roland DXY-880 and the HP-7475, both respond to the same commands for graphics input, since to make the DXY-880 plotter compatible with a wider range of graphics software, Roland made it respond to the two-letter commands of the Hewlett-Packard Graphics Language (HP-GL) as well as the Roland plotter language. Three of the two-letter plotter commands are of interest here, namely the HP-GL commands that allow graphics input from the plotter to the host computer. If the following six characters are sent to the plotter:

    DP;OD;

then the *dcx* and *dcy* coordinates and pen status (up or down) will be sent to the host computer which should issue a read instruction to receive them. The coordinates are sent to the host as ASCII strings of digits. Notice that two HP-GL commands are necessary to obtain graphics input: the DP and OD commands, and that HP-GL commands are (normally) terminated by a semicolon. The DP command stands for digitize point, and puts the plotter into digitizing mode. In digitizing mode, the user can move the pen around the plot area by use of arrow keys on the front panel of the plotter. After the plotter pen has been moved to the desired location, the enter key (also on the front panel of the plotter) is pressed to signal the plotter to record the current position of the pen. The OD instruction tells the plotter to transmit the current contents of the register holding the digitized *x* and *y* coordinates and the pen status (0 = up and1 = down), with commas separating the parameters and terminated by the carriage-return character, as an ASCII string. If the software does not wait for the user to finish moving the pen before it sends the OD command to the plotter, then invalid data will be transmitted to the host. The host can tell when the user has finally pressed enter on the plotter by another HP-GL command called OS which outputs the plotter status information to the host. If the command:

    OS;

is sent to the plotter, the plotter responds by immediately transmitting the status byte to the host. Bit 2 (the third least significant bit) of the plotter's status byte tells whether a digitized point is available or not. (0 = not yet ready, 1 = ready.) Therefore the following routine can be used to get digitized point data from such a plotter:

```
procedure plotter_getpoint(var code, dcx, dcy : integer);
{Put the plotter into graphics input mode where the host will wait for the user
to set the pen position and then the plotter will transmit its device
coordinates to the host.}
const
    semicolon = 59;
var
    status,bit,terminator,pen : integer;
```

```
begin
    write_output(plotter, ord('D'));
    write_output(plotter, ord('P'));
    write_output(plotter, semicolon);
    repeat
        write_output(plotter, ord('O'));
        write_output(plotter, ord('S'));
        write_output(plotter, semicolon);
        read_input(plotter, status);
        read_input(plotter, terminator); {ignore carriage return}
        bit := (status div 4) mod 2;
    until bit <> 0;
    write_output(plotter, ord('O'));
    write_output(plotter, ord('D'));
    write_output(plotter, semicolon);
    read_integer(plotter, dcx, terminator);
    if chr(terminator) <> comma then error('Expected a comma');
    read_integer(plotter, dcy, terminator);
    if chr(terminator) <> comma then error('Expected a comma');
    read_integer(plotter, pen, terminator);
    if chr(terminator) <> cr then error('Expected a carriage return');
    code := pen; {output the pen status as the 'hit code'}
end;
```

The routine 'read_integer' interprets bytes received from the specified device as the digits making up an integer, and returns the integer value. A nondigit after the first digit is interpreted as a terminator of the digit and this character is returned too. The 'read_integer' routine is analogous to the 'write_integer' routine for outputs. It may be implemented as follows:

```
procedure read_integer(device : device_names;
        var value, terminator : integer);
{Wait for a string of digits to be entered. A nondigit signals the end of
the input integer.}
const
    space = 32; {ASCII code for a space character}
var
    digit_string : string[6];
    i : integer;
begin
    repeat {Skip leading blanks}
        read_input(byte);
    until byte <> space;
    i := 1;
    while char_type(byte) <> digit do
```

```
begin
    read_input(byte)
    while char_type(byte) = digit do
    begin
        digit_string[i] := chr(byte);
        i := i+1; if i>6 then error('Input number is too long');
        read_input(byte);
    end;
    terminator := byte;
    value := string_to_integer(digit_string);
end;
end;
```

The routines 'char_type' and 'string_to_integer' detect the ASCII character code type, and convert a six-character string to a digit respectively. The Pascal code for these routines is easily written (see Appendix A).

These routines demonstrate graphics input from a plotter. Graphics input from a Tektronix terminal is now considered.

The computer can use the Tektronix 4010 for graphics input as well as output. For the computer to obtain the location of the alpha (i.e. text) cursor it must send the escape sequence ESC,ENQ to the 4010. This command can equally well be given by the user manually from the keyboard. The Tektronix terminal responds to this escape sequence by sending:

status byte, high x , low x , high y , low y , cr, and EOT.

The status byte reports information such as whether the associated hard-copy unit is on, whether the text is currently using the center margin, and so forth. This mode of operation is demonstrated in the following routine which returns the current cursor location for the Tektronix 4010:

```
procedure tek4010_get_cursor_location(var x, y : integer);
{Use the Tektrix 4010s alpha cursor graphics input mode to obtain the cursor
position in device coordinates (x, y).}
const
    esc = 27; enq = 5; cr = 13; eot = 4; {ASCII codes}
var
    status,high_x,low_x,high_y,low_y : integer;
begin
    write_output(tek4010, esc); write_output(tek4010, enq);
    read_input(tek4010, status);
    read_input(tek4010, high_x); read_input(tek4010, low_x);
    read_input(tek4010, high_y); read_input(tek4010, low_y);
    read_input(tek4010, cr); read_input(tek4010, eot);
    high_x := high_x mod 32; low_x := low_x mod 32;
    x := 32*high_x + low_x;
```

```
        high_y := high_y mod 32; low_y := low_y mod 32;
        y := 32*high_y + low_y;
    end;
```

The cross-hairs cursor positioning submode places non-storing cross hairs on the Tektronix screen at the current beam position and allows the user to move the cross hairs to any desired point on the screen. The cross hairs consist of a vertical line from the top of the screen to its bottom, and a horizontal line from the left hand side of the screen to the right hand side. Where these two lines intersect is the point currently referred to. By rolling one thumb wheel on the keyboard, the vertical line can be shifted left or right. Another thumb wheel moves the horizontal line up or down. Once the cross hairs have been adjusted to indicate the desired point, the pressing of any other key on the keyboard (called a 'hit key') transmits the hit-key code and coordinates of the cross hairs to the host computer, disables the cross hairs, and returns to alpha mode. The following routine makes use of this graphics cursor position input mode of the Tektronix 4010 terminal:

```
procedure tek4010_getpoint(var hit_code, dcx, dcy : integer);
{Use the Tektronix 4010 cross hairs positioning graphics input mode to get
the device coordinates of a user selected point on the screen.}
const
    esc = 27; sub = 26; cr = 13; eot = 4; {ASCII codes}
var
    high_x,low_x,high_y,low_y : integer;
begin
    write_output(tek4010, esc); write_output(sub);
    read_input(tek4010, hit_code);
    read_input(tek4010, high_x); read_input(tek4010, low_x);
    read_input(tek4010, high_y); read_input(tek4010, low_y);
    read_input(tek4010, cr); read_input(tek4010, eot);
    high_x := high_x mod 32; low_x := low_x mod 32;
    dcx := 32*high_x + low_x;
    high_y := high_y mod 32; low_y := low_y mod 32;
    dcy := 32*high_y + low_y;
end;
```

The hit code is the ASCII code for the key that the user struck to exit from graphics input mode. It usually has special significance in the graphic software. For example, a hit code of ord('A') could indicate the first point to draw an arc from, or ord('P') could indicate the start of a polyline, and so forth. The meaning of the hit code is software dependent (i.e. programmable).

The current beam position in graphics output mode can also be obtained without the need for the user to strike a key by entering the current-beam-position graphics input mode which has a similar escape sequence and terminal response to the above two graphics input modes. The following routine inputs the CP using this mode:

```
procedure tek4010_get_cp(var dcx, dcy : integer);
```

```
const
    esc = 27; sub = 26; enq = 5; nul = 0; cr = 13; eot = 4; {ASCII codes}
var
    high_x,low_x,high_y,low_y : integer;
begin
    write_output(tek4010, esc); write_output(tek4010, sub);
    write_output(tek4010, esc); write_output(tek4010, enq);
    read_input(tek4010, high_x); read_input(tek4010, low_x);
    read_input(tek4010, high_y); read_input(tek4010, low_y);
    read_input(tek4010, cr); read_input(tek4010, eot);
    high_x := high_x mod 32; low_x := low_x mod 32;
    dcx := 32*high_x + low_x;
    high_y := high_y mod 32; low_y := low_y mod 32;
    dcy := 32*high_y + low_y;
end;
```

The general-purpose routine 'get_point(key, px, py)', for reading graphics input data from the currently selected input device, operates as follows. The routine waits for the device coordinates and a key code to be transmitted from the currently selected graphics input device to the host computer. The device coordinates are then transformed by 'inp_to_phys' for output as physical coordinates. The routine based on the two graphics input routines already shown is:

```
procedure get_point(var code : integer; var px, py : real);
{Wait for graphics input from a graphics device and return the 'hit code' in
key and the physical coordinates of the digitized point returned in (px, py).}
var
    dcx,dcy,pen,key : integer;
begin
    case cur_inp_dev of
        plotter:
        begin
            plotter_getpoint(pen, dcx, dcy);
            key := ord('D'); {any code would do, here D stands for Down};
            if pen = 1 then key := ord('U'); {and U stands for pen Up}
        end
        tek4010:
            tek4010_getpoint(key, dcx, dcy);
    end;
    inp_to_phys(dcx, dcy, px, py);
end;
```

Problems

2.1   Write machine code to draw a triangle with vertices at (400, 400), (600, 600), and (800, 400) in physical coordinates and label these vertexes A, B, and C respectively. Optimize the machine codes according to the rules given in Section 2.6.

2.2   Write optimized machine code to draw a labelled rectangle ABCD whose width is 100, height 50, with lower left corner at (80, 80) in physical units.

2.3   Write a procedure to input physical coordinates, convert them to byte values given xmin, xmax, ymin, and ymax, and output the codes to a Tektronix 4010 terminal as console device (i.e. via Pascal write statements). Use the physical-to-device coordinate transformation equations of Chapter 1 to implement 'phys_to_out'.

2.4   Write a program to draw a regular polygon (i.e. a polygon whose sides are all equal in length and whose internal angles are all equal) with radius equal to one third of the height of the screen and center at the center of the screen. The program should ask for n, the number of vertexes. Note that if polygons were drawn of fixed side length, as n increased they would soon be too big to display on the screen.

2.5   Modify the program in problem 2.4 to also ask for the radius r of the circle which encloses the regular polygon. Using your program, estimate the number n required to make the polygon look like a 'good enough' approximation to a circle for various radii values. Using the *ndh*, *ndv*, *width*, and *height* parameters for the device (see Table 1-1) obtain a theoretical relationship between n and r for approximating circles by polygons.

2.6   Modify the program in problem 2.4 to draw star shapes by asking for a second input l, the link to point number. If l = 1 then a regular polygon is drawn. If l = 2 then lines are drawn connecting every second vertex rather than every next vertex, and so forth. This can give rise to several polygons having to be drawn. For example, the case n = 6 and l = 2 gives the 'Star of David' which consists of two triangles. For n = 6 and l = 3, a star shape consisting of three line segments is formed. How many different shapes can be obtained in this manner for a given n ?

2.7   Construct a compilation unit called 'dev_driver' for each graphics device on your system (where 'dev' is replaced by an abbreviation for each device). If no devices are available, use the devices described in this chapter, that is, the plotter and tek4010, and make the compilation units 'plotter_driver' and 'tek4010_driver'. Each device driver compilation unit is to provide the following four basic functions:

```
dev_clear
dev_move_to(dcx, dcy : integer);
dev_draw_to(dcx, dcy : integer);
dev_getpoint(var k : char; var dcx, dcy : integer);
```

Note that clearing the Tektronix 4010 is achieved by sending the ASCII characters ESC,FF. The nearest equivalent for a plotter is to send the print head to its home position. This is achieved by sending the letter H and then a new line to the plotter. The four characteristic numbers of each device should be global values exported from each device-driver compilation unit. The data type is called 'device' as in Chapter 1. Thus 'tek4010_driver' exports a record 'tek4010' with components:

```
tek4010.ndh := 1024; tek4010.ndv := 781;
tek4010.width := 188.5; tek4010.height := 138.5
```

and so forth.

2.8   Write a compilation unit called 'g2d_driver' which combines all device drivers from question 2.7 with a physical coordinate user interface. The graphics routines provided in this compilation unit are:

```
clear;
move_to(px, py : real);
draw_to(px, py : real);
get_point(var k : char; var px, py : real);
```

The following procedures should also be supplied in this compilation unit:

```
select_input_device(dev : device_names);
select_output_device(dev : device_names);
```

as discussed in Chapter 1. The following procedures should be internal to the 'g2d_driver' compilation unit:

```
inp_to_phys(dcx, dcy : integer; var px, py : real);
phys_to_out(px, py : real; var dcx, dcy : integer);
```

as discussed in Chapter 1. This compilation unit forms the basis of G2D, the two-dimensional graphics package described in the following chapters up to Chapter 8.

2.9   Given a graphics device-driver compilation unit for some microcomputer-based graphics VDU called 'vdu_driver' with all the functions and external data values as discussed in problem 2.7, write a Tektronix 4010 emulator. This is a program that receives bytes from the serial communications port and interprets them the way a Tektronix 4010 terminal does. In this first version of a Tektronix emulator, aim at only emulating the alpha mode, move-to and draw-to. (This alpha mode emulation need not allow text characters to be written at the CP.) When a 1D hex byte is received the emulator program should read in the next four bytes, interpret them as a Tektronix 4010 device coordinate address, convert them to the VDU's device coordinates and execute a move-to. Subsequent sets of four bytes are similarly interpreted and cause the program to execute a draw-to until a 1F hex byte is received. After a 1F hex byte is received, all subsequent bytes are echoed as text to the VDU screen until the next 1D hex byte is received.

2.10 Extend the Tektronix 4010 terminal emulation program of the previous problem in the following ways. Firstly, have it correctly respond to the Tektronix 'clear the screen' escape sequence. Secondly allow text characters to be drawn in graphics at the most recent CP. Thirdly implement the graphics input mode so that it sends the typical Tektronix escape sequence back to the host. Fourthly allow the emulator to recognize optimized machine codes where coordinates can be expressed in fewer than the usual four bytes. Fifthly respond to a hard-copy escape sequence by implementing a screen dump routine (see Chapter 3).

3

Dot oriented graphics equipment

3.1 Bit image graphics printers

In contrast to the uniform smooth lines produced by line graphics equipment, dot graphics equipment may produce chunky, jagged, or staircase lines of varying width depending on the direction of the line. Where a digital plotter can draw a straight line between two finite grid points, the dot-oriented printer can only place dots at a finite number of grid points and builds lines by the close placement of a linear sequence of dots.

An example of a dot graphics hard-copy device is one of the low-cost Epson 160 characters per second (cps) series of printers with 'bit image graphics'. This is a dot matrix printer whose print-head has nine pins in a vertical column. Each pin can be individually switched on and off up to 1920 times as the print-head sweeps across the paper. An example of an expensive dot graphics hard-copy device is the FACIT 4544 color printer.

In order for any of these printers to print graphics patterns in dots rather than the normal printing function of text characters, they must first be put into bit-image mode. This is done by a special escape sequence that may vary with different printers. The graphics output pixel data must then be coded into bytes and sent to the printer.

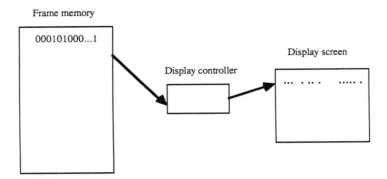

Figure 3-1 A row of bits in frame memory is converted to a row of dots on the display screen.

3.2 **Raster graphics VDUs**

The most popular method for graphics display today takes advantage of there being literally hundreds of millions of TVs in the world. The black-and-white TV has been used as an alphanumeric terminal for a long time and with a little modification (mainly the addition of pixel memory – Figure 3-1) it can be readily extended to serve as a graphics output display device. To make a simple graphics terminal requires only:

1. a digital (pixel) memory or frame buffer in which the displayed image is stored as a matrix of intensity values;
2. a TV without tuning and receiving electronics (or else these are by-passed and the video output signal is fed directly to the TV's video amplifier); and
3. a simple interface called the display controller that passes the contents of the frame buffer (converting it to the appropriate video output signal) to the monitor. The image must be passed repeatedly to the TV monitor at least 15 times a second in order to maintain a steady picture on the screen and reduce screen flicker.

All TVs rely on a technique called raster scanning. In raster scanning the CRT beam is deflected in a weaving pattern that sweeps across, and gradually works its way down, the screen many times per second. (See Figure 3-2). This pattern for generating a display on the screen is called a *raster*.

A TV broadcasting station sends a signal to the TV that contains audio and video information plus synchronizing (sync) pulses (Figure 3-3). Circuits in the TV use the sync pulses to get in step with the transmitted signal. There are horizontal sync pulses for starting the horizontal sweep of the beam and vertical sync pulses for starting the vertical retrace. In between the horizontal sync pulses is the video information for that line. The video image that is displayed between sequential vertical sync pulses is called a *field*. On a TV the image can appear to be animated because it consists of many still *frames* displayed rapidly one after the other. TV sets use *interlacing* in displaying pictures. This means that the scan lines displayed in one field are only the even line numbers and in the next field

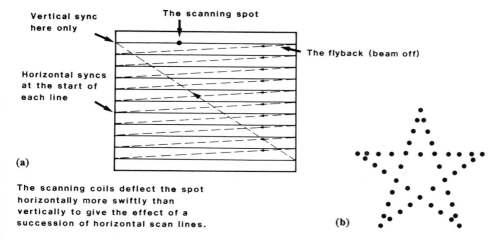

(a)

The scanning coils deflect the spot
horizontally more swiftly than
vertically to give the effect of a
succession of horizontal scan lines.

(b)

Figure 3-2 Raster scanning. (a) The raster scanned CRT. The electron beam (scanning spot) zig-zags down the screen drawing dots (pixels) during horizontal sweeps from left to right. (b) A star shape made from 5 straight line segments is represented on a raster CRT by dots at the closest available positions.

are the odd line numbers. A pair of fields one after the other therefore make one frame of the picture. Many raster graphics VDUs have this interlace mode of operation: it allows double the vertical resolution for the same scan rate. However, interlace mode means that the frame rate is half the field display rate, and this may cause the picture to flicker. When a VDU operates in *noninterlaced mode* each field uses all scan lines, and the frame rate

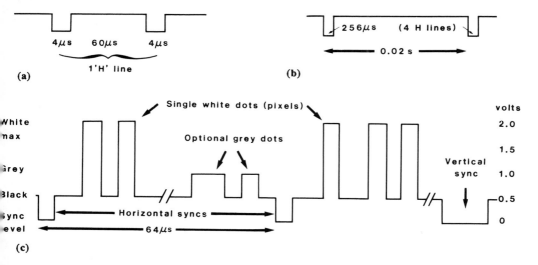

Figure 3-3 Monochrome raster CRT video signals. (a) The horizontal synchronization pulses. (b) The vertical sync pulses. (c) The composite video signal for a monochrome raster CRT combines horizontal and vertical sync pulses and pixel intensity pulses.

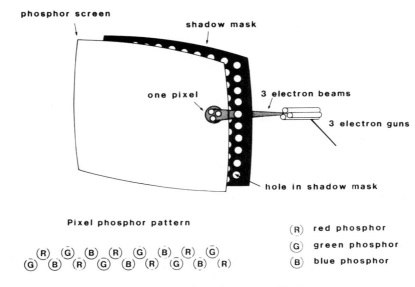

Figure 3-4 Schematic representation of a color raster CRT.

equals the field rate, giving flicker-free animation. The refresh rate for raster VDUs is the time to draw all scan lines and hence is equal to the frame rate.

In the case of black-and-white TV transmission, the video information on a line is an analog signal to allow an almost infinite variety of grey shades on the TV screen. However to make up a single horizontal line of pixels (pels, picture elements or picture dots) on the display screen of a computer terminal, this video information can also be in the form of pulses. If there is one bit of frame memory per pixel on the screen, then the pixel can only be in one of two states: on or off. This *bilevel* display is sufficient for simple graphics and alphanumeric terminals. For more advanced graphics output, however, it is necessary to have more than one bit per pixel so that the pixels can be displayed in a range of intensity levels. For example, if the frame memory stores eight bits per pixel, then each pixel has 256 possible intensity levels from off (black) through greys to white (full on). The number of bits assigned to each pixel by the frame memory is called the pixel depth of the graphics terminal.

Figure 3-3 shows the composite video signal input to a black-and-white TV for use as a computer VDU. Most of the time the beam is off. If the computer is properly synchronized to the sweeping beam, it can turn the beam on at any point in the display's *x* -*y* plane and there form a dot (or pixel). The raster-scanned VDU can be thought of as a dense matrix of pixels refreshed rapidly that corresponds to certain bits in the frame buffer and if so, the screen is *memory mapped*.

Raster scanning technology eliminates the need for expensive analog circuitry. However it means that all the dots that make up a shape must be stored, rather than just the end points of vectors as in vector graphics – raster graphics requires much more frame memory. The price of digital memory is nearly halving every year so that raster graphics with very high resolution is becoming cheaper and more accessible.

Since raster graphics displays color better than vector graphics, the raster technique is today the more popular method for color graphics VDUs (a color monitor like a color TV is used). In monochrome monitors, the whole surface of the screen is uniformly coated with the same type of phosphor and the electron beam can be aimed at any point on the screen by analog x - y voltages. In contrast to this, the pixels on the screen of a color monitor or color TV are a triad of three phosphors that produce the red, green, and blue colors; and instead of one electron gun there are three (see Figure 3-4), each assigned to one color of phosphor. Between the phosphor-dotted screen surface and the electron guns is a metal barrier, called the *shadow mask*, that with a hole at the right location behind each pixel ensures that the electron guns cannot fire at the wrong color phosphor. (Now red, green, and blue are the primary colors for color addition; that is, by adding the separate intensities of the red, green, and blue lights, nearly all the colors that the human eye can perceive may be imitated. Recall that when two different colored lights shine on a surface, the colors add together. If dyes of different colors are mixed, color subtraction is performed. The primary colors for color subtraction - red, green, and yellow (used in color printers) – are different from those for color addition.) By varying the intensity of each electron beam, which varies the intensity of the glow of the phosphors, visually different colors are formed. Like the single electron gun in a monochrome monitor, each electron gun in a color monitor (also called an RGB monitor) has an assigned number of bits in the frame memory of the graphics terminal that determines the intensities of the red, green, and blue (RGB) phosphors. With one bit plane per gun (and hence three bits of graphics display RAM per pixel), eight colors are possible as shown in Table 3-1. The number of bit planes is also known as *pixel depth*.

With p bit planes per gun, 2^{3p} colors are possible. Some graphics terminals have four bit planes where the first three give R, G, and B bit values as in the above table, and the fourth bit plane is for the brightness or total intensity of the displayed color. This results in $2^4 = 16$ possible colors for every pixel. When a bit from this fourth bit plane is zero, the eight colors in Table 3-1 are produced. When the brightness bit equals one another eight colors are displayed (bright versions of the colors in Table 3-1). (Note that 'bright black' should be a grey color although some graphics terminals leave all guns off in this case too which means that only 14 true colors are displayable.) Other systems have different numbers of bit planes with different meanings for the bit planes.

Table 3-1 Three bit RGB colors.

| Electron Gun Values | | | Binary | Color |
R	G	B	value	name
0	0	0	0	black
0	0	1	1	blue
0	1	0	2	green
0	1	1	3	cyan (ie turquoise)
1	0	0	4	red
1	0	1	5	magenta (ie purple)
1	1	0	6	yellow
1	1	1	7	white

If a typical color TV is measured, figures similar to the following are obtained: width 42 cm, height 31 cm (providing an aspect ratio of roughly .75), with 546 pixels horizontally and 434 pixels vertically. This results in a pixel aspect ratio close to unity; that is, the tube has nearly square pixels.

It is interesting to compare the resolution of a typical color TV with a high-resolution color graphics terminal. Although the graphics terminal usually has thousands more pixels than the TV, TV quality pictures cannot be produced on the graphics terminal. The reason is that the computer supplies each electron gun with only a limited discrete set of voltage levels whereas the TV signal provides a smooth analog (infinite) range of voltages. When only a small discrete range of colors are available per pixel and the resolution is low (so that individual pixels are discernible as for a TV) then straight lines other than horizontal and vertical lines can appear jagged, like a staircase. This effect is called *aliasing* because a true straight line is alternatively represented as a jagged line (its 'alias'). In the case of a TV, the smooth range of signals to the electron guns allow neighbouring pixels to blur the edges of straight lines and then the eye ignores the blurring and identifies perfectly straight edges without a strong appearance of jaggedness that only a discrete range of pixel colors would cause. Thus because of the large number of possible colors for a TV a blurring effect can be displayed to overcome the sharp changes in color from one pixel to another.

The straight-line-drawing algorithms given in Section 3.4 all set selected pixels to the same pixel value even though not all of these pixels are 100 percent centered on the true line. This causes the staircase-effect of the line's alias. The above consideration of how a TV displays a straight line in the same raster grid size shows a method that can be used to overcome line aliasing. By using sampling theory, the proportion of a line of given thickness that occupies each graphics grid cell (pixel location) can be estimated and then if each pixel involved is set to an average of the line color and the background color in this proportion (different for every pixel) then the line will actually be represented as blurred. From a distance the eye accepts and corrects this visual information and recognizes a straight line. This technique is called *antialiasing* since it removes the effect of the aliased line. For this effect to work there must be a sufficient number of shades between the foreground line color and the background color per pixel. The antialiasing algorithm can be implemented by the user in software and on some graphics terminals it is provided in the hardware routine for line drawing.

If D is the pixel depth, then the actual number of colors displayable at one time on a color raster graphics VDU is 2^D. However the total number of different colors displayable (known as the *palette range*) can be much more than this. By using the pixel value from the graphics RAM as an index into a color look-up table rather than as a color, a much larger selection of colors becomes available. A *palette* or *logical color* is one of the possible pixel values. Thus there are 2^D palettes or logical colors and they are called palette 0 through to palette number $2^D - 1$. Each palette is an index into a hardware color look-up table (CLUT). The user's software can write selected physical color values into the color look-up table entries to correspond to a palette (or logical colour). The color table is a fixed area of RAM with 2^D entries often 24 bits wide: eight bits for each gun so that each electron gun can have any of 256 intensity levels. This makes 16 million possible colors to choose from, but only 2^D are simultaneously displayable on the screen. The palette range is then said to be 16 million.

3.3 Software primitives for dot oriented graphics

It will be assumed that the graphics system used has an intrinsic function for plotting at a given (*dcx*, *dcy*) point. In the most general case, this function has the form:

    write_pixel(frame_nr,dcx,dcy,pixel_value : integer)

The 'frame_nr' parameter is the number of the frame RAM. A frame RAM is the graphics display RAM used to store the pixel information for one screen of graphics. Many raster graphics systems cater for multiple frame RAMs. They can be used in graphics animation applications: while one frame is being displayed on the screen, the computer is entering graphics data into the next frame RAM.

Since raster graphics has a read-write graphics RAM area, the converse primitive should also be available:

    read_pixel(frame nr,dcx,dcy : integer; var pixel_value : integer)

Often it will be assumed that there are no alternative frames, and the primitives will be used as 'write_pixel(dcx,dcy,pixel_value)', and 'read_pixel(dcx,dcy,pixel_value)'. Additionally, the programmer needs access to the hardware color look-up table. This is provided by the following two primitives:

    write_CLUT(pixel_value,R,G,B : integer)
    read_CLUT(pixel_value : integer; var R,G,B : integer)

From these four raster graphics primitives it should be possible to build up all necessary graphics commands. Examples of doing this are shown throughout this book.

For a lot of useful computer graphics color, shading, or alternative screen frames are not needed. Also, there may be no CLUT, or else it is initialized to the colors wanted and the programmer may not need to vary them. In these circumstances, the raster graphics primitives may be reduced simply two routines:

    dot_on(dcx,dcy)

and:

    dot_off(dcx,dcy)

which are special cases of the first primitive above. These routines set the pixel, addressed by device coordinates *dcx* and *dcy*, on and off respectively. Although these subroutines use screen coordinates (*dcx*, *dcy*) to address the dots, higher level routines would call the viewing transformation to convert user coordinate values to screen dots.

3.4 Line-drawing algorithms

One of the most basic geometric elements to be drawn on a graphics terminal is a line segment. Usually nowadays, line-drawing routines are provided in the hardware by graphics controller chips. The chip is given the end-points' pixel addresses and works out which pixels to set in between. This process of converting vector graphics end point data to raster information is called *rasterizing*. Meanwhile the host processor can continue with other computations. Complicated graphics drawing requires a large number of line segments to be drawn and speed is important. The hardware solution via a graphics controller chip provides the fastest possible line-drawing method. When this function is not available as a hardware command and has to be implemented in software, ideally the routine should be written in efficient machine code for maximum speed. However it is instructive to look at some algorithms for line drawing presented in a high-level language to gain an appreciation of the programming steps required and to show how the approaches to drawing of any given mathematical curve may be generalized. Mathematical curve drawing is considered in more detail in Chapter 4.

One method of forming a raster graphics plot is to compute *all* the coordinates of the pixels to be plotted, store them, and finally plot the points. This approach may be applicable to plotting on a bit-image graphics printer but it is not necessary in raster screen plotting – it can use up too much memory (main memory not screen refresh memory). Instead incremental computing techniques can be used. These are a form of iterative computation in which each iterative step is simplified by maintaining a small amount of state or memory about the progress of the computation. Starting at one end of a line and using this technique, the next point is computed and plotted in a loop until the other end of the line is plotted. Before some incremental line-drawing algorithms are considered, a few general points must be raised.

Newman and Sproull (1979, p. 21) have identified the following requirements for acceptable raster line-drawing algorithms :

1. Lines should appear to be straight. Point plotting techniques are fine for lines parallel or at 45 degrees to the x or y axes. Other oblique lines raise difficulties in choosing which pixels to set.
2. Lines should terminate accurately. Small gaps at the end of one line segment and the start of the next have a bad appearance. Some algorithms cause this gap to grow cummulatively. This problem is call 'end-point paranoia'.
3. Lines should have constant density. The line density is the number of dots displayed per unit length of line.
4. Line density should be independent of line length and angle.
5. Lines should be drawn rapidly.

Essentially the problem is to fit a curve, in this case a straight line, which is accurately defined by *real* coordinates, to a lattice or grid of *integer* coordinate values. This can be done by following the line in its real coordinates and placing the pixels at the nearest grid point (dcx, dcy) by rounding or truncating the real coordinate values (x, y) to integers. Any line-drawing algorithm can be tested in respect to each of the five requirements previously stated. For requirement 1, the sum of the squares of the deviations of each pixel (dcx, dcy) from the true line positions (x, y) can be calculated. The best line algorithm will have the smallest total deviation. Requirement 2 is only of concern when the line's end-points are specified in user coordinates. For requirement 3, the number of pixels turned on are counted and divided by the length of the line. Requirements 4 and 5 can only be determined by running several benchmark tests on each algorithm.

The simple digital differential analyser (DDA) algorithm

The DDA is a general algorithm that generates a curve from its differential equation. In this algorithm, the derivative is approximated by the ratio of a small change Δy of the y values to a small change Δx of the x values. If one of Δy or Δx is known, the other can be computed, and these are then used as increments in the x and y directions to locate the next pixel to be set. In the case of a straight line, the differential equation is trivial:

$$dy \, / \, dx = m \; = \Delta y \, / \, \Delta x$$

where the slope m is a given constant. If the line to be drawn is from the point ($dcx1$, $dcy1$) to the point ($dcx2$, $dcy2$) in device coordinates then the slope is the real number:

$$m \; = (dcy2 - dcy1) \, / \, (dcx2 - dcx1)$$

and hence the increments in x and y are related by:

$$\Delta y \; * \; (dcx2 - dcx1) = \Delta x \; * \; (dcy2 - dcy1) \qquad (3.1)$$

Using the real variables x and y to represent true points on the line, the algorithm starts with the initial values $x = dcx1$, and $y = dcy1$. These coordinates are rounded to integers and a pixel is set at the resulting device coordinate position. The real coordinates are then incremented by Δx and Δy respectively to find the next device coordinate location for the next pixel. If the projection of the line along the x axis, the absolute value of $dcx2 - dcx1$, is greater than or equal to the projection of the line along the y axis, the absolute value of $dcy2 - dcy1$, then Δx is chosen to be plus or minus one depending on whether $dcx2 - dcx1$ is positive or negative and Δy is computed from equation 3.1. If the x axis projection is less than the y axis projection then Δy is taken as plus or minus one depending on the sign of $dcy2 - dcy1$ and Δx is computed from equation 3.1. In either case the new true coordinates are rounded to integers and a pixel is set at that point. This step is repeated until the second end point ($dcx2$, $dcy2$) is reached. A procedure that performs this algorithm is shown in Box 3-1.

An alternative to rounding is truncation. This is obtained by replacing the 'round' functions in Box 3-1 with 'trunc' functions. The result is a different set of pixels are set to represent the same line.

This algorithm can be modified for implementation in machine code on a processor without hardware division instructions by replacing 'nr_pixels' by the nearest power of 2. Higher precision integer numbers can be used rather than real numbers. Division by

Box 3-1 Straight line algorithm #1.

```
procedure raster_line_1(dcx1, dcy1, dcx2, dcy2 : integer);
{Algorithm #1 to draw a straight line segment from the point (dcx1,dcy1) to the
point (dcx2,dcy2) in device coordinates.}
var
    i,dcx,dcy,nr_pixels : integer;
    len,x,y,delta_x,delta_y : real;
begin
    {determine the maximum pixel length of the line :}
    nr_pixels := abs(dcx2-dcx1);
    if abs(dcy2-dcy1) > nr_pixels then nr_pixels := abs(dcy2-dcy1);
    {set up the differential increments :}
    delta_x := (dcx2-dcx1)/nr_pixels;
    delta_y := (dcy2-dcy1)/nr_pixels;
    {initialize the real variables along the line segment :}
    x := dcx1; y := dcy1;
    for i := 1 to nr_pixels do
    begin
        dcx := round(x); dcy := round(y);
        dot_on(dcx,dcy);
        x := x + delta_x; y := y + delta_y;
    end;
end;
```

'nr_pixels' is then rapidly done by right shifting by the appropriate number of bits. This is called the symmetrical DDA algorithm (Newman & Sproull, 1979, p. 22) and it produces lines as acceptable as the simple DDA algorithm though different dots are turned on. The symmetrical DDA generates accurate lines since the displacement of a displayed dot from the true line is never greater than one half a screen unit. (See Figure 3-5.)

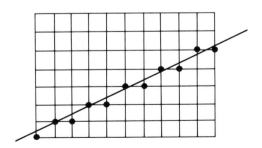

Figure 3-5 The significance of the error term 'err' in the symmetrical DDA.

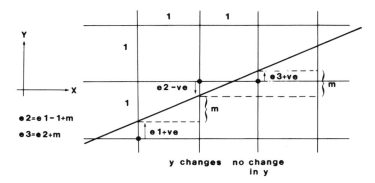

Figure 3-6 The significance of the error term 'err' in the Bresenham algorithm.

Bresenham's algorithm

Like the DDA algorithms, each iteration in Bresenham's algorithm changes one of the coordinate values by ±1 but the other coordinate may or may not change depending on the value of an error term maintained by the algorithm. The error term is the distance measured perpendicular to the axis of greatest movement between the exact path of the line and the actual dots generated. This is illustrated in Figure 3-6. Assume for simplicity that the slope of the line is m with:

$$0.25 < m \ < 0.5$$

and end-point 1 has $dcx1 < dcx2$. First a dot is placed at (dcx, dcy) where $dcx = dcx1$ and $dcy = dcy1$. This is the exact end-point so there is no error in placing this point. Now move along the x axis to the next vertical grid line; that is, the line $dcx = dcx1 + 1$. The true y coordinate here is $dcy1 + m$ and this is closer to $dcy1$ than to $dcy1 + 1$, so for the second pixel select the point (dcx, dcy) where $dcx = dcx1 +1$ and $dcy = dcy1$. The error in this pixel is the true y value minus the approximate y value which is $err = m$. Moving along the x axis to the next vertical grid line gives $dcx = dcx1 +2$ and the true y coordinate is now $dcy1 + 2m$. Since $2m > 0.5$ (as seen in Figure 3-6), the next y grid line gives the closer y coordinate value. So for the third pixel select the coordinate $dcy = dcy1 +1$. The error in y is again computed as the true y value minus the approximate value used which gives $err = 2m - 1$. This process is continued until the other end point is reached. At each new dcx value a new error is computed by adding m to the last error value; and if the result is greater than a half, the y coordinate is bumped up which takes 1 from the error term. This algorithm can be expressed simply as shown in Box 3-2.

Note: this routine (and also 'raster_line_1') will not perform correctly for all lines. It assumes that $dcx1 < dcx2$ and $dcy1 < dcy2$. These exception cases can be covered by introducing x and y increment variables as in Box 3-3.

For fast machine-code implementation, floating-point variables and operations and in particular divisions should be avoided. In 'raster_line_3' (Box 3-3), there are two floating-point variables: 'slope' and 'err'. It is possible to convert these to integer equivalents by multiplying through by 2*'x_change'. The factor of 2 eliminates the need for a floating-point comparison with 0.5. It is also preferable for integer comparisons to be made

Box 3-2 Straight line algorithm #2.

```
procedure raster_line_2(dcx1, dcy1, dcx2, dcy2 : integer);
{Simple algorithm to draw a raster line from (dcx1,dcy1) to (dcx2,dcy2).}
var
    dcx, dcy, x_change, y_change : integer;
    err, slope : real;
begin
    dcx := dcx1; dcy := dcy1;
    x_change := dcx2 - dcx1; y_change := dcy2 - dcy1;
    slope := y_change / x_change; err := 0.0;
    for dcx := dcx1 to dcx2 do
    begin
        dot_on(dcx,dcy);
        if err > 0.5 then
        begin
            dcy := dcy + 1 ; err := err - 1.0 ;
        end;
        err := err + slope;
    end;
end;
```

Box 3-3 Straight line algorithm #3.

```
procedure raster_line_3(dcx1, dcy1, dcx2, dcy2 : integer);
{Algorithm to draw a raster line from (dcx1,dcy1) to (dcx2,dcy2) in
device coordinates.}
var
        i, dcx, dcy, x_change, y_change : integer;
        err, slope : real;
begin
    dcx := dcx1; dcy := dcy1;
    x_change := dcx2 - dcx1; y_change := dcy2 - dcy1;
    x_increment :=1; if x_change < 0 then x_increment := -1;
    y_increment :=1; if y_change < 0 then y_increment := -1;
    slope := y_change / x_change; err := 0.0;
    for i := 1 to abs(x_change) do
    begin
        dot_on(dcx,dcy);
        if err*y_increment > 0.5 then
        begin
            dcy := dcy + y_increment ; err := err - y_increment ;
        end;
```

```
        err := err + slope*x_increment;
        dcx := dcx + x_increment;
    end;
end;
```

against zero rather than any other integer value and so this constant should be removed from the error variable by another change of variables. After changing to these integer variables, an improved version is obtained which is Bresenham's algorithm. It is shown in Box 3-4.

This algorithm can be improved further by first finding whether to compute along the *x* axis as done in Box 3-4, or along the *y* axis in a similar manner. It should also catch the case where 'x change' or 'y change' is zero.

Box 3-4 Straight line algorithm #4.

```
procedure raster_line_4(dcx1, dcy1, dcx2, dcy2 : integer);
{Bresenham's algorithm to draw a raster line from (dcx1,dcy1) to (dcx2,dcy2).}
var
    i, dcx, dcy, x_change, y_change, integer_err ,n,m: integer;
begin
    dcx := dcx1; dcy := dcy1;
    x_change := dcx2 - dcx1; y_change := dcy2 - dcy1;
    x_increment :=1; if x_change < 0 then x_increment := -1;
    y_increment :=1; if y_change < 0 then y_increment := -1;
    n := abs(x_change); m := abs(y_change);
    if (n > m) then
    begin
        integer_err := (2*y_change - x_change)*x_increment;
        for i := 1 to n do
        begin
            dot_on(dcx,dcy);
            if integer_err > 0 then
            begin
                dcy := dcy + y_increment ;
                integer_err := integer_err - 2*x_change*x_increment ;
            end;
            integer_err := integer_err + 2*y_change*x_increment;
            dcx := dcx + x_increment;
        end;
    end
    else
```

```
begin
    integer_err := (2*x_change - y_change)*y_increment;
    for i := 1 to m do
    begin
        dot_on(dcx,dcy);
        if integer_err > 0 then
        begin
            dcx := dcx + x_increment ;
            integer_err := integer_err - 2*y_change*y_increment ;
        end;
        integer_err := integer_err + 2*x_change*y_increment;
        dcy := dcy + y_increment;
    end;
end;
end;
```

3.5 Vector graphics on raster hardware

Straight line segments (i.e. vector graphics) are used a great deal in computer-generated pictures, for example, block diagrams, bar charts, engineering drawings, logic schematics, architectural plans, and so forth. Raster graphics, though, is more flexible and all vector graphics type output can be achieved on raster graphics VDUs by using lines made up of closely placed pixels.

In the past there has been considerable investment in the then more popular vector graphics terminals. This software should continue to be available on more modern graphics terminals. Many modern raster graphics terminals have Tektronix emulation modes so that vector graphics software packages originally designed for Tektronix terminals will also function on these newer terminals. (See also the Tektronix emulator program of problem 2.10.) Many concepts from vector graphics such as the CP and the display file are important to understanding the design of graphics software packages (these are discussed further in Chapter 5) have continued to be used by computer graphics developers and incorporated into graphics standards. For all these reasons there is a need to be able to simulate vector graphics on raster hardware.

To implement vector graphics software on a raster graphics VDU, the vector graphics primitives, 'move_to' and 'draw_to', must be implemented via the raster graphics primitives 'dot_on' and 'dot_off'. Satisfactory simulation of vector graphics output is not always achieved by raster graphics equipment. In particular the lines have visible steps even at the best resolutions, and the lines are not uniformly thick for every slope. A hardware technique, mentioned earlier, called antialiasing has been used to smooth lines on raster screens. (See also Foley & Van Dam, 1982, p. 436.) This is achieved by allowing variable intensity on neighboring pixels to blur out the sharp edges of angled lines.

The raster algorithm for 'move_to' requires no calls to the raster graphics primitives and simply updates the current beam position. The current beam position must be a data structure that is global to the primitives to be simulated (as in Section 2.4):

```
type pen_conditions = (up,down);
var cp = record {Define the current position as a global data structure}
     x,y : integer; { device coordinates are integers}
     pen_status : pen_conditions;
     end;

procedure init_cp;
{Initializes the data in the cp data structure. This simulates switching
on the vector graphics terminal.}
begin
     cp.x := 0;
     cp.y := 0;
     cp.pen_status := up;
end;

procedure move_to(dcx, dcy : integer);
{Routine to implement the vector graphics primitive function to move to a
point on a raster graphics VDU. (dcx,dcy) = point to move to in device
coordinates.}
begin
     cp.x := dcx;
     cp.y := dcy;
     cp.pen_status := up;
end;
```

The algorithm used to make 'draw_to' requires a raster line-drawing routine 'raster_line' which calls 'dot_on'. Several algorithms for a 'raster_line' routine have already been discussed.

```
procedure draw_to(dcx, dcy : integer);
{Routine to implement the vector graphics primitive function of drawing a line
to a point (dcx,dcy) in device coordinates ('rasters') on a raster VDU.}
var
     x1,y1,x2,y2 : integer;
begin
     {set up the endpoints of the line to be drawn :}
     x1 := cp.x;
     y1 := cp.y;
     x2 := dcx;
     y2 := dcy;
     {use a suitable algorithm for drawing the line segment ;}
     raster line(x1,y1,x2,y2);
```

```
      {update the current beam position :}
      cp.x := dcx;
      cp.y := dcy;
      cp.pen_status := down;
   end;
```

3.6 Screen dump routines

To 'dump' the raster screen to a printer means obtaining a hard copy of the image currently on the screen. This requires that all the pixel values currently set on the screen must be read and converted to the format needed to set the dot-matrix printer's pins and then this information is transmitted to the printer for line after line of dots until the whole screen is done. The printer must first be set into bit-image mode with the right dot density corresponding to the resolution of the screen. In the case of the Apple Imagewriter printer, dumping a raster screen with resolution 512 x 342, the following escape sequences should be sent:

1. ESC c (to reset the printer to its default status; for example switch off underlining and
   double-width characters, and so forth);
2. ESC n (to set the horizontal dot density to 0.28 dots per mm, that is,. 72 dots per inch);
3. ESC T 1 6 (to set the vertical dot density to 0.28 dots per mm, that is,. 72 dots per inch).

While it would be possible to implement a routine 'printer_dot_on(dcx,dcy)' for the Imagewriter, printing graphics one dot at a time is not the most efficient usage of the hardware. There are eight pins on the Imagewriter print head and so a column of eight pixels can be printed at a time. The screen dump routine should therefore read pixels from top to bottom of the raster screen in rows of eight pixels. The following escape sequence sends the pixel data for a whole row to the Imagewriter in graphics mode:

$$\text{ESC G 5 1 2 } B_1 \ B_2 \ B_3 \ ... \ B_{512} \text{ cr lf}$$

where B_1, B_2, and so forth are the byte values calculated for the first column of eight pixels, the second column, etc. The topmost pixel in each column of eight pixels is bit zero of each B_i and the bottom most pixel is bit seven in each B_i. The routine shown in Box 3-5 performs this function.

Note that this algorithm prints a dot for every pixel on the screen whose pixel value is nonzero. This part of the algorithm could be easily changed to print the 'negative' of the screen image. Alternatively, the screen printing routine could select a specific color only for printing. Using colored ink ribbons in the printer enables colored hard-copies to be printed by printing the same screen several times - once for each subtractive primary ink color.

Box 3-5 Graphics screen printouts.

```
procedure screen_dump(frame_nr : integer);
{ Read a raster screen which has resolution 512 x 342, convert the pixels to pin
values and send to the Apple Imagewriter printer.}
const
    nr_dots_horiz = 512;
    nr_dots_vert = 342;
    lf = 10; cr = 13; esc = 27;
var
    i,row,max_row,dcx,dcy,byte,value : integer;
    int_string : string[6];

    procedure set_up_the_printer;
        {Put it into graphics bit image mode with 72 dots per inch both
        horizontally and vertically.}
    begin
        {Software reset : initialize the printer to its defaults :}
        write_output(printer,esc); write_output(printer,ord('c'));
        {Set 9 characters (= 8 bits wide) per inch (horizontally) :}
        write_output(printer,esc); write_output(printer,ord('n'));
        {Set vertical line spacing to 16 * 1/144 ths = 1/9 inch}
        {so that each character (8 bits high) makes 72 dots per inch}
        {vertically :}
        write_output(printer,esc); write_output(printer,ord('T'));
        write_output(printer,ord('1')); write_output(printer,ord('6'));
    end;

    procedure print_graphics_header;
    {Send the start of graphics data header for each row, ie :}
    {    ESC G 512}
    var
        i : integer;
    begin
        {Escape sequence to set the next print line as 'G'raphics bytes}
        {rather than ASCII character bytes :}
        write_output(printer,esc); write_output(printer,ord('G'));
        for i := 1 to 4 do
        begin
            byte := ord(int_string[i+2]);
            write_output(printer,byte);
        end;
    end;
```

```
begin
    set_up_the_printer;
    int_string := integer_to_string(nr_dots_horiz);
    max_row := nr_dots_vert div 8;
    if nr_dots_vert mod 8 > 0 then max_row := max_row + 1;
    for row := 1 to max_row do
    begin
        print_graphics_header;
        dcy := (max_row-row+1)*8 - 1;
        for dcx :=0 to nr_dots_horiz-1 do
        begin
            byte := 0;
            read_pixel(frame_nr,dcx,dcy,value);
            if value>0 then byte := 1;
            read_pixel(frame_nr,dcx,dcy-1,value);
            if value>0 then byte := byte +2;
            read_pixel(frame_nr,dcx,dcy-2,value);
            if value>0 then byte := byte + 4;
            read_pixel(frame_nr,dcx,dcy-3,value);
            if value>0 then byte := byte + 8;
            read_pixel(frame_nr,dcx,dcy-4,value);
            if value>0 then byte := byte + 16;
            read_pixel(frame_nr,dcx,dcy-5,value);
            if value>0 then byte := byte + 32;
            read_pixel(frame_nr,dcx,dcy-6,value);
            if value>0 then byte := byte + 64;
            read_pixel(frame_nr,dcx,dcy-7,value);
            if value>0 then byte := byte + 128;
            write_output(printer,byte);
        end;
        write_output(printer,cr); write_output(printer,lf);
    end;
end;
```

3.7 Graphics input methods

The digitizer tablet is the most common method of digital graphics input today. A digitizer tablet consists of a flat drawing board and a pen stylus or cross-hairs puck connected by wires to the computer. Whenever the stylus is near the drawing board surface the pen position on the board is detected electromagnetically and can be transmitted to the host computer at any time. The stylus and puck have microswitches on them which allow information to be transmitted to the host.

An example of a low-cost digitizer is the Graphtek KD4030. With an A3-sized drawing board, any A3 or smaller sheet of paper with a graphics pattern to be digitized can be fastened to the digitizer's surface. Even books up to 2 cm thick can be placed on the digitizer and then traced over by the stylus as the tablet works by magnetic induction of sufficient sensitivity. The effective digitizable area is 380 mm horizontally by 260 mm vertically with a resolution of 0.1 mm; and up to 110 positions per second can be registered. The tablet's functions are activated by simple single-character ASCII commands sent by the host computer. For example, if the host sends 'P', the digitizer is put into *point mode* where it transmits point coordinates to the host every time the user presses a button on the stylus or cross-hairs puck. Two other useful modes are the *stream mode* and the *switch stream mode*. In the former, the coordinates of the stylus are sent to the host at regular (programmable) intervals from 2 to 110 coordinate pairs a second. The latter mode does the same thing as long as one of the buttons is depressed, and once all buttons are released the transmission of point data ceases. These modes are very useful for entering freehand drawings into the computer. Another command tells the digitizer not to retransmit coordinates which are equal to or within a certain (programmable) distance from the last point transmitted. The format for transmission of coordinate data from the digitizer to the host is either done in ASCII text format or squashed into binary numeric value format. The ASCII format is:

X X X X , Y Y Y Y , F cr lf

where X X X X is the four-digit right-justified ASCII representation of the *dcx* coordinate value (multiples of 0.1 mm) and Y Y Y Y the representation for the *dcy* coordinate value. *F* is the code for the function key that was pressed. It equals 1, 2, 4, or 8 depending on whether button Z, 1, 2, or 3 was pressed. The following routine shows a sample usage of this digitizer in the point mode.

```
procedure digitizer_getpoint(var hit_code, dcx, dcy : integer);
{Read one digitized point from the KD4030 digitizer.}
var
    byte,pen_nr : integer;
begin
    write_output(digitizer,ord('P'));
    read_integer(digitizer,dcx);
    read_input(digitizer,byte); {skip over the comma}
    read_integer(digitizer,dcy);
    read_input(digitizer,byte); {skip over the second comma}
    read_integer(digitizer,pen_nr);
    read_input(digitizer,byte); {remove the cr from the input stream}
    read_input(digitizer,byte); {remove the lf from the input stream}
    hit_code := pen_nr;
end;
```

Most bit-image graphics printers do not enable graphics input to be taken from the printed hard copy. However there is at least one printer type that has its print head

Figure 3-7 Screen digitization using movable cross hairs.

mechanism replaced by an optical scanner which detects a column of dots at a time and sends their byte value back to the host computer. With this system, photographs can be inserted in the 'print' platen and optically digitized. The host can then do image processing on the digitized picture and display the results on a graphics screen.

It is not difficult to use a graphics VDU screen for digitizing data – see Figure 3-7. What are required are routines to place and move the cross hairs on the VDU screen, and a routine to read direction commands from the keyboard without echo. If the routine 'place_cross_hair(dcx, dcy)' draws the small cross hairs on the screen centered at the pixel with device coordinates (*dcx, dcy*) by XORing with the background and the routine 'read_input(keyboard,byte)' waits for a key press on the keyboard and returns the ASCII byte value of the key that was pressed, then the following routine will allow the user to digitize points from the graphics screen.

```
procedure screen_getpoint(var hit_code, dcx, dcy : integer);
{Get a digitized point from the VDU. This routine displays the cross hairs at the
origin, and waits for the user to move it. Once the position is selected, any
alphanumeric   key (called the 'hit key') pressed will exit this routine with the
device coordinates of the chosen point.}
const
    {Suitable keys can be set here e.g. arrow or function keys :}
    right = 18; up = 21; left = 12; down = 4;
    faster = 6; slower = 19; brake = 2; home = 8;
```

```
    var
        key_pressed, delta,delta_max : integer;
    begin
        delta := 1;
        delta_max := nr_dots_vert div 2;
        if nr_dots_horiz div 2 < delta_max then
            delta_max := nr_dots_horiz div 2;
        dcx := 0; dcy := 0; place_cross_hairs(dcx,dcy);
repeat
    read_input(keyboard,key_pressed);
    case key_pressed of
        right :
            begin
                dcx := dcx + delta;
                if dcx > nr_dots_horiz-1 then dcx := nr_dots_horiz-1;
            end
        up :
            begin
                dcy := dcy + delta;
                if dcy > nr_dots_vert-1 then dcy := nr_dots_vert -1;
            end;
        left :
            begin
                dcx := dcx - delta;
                if dcx < 0 then dcx := 0;
            end;
        down :
            begin
                dcy := dcy - delta;
                if dcy < 0 then dcy := 0;
            end;
        faster :
            begin
                delta := 2 * delta;
                if delta > delta_max then delta := delta_max;
            end;
        slower :
            begin
                delta := delta div 2;
                if delta < 1 then delta := 1;
            end;
        home :
            begin
                dcx := 0; dcy := 0;
            end;
        brake :
```

```
            delta := 1;
    end;
    place_cross_hairs(dcx,dcy);
until (char_type(key_pressed) = digit) or
    (char_type(key_pressed) = upper_case) or
    (char_type(key_pressed) = lower_case);
hit_code := key_pressed;
    end;
```

If a line drawing routine that draws by XORing with the current values in pixel memory is not available then 'place_cross_hairs' can be implemented by direct calls to the raster primitives in the following way:

```
procedure place_cross_hairs(dcx, dcy : integer);
{Draw cross hairs at the device coordinates (dcx,dcy) nondestructively.}
const
    frame_nr = 0; {Work in the default frame memory}
    half_length = 10; {To make a 20x20 cross - any visible size will do.}
var
    x,y,old_value,temp, new_value : integer; {pixel values}
begin
    y := dcy;
    for x := dcx - half_length to dcx + half_length do
    begin
        read_pixel(frame_nr,x,y,old_value);
        temp := 1 - old_value mod 2; {invert the lowest bit}
        new_value := 2*(old_value div 2) + temp; { XOR with 1}
        write_pixel(frame_nr,x,y,new_value);
    end;
    x := dcx;
    for y := dcy - half_length to dcy + half_length do
    begin
        read_pixel(frame_nr,x,y,old_value);
        temp := 1 - old_value mod 2; {invert the lowest bit}
        new_value := 2*(old_value div 2) + temp; { XOR with 1}
        write_pixel(frame_nr,x,y,new_value);
    end;
end;
```

Problems

3.1   Answer the following questions concerning the PAL (Phase Alternation by Line) system for encoding video information given that in the PAL system one horizontal line (a 'H line') takes 64 microseconds, the line frequency (screen refresh rate) is 50 Hertz, and each complete picture frame requires two vertical scans (due to interlacing):

(a) How many lines are scanned per second on a PAL TV set?
(b) How many lines are scanned in one vertical sync time?
(c) How many picture frames are shown on a PAL TV per second?

Redo these questions for the NTSC (National Television Systems Committee) video system where the screen refresh rate is 60 Hz (and the other parameters are the same).

During the vertical retrace period when the scanning spot moves from the bottom right to the top left corner of the screen and waits for synchronization, no video information is received for displaying. This time interval is slightly less than 10 percent of the time needed to scan the whole screen and consequently roughly 10 percent of the number of scan lines calculated above (625 for PAL and 525 for NTSC) are not active. For the PAL system there are actually 585 visible scan lines on the screen and for the NTSC system there are 480. Both systems use the same screen physical aspect ratio of 3/4. NTSC monitors therefore cannot provide as high a resolution as PAL monitors.

3.2   Compute the screen and pixel aspect ratios, and the horizontal, vertical and area resolutions (pixel densities) from the sample data given for a typical color TV in Section 3.2. Rate this as a graphics terminal by comparison with the corresponding values for the devices listed in Table 1-1.

3.3   Show carefully what change of variables and assumptions allow us to go from the algorithm described in the routine 'raster_line_3' to the version of Bresenham's algorithm presented in the routine 'raster_line_4'. Write code that will check the five requirements for a good raster line algorithm as given in Section 3.4, and apply to the line algorithms discussed in that section.

3.4   Write an improved Bresenham routine for drawing straight lines by allowing the software to choose whether to loop by increments along the x axis or along the y axis. Have your routine check for the exception cases such as a line parallel to the x axis.

3.5   The 'screen_dump' routine in Section 3.6 assumes that the routine 'read_pixel' returns a pixel value of zero when it is given device coordinates out of range (i.e. off the display rectangle). It wastes time attempting to read pixels for negative values of dcy when 'nr_dots_vert' is not an exact multiple of eight. Write a similar algorithm that does not need this requirement. The new version should have an outer loop taking *dcy* as loop index from 'nr_dots_vert -1' down to 0. An inner loop takes *dcx* from 0 to 'nr_dots_horiz - 1' reading pixels and filling a byte array at increasing bit positions. After every eighth *y* line the byte array is sent to the printer.

3.6 Modify the 'screen_dump' routine of Section 3.6 to have an extra input parameter which tells the routine to print the positive screen image or the negative screen image, or to print only a selected color. Assume that there are only the eight colors of Table 3-1 available on the screen. The new parameter can be an integer whose value modulo eight is the color to select for printing. If the value is negative then a dot is printed whenever the current pixel does not have the specified color.

3.7 Using routines from Chapter 1 and this chapter, write the code for 'set_window' which sets up user coordinate ranges in global variables and for a procedure 'plot_line' which takes as parameters the end points of the line in user coordinates and draws the line connecting them. This procedure must draw a line between the two points in user coordinates on whatever sort of device is the currently selected output graphics device.

3.8 The version of 'place_cross_hairs' given in Section 3.7 does not avoid writing past the edges of the display rectangle. Improve the routine by preventing this from occurring. Introduce four new variables $dcx1$, $dcx2$, $dcy1$, and $dcy2$ for the end points of the *x* and *y* loops respectively where $dcx1 = dcx - half\_length$ etc. Check that $dcx1$ and $dcy1$ are greater than or equal to zero and if not then set them to zero. Similarly check that $dcx2$ and $dcy2$ are less than 'nr_dots_horiz' and 'nr_dots_vert' respectively, and if not set them to the maximum values allowed. The routine should also start with a check to see if the point (dcx, dcy) is within the display rectangle. If it is not within the display rectangle, no drawing should be attempted and control should immediately return from this routine.

3.9 Using routines from Chapter 1 and this chapter, write code for 'set_window' to set up user coordinates and a procedure 'read_point' which ultimately calls 'digitizer_getpoint' or 'screen_getpoint' depending on the currently selected input device, and returns the hit code and the coordinates of the point on the graphics input device selected by the user in user coordinates. Write code using this routine and the routine 'plot_line' from problem 3.6 to loop digitizing two points, the first with hit code corresponding to the 'P' key and the second with hit code 'Q', and then draw a straight line segment joining the two points P and Q together. Hit codes other than 'P', 'Q', and ESC should be ignored. On pressing the ESC key, the line drawing loop should terminate.

3.10 Using the 'read_point' and 'draw_line' routines from problem 3.9, show how a square of 5 cm on each side is input from a device into physical coordinates and then output to the currently selected output device without distortion of size or proportions.

3.11 It is advantageous for line-drawing algorithms to use only integer variables so that the algorithm runs faster, as in the Bresenham algorithm (see Box 3-4). A new integer-only line-drawing algorithm is shown in Box 3-6. This is based on the Euclidean algorithm for finding the greatest common divisor of two numbers. Implement all of the line-drawing algorithms in Boxes 3-1 to 3-4 and Box 3-6. Generate some random end points in device coordinates, and compare the speeds of drawing the line segments for each algorithm.

Box 3-6 Straight line algorithm #5.

```
procedure raster_line_5(dcx1,dcy1,dcx2,dcy2 : integer);
{A new line drawing algorithm based on Euclid's algorithm
for finding the greatest common divisor of two numbers.}
var
        deltax,deltay,xrange,yrange,xincr,yincr,dcx,dcy,i,xr,yr,n: integer;
begin
        deltax := dcx2 - dcx1; xrange := abs(deltax);
        deltay := dcy2 - dcy1; yrange := abs(deltay);
        xincr := 1; if (deltax < 0) then xincr := -1;
        yincr := 1; if (deltay < 0) then yincr := -1;
        dcx := dcx1; dcy := dcy1;
        xr := xrange; yr := yrange;
        n := xrange + yrange;
        for i := 1 to n do
        begin
                dot_on(dcx,dcy);
                if (xr >= yr) then
                begin
                        dcx := dcx + xincr; xr := xr - yrange;
                end
                else
                begin
                        dcy := dcy + yincr; yr := yr - xrange;
                end;
        end;
end;
```

4

Curve drawing

4.1 Circle and arc generation

Circles and circular arcs are frequently required in graphics outputs. Various nonincremental and incremental algorithms for implementing a 'draw_circle' procedure exist. Some methods are faster than others but may only be suitable for drawing circles not arcs or for generalizing to spirals and ellipses.

The equation of a circle, whose centre is (x_0, y_0) and radius is a, in Cartesian coordinates is:

$$(x - x_0)^2 + (y - y_0)^2 = a^2 \qquad (4.1)$$

In nonincremental methods a regular polygon of n sides usually approximates the circle. The vertices of the polygon are computed by:

```
x[i] := x0 + a*cos(2*pi*i / n)          (4.2a)
y[i] := y0 + a*sin(2*pi*i / n);         (4.2b)
```

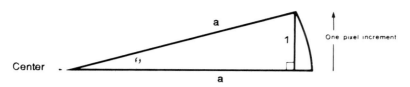

Figure 4-1 Computation of the number of line segments n for polygonal approximation.

and the length of the side is given by:

$$s = 2a \, \cos(p / n)$$

The sides are drawn by line drawing routines as discussed in Sections 2.4 and 3.5. To improve the accuracy of the representation of a circle, s must be small in comparison with the radius a; the latter formula providing the value of n. A simpler method for determining n is as follows.

For a circle to look round, rather than like a regular polygon, n must be chosen sufficiently large. If adjacent dots are to be on sequential horizontal scan lines at the ends of the horizontal diameter then the following formula produces n :

$$n = 2\pi / \sin^{-1}(d / a)$$

where d is the distance between scan lines:

$$d = height / ndv$$

The basis of this calculation can be seen in Figure 4-1. For a large radius a compared with the dot spacing d , this formula gives the approximation:

$$n \approx int(2\pi a / d)$$

When a large enough n is used however, the amount of computation involved in finding the vertexes by equations 4.2a and 4.2b slows down the algorithm. This load can be reduced by recognizing that a circle is symmetrical: for every vertex in the first quadrant, corresponding vertexes in the other three quadrants can be obtained by reflection about the axes centered on $(x0,y0)$. Thus if (x,y) is a point on the circumference, then so are $(2x_0 - x, y)$, $(2x_0 - x, 2y_0 - y)$, and $(x, 2y_0 - y)$. This reduces vertex calculations by a factor of four. Similarly through the use of reflection symmetry about the line of unit slope through (x_0,y_0), it is known that if (x,y) is on the circumference of the circle then its reflection about this line, namely $(y - y_0 + x_0, x - x_0 + y_0)$ is also on the circle. This further reduces vertex computations to only $n / 8$.

Another way of saving processor time in the computations in equations 4.2a and 4.2b is to use table look-up (with linear interpolation if necessary) in place of the time consuming trigonometric functions. The sine table has to be set up previously by the software or read from disk. The cosine value for any angle θ is determined by using the sine table look-up for $\pi / 2 - \theta$. Another approach is to use the square root function rather than the trigonometric function:

$$y = y_0 + \sqrt{[a^2 - (x - x_0)^2]}$$

and loop from $x = 0$ to $x = a$ using symmetry rules to determine the vertexes in the other quadrants. (See problem 4.1.)

There are a number of incremental methods for plotting circular arcs which are often faster. These methods compute points on the circumference of the circle one at a time and draw straight line segments joining them using the line-drawing functions of the graphics device, or simply set the pixels if the increments are designed to be one pixel at a time.

If the differentials of equation 4.1 are taken, (remembering that 'x0', 'y0', and 'a' are constants) then:

$$(x - x_0)\delta x + (y - y_0)\delta y = 0$$

or in terms of the usual derivative:

$$dy / dx = - (x - x_0) / (y - y_0) \tag{4.3}$$

The latter equation is used in the circle-generating DDA. Recall from Section 3.5 that a DDA or digital differential analyser is an algorithm for selecting a sequence of neighboring pixels, to turn on in a digital lattice, that make a best approximation to the desired curve. A DDA uses the differential equation of the curve such as equation 4.3 for circles to generate the digital pixels to set. Let us consider how the DDA algorithm of Section 3.5 works for circle drawing.

The DDA computes the next coordinate (x, y) from the displacements $(\Delta x, \Delta y)$ which in turn come from the differential equation (D.E.) of the curve. The (x, y) coordinates are then rounded to integers and the lines connected. In the case of a circle, equation 4.3 gives the formulas for Δx and Δy. By setting:

$$dy / dx \approx \Delta y / \Delta x$$

and multiplying through by Δx to obtain:

$$\Delta y = - \varepsilon \ (x - x_0) \tag{4.4}$$

where ε is a small quantity given by:

$$\varepsilon = \Delta x / (y - y_0) \tag{4.5}$$

Equation 4.5 can be rearranged as:

$$\Delta x = \varepsilon \ (y - y_0) \tag{4.6}$$

Equations 4.4 and 4.6 thus provide the formulas for $(\Delta x, \Delta y)$ at any coordinate location (x, y). Note firstly that the displacement vector, $(\Delta x, \Delta y)$, depends on the parameter ε which is to be regarded as a small constant, provided to the algorithm by the user. The smaller ε is chosen to be, the closer together the output coordinates will be, that is, the better the digital approximation to the circle would be. Secondly note that unlike the case of a straight line, the displacement vector changes with the (x, y) value.

The Δx and Δy are the displacements from one knot point to the next, that is:

$$x_{i+1} = x_i + \Delta x$$
$$y_{i+1} = y_i + \Delta y$$

so in this method a difference equation is effectively used as an approximation to the differential equation 4.3:

$$x_{i+1} = x_i + \Delta y$$
$$y_{i+1} = y_i - \Delta x$$

To the extent that the difference equation is only an approximation to the differential equation the resulting output will be faulty. In particular, this difference equation results in a spiral rather than an arc – each step is made in the direction perpendicular to a radius of the circle so each point will be farther from the centre than the point before. The following pair of difference equations eliminate this problem:

$$x_{n+1} = x_n + \varepsilon\, y_n$$
$$y_{n+1} = y_n - \varepsilon\, x_{n+1}$$

To draw circular arcs, the circle parameters (x_0, y_0) and two angles θ_1 and θ_2, indicating the start and end of the arc, are required. The first circle algorithm above can be easily adapted to arc drawing, by using equations 4.2a and 4.2b to compute only those vertexes whose trigonometric argument θ lies between θ_1 and θ_2.

4.2 Mathematical curve drawing

Apart from displaying circles or parts of circles, many other mathematical curves may need to be generated. But instead of writing a new routine for every new mathematical function, it is preferable to have a general purpose routine called 'draw_curve', say, which will generate any mathematical shape:

$$y = f(x) \tag{4.7}$$

The function f must clearly be passed to the routine 'draw_curve', as well as the start and end points of the curve to be displayed. The definition of the curve as given in equation 4.7 is called the *explicit* form of the curve. The explicit form is not adequate since computer languages require that any function f be single valued. An example of a double-valued function (for most values of x) is:

$$f(x) = \pm\sqrt{(a^2 - x^2)}$$

A general purpose 'draw_curve' routine could not accept a function like this as a parameter. A superior approach to the explicit form is the parametric form of the equations of the curve:

$$x = fx(t) \tag{4.8a}$$
$$y = fy(t) \tag{4.8b}$$
$$t_1 \leq t \leq t_2 \tag{4.8c}$$

Eliminating t between equations 4.8a and 4.8b results in the original form of the curve (equation 4.7). The latter form is better for computer languages since both of the functions fx and fy are single-valued functions. This means that instead of passing one

Box 4-1 A simple curve drawing algorithm using equal parameter increments.

```
procedure draw_curve1(function xfn(t : real) : real;
                      function yfn(t : real) : real;
                      t1,t2 : real; n : integer);
{Draw the curve defined by :
    x = xfn(t)
    y = yfn(t)
for
    t1 ≤ t ≤ t2
by using n straight line segments.}
var
    i : integer;
    t_increment,x1,y1,x2,y2 : real;
begin
    t_increment := (t2 - t1)/n;
    x1 := xfn(t1); y1 := yfn(t1);
    for i := 1 to n do
    begin
        t := t1 + (i-1)*t_increment;
        x2 := xfn(t); y2 := yfn(t);
        plot_line(x1,y1,x2,y2);
        x1 := x2; y1 := y2;
    end;
end;
```

function to 'draw_curve' we pass two. For instance, in the example of the circle this gives:

$$x = r \, \cos(\theta)$$
$$y = r \, \sin(\theta)$$
$$0 \le \theta \le 2 \, \pi$$

Let us next consider how 'draw_curve' should function internally. A smooth curve can be approximated by a sequence of joined straight line segments. One way of implementing a routine to draw mathematical parametrized curves is to consider it as consisting of a sequence of straight line segments determined by equal increments of the curve's parameter t. This involves a loop through the available t values t_1 to t_2 as shown in Box 4-1. However the line segments generated in this algorithm will in general be of unequal lengths. In particular, it is not guaranteed that the smaller line segments will occur at the points on the curve of higher curvature. This means that the generated curve can be a very poor approximation to the true curve. It is always possible to improve the approximation by increasing the number of straight line segments to be used. But because line segment length is not necessarily tied to curvature, this could turn out to be a very inefficient method of generating the curve to the required level of approximation.

An ideal method here is to reparametrize the curve using arc length s along the curve in place of parameter t. A call to this curve-drawing routine would assure that equal intervals in the parameter would result in roughly equal length line segments. The arc length is found as a function of t by the integral equation:

$$\sigma \equiv \sigma(t) = \int_{t_1}^{t} \sqrt{[(dx \, / \, dt \,)^2 + (dy \, / \, dt \,)^2]} \, dt \qquad (4.9)$$

Unfortunately this equation cannot usually be expanded in closed form. For instance in the simple case of the ellipse, the function $\sigma(t)$ can only be expressed in the so called incomplete elliptic integral of the second kind for which values have to be determined by numerical methods. Another method will have to be sought to overcome this problem.

If the number of line segments is increased, while at the same time their lengths are reduced, then the approximation will come closer and closer to the true curve. Since a graphics output device has a finite nonzero resolution, there is no point in carrying this limiting process beyond the device's resolution. The algorithm for 'draw_curve' given in Box 4-2 uses these ideas and allows the user to choose the approximation level by passing as a parameter the maximum number of device resolution points (dots) required.

This routine requires the user to set up four external routines to implement the functions 'xfn', 'yfn', 'xderiv', and 'yderiv', where 'xderiv' and 'yderiv' are the derivatives of the functions 'xfn' and 'yfn' respectively. If a mistake is made in differentiation or in implemention, then 'draw_curve' will produce erroneous graphics output. The burden on the user can be lessened by allowing the curve-generating routine to approximate the derivative functions by taking small changes in the arguments. (See problem 4.2.)

Box 4-2 An algorithm for uniform curve approximation using curve tangent functions.

```
procedure draw_curve(function xfn(t : real) : real;
                     function yfn(t : real) : real;
                     function xderiv : real; function yderiv : real;
                     lambda1,lambda2 : real; dhmax,dvmax : integer);
{   INPUTS:          xfn the external function
                     yfn the external function
                     xderiv the derivative of xfn with respect to the parameter
                     yderiv the derivative of yfn with respect to the parameter
                     lambda1 the first value of the parameter on the curve
                     lambda2 the last value of the parameter on the curve
                     dhmax the maximum desired pixel increment along the
                     horizontal axis of the screen between knot points
                     dvmax the maximum desired pixel increment along the
                     vertical axis of the screen between knot points.}
var
    x1,y1,lambda,xder,yder,dlambda : real;
    h1,v1,h2,v2 : integer;
begin
{Determine the initial point of the curve :}
    lambda := lambda1;
    x1 := xfn(lambda);
    y1 := yfn(lambda);
    viewing_transformation(x1,y1,h1,v1);
{loop to draw the sequence of vectors :}
    while lambda < lambda2 do
    begin
        xder := abs(xderiv(lambda));
        yder := abs(yderiv(lambda));
        if (xder > yder) then
            dlambda := (xmax-xmin)/(hmax-hmin)/xder*(dhmax)
        else
            dlambda := (ymax-ymin)/(vmax-vmin)/yder*(dvmax);
        lambda := lambda+dlambda;
        x := xfn(lambda);
        y := yfn(lambda);
        viewing_transformation(x,y,h2,v2);
        plot_line(h1,v1,h2,v2);
        h1 := h2;
        v1 := v2;
    end;
end;
```

4.3 Spirographics

A Sprirograph^{TM} is a pattern drawing, educational toy originally made in England by Denys Fisher (Eng.). This invention enables one to draw fascinating graphics patterns by using plastic revolving stencils and any colored ball point pen on a sheet of paper. Seventeen different-sized wheels, two different-sized rings, and two different-sized racks are provided in the kit. To make a simple spirograph pattern one selects one of the wheels and a ring stencil. The wheel stencil has holes at various distances from the center of the wheel through which the ball point is inserted and a certain number of teeth on its circumference. The ring stencil has teeth on the inside and the outside of the ring. By placing the wheel inside or outside the ring, meshing the teeth of each together, and following the path of the wheel several times around the ring, the pen will mark out a spirograph pattern on a sheet of plain paper. The rack stencil is an alternative to using the ring. It is straight like a ruler, but with semicircular ends, and also has teeth around its perimeter. It is clear that on the straight section of the rack, the locus of the pen will mark out a cycloid curve. The curves from using the rings are therefore circularly distorted cycloids with periods depending on the ratio of the number of teeth on the wheel to the ring. But what are the actual mathematical equations of the spirograph patterns.

Let us first consider the curves formed by having a wheel of radius r_W move around the outside of a ring whose radius is r_R with the pen at distance r_P from the centre of the wheel. Let the center of the ring be the origin of coordinates O, the centre of the wheel W, and the position of the pen be P. The point W is determined by the equations:

$$x_W = (r_R + r_W) \cos \theta \qquad (4.10)$$
$$y_W = (r_R + r_W) \sin \theta \qquad (4.11)$$

where θ is the angle of W above the x axis with respect to the origin O. Equations 4.10 and 4.11 above give the coordinates (x_W, y_W) of the vector OW. The components of the vector WP are given by:

$$u_P = r_P \cos \phi \qquad (4.12)$$
$$v_P = r_P \sin \phi \qquad (4.13)$$

where ϕ (phi) is the angle P makes about W with respect to the x direction. Because the wheel and ring are geared together, there is no slip between them and so:

$$r_W \, \phi = r_R \, \theta \qquad (4.14)$$

The locus of the point P is given by the vector:

$$OP = OW + WP \qquad (4.15)$$

By combining equations 4.10 to 4.15 the components of OP, (x, y), can be found, which are the Cartesian coordinates of P, as:

$$x = (r_R + r_W) \cos \theta + r_P \cos((r_R / r_W) \theta) \qquad (4.16)$$

$$y = (r_R + r_W) \sin \theta + r_P \sin((r_R / r_W) \theta) \qquad (4.17)$$

These two equations define the spirograph curve in Cartesian coordinates with parameter θ. It is easy to see that the equations for the spirograph using a wheel on the inside of the ring instead of on the outside is given by:

$$x = (r_R - r_W) \cos \theta + r_P \cos((r_R / r_W) \theta) \qquad (4.18)$$

$$y = (r_R - r_W) \sin \theta + r_P \sin((r_R / r_W) \theta) \qquad (4.19)$$

An advantage of computer-developed graphics over mechanically developed graphics, such as by means of the spirograph equipment, is that the computer is not limited by the physical design of the equipment. Thus the computer can plot the more general spirographics curve:

$$x = A \cos \theta + B \cos(C \theta) \qquad (4.20)$$

$$y = A \sin \theta + B \sin(C \theta) \qquad (4.21)$$

where A and B are real parameters and C is a ratio of integers (i.e. a rational number). As examples, it is physically impossible to have $r_P \geq r_W$ or $r_W \geq r_R$ in the wheel inside the ring case when using the Spirograph equipment. The computer however can simulate these and many other cases: the computer is a more flexible spirographics device. Examples of computer spirographs and their parameters according to equations 4.20 and 4.21 are presented in the accompanying figure. (See Figure 4-2.) By superimposing several of these spirographs in different colors many different artistic patterns can be developed.

The principles of spirographics can be extended to other mathematical curves to produce artistic patterns. The idea is that the constants appearing in the parametric equations for a mathematical curve are converted to slowly varying functions of the curve parameter. When the new equations are plotted, a family of closely spaced shapes of the original mathematical curve appears with each shape smoothly joined to its neighbour in the family. As an example of this extension of the spirographics concept consider taking as a base shape, the ellipse. The equation of a horizontal ellipse is:

$$(x - x_0)^2 / a^2 + (y - y_0)^2 / b^2 = 1 \qquad (4.22)$$

which can be written in parametric form as:

$$x = x_0 + a \cos(\theta) \qquad (4.23a)$$

$$y = y_0 + b \sin(\theta) \qquad (4.23b)$$

$$0 \leq \theta \leq 2\pi \qquad (4.23c)$$

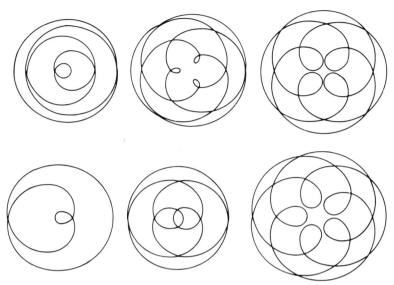

Figure 4-2 Spirographic plots.

and where x_0, y_0, a, and b are constants. By combining equations 4.23a, b, and c with:

$$a = a_0 + a_1 \theta \qquad (4.24a)$$

$$b = b_0 + b_1 \theta \qquad (4.24b)$$

$$0 \leq \theta \leq \infty$$

where the curve parameter θ is now allowed to increase from zero indefinitely, a family of varying ellipses, all smoothly joined in sequence, is created. Of course in any given plot a stopping point is selected as an upper limit for θ. Similarly, the new constants a_0, a_1, b_0, and b_1 need to be specified. The program should ask for 'a0', 'a1', 'b0', 'b1', and 'dtheta' (the angle increment per iteration) and then loop forever computing 'a' and 'b', and then 'x' and 'y' by the formulas above, and plot the line segments. The result is that the initial ellipse squishes to a new elliptic shape and then retaining this last shape expands forever.

To create a family of joined rotating ellipses, another programming approach is needed. The equation for a rotated ellipse is:

$$A x^2 + 2 h x y + B y^2 + C = 0 \qquad (4.25)$$

where $A B - h^2 > 0$. To get a family of rotating connected ellipses these parameters may be varied as follows:

$$A = a^2 \sin^2 \phi + b^2 \cos^2 \phi \qquad (4.26a)$$

$$B = a^2 \cos^2 \phi + b^2 \sin^2 \phi \qquad (4.26b)$$

$$h = (a^2 - b^2) \sin \phi \cos \phi \qquad (4.26c)$$

$$C = -a^2 b^2 \qquad (4.26d)$$

where a and b are held constant, and ϕ, the angle of the ellipse to the x axis, is varied over the range zero to infinity. The parametric representation can again be used for the plotting:

$$x = x_0 + a \cos \theta \cos \phi + b \sin \theta \sin \phi \qquad (4.27)$$
$$y = y_0 - a \cos \theta \sin \phi + b \sin \theta \cos \phi \qquad (4.28)$$

and ϕ should be a slowly varying function of θ such as:

$$\phi = \phi_0 + \phi_1 \theta \qquad (4.29)$$

Sample graphics output using these formulas for various values of these parameters are shown in Figure 4-3.

4.4 Data plotting

Often it is wished to display a set of data points as a neat line graph. The data points may have come from scientific laboratory experiments, census surveys, computer performance statistics, and so forth. In these curve-fitting methods the assumption is that the point data is held in a data structure of the following defined type :

```
const
    max_nr_data_points = 200;
type
    data_points = record
        n : integer;
        x,y : array[1 .. max_nr_data_points] of real;
        end;
```

The data may be read in to the program by a procedure such as the following routine:

```
procedure input_data_points(var data : data_points);
{Read in the data points from the keyboard (or a file).}
var
    i : integer;
begin
    write('Number of data points?');
    readln(data.n);
    for i := 1 to data.n do
```

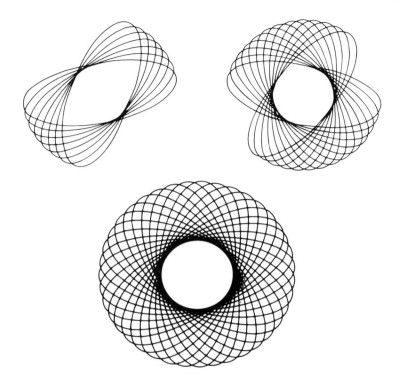

Figure 4-3 Ellipses with slowly varying parameters.

```
      begin
          write('x[',i:3,'], y[',i:3,'] = ?');
          readln(data.x[i],data.y[i]);
      end;
  end;
```

Now a routine is needed to plot this data as a line graph, for example:

plot_data(data:data_points; heading,x_title,y_title : str40)

The parameters 'heading', 'x_title', and 'y_title' are character strings which give a title for the graph and labels for the x and y axes. They have the type 'str40' which is a user-defined type consisting of a packed array of 40 characters.

This routine will need to perform the following tasks:

1. Determine a suitable window size.
2. Set the window size (by 'set_window(xmin,ymin,xmax,ymax)').
3. Draw a pair of axes with tick marks suitably placed on them.
4. Sort the data pairs by x value.

5. Draw a polyline through the data points.
6. Write the graph heading.
7. Label the x axis.
8. Label the y axis.

To determine a suitable window size, first determine the maximum and minimum x and y values in the coordinate arrays. Call these 'x_value_max', 'x_value_min', 'y_value_max', and 'y_value_min'. These then give the ranges of values in the x and y data value coordinates:

```
x_range := x_value_max - x_value_min;
y_range := y_value_max - y_value_min;
```

Naturally the graph will not occupy the entire display rectangle. Let a margin be set of 10 percent around the graph. Then the parameters of the graphics window are:

```
xmin := x_value_min - 0.1*x_range;
ymin := y_value_min - 0.1*y_range;
xmax := x_value_max + 0.1*x_range;
ymax := y_value_max + 0.1*y_range;
```

The window size is specified to the graphics system now by the call:

```
set_window(xmin,ymin,xmax,ymax)
```

To draw the axes, two calls to the line-drawing routine are made and then the tick marks are added. Therefore a routine such as:

```
draw_axes(dxpdiv,dypdiv,tick_size : real)
```

may be required, where 'dxpdiv' is the x increment per tick along the x axis, 'dypdiv' is the required y increment per tick along the y axis and 'tick_size' is the length of the tick marks (perpendicular to each axis). This routine could draw the axis lines by:

```
draw_line(xmin,0,xmax,0);
draw_line(0,ymin,0,ymax);
```

However, since the (x , y) origin $(0,0)$ may not be included in the range of data, the most suitable lines must be selected to be drawn as axes:

```
yaxis = 0;
if yaxis < y_value_min then yaxis = y_value_min;
if yaxis > y_value_max then yaxis= y_value_max;
draw_line(x_value_min,yaxis,x_value_max,yaxis);
xaxis = 0;
if xaxis < x_value_min then xaxis = x_value_min;
```

```
if xaxis > x_value_max then xaxis= x_value_max;
draw_line(xaxis,y_value_min,xaxis,y_value_max);
```

To place tick marks on these axes, the positions of the first tick marks must be found and then all the tick positions visible on the graph should be computed and drawn. The tick marks could start at the origin (0,0) but this may not be on the graph. If the interval along the x axis between tick marks is 'dxpdiv', then the first tick mark should be placed at ('x','yaxis') where 'x' is the first value greater than 'x_value_min' that is a whole number times 'dxpdiv'. One tick is placed by the calls:

```
user_to_phys(x,yaxis,px,py);
move_to(px,py);
draw_to(px,py+tick_size);
```

and then the next tick position is determined by:

```
x := x + dxpdiv;
```

Similar steps are required for placing ticks along the y axis.

In many cases it is necessary that data be sorted according to its x component values. A routine to do this would have the following form (see problem 4.4):

```
procedure sort_data_values(data : data_points);
{Sort the (x,y) points by their x value in ascending order.}
```

To emphasize the relationship between the data points, a polyline could be used. A *polyline* is simply a series of connected straight lines and it would require a polyline-drawing procedure with the form:

```
draw_polyline(nr_pts,x_values,y_values)
```

where the expected input is an integer count of data points, and two arrays containing their values. This routine basically loops through the following statements:

```
x1 := x_values[i];
y1 := y_values[i];
x2 := x_values[i+1];
y2 := y_values[i+1];
draw_line(x1,y1,x2,y2);
```

for 'i = 1' to the value 'i = nr_pts - 1'.

Finally the data plot must be labeled. This can be achieved by suitable calls to the graphics output primitive:

```
draw_text(x_start,y_start, text_string)
```

which draws the desired label, stored in the 'text_string' character array, starting from the point ('x_start','y_start') in user coordinates. How this procedure can be made is explained in Section 8.6. Two related routines are also needed. They are:

```
text_angle(degrees)
```

which sets the default direction, and:

```
text_scale(x_scale_factor,y_scale_factor)
```

which sets the x and y scale factors for the displayed text. These procedures could be used as follows:

```
{Draw the heading on the plot :}
x1 := x_value_min;
y1 := 0.5*(y_value_max + ymax);
draw_text(x1, y1, heading);
{Draw the label on the horizontal x-axis :}
x1 := 2 / 3*(xmax-xmin);
y1 := 0.5*(y_value_min + ymin);
text_scale(0.5,0.5);
draw_text(x1,y1,x_label,x1,y1);
{Draw the label on the vertical y-axis :}
x1 := 0.5*(x_value_min + xmin);
y1 := y_value_max;
text_angle(90.0);
draw_text(x1,y1,y_label);
```

Two examples of the use of this 'plot_data' routine are shown in Figure 4-4.

(*Note* : When a lot of statistical data is given in a 'data_points' structure and when there is no wish to draw one polyline that goes through each point, it is useful in these cases to display the data as a scattergram. A procedure:

procedure scatter_gram(data:data_points;heading,x_title,y_title : str40)

could therefore be constructed in analogy to the procedure 'plot_data'. Instead of calling the procedure 'plot_polyline', the 'scatter_gram' procedure calls 'plot_polypoint(nr_pts, x_values, y_values)'. This procedure (sometimes known as the *polymarker* display procedure) displays every point in the array on the graph as a small marker such as a small plus sign. To draw a plus sign marker 1 mm in size at the user coordinate point (x ,y) the following calls could be made:

```
user_to_phys(x,y,px,py);
move_to(px,py-0.5);
draw_to(px,py+0.5)
move_to(px-0.5,py)
draw_to(px+0.5,py)
```

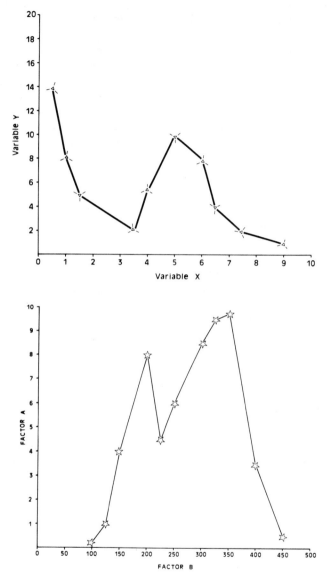

Figure 4-4 Line plots generated by the 'plot_data' procedure.

Other marker symbols can just as easily be made. A procedure called 'set_point_style(i)' allows the programmer to change the marker symbol to symbol number 'i' where 'i' is an integer.)

The problem of fitting a smooth curve to a set of data points is an old and common problem in the sciences. Curve fitting is used to find mathematical relationships between observable quantities and to perform interpolation and extrapolation of values to regions where measurements have not been and possibly could not have been done. The method of least squares linear regression has been known for a long time. It essentially consists of finding the line of best fit to the data points by minimizing the sum of the squares of the distances of the points from each test line. Likewise the use of nonlinear axis scales, nonlinear regression, and polynomial curve fitting have been known and practiced for a long time before computer graphics was widely available. With the advent of the computer, the arduous number-crunching aspect of these problems has been eliminated. And now with the advent of computer-generated graphic images, the tables of printed results and manually drawn curves have been replaced with the immediate visual impact of computer-drawn curves of best fit. Several curve-fitting techniques will now be dealt with in detail in the next three sections.

4.5 Least squares curve fitting

Least squares formulas and their explanation can be found in many books on numerical analysis. (See Kuo, 1972; Hornbeck, 1975; Ralston & Rabinowitz, 1978; Atkinson, 1978.) The data points used here are assumed to have been ordered as described in the previous section. To fit the supplied data, test lines described by their end points, called '(x1,y1)' and '(x2,y2)', can be plotted where:

    x1 := data.x[1]

and:

    x2 := data.x[data.n]

that is, a line joining these end points stretches the entire span of the data points. The aim is to select the most suitable values for 'y1' and 'y2' so that the resulting line appears closest to the experimental data. In the least squares method, the sum of the squares of the vertical distance of each data point from the line is calculated:

$$S = \sum_{i=1,n} (Y_i - \{y_1 + (X_i - x_1) m \})^2 \qquad (4.30a)$$

where:

$$m = (y_2 - y_1) / (x_2 - x_1) \qquad (4.30b)$$

is the slope of the current test line from (x_1, y_1) to (x_2, y_2). (It is safe to assume that $x_2 \neq x_1$.) The function S in equation 4.30a is the objective function to be minimized. It is a function of y_1 and y_2 only. However it is more convenient to use m as the second variable of S rather than y_2. To minimize $S = S(y_1, m)$ the partial derivatives are taken and the results set to zero:

$$\partial S / \partial y_1 = a\ y_1 + b\ m - e = 0 \qquad (4.31a)$$
$$\partial S / \partial m = c\ y_1 + d\ m - f = 0 \qquad (4.31b)$$

where the constants are:

$$a = \Sigma 1 \equiv n$$
$$b = \Sigma(X_i - x_1)$$
$$c = b$$
$$d = \Sigma(X_i - x_1)^2$$
$$e = \Sigma Y_i$$
$$f = \Sigma Y_i\ (X_i - x_1)$$

The solution to equations 4.31a and b is via the usual Kramer rule:

$$y_1 = (e\ d - b\ f) / (a\ d - b\ c)$$
$$m = (a\ f - e\ c) / (a\ d - b\ c)$$

Finally y_2 is obtained from the latter equations as:

$$y_2 = y_1 + m\ (x_2 - x_1)$$

A procedure to implement this algorithm is given in Box 4-3.

Having determined the end points of the optimal line by the least squares method, a plot of this line of best fit can be made by the call:

draw_line(x1,y1,x2,y2)

The least squares method extends to finding the closest curve that fits the data points in a family of curves other than straight lines. It is easy to generalize the above algorithm to find the best polynomial, of specified degree p, that fits the data. If $p \geq n$, that is, the degree of the fitting polynomial equals or exceeds the number of data points, an exact fitting polynomial can be found and this is discussed in the next section. Here the generalization of the above formulas is considered for a polynomial of degree $p < n$. Let the fitting polynomial be given by:

$$y = P(x) = a_0 + a_1 x + a_2 x^2 + a_3 x^3 + \ldots + a_p x^p$$

and the problem is to determine the constants a_j for $j = 0$ to $j = p$ which make P the

Box 4-3 Determining the line of best fit.

```
procedure least_squares_line(data : data_points; var x1,y1,x2,y2 : real);
{Determine the endpoints (x1,y1) and (x2,y2) of the line of closest fit
 to the data points.}
var
    i : integer;
    a,b,c,d,e,f,m : real;
begin
    x1 := data.x[1]; x2 := data.x[2];
    a := 0.0; b:= 0.0; c := 0.0; d:= 0.0; e := 0.0; f := 0.0;
    for i := 1 to data.n do
    begin
        b := b + (data.x[i] - x1);
        d := d + (data.x[i] - x1) * (data.x[i] - x1);
        e := e + data.y[i];
        f := f + data.y[i] * (data.x[i] - x1);
    end;
    a := n; c:= b;
    y1 := (e*d - b*f)/(a*d - b*c);
    m := (a*f - e*c)/(a*d - b*c);
    y2 := y1 + m*(x2 - x1);
end;
```

best fitting polynomial. The objective function in this case is:

$$S = \sum_{i=1,n} (Y_i - P(X_i))^2 \qquad (4.32)$$

which is a function of the parameters a_j alone. To optimize the objective function, the partial derivatives of S are taken with respect to its arguments, the coefficients a_j, and the answers are set to zero:

$$\partial S / \partial a_j = \sum (Y_i - P(X_i)) X_i^j = 0 \qquad (4.33)$$

Equation 4.33 is $p+1$ simultaneous linear equations in the $p+1$ unknowns a_j for $j = 0$ to $j = p$:

$$a_0 \sum X_i^j + a_1 \sum X_i^{j+1} + ... + a_p \sum X_i^{j+P} = \sum Y_i X_i^j \qquad (4.34)$$

or in matrix form:

$$C\ a = R \qquad (4.35)$$

where the coefficient matrix is:

$$C = (c_{kl}) \text{ and } c_{kl} = \sum_{i=1,n} X_i^{k+1}$$

and the column matrix of the right-hand side constants is given by:

$$R = (r_k) \text{ with } r_k = \sum_{i=1,n} Y_i X_i^k$$

Notice that the C matrix is symmetric, that is, $c_{kl} = c_{lk}$.

These simultaneous linear equations can be solved in any standard way such as by Cramer's Rule. The procedure given in Box 4-4 determines the coefficient matrix for the

Box 4-4 Determination of matrices for polynomial least squares.

```
procedure least_sq_poly_matrices(data : data_points; p : integer;
    var cmatrix : array[0 .. p, 0 .. p] of real;
    var rmatrix : array[0 .. p] of real);
{Determines the coefficient & right hand side matrices C and R for
 equation [8] which is used to get the coefficients of the fitting
 polynomial.}
var
    i,k,l : integer;
    sum : real;
begin
    for k := 0 to p do
    begin
        for l := 0 to p do
        begin
            sum := 0.0; pow := k+l;
            for i := 1 to data.n do
                csum := sum + power(data.x[i],pow);
            c[k,l] := sum;
        end;
        for k := 0 to p do
        begin
            sum := 0.0; pow := k;
            for i := 1 to data.n do
                sum := sum + data.y[i]*power(data.x[i],pow);
            rmatrix[k] := sum;
        end;
    end;
end;
```

left-hand side of equation 4.35 and the right-hand side column matrix of equation 4.35.

A routine is now required to solve the matrix equation in equation 4.35. Although Cramer's Rule is a useful algebraic method for matrix equations of low order, it is not the most efficient method for computer solution of simultaneous equations for larger numbers of equations. The Gauss-Jordan elimination routine is more suitable for this problem. (See problem 4.6.)

4.6 Polynomial curve fitting

An alternative approach is to fit a polynomial to the data points. Again the points must be sorted on the X_i values but this time the reason is to permit the fitting of a single-valued polynomial function. In general if there are n data points (X_i, Y_i) (with n distinct X_i values), then a polynomial of degree $n-1$ can be fit. The algorithm to determine the polynomial is called Lagrange polynomial interpolation. Let the polynomial be given by:

$$y = P(x) \tag{4.36}$$

Then it must satisfy:

$$Y_i = P(X_i) \tag{4.37}$$

for $i = 1$ to $i = n$. The solution is:

$$P(x) = \sum_{i=1,n} L_i(x) Y_i \tag{4.38a}$$

where:

$$L_i(x) = \prod_{k=1,n \ \& \ \neq i} (x - X_k) / (X_i - X_k) \tag{4.38b}$$

It can easily be seen that:

$$L_i(X_j) = \delta_{ij} \tag{4.39}$$

the Kronecker delta function which equals 1 if $i = j$ but otherwise equals zero. Because of this property of the Lagrange polynomials $L_i(x)$, it is clear that the n conditions in equations 4.37 are satisfied. This polynomial solution $P(x)$ is then computed for small steps in x and short line segments are drawn between the computed values $(x, P(x))$ to give the appearance of a smooth curved line fit to the data points.

A function to implement the polynomial fitting is as follows:

```
function poly_fit(data : data_pts; x : real);
{Determines the value y = P(x) where P is the polynomial which fits the
 data points given in the data parameter.}
var
    i,k : integer;
    y, Li : real;
begin
    y := 0.0;
    for i := 1 to data.n do
    begin
        Li := 1.0;
        for k := 1 to data.n do
            if k <> i then
                Li := Li * (x - data.x[k]) / (data.x[i] - data.x[k]);
        y := y + Li*data.y[i];
    end;
    poly_fit := y;
end;
```

This routine recalculates the polynomial every time an interpolation or extrapolation is called for. It is useful therefore if only a few points need interpolating or extrapolating. For a large number of points this could involve considerable computation time especially when the values of y are computed corresponding to many values of x, as for example, when it is necessary to plot the polynomial curve. A simpler approach is to compute the polynomial once and store the coefficients in its expansion. Then every time it is wished to evaluate $P(x)$ we simply refer to the table holding the polynomial coefficients and build the answer from them.

For large values of n the computation of the polynomial fit function and the plotting becomes slow and onerous. A simpler approach for these cases is to do piecewise polynomial interpolation. That is, the n data points are split up into groups of smaller size say m, and $(m-1)$th degree polynomials are then found to fit each group of data points. To plot a smoothly fitting curve to the data the $(m-1)$th degree polynomials are plotted in sequential order until all the data points have been considered.

4.7 Spline curve fitting

The task of fitting a smooth curve to a set of points in a plane was achieved in the earlier days of drafting by means of mechanical drawing splines. A spline is simply a long strip of flexible material (such as lead encased in plastic) with a drawing edge like a ruler and with a certain amount of stiffness. As a 'flexible ruler' it can be easily shaped to join points on a graph that are not too widely scattered. This manual process can now be done by computer-generated graphics using a mathematical approach similar to that discussed in the previous paragraph. The most common method uses cubic spline functions to join adjacent points (rather than using straight line joins). Because the cubic spline functions are two degrees higher than simple line fit curves, there are two extra parameters to be adjusted to simulate the smoothness of mechanical splines. These two degrees of freedom are used up by requiring continuity in the first and second derivatives between adjacent spline functions. More information on spline curve fitting can be found in Hornbeck, 1975, Ralston & Rabinowitz, 1978, and Atkinson, 1978.

Let us now study the mathematics of splines by considering firstly the less commonly used parabolic splines. The data structure of type 'data_points' as described earlier, is still used, but without the assumption that this data has been sorted, as this will allow loops to be drawn. The functions plotted may thus be multivalued in contrast to the restriction in the previous section to single valued plot curves.

Parabolic splines

For parabolic splines a parabola is fitted through the first three points $P1$, $P2$, and $P3$ of the data array of knot points. Then a second parabolic arc is found to fit the sequence of points $P2$, $P3$, and $P4$. This continues in this way until a parabolic arc is fitted through Pn -2, Pn -1, and Pn. The final plotted curve is a meshing together of all of these parabolic arcs. This description of a parabolic spline will have to be slightly modified as will be shown later.

To find the formulas for the parabolic arcs, assume the equation:

$$y = a\ x^2 + b\ x\ + c \tag{4.40}$$

and substitute into this equation the three points through which it passes:

$$P1 = (x1, y1)$$
$$P2 = (x2, y2)$$
$$P3 = (x3, y3)$$

This gives us a linear set of equations for a, b, and c :

$$V \begin{pmatrix} a \\ b \\ c \end{pmatrix} = \begin{pmatrix} y1 \\ y2 \\ y3 \end{pmatrix}$$

where V is the Vandermonde matrix:

$$V = \begin{pmatrix} x1^2 & x1 & 1 \\ x2^2 & x2 & 1 \\ x3^2 & x3 & 1 \end{pmatrix}$$

By algebraically inverting this matrix we can solve for a, b, and c. If this is done again for the points $P2$, $P3$, and $P4$ a second parabolic arc is obtained with parameters a', b', and c'. By drawing part of the first parabolic arc from $P1$ to $P2$, and part of the second parabolic arc from $P2$ to $P3$, and so on, the whole curve can be drawn. However the slopes at $P2$ are:

$$m = 2 a \, x2 + b$$

and:

$$m' = 2 a' x2 + b'$$

for the two adjoining parabolic arcs, and these are not necessarily equal. Patching a curve together in this manner will in general produce a nonsmooth curve (i.e. the first derivative is not continuous). A better approach is to determine a, b, and c as above, draw the arc from $P1$ to $P2$, and then compute the slope m at $P2$. The next parabolic arc is determined as the parabola passing through $P2$ and $P3$ with slope m at $P2$. Subsequent parabolic arcs are found in a similar way and patching these together results in a smooth spline. The equations to solve for a', b', and c' are now:

$$y2 = a' x2^2 + b' x2 + c'$$
$$y3 = a' x3^2 + b' x3 + c'$$
$$m = 2 a' x2 + b'$$

These alternative linear equations are easily solved algebraically.

Another problem arises with parabolic splines. This problem is shown in Figure 4-5 where the third parabola heads off backwards instead of forwards from point $P3$. The algorithm described above allows cusps to occur in the output as shown in this example. To avoid a cusp we should 'reflect' the parabolic arc with respect to the line joining its end points. The 'reflection' is done along lines of slope m (where m is the arc slope at the first endpoint) rather than perpendicular to the straight line join of the arc's end points.

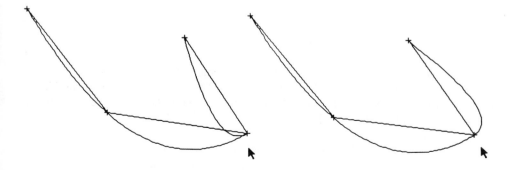

Figure 4-5 A problem with parabolic splines - occurrence of cusps.

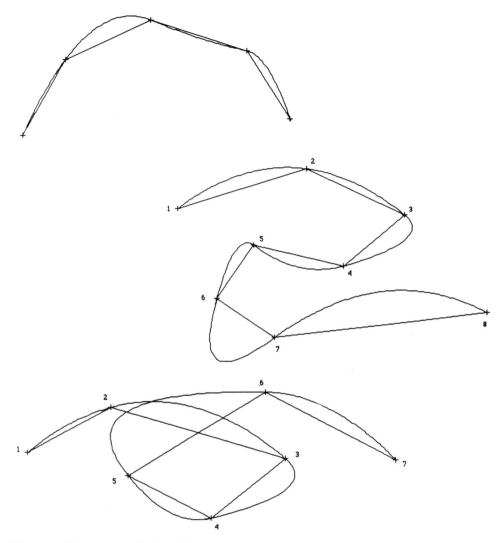

Figure 4-6 Sample parabolic splines.

To 'reflect' an arc, a formula is needed and this formula can be described as follows. Suppose that there is a need to reflect the arc from $P2$ to $P3$, then each point on this arc must be transformed to a new position. In particular, the point (x, y) on the arc between $P2$ and $P3$ is moved to $(xrefl, yrefl)$ where:

$$xrefl = [(y - m\ x) - (y2 - M\ x2)] / (M - m)$$
$$yrefl = [M\ (y - m\ x) - m\ (y2 - M\ x2)] / (M - m)$$

In these equations, M is the slope of the line joining $P2$ to $P3$, that is:

$$M = (y3 - y2) / (x3 - x2)$$

When should we reflect a parabolic arc? The cusps occur whenever there is a reversal in x values of consecutive knot points and this can be easily detected as the spline curve is developed. The results of these corrections are shown in sample parabolic splines in Figure 4-6.

Cubic splines

Cubic splines are a straight forward extension of the concepts underlying parabolic splines. The total curve in this case is a sequence of arcs of cubics rather than parabolic curves. Each cubic satisfies:

$$y = a \ x^3 + b \ x^2 + c \ x + d \qquad (4.41)$$

rather than equation 4.40. A cubic curve requires four points $P1$, $P2$, $P3$, and $P4$ to define it rather than three as for parabolas. There must be at least four knot points for a cubic spline to be drawn. Using four point coordinates in equation 4.41 results in a system of four simultaneous linear equations for a, b, c, and d. Again there is a Vandemonde matrix on the left-hand side of the equation and a column vector of y values $(y1, y2, y3, y4)^T$ on the right.

If these four equations are solved for a, b, c, and d, and the cubic arc plotted from $P1$ to $P2$, and then solved the equations for another four parameters a', b', c', and d' relating to the points $P2$, $P3$, $P4$, and $P5$, and drew the new cubic arc from $P2$ to $P3$, and so forth, then the same problem mentioned for parabolic splining, still exists, namely a lack of smoothness between cubic arc sections. Therefore the requirements for selecting the cubic arcs should be changed. Instead of requiring the arc to pass through four knot points, it is only required to pass through the first two and have the gradients at these two end points match from arc to arc. This would mean solving for a, b, c, and d from the four linear equations:

$$a \ x1^3 + b \ x1^2 + c \ x1 + d = y1$$
$$a \ x2^3 + b \ x2^2 + c \ x2 + d = y2$$
$$3 \ a \ x1^2 + 2 \ b \ x1 + c = m1$$
$$3 \ a \ x2^2 + 2 \ b \ x2 + c = m2$$

However we do not know the $m1$ and $m2$ slope values ab initio.

A solution to this problem which is a generalization of the parabolic spline previously discussed is as follows. Take the first four points $P1$, $P2$, $P3$, and $P4$ and solve for the cubic (a, b, c, d) passing through them as earlier descibed. Plot the part of the cubic from $P1$ to $P2$ only. Now compute the first and the second derivative values at $P2$. These could be called m and s to continue the generalization of the parabolic formulation. Now four equations are still required to determine the next cubic arc. These are obtained by requiring the second arc to pass through $P2$ and $P3$ and start with slope m and second derivative s. Once the coefficients (a', b', c', d') are computed from these equations the cubic arc is drawn from $P2$ to $P3$ and the slope m and second derivative s at the end point $P3$ are computed for the next cubic (if any) in the sequence.

The equations for the second cubic arc coefficients are therefore:

$$a' x2^3 + b' x2^2 + c' x2 + d' = y2 \tag{4.42a}$$
$$a' x3^3 + b' x3^2 + c' x3 + d' = y3 \tag{4.42b}$$
$$3 a' x2^2 + 2 b' x2 + c' = m \tag{4.42c}$$
$$6 a' x2 + 2 b' = s \tag{4.42d}$$

Similar equations apply to the third and subsequent cubic arcs. These equations are simplified by subtracting equation 4.42b from equation 4.42a and dividing through by ($x3$ -$x2$). If equation 4.42c is subtracted from this derived equation, then coupled with equation

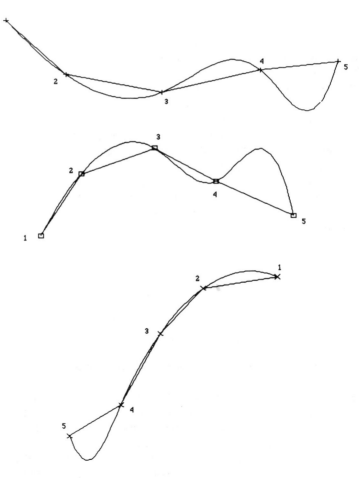

Figure 4-7 Sample cubic splines.

4.42d we have a pair of equations in a' and b' alone. These are easily solved and the result is as follows:

$$a' = [(M - m) / \Delta - s / 2] / \Delta$$
$$b' = s / 2 - 3 a' x2$$
$$c' = m - 3 a' x2^2 - 2 b' x2$$
$$d' = y2 - a' x2^3 - b' x2^2 - c' x2$$

where:

$$\Delta = x3 - x2$$
$$M = (y3 - y2) / \Delta$$

Figure 4-7 shows some cubic splines generated by these formulas. It can be seen that cubic splines do not oscillate about the straight polyline connections as much as the parabolic splines do. In fact the cubic splines are a truer representation of the drafting spline than are parabolic splines. In computer graphics without the physical limitations of a real spline device, the generalization of a drafting spline can be done in many ways. Many different kinds of mathematical splines have been defined in this way and many of these have particularly useful properties. One desirable property is 'local control'. This means that if a knot point is moved interactively then the whole spline curve doesn't have to be recomputed and redrawn, but only the spline sections connected to that point. Another desirable feature in spline functions is a reduction in computational overhead. The fewer floating-point operations that must be performed to produce a given spline curve, the faster the curve can be drawn. Many different spline functions can be found described in works on numerical methods for computation (such as Atkinson, 1978; Conte & deBoor, 1980; Ralston & Rabinowitz, 1978; Hornbeck, 1975; Plastock & Kalley, 1986). A brief summary of the cubic splines often used in computer graphics can also be found in Section 9.2.

4.8 Special curves for computer graphics

The method for defining splines in the previous section depended on them being represented in the *explicit function form* of piecewise polynomials $y = f(x)$. This form is most useful in areas where mathematical interpolation and extrapolation are needed; for given any value of x the corresponding y value is readily estimated. As noted in Section 4.2, the explicit function form is not the most applicable for computer graphics since f must be single valued and therefore loops cannot be included in the curve. The more general *parametric function form* given by equations 4.8a to 4.8c are appropriate to computer graphics. This latter parametric form allows y to be a multivalued function of x and still be representable in computer languages. It is suitable to computer graphics where arbitrarily shaped curves are used. It is not suited to the problem of interpolation and extrapolation of values of y for given values of x especially when the x function cannot be inverted in closed form. A third form for representing curves in two dimensions is the *implicit function form* :

$$F (x ,y) = 0$$

This is the most general form for representing curves in two dimensions in that it encompasses more curves than the other forms in a single equation. However it is not directly suited to computer graphics because it is difficult to derive the coordinates (x ,y) of points on the curve from it. The implicit form can be differentiated to yield a pair of coupled differential equations that can then be integrated (by an accurate Newton-Raphson method, for example) step by step to trace a curve from a given initial point on the curve. The difficulties here are in first finding a point on the curve and then making sure that all parts of the curve have been plotted. For example, the implicit form may represent the two sheets of an hyperbola so that in this case the curve must be drawn from two seed points - one from each sheet. Furthermore with infinite curves, as in this example, integration must be done both forwards and backwards from the seed point on each curve.

There is an interesting theorem one can easily prove concerning the relationship between explicit, parametric, and implict forms when the functions involved are (finite integer) polynomials. This is that if in the parametric form, fx is a polynomial in t of degree m and fy is a polynomial in t of degree n , then one can combine ('implicitize') these to give an implicit function form which is a bivariate polynomial of degree n in x and m in y . The converse to the theorem is also easily proved (by counterexample). This is that the general implicit function which is a bivariate polynomial of degree n in x and m in y cannot always be cast ('parametrized') into the parametric form. In fact one can show that quadratic polynomials (m = n = 2) in the parametric form can only represent parabolas. The general conic cannot be represented by polynomial functions in the parametric form, but only in the implicit form. These theorems show that the implicit form is more powerful than the parametric form which in turn is more powerful than the explicit form (since the explicit form is a special case of the parametric form viz where fx (t) = t). In spite of the restrictions of the parametric form it is widely used in computer graphics and as such we shall look at two smooth curves obtained by piecing together polynomial parametric function segments, Bezier curves and then B-splines.

A Bezier curve in two dimensions is a smooth curve which is defined by n points $(x_i$,y_i) for i = 1 to i = n . It is given by the equations:

$$x (u) = \Sigma_k {}_{=0,m} \ B_{k,m} (u) x_{k +1}$$
$$y (u) = \Sigma_k {}_{=0,m} \ B_{k,m} (u) y_{k +1}$$

where m = n - 1 and the Bezier blending coefficients $B_{k,m} (u)$ are simply the Bernstein polynomial basis functions:

$$B_{k,m} (u) = m ! / k ! / (m -k)! \ \ u^k \ \ (1-u)^{m -k}.$$

It can be readily seen from these equations that:

$$x(0) = x_1 \qquad x(1) = x_n$$
$$y(0) = y_1 \qquad y(1) = y_n$$

that is, the curve starts at the first point in the array and ends at the last. The Bezier curve does not necessarily pass through any of the other points of the array. However it does have the property of remaining within the convex hull defined by the array of points. The convex hull is the polygon formed when a rubber band is stretched around the control points.

A procedure 'plot_Bezier_curve(n,xa,ya)' will be needed that will take as inputs the number of points 'n' and their coordinates in the arrays 'xa' and 'ya'. One way of doing this is to write three supporting procedures. The first called 'compute_Bez_coefficients(m,Bez_coeff)' takes as input 'n-1' and outputs the array 'Bez_coeff[0 .. m]'. This array simply holds the constants:

$$Bez\_coeff[k] = m! / k! / (m-k)!$$

They are created by a suitable loop:

```
for k := 0 to m do
begin
    Bez_coeff[k] := 1.0;
    for j := m downto k+1 do
        Bez_coeff[k] := Bez_coeff[k] * j;
    for j := m - k downto 2 do
        Bez_coeff[k] := Bez_coeff[k] / j;
end;
```

The second procedure uses these coefficients in computing the blending values for each point. It is in fact a function called 'Bez_blending_value(m,k,u,Bez_coeff)' which takes integers 'm' and 'k', real value 'u', and real array 'Bez_coeff' as inputs and returns the corresponding blending value that is to multiply 'xa[k+1]'. This is simply a matter of multiplying 'Bez_coeff[k]' by 'u' k times and by '(1-u)' $m-k$ times. The third procedure 'comp_Bez_pt(n,xa,ya,u,Bez_coeff,x,y)' computes a point at parameter position 'u' along the Bezier curve. The first five parameters are inputs and the last two are output real values - the coordinates of the point on the Bezier curve corresponding to parameter value 'u'. The coding is essentially:

```
x := 0.0;
y := 0.0;
m := n - 1;
for k := 0 to m do
begin
    bv := Bez_blending_value(m,k,u,Bez_coeff);
    x := x + xa[k+1]*bv;
    y := y + ya[k+1]*bv;
end;
```

With these three support routines the 'plot_Bezier_curve' procedure is easily constructed. This routine must first call 'compute_Bez_coefficients' to set up the array 'Bez_coeff'. It then moves to the first point on the curve (corresponding to 'u = 0') and then computes points along the curve at equal intervals of 'u' up to 'u = 1' drawing straight line segments between each pair of points.

If the above algorithm is analysed, it is apparent that computing each Bezier blending value takes m multiplications and so to compute a point on the Bezier curve takes $n \times m$ floating-point multiplications. Box 4-5 shows a more efficient program to plot Bezier curves. This version has two fewer procedures and does not need the array 'Bez_coeff'. It uses the fact that in the sequence of blending values from $k = 0$ to $k = m$ each blending value can be quickly computed from the one before:

$$bv_k = bv_{k-1} \quad (m - k + 1) / k \quad u / (1-u)$$

The improved algorithm therefore only requires $3 m$ multiplications and m divisions and runs considerably faster.

Box 4-5 A procedure to plot two-dimensional Bezier curves.

```
program Bezier_curve(input,output);
const
    POLY_MAX = 100;
type
    real_array = array[0..POLY_MAX] of real;
var
    n : integer;
    xa, ya : real_array;
    Bezier : record
        ax, bx, cx, dx : real;
        ay, by, cy, dy : real;
        end;
    xmax, xmin, ymax, ymin : real;
    Bez_coeff : real_array;
    nr_steps : integer;

procedure initializations;
begin
    writeln('Enter range of x values :');
    write('xmin = ');
    readln(xmin);
    write('xmax = ');
    readln(xmax);
    writeln('Enter range of y values :');
    write('ymin = ');
    readln(ymin);
    write('ymax = ');
```

```
        readln(ymax);
        write('Number of steps in the Bezier curve? (eg 10) ');
        readln(nr_steps);
        init_G2D;
        set_window(xmin,ymin,xmax,ymax);
end;

procedure input_the_points;
var
        i : integer;
begin
        write('Number of points?');
        readln(n);
        for i := 1 to n do
        begin
            write('Enter x[', i : 1, '] y[', i : 1, '] ');
            readln(xa[i], ya[i]);
            plot_point(xa[i], ya[i]);
        end;
end;

procedure compute_Bez_coefficients (nm1 : integer;
var Bez_coeff : real_array);
var
        k, j : integer;
begin
        for k := 0 to nm1 do
        begin
            Bez_coeff[k] := 1.0;
            for j := nm1 downto k + 1 do
                Bez_coeff[k] := Bez_coeff[k] * j;
            for j := nm1 - k downto 2 do
                Bez_coeff[k] := Bez_coeff[k] / j;
        end;
end;

function Bez_blending_value (nm1, k : integer; u : real;
Bez_coeff : real_array) : real;
var
        bv, v : real;
        i : integer;
begin
        bv := Bez_coeff[k];
        for i := 1 to k do
            bv := bv * u;
        v := 1 - u;
```

```
        for i := 1 to nm1 - k do
            bv := bv * v;
        Bez_blending_value := bv;
    end;


procedure comp_Bez_pt (n : integer; xa, ya : real_array; u : real;
        Bez_coeff : real_array; var x, y : real);
var
    k, nm1 : integer;
    bv : real;
begin
    x := 0.0;
    y := 0.0;
    nm1 := n - 1;
    for k := 0 to nm1 do
    begin
        bv := Bez_blending_value(nm1, k, u, Bez_coeff);
        x := x + xa[k + 1] * bv;
        y := y + ya[k + 1] * bv;
    end;
end;


procedure plot_Bezier_curve (n : integer; xa, ya : real_array);
var
    i, nm1 : integer;
    x1, y1, x2,y2,u : real;
begin
    nm1 := n - 1;
    compute_Bez_coefficients(nm1, Bez_coeff);
    comp_Bez_pt(n, xa, ya, 0.0, Bez_coeff, x1, y1);
    for i := 1 to nr_steps do
    begin
        u := i / nr_steps;
        comp_Bez_pt(n, xa, ya, u, Bez_coeff, x2, y2);
        plot_line(x1,y1,x2,y2);
        x1 := x2; y1 := y2;
    end;
end;


begin
    initializations;
    input_the_points;
    plot_Bezier_curve(n, xa, ya);
end.
```

Some samples of Bezier curve plots can be seen in Figure 4-8. From the figures it can be seen that Bezier curves do not have the unstable oscillatory nature of higher degree polynomial fits.

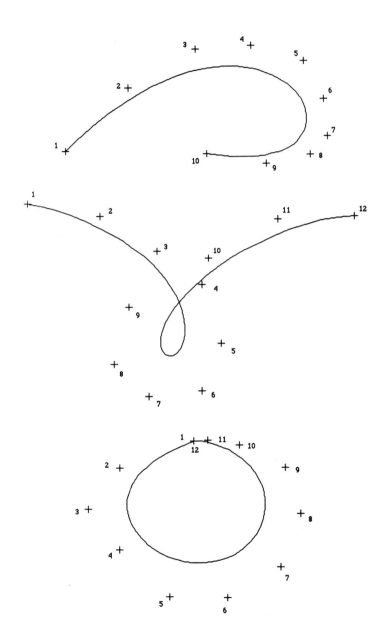

Figure 4-8 Sample two-dimensional Bezier curve plots.

Another smooth curve based on a set of control points is the two-dimensional cubic B-spline. This curve consists of piecewise cubic polynomials in parametric form:

$$x(t) = a_x\ t^3 + b_x\ t^2 + c_x\ t + d_x$$
$$y(t) = a_y\ t^3 + b_y\ t^2 + c_y\ t + d_y$$

The i th cubic passes from (x_i, y_i) at $t = 0$ to (x_{i+1}, y_{i+1}) at $t = 1$ and uses the coordinates of the points at $i-1$, i, $i+1$, and $i+2$ in computing the coefficients in the cubics above. Since each cubic piece uses the coordinates of the point before the piece and the point after the piece it is clear that the B-spline draws a smooth curve from the second-point to the second last point in the control array with the end points being used in the computations of coefficients. The coefficients are computed by a straightforward matrix product:

$$\begin{pmatrix} a_x \\ b_x \\ c_x \\ d_x \end{pmatrix} = \begin{pmatrix} -1 & 3 & -3 & 1 \\ 3 & -6 & 3 & 0 \\ -3 & 0 & 3 & 0 \\ 1 & 4 & 1 & 0 \end{pmatrix} \begin{pmatrix} x_{i-1} \\ x_i \\ x_{i+1} \\ x_{i+2} \end{pmatrix} / 6$$

A similar matrix equation applies to the computation of the four coefficients in the parametric cubic for y:

$$\begin{pmatrix} a_y \\ b_y \\ c_y \\ d_y \end{pmatrix} = \begin{pmatrix} -1 & 3 & -3 & 1 \\ 3 & -6 & 3 & 0 \\ -3 & 0 & 3 & 0 \\ 1 & 4 & 1 & 0 \end{pmatrix} \begin{pmatrix} y_{i-1} \\ y_i \\ y_{i+1} \\ y_{i+2} \end{pmatrix} / 6$$

Procedures for plotting B-splines using this fast technique can be found in Box 4-6.The routine to plot the B-spline takes as inputs 'n', the number of control points, and the arrays 'xa' and 'ya' of coordinate values of these points. The routine has a loop for each cubic piece of the B-spline, computing the coefficients in the cubic, and then plotting the cubic. Note that in the case of the B-spline program separate Pascal functions are provided to evaluate the x function and the y function at a given t value. In the case of the Bezier curves, a single procedure computed x and y simultaneously for a given u parameter value. In the Bezier curve case, it is much more efficient to compute x and y together; whereas in the B-spline case, there is no advantage in computing x and y together in the one routine. Some samples of B-spline plots can be seen in Figure 4-9. From the figures it can be seen that B-splines do not have the unstable oscillatory nature of higher degree polynomial fits. Furthermore they have the property of local control. This means that moving one of the control points does not alter the curve far from that control point - only the local cubic pieces that use the moved point need to be recalculated and redrawn. This property makes the B-splines very useful for modeling arbitrary smooth shapes as easily as altering the outline made by a piece of putty.

In Chapter 9 Bezier and spline functions are encountered again both as curves and as surfaces in three-dimensional space.

Box 4-6 A program to plot two-dimensional B-splines.

```pascal
program B_spline(input,output);
const
    nr_steps = 5;
type
    real_array = array[1..100] of real;
var
    n : integer;
    xa, ya : real_array;
    B_spline : record
        ax, bx, cx, dx : real;
        ay, by, cy, dy : real;
    end;

procedure initializations;
begin
    init_G2D;
    set_window(0,0,100,100);
end;

procedure input_the_points;
var
    i : integer;
begin
    write('Number of points?');
    readln(n);
    for i := 1 to n do
    begin
        write('Enter x[', i : 1, '] y[', i : 1, '] ');
        readln(xa[i], ya[i]);
    end;
end;

function B_spline_x (t : real) : real;
begin
    with B_spline do
        B_spline_x := (ax * t * t * t + bx * t * t + cx * t + dx)/6;
end;

function B_spline_y (t : real) : real;
begin
    with B_spline do
        B_spline_y := (ay * t * t * t + by * t * t + cy * t + dy)/6;
end;
```

```pascal
procedure compute_B_spline_coefficients (i : integer);
begin
    with B_spline do
    begin
        ax := -xa[i - 1] + 3 * xa[i] - 3 * xa[i + 1] + xa[i + 2];
        bx := 3 * xa[i - 1] - 6 * xa[i] + 3 * xa[i + 1];
        cx := -3 * xa[i - 1] + 3 * xa[i + 1];
        dx := xa[i - 1] + 4 * xa[i] + xa[i + 1];
        ay := -ya[i - 1] + 3 * ya[i] - 3 * ya[i + 1] + ya[i + 2];
        by := 3 * ya[i - 1] - 6 * ya[i] + 3 * ya[i + 1];
        cy := -3 * ya[i - 1] + 3 * ya[i + 1];
        dy := ya[i - 1] + 4 * ya[i] + ya[i + 1];
    end;
end;
procedure plot_curve (t1, t2 : real; s : integer);
var
    t, delta_t, x1, y 1,x2,y2: real;
    i : integer;
begin
    x1 := B_spline_x(t1);
    y 1:= B_spline_y(t1);
    delta_t := (t2 - t1) / s;
    for i := 1 to s do
    begin
        t := t1 + i * delta_t;
        x2 := B_spline_x(t);
        y 2:= B_spline_y(t);
        plot_line(x1,y1,x2,y2);
        x1 := x2; y1 := y2;
    end;
end;
procedure plot_B_spline (n : integer; xa, ya : real_array);
var
    i : integer;
begin
    for i := 2 to n - 1 do
    begin
        compute_B_spline_coefficients(i);
        plot_curve(0.0, 1.0, nr_steps);
    end;
end;
begin
    initializations;
    input_the_points;
    plot_B_spline(n, xa, ya);
end.
```

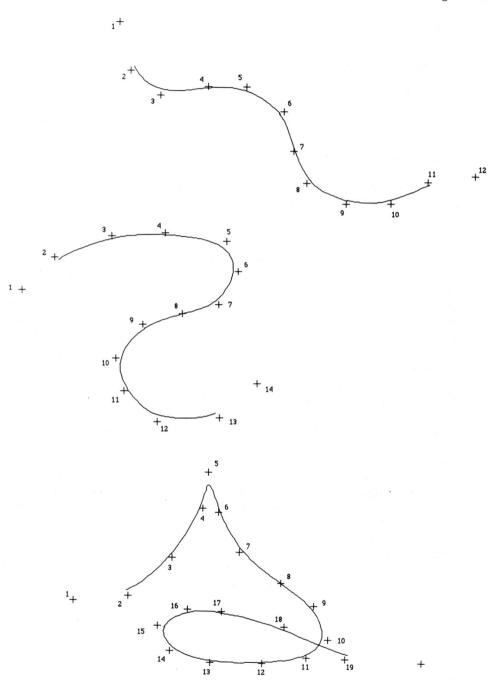

Figure 4-9 Sample two-dimensional B-spline plots.

Problems

4.1   Write seven procedures:

      procedure draw_circle1(xc,yc,r : real)

to:

      procedure draw_circle7(xc,yc,r : real)

according to the algorithms for drawing circles given in Section 4.1. Time them on an available graphics VDU and comment on the results that you get.

4.2   Write and test a procedure:

      procedure draw_arc(xc,yc,r,theta1,theta2: real)

to draw a circular arc. Consider how this could be generalized to draw elliptic arcs and spirals. (For spirals, in place of the parameter 'r' use two inputs 'r1' and 'r2' where 'r1' is the distance of the start of the spiral curve from the centre '(xc,yc)', and 'r2' is the distance at the end of the spiral corresponding to q = 'theta2'. Any radius in between the end points of the spiral is determined from 'r1' and 'r2' in linear proportion to the angle θ from 'theta1' to 'theta2'.)

4.3   Write the spirograph program using a call to a procedure:

      procedure spirograph(rr,rw,rp : integer)

The main routine should ask for the values of the parameters 'rr', 'rw' and 'rp' which should be integers. Allow for spirograms inside the ring by detecting if 'rw' is negative and adjusting the formula as necessary. Use your program to reproduce the spirographics in Figure 4-2 with the parameters given in that figure.For integer input parameters, the spirograph is a closed curve, that is, the functions in equations 4.20 and 4.21 are periodic. Express the period Θ of these functions in terms of the parameters of the spirograph. To always draw completed spirographs allow the curve parameter θ to vary from 0 to Θ. What effect does allowing the parameters 'rr', 'rw' and 'rp' to be real in the above procedure have?

4.4   Write the procedure:

      procedure draw_axes(dxpdiv,dypdiv,tick_size : real)

as described in the text. Also write the procedure:

      procedure draw_polyline(n:integer; xa,ya : array_of_200_reals) as described in the text. Write also the 'sort_data_values' procedure. Put your results together to make the 'plot_data' procedure described in Section 4.4. Test this procedure on a set of real data.

4.5   Write the procedure:

procedure scatter_gram(data:data_points;heading,x_title,y_title : str40)

as described in the text. Write a program to test this procedure on a set of real data.

4.6   Constructing the user types:

```
const
    p = 40;
type
    square_matrix = array[0..p,0..p] of real;
    column_matrix = array[0..p] of real;
```

write the procedure for Gauss-Jordan elimination with the heading:

procedure gauss_jordan(c : square_matrix; r : column_matrix; **var** a : column_matrix);
{This solves the matrix equation C*A = R where C is a ('p'+1) x ('p'+1) matrix, A is ('p'+1) x 1 matrix and R is ('p'+1) x 1 matrix for the matrix A, given C and R, by the Gauss-Jordan elimination method.}

Note that to match the problem definition given in Section 4.5 the rows and columns of these matrices start numbering from zero.
Use your procedure, and the procedure 'least_sq_poly_matrices' to make a procedure:

procedure least_squares_polygon(data:data_points; p : integer;
    var a : column_matrix)

which generalizes the procedure 'least_squares_line' given in the text.

4.7   Write a program to generate random data for the 'data_points' data structure used in the text. Have the program then ask the user whether a least squares line or polynomial fit to the data is required. The program should then call the appropriate procedure (see Section 4.5 and problem 4.5) and finally plot the curve on a scattergram.

4.8   Write a program called 'parabolic_spline1' to draw a parabolic spline through graphics points entered by screen digitization (i.e. the use of a moving cross hairs on the screen and arrow keys). Draw a polyline through the knot points as well so that it is clear where the knot points are. The main routine should be similar to the following code:

```
initialize_graphics;
set_window(0,0,100,100);
enter_points;
plot_polyline(n,xarray,yarray);
parabolic_spline1(n,xarray,yarray);
```

Your 'parabolic_spline1' procedure should call a 'draw_parabolic_arc' procedure which has the heading:

procedure draw_parabolic_arc(a,b,c,x1,x2 : real);

4.9 Write a program called 'parabolic_spline2' to draw a parabolic spline through graphics points digitized from the screen as in problem 4.8. Draw a polyline through the knot points as well so that it is clear where the knot points are. The main routine should be similar to the following code:

```
initialize_graphics;
set_window(0,0,100,100);
enter_points;
draw_polyline(n,xarray,yarray);
parabolic_spline2(n,xarray,yarray);
```

Your parabolic_spline2 procedure should call a draw_parabolic_arc procedure which has the heading:

procedure draw_parabolic_arc(a,b,c,x1,x2 : real);

and a routine to draw a reflected parabolic arc having the heading:

procedure inverted_parabolic_arc(a,b,c,x1,x2 : real);

Be careful to provide the correct end slope of the reflected parabolic arc for the next parabolic arc.

4.10 Write a program similar in structure to the program in problem 4.8, to draw cubic splines. Modify both programs to optionally read knot point data from a file. Using the same data file run the two programs and compare the spline curves produced.

4.11 For any curve $y = f(x)$ in two dimensions derive the following formulas for the tangent and curvature vectors:

$$\tau \equiv d\mathbf{r} \ / \ d\sigma = (1, m) \ / \ \sqrt{(1+m^2)}$$

$$\kappa \equiv d\tau \, / \, d\sigma = (-m, 1) \, s \, / \, (1+m^2)^2$$

where:

$$m \equiv dy \, / \, dx \equiv f\,'(x)$$
$$s \equiv dm \, / \, dx \equiv f\,''(x)$$

and σ measures arc length along the curve. (See for example Kreyszig, 1972.) Hence prove that for the cubic spline method given in Section 4.7 that the tangent and curvature vectors, τ and κ, are continuous across spline sections. The curvature $\kappa \equiv |\kappa|$ and radius of curvature $\rho \equiv 1 \, / \, \kappa$ are therefore also continuous across cubic spline sections.

4.12   Generalize the spline concepts of Section 4.7 to apply to quartic splines. Use continuity of the first, second, and third derivatives, m, s, and t of the quartic curve equation $y = f(x)$ in determining the second and subsequent spline segments. Write a program, similar in structure to the program in problem 4.10, to draw quartic splines. Using the same data file run the three programs for parabolic (problem 4.8), cubic (problem 4.10), and quartic splines and compare the spline curves produced and execution times.

4.13   Lissajous curves are displayed on a cathode ray oscilloscope when the horizontal sweep voltage (x) and the vertical voltage (y) both vary sinusoidally with time. The two sinusoidal signals may have different amplitudes $(A_x$ and $A_y)$, periods $(T_x$ and $T_y)$ and phase angles $(\phi_x$ and $\phi_y)$. Sample Lissajous curves are shown in Figure 4-10. The general parametric equations for Lissajous curves are (Resnick & Halliday, 1966, page 379):

$$x = A_x \, \sin(2 \, \pi \, t \, / \, T_x + \phi_x)$$
$$y = A_y \, \sin(2 \, \pi \, t \, / \, T_y + \phi_y)$$

Write a program to display Lissajous curves.

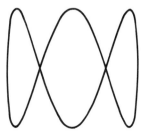 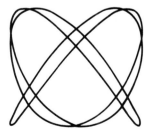

Figure 4-10 Sample Lissajous figures.

5

Two-dimensional graphics objects

5.1 Basic geometrical elements for graphics

A *basic geometrical element* (or *entity*) is defined for the purpose of this book as a simple unit of geometry that is frequently needed in computer graphics. The most obvious examples of these are points and lines. A *basic graphical element* is a *realization* of a geometrical element for actual use in a graphics system, that is, the implementation of a geometrical element used in the display of complex pictures. (See Figure 5-1.) The realization of a geometrical element is the mapping from geometry to a particular graphics output device. This mapping can be done in a variety of ways. Thus a line can be realized on a graphics screen in different colors, line thicknesses, and styles (solid, dashed, etc.). These alternatives (color, size, and style) are called the *attributes* of the graphical element. A graphics picture then is considered to be composed in general of multitudes of the various basic graphical elements with varying attributes. The number of different basic graphical elements and their possible attributes which are available to the user for construction of pictures can be taken as an indicator of the utility, flexibility, and power of the graphics system.

Consider now what elements of two-dimensional geometry could be useful to a two-dimensional graphics system. The most obvious geometrical figures needed within a graphics system are line segments and circular arcs. However other geometrical shapes may also be useful in particular applications. For each geometrical element we need to know its defining equation and what the parameters are in its defining equation. The normal defining parameters which are used in geometry may not be (and in general will not be) adequate for use in computer graphics. Alternative equations and sets of parameters must always be considered. Some alternatives are more natural for the user and some alternative definitions are more general and suitable to the software. In particular since graphics input devices read points in cartesian coordinates the *aim will be to redefine all geometrical elements by means of suitably selected points*. This will be advantageous when we come to transforming graphics elements as we shall see in the next chapter. Examples of useful basic graphical elements are listed below together with their usual geometrical definitions and their definitions in terms of points.

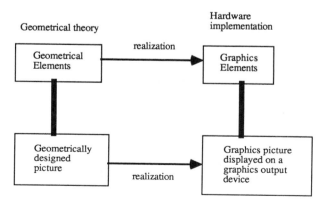

Figure 5-1 The mapping from geometry to computer graphics.

Points

The point is the most basic graphical element and is completely defined by a pair of user coordinates (x, y). Alternatives here are the usage of other coordinate systems such as polar coordinates (r, θ) where:

$$x = r \, \cos(\theta)$$
$$y = r \, \sin(\theta)$$

and:

$$r = \sqrt{(x^2 + y^2)}$$
$$\theta = \arctan(y/x)$$

The next chapter will show that it is better and simpler for the underlying software to operate in Cartesian coordinates (x, y). Therefore if polar coordinates or some other curvilinear coordinate system is desired by the user, they should only appear at the user interface below which the coordinates are immediately converted to Cartesian coordinates. (See problem 5.1.) A geometrical point strictly has no size, but it may be realized in a graphics system as a dot of one or more pixels switched on in the display rectangle. The attributes for the realization of a point are the color, the number of pixels used (the size), and the style such as various marker symbols. These are especially useful in data plotting. See problem 5.11 for examples of markers.

Lines

A line is of infinite extent and can be defined by an angle of slope, θ, and one point on the line $P = (PX, PY)$. This definition requires three real numbers. However angles are not good parameters for defining graphics elements because of the seam connecting $\theta = 0$ and $\theta = 2\pi$. The line can also be defined by only two parameters m the slope $(\tan(\theta))$ and c (the y intercept) as in the usual formula:

$$y = m \, x + c$$

This definition breaks down and is not valid for the line $x = 0$ (where $\theta = \pm\pi/2$). The more useful definition of a line is a linear parametric equation for x and a similar equation for y. This form can also be defined by points:

$$x = a_x + t \, b_x$$
$$y = a_y + t \, b_y$$

The line passes through the point (a_x, a_y) in the direction of (b_x, b_y) and the parameter t extends from negative infinity to positive infinity. The parameter may be rescaled to represent length along the line from the point (a_x, a_y) by dividing it by $\sqrt{[b_x^2 + b_y^2]}$. A routine to produce a line on a graphics output device would normally need a parameter to specify the required thickness of the line. Other parameters may specify if the line is to be a broken line made up of dots and/or dashes, and in what arrangement. These additional parameters are the attributes of the line graphics element.

Rays

A ray is a semi-infinite line. It can be defined by the finite end point (RX, RY) and its slope m or better its angle θ. Alternatively the parametric equations above could be used with the restriction that $0 \leq t \leq \infty$. All the comments for lines therefore apply to rays as well. An additional attribute can be used to describe the shape of the finite end point of the ray – is it square or round, for instance. Rays are often used in geometrical constructs in proving theorems or testing conditions such as whether a point is inside a closed polygon or not. Obviously lines and rays being infinite cannot 'fit' onto the graphics screen – they will be clipped to size. Although the result is a finite line segment, the geometrical concepts of lines and rays can have sufficient importance in some applications to require them to be available as graphical elements to the graphics programmer.

Line segments

A line segment is a finite connected subset of a line and therefore can be uniquely specified by the parametric equation of the line, but with specified limits on its parameter:

$$t_1 \leq t \leq t_2$$

In this method the six real numbers a_x, a_y, b_x, b_y, t_1, and t_2 define the line segment. The natural way to define a line segment however is to specify only the two end points $(X1, Y1)$ and $(X2, Y2)$ and the equations:

$$x = \lambda X1 + (1-\lambda) Y1$$
$$y = \lambda X2 + (1-\lambda) Y2$$
$$0 \leq \lambda \leq 1$$

This is clearly a special case of the former method. All the attributes of lines are applicable to line segments. In addition, there can be an attribute to specify the style at both ends of the line segment, for example, square, oblique, outward 'V', inward 'V', inward semicircle, outward semicircle, bevelled, rounded, and so forth. Sometimes we will loosely use the word 'line' when we really mean a finite line segment.

Arrows

An arrow is a line segment with an arrow head at one end. This is defined by a line segment with the assumption that the arrow head is at $(X2, Y2)$. Arrows are frequently needed in diagrams such as for overhead transparencies, and in flow charts, engineering drawings, and so forth. The points S and T for drawing the line segments for the arrow

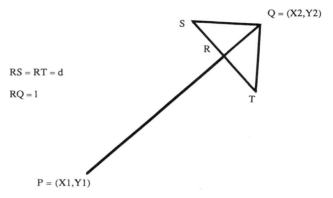

Figure 5-2 Features of an arrow symbol.

head are equidistant from the arrow shaft line segment PQ. See Figure 5-2. One algorithm for determining the coordinates of S and T is as follows. From the diagram, if $Q_x = P_x$ then:

$$S_x, T_x = R_x \pm d$$
$$T_y, S_y = R_y$$

otherwise the slope of PQ must be found:

$$m = (Q_y - P_y) / (Q_x - P_x)$$

and then:

$$S_x, T_x = R_x \pm d\, m\, / \sqrt{[1+m^2]}$$
$$T_y, S_y = R_y + R_x\, / m \pm d\, / \sqrt{[1+m^2]}$$

For an alternative approach see problem 5.12. In these formulas:

$$R_x = \lambda_1 P_x + (1-\lambda_1) Q_x$$
$$R_y = \lambda_1 P_y + (1-\lambda_1) Q_y$$

The length of the arrow head is given by:

$$l = (1-\lambda_1) \sqrt{[(Q_x - P_x)^2 + (Q_x - P_x)^2]}$$

Therefore the following parameters are required to draw this arrow: P_x, P_y, Q_x, and Q_y.

The parameters l and d may be regarded as attributes of the arrow shape; that is, they have default values that can only be changed by a call to a special routine. All the attributes of line segments are again applicable to arrows. Additional attributes may be the shape, the style (straight or curved edges, open, closed, or filled in), and the size of the arrow head.

Rectangles

Rectangles with sides parallel to the coordinate axes (i.e. with sides that are horizontal and vertical only) are used extensively within computer graphics. It is handy to refer to this sort of rectangle as a (two-dimensional) box. One way of specifying a box is to give a corner, say the lower left corner, and then state the width and height of the box in user coordinate units. A box can alternatively be specified uniquely by just two points: the diagonally opposite corners such as the lower left point (XLL, YLL) and the upper right point (XUR, YUR). The general rectangle can then be defined by the chosen box parameters plus an angle of rotation away from the x axis. Alternatively, the rectangle can be specified by two adjacent corners representing one side of the rectangle, say the bottom side, and the perpendicular height of the rectangle. Both of these methods require five real numbers. Another approach is to give the coordinates of three corners of the rectangle – six real numbers. To summarize: in order to define a box shape from a graphics input device two points must be read in, and in order to specify a general rectangle from a graphics input device three points must be read in.

Circles

A circle is defined by its centre (x_c, y_c) and its radius r in user coordinate units. The equation of the circle is:

$$(x - x_c)^2 + (y - y_c)^2 = r^2$$

This definition therefore uses three real parameters. Another algebraic way of representing a circle is by the three real numbers (g, f, c) where the equation of the circle is:

$$x^2 + y^2 + 2gx + 2fy + c = 0$$

(See D. Pedoe, 1979.) Clearly these parameters are related to the previous three by:

$$x_c = -g$$
$$y_c = -f$$
$$r = \sqrt{(f^2 + g^2 - c)}$$

To interactively define circles using graphics input, circle definitions by means of points are preferred. One technique is to specify a diameter by its two end points, say

(X1,Y1) and (X2,Y2), and then the circle is again uniquely defined, but this time by using four real parameters rather than three. To obtain the usual parameters for a circle:

$$x_c = (X1 + X2) / 2$$
$$y_c = (Y1 + Y2) / 2$$
$$r = \sqrt{[(X2 - X1)^2 + (Y2 - Y1)^2]} / 2$$

A second point definition method for circles is described in problem 5.3.

Ellipses

An ellipse can use the same parameters, x_c, y_c, and r, as a circle, in addition to the eccentricity e. The equation for the ellipse then becomes:

$$((x - x_c) / a)^2 + ((y - y_c) / b)^2 = 1$$

where the semimajor axis (a), semiminor axis ($b <= a$) and eccentricity (e) are related by:

$$a = r \ ^4\sqrt{(1 - e^2)}$$
$$b = r / \ ^4\sqrt{(1 - e^2)}$$

The eccentricity is given by $e = \sqrt{(1 - b^2/a^2)}$ where a is assumed to be the semiminor axis (ie $a \geq b$).

Clearly, from these formulas an alternative (and more usual) set of parameters for defining an ellipse are the four real numbers x_c, y_c, a, and b. The ellipse is also uniquely defined by any four points on its circumference. This approach requires eight real numbers. If two of these points are specified as being extremities of the major (or minor) axis then only three points are required. The formula for the ellipse given above only applies when the major and minor axes of the ellipse align with the x-y axes. An angle parameter may be included to give the angle of the major axis anticlockwise from the x axis. Alternatively the coefficients in the expanded quadratic form (below) may be used.

Parabolas and hyperbolas

These other conic sections may likewise be defined and used in the graphics system. They correspond to special cases of the general quadratic form:

$$a x^2 + 2 b x y + c y^2 + d x + e y + f = 0$$

For the parabola:

$$(y - y_c)^2 = 4 a (x - x_c)$$

and the hyperbola:

$$(x - x_c)^2 / a^2 - (y - y_c)^2 / b^2 = 1$$

The shapes can alternatively be put into parametric form. The so called 'freedom-equations' for the parabolas are:

$$x = x_c + a\ t^2$$
$$y = y_c + 2\ a\ t$$

and the freedom-equations for the hyperbolas are:

$$x = x_c + a\ (1+t^2)\ /\ (1-t^2)$$
$$y = y_c + 2\ b\ t\ /\ (1-t^2)$$

These geometrical shapes are used less frequently in computer graphics and it is easy for the user to write the appropriate routines when needed.

Arcs of circles

An arc is a subset of the points of a circle between two specified points on the circumference. An arc is simply defined by the coordinates of the centre (x_c, y_c), the radius r as previously, plus the bounding angles θ_1 and θ_2. The points (x, y) in the arc satisfy:

$$x = r\ \cos(\theta)$$
$$y = r\ \sin(\theta)$$

where:

$$\theta_1 \le \theta \le \theta_2$$

To uniquely define an arc by a minimum number of points, the end points of the arc can be taken plus any point intermediate between them on the arc. Some short calculations show that if $(X1,Y1)$ and $(X3,Y3)$ are the end points of an arc and $(X2,Y2)$ is some point on the arc between the end points, then normal arc parameters are given by the following equations (see problem 5.2):

$$x_c = det1\ /\ det/2$$
$$y_c = det2\ /\ det/2$$
$$r = \sqrt{[(X1 - x_c)^2 + (Y1 - y_c)^2]}$$
$$\theta_1 = \arctan[(X1 - x_c)\ /\ (Y1 - y_c)]$$
$$\theta_2 = \arctan[(X3 - x_c)\ /\ (Y3 - y_c)]$$

where:

$$det1 = (X2^2-X1^2+Y2^2-Y1^2)\,(Y3-Y1) - (Y2-Y1)\,(X3^2-X1^2+Y3^2-Y1^2)$$
$$det2 = (X2-X1)\,(X3^2-X1^2+Y3^2-Y1^2) - (X2^2-X1^2+Y2^2-Y1^2)\,(X3-X1)$$
$$det = (X2-X1)\,(Y3-Y1) - (Y2-Y1)\,(X3-X1)$$

Again note that the six real parameters $X1$, $Y1$, $X2$, $Y2$, $X3$, and $Y3$ are not unique for the second point can lie anywhere on the arc between the first two points. This non-uniqueness is because only five parameters rather than six are required in defining the arc. However the six parameters do define a unique arc.

Arcs of ellipses

Similarly an arc of an ellipse is defined by (x_c, y_c), r, e, θ_1, and θ_2. The points (x, y) on an elliptic arc satisfy:

$$x = a\ \cos(\theta)$$
$$y = b\ \sin(\theta)$$

where:

$$\theta_1 \le \theta \le \theta_2$$

Surprisingly, just three points in the two-dimensional plane can determine a unique elliptic arc. Given the two end points of the elliptic arc as $(X1,Y1)$ and $(X2,Y2)$ and given that the third point is the center of the ellipse which is assumed to have axes parallel to the x and y user axes we can deduce that:

$$x_c = X3$$
$$y_c = Y3$$
$$a = \sqrt{[det\ /\ det1\,]}$$
$$b = \sqrt{[det\ /\ det2\,]}$$
$$\theta_1 = \arctan[(Y1-Y3)\ /\ (X1-X3)\ b\ /\ a\,]$$
$$\theta_2 = \arctan[(Y2-Y3)\ /\ (X2-X3)\ b\ /\ a\,]$$

where:

$$det1 = (Y2-Y3)^2 - (Y1-Y3)^2$$
$$det2 = (X1-X3)^2 - (X2-X3)^2$$
$$det = (X1-X3)^2\,(Y2-Y3)^2 - (Y1-Y3)^2\,(X2-X3)^2$$

Arcs of parabolas and arcs of hyperbolas

These may likewise be defined by taking a finite subrange on the parameter t in the respective freedom-equations given above. The choice of a minimum set of points for uniquely specifying each type are left as problems for the reader. (See problems 5.5 and 5.7.)

Sectors

A sector, also called a wedge, is a closed curve consisting of two radii of a circle and the arc of the circumference between the radii. The same parameters as for arcs of circles are required.

Polygons

A polygon is any closed continuous sequence of line segments, that is, a polyline whose last knot point is the same as its first knot point. The line segments are the sides of the polygon and their points of intersection are the vertexes of the polygon. In the case of a regular polygon the sides are of equal length. To define a polygon, a program requires the number of vertexes 'n' and two arrays containing the coordinates of the vertexes 'xa(1..n)' and 'ya(1..n)'. The procedure 'plot_polyline(n+1,xa,ya)' will produce the same result as 'plot_polygon(n,xa,ya)' if 'xa[n+1]' = 'xa[1]' and 'ya[n+1]' = 'ya[1]'. However the 'plot_polygon' procedure also has an area fill attribute not available to the 'plot_polyline' procedure. This attribute says whether the polygon is to be drawn hollow or filled in. Other attributes for polygons are the area fill style and color. The style attribute describes whether the area is filled uniformly with a color, by hatching, or by some other pattern. Refer also to Chapter 4.

Polynomial fits and splines

These are two methods for fitting smooth curves between a sequence of points. Both require 'n', the number of points to fit a curve to, and two arrays 'xa(1..n)' and 'ya(1..n)' containing the coordinates of these points. They have been discussed in the Chapter 4.

Text labels

Frequently there is a wish to label parts of the graphics output. A label requires a location (x, y) and a string of characters to be displayed. Some languages which do not cater for dynamic strings would instead require the number of characters 'nchar' and the characters in an array 'chars(1..nchar)'. More generally knowledge may be required of the angle 'theta' and the size 'size' at which to write the characters. These are attributes for text labels. Graphics-generated text will be discussed more fully in Section 8.6.

5.2 Graphical element display routines

For every basic graphical element available in the graphics system, there must be a routine to display the element on the graphics output device. These routines must take as inputs the defining parameters of the corresponding graphical element as described in the previous section or else an equivalent set. Intelligent graphics hardware systems have some of these routines built into the hardware and thus are already available by simple calls. For example, most digital plotters have circular arc drawing routines in ROM (read only memory or firmware). In the case of one make of plotter, for example, a circular arc is plotted when it receives the following character stream:

$$\text{'C'} \ x \ \text{','} \ y \ \text{','} \ r \ \text{','} \ t_1 \ \text{','} \ t_2$$

where the parameters x, y, r, t_1, and t_2 are as discussed in the previous section, and are transmitted to the plotter as the string of characters in their decimal representation. The parameters x, y, and r are in the device coordinate units of tenths of a millimeter, and t_1 and t_2 are in degrees between 0 and 360. Most other plotters and graphics VDUs have similar commands directly available to the software.

Wherever these graphics commands are not available in the hardware or firmware, the drawing algorithms have to be implemented as software routines. The latter routines will ultimately call the hardware primitives – the graphics commands actually supplied to control the hardware. The graphics elements or their display routines which are available in a given graphics system are often called *graphics output primitives* in the literature. These are 'primitives' in the sense of software engineering (i.e. the lowest single function modules in the software) in contrast to the hardware primitives (e.g. 'moveto' and 'drawto'); though as seen in the plotter example, the graphics output primitives of a software system may in fact be provided directly by the hardware.

A suitable general approach to making each of these routines is to call 'draw_curve' (see Chapter 4) with the appropriate functions and parameters. This routine allows the t parameter increment Δt to vary in such a way as to make line segment length vary inversely with the local curvature on the locus of the curve to be plotted. It generates the best possible approximation to the true curve for the given number of line segments.

The parameters which are passed as inputs to the display routines are the defining parameters of the graphics elements as discussed in the previous section. However, for the interactive user of a graphics system, parameters like slopes, angles, eccentricities, and so forth needed to produce the desired visual shape are not readily known to the user at the time. These sorts of parameters are also difficult to deal with uniformly since they have their own peculiarities such as the cases of positive and negative infinite slopes, the seam at 2π that angles wrap around, and the need to keep eccentricities nonnegative. In comparison, the advantages of point definitions of geometric elements are easily seen: they are simple to enter interactively to obtain the curve that the user wants visually, they transform nicely under point transformations (as shown in the next chapter), and finally they, having all the same data type, do not have the individual peculiarities of the usual parameters like slopes and angles and so can be treated uniformly. A convention used in this book is that graphics element display routines which use point definition parameters have routine names prefixed by 'plot' (e.g. 'plot_circle(x1,y1,x2,y2)'), while graphics element display routines which use the normal parameters of geometry for parameters are prefixed by 'draw' (e.g. 'draw_circle(xc,yc,r)'). Again note that point definitions of graphics elements usually involve more parameters than the usual definitions. For example, the point definition of a circle takes four real parameters whereas the geometric definition requires only three real parameters. This leads to some arbitrariness in the choice of points to define each graphics element. Although the choice of points for parameters is not unique, the graphics element they define is unique, defined by the specification of the mathematical relationship of the point coordinates to the usual geometrical parameters that define the graphics element.

A simple example is to draw a standard ellipse centred at (x_c, y_c) with semimajor axis a and semiminor axis b. Using the general 'draw_curve' procedure of the previous chapter the following procedure can be written to draw this graphics element:

```
procedure draw_ellipse(xc,yc,a,b : real);
{Draw an ellipse with centre at (xc,yc) and semi-major and minor axes as
a and b in user coordinates.}
const
    pi = 3.1415926;
    function xellipse(theta) : real;
    begin
        xellipse := xc + a * cos(theta);
    end;
    function yellipse(theta) : real;
    begin
        yellipse := yc + b * sin(theta);
    end;

begin
    draw_curve(xellipse,yellipse,0,2*pi);
end;
```

(Compare this with problem 5.13 where the corresponding 'plot_ellipse' procedure is defined.)

Some of the geometric elements that are of interest have an infinite extent, for instance, lines, rays, parabolas, and so forth. It may seem strange for graphics display routines to be needed for geometric elements that are infinitely long: the screen is finite after all. Nevertheless infinite geometric elements are found to be useful in computer graphics. An example of where (infinite) lines are needed is in drawing axes. When a picture is scaled down, the visible limits of the axes should not also be scaled down – the axes must still reach to the extremities of the display area.

Attributes may be set explicitly by passing them as parameters or implicitly by accessing them through global data structures (COMMONs in the FORTRAN language). The latter approach is usually adopted so as to unclutter the parameter passing for the user. This means that the system provides default attributes for the user, and if the user wants other values for the attributes then a call to explicit routines will change the default attribute values. Attribute parameters are almost invariably nonnegative integers. Integers are used because the types of attributes available are often a discrete set of nondescript possible styles for graphics output. There is no inherent ordering in the possible styles so a numbering is arbitrarily given to them. The integer value zero is often the default attribute value but sometimes zero is used to mean that the graphics element is not to be displayed and the default corresponds to attribute index value of one. Negative attribute values or values beyond the number available are errors and can be reported as such by the software. The attributes available for each output primitive are often hardware dependent. When the desired attribute is not available in the graphics hardware, *attribute programming* must be undertaken; that is, the attributes are implemented in software. Some attribute-setting procedures based on graphics elements mentioned in Section 5.1 are:

    'set_point_style(i)'
    'set_point_size(s)'
    'set_line_style(i)'
    'set_line_dash_length(s)'
    'set_line_thickness(i)'

where 'i' is the attribute index (an integer) and 's' is a real number measuring length in millimeters. Procedures such as these are needed for every attribute of every graphics element implemented in a graphics software package.

5.3 Graphic objects

All graphics pictures are built up from the basic graphical elements as discussed in Section 5.1. However, there is a need to be able to build within a graphics display picture named and identifiable units that can be independently manipulated. These units are termed graphics objects, and the notion of writing graphics programs using graphics objects is called graphics object oriented programming. A graphics object is an incorporation of

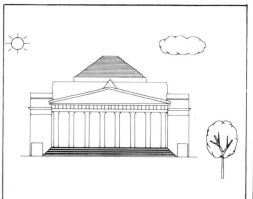

Figure 5-3 Computer-drawn pictures consisting of many graphics objects. (Note that two-dimensional graphics objects may be used in composing three-dimensional scenes such as these, however they cannot be transformed to produce new three-dimensional views.)

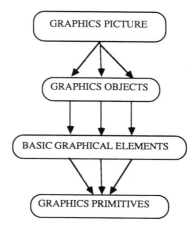

Figure 5-4 Graphics picture structure.

many basic graphical elements into a single identifiable unit and as such consists of lists of graphical elements. A graphics picture will in general consist of many graphics objects. (See Figure 5-3.) Figure 5-4 shows the hierarchical relationship between graphics pictures, objects, entities, and primitives.

There are two approaches to implementing graphics objects within a program : the *procedural* approach and the *data-driven* approach. In the former method, for every graphics object that the user wishes to place in a picture there is a procedure that draws the particular object based on only a few configurational parameters: every graphics object has its own display routine. In the latter approach, graphics objects are specified by named data structures that are individually passed to the one general drawing routine: one display routine is used for every possible graphics object.

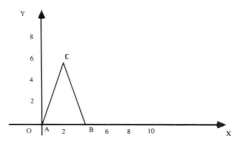

Figure 5-5 An elementary graphics object.

As a simple example, a triangle is a two-dimensional graphics object consisting of three line segments. Triangle ABC is shown in Figure 5-5. The data structure to represent it in software is the following list of line segments:

AB, BC, CA

Figure 5-6 shows some other graphics objects. These are the five symbols used in flowchart diagrams: start, stop, and continuation bubbles, process boxes, decision boxes, and input and output boxes. Each of these can be stored in the computer memory as a graphics object as lists of line segments, arcs, and circles. For instance, the bubble is a single graphical element, a circle (or else two arcs, say, top half and bottom half). The decision box is a list of line segments:

AB, BC, CD, DE, EF, FA

(or else a single polygon). The printout symbol consists of a list of line segments:

EF, FG, GA

and a list of arcs:

ABC, CDE

In the procedural approach to graphics objects, a procedure would be written to draw the general triangle ABC given the coordinates of its vertexes A, B, and C. A different procedure would be used to draw rectangles such as in Figure 5-6(b) or decision boxes as in Figure 5-6(c).These procedures would then only be relevant to flowcharting. In the data-driven approach to graphics objects, the data of each graphics object is fed into the same display routine. This display routine can be one of the library of graphics routines provided to the programmer in a graphics software package. It is equally useful for a very wide range of graphics objects. The data-driven approach to programming graphics objects is taken in this book because of its greater generality.

The picture units, or graphics objects, within any flowchart are obvious. However in general, the separation of an arbitrary picture into graphics objects is not a unique process. There is no right or wrong choice here: the decision is entirely up to the user of the system.

The user will normally design graphics objects one at a time and save each one onto a disk file. Some time later will come the composition of one or more complete pictures using the library (or libraries) of graphics objects that have been built up. In the flowchart symbols example, a library of five graphics objects representing the five flowchart symbols is stored, and this allows a program to draw any desired flowchart easily.

Graphics object libraries should allow for flexibility. Users may wish to edit the graphics objects by adding to or removing from the lists of graphics elements in each graphics object. This point is covered in Section 5.6. However, first will be a description of a simple data structure for a limited graphics object concept and procedures for handling this concept.

5.4 Data structures for graphics objects

In designing graphics package software for the graphics object concept, two key decisions must be made: what graphics elements may be members of graphics objects and what data

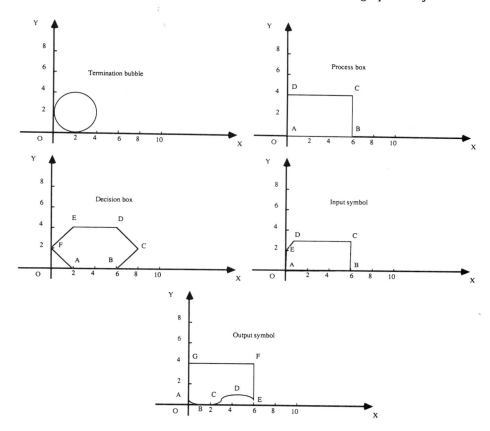

Figure 5-6 Graphics objects suitable for making flowcharts. (a) Termination bubble.
(b) Process box. (c) Decision box. (d) Input symbol. (e) Output symbol.

structures are used to hold them. The simplest choice for graphics objects would be lists
of line segments only. The problem with this design is that often too many line
segments would be needed, especially to form smooth curves. The small amount of data
used to define often needed curves like circles and arcs is a great saving in line segment
counts. So a better type of graphics object is one that consists simply of line segments,
circles, and circular arcs. This can be represented by three lists: a list of line segments, a
list of circles, and a list of arcs. In the more general case, lists could come from any of
the selection of graphics elements discussed in Section 5.1. In any case there is a need for
a lot of list-type data structuring.

In a language with static data structures only, a list is represented by an integer
giving the number of elements in the list, and an array (or several) containing the data for
each entry in the list. For example, for graphics objects that consist of only line
segments and arcs (with no more than 200 line segments and 100 arcs), the following
Pascal data structuring is suitable:

```
const
    max_nr_line_segs = 200;
    max_nr_circles = 100;
    max_nr_arcs = 100;
type
    line_segment_type = record
        x1,y1,x2,y2 : real;
        end;
    circle_type = record
        x1,y1,x2,y2 : real;
        end;
    arc_type = record
        x1,y1,x2,y2,x3,y3 : real;
        end;
    graphics_object = record
        name : string[40];
        nr_line_segs : integer;
        line : array[1.. max_nr_line_segs] of line_segment_type;
        nr_circles : integer;
        circle : array[1.. max_nr_circles] of circle_type;
        nr_arcs : integer;
        arc : array[1.. max_nr_arcs] of arc_type;
        end;
```

Graphics objects are generally dynamic entities. They may have parts added to them or deleted from them and will vary in the numbers and types of graphics elements included in them. Therefore static data structures such as those above are too limiting. Pascal allows for dynamic data structures through the use of pointers (anonymous variables), and the procedures 'new' and 'dispose'. It also has the variant record type so that the same record type can be used to hold line segment, arc, and circle parameters for instance. In this case the following data structuring is suitable:

```
type
    graphics_element_node_ptr = ^graphics_element_node;
    graphics_element_node = record
        next,prev : graphics_element_node_ptr;
        graphics_element_type : (line_type,arc_type,circle_type);
        case graphics_element_type of
            line_type : (x1,y1,x2,y2 : real);
            arc_type : (x1,y1,x2,y2,x3,y3 : real);
            circle_type : (x1,y1,x2,y2 : real);
        end;
```

Dynamic data structures for general two-dimensional shapes are considered in Chapter 7.

Note that as shown before arcs could have been defined by the center coordinates, a radius, and two angles. However, since a subsequent primary interest is the manipulation, and in particular the linear transformation, of graphics objects, these parameters cannot be handled in a uniform and simple way. The linear transformation equations for points and hence line segments are well-known and straightforward. (See Chapter 6.) But the scalars called r, θ_1, and θ_2 of the alternative method do not transform uniformly among all linear transformations. It is clearly far better to have all basic graphical elements defined in terms of points (x, y) as these have easy transformation rules. It may be that the definition of a basic graphical element contains more parameters when expressed in this way, but this is not so important, and the computer is capable of carrying the extra data. With less variety in the parameter types to be stored for graphics objects, the list structuring is also made easier.

Another advantage in storing basic graphical elements as point data is that it makes possible graphics screen input of the graphics element. Points are easily entered from a graphics screen or digitizer and hence all basic graphical elements can be defined interactively from the graphics input device. (Note that a graphics screen is ordinarily considered to be an output device only. Yet through the use of cross-hairs graphics cursors and software that keeps track of the current location of the cross hairs, and by using single nonechoed keystroke input from the keyboard as an indicator to the software, the screen may be viewed as a graphics input device. See Section 3.7.)

More general data structuring allows for other graphics elements to be present in the graphics object and uses dynamic data structures. Since it has been agreed that all graphics elements be defined in terms of points, and all graphics input and output primitives operate on point coordinates, it is preferable to hold a list of coordinate data in memory for any graphics object and have graphics elements index into the points table for actual coordinate values. Furthermore, the Pascal 'new' and 'dispose' functions could be used to make the lists truly dynamic. Each graphics element will then be represented by a record containing the right number of integers which are indexes into the points table, together with a pointer to another record of the same kind. The graphics object itself is then a list of pointers to the types of graphics elements catered for. (See problem 5.14.)

5.5 Displaying graphics objects

Only one routine is required to display the wide variety of possible graphics objects. Since any graphics object simply consists of lists of the various available graphics elements, the display routine will essentially loop through all line segments calling the line segment display routine, and then loop through all circular arcs calling the arc display routine, and so forth. The display routine must be passed the entire data structure for any given graphics object. It may also have to convert the defining parameters to those required for the graphical element display routines. In the example of the arc from the previous section, the display routine must translate each '(arc[i].x1, arc[i].y1, arc[i].x2, arc[i].y2, arc[i].x3, arc[i].y3)' set into the '(xcent, ycent, radius, theta1, theta2)' form for a low-level arc display routine. Note that the low-level arc display routine provided in firmware often uses the former list of inputs because they are the more natural defining set of data and they define arcs uniquely. The other basic graphical element display routines provided by the hardware may use parameters that need to be derived from the parameters in the graphics object data structure.

Some graphics software packages cause each graphic element to be drawn as it is being added to the graphics object list structures. A graphics object display routine is still necessary however, for if the screen is cleared the user must be able to redraw the graphics object without repeating calls to draw its constituent elements. Some other graphics software packages do not explicitly provide the graphics object display routine to the programmer. However, this routine will still exist within the graphics software package

Box 5-1 The display_graphics_object procedure.

```
var
    current_go : graphics_object;

procedure display_graphics_object;
{Procedure to display the data stored in the current graphics object data
structure.}
var
    i : integer;
    x1,y1,x2,y2,x3,y3 : real;
    xc,yc,radius,theta1,theta2 : real;
begin
    with current_go do
    begin
        for i := 1 to nr_line_segments do
        begin
            x1 := line[i].x1; y1 := line[i].y1; x2 := line[i].x2; y2 := line[i].y2;
            plot_line(x1,y1,x2,y2);
        end;
        for i := 1 to nr_circles do
        begin
            x1 := circle[i].x1; y1 := circle[i].y1;
            x2 := circle[i].x2; y1 := circle[i].y2;
            convert_circle(x1,y1,x2,y2,xc,yc,radius);
            draw_circle(xc,yc,radius);
        end;
        for i := 1 to nr_arcs do
        begin
            x1 := arc[i].x1; y1 := arc[i].y1;
            x2 := arc[i].x2; y2 := arc[i].y2;
            x3 := arc[i].x3; y3 := arc[i].y3;
            convert_arc(x1,y1,x2,y2,x3,y3,xc,yc,radius,theta1,theta2);
            draw_arc(xc,yc,radius,theta1,theta2);
        end;
    end;
end;
```

and this enables the package to automatically redraw the graphics object after a change such as when the user calls the clear screen routine. If the current attributes of each graphics element are also stored in the graphics object within graphics element data, then the graphics object display routine should extract each element's attributes at the same time as its parameters. This means that graphics objects may consist of solid lines, dashed lines, arcs of single and double pixel thickness, circles in various colors, and so forth. In addition to the components of graphics objects having individual attributes, the graphics object as a whole may have global attributes. Typical attributes for a graphics object are whether it is to be displayed (its *visibility* attribute), whether it is to be displayed highlighted in some way (such as by being brighter than usual or by having it flashing on and off) (its *highlighting* attribute), whether it can be selected with a pointing device (such as a mouse, light pen, or cross hairs) (its *detectability* attribute), what is its drawing order relative to other graphics objects (its *priority* attribute), and what is its position, scaling, and orientation. A header record for the list could store these attributes, and the graphics object display routine would first look into the header record to take note of these global attributes.

For the simple static graphics object design presented in the previous section, the routine 'display_graphics_object' in Box 5-1 would suffice as a graphics object display routine.

5.6 Loading and saving graphics objects

Loading a graphics object means reading it in from disk or other secondary storage medium. Saving is the opposite operation namely that of writing the data definition of the graphics object out to disk. This leads to a consideration of what file data structure is appropriate to hold the graphics object. The file data are a copy of the memory data structure for the graphics object plus possible check data which are redundant information. A suitable decision is to store the graphics object data in text files which will mean that the data can be created and modified via an ordinary text editor. In designing the layout for the graphics object files, the user should be kept in mind and the format made as readable as possible. Comments and keywords are therefore allowed. Computer graphics deals with large amounts of data so when there are errors in the data they tend to be painfully obvious when the graphics is displayed but extremely difficult to locate in the data file. Adequate and accurate commenting within the source file should enable the bugs to be more easily found. It is also convenient to have many (related) graphics object data structures stored within the one data file. This means that the graphics objects will be accessed by the sequential access method. This results in a slower and less flexible way of loading graphics data. However it is suitable for the initial setup of graphics data until it is verified bug free. After that stage the data could be transferred to a direct access binary file.

An appropriate file data structure for the simple line segment, circle, and arc graphics object is for the start of data for a graphics object to be indicated by the keyword 'NAME'. Following this keyword and on the same line is the text string name of the graphics object enclosed in single quotes. Subsequent lines shall start with the key words 'LINE', 'CIRCLE ', or 'ARC ' with the appropriate coordinate data following on the same line. These three kinds can be intermingled in any order. The end of the graphics data for this graphics object is signified by the keyword 'END ' at the start of a line. After this keyword there would be either another graphics object data layout or the end of file. Comments may also be freely sprinkled throughout the data file. Any line starting with an asterisk is counted as a comment only. Comments can also be added at the end of the other sorts of valid lines after all the data for the keyword of that line has been specified. To make it easier on the user, lower case letters are allowed in the keywords, and the keywords can be abbreviated to a single letter. At least one space must follow the abbreviated keyword letter.

As an example, the triangle in Figure 5-5 could be stored in a file as follows:

```
* Graphics object data definition for the triangle in Figure 5-5:
NAME 'triangle'
LINE 0 0 4 0                        -- the line AB
LINE 4 0 2 6                        -- the line BC
LINE 2 6 0 0                        -- the line CA
END
* end of data.
```

Note the use of comments in this file. In this structure the first character on each line tells the computer the purpose of the line. A line starting with 'N' or 'n' is the first line of a graphics object, and the definition is complete when 'E' or 'e' is encountered as the first character on a line. Also quotes are not necessary on the name string if it has no imbedded space characters. The file may therefore be abbreviated to the form:

```
n triangle
l 0 0 4 0
l 4 0 2 6
l 2 6 0 0
e
```

but this style would be less helpful in locating data errors (especially in larger files).

The graphics data file consists then of multiple copies of this kind of record. Of course more sophisticated graphics data bases (often multilevel ISAM databases) occur in professional graphics systems. In particular the file would be indexed on the name of the graphics object, and contain information on the relationships between graphics objects within a graphics picture. As stated earlier, these data structures can be used after the data are typed in in the above format, and checked on a graphics output device using the 'display_graphics_object' routine.

Having decided on a structure, routines are now needed to load and save the graphics objects from files with this format using industry-extended Pascal. These are easy to write, and an example is shown in Box 5-2.

Another way of creating a graphics object is by the interactive usage of a graphics input device such as a digitizer or a movable cross hairs on the graphics screen. It will be

Box 5-2 Graphics object load and save procedures.

```
{Global file identifiers :}
var
    go_out_file, go_in_file : text;
    current_go : graphics_object;

procedure select_output_go_file(filename : string);
{Implementation dependent routine to open the disk file specified in filename
as the current graphics object output file. This routine should be modified to
see if the file to be created already exists. If so the routine could ask the user if
he wants to erase the old file or not before proceeding. If not then the file
should be opened in append mode so that new graphics object data will be
added at the end of a currently existing graphics object file.}
begin
    rewrite(go_out_file,filename);
end;

procedure select_input_go_file(filename : string);
{Implementation dependent routine to open the disk file specified in the string
filename as the current graphics object input file. If the file to be opened does
not exist the error should be reported and processing continue rather than
have the program abort because of a file name error.}
begin
    reset(go_in_file,filename);
end;

procedure save_graphics_object(name : string);
{Saves the current graphics object to the currently opened graphics object
output file.}
const
    quote = 39; {ASCII code for the single quote character}
var
    i : integer;
begin
    with current_go do
    begin
        writeln(go_out_file,'NAME ',chr(quote),name,chr(quote));
        for i := 1 to nr_line_segs do
            writeln(go_out_file,'LINE ',line[i].x1,line[i].y1,line[i].x2,line[i].y2);
        for i := 1 to nr_circles do
            writeln(go_out_file,'CIRCLE ', circle[i].x1, circle[i].y1,circle[i].x2,
                circle[i].y2);
        for i := 1 to nr_arcs do
            writeln(go_out_file,'ARC ',arc[i].x1,arc[i].y1,arc[i].x2,arc[i].y2,
```

```
                arc[i].x3,arc[i].y3);
        end;
        writeln(go_out_file,'END ');
 end;

 procedure load_graphics_object;
 {Loads the next graphics object in the currently opened graphics object input
 file as the new current graphics object.}
 var
        exit : boolean;
        ch : char;
        i : integer;

        procedure skip_to_spaces;
        {This routine reads characters from the current text line of the file
        go_in_file to skip the keyword looking for the separating space(s)
        or tab(s).}
        const
            tab_char = 9; {ASCII code for a horizontal tabulation character}
        var
            ch : char;    {Local variable only}
        begin
            while (ch <> ' ') and (ord(ch) <> tab_char) do
                read(go_in_file,ch);
        end;

 begin
        exit := false;
        with current_go do
        begin
            nr_line_segs := 0;
            nr_circles := 0;
            nr_arcs := 0;
            while not eof(go_in_file) and not exit do
            begin
                read(go_in_file,ch); skip_to_spaces;
                case ch of
                    '*' :
                        readln(go_in_file,comment); {ignore comments}
                    'n', 'N' :
                        readln(go_in_file, name);
                    'l', 'L' :
                    begin
                        i := nr_line_segs + 1;
                        readln(go_in_file,line[i].x1,line[i].y1,line[i].x2,line[i].y2);
```

```
                    nr_line_segs := i;
            end;
            'c', 'C' :
            begin
                i := nr_circles + 1;
                readln(go_in_file,circle[i].x1,circle[i].y1,
                circle[i].x2,circle[i].y2);
                nr_circles := i;
            end;
            'a', 'A' :
            begin
                i := nr_arcs + 1;
                readln(go_in_file,arc[i].x1,arc[i].y1,arc[i].x2,arc[i].y2,
                arc[i].x3,arc[i].y3);
                nr_arcs := i;
            end;
            'e', 'E' :
                exit := true;
            otherwise
                error('**invalid line in graphics object input file **');
        end;
      end;
    end;
  end;
```

handy to have a routine that can read in graphics object data directly from the graphics input device using special key codes to interpret the meanings of the points being read in. For example, one particular digitizer has four buttons on a puck with cross hairs that can be moved precisely over any point on the digitizing tablet surface. The buttons are labelled 'Z' (zero), '1', '2', and '3' and return hit codes of 1, 2, 4, and 8 respectively. Combinations of these could be used in any desired manner. For instance: 'Z' to end the graphics object data, '1' on all points for lines, '2' on all points for circles, and '3' on all points for arcs. Thus '1' signifies the start point or end point of a line segment wherever the software is up to in reading points. Another approach is to use different buttons for the different points in a graphics element. For example : 'Z' means exit. If a '1' occurs as the first hit code then a line segment is being defined and the second point is given with button code '2'. If a '2' occurs first then a circle is being defined and the second point must be a '3'. If a '3' arrives as the first hit code of a graphics element then an arc is meant and the other two points are signified by '1' and '2' respectively. This approach is probably more prone to error than the former method. Other combination schemes can be devised, but a different approach again is to ignore the button code from the digitizer and operate under console keyboard control. That is, the user types characters at the keyboard indicating what graphics element is now being entered. This approach could be accompanied by a menu of choices (exit, line segment, circle, or arc) on a text screen. The procedure in Box 5-3 is illustrative of these ideas. The actual hit code scheme implemented in this version is the first one mentioned above. Note that it may not be

Box 5-3 Procedure to digitize a graphics object.

```
procedure read_graphics_object(go_name : string[40]);
{Reads a graphics object from the currently selected graphics input device as
the new current graphics object.}
var
    exit : boolean;
    ch : char;
    hit_code,i : integer;
begin
    exit := false;
    with current_go do
    begin
        nr_line_segs := 0;
        nr_circles := 0;
        nr_arcs := 0;
        name := go_name;
        while not exit do
        begin
            read_point(hit_code,x1,y1); ch := chr(hit_code);
            case ch of
                '2' :
                begin
                    i := nr_line_segs + 1;
                    read_point(hit_code,x2,y2);
                    line[i].x1 := x1; line[i].y1 := y1;
                    line[i].x2 := x2; line[i].y2 := y2;
                    nr_line_segs := i;
                end;
                '4' :
                begin
                    i := nr_circles + 1;
                    read_point(hit_code,x2,y2);
                    circle[i].x1 := x1; circle[i].y1 := y1;
                    circle[i].x2 := x2; circle[i].y2 := y2;
                    nr_circles := i;
                end;
                '8' :
                begin
                    i := nr_arcs + 1;
                    read_point(hit_code,x2,y2);
                    read_point(hit_code,x3,y3);
                    arc[i].x1 := x1; arc[i].y1 := y1;
                    arc[i].x2 := x2; arc[i].y2 := y2;
                    arc[i].x3 := x3; arc[i].y3 := y3;
```

```
                    nr_arcs := i;
           end;
           '1' :
                    exit := true;
           otherwise
                    error('**invalid hit code on reading a point **');
           end;
       end;
   end;
end;
```

suitable for screen input if the numeric keypad (and hence the digits '0', '1', '2' and '3') is being used to direct the cross hairs around on the screen. Minor modifications are necessary for alternative schemes.

The similarity of this routine to the graphics object load routine is obvious. It is also clear how to change the routine to make it suit any set of hit codes that the graphics programmer may wish to implement. All that would have to be done would be to change the character selectors in the case statement and possibly add some checking for valid hit codes on the second and third points read in for a graphics element. The above routine does no checking on the second and third hit codes but to include checks may be thought useful. As with the graphics object loading procedure sample code, no checking was done on whether too many line segments, circles, or arcs were being loaded for the size of the (static) array structures. This sort of check should also be incorporated in both of these procedures.

5.7 Examples of graphics objects

The data for two graphics objects are presented in Box 5-4. They are stored in a text file with a file name suited to the operating system such as 'ART.DATA'. The objects are displayed in Figure 5-7. The procedural calls to produce this graphics output are as follows:

```
set_window(0,0,100,100);
open_input('ART.DATA');
load_graphics_object;
display_graphics_object;
write('Ready for next object?'); readln(ans);
clear_screen;
set_window(0,0,10,10);
load_graphics_object;
display_graphics_object;
close_input;
```

The file listed in Box 5-5 and called something like 'ELECTRONIC.SYMBOLS' (or an abbreviation depending on operating system naming restrictions) holds graphics object data definitions for ten symbols used in electronic circuit diagrams. This data file is used in sample applications later in this book. The graphics objects in this file are displayed in Figure 5-8. Procedure calls to display these objects are similar to those for the previous example. The graphics objects of Box 5-5 are all defined within user coordinate (window) limits of (0,0) to (10,10).

Box 5-4 Two sample graphics objects.

```
* Start of a graphics object text file.
* First graphics object is a shed :
NAME 'SHED'
* the shed consists of 9 line segments :
LINE      10 10 40 10
LINE      40 10 40 40
LINE      40 40 25 50
LINE      25 50 10 40
LINE      10 40 10 10
LINE      10 40 40 40
LINE      20 10 20 30
LINE      20 30 30 30
LINE      30 30 30 10
END            -- no arcs or circles.

* The second graphics object is a simple Christmas tree design :
NAME 'CHRISTMAS TREE'
* consisting of 16 line segments :
LINE      5.0 9.0 6.0 7.5
LINE      6.0 7.5 5.5 7.5
LINE      5.5 7.5 6.5 6.0
LINE      6.5 6.0 6.0 6.0
LINE      6.0 6.0 7.0 4.0
LINE      7.0 4.0 3.0 4.0
LINE      3.0 4.0 4.0 6.0
LINE      4.0 6.0 3.5 6.0
LINE      3.5 6.0 4.5 7.5
LINE      4.5 7.5 4.0 7.5
LINE      4.0 7.5 5.0 9.0
LINE      5.2 4.0 5.2 2.5
LINE      4.8 2.5 4.8 4.0
LINE      3.5 2.5 6.5 2.5
LINE      6.5 2.5 5.8 1.0
LINE      5.8 1.0 4.2 1.0
LINE      4.2 1.0 3.5 2.5
*there are no arcs in the Christmas tree :
END
* < End of File>
```

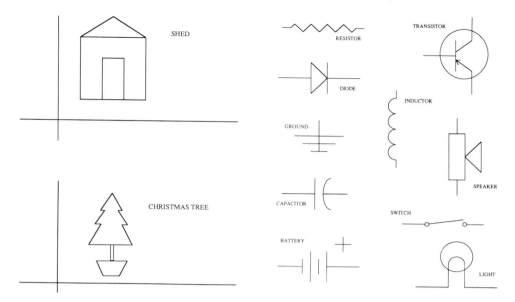

Figure 5-7 Graphics objects from Box 5-4.   **Figure 5-8** Graphics objects from Box 5-5.

Box 5-5 Electronic circuit symbols.

```
* First electronic circuit component graphics object
NAME 'RESISTOR'
LINE     0 0 1.0 0
LINE     1.0 0 1.5 0.5
LINE     1.5 0.5 2.5 -0.5
LINE     2.5 -0.5 3.5 0.5
LINE     3.5 0.5 4.5 -0.5
LINE     4.5 -0.5 5.5 0.5
LINE     5.5 0.5 6.5 -0.5
LINE     6.5 -0.5 7.5 0.5
LINE     7.5 0.5 8.5 -0.5
LINE     8.5 -0.5 9.0 0.0
LINE     9.0 0.0 10.0 0.0
END
*
* 2nd graphics object :
NAME 'DIODE'
LINE     0 0 4 0
LINE     4 -2 4 2
LINE     4 2 6 0
LINE     6 0 4 -2
LINE     6 -2 6 2
```

```
LINE    6 0 10 0
END
*
* 3rd graphics object :
NAME 'GROUND'
LINE 0 0 0 -2
LINE -3 -2 3 -2
LINE -2 -3 2 -3
LINE -1 -4 1 -4
END
*
* 4th graphics object :
NAME 'CAPACITOR'
LINE    0 0 4 0
LINE    4 -2 4 2
LINE    5 0 10 0
ARC     6 -2 5 0 6 2
END
*
* 5th graphics object :
NAME 'BATTERY'
LINE 0 0 3 0
LINE 3 -1 3 1
LINE 4 -2 4 2
LINE 5 -1 5 1
LINE 6 -2 6 2
LINE 6 0 10 0
LINE 7 3 9 3
LINE 8 4 8 2
END
*
* 6th graphics object :
NAME 'INDUCTOR'
LINE 0 0 0 -1
LINE 0 -9 0 -10
ARC 0 -1 -1 -2 0 -3
ARC 0 -3 -1 -4 0 -5
ARC 0 -5 -1 -6 0 -7
ARC 0 -7 -1 -8 0 -9
END
*
* 7th graphics object :
NAME 'TRANSISTOR'
LINE    0 0 4 0
LINE    6 -5 6 -2
LINE    6 5 6 2
```

```
LINE     4 2 4 -2
LINE     4 0.5 6 2
LINE     4 -0.5 6 -2
LINE     4 -0.5 4.8 -0.5
LINE     4 -0.5 4.5 -1.2
CIRCLE  2 0 8 0
END
*
* 8th graphics object :
NAME 'SWITCH'
LINE 0 0 3 0
LINE 3.5 0 7.5 1
LINE 8 0 10 0
CIRCLE 3 0 3.5 0
CIRCLE 7.5 0 8 0
END
*
* 9th graphics object :
NAME 'SPEAKER'
LINE 0 0 0 -2
LINE -1 -2 1 -2
LINE 1 -2 1 -8
LINE 1 -8 -1 -8
LINE -1 -8 -1 -2
LINE 1 -5 3 -3
LINE 3 -3 3 -7
LINE 3 -7 1 -5
LINE 0 -10 0 -8
END
*
* 10th and last graphics object for electronic circuits :
NAME 'LIGHT'
LINE 0 0 4 0
LINE 4 0 4 3
LINE 6 3 6 0
LINE 6 0 10 0
ARC 4 3 5 4 6 3
CIRCLE 3 4 7 4
END
*<End of File>
```

5.8 Generalized graphics objects

The graphics objects described in Sections 5.4 to 5.7 are limited to a quota of line segments, circles, and arcs. A more powerful design for grouping graphics elements than this is usually required. One obvious improvement is to allow any of the graphics output primitives available in the software to be included in the graphics object. Another improvement is to implement dynamic listing so that any number of output primitives can be used (subject ultimately to main memory limitations). The simple static list design for graphics objects of Section 5.4 can also be improved by incorporating attribute values with each element in the object, and also global attributes for the graphics object as a whole as discussed in Section 5.5. A still more general kind of graphics object is possible: the *generalized graphics object* allows other graphics commands apart from graphics element display and attribute setting commands to be grouped into one object.

Many graphics systems maintain a *display list* , an ordered list of all the graphics commands associated with a particular unit or units within the picture. The purpose of this is twofold. Firstly it saves a condensed form of the output graphics, and secondly if something is erased from the output screen other picture units can readily be restored from the display list memory. The display list on such devices is a feature of the hardware and there is a special memory area called the display list memory. For those graphics devices without a display list memory, it can be simulated in software. This idea can be applied here so that a generalized graphics object is then simply a list of graphics commands (procedure calls) in chronological sequence. The file structure for holding these generalized graphics objects can be an extension to the file structure holding the simple style of graphics objects. Then all available graphics procedure calls such as clearing the screen, and window and viewport setting can be included as well in the graphics object file. Again there is no need to place parentheses around the parameters on each line of the file. The software can accept lower case as well as upper case procedure names. The procedure names could also be abbreviated, for instance, allowing 'ARROW ' as well as 'PLOT_ARROW '. Some lines in the generalized graphics object file such as 'NAME ', comment, and 'END ' lines, do not correspond to graphics procedures. They are nevertheless useful and necessary to keep in the file.

A simple memory data structure can also be provided. When a generalized graphics object is loaded from file it can be stored in main memory as a Pascal internal file with exactly the same format as the external disk file. Although as a rule this is not an efficient usage of memory (for example, comments need not be retained, procedure names could be coded, and parameter values converted to binary equivalents), this internal data structure does provide maximum flexibility in a simple way. It also means that if the graphics object is edited within the program, or appended to, then on saving it again to a disk file, the old comments will reappear.

With these choices for the generalized graphics object file structure and memory resident data structure, loading a graphics object and saving one are simple operations of copying one sort of sequential text file to the other (external to internal, and vice versa). Displaying a graphics object on the other hand now involves 'interpreting' the internal file of graphics commands. That is, the display routine must look at the file line by line. On each line the routine must discover which procedure it is required to call, extract the required number of parameters from the rest of that line, and then call the appropriate procedure with these parameter values. (Graphics interpreters are discussed in more detail in Chapter 15.)

The style of graphics object presented in this section allows for much more flexible graphics programming than that of previous sections. Note that the graphics elements are now called in the order in which they are found in the data file, rather than by doing all line segments first, followed by all circles, and then all arcs as in the simpler style of graphics object. More importantly with this generalized graphics object, hierarchical object structures are possible. That is, the graphics objects can be nested to any depth within other graphics objects. This is possible because the command 'load_object' (and similar ones for modifying generalized graphics objects as discussed below) is a valid possible command line in a generalized graphics object data file. Another useful feature of generalized graphics objects is that being files they are easily merged. A program can read in several graphics objects into memory simultaneously by opening several internal files (up to the number allowed by the compiler and operating system), and any pair of these can be merged into another internal file, displayed, or written to disk.

In summary then the simple procedures listed below are required to manipulate generalized graphics objects. Two special data types are used in these procedures. They are defined as:

```
type
     str40 = string[40];
     text_ptr = ^text;
```

Additionally the simple idea of a (single) current graphics object on which all operations act will continue to be used. For generalized graphics objects, this takes the form:

```
var
     current_object : text;
```

The implementation of these routines as Pascal code is left as an exercise. (See problems 5.11 and 5.12.)

Note firstly that the two routines discussed in Section 5.6 that open a nominated external disk file for reading and writing can still be used. The other graphics object handling procedures of that section need modification to the following form:

1. 'load_object' – reads the next generalized graphics object in the currently open graphics object file into main memory as the 'current' graphics object called 'current_object'.
2. 'display_object' – reads through all the lines in the 'current_object' file, determines the required graphics function of each line and then performs each function.
3. 'save_object' – writes the current generalized graphics object stored in the 'current_object' internal file to the currently open graphics object output file by appending to the end of the sequential file.

Additional procedures can now be added to the list of generalized graphics object handling procedures to take advantage of the flexibility provided by the generalized graphics objects. These procedures are :

1. 'store_object(**var** obj : text_ptr)' – Copies the 'current_object' internal file to a new internal file pointed to by the pointer 'obj'.
2. 'restore_object(obj : text_ptr)' – Copies the internal file pointed to by the pointer 'obj' to become the 'current_object' internal file overwriting any previous contents of that file.
3. 'zero_object' – Empties the 'current_object' internal file.
4. 'open_object' – Opens the 'current_object' internal file for appending further graphics commands. Any subsequent graphics calls are written to this file rather than being executed immediately.
5. 'close_object' – Closes the 'current_object' internal file so that further graphics procedure calls are executed in the normal manner rather than being appended to the end of the 'current_object' file list of graphics commands.
6. 'merge_object(obj : text_ptr)' – Appends a copy of the generalized graphics object pointed to by the pointer 'obj' to the end of the 'current_object' file.
7. 'edit_object' – Allows editing of the current graphics object from within an executing application program.

This last routine could be implemented in a number of ways. In one method the routine steps through each line of 'current_object', performs each line, and copies the lines to a new version of 'current_object'. After each line the routine waits for a keypress command from the user. A return key or space bar causes the next line to be performed. If 'D' is pressed by the user then the last line is not copied into the new version of 'current_object'. If 'I' is pressed then new lines may be inserted at this point in the object. Inserting can be done by typing in the line from the keyboard and/or using screen digitizing to enter the point coordinates. If 'E' is pressed then the command of the last line is copied to the new 'current_object' file but the coordinates of the points used as parameters can be changed by use of the screen digitizing routine. When new command lines are inserted or points are edited in this way the new version of the lines are also displayed. Other edit object commands are available to the user such as 'C' to convert from single stepping through the object to continuous mode and 'S' to stop continuous mode and revert to single stepping through the lines of the current object file. The 'C' and 'S' edit commands are useful for speeding through graphics objects that are very large. Once the data bug is seen on the screen the 'S' command can be used and then the other editing commands. Another edit command that would be useful is 'B' to go backwards from a certain point in the file. This is a little difficult for sequential files of variable record length.

Problems

5.1   Some mathematical curves are better expressed in polar coordinates than Cartesians. For instance, the equations may be single valued in polars but not in Cartesians. Write routines 'polar_to_cartesian' and 'cartesian_to_polar' for converting polar coordinates ('r','theta') to Cartesian coordinates ('x','y') and vice versa. Use one of these routines and 'plot_line' to plot the curve of a cardioid given by

$$r = a \ (1 + \cos(\theta))$$

by line segments between n equal increments of θ from 0 to 2π.

5.2   Compute the values of x_c, y_c, r, θ_1, and θ_2 for an arc given the three defining points (x_1, y_1), (x_2, y_2), and (x_3, y_3) and so verify the formulas in Section 5.1.

5.3   For screen input, circles can be defined by just two points. Two definitions are possible. In the first, the two points are the center and a point on the circumference. In the second the points are the end points of a diameter. For each of these methods, derive the equations relating the normal circle definition parameters (center coordinates and radius) to the coordinates of the two points. Check your formulas for the second method with the formulas given in Section 5.1. Now using routines previously defined in this book, write two Pascal programs to display a circle from screen input via movable cross hairs for the two methods. Comment on which method you think that the user might find more useful in a typical application.

5.4   Prove that an ellipse with major and minor axes parallel to the coordinate axes can be uniquely determined by four points on its circumference. Substitute the known constants (x_i, y_i) for $i = 1$ to $i = 4$ into the Cartesian equation of an ellipse and solve the resulting four simultaneous equations for the ellipse parameters x_c, y_c, a, and b.

(*Hint* : Subtract the first equation from the other three to form three new equations. Divide the first of the latter set of equations into the remaining two of this set giving two rational linear equations for x_c and y_c alone. These equations can be rearranged into lineo-linear form[†] , that is, each being a sum of a constant term, a multiple of x_c, a multiple of y_c, and a multiple of the product $x_c\,y_c$. Use the first of these to express y_c in terms of x_c and substitute into the second. Having obtained x_c and y_c, substitute into the first and second of the original

---

[†] A relation between variables x and y of the form $a\,x + b\,y + c\,x\,y = d$ is called a *lineo-linear* relationship. (See Sommerville, 1956, page 223.)

four equations. Subtracting these will give the ratio of b to a and by substituting for b in the first equation a can be found, and hence b .)

5.5   Write a routine called 'draw_parabolic_arc' which draws a short continuous section of a parabola using the parameters 'xc' , 'yc' , 'a' , 't1', 't2', and 'n'. Here ('xc','yc') is the parabolic center, 'a' is the standard parabolic parameter, 't1' is the initial t value, 't2' its final value, and 'n' is the number of line segments to use for making the approximation to the smooth curve. The parabola is another example of a geometrical element of infinite extent so now write a routine 'draw_parabola' to display as much of a parabola as is visible within the current window. This routine should refer to the window limits to determine 't1' and 't2' so that the curve does not go outside of the current user coordinate window and then call 'draw_parabolic_arc'.

5.6   Determine the minimum number of points and the appropriate choices for a set of points that can uniquely define a parabola. Work out the mathematical formulas relating the coordinates of these points to the standard parameters of a parabola as given in Section 5.1. Use your answer to design a Pascal routine calling other routines defined already to read in points from the screen to define a parabola, and then display the parabola via the procedure 'draw_parabola' of problem 5.5.

5.7   Write a routine called 'draw_hyperbolic_arc' which draws a short continuous section of a hyperbolic curve using the parameters 'xc', 'yc', 'a', 'b', 't1', 't2', and 'n'. Here 'xc', 'yc', 'a', 'b' are the standard hyperbolic parameters, 't1' is the initial t value, 't2' its final value, and 'n' is the number of line segments to use for making the approximation to the smooth curve. Assume that if 'a' and 'b' are the same sign (positive) then the arc is a piece of the right-hand curve and if they are of opposite sign then the arc should be from the left-hand curve of the hyperbola. Now write a routine 'draw_hyperbola' to display as much of both curves of the hyperbola (which is infinitely long) as is visible within the current window. This routine should refer to the window limits to determine 't1' and 't2' so that the curve does not go outside of the current user coordinate window, and then call 'draw_hyperbola_arc'.

5.8   Determine the minimum number and appropriate choices for a set of points that can uniquely define an hyperbola. Work out the mathematical formulas relating the coordinates of these points to the standard parameters of hyperbolas as given in Section 5.1. Use your answer to design a Pascal routine calling other routines defined so far in the book to read in points from the screen to define a hyperbola, and then display the hyperbola via the procedure 'draw_hyperbola' of problem 5.7.

5.9   Write a procedure that draws an asteroid of radius r centered at (x_c , y_c) where one axis of the figure make an angle ϕ with the positive x axis.
The parametric form of the asteroid is (for $\phi = 0$ and centered at the origin):
$$\{(r \cos^3(\theta), r \sin^3(\theta)) : 0 < \theta < 2\pi \}$$

5.10   Change the procedure 'save_graphics_object' so that it will insert the string ' TO ' between coordinate pairs in the output file. Correspondingly change the 'load_graphics_object' procedure to ignore the presence or absence of the word ' TO ' between coordinate pairs. Note that lines and circles have only two coordinate pairs so that only one occurrence of ' TO ' should be expected, for example:

LINE 0 0 TO 4 0

On the other hand, arcs have three coordinate pairs so that at most two ' TO ' strings could be expected as in:

ARC 6 -2 TO 5 0 TO 6 2

Next consider what is involved in relaxing the syntax further by allowing parentheses and commas to be inserted in graphics object files as, for example, in the line:

ARC (6,-2) TO (5,0) TO (6,2)

The load routine should not worry about error checking for matching parentheses. Allowing upper and lower case letters (with lower case letters folding to upper case on reading in) equally, these mean that the following command line style is also acceptable:

LINE(0,0,4,0)

Finally allow indenting by making the loading routine skip initial spaces and tab characters on the command line. These changes allow for highly readable graphics object data files.

5.11   Implement the routines: 'load_object', 'save_object', 'store_object', 'restore_object', 'zero_object', and 'merge_object' as discussed in Section 5.8. Allow the flexibility in graphics object file structure that is discussed in problem 5.10. Write the general design for the procedure 'display_object' and give a specific instance of this routine that uses the procedures: 'window', 'plot_line', 'plot_circle', 'plot_arc', 'plot_arrow', and 'plot_ellipse', as well as all the graphics object manipulation routines mentioned in Section 5.8.

5.12   Implement the procedure 'edit_object' as discussed in Section 5.8. Use the procedure 'display_object' (see problem 5.11) as a basis.

5.13   Construct the procedures 'plot_point(x,y : real)' and 'point_style(index : integer)' to plot 10 marker symbols selected from those shown in Figure 5-9. The former procedure should call the 'user_to_phys(x,y,px,py)', 'move_to(px,py)' and 'draw_to(px,py)' routines. If the index is between 0 and 9 then the markers selected from Figure 5-9 should be displayed at (x,y) where marker 0 is the single pixel say and the other markers are 2 mm by 2 mm. If the index parameter for 'point_style' is greater than 9 then the digits to the left of the lowest in the decimal form of the number are the scaling factors. Thus 'point_style(43)', will result in points being plotted as marker symbol 3 in a square 8 mm x 8 mm centered on the desired point (x ,y) in the output graphics.

5.14   Create a graphics object file consisting of all the flowchart symbols as shown in Figure 5-6. Using either the simple graphics object manipulation routines or the generalized graphics object routines show the way that any flow chart can be drawn with this data.

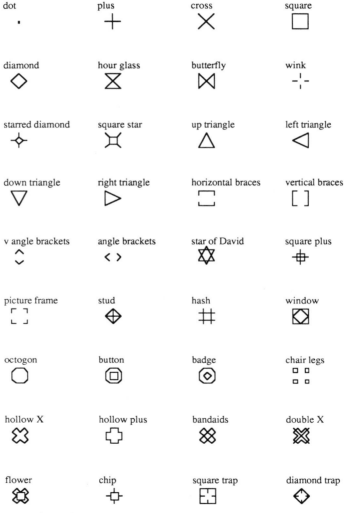

Figure 5-9 A selection of marker symbols useful for representing key points in curve plots.

6

Two-dimensional transformations

6.1 Active and passive transformations

All geometry and graphics is based upon points. To transform a geometrical picture therefore implies that each point of the picture is to be transformed in some defined way. The geometrical picture is realized on a graphics screen (or other graphics output device) by pixels with each geometrical point realized by a pixel (in a many to one relationship). A transformation on the geometrical points making up the picture then induces a transformation on the pixels in the graphics realization of the picture. (See Figure 5-1.) The relationship between points and pixels is determined by the viewing transformation. Recall that the routine 'select_user_coords' or 'set_window' sets up user coordinate space with a window and 'set_viewport' sets up a viewport on the output rectangle to correspond to the window in user coordinates. Transformations will be done in user coordinates and the effects induced on the pixels by the viewing transformation will be noted.

The general two-dimensional point transformation is given by a pair of equations:

$$x' = f_1(x, y) \tag{6.1}$$
$$y' = f_2(x, y) \tag{6.2}$$

where f_1 and f_2 are functions that are not necessarily linear in their arguments. A more compact notation for the general transformation is:

$$X' = F(X) \tag{6.3}$$

where X, F, and X' are two-dimensional column vectors, that is, 2×1 matrices:

$$X \equiv (x, y)^T \qquad F \equiv (f_1 f_2)^T \quad X' \equiv (x', y')^T$$

(The superscript T means take the transform, that is, convert a row matrix into a column matrix.) The coordinates in X and X' are user coordinates which are transformed by F. There are two opposing ways to interpret the transformation expressed in the equation above. It can be viewed as an active transformation or as a passive transformation.

Active transformations

In the active transformation X and X' represent different points in the same coordinate system. The transformation causes points to move, so that if all points are operated upon by the same active transformation then the shape defined by the original points will be distorted. For example, if:

$$x' = 2x$$
$$y' = 2y$$

represents an active transformation applied to all points in two-dimensional space then the (x, y) space will be expanded like a piece of rubber by a factor of two equally in all directions. The transformation has actively moved points to new physical positions. The physical coordinates of (x, y) and (x', y') are different.

Passive transformations

In a passive transformation X and X' represent the same point in space but in a different coordinate system. In this interpretation

$$x' = 2x$$
$$y' = 2y$$

is simply a renaming of all points in space due to a change of user coordinates. For this transformation, the coordinate scales (distances between the tick marks on the axes) are halved thereby causing all coordinate values to double. The coordinates of a point change not because of a shifting of the point through space but because of the use of a new coordinate system (i.e. a new set of axes) to relabel points. The physical coordinates corresponding to (x,y) and (x',y') are the same.

Another way of looking at the difference between active and passive transformations is that active transformations operate on points (moving them) while passive transformations operate on the coordinate axes (thereby implicitly affecting all points). An active transformation may effect only a few selected points whereas a passive transformation implicitly effects all points.

The transformation equations can be interpreted equally well as an active transformation or as a passive transformation. However the interpretation can effect the graphics output or the manner of using the transformation routines. Thus if the graphics package is built on the assumption that all transformations are active, then plotting the point X and next the point X' produces two different points on the screen. If however the package assumes all transformations are passive then plotting X, computing the transformation and plotting X' may cause the same point to be plotted on the output – that is, no change in the graphics output. If instead of plotting X' as the second point the programmer chose to plot X again, then a new point would be plotted on the output rectangle. In fact plotting X, doing a passive transformation, and then plotting X again produces the same result as plotting X, using the inverse active transformation, and plotting X'.

It is possible for the graphics package to have a different implementation style for passive transformations. Supposing that the transformation does not transform the window limits then the passive transformation will move points like an active transformation, but unlike an active transformation, it will move all points by the same transformation equations simultaneously.

Thus it is important to note that some graphics software is built on the assumption of passive transformations, and others use active transformations. In the equations and routines throughout this book the assumption will be made that all transformations are active. Since points in user coordinate space are realized as pixels on the graphics output screen, the active transformation (usually) results in a different selection of pixels. In the case of a passive transformation on any graphics picture, all the displayed pixels move rather than just the few that have been operated upon. The pixels move because the window limits are not affected by the transformation.

6.2 Two-dimensional transformation groups

A group in the sense of Pure Mathematics is a set T together with a binary operator '*' on the elements of T such that:

1. $a*b \in T$ whenever a and b are elements in T (closure under *).
2. T contains an identity element e such that $e*a = a*e = a$ for all elements a in T (existence of an identity).

3. $(a*b)*c = a*(b*c)$ for all elements $a, b, c \in T$ (associativity rule).

4.   For every element $a \in T$ there is an inverse element a^{-1} for which $a*a^{-1} = e = a^{-1}*a$ (existence of an inverse).

The set of all possible two-dimensional transformations F forms a mathematical group in this sense under functional composition. This means that if $F \equiv (f_1, f_2)$ and $G \equiv (g_1, g_2)$ are two-dimensional transformation functions in this notation, then so is their group 'product' $H = F*G$ where:

$$H = (h_1, h_2)$$

and h_1 and h_2 are obtained by function composition:

$$h_1 = f_1(g_1, g_2)$$
$$h_2 = f_2(g_1, g_2)$$

Thus if F maps X to X', and G maps X' to X'', then the product $F*G$ maps X to X'' via:

$$x'' = h_1(x, y) \equiv f_1(g_1(x, y), g_2(x, y))$$
$$y'' = h_2(x, y) \equiv f_2(g_1(x, y), g_2(x, y))$$

Of interest here are the subgroups of the group of all two-dimensional transformations – that is, those subsets of the total transformation group whose members form a group among themselves. When the elements of a subgroup are represented by equations of the same form differing only by different values of parameters in the equations, as in:

$$X' = F(X; A) \tag{6.4}$$

where:

$$A \equiv (a_1, a_2 \ ...) \tag{6.5}$$

are the group parameters, the subgroup is called a continuous parametrized group or Lie group. Each set of values for the group parameters, A, uniquely specifies one of the transformations of the group. The product of two group elements (i.e. transformations of the group) having parameters A and B respectively produces a group element with parameter C which depends on A and B:

$$X'' = F(X'; B) = F(F(X; A); B) \equiv F(X; C)$$

$\Rightarrow$

$$C = \phi(A, B)$$

The functions in ϕ are called the group composition functions: they are the 'multiplication table' of the group. These relationships are explored in the Lie group examples that follow. The Lie groups of most interest in two-dimensional graphics have mathematically simple transformation equations.

6.3 Two-dimensional transformation of graphics elements

It was explained in Section 5.1 how geometrical elements such as line segments, polylines, conics, and arcs of conics, each of which consists of an infinite number of points, can be defined by means of a finite set of points. A geometrical element is transformed by applying the transformation function F to each of its constituent points. This means applying F an infinite number of times, a practical impossibility. Another approach is to apply F to each point in the finite point set used to define the geometrical element, and then use these transformed points to generate another instance of the geometrical element. This latter instance of the geometrical element may unfortunately not be identical to the transformed geometrical element. A geometrical element is said to be *invariant* under a group if the set of points obtained by applying any transformation F to all the points of a geometrical element is the same as that generated after applying F to the finite set of points that define the geometrical element.

Consider the effect of the general transformation of the previous section applied to a line segment. Let the line segment have end points $X_1 = (x_1, y_1)^T$ and $X_2 = (x_2, y_2)^T$. Any point X where:

$$X = (x, y)^T$$

on the line segment satisfies the equation of a line segment. That is, there exists a λ such that:

$$X = \lambda X_1 + (1-\lambda) X_2 \qquad (6.6)$$
$$0 \le \lambda \le 1. \qquad (6.7)$$

After the transformation $X' = F(X)$ is applied to all points of the line segment, what shape is produced? If the transformed points X_1', X_2', and X' satisfy the same line segment equation for the same λ value then the result will be a line segment. This property will not always be true of the general transformations F of the previous section.

However line segments are preserved as line segments under first-degree polynomial transformations, that is, where the function $F(X)$ takes the form:

$$X' = A *X + B \qquad (6.8)$$

where A is a constant 2 x 2 invertible matrix and B is a constant 2 x 1 column matrix. This group is called the affine group. Thus the category of line segments is invariant under the affine group. This assertion is easily seen to be true for line segments by applying the transformation in equation 6.8 to equation 6.6. The result is the same equation with X', X_1', and X_2' in place of X, X_1, and X_2. In other words, after the transformation, the equation is still that for a line segment and corresponding points on the line segment even have the same λ values. For the results of transforming some other geometrical elements refer to the problems 6.2, 6.9, and 6.10.

Furthermore, transformations of this kind are a subgroup of the group of all two-dimensional transformations (see problem 6.3). Henceforth only these linear inhomogeneous transformations in user coordinate space will be considered. In expanded (nonmatrix) form these equations are:

$$x' = a_{11} x + a_{12} y + b_1 \qquad (6.9)$$
$$y' = a_{21} x + a_{22} y + b_2 \qquad (6.10)$$

The parameters of this group are the six coefficients in the matrices A and B as shown in these equations. The functions $f \equiv (f_1, f_2, ...f_6)$ which relate parameters in a product of transformations can easily be deduced. (See problem 6.4.)

A closer look can now be taken of the well-known subgroups of the general first-degree transformation group. The four different kinds of first-degree transformations are special cases of the equations above. For example, if A is the identity matrix then the equations represent a translation with b_1 and b_2 the displacements in the x and y directions. If on the other hand B is zero and A is a multiple of the unit matrix the transformation is a dilatation (uniform expansion), and if more generally A is only diagonal this is the subgroup of scalings. If B is zero and A satisfies

$$A^T A = I$$

then A is a rotation matrix and the transformation is a rotation of points about the origin. The final useful kind of transformation occurs when A is triangular with unit determinant and B is zero (i.e. $b_1 = b_2 = 0$) and this kind is called a shear transformation. For all of these subgroups, the identity transformation occurs when A is the identity matrix and B is zero.

The linear transformations are therefore any combination of only four kinds:

1. translation;
2. scaling;
3. rotation; and
4. shears.

Each of these kinds of transformation will be dealt with in more detail. For each transformation subgroup, a Pascal routine must be written to perform the transformation expressed in equation 6.8. In order to visualize the actions of a group better, the transformation will be applied to a simple graphics object: the unit square *ABCD* as shown in Figure 6-1, where $A = (0,0)$, $B = (1,0)$, $C = (1,1)$ and $D = (0,1)$. The transformation is applied to each vertex of the square resulting in a new quadrilateral *A'B'C'D'*.

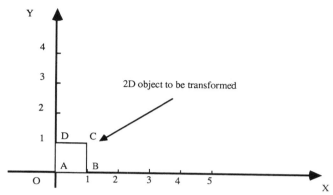

Figure 6-1 The unit square - a simple graphics object to demonstrate transformations.

Translation of graphics objects

As stated above, the transformations expressed by equation 6.8 are translations when *A* is the identity matrix. To translate the complete graphics object, every point (x,y) in the graphics object must undergo a displacement to a new point (x',y'):

$$(x,y) \rightarrow (x',y')$$

according to:

$$x' = x + t_x$$
$$y' = y + t_y$$

This is a two-parameter Lie group where the parameters are given by $A = (t_x, t_y)$ the displacement vector for translating a point. The identity transformation is the case where the parameters are zero, that is, $A = (0,0)$. The inverse of the translation defined by the parameters $A = (a_1, a_2)$ is the one defined by the parameters $A = (-a_1, -a_2)$. If the translation defined by the parameters $A = (a_1, a_2)$ is applied to $X = (x, y)^T$, followed by a translation with displacement parameters $B = (b_1, b_2)$ then the result is equivalent to the single translation with parameters $C = (c_1, c_2)$ where:

$$c_1 = a_1 + b_1$$
$$c_2 = a_2 + b_2$$

or in matrix form:

$$C = \phi\,(A,B\,) = A + B$$

These two equations embody the composition functions for the translation group: the resultant displacement of two translations is the vector sum of the separate displacement vectors.

The two-dimensional translation group has many subgroups. An example of a two-parameter subgroup is the case where t_x and t_y are restricted to integral values rather than real values. If t_x and t_y are functions of another parameter say t as in:

$$t_x = t_x\,(t\,)$$
$$t_y = t_y\,(t\,)$$

then this is a one-parameter subgroup of the translation group. For example the functions:

$$t_x = a\;t$$
$$t_y = b\;t$$

where a and b are constants provides an interesting class of subgroups. When b is zero, the set of transformations is a subgroup that moves points parallel to the x axis. When a is zero, the set of transformations is another subgroup, that which moves points parallel to the y axis, and so forth.

To translate a graphics object the following procedure must be applied to every coordinate pair in the graphics object data structure:

procedure translate_point(tx,ty : real; **var** x,y : real);
{Perform the translation of point P = (x,y) in user coordinates by the

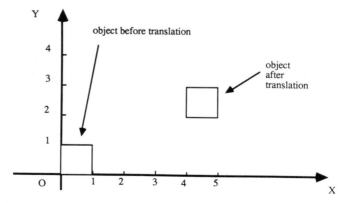

Figure 6-2 Translation of the unit square of Figure 6-1.

displacement vector (tx,ty)}
begin
    x := x + tx;
    y := y + ty;
end;

As an example take 'tx'=2 and 'ty'=3 and apply this routine to the four vertexes A, B, C, and D of the unit square. The result is $A' = (2,3)$, $B' = (3,3)$, $C' = (3,4)$, and $D' = (2,4)$. The transformed square is shown in Figure 6-2. The unit square has been shifted without distortion of shape or size: its area is still equal to 1.

Rotation of graphics objects

Every point $P = (x, y)$ in the graphics object is moved to a new point $P' = (x', y')$ by rotating the line OP from the origin to the point through a counterclockwise angle of a radians to the new line OP'. The transformation:

$$(x, y) \rightarrow (x', y')$$

is more easily seen from polar coordinates. The polar coordinates of P are (r, θ) and the polar coordinates of P' are (r', θ'). It is clear that in polar coordinates the rotation transformation equations are:

$$r' = r$$
$$\theta' = \theta + a$$

Since:

$$x' = r' \cos(\theta') = r \cos(\theta+\alpha)$$
$$y' = r' \sin(\theta') = r \sin(\theta+\alpha)$$

and the compound angle formulas are:

$$\cos(\theta+\alpha) = \cos(\theta) \cos(\alpha) - \sin(\theta) \sin(\alpha)$$
$$\sin(\theta+\alpha) = \sin(\theta) \cos(\alpha) + \cos(\theta) \sin(\alpha)$$

the Cartesian coordinates transform according to the formulas:

$$x' = \cos(\alpha) x - \sin(\alpha) y$$
$$y' = \sin(\alpha) x + \cos(\alpha) y$$

This is a one parameter group where the parameter is α. The identity transformation is the case $\alpha = 0$. The rotation transformation inverse to the one for angle α is the transformation with parameter $-\alpha$. If a point $P = (x, y)$ is rotated about the origin by α radians to P', and then P' is rotated about the origin by β radians to P'' then the total transformation from P to P'' is the same as a single transformation through γ radians where:

$$\gamma \equiv \phi\,(\alpha,\beta) = \alpha + \beta$$

is the composition function for the two-dimensional rotation group. Note however that all angles are meant to be modulo $2\,\pi$. Finite subgroups of this group can be found when α is restricted to multiples of $2\,\pi\,/\,n$ where n is the order of the subgroup, that is, the number of distinct elements (rotation transformations) in it.

To rotate a graphics object the following procedure must be applied to every coordinate pair in the graphics object data structure:

```
procedure rotate_point(alpha : real; var x,y : real);
{Perform a rotation transformation on the point P = (x,y) in
user coordinates about the origin     through alpha radians.}
var
    xtemp,ytemp,sine,cosine : real;
begin
    xtemp := x; ytemp := y;
    cosine := cos(alpha); sine := sin(alpha); {more efficient to use locals}
    x := cosine*xtemp - sine*ytemp;
    y := sine*xtemp + cosine*ytemp;
end;
```

As an example take $\alpha = \pi\,/\,6$ and apply this routine to the four vertexes $A, B, C,$ and D of the unit square. The result is $A' = (0,0), B' = (0.866,0.5), C' = (0.366,1.366),$ and $D' = (-0.5,0.866)$. The transformed square is shown in Figure 6-3. The unit square has been rotated without distortion of shape or size: its area is still equal to 1.

Scaling graphics objects

Every point $P = (x, y)$ in the object is moved to a new point $P' = (x', y')$:

$$P = (x, y) \rightarrow P' = (x', y')$$

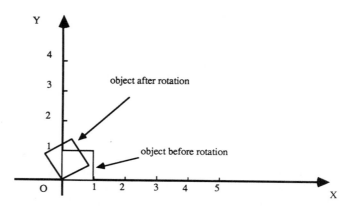

Figure 6-3 Rotation of the unit square of Figure 6-1.

according to:

$$x' = s_x \ x$$
$$y' = s_y \ y$$

This is a two-parameter group where the parameters are given by $A = (s_x, s_y)$. The identity transformation corresponds to $A = (1,1)$. The inverse group element to the transformation for $A = (s_x, s_y)$ is the scaling transformation corresponding to parameters $A = (s_x^{-1}, s_y^{-1})$. The group composition functions ϕ are clearly:

$$c_1 = a_1 \ b_1$$
$$c_2 = a_2 \ b_2$$

If s_x and s_y are unequal then the transformation results in a distortion of the x -y proportions of the original shape. If one value is +1 and the other -1 then the object will be reflected about an axis. Reflections, where $s_x = \pm 1$ and $s_y = \pm 1$ form a finite subgroup of the scaling group. One-parameter subgroups can be found by setting s_x and s_y to functions of a single parameter, t say. Two important one parameter subgroups are the x -scaling and y -scaling subgroups which correspond to $s_y = 1$ and $s_x = 1$ respectively. Another important one-parameter subgroup is when both parameters are equal. These transformations are call dilatations and either uniformly expand or contract graphics objects with respect to the origin.

To scale a graphics object the following procedure must be applied to every coordinate pair in the graphics object data structure:

```
procedure scale_point(sx,sy : real; var x,y : real);
{Perform a scale transformation on the point P = (x,y) in
user coordinates using the scale     parameters sx and sy.}
begin
    x := sx*x;
    y := sy*y;
end;
```

As an example take 'sx' = 2 and 'sy' = 3 and apply this routine to the four vertexes A, B, C, and D of the unit square. The result is $A' = (0,0)$, $B' = (2,0)$, $C' = (2,3)$, and $D' = (0,3)$. The transformed square is shown in Figure 6-4. The unit square has been enlarged with distortion of shape: its area is now equal to 6, which comes from the product of the determinant of the transformation matrix A and the area of the square before the transformation was applied.

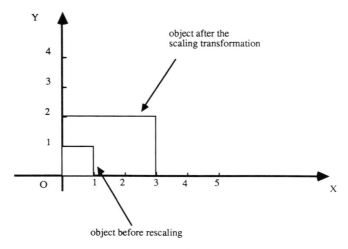

Figure 6-4 Rescaling of the unit square of Figure 6-1.

Shear transformations

When matrix B = 0 in equation 6.8 and matrix A has the form:

$$A = \begin{pmatrix} 1 & a \\ 0 & 1 \end{pmatrix}$$

the x -shear transformations are obtained. These make a one-parameter Lie group. The identity transformation occurs for a = 0, the inverse of element a is the transformation with parameter $-a$ and the composition function is:

$$c \equiv \phi(a, b) = a + b$$

To perform an x -shear operation on a graphics object the following procedure must be applied to every coordinate pair in the graphics object data structure:

```
procedure x_shear_point(a : real; var x,y : real);
{Perform the x-shear group operation on the point P=(x,y) in
user coordinates using shear parameter a.}
begin
    x := x + a*y;
end;
```

When matrix B = 0 in equation 6.8 and matrix A has the form:

$$A = \begin{pmatrix} 1 & 0 \\ a & 1 \end{pmatrix}$$

the x-shear transformations are obtained. These make a one-parameter Lie group. The identity transformation occurs for $a = 0$, the inverse of element a is the transformation with parameter $-a$ and the composition function is:

$$c \equiv \phi(a, b) = a + b$$

To perform an x-shear operation on a graphics object the following procedure must be applied to every coordinate pair in the graphics object data structure:

```
procedure y_shear_point(a : real; var x,y : real);
{Perform the y-shear group operation on the point P=(x,y) in
 user coordinates using shear parameter a.}
begin
    y := a*x + y;
end;
```

As an example take 'a' = 2 and apply the x-shear routine to the four vertexes A, B, C, and D of the unit square. The result is $A' = (0,0) \equiv A$, $B' = (1,0) \equiv B$, $C' = (3,1)$, and $D' = (2,1)$. The transformed square is shown in Figure 6-5. The unit square has been distorted in its shape but its area is still equal to 1. It should be noted that the determinant of all shear transformation matrices A is equal to 1.

6.4 Algebraic versus matrix formulation

The routines of the previous section enable useful transformations to be applied to the points that define graphics objects. Because the transformations are groups, each transformation can be referred to by its parameters which are fewer than the number of

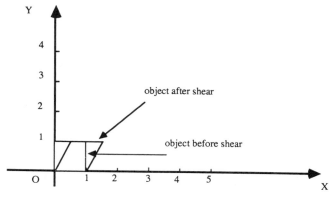

Figure 6-5 Shear distortion of the unit square of Figure 6-1.

matrix elements involved in the most general linear transformation as in equation 6.8. The routines adopt a straight forward algebraic equation approach to each transformation. An alternative approach is to write extra procedures that set up the matrices A and B as array data structures in the software given the group type and its parameters. After making the matrices, another routine could be called to perform the matrix product and sum occurring in equation 6.8 and finally obtain the transformed point as the column matrix X'. This approach seems like a lot of extra code to do the same thing as the straightforward algebraic approach given in the routines above. However there are good reasons for taking the matrix approach.

The transformations presented in all the routines above except for translations operate with respect to the origin of user coordinates. For example, suppose that the window is set up by:

set_window(100,100,150,150)

then the user coordinate origin is not visible. If a graphics object in this window is rotated by say 45 degrees with respect to the origin, it will be transformed out of view. What is needed is to be able to rotate, scale, and so forth around an arbitrarily set center. This can be done by a change of coordinate system so that the desired center point, say (x_c, y_c), is the new origin of coordinates. Then apply the appropriate transformation in the new coordinate system and finally restore the old coordinate system. This change of coordinate system is a passive transformation equivalent to a translation with parameters:

$$t_x = -x_c$$
$$t_y = -y_c$$

The following calls therefore rotate the point $P = (x, y)$ about the center $C = (x_c, y_c)$:

```
tx := -xc; ty := -yc;
translate_point(tx,ty,x,y);
alpha := pi / 4;
rotate_point(alpha,x,y);
tx := xc; ty := yc;
translate_point(tx,ty,x,y);
```

Similar code segments would be required to perform scalings or shearings centered on C rather than the origin.

In computer graphics, there is a need to apply these sorts of transformations a large number of times in forming graphics pictures – at least once for each point in each graphics object. If a graphics object contains n points then by the algebraic approach a rotation about C requires $3n$ calls to the algebraic point transformation routines as the above code segment indicates. The matrix approach provides a slightly less compact representation of each transformation (since in the matrix approach all matrix components are to be retained rather than just the group parameters to which they correspond), but it allows the concatenation of transformations by matrix multiplications. After the concatenated matrices are formed only n calls to a point transformation routine are needed to transform the graphics object in the matrix approach.

These remarks about saving processing effort by the use of matrices also apply to those cases where a string of transformations are to be applied to the same graphics object data before it is displayed on the output device. In a batched environment or where a graphics picture is being developed without user interaction under the control of commands coming from a file, quite clearly the display of the results of intermediate transformations is not wanted. In an interactive environment one usually likes to see the results of each transformation immediately. However if the screen is a storage screen or has selective erasure difficulties it may again be undesirable to see the results of intermediate transformations. In these cases and to reduce the processing for transformations about an arbitrary center C the matrix approach should be used. In this approach the concatenated matrices for equation 6.8 are computed rather than the new graphics object data values after each transformation. When the final matrix is concatenated, the matrix equation 6.8 is evaluated for each point and this is when the graphics object data values are changed.

If it were not for translations, that is, the matrix B in equation 6.8, a sequence of transformations would be concatenated by simply multiplying the matrices of the transformations. The 2 x 1 translation matrix B spoils this simple concatenation formulation since the translations operate by addition rather than multiplication. The 3 x 3 matrix method explained below shows how all transformation types in equation 6.8 can be treated in the uniform manner of matrix multiplication.

When large numbers of points have to be transformed then the transformations may conveniently be stored as 3 x 3 matrices and then all transformations can be treated identically as matrix multiplications with different matrices. In this three-dimensional representation of the transformations a point in two-dimensional space is represented by a 3 x 1 column vector:

$$ H = \begin{pmatrix} H_1 \\ H_2 \\ S \end{pmatrix} $$

These are termed *homogeneous coordinates* in two dimensions. The two-dimensional Cartesian coordinates (x, y) are related to the homogeneous coordinates by:

$$ x = H_1 / S $$
$$ y = H_2 / S $$

S can be thought of as a uniform scaling factor. Usually $S = 1$ so that $H_1 \equiv x$ and $H_2 \equiv y$. However homogeneous coordinates have the nice feature that they can label points on the circle at infinity by having $S = 0$. Being able to refer precisely to the various points at infinity resulted in many new theorems and researches in projective geometry.

In homogeneous coordinates all three kinds of linear two-dimensional transformations have the matrix form:

$$H' = C * H$$

where:

$$H' = \begin{pmatrix} x' \\ y' \\ 1 \end{pmatrix}$$

$$H = \begin{pmatrix} x \\ y \\ 1 \end{pmatrix}$$

$$C = \left(\begin{array}{cc:c} A & & B \\ \hdashline 0 & 0 & 1 \end{array} \right)$$

C is a 3 x 3 augmented matrix constructed from the 2 x 2 square matrix A and 2 x 1 column matrix B.

6.5 Routines to create the matrices

Here are the routines that produce the 3 x 3 matrix C of the active transformations using homogeneous coordinates with scaling $S = 1$.

```
type
    matrix = array[1..3, 1..3] of real;
    point = array[1..3] of real;

procedure zero_matrix(var a : matrix);
{Set a to equal the zero matrix.}
var
    i,j : integer;
begin
    for i := 1 to 3 do
        for j := 1 to 3 do
            a[i,j] := 0.0;
end;

procedure identity_matrix(var a : matrix);
{Set matrix a to equal the identity matrix.}
var
    i : integer;
```

```
begin
    zero_matrix(a);
    for i := 1 to 3 do
        a[i,i] := 1.0;
end;


procedure translation_matrix(tx,ty : real; var a : matrix);
{Set matrix a to be the translation matrix for translation parameters tx and ty.}
begin
    identity_matrix(a);
    a[1,3] := tx;
    a[2,3] := ty;
end;


procedure rotation_matrix(theta : real; var a : matrix);
{Set matrix a to be the rotation matrix for angle theta.}
begin
    identity_matrix(a);
    a[1,1] := cos(theta); a[1,2] := -sin(theta);
    a[2,1] := sin(theta); a[2,2] := cos(theta);
end;


procedure scale_matrix(sx,sy : real; var a : matrix);
{Set matrix a to be the scale transformation matrix for the parameters sx and
sy.}
begin
    identity_matrix(a);
    a[1,1] := sx;
    a[2,2] := sy;
end;


procedure x_shear_matrix(p : real; var a : matrix);
{Set the matrix a to be the x-shear transformation matrix for the group
parameter p.}
begin
    identity_matrix(a);
    a[1,2] := p;
end;


procedure y_shear_matrix(p : real; var a : matrix);
{Set the matrix a to be the y-shear transformation matrix for the group
 parameter p.}
begin
    identity_matrix(a);
    a[2,1] := p;
end;
```

```
procedure matrix_multiply(a,b : matrix; var c : matrix);
{Perform the matrix multiplication A*B to give C as output matrix.}
var
    i,j,k : integer;
    sum : real;
begin
    for i := 1 to 3 do
        for j := 1 to 3 do
        begin
            sum := 0.0;
            for k := 1 to 3 do
                sum := sum + a[i,k]*b[k,j];
            c[i,j] := sum;
        end;
end;
```

```
procedure transform_point(a : matrix; xold : point; var xnew : point);
{Apply the 3x3 active transformation matrix a to the old point xold and obtain
the coordinates of the transformed point xnew according to the matrix
equation : a*xold = xnew.}
begin
    for row := 1 to 3 do
    begin
        sum := 0.0;
        for col := 1 to 3 do
            sum := sum + a[row,col]*xold[col]
        xnew[row] := sum;
    end;
end;
```

These routines can be used to transform any graphics object by simply transforming all the points which define the graphics object (and assuming group invariance of the constituent geometrical elements). It is possible to simplify the programmer interface on this last procedure so that it takes the form:

```
procedure transform_point(a : matrix; var x,y : real);
```

Here 'x' and 'y' are input as the old coordinates and then output as the transformed coordinates. In this form, the programmer no longer has to set up homogeneous coordinates. The internal code however will convert 'x' and 'y' into homogeneous coordinate form, and then extract the output coordinate values from the 'xnew' homogeneous coordinates.

6.6 Transformation of graphics objects

As previously shown in Section 6.4, the advantage in using matrices over the algebraic approach of Section 6.2 comes about when it becomes necessary to transform large numbers of points as found in a typical graphics object, and when these transformations are done about a point other than the origin. All the graphics elements, as discussed in Section 5.3, are defined by certain point coordinates, and as the transformations covered here are of the first degree, they can be used to transform graphics elements. The following routines transform graphics objects by transforming all the graphics elements in the graphics object.

```
var
    center : record
        x,y : real;
    end;
procedure set_center(cx,cy : real);
{Procedure to change the default center of the transformation.}
begin
    with center do
    begin
        x := cx;
        y := cy;
    end;
end;
procedure transform_graphics_object(a : matrix);
{Apply the 3x3 transformation matrix to all points in the current graphics
object in homogeneous coordinates.}
var
    i : integer;
    x,y : real;
begin
    with current_go do
    begin
        for i := 1 to nr_line_segs do
        begin
            x := line[i].x1; y := line[i].y1;
            transform_point(a,x,y);
            line[i].x1 := x; line[i].y1 := y;
            x := line[i].x2; y := line[i].y2;
            transform_point(a,x,y);
            line[i].x2 := x; line[i].y2 := y;
        end;
        for i := 1 to nr_circles do
        begin
            x := circle[i].x1; y := circle[i].y1;
            transform_point(a,x,y);
            circle[i].x1 := x; circle[i].y1 := y;
            x := circle[i].x2; y := circle[i].y2;
            transform_point(a,x,y);
            circle[i].x2 := x; circle[i].y2 := y;
        end;
        for i := 1 to nr_arcs do
```

```
      begin
         x := arc[i].x1; y := arc[i].y1;
         transform_point(a,x,y);
         arc[i].x1 := x; arc[i].y1 := y;
         x := arc[i].x2; y := arc[i].y2;
         transform_point(a,x,y);
         arc[i].x2 := x; arc[i].y2 := y;
         x := arc[i].x3; y := arc[i].y3;
         transform_point(a,x,y);
         arc[i].x3 := x; arc[i].y3 := y;
      end;
   end;
end;

procedure translate_graphics_object(tx,ty);
{Translate the current graphics object by the parameters given.}
begin
   translation_matrix(tx,ty,a);
   transform_graphics_object(a);
end;

procedure rotate_graphics_object(alpha : real);
{Rotate the current graphics object by the angle alpha in degrees about the
center set by the  set_center routine.}
const
   pi = 3.1415926;
var
   tx,ty : real;
   a,b,c,d : matrix;
begin
   tx := -center.x; ty := -center.y;
   translation_matrix(tx,ty,a);
   alpha := alpha*pi / 180.0 {convert degrees to radians}
   rotation_matrix(alpha,b);
   matrix_multiply(b,a,c);
   tx := center.x; ty := center.y;
   translation_matrix(tx,ty,a);
   matrix_multiply(a,c,d);
   transform_graphics_object(d);
end;

procedure scale_graphics_object(sx,sy : real);
{Scale the current graphics object by the factors sx and sy about the center
set by the  set_center routine.}
var
   tx,ty : real;
   a,b,c,d : matrix;
```

```
begin
    tx := -center.x; ty := -center.y;
    translation_matrix(tx,ty,a);
    scale_matrix(sx,sy,b);
    matrix_multiply(b,a,c);
    tx := center.x; ty := center.y;
    translation_matrix(tx,ty,a);
    matrix_multiply(a,c,d);
    transform_graphics_object(d);
end;
```

```
procedure x_shear_graphics_object(p : real);
{Shear the current graphics object by the parameter p in the x direction about
the center set by  the set_center routine.}
var
    tx,ty : real;
    a,b,c,d : matrix;
begin
    tx := -center.x; ty := -center.y;
    translation_matrix(tx,ty,a);
    alpha := alpha*pi / 180.0          {convert degrees to radians}
    x_shear_matrix(p,b);
    matrix_multiply(b,a,c);
    tx := center.x; ty := center.y;
    translation_matrix(tx,ty,a);
    matrix_multiply(a,c,d);
    transform_graphics_object(d);
end;
```

```
procedure y_shear_graphics_object(p : real);
{Shear the current graphics object by the parameter p in the y direction about
the center set by  the set_center routine.}
var
    tx,ty : real;
    a,b,c,d : matrix;
begin
    tx := -center.x; ty := -center.y;
    translation_matrix(tx,ty,a);
    alpha := alpha*pi / 180.0          {convert degrees to radians}
    y_shear_matrix(p,b);
    matrix_multiply(b,a,c);
    tx := center.x; ty := center.y;
    translation_matrix(tx,ty,a);
    matrix_multiply(a,c,d);
    transform_graphics_object(d);
end;
```

6.7 **Instancing**

When computer graphics is used to draw electronic circuit diagrams, symbols such as the transistor will be needed over and over again. Likewise in plotting flowcharts a symbol such as a decision box will be used many times within the one diagram. Each occurrence of a particular symbol is called an *instance* of the symbol. To create a diagram the user must select a symbol, and transform and display an instance of it on the graphics output display. This process is called 'instancing' and the transformations on instances of symbols are sometimes called 'instance transformations'. (See Newman & Sproull, 1979.) The general procedure is to load a graphics object (the selected symbol for display), apply the appropriate transformation routines given in the previous section, and then call the display routine 'display_graphics_object'. In order to place the second instance of the symbol, all the transformations done on the first one would have to be undone so that the original data is available for transformation again. Systems that use passive transformations have an advantage here in that they do not actually change the data stored in the current graphics object. They instead accummulate the sequence of transformations performed in a single matrix called the current transformation matrix (CTM). When all necessary transformations have been called, the display routine applies the result to the coordinate system and the graphics object is drawn using its original (unchanged) data. This results in the graphics object appearing as it should, and by simply resetting the CTM back to the identity matrix the software is ready for the next transformation. Note that the data in the graphics object never changes and that the coordinate system is manipulated for each instance but restored to the original user Cartesian coordinate system after displaying the instance.

A method of recovering the original graphics data when active transformations are used is to invent a copying routine. This routine fills a new data structure with the data in the current graphics object. Another routine is needed to restore the data into the current graphics object data structure after placing the instance. A simple pair of routines for achieving this is as follows:

```
var
    hold : graphics_object;

procedure hold_graphics_object;
{Routine to take a copy of the current graphics object data.}
begin
    with current_graphics _object do
    begin
        hold.nr_lines := nr_lines;
        for i := 1 to nr_lines do
        begin
            hold.line[i].x1 := line[i].x1;
            hold.line[i].y1 := line[i].y1;
            hold.line[i].x2 := line[i].x2;
            hold.line[i].y2 := line[i].y2;
        end;
```

```
          hold.nr_arcs := nr_arcs;
          for i := 1 to nr_arcs do

          begin
              hold.arc[i].x1 := arc[i].x1;
              hold.arc[i].y1 := arc[i].y1;
              hold.arc[i].x2 := arc[i].x2;
              hold.arc[i].y2 := arc[i].y2;
              hold.arc[i].x3 := arc[i].x3;
              hold.arc[i].y3 := arc[i].y3;
          end;
      end;
  end;

procedure unhold_graphics_object;
{Routine to restore the current graphics object data from that stored in the
hold data  structure.}
begin
    with current_graphics _object do
    begin
        nr_lines := hold.nr_lines;
        for i := 1 to nr_lines do
        begin
            line[i].x1 := hold.line[i].x1;
            line[i].y1 := hold.line[i].y1;
            line[i].x2 := hold.line[i].x2;
            line[i].y2 := hold.line[i].y2;
        end;
        nr_arcs := hold.nr_arcs;
        for i := 1 to nr_arcs do
        begin
            arc[i].x1 := hold.arc[i].x1;
            arc[i].y1 := hold.arc[i].y1;
            arc[i].x2 := hold.arc[i].x2;
            arc[i].y2 := hold.arc[i].y2;
            arc[i].x3 := hold.arc[i].x3;
            arc[i].y3 := hold.arc[i].y3;
        end;
    end;
end;
```

These two procedures 'hold_graphics_object' and 'unhold_graphics_object' allow a *one-level stack* only; that is, a second hold wipes out the previous hold. This is sufficient to cover the general sequence of calls for instancing as can be seen in the following procedure. This procedure reads symbols from the file called 'cad_data' and instancing commands from a file called 'cad_file'. These two file names are assumed to be global to this procedure.

```
procedure display_instances;
{Procedure to demonstrate instancing for Computer Aided Design.}
var
     symbol,instance,nr_symbols,nr_instances : integer;
     alpha,sx,sy,tx,ty : real;
begin
     select_input_file(cad_data);
     readln(cad_file,nr_symbols);
     {Loop for each symbol :}
     for symbol := 1 to nr_symbols do
     begin
          load_graphics_object;
          hold_graphics_object;
          readln(cad_file,nr_instances);
          {Loop for each instance of the symbol :}
          for instance := 1 to nr_instances do
          begin
               readln(cad_file,alpha,sx,sy,tx,ty);
               rotate_graphics_object(alpha);
               scale_graphics_object(sx,sy);
               translate_graphics_object(tx,ty);
               display_graphics_object;
               unhold_graphics_object;
          end;
     end;
end;
```

A more powerful graphics software design allows for holding several different graphics objects or transformations of the same graphics object simultaneously in memory. This is achieved by using pointers to graphics object data structures. The pointer variable becomes the identifying name of an instance of a graphics object as far as the user of the graphics system is concerned. To save an instance, the standard Pascal function 'new' is called with the desired pointer variable, and then the components of the graphics object data structure, which is now pointed to, is filled up from the current graphics object data. This can be done by a procedure with a declaration:

```
procedure save_graphics_object(var go_ptr : go_pointer_type);
```

where 'go_pointer_type' is a user defined type, which is a pointer to the graphics object data type given in Chapter 5. To recall the instance at any time, the user must call a procedure to copy from a specified graphics object pointer data to the current graphics object data structure of the graphics package. A suitable procedure declaration for this procedure is:

```
procedure copy_graphics_object(go_ptr : go_pointer_type);
```

When the user is finally finished with a particular instance saved in this manner, the user can call the Pascal 'dispose' function to release the memory used.

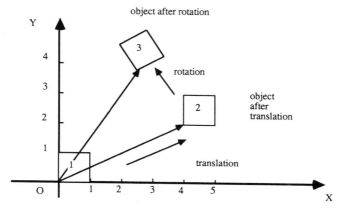

object after rotation

Figure 6-6 The unit square at position (1) is translated to position (2) by the translation of Figure 6-2 and then rotated about the origin to position (3) by the rotation transformation of Figure 6-3.

6.8 Examples of graphics object transformations

Three examples of using the transformations taught in this chapter follow. Use is made of the graphics object data files presented in Section 5.7.

Example : Translate the graphics object of Figure 6-1 by 2 units along the x axis and 3 units along the y axis, and then perform a rotation about the origin through 30 degrees. Is this the same resulting shape, if these transformations are performed in the reverse order?

Solution : The unit square from Figure 6-1 is repeated in Figure 6-6 and shown as position (1). First, a translation is done with $t_x = 2$, and $t_y = 3$, and this results in position (2) shown in Figure 6-6. Each point X of the graphics object has been moved to $X' = X + T$. Next a rotation transformation is applied with the matrix:

$$R = \begin{pmatrix} 0.8660 & -0.5 \\ 0.5 & 0.8660 \end{pmatrix}$$

and the result of this is shown as position (3) in Figure 6-6. Each new point X' of the translated graphics object is transformed to:

$$X'' = R * X'$$

The combined effect is therefore:

$$X'' = R * (X + T) = R * X + R * T$$

Note : in general these transformations are order-dependent. If R is performed first and then the translation by T, the result would be different:

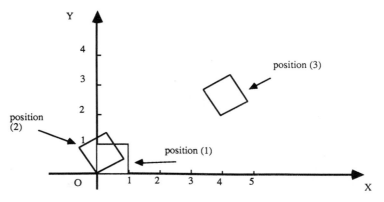

Figure 6-7 The transformations of Figure 6-6 in reverse order produce a different final result. A rotation takes the unit square from position (1) to position (2') then the object is translated to position (3').

$$X''' = R * X + T$$

The effect of this ordering is shown in Figure 6-7.

Example : Cause the computer to draw the simple electronic circuit diagram shown in Figure 6-8 as circuit 1.

Solution : A program to do this follows:

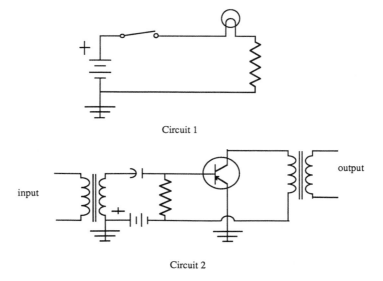

Figure 6-8 Electronic circuits drawn with the symbols of Figure 5-8 as graphics objects.

```
program Circuit1;
{$I G2D.EXT   include the file of G2D external declarations}
begin
    initialize_G2D; {initializations for 2D graphics}
    set_window(0.0,0.0,50.0,50.0);
    select_input_file('ELECTRONIC.SYMBOLS');
    load_graphics_object; {load the resistor symbol}
    rotate_graphics_object(-90.0);
    translate_graphics_object(30.0,20.0);
    display_graphics_object;
    load_graphics_object; {skip the diode symbol}
    load_graphics_object; {load the ground symbol}
    translate_graphics_object(10.0,10.0);
    display_graphics_object;
    load_graphics_object; {skip the capacitor symbol}
```

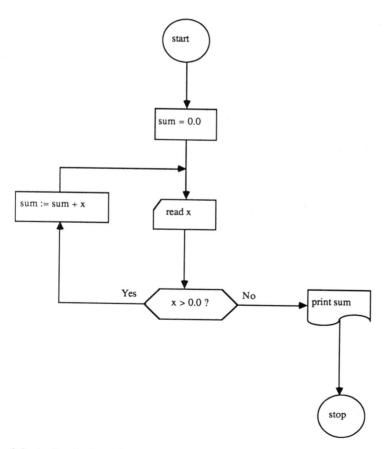

Figure 6-9 A simple flowchart using the symbols of Figure 5-6 as graphics objects.

```
        load_graphics_object; {load the battery symbol}
        rotate_graphics_object(90.0);
        translate_graphics_object(10.0,10.0);
        display_graphics_object;
        load_graphics_object; {skip the inductor symbol}
        load_graphics_object; {skip the transistor symbol}
        load_graphics_object; {load the switch symbol}
        translate_graphics_object(10.0,20.0);
        display_graphics_object;
        load_graphics_object; {skip the speaker symbol}
        load_graphics_object; {load the light symbol}
        translate_graphics_object(20.0,20.0);
        display_graphics_object;
        plot_line(10.0,10.0,30.0,10.0);
        terminate_G2D; {close off the 2D graphics package properly}
    end.
```

Example : Have the computer draw the flowchart shown in Figure 6-9.

Solution : A program that produces this diagram is given below. The data file for the flowchart symbols is also included.

```
    program flow_charter;
    {$I G2D.EXT   include the file of G2D external declarations}
    var
        cad_file : text;
    begin
        initialize_G2D; {initializations for 2D graphics}
        set_window(0.0,0.0,40.0,40.0);
        select_input_file('FLOWCHART.SYMBOLS');
        reset(cad_file,'FLOWCHART.CAD');
        {place all of the symbols :}
        display_instances;
        {connect all of the symbols with lines :}
        plot_line(20.0,31.0,20.0,29.0);
        plot_line(20.0,25.0,20.0,22.0);
        plot_line(20.0,19.0,20.0,17.0);
        plot_line(16.0,15.0,9.0,15.0);
        plot_line(9.0,15.0,9.0,19.0);
        plot_line(9.0,23.0,9.0,24.0);
        plot_line(9.0,24.0,20.0,24.0);
        plot_line(24.0,15.0,28.0,15.0);
        plot_line(31.0,13.5,31.0,11.0);
        terminate_G2D; {close off the 2D graphics package properly}
    end.
```

The file 'FLOWCHART.SYMBOLS' consists of the flowchart graphics objects discussed in Section 5.3. (See also problem 5.14.) The flowchart CAD file called 'FLOWCHART.CAD', is a textfile with the following contents:

```
5    {number of symbols to use}
2    {number of termination instances required}
0.0 1.0 1.0 18.0 31.0 {angle, scale, and translation parameters for the first instance}
0.0 1.0 1.0 29.0 7.0  { ditto for the second instance}
2    {number of process instances required}
0.0 1.0 1.0 17.0 25.0
0.0 1.0 1.0 6.0 19.0
1    {number of decision instances required}
0.0 1.0 1.0 16.0 13.0
1    {number of input instances required}
0.0 1.0 1.0 17.0 19.0
1    {number of output instances required}
0.0 1.0 1.0 28.0 13.0
```

Problems

6.1 Prove that the group $(F,*)$ of two-dimensional transformations has the associative property using the notation $F \equiv (f_1, f_2)$ for transformation functions as in Section 6.1. That is, demonstrate that:

$$F * (G * H) \equiv (F * G) * H$$

by using $L = G * H$ and $M = F * G$ as intermediate terms.
Derive the equations for f_1 and f_2 for the (nonlinear) circle inversion transformation. Note that given a fixed circle of radius r and center $C = (x_c, y_c)$ the inversion of a point P inside the circle but not coinciding with the center C is the point P' outside of the circle such that P is in the line segment CP' and triangles CPT and CTP' are similar where TP' is a tangent to the circle. Do circle inversions form a group?

6.2 Show that the linear inhomogeneous transformations:

$$F(X) = A * X + B$$

preserve line segments as line segments as stated in the text. Show that circles are invariant under rotations, dilatations, and translations, but not unequal scalings (which convert them into ellipses). Likewise show that the various conics and their arcs are invariant in their kinds under rotations, dilatations, and translations.

6.3 Show that the linear inhomogeneous transformations:

$$F(X) = A * X + B$$

form a Lie group by having the usual group properties:
(a) The product of two transformations is another transformation of the same kind.
(b) The identity transformation $X' = X$ is a special case of these transformations.
(c) Every transformation has an inverse transformation that is of the same kind.
(d) Products of the transformations are associative.

6.4 With reference to the affine transformation group in two dimensions (the transformations of equation 6.8), determine the functions f relating the 12 parameters of two transformations to the 6 parameters of the transformation representing the product of the two transformations.

6.5 If in equation 6.8 the matrix B is zero and the 2 x 2 matrix A is symmetric and tracefree (i.e. the sum of its diagonal elements is zero) then this represents a shear transformation. Equations 6.9 and 6.10 reduce to:

$$x' = a \, x + b \, y$$
$$y' = b \, y - a \, x$$

Show that these transformations do not form a group on their own since the product of two shear transformations is not another shear transformation. Show however that triple products rather than double products of shear transformations turn out to be shear transformations. The shear transformations do not include the identity (whose trace is 2). However, they do include their inverse. Prove that the inverse of the shear transformation with parameters $A = (a, b)$ is the shear with parameters $A = (-a / (a^2 - b^2), b / (a^2 - b^2))$. Write a procedure 'shear_point(a,b : real; **var** x,y : real)' to perform a shear transformation on the point $P = (x, y)$ in user coordinates by the parameters a and b.

6.6 The transformations when matrix $B = 0$ in equation 6.8 and matrix A has the form:

$$A = \begin{pmatrix} 1 & a \\ b & 1 \end{pmatrix}$$

generalize the x and y shear transformations. Do these transformations form a group?

6.7 The transformations when matrix $B = 0$ in equation 6.8 and matrix A has the form:

$$A = \begin{pmatrix} a & b \\ -b & a \end{pmatrix} \equiv a*I + b*E$$

generalize the rotation transformations. (The latter identity defines the 2 x 2 matrix E. The 3 x 3 version of this matrix is defined in problem 6.14.) Do these transformations form a group? (Yes.) Derive the composition functions:

$$a" = a\ a' - b\ b'$$
$$b" = a\ b' + b\ a'$$

Show that the parameters for the inverse transformation are given by:

$$a' = a\ /(a^2 + b^2)$$
$$b' = -b\ /(a^2 + b^2)$$

6.8 Assume that the following graphics commands have been executed:

```
set_window(-1.5, -1.0,20.5, 15.75);
plot_circle(8.0,5.0,12.0,9.0);
plot_line(8.0,5.0,12.0,9.0);
```

Suppose that the user wishes to issue the following passive transformation:

```
move the origin to (1,0)
rotate the axes through π / 4 radians, and
change the x scale by a factor of 2
```

and then draw the circle and line again with the original coordinate values but in the new coordinate system. Show a sequence of active transformations and calls to 'plot_circle' and 'plot_line' that will produce the same effect.

6.9 Prove that the equation:

$$A\ (x - x_c)^2 + B\ (x - x_c)\ (y - y_c) + C\ (y - y_c)^2 = 1$$

represents an ellipse whose semimajor axis is a with angle α to the x axis, and whose semiminor axis is b and whose center is (x_c, y_c), where:

$$\alpha = \tan^{-1}[B\ /\ (A - C)]\ /\ 2$$
$$a = \sqrt{[\cos(2\ \alpha)\ /\ \{\cos^2(\alpha)\ A - \sin^2(\alpha)\ C\ \}]}$$
$$b = \sqrt{[\cos(2\ \alpha)\ /\ \{\cos^2(\alpha)\ C - \sin^2(\alpha)\ A\ \}]}$$

Use these formulas to write a procedure to draw an ellipse with center (x_c, y_c), major axis a, minor axis b, in which the major axis makes an angle of a with the positive x axis.

6.10 Write a program to draw a polygon of n sides and distort it so that it is twice as high as it is wide. Prove that under an unequal scaling transformation (i.e. with $s_x \neq s_y$), a circle of radius r centered at (x_c, y_c) is transformed into an ellipse centered at $(s_x x_c, s_y y_c)$ with semimajor and semiminor axes lengths as:

$$a = s_x r$$
$$b = s_y r$$

The axes of this ellipse are parallel to the coordinate axes. Use the results of problem 6.9 to interpret the shape resulting from an x-shear transformation operating on the above circle.

6.11 It is possible to use only 2 x 3 arrays instead of the 3 x 3 matrix arrays used in Section 6.4. This is because row 3 of A doesn't hold any useful data. It is always $(0,0,1)$ and it simply transforms 1 (the 3rd element of X) into 1 (the third element of X '). Therefore a saving on memory requirements can be made by using only 2 x 3 arrays and changing the transformation routines appropriately. Show what changes are required in the routines in Section 6.5 to achieve this idea.

6.12 The commutator of two square matrices A and B is the matrix denoted $[A,B] = A B - BA$. A matrix group is called *abelian* if all of its elements commute, that is, if the commutator of any pair of matrices in the group is the zero matrix. Show that the group of 3 x 3 rotation matrices (in homogeneous coordinate space) is abelian. Likewise show that the group of 3 x 3 scale transformations in homogeneous space and the group of 3 x 3 translations in homogeneous space are abelian groups. Show that the nontrivial 3 x 3 rotation matrices do not commute with the nontrivial 3 x 3 scale matrices. Likewise show that rotation matrices do not commute with translation matrices, and scale matrices do not commute with translation matrices. Also show that the product of a 3 x 3 rotation matrix with a 3 x 3 scale matrix is neither a rotation matrix nor a scale matrix. This means that the combined set of rotation and scale matrices does not form a group. Likewise show that the combined set of rotation and translation matrices, and the combined set of scale and translation matrices respectively do not form groups.

6.13 Calculate the general form of the 3 x 3 matrix for rotation about a point $C = (x_c, y_c, 1)^T$ in homogeneous coordinates. The formula from which to calculate this 3 x 3 matrix can be seen from the text to be:

$$R_C(x_c, y_c, \theta) = T(x_c, y_c) R(\theta) T(-x_c, -y_c)$$

Show that the set of matrices of this kind form a Lie group.
Also calculate the general form of the 3 x 3 matrix for scaling about a point C in homogeneous coordinates. A similar formula to compute this matrix can be derived from the text:

$$S_C (x_C, y_C, s_x, s_y) = T (x_C, y_C) S (s_x, s_y) T (-x_C, -y_C)$$

Show that the set of matrices of this kind form a Lie group.

6.14 The *group generators* of a Lie group are the derivatives of the generic group element with respect to each of the group parameters and evaluated at the parameter value for the identity of the group. For example, the Lie group of 3 x 3 (two-dimensional) rotation matrices in homogeneous coordinates has only one parameter q and it equals zero for the identity matrix. Therefore this Lie group has only one generator and it is the matrix:

$$E = [\partial R (\theta) / \partial \theta]_{\theta=0}$$
$$= \begin{pmatrix} 0 & -1 & 0 \\ 1 & 0 & 0 \\ 0 & 0 & 0 \end{pmatrix}$$

Show that the general 3 x 3 rotation matrix can be computed from the generator by the equation:

$$R (\theta) = e^{\theta E}$$

Derive the two generaors T_x and T_y for the translation group in the same way and show that:

$$T (t_x, t_y) = \exp(t_x T_x + t_y T_y) = \exp(t_x T_x) . \exp(t_y T_y)$$

Repeat these types of calculations for the group of 3 x 3 scale transformations. In this case use as group parameters $p = \ln (s_x)$ and $q = \ln (s_y)$ for which the group identity occurs when $p = 0$ and $q = 0$.

7

Two-dimensional graphics algorithms

7.1 Types of algorithms required

Computer graphics is a new and quickly expanding field of computer science. It has its own terminology, methods, and hardware. New algorithms for new problems in graphics are continually arising. Techniques are currently being developed to create improved user-friendly interfaces to graphics systems for noncomputer professionals, in particular for artists. Another current area of research and development is the improvement of algorithms to speed up graphics display. Coupled with this problem are far more comprehensive problems in graphics research related to new intelligent graphics database designs which incorporate associativity of graphics objects. Current standard database designs are not particularly suited to handling the enormous amounts of data required in computer graphics. These are only some of the developing fields, and undoubtably many new and intriguing areas of research in computer graphics will open up in the future.

    The clipping algorithms are some of the most frequently required algorithms in computer graphics. Clipping means cutting a graphics display to neatly fit a predefined graphics region on the output display surface, the viewport. A viewport is (virtually always) a rectangular subarea of the graphics display rectangle with sides parallel to the display rectangle's sides. The purpose of viewporting is to give the effect of having several graphics display surfaces that can be viewed simultaneously. The user simply needs the command:

set_viewport(pxmin,pymin,pxmax,pymax)

to define a viewport on the screen by physical coordinate limits. Subsequent graphics output has to be limited to this user-selected rectangle only (or rather to the intersection of this rectangle and the device's display rectangle). The user can specify a Cartesian coordinate system for the viewport area by using the 'set_window' procedure which always applies to a particular viewport. Having set up a user Cartesian coordinate system inside the selected viewport, the user can then proceed to draw all desired graphics in terms of these user coordinates. The graphics produced must only appear inside the nominated viewport – it must be clipped to this current viewport. The user may at any time define a new viewport on the screen and then define user coordinates for that viewport and place graphics in it as well. In this way many viewports with associated windows and graphics may appear on the screen at once as in Figure 7-1.

Some graphics software systems allow the programmer to define almost any number of viewports and windows at the outset before any graphics drawing is done. These systems need to have identification numbers to associate windows to viewports and declare which combination is currently the target for graphics drawing commands. The simpler approach adopted here in the graphics package G2D is to have only one viewport and one window defined at any time. By calling 'set_window' a default viewport is also set up. This default viewport is the entire display rectangle. This relieves the user from the need to know about viewports and the 'set_viewport' procedure until there is a desire to use them. However if the programmer does want to use viewports then subsequent to a call to 'set_window' would be a call to the 'set_viewport' procedure. The Cartesian coordinate limits set up by the 'set_window' call then apply to the area inside the last viewport set by the 'set_viewport' procedure. As soon as the next viewport is declared the G2D software forgets about the previous viewport limits: G2D only maintains one viewport, the currently active one.

An example of using the viewporting idea is when there is a wish to plot several different graphs on the screen, for example, a pie chart on the top half of the screen and a bar chart in the bottom half. Then the top half of the screen can be defined as one viewport and show the results of commands that draw pie segments. The bottom half of the screen could be divided into two viewports: the left-hand side viewport to show the bar chart with labelled axes, and the right-hand viewport to display command and menu information. Viewporting provides greater convenience to the user. Instead of a need to ensure that the resultant graphics neatly fits the whole screen, all there is to worry about is that each individual graphics picture fits as wanted within its own window.

Every graphics picture is (ultimately) constructed from graphics elements (points, lines, arcs, polygons, etc.). The clipping algorithm must divide each graphics element into its visible and invisible portions, and discard the invisible portion. So each graphics output routine for the various available graphics elements such as 'plot_line' and 'plot_arc' will need to have a clipping algorithm associated with it to ensure that the graphics elements are only produced within the current viewport area. Thus there is a need to consider clipping routines for each graphics element, that is, 'clip_line', 'clip_arc', and so forth.

So far windows, and the viewports to which they are mapped, have always been chosen as rectangles with sides parallel to the sides of the output rectangle. However, clipping may be performed to some more general shapes; for example, a picture may be clipped to neatly fit a tilted rectangle (e.g. a diamond shape as in some portraits), a circle, or an ellipse, and so forth. Most clipping algorithms apply to line segments, but there is a need for other clipping routines, such as routines for the clipping of circular arcs or ellipses, as well as a need to clip these to the most general irregular closed polygon shape or graphics objects that are multiply connected (i.e. consist of more than one closed shape).

The logical inverse of clipping is the covering process whereby graphics elements are cut so as to neatly fit around a predefined closed graphics object. A typical application is the leaving of room for labels on a diagram. There are already standard routines for covering lines and line segments by rectangles but in the future more general algorithms will be needed. As with clipping it may be required to generalize the covering algorithms to cater for more general shapes than rectangles with sides parallel to the axes. For example, the covering area may be an arbitrary polygon possessing any amount of convexity and concavity.

Area filling for two-dimensional monochrome graphics is is best done by *hatching*. Hatching means filling a predefined shape with a family of equidistant parallel lines. This is easily achieved for rectangles and circles, but the hatching of general sectors (of circles) is a slightly more difficult task because of the possibility of concavity in sectors. A more general requirement could be to use families of circles or ellipses and so forth, with varying separations to fill the most general closed graphics object shapes. The varying distances can give a three-dimensional effect. When color is added to the hatching (by hatching with colored lines) the colors can tend to mix in the eye and thereby extend the effective range of colors available and enhance the impact of the graphics output. (This effect (called *dithering*) is discussed in Chapter 13.) A method more general than hatching is that of pattern filling. A simple application of pattern filling is where a map shows a swamp area as a region uniformly filled with the usual cartographic symbol for a swamp. General pattern filling algorithms are and will continue to be an area for graphics research and development.

Figure 7-1 Viewports and their associated windows.
(a) The viewing transformation maps user-coordinate data in windows to device coordinate data in viewports on the output display rectangle.
(b) Graphics output must be clipped to the current viewport so that no graphics is drawn outside the current viewport on the output display rectangle.
(c) The large rectangle on the left shows a picture consisting of a stick figure and x and y axes in two-dimensional space. Two windows have been defined on the picture and they are represented by two rectangles within the larger one. On the right is a representation of the graphics display rectangle (such as a VDU screen). Only parts of the picture have been mapped to this rectangle. The two rectangles within this display rectangle are the viewports, one for each window in the picture space. The graphics within each window is mapped one-to-one and onto its corresponding viewport.

A graphics picture for display (e.g. architectural plans) –:

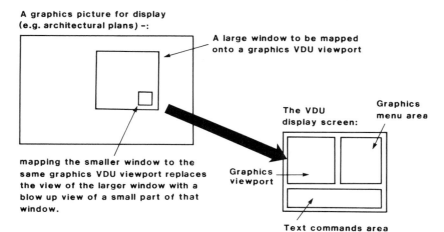

A large window to be mapped onto a graphics VDU viewport

The VDU display screen:

Graphics menu area

Graphics viewport

mapping the smaller window to the same graphics VDU viewport replaces the view of the larger window with a blow up view of a small part of that window.

(a)

Text commands area

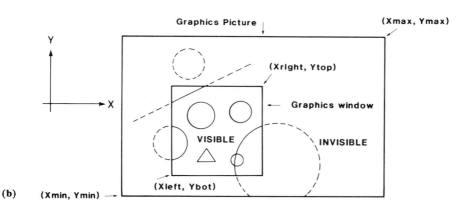

(b)

(c)

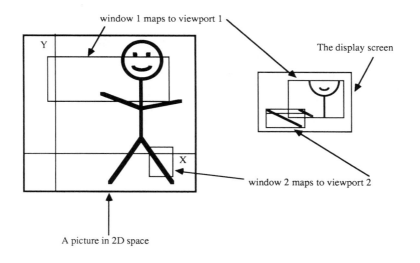

7.2 A simple line clipping algorithm

As already mentioned, clipping is the process of drawing (or reducing the graphics to be drawn to) only those parts of a graphics picture that lie within the specified clipping area. The clipping areas to be considered in this section are rectangles with vertical and horizontal sides. Therefore the data structure for a rectangle will often be required, and it will be defined by the following:

type
    rectangle_type = **record**
        xmin,ymin,xmax,ymax : real;
    end;

In this data structure, ('xmin','ymin') is the lower left corner of the rectangle and ('xmax','ymax') is the upper right corner. This is similar to the data structure of windows and viewports. The algorithm here therefore is the basic line clipping algorithm needed to implement the viewporting concept in graphics packages. (Since all graphics could be constructed from a line drawing routine alone, and since lines are the simplest curve to handle, this chapter starts by describing a line clipping algorithm. Similarly, while there are many methods of line clipping, this section will consider a simple solution to the problem.) The clipping algorithm chosen must make the part of the picture outside of the clipping rectangle 'invisible' but must nevertheless keep track of where the lines go. Thus in the case of a polyline, there may well be many line segments outside of the clipping rectangle that are not to be drawn. The graphics system needs to keep track of the invisible part of the polyline so that when it reenters the clipping rectangle it does so at the correct point on the border of that rectangle.

Even if the viewport is the whole screen, plotting graphics outside of the viewport area is undesirable for at least two reasons. Firstly CPU time is wasted attempting to draw the invisible portion, and secondly it can cause totally incorrect graphics output. Many screens have the wraparound feature so that lines drawn off the screen on one side reappear on the screen from the opposite side. This can obviously cause troublesome unidentifiable graphics outputs. For many other screens however attempting to draw a line where the end points of the line are outside the screen limits results in no line being plotted at all. This also results in incorrect graphics displays. In some computers (such as the Amiga), which have flexible pixel RAM permitted to lie anywhere in the computer's main memory, if clipping is not done then drawing out of the pixel RAM area will corrupt other programs and software lying in memory.

The basis for the clipping is that the point (x, y) in user coordinates is visible iff (mathematical abbreviation for 'if and only if'):

$$rect.xmin \leq x \leq rect.xmax$$
$$rect.ymin \leq y \leq rect.ymax$$

(This is essentially the point clipping algorithm for rectangles.) It would however take too much time to check every point of a picture with these inequalities and also it is inappropriate to convert graphics displays to points for line drawing vector graphics terminals. Therefore clipping algorithms are required that work on graphics objects more general than single points. In this section the Pascal code is developed to do the line-to-rectangle clipping suitable for a graphics package. The design techniques are subsequently built into the simple graphics demonstration package G2D described more fully in Chapter 8.

There are four possibilities for picture lines in relation to a viewport:

1. Both end points of the line lie inside the window.
2. One end point is within the window and the other is outside.
3. Both end points of the line are outside the window but the line passes through the window.
4. Both end points of the line are outside the window and the line does not pass through the window.

All but case 1 need clipping. The visible part of the lines for each case are:

1. The whole line;
2. From the end point within the window to where the line cuts the window boundary;
3. Between the two points where the line cuts the window boundaries;
4. No part visible.

In general (see Figure 7-2), the aim is to find the segment $R1R2$, of a line $P1P2$ within a picture, that crosses a window at $Q1$ and $Q2$ and the clipping rectangle within the window at points $R1$ and $R2$. The line segments $P1R1$ and $R2P2$ are to be deleted while the segment $R1R2$ is to be displayed. The problem is to determine $R1$ and $R2$ given $P1$ and $P2$.

The first step in the line clipping algorithm is to decide the nature of the given end points of the line. For this purpose the picture is divided into nine regions as shown in Figure 7-3. Each point (x, y) in the picture can now be classified by two integer parameters ax and ay where:

$$
\begin{array}{llll}
x & < & rect.xmin & \Rightarrow\ ax\ =\ -1 \\
rect.xmin & \leq x\ \leq rect.xmax & \Rightarrow\ ax\ =\ 0 \\
x & > & rect.xmax & \Rightarrow\ ax\ =\ 1 \\
y & < & rect.ymin & \Rightarrow\ ay\ =\ -1 \\
rect.ymin & \leq y\ \leq rect.ymax & \Rightarrow\ ay\ =\ 0 \\
y & > & rect.ymax & \Rightarrow\ ay\ =\ 1
\end{array}
$$

The (ax, ay) pair are together called the area code. The values of -1, 0, and 1 are simply useful arithmetic values for determining the status of points within the simple line clipping algorithm. The procedure in Box 7-1 is a simple routine that determines ax and ay for any given point (x, y).

Note the use of an explicit parameter called 'rect' to hold the coordinates of the lower left and upper right points of the rectangular region for clipping. The variables in 'rect' must be initialized to the window limits. This procedure will be called for both end points of the line:

find_area_code(rect,x1,y1,ax1,ay1);
find_area_code(rect,x2,y2,ax2,ay2);

Next consider the possible combinations of 'ax1', 'ay1' and 'ax2', 'ay2' in turn. The possibilities are related to the four cases of lines discussed above. Instead of directly programming for these four cases, a first check is made for picture lines that could not possibly pass through the window and these lines are rejected. Secondly, an attempt is made to shift the end points to the nearest window boundary if the points lie outside the window. Thirdly if the resultant points are coincident, this means that the original line did

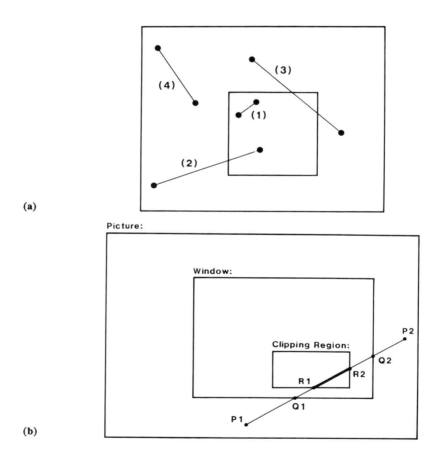

Figure 7-2 Clipping a line through a window to a given rectangle.
(a) In clipping line segments there are four possible cases to consider (1) to (4) where the line segments are partially or totally inside or outside of the current window.
(b) The line segment $P1P2$ is to be clipped to a clipping rectangle within a window. The result should be the line segment $R1R2$ highlighted.

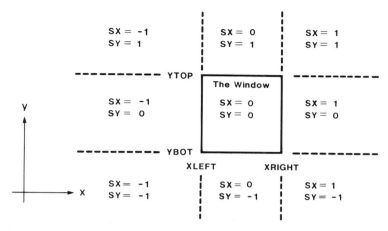

Figure 7-3 Line endpoints can be in any of the nine sectors about the rectangle.

not pass through the window, then this case is rejected. Finally, the clipped line is plotted. Line interpolation is done by the following formula:

$$y' = y + m \ \Delta x$$

where:

$$m = (y2 - y1) / (x2 - x1)$$

is the slope of the line and:

$$\Delta x = x' - x$$

is the change in x value. Linear interpollation is illustrated in Figure 7-4.

Box 7-1 A procedure for determining the area code numbers 'ax' and 'ay' for the simple line clipping algorithm.

```
procedure find_area_code(rect : rectangle_type; x,y : real; var ax,ay :
integer);
{Determine the area code (ax,ay) of a point (x,y) in user coordinates}
{with respect to the rectangle rect.}
begin
    ax := 0; ay := 0; {initialize the outputs}
    if x < rect.xmin then ax := -1;
    if x > rect.xmax then ax := 1;
    if y < rect.ymin then ay := -1;
    if y > rect.ymax then ay := 1;
end;
```

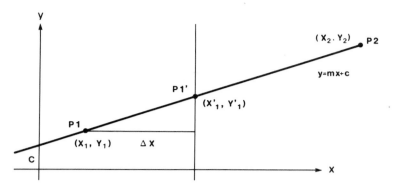

Figure 7-4 When a point such as *P*1 is outside of a window linear interpolation is used to move it to *P*1' on the nearest edge of the window.

Ordinarily the clipping region in a clipping process is the whole of the currently active graphics window, so that all graphics output is clipped to the size of the window for displaying on a viewport. In that case it is possible to construct a line clipping routine that would directly access the current window record structure, eliminating the need to pass a rectangle record to the clipping routine. However for greater generality at this time, the coordinate limits (i.e. lower left corner and upper right corner coordinates) of the clipping rectangle will be passed through a parameter called 'rect'. To perform ordinary line clipping to windows, simply ensure that the components of 'rect' have been initialized to the window limits. It will help to study the pseudocode for this simple line clipping algorithm before reading the Pascal code. The pseudocode is shown below:

The simple line clipping algorithm
Purpose: To draw the part of a line connecting two given points
            that passes through a given rectangle.
Inputs: ('x1','y1') and ('x2','y2') – the given end points
            'rect' – the record containing the clipping edges.
Outputs: None
Pseudocode:
    1. Determine the area codes of both end points.
    2. If the end points lie in the same area outside the rectangle then exit.
    3. If end point 1 is to be moved then:
        3.1 Move end point 1 to the nearer *x* edge.
        3.2 Compute the area code of the new point 1.
        3.3 If still outside the rectangle then:
            3.3.1 shift again to the nearer *y* boundary.
    4. If end point 2 is to be moved then:
        4.1 Shift end point 2 to the nearer *x* edge.
        4.2 Compute the area code of the new point 2.
        4.3 If another shift is required then:
            4.3.1 Shift point 2 to the nearer *y* boundary.
    5. If the end points now coincide then exit.

6. Draw a line from the new end point 1 to the new end point 2.
7. Exit.

This pseudocode draws the clipped line in step 6. A more flexible routine would output the new end point coordinates to be used as the user wishes. This is what the implementation of this algorithm as shown in Box 7-2 does. Note that the clipped lines are output from 'clip_line' in the last four parameters. An alternative is to reuse the first four parameters having them as 'var' parameters.

Box 7.2 A simple line clipping algorithm.

```
procedure clip_line(x1,y1,x2,y2 : real; rect : rectangle_type;
    var x1clipped,y1clipped,x2clipped,y2clipped : real);
{Clip the line joining (x1,y1) to (x2,y2) to the given rectangle in rect. The output
parameters are the endpoints of the clipped line segment.}
const
    eps = 1e-6;
var
    xedge,yedge,xprime,yprime : real;
    ax1,ay1,ax2,ay2 : integer;
begin
    {determine the area codes of both endpoints :}
    find_area_code(rect,x1,y1,ax1,ay1);
    find_area_code(rect,x2,y2,ax2,ay2);
    {if the endpoints are in the same area outside of the rectangle then}
    {exit without plotting the line :}
    if not ((ax1*ax2 = 1) or (ay1*ay2 = 1)) then
    begin
        {do we need to shift endpoint 1?}
        if ax1 <> 0 then
        begin
            {okay, move endpoint 1 to the nearer x edge of the rectangle :}
            {getting the nearer x edge}
            xedge := rect.xmin; if ax1 = 1 then xedge := rect.xmax;
            {linear interpolation :}
            xprime := xedge; yprime := y1 + (y2-y1)/(x2-x1) * (xprime-x1);
            {shift endpoint 1 to the new point :}
            x1 := xprime; y1 := yprime;
            {recompute the area code for the shifted endpoint :}
            find_area_code(rect,x1,y1,ax1,ay1);
        end;
        {if ay1 is non-zero then a second shift is required :}
        if ay1 <> 0 then
        begin
            yedge := rect.ymin; if ay1 = 1 then yedge := rect.ymax;
            yprime := yedge; xprime := x1 + (x2 - x1)/(y2 - y1) * (yprime-y1);
```

```
            x1 := xprime; y1 := yprime;
        end;
        {does the second endpoint need to be shifted to the rectangle edge?}
        if ax2 <> 0 then
        begin
            {shift point 2 to the nearest x edge of the rectangle :}
            xedge := rect.xmin; if ax2 = 1 then xedge := rect.xmax;
            xprime := xedge; yprime := y1 + (y2-y1)/(x2-x1) * (xprime - x1);
            x2 := xprime; y2 := yprime;
            find_area_code(rect,x2,y2,ax2,ay2);
        end;
        {Next see if another shift is required :}
        if ay2 <> 0 then
        begin
            yedge := rect.ymin; if ay2 = 1 then yedge := rect.ymax;
            yprime := yedge; xprime := x1 + (x2-x1)/(y2-y1) * (yprime - y1);
            x2 := xprime; y2 := yprime;
        end;
        x1clipped := x1; y1clipped := y1;
        x2clipped := x2; y2clipped := y2;
    end;
end;
```

This procedure can now be used on every line in the picture to be clipped to fit a given rectangle in the user coordinate window. The algorithm is essentially a version of the Cohen-Sutherland algorithm [see Newman & Sproull, 1979, and cf. Angell, 1982]. In order to plot a clipped line the following sequence of calls can be used:

```
{Define and draw the clipping rectangle by digitizing opposite vertexes :}
read_point(key,x1,y1); read_point(key,x2,y2);
set_rectangle(x1,y1,x2,y2,rect);
draw_rectangle(rect);
{Digitize two points to draw a line :}
read_point(key,x1,y1); read_point(key,x2,y2);
clip_line(rect,x1,y1,x2,y2,x1c,y1c,x2c,y2c);
{Are the clipped endpoints non-coincident? :}
if (abs(x2-x1) > eps) or (abs(y2-y1) > eps) then
    plot_line(x1c,y1c,x2c,y2c);
```

In order for the lines drawn by 'plot_line' to be properly clipped to the current viewport, the 'clip_line' routine should be called by 'plot_line' before any other statements are performed. The 'rect' parameter for this call is just the window record.

7.3 A simple line covering algorithm

Having looked at a simple line clipping algorithm, a simple line covering algorithm will now be described. Covering is the opposite of clipping – for clipping, the lines outside a rectangle are deleted; and for covering, the lines inside a rectangle are deleted. Covering is normally used when messages are to be written over parts of a complicated diagram. Text and graphics superimposed often result in confusion. Therefore part of the graphics picture is firstly blanked out by the covering routine and then the required message is written inside the covering area. Since the concepts of clipping and covering are opposites, the algorithms would be expected to be very similar. The algorithms could also be expected to share common subroutines. In general, as shown in Figure 7-5, the aim is to find the segments $Q1R1$ and $Q2R2$ of a line $P1P2$, within a picture, that crosses a window at $Q1$ and $Q2$ and the covering rectangle within the window at points $R1$ and $R2$.

The line segments $Q1R1$ and $R2Q2$ are to be displayed while the segment $R1R2$ is to be deleted. The problem is again to determine $R1$ and $R2$ given $P1$ and $P2$. The simplified case, where $P1$ and $P2$ are both within the user window, is covered here. For this routine, it will be assumed that the coordinate limits (i.e. lower left corner and upper right corner coordinates) of the covering rectangle are contained in the 'rect' rectangle record and that these parameters have been previously initialized. The pseudocode for the line covering routine follows:

The simple line covering algorithm
Purpose: To draw the part of a line connecting two given points
              that lies outside of a given rectangle.
Inputs: ('x1','y1') and ('x2','y2') - the given endpoints
              'rect' - the record containing the cover edges.
Outputs: None
Pseudocode :
    1. Determine the area code of both end points.

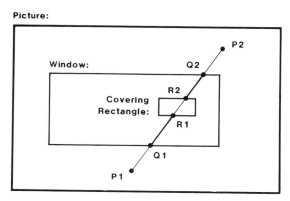

Figure 7-5 The problem of covering a line segment such as $P1P2$ with a given rectangle within a window is similar to the line clipping problem. It results in drawing only the line segments $Q1R1$ and $R2Q2$.

2. If both end points of the line are on the same side of one pair of extended covering rectangle edges then:

    2.1 Draw the entire line (since it is outside the cover).

    2.2 Exit.

3. If $(x1, y1)$ is not between x edges then:

    3.1 Locate the point $R1 = (x', y')$ on the line at the nearer x edge

    3.2 Compute the area codes for $R1$.

4. If $R1$ is not between y edges then move it along the line to the nearer y edge.

5. If $P1$ and $R1$ coincide then goto 7.

6. Draw the line $P1$ to $R1$.

7. Repeat steps 3, 4, 5, and 6 for the second endpoint $P2$.

This pseudocode can be implemented as shown in Box 7-3. This routine covers a rectangular area from lines with given end points. This is suitable for placing text labels onto diagrams since these would usually take a rectangular area. In general, both the end

Box 7-3 A simple line covering algorithm.

```
procedure cover_line(x1,y1,x2,y2 : real; rect : rectangle_type);
{Routine to plot the line joining (x1,y1) to (x2,y2) with the part within the
rectangle defined in rect blanked out.}
const
    eps = 1e-6;
var
    ax1,ay1,ax2,ay2 : integer;
    xedge, yedge : real;
begin
    {Determine the area code of both end points : }
    find_area_code(rect,x1,y1,ax1,ay1);
    find_area_code(rect,x2,y2,ax2,ay2);
    {If both endpoints are on the same side of a pair of cover edges
    then draw the line and exit :}
    if ((ax1*ax2 = 1) or (ay1*ay2 = 1) then
        plot_line(x1,y1,x2,y2)
    else
    begin
        {** Calculate the point R1 **
        If P1 is not between x edges then locate R1 on the line
        at the nearer edge : }
        {initialize R1 = P1 :}
        xprime := x1; yprime := y1;
        if (ax1 <> 0) then
        begin
            {Compute the nearer x edge : }
            xedge=rect.xmin; if ax1 = 1 then xedge=xmax;
```

```
          {Locate R1 as (X1P,Y1P) :}
          xprime := xedge;
          yprime := y1+(y2-y1)/(x2-x1)*(xprime - x1);
          {Find the area codes of R1 : }
          find_area_code(xprime,yprime,ax1,ay1);
     end;
     {If R1 is not between y edges then shift it to the nearer y edge :}
     if ay1 <> 0 then

     begin
          {Compute the nearer y edge :}
          yedge := rect.ymin; if ay1 = 1 then yedge := rect.ymax;
          {Locate R1 :}
          yprime := yedge;
          xprime := x1+(x2-x1)/(y2-y1)*(yprime-y1);
     end;
     {If P1 and R1 don't coincide then draw the line segment P1R1 :}
     if (abs(xprime-x1) > eps) or (abs(yprime-y1) > eps) then
                    plot_line(x1,y1,xprime,yprime);
     {** Repeat the above process for P2 **}
     {initialize R2, i.e. R2 = P2 :}
     xprime := x2; yprime := y2;
     {Is P2 between x edges? :}
     if (ax2 <> 0) then

     begin
          {Find the nearest edge :}
          xedge := rect.xmin; if ax2 = 1 then xedge := rect.xmax;
          { * Calculate the point R2 * :}
          xprime := xedge; yprime := y1 + (y2-y1)/(x2-x1)*(xprime-x1);
          {Find the area codes of R2 :}
          find_area_code(rect,xprime,yprime,ax2,ay2);
     end;
     {If P2 is not between y edges then move it :}
     if ay2 <> 0 then

     begin
          {Compute the nearer y edge :}
          yedge := rect.ymin; if ay2 = 1 then yedge := ymax;
          {Locate R2 :}
          yprime := yedge; xprime := x1 + (x2-x1)/(y2-y1)*(yprime - y1);
     end;
     {If  R2 <> P2 then draw the line segment R2P2 :}
     if (abs(x2-xprime) > eps) or (abs(y2-yprime) > eps) then
                    plot_line(xprime,yprime,x2,y2);
     end;
end;
```

points $P1$ and $P2$ of the line segment will not always be inside the user coordinate space (the window) so that clipping is required in addition to the covering. This can easily be done by first calling the 'clip_line' routine and then passing the clipped end points of the line on to the above 'cover_line' routine. The following code fragment illustrates these ideas:

```
{Define and draw the clipping rectangle by digitizing opposite vertexes :}
read_point(key,x1,y1); read_point(key,x2,y2);
set_rectangle(x1,y1,x2,y2,rect1);
draw_rectangle(rect);
{Define and draw the covering rectangle by digitizing opposite vertexes :}
read_point(key,x1,y1); read_point(key,x2,y2);
set_rectangle(x1,y1,x2,y2,rect2);
draw_rectangle(rect);
{Digitize two points to draw a line :}
read_point(key,x1,y1); read_point(key,x2,y2);
clip_line(rect,x1,y1,x2,y2,x1c,y1c,x2c,y2c);
{Are the clipped endpoints non-coincident? :}
if (abs(x2-x1) > eps) or (abs(y2-y1) > eps) then
    cover_line(x1c,y1c,x2c,y2c,rect2);
{Now enter a text label into rect2}
```

However it is likely that more than one label per graphics diagram is wanted and this means covering graphics output using many variously sized rectangle covers. Furthermore, covering could be done using more general complex shapes such as concave polygons or a closed shape with one or more 'holes' inside through which the original graphics display can be seen suitably clipped. Such general covering routines are more difficult to design and will be considered in Section 7.7.

7.4 General two-dimensional data structuring

Many fast graphics algorithms apply to rectangles but cannot be generalized. To turn to graphics algorithms that apply to two-dimensional geometrical shapes more general than the rectangle, first a suitable data structuring must be defined, in place of 'rectangle_type' of Section 7.2, to represent the more general shapes.

A simple space-saving method for holding the vertex data for all graphics objects to be displayed is to place the (x, y) coordinates into a table. A point is then defined as an integer, and its coordinates are obtained by table lookup using the integer value as an index. The data structure for a line segment is then an integer array of dimension two which stores the indexes for each end point. Polylines and polygons may be represented by integer arrays plus integers to define the size of the arrays. However to improve vertex insertion and deletion times, list structures (with single pointers) can be employed. To represent broken polylines and unions of polygons, dynamic list structures with heavy

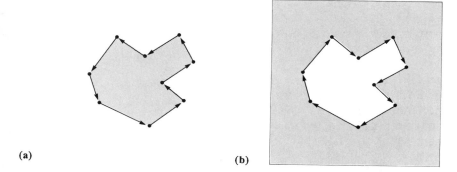

Figure 7-6 The finite area defined by a polygon with vertexes listed in the anticlockwise sense (a) and the infinite area defined by a polygon with vertexes in the clockwise sense (b).

use of pointer variables are suitable. A region of two-dimensional space can be defined by set unions and intersections of the interiors of polygons. By convention, the finite area inside a polygon F is referred to as its 'interior' if the vertexes are listed in anticlockwise order. If the list of vertexes for a polygon is in clockwise order then the finite area enclosed by the polygon is referred to as the 'exterior' of the polygon. (See Figure 7-6.)

Now a polygon is a list of vertexes and a two-dimensional space region can be represented as a list of polygons, therefore, in general, two-dimensional shapes usually involve lists of many geometrical elements (cf. Section 5.1). A programming language with inbuilt list processing statements (such as LISP) would serve well here. However Pascal (with a properly functioning dispose function) can handle dynamic lists, and much of the inner list parameter handling can be kept tucked away inside list manipulation procedures so that the user need not be bogged down by keeping track of pointers and other inner list handling problems when there are more important high-level geometrical problems.

For example, using Pascal, the following data structure types and variables would be adequate to represent points, line segments, polygons, and general two-dimensional regions:

```
const
    max_nr_points = 200;
type
    point_type = record
        x,y : real;
        end;
    line_segment_type = record
        pt1,pt2 : integer;
        end;
    vertex_node = record
        pt : integer;
```

```
            next : ^vertex_node;
            end;
        polygon_header = record
            nr_vertexes : integer;
            first : ^vertex_node;
            end;
        polygon_type = ^polygon_header;
        polygon_node = record
            polygon : ^polygon_type;
            next : ^polygon_node;
            end;
        region_header = record
            nr_polygons : integer;
            first : ^polygon_node;
            end;
        region_type = ^region_header;
    var
        nr_points : integer;
        point_table : array[1..max_nr_points] of point_type;
```

In actual Pascal implementations, additional pointers should be added to the vertex and polygon lists – it would be better to have doubly linked list structures rather than simple single-linked lists. A pointer in the head of each of these lists should point to the last entry (as well as having a first entry pointer), and each item of the list could have a backward pointer (as well as its 'next' pointer). These are helpful for the delete operations on lists (described below), so that lists need not be traversed only in the forward direction by the software.

Routines are required to provide controlled access to these data structures. These are the typical routines of list processing. A set of the nine basic list manipulation routines is presented in Box 7-4 by their first lines to show how they are defined and used. The type 'list_type' is a generic name for a pointer to a list header. Figure 7-7 shows the general list structure. Special cases of this structure are the 'polygon_type' and

Box 7-4 The nine basic list processing functions.

```
procedure    new_list(list : list_type);
procedure    append_item(item : item_type; list : list_type);
function     list_size(list : list_type) : integer;
function     item_number(item : item_type; list : list_type) : integer;
procedure    insert_item_after(item_nr : integer; item : item_type;
                 list : list_type);
procedure    delete_item_number(item_nr : integer; list : list_type);
procedure    delete_last_item(list : list_type);
procedure    delete_list(list : list_type);
function     get_item(item_nr : integer; list : list_type) : item_type;
```

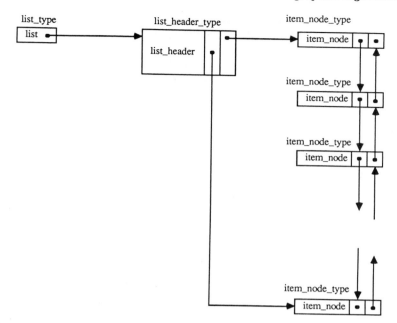

Figure 7-7 Data structuring for a general list.

'region_type' above which are illustrated in Figure 7-8. Figure 7-9 shows two examples of such regions. The first routine 'new_list' creates and initializes a new record for the pointer 'list'. The user must call this routine first to create a list. The second routine allows the entry of items into the list. The user must supply the item value in the parameter 'item' that has the generic (general-purpose) type name 'item_type'. The 'append_item' procedure could also check that the item to be appended is not already in the list. For the case of polygons and regions, list entries must be unique. The function 'list_size' returns the number of items currently in the specified list to the user. The 'item_number' function returns the first position number in the list where a specified item matches. The procedure 'insert_item_after' allows the user to put entries into the list at any position in the list rather than only at the end as 'append_item' does. If the specified list position (as given in the parameter 'item_nr') is zero then the new item is added at the top of the list. If 'item_nr' is less than zero or greater than the number of entries currently in the list then an error message is returned to the user. The procedure 'delete_item_number' allows the user to cancel a previous 'insert_item_after' and take any item from any valid position in the list. The next procedure 'delete_last_item' is the opposite of the 'append_item' routine in that it removes the last list entry. The procedure 'delete_list' empties the list entirely. With all delete functions the Pascal dispose function is used which should properly release the memory used by the list on the heap. The function 'get_item' is for reading list items back to the user.

Pascal, even when extended to have separate compilation units, does not provide fully for the software engineering concept of *data abstraction*. With data abstraction, a data structure and operations can be provided to the user with the base type(s) unspecified so

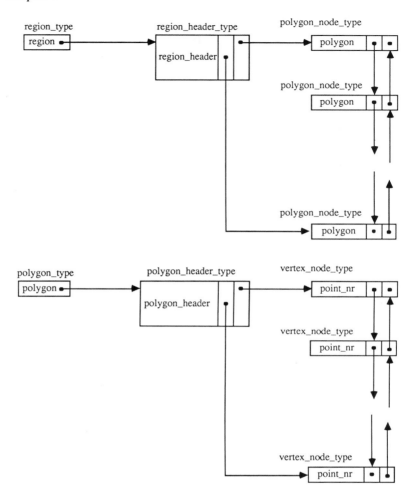

Figure 7-8 The data structure for a region as a list of polygons each of which is a list of vertexes.

that the same structure and operators can be applied to structures built on various base types. For example, the list structure and its nine operators described above may be set up for a base type ('item_type') of 'polygon_type' so that the lists will be regions. If data abstraction we available, the same set of routines could then be used for the polygon vertex lists. However in Pascal, another set of almost identical code must be set up giving a total of eighteen list processing procedures. Additionally, the following four routines would be useful for setting up and using the points table in a structured and controlled way:

1. **procedure** init_data
    – sets 'nr_points' to zero and sets all pointers to 'nil'.

2. **procedure** enter_point(x,y : real)
   – first tests to see if ('x','y') is already in the table, and if not it increments 'nr_points' and if 'nr_points' is not greater than the maximum allowed, the coordinates are stored at the 'nr_points' location.
3. **function** get_point_id(x,y : real) : integer;
   – returns the (positive) integer identification number for the specified point if it is in the table, otherwise it returns zero.
4. **procedure** change_point(id : integer; x,y : real)
   – changes the coordinates of the point in the points table with identification number 'id' to the new coordinate values of 'x' and 'y' if such a point exists in the table.

The following routines are needed to display the data held in the list structures:

1. **procedure** draw_polygon(f : polygon_type)
   – draws the polygon 'f' using the data in the specified polygon.
2. **procedure** draw_region(r : region_type)
   – draws the region 'r' using the data in the specified region structure.

If the region is multiply connected or has holes then the 'nr_polygons' member will be greater than one. The data for a region should be tested for consistency: a region should:

1. consist of at least one polygon;
2. ensure that none of the polygons are self intersecting;
3. ensure.that none of the polygons intersect any other polygon;
4. label nested polygons in alternating directions;
5. have the outermost polygon labelled in the anticlockwise sense.

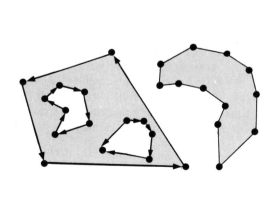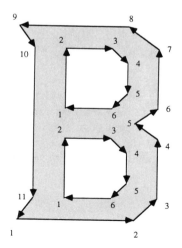

Figure 7-9 Two examples of two dimensional regions.

An alternative data structure called a quadtree has been used also to represent arbitrary two-dimensional regions. A quadtree is a tree data structure with zero to four branches from each node. Each terminal node represents a rectangle totally contained within the region. It is constructed by dividing the display rectangle up into quadrants which are similar rectangles but at half the scale. For every quadrant that the region intersects there is a branch to a new node from the quadtree root node. The quadrants are next subdivided into quadrants themselves and new branches are added to the tree wherever the region intersects a subquadrant. This process continues until further subdivision is not required because the rectangles represented by the terminal nodes are entirely within the region. (The subdivision process also need not go further than the display pixels themselves.) Quadtrees, however, do not readily yield border data required for some of the algorithms considered in this chapter, and for regions whose edges are not all parallel to the axes, they will generally consume more memory.

7.5 Useful two-dimensional support routines

A number of basic algorithms are required to support the containment, clipping, covering, and hatching algorithms discussed in the following sections. One of the most basic support routines is the routine to test two line segments for intersection. This routine is needed so many times that it will be carefully discussed first.

The algorithm for finding line segment intersections is straight forward. The routine must return a logical flag and the line segment parameter value λ at the point of intersection. Let (x_i, y_i) for $i = 1$ and $i = 2$ be the end points of the first edge, and for $i = 3$ and $i = 4$ the end points of the second. The algorithm must first check for the cases:

$$\max\{x_i\} < \min\{x_j\} \quad \text{or} \quad \min\{x_i\} < \max\{x_j\}$$

or:

$$\max\{y_i\} < \min\{y_j\} \quad \text{or} \quad \min\{y_i\} < \max\{y_j\}$$

where $i = 1, 2$ and $j = 3, 4$; and if any of these conditions are true then the routine immediately returns with the intersection flag set to false. This is an example of *minmax testing* . Now let the parameter for the first edge be λ and that for the second be μ. The simultaneous edge equations reduce to two simultaneous linear equations for λ and μ. When the determinant of these equations is nonzero the lines are nonparallel and a solution for λ and μ can be found:

$$\lambda = \{(x_3 - x_1)(y_4 - y_3) - (x_4 - x_3)(y_3 - y_1)\} \, / \, det$$
$$\mu = \{(x_3 - x_1)(y_2 - y_1) - (x_2 - x_1)(y_3 - y_1)\} \, / \, det$$

provided:

$$det \equiv \{(x_2 - x_1)(y_4 - y_3) - (x_4 - x_3)(y_2 - y_1)\} \neq 0$$

For the edges to actually intersect, there is a further requirement that both the edge parameter values lie in the interval [0,1]. This routine will be referred to by the definition:

function intersects(seg1,seg2 : line_segment_type;
    var lambda : real) : boolean;

where 'seg1' and 'seg2' are two line segments using the 'line_segment_type' presented in the previous section. This procedure could have easily had line parameters, 'lambda' and 'mu', for the intersection point as output parameters. However, in practice, both intersection line parameters, 'lambda' and 'mu', are never needed and the parameter 'mu' is unnecessary. Note that the 'lambda' parameter belongs to 'seg1' not 'seg2'. Of course, if 'seg2's parameter were the one wanted then the call would be made with the order of the parameters 'seg1' and 'seg2' reversed.

The problem of 'end point paranoia' must be cared for in this algorithm and in many similar ones. The problem will be mentioned here but applies to the many other areas such as containment testing in two dimensions and edge visibility testing in three dimensions. The end point paranoia problem arises from two facts. The first is that objects in the real world, and mathematical abstractions of them, are ultimately defined in terms of real numbers and so it is familiar to use real numbers for the coordinates of points. The second fact is that computers store real numbers reliably to only a given finite precision. An end point may actually touch another line but the computer records the intersection 'lambda' parameter value as differing from its end-point value of 1 by, say, 1e-20 (or by, say, -1e-21 away from $\lambda = 0$ for the other end point). This extremely small difference caused by cumulative approximations in floating-point operations done to a finite precision would then cause the software to think that lines that actually do touch do not touch (or vice versa) and so the graphics output will be wrong! Because line segment intersection is a support routine for many high-level graphics routines (three-dimensional as well as two-dimensional routines) this neglible numerical error will therefore have unexpected macroscopic effects in the output graphics. The remedy is to use the 'epsilon' constant (say epsilon = 1e-6) and test real numbers to within 'epsilon' of their test values. Its a good idea to have the constant 'epsilon' defined globally within the compilation unit so that all routines that need it work to the same precision.

The minmax test has been mentioned above in relation to the question of intersection of two line segments. The minmax test applies far more widely than this. It is of importance in the question of the intersection of any two regular or irregular two-dimensional geometrical shapes. Given any (finite) geometrical object there is a minimal rectangle that encompasses the object. The lower left corner of this rectangle has the minimum x value of all points in the object for its x coordinate, and the minimum y value of all points in the object for its y component: $(xmin, ymin)$. Similarly the upper right corner of this minimal bounding rectangle has coordinates $(xmax, ymax)$ being the maximum x and y values of all points in the object. The second object has a similar bounding rectangle. Let us call these two rectangles 'rect1' and 'rect2' which are of type 'rectangle_type' as discussed in Section 7.2. The support routine for minimax testing is then of the form:

function rectangle_overlap(rect1,rect2 : rectangle_type) : boolean;

which returns a boolean result saying whether the two specified rectangles 'rect1' and 'rect2' overlap or not. It is not easy to see the criterion for when the overlap of the two rectangles occurs. The inverse criterion, that of determining when they do not overlap is more immediate: namely there is no overlap if the minimum x component of the second is greater than maximum x of the first, or if the maximum x of the second is less than the minimum x of the first, or if the minimum y of the second is greater than the maximum y of the first, or if the maximum y of the second is less than the minimum y of the first rectangle. Using this logic, the overlap criterion can be written in Pascal as:

```
overlap := true;
if   (rect2.xmin > rect1.xmax) or
     (rect2.xmax < rect1.xmin) or
     (rect2.ymin > rect1.ymax) or
     (rect2.ymax < rect1.ymin)
then       overlap := false;
```

Determining the minimal bounding rectangle or *minmax box* for every possible graphics element is an intriguing problem. For example, the minmax box for a circle defined by two points $(x1, y1)$ and $(x2, y2)$ (the ends of a diameter as before) is given by:

$$xmin = xc - r$$
$$ymin = yc - r$$
$$xmax = xc + r$$
$$ymax = yc + r$$

where:

$$xc = (x1 + x2) / 2$$
$$yc = (y1 + y2) / 2$$
$$r = \sqrt{[(xc - x1)^2 + (yc - y1)^2]}$$

The more intriguing problem of determining the minmax box for an arc in terms of its point definition parameters $(x1, y1)$, $(x2, y2)$ and $(x3, y3)$ is left as an exercise. Note that two further routines should be provided in the package:

procedure set_rectangle(x1,y1,x2,y2 : real; **var** rect : rectangle_type);

which uses two points to set up a rectangle record where the two points are assumed to be opposite vertexes (of either diagonal). The second useful procedure in this area is:

procedure draw_rectangle(rect : rectangle_type);

which simply makes four calls to the 'plot_line' routine.

Simple algorithms are required to compute polygon angles and areas, and validate polygon data, and find if and where two line segments intersect. The exterior angles of the polygon $F = P_1 P_2 P_3 \ldots P_n$ are defined by inner products of consecutive edge vectors:

$$\phi_i = \cos^{-1}\{s_i . s_{i'} \, / \, |s_i| \, / \, |s_{i'}|\} \tag{7.1}$$

where:

$$|s_i| = \sqrt{[s_{ix}^2 + s_{iy}^2]}$$

is the length of the vector s_i , the length of side i, $P_i P_{i'}$, of the polygon. (Here i' is the cyclically next vertex in the list, that is, $i' = (i \mod n) + 1$.)

Polygon algorithms are greatly simplified if it is known that the polygon is convex. A polygon F is defined as being *convex* if:

$Q , R \in F \Rightarrow QR$ is a subset of the interior of F

If the polygon is not convex then it is called *concave*. In other words, for a polygon to be convex, every point along the line segment joining any pair of points inside F must also be contained inside F otherwise the polygon is concave. This however is not a practical definition for testing convexity of any given polygon F. A more practical method is based on angle determinations.

For every vertex P of the polygon F, the interior angle is defined by:

$$\psi_i = \pi - \phi_i \tag{7.2}$$

A useful concept derived from interior angles is that of a *point of concavity* . A vertex P_i of a polygonal figure F is called a point of concavity iff the interior angle at P_i is strictly greater than π radians, otherwise it may be called a point of convexity. Equivalently a vertex P_i of a polygonal figure F is a *point of convexity* iff the exterior angle at P_i is strictly greater than π radians, otherwise it is a point of concavity. The maximum number of consecutive points of concavity can be called the recursive order of concavity of the polygon. Similarly, the order of convexity of a polygon is the maximum number of consecutive points of convexity of the polygon. If the order of concavity is zero or equivalently the order of convexity equals the number of vertexes in the polygon then the polygon is *convex*.

Formula 7.1 involves considerable computation time in its evaluation owing to the square root function implicit in $|s_i|$ and the inverse cosine function. The inverse cosine function is multivalued and computer implementations of it generally only return valid angles when the argument is in the semi-open interval [0,1). The valid range of angles returned is only 0 to $\pi / 2$ radians. It is therefore preferable to invent a real function called 'angle(deltax,deltay)' which returns the angle of a vector with components ('deltax','deltay') with tail at the origin and result in the range [0,2π). This is easily achieved by using the ubiquitously implemented 'arctan' function taking cases for the four quadrants. This routine is then used to form the angles:

$$\theta_i = \text{angle}(s_i)$$

The external angles are easily obtained from these angles by taking differences in pairs.

Since the polygon is closed, from elementary geometry the following equality holds:

$$\Sigma \phi_i = 2\pi (\chi + 1)$$

In this formula χ is an integer which equals zero if the polygon has no self-crossings. It is assumed that polygon crossings are the result of data errors, and a routine is required that will locate the vertexes between which the polygon self-overlaps. This is easily done if there are no points of concavity by stopping the summation when it first exceeds 2π and noting the corresponding polygon vertex number i. Failing this, all line segments could be tested for intersection against all others. For a polygon of n sides, this would mean $n (n-1) / 2$ calls to the 'intersects' routine.

The area of a polygon can easily be found by summing the areas of the subtended trapeziums. Two points $P = (x_1, y_1)$ and $Q = (x_2, y_2)$ form a trapezium with the x axis whose area is:

$$A = (y_2\text{-}y_1)\,(x_2\text{-}x_1) / 2$$

Therefore the formula for the area of a polygon is simply:

$$A(F) = (\Sigma(y_{i'} + y_i)\,(x_{i'} - x_i)) / 2$$

This formula can be used to test the vertex sequence of a polygon since if this sum is negative then the vertexes are labeled in the clockwise sense rather than the anticlockwise sense. This formula can also be used to derive the area that an edge subtends at a point. If the latter sum yields a negative answer for a test point in relation to a polygon edge, then the point is on the inside side of the edge.

7.6 The general containment problem

A polygonal figure:

$$F = \bigcup_{i=1}^{n} P_i P_{i'}$$

where each vertex P_i is distinct, partitions the real plane R^2 into three disjoint sets: inside F, the boundary (which equals F), and outside F. Workable criteria are needed for

Color graphics VDU with a two-button mouse and color hard-copy output. Courtesy of Tektronix Australia.

Graphics hardcopy output devices. Courtesy of Tektronix Australia.

The Apple Macintosh graphics microcomputer. Courtesy of Apple Computer Australia.

The Apple Laserwriter for high quality (300 dots per inch) graphics output. Courtesy of Apple Computer Australia.

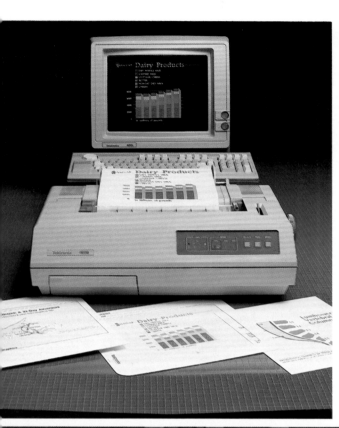

Data plots with hard-copy output.
Courtesy of Tektronix Australia.

A typical drum plotter used in batch
processing on a mainframe.
Courtesy of Silicon Graphics.

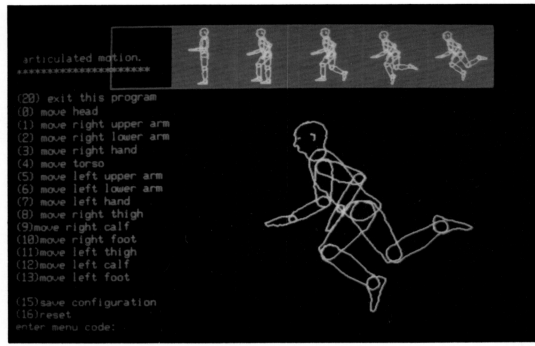

A graphics program to display motion of the human body.

Color VDUs used for CAD. Courtesy of Tektronix Australia.

CAD station. Courtesy of Tektronix Australia.

Circuit design using a color graphics package called ECAD from The Mentor Graphics running on an Apollo DN3000. Courtesy of Domain Computers.

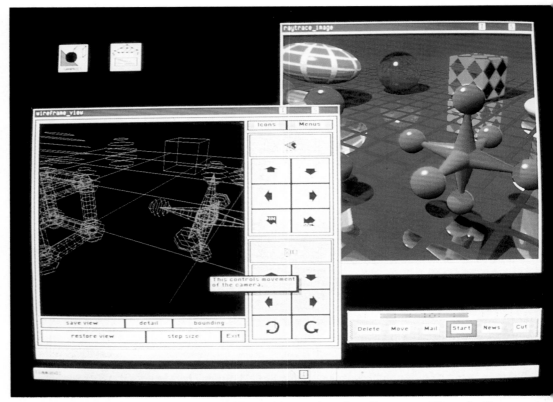

The windowing environment on a DN3000 graphics workstation. Courtesy of Domain Computers.

Three-dimensional bar charts created by the Plot 10 GDI software.
Courtesy of Tektronix Australia.

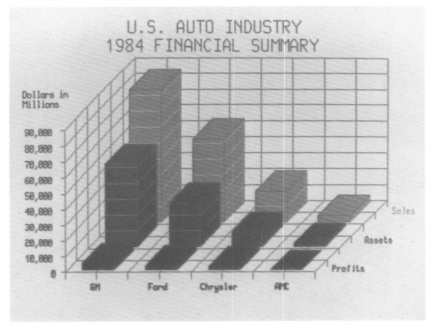

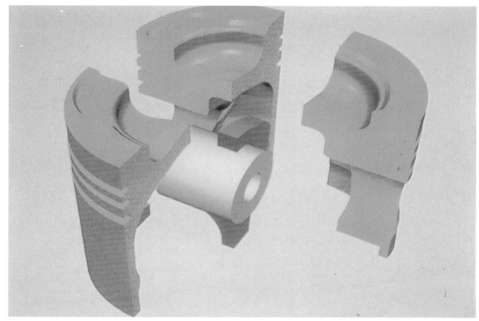

Three-dimensional CAD. Courtesy of Silicon Graphics.

Interactive three-dimensional CAD. Courtesy of Silicon Graphics.

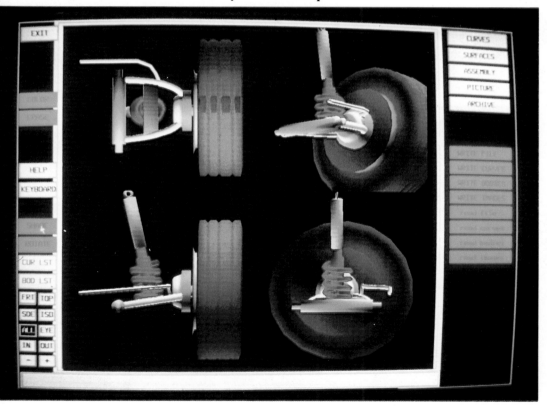

CAD/CAM. A shape designed on a computer graphics screen (CAD) is cut out by NC (Numerically Controlled) machinery (CAM) attached to the same host computer. Courtesy of Tektronix Australia.

Analysis of aerodynamic stability using a color graphics workstation. Courtesy of Silicon Graphics.

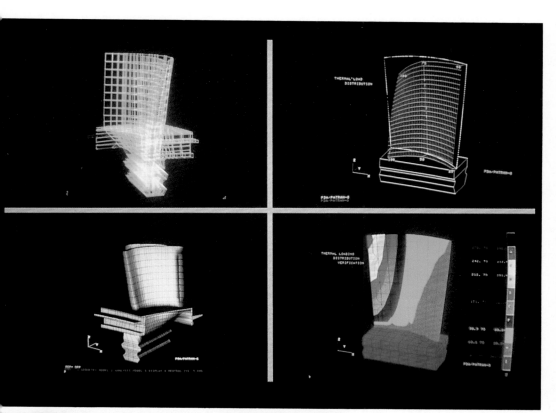

Different displays generated by
a finite element analysis and
modelling package.
Courtesy of Domain Computers.

Solid Modelling using an
Integraph workstation.
Courtesy of Domain Computers.

Molecular modelling on the Iris
three-dimensional graphics workstation
Courtesy of Silicon Graphics.

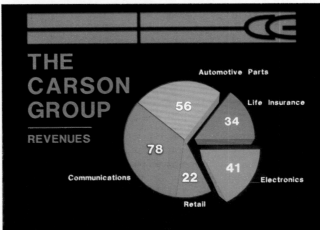

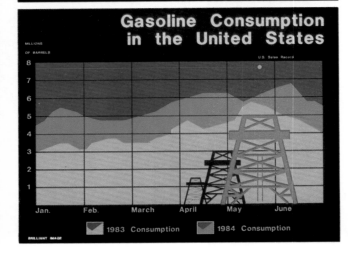

The use of computer graphics to
display color charts.
Courtesy of Zenographics.

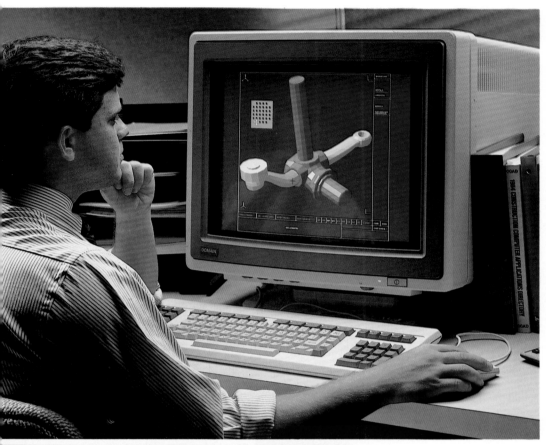

Solid rendering of a mechanical linkage using a DN590 graphics workstation.
Courtesy of Domain Computers.

The appearance of three-dimensional depth and spherical surfaces using computer graphics.

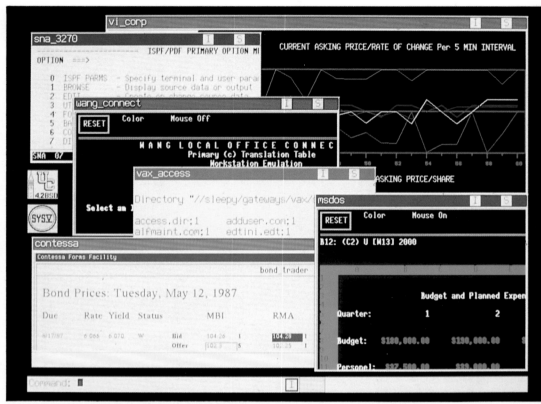

Screen images generated by Intelligent Light running on a DN590T.
Courtesy of Domain Computers.

Realistic fish tank color image scene generated by computer graphics.
Courtesy of Silicon Graphics.

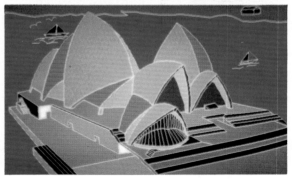

Yachts animated behind the Sydney Opera House using triple buffering.

deciding when a test point $P^* = (x^*, y^*)$ belongs or does not belong to any of these sets associated with a polygon. One test [Giloi, 1978] is to sum the angles subtended by the edges of F at P^*. For points inside or on the boundary of the polygon, the sum should be 2π; while for test points outside the polygon, the sum should be zero. This algorithm is called the *angle sum test* for containment. However as noted in the previous section, angle determination involves considerable processing and for this test it must be done n times. Another more commonly used algorithm for determining containment is known as the *ray test* [e.g. Harrington, 1983]: a point P^* is within the polygon iff a ray starting at P^* intersects in an odd number of points of the boundary F without intersecting any of the vertexes. This is because each such intersection of the ray with the boundary corresponds to moving from inside F to outside F, or vice versa, as a point moves along the ray from P^* and so an odd number of crossings means that the point started from, P^*, must have been inside F. Since n is finite, it is always possible to choose a ray which does not intersect any of the vertexes $P_1, P_2, \ldots P_n$.

Reference to Figure 7-10 will show why this restriction is required. Sometimes a vertex intersection counts effectively as two intersections and sometimes as one. Because there are only a finite number of vertexes it is always possible to arrange the test ray construction to avoid them. However, this restriction can be lifted if the nature of the vertexes intersecting the ray is carefully noted. What really needs to be counted is the number of border crossings rather than all intersections with the border of the polygon. In particular if the previous and the next vertexes to a vertex which intersects the ray are on the same side of the ray then that intersection should not be counted – it is not a crossing. If the previous and next vertexes are on opposite sides of the ray then the intersection counts like all other nonvertex intersections of the ray with the polygon, on one side of the intersection the ray is outside of the polygon and on the other side of the point of intersection the ray is inside the polygon. In this case the intersection is in fact a crossing, that is, the ray actually crosses the polygon border. A simple way to tell if the previous and next vertexes are on the same or opposite sides of the ray is to see if the imaginary line joining the previous and the next vertex would intersect the ray or not. Sample cases of these considerations are shown in Figure 7-11.

Furthermore, an infinite ray need not be used, but rather a line segment from P^* to a point Q known to be outside of F. For example, the line segment from P^* to the point $Q = (xmin, y^*)$ where $xmin$ is the minimum vertex x component in F. This algorithm also requires a loop through all edges 1 to n but this time testing each edge for intersection with the line segment P^*Q which is less onerous than angle determination. If the test line segment P^*Q strikes a vertex (to within 'epsilon' as discussed before) then an imaginary line segment from the previous to the next vertexes is constructed and this is tested for intersection with P^*Q by a call to 'intersects'. The boolean result is ignored; the first parameter has to be the constructed line segment, the second parameter being the line segment P^*Q. This means that the 'lambda' value corresponds to the constructed line segment (rather than the test line segment), and only if its value is within [0,1] (to an error of 'epsilon') does the intersection count as a border crossing. Note that the lambda value for the test line segment P^*Q is irrelevant and for the purposes of this test P^*Q may be extended to an infinite straight line.

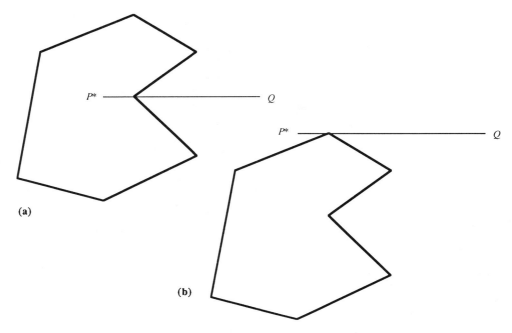

Figure 7-10 Problem cases in determining polygon boundary crossings.

The second algorithm can however be optimized by use of the observation that the edges of F far from P^*Q cannot intersect with P^*Q. To implement this idea, whenever a polygon is defined the program should precompute, in addition to the polygon's angles as mentioned in Section 7.5 the following arrays:

exmin[1..n], exmax[1..n], eymin[1..n], eymax[1..n]
ixmin[1..n], ixmax[1..n], iymin[1..n], iymax[1..n]

The array 'exmin[]' is the sorted array of minimum x components for each of the n edges of the polygon, and 'ixmin[]' is the array of corresponding edge numbers. Thus 'exmin[j]' is the j th smallest x component of all the n edges and it corresponds to edge $P_i P_{i'}$ where 'i = ixmin[j]'. The other arrays are set up similarly. The arrays 'exmin[1..n]', 'exmax[1..n]', 'eymin[1..n]', and 'eymax[1..n]' are sorted in increasing order. By choosing a pair of these arrays, it is possible to reduce the number of intersections that have to be tested. Thus for the choice $Q = (xmin, y^*)$, the program must use the 'exmin[]' and 'ixmin[]' pair of arrays. The following pseudocode shows how they are used:

initialize intersection counter to zero
j ← 1
while exmin[j] ≤ x^* and j ≤ n
    i ← ixmin[j]

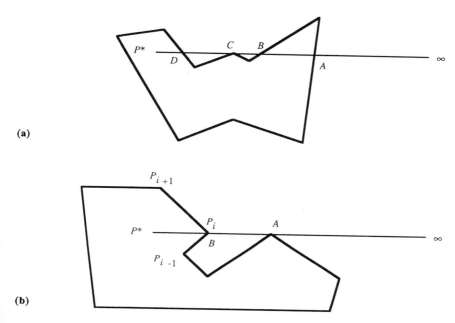

Figure 7-11 An intersection of the ray with an edge of the polygon is counted as a crossing if $0 < \lambda < 1$ as in points A, B, and D in case (a), or if $\lambda = 0$ and P_{i-1} and P_{i+1} are on opposite sides of the ray as for point B of case (b). Thus there are 3 crossings in (a) and 1 in (b).

```
if edge P_iP_i, intersects P*Q then
        increment the intersection counter
    increment j
if the number of intersections is odd then
        return TRUE
else
        return FALSE.
```

The other arrays 'exmax[1..n]', 'eymin[1..n]', and 'eymax[1..n]' apply to other choices for Q namely $Q = (xmax, y^*)$, $Q = (x^*, ymin)$, and $Q = (x^*, ymax)$ where $xmax$, $ymin$, and $ymax$ are the maxima and minima in vertex components. The algorithm expressed in the above pseudocode can then be further modified to determine which of these four choices for Q (left, right, up, or down from P^*) leads to the least number of edges of F to test for intersection with P^*Q.

Simpler containment tests can be developed based upon the areas subtended by edges of the polygon at the test point. Area computations consume considerably less processing effort. The case when the polygon F is convex is very simple. If F is convex then P^* is inside F if and only if:

$$\sum_{i=1}^{n} |A_i| = A$$

where A_i is the (signed) area subtended by side i of F at P^*, and A is the total area of the polygon. For concave polygons the following area test determines containment: P^* is inside F iff the area subtended by the nearest edge to P^* is negative. Determining the nearest edge however requires looping through all vertexes of F seeing if the perpendicular from P^* to each edge intersects the edge and if so computing the distance of P^* and keeping track of the minimum value. An alternative to searching for the nearest edge is to select any neighboring edge where a neighboring edge is defined as one which contains a point M such that P^*M does not intersect any other edge of F. (If F is convex and P^* is inside F then all edges are neighboring to P^* in this sense.) A neighboring edge can be found by applying the above pseudocode to the line segment P^*Q and replacing the step which says 'increment intersection counter' (in line 6) with 'save the edge number for the smallest λ'. At the end of the loop if P^* is on the inside of the neighboring edge (i.e. $y_{i'}$ < y_i) then P^* is inside F. This therefore represents roughly the same amount of processing as the modified ray test method. However a further improvement can be applied when searching for the neighboring edge in the P^*Q direction. Rather than compute and minimize λ values, instead compute the x coordinates of intersection and maximize these. The improvement is that the algorithm need not compute line intersections for edges of F whose maximum x component is less than the maximum x intersection value found to date.

The comments above regarding improving the modified ray test algorithm by testing which of the four directions reduces the processing load apply equally well to the above neighboring edge method. Of course, all containment algorithms first test that P^* is within the rectangle defined by the minima and maxima in vertex coordinates. (This is called the minmax test as mentioned before.) In the following sections the containment testing routine is denoted 'contains(F, P^*)'. Both the modified ray test and the neighboring edge containment tests are easily generalized to regions provided the constituent polygons have been data checked as described earlier. This is because both algorithms only need to know the total list of directed edges to work correctly. This generalized containment routine will be called 'contains_region(P, S)' where 'P' is the test point and 'S' a region.

7.7 Generalized two-dimensional clipping and covering

First consider clipping a line to a general polygonal figure. The simple algorithm presented in Section 7.2 clips a line segment to a rectangle. The method used there breaks down when a line segment is to be clipped to any other shape such as a circle, a triangle, or a general polygon shape. The 'find_area_code' routine is no longer relevant to these more general clipping shapes. A more general algorithm is outlined below for the case of line (whether finite, semi-infinite, or infinite) clipping to a general polygon which may have any degree of convexity or concavity. The general method could be called the λ-*clipping algorithm* . Basically what is of concern is the intersection of line segments. The parametric form of the line is more useful in this particular problem:

$$x = x1\ (1-\lambda) + x2\ \lambda$$
$$y = y1\ (1-\lambda) + y2\ \lambda$$

At the $(x1,y1)$ end point of the line segment, $\lambda = 0$, and at the $(x2,y2)$ end point to the line segment, $\lambda = 1$. Any point (x,y) is a valid point on the line segment from $(x1,y1)$ to $(x2,y2)$ provided it satisfies the above equations for some value of λ with:

$$0 < \lambda < 1$$

When the line to clip (represented by the equations above) intersects any side of the polygon, the λ value for the intersection is computed. Note carefully that this λ value is the parameter on the line to be clipped – not the parameter for the polygon side. If λ is between 0 and 1, the 'lambda' of the point of intersection is saved in a table. Points on the line segment to be clipped with these 'lambda' values (not 0 or 1) are called *critical points* in the algorithm. After running through all sides of the polygon the points of intersection are then sorted by their λ value and any duplicate λ values are tossed out. Finally lines are drawn between alternate pairs of the points of intersection starting from the least λ value. As with the containment test, vertex intersections must be treated carefully – they represent either one or two intersections as discussed earlier. The case when one or more edges of the polygon coincide with the line to be clipped are catered for by storing the 'lambda' for the end point of lower index i of the side as the point of intersection of the coinciding line.

A general method of clipping a line segment to an arbitrary polygon using this method is presented in Box 7-4 where it is assumed that the line segment is 'seg=MN'. The 'enter_lambda' procedure in this algorithm simply stores the intersection 'lambda' values in a table for later use. The algorithm requires a sort routine (called 'sort' in Box 7-4) to sort the 'lambda' values in increasing order between 0 and 1. If any two or more lambda values are equal (to within 'epsilon') then the duplicate values should be discarded from the table and the table size parameter 'nr_lambda' reduced correspondingly. (Another method is to have procedure 'enter_lambda' enter 'lambda' values in sorted order and not enter 'lambda' values already in the table.)

To clip a polyline the above algorithm is simply applied to each line segment of the polyline as shown in the following code.

Box 7-5 An algorithm to clip a line segment to an arbitrary polygon.

```
procedure segment_clip(seg : line_segment_type; poly : polygon_type);
const
    table_size = 100;
var
    M,N : point_type;
    i, j : integer;
    max_seg_x,x1,y1,x2,y2 : real;
    n,nr_lambda : integer;
    lambda_table : array [1 .. table_size] of real;

procedure enter_lambda(lam_val : real);
{Enter the input lambda value as the next element in the lambda table.}
begin
    nr_lambda := nr_lambda+1;
    if (nr_lambda > 0) and (nr_lambda <= table_size) then
        lambda_table[nr_lambda] := lam_val
    else
        error('too many line intersections');
end;

begin
    n := poly^.nr_vertexes;
    nr_lambda := 0;               {initialize the lambda table to empty}
    M := seg.pt1; N := seg.pt2; {extract the line segment endpoints}
    max_seg_x := M.x;            {find the maximum x value in the line segment}
    if N.x > max_seg_x then max_seg_x := N.x;
    {does the line segment start from inside the polygon?}
    if contains(M,poly) then
        enter_lambda(0);
    j := 1;
    while (exmin[j] <= max_seg_x) and (j <= n) do
    {looking for crossings at points between M and N:}
    begin
        i := ixmin[j];
        if intersects(seg, side[i], lambda) then
            enter_lambda(lambda);
        j := j+1;
    end;
    {does the line segment terminate inside the polygon?}
    if contains(N,poly) then
        enter_lambda(1);
    {sort the crossing points - throw away duplicates:}
    sort(nr_lambda,lambda_table);
    i := 1;
    while i <= nr_lambda do
```

```
    {draw line segments between alternate pairs of crossings}
    begin
        lambda := lambda_table[i];
        x1 := M.x*(1-lambda) + N.x*lambda;
        y1 := M.y*(1-lambda) + N.y*lambda;
        lambda := lambda_table[i+1];
        x2 := M.x*(1-lambda) + N.x*lambda;
        y2 := M.y*(1-lambda) + N.y*lambda;
        plot_line(x1,y1,x2,y2);
        i := i+2;
    end;
end;
```

```
procedure polyline_clip(pline : polyline_type; poly : polygon_type);
var
    i,m : integer;
begin
    m := pline.nr_vert;
    for i := 1 to m-1 do
        segment_clip(pline.edge[i],poly);
end;
```

This routine can likewise be applied to clipping of polygons by polygons with output being the displayed broken polyline.

To cover a segment by a polygon, all parts of the line segment must be displayed except those inside the polygon. The algorithm is very similar to the 'segment_clip' algorithm above. It is shown in Box 7-6 for completeness. Notice that the difference between 'segment_clip' and 'segment_cover' code is that the containment conditions are inverted.

To cover a polyline as done for clipping, call 'segment_cover' for each segment of the polyline. Both of these segment clipping and covering algorithms can be modified to use all four arrays 'exmin[]', 'exmax[]', 'eymin[]', and 'eymax[]' to dynamically determine which condition for the while-loop will reduce the number of edges of the polygon F that must be investigated for intersections. The modified algorithms would therefore initially compute the maximum and minimum line segment x and y components to be used in the while conditions. The additional code must work out the number of irrelevant edges of the polygon in the four cases and continue working with the arrays that maximized the number of irrelevant edges.

A surprising feature of these clipping and covering algorithms is that they not only work for polygons, but also for general two-dimensional regions (as defined in Section 7.4). These algorithms for polygon areas really only need to be given a list of line segments to work and they do not depend on how the line segments fit together. The clipping and covering algorithms above therefore are easily extended to work for regions which are unions of polygons. (These are again naturally presumed to be data checked as discussed before.) This is done by regarding a region as simply a large list of edges for which the intersections with a line segment are required. Clipping and covering only differ

Box 7-6 An algorithm to cover a line segment with an arbitrary polygon.

```
procedure segment_cover(seg : line_segment_type; poly : polygon_type);
const
    table_size = 100;
var
    M,N : point_type;
    i, j : integer;
    max_seg_x,x1,y1,x2,y2 : real;
    n,nr_lambda : integer;
    lambda_table : array [1 .. table_size] of real;

procedure enter_lambda(lam_val : real);
{Enter the input lambda value as the next element in the lambda table.}
begin
    nr_lambda := nr_lambda+1;
    if (nr_lambda > 0) and (nr_lambda <= table_size) then
        lambda_table[nr_lambda] := lam_val
    else
        error('too many line intersections');
end;

begin
    n := poly^.nr_vertexes; nr_lambda := 0;
    M := seg.pt1; N := seg.pt2;
    max_seg_x := M.x;
    if N.x > max_seg_x then max_seg_x := N.x;
    if not contains(M,poly) then
        enter_lambda(0);
    j := 1;
    while (exmin[j] <= max_seg_x ) and (j <= n) do
    begin
        i := ixmin[j];
        if intersects(seg, side[i], lambda) then
            enter_lambda(lambda);
        j := j+1;
    end;
    if not contains(N,poly) then
        enter_lambda(1);
    sort(nr_lambda,lambda_table);
    i := 1;
    while i <= nr_lambda do
    begin
        lambda := lambda_table[i];
        x1 := M.x*(1-lambda) + N.x*lambda;
```

```
        y1 := M.y*(1-lambda) + N.y*lambda;
        lambda := lambda_table[i+1];
        x2 := M.x*(1-lambda) + N.x*lambda;
        y2 := M.y*(1-lambda) + N.y*lambda;
        plot_line(x1,y1,x2,y2);
        i := i+2;
    end;
end;
```

then in how they treat the end points M and N of the given line segment. The *complement of a region* is obtained by reversing the direction of vertex labeling in all the constituent polygons. A region and its complement are disjoint sets and their union is R^2. The clipping of a polyline to a region is equivalent to covering the polyline by the complement of that region and vice-versa. Also since clipping and covering use opposite pairs of intersection vertexes in displaying the output broken polyline, they are complementary sets within the input polyline – their union is the original polyline:

```
pline = polyline_clip(pline, region) U
        polyline_cover(pline, region)
```

Having built algorithms to generalize clipping from simple line clipping to one rectangle to polyline clipping to any polygon-defined two-dimensional region, it is now worthwhile to consider the clipping of graphics elements other than line segments.

Circle Clipping

Consider the problem of clipping circles and arcs of circles to rectangular viewports on the display surface. The rectangle is again defined by the coordinates ('xmin','ymin') of the lower left corner and the coordinates ('xmax','ymax') of the upper right corner and it will be considered as consisting of four edges:

1. plot_line(xmin,ymin,xmax,ymin);
2. plot_line(xmax,ymin,xmax,ymax);
3. plot_line(xmax,ymax,xmin,ymax);
4. plot_line(xmin,ymax,xmin,ymin);

The circle is defined geometrically by its centre (xc, yc) and radius r.

To solve the problem, test for intersections of edges 1 to 4 in turn against the circle. The equation for the circle is:

$$(x - xc)^2 + (y - yc)^2 = r^2 \qquad (7.3)$$

The equation for the general edge from $(x1, y1)$ to $(x2, y2)$ is parametrically:

$$x = x1 \; (1-\lambda) + x2 \; \lambda \qquad\qquad (7.4a)$$
$$y = y1 \; (1-\lambda) + y2 \; \lambda \qquad\qquad (7.4b)$$

where:

$$0 \le \lambda \le 1 \qquad\qquad (7.4c)$$

To find intersections of the general line segment with the circle, substitute equations 7.4a and 7.4b into equation 7.3 and solve the subsequent quadratic equation for λ. This quadratic equation is called Joachimsthal's ratio equation (for a circle). The roots of this equation are:

$$\lambda = [-a \pm \sqrt{\{a^2 - b \; c\}}] \; / \; b \qquad\qquad (7.5)$$

where:

$$a \equiv \Delta x \; (x1 - xc) + \Delta y \; (y1 - yc)$$
$$b \equiv (\Delta x)^2 + (\Delta y)^2$$
$$c \equiv (x1 - xc)^2 + (y1 - yc)^2 - r^2$$
$$\Delta x \equiv x2 - x1$$
$$\Delta y \equiv y2 - y1$$

Substitute the appropriate pair of vertexes from sides 1 to 4 for the parameters $x1$, $y1$, $x2$, and $y2$ in the condition equations. If either of the solutions λ_+ and λ_- of equation 7.5 satisfies:

$$0 \le \lambda \le 1$$

then there is a corresponding intersection for that line segment and the circle at the point(s) (x, y) obtained by substituting the λ value into equations 7.4a and 7.4b. If the roots λ_+, λ_- are distinct then these intersections are actually crossings, on one side of which the arc is outside the viewport and on the other side the arc is inside the viewport. When the radical in equation 7.5 vanishes the λ roots are equal and the circle kisses (grazes) the viewport. Kissing points are noncritical (they are not crossings) and so these are ignored – only crossings are relevant, not all intersections.

Recalling that the 'lambda' values wanted for storage are those along the graphics element to be clipped – and not the 'lambda' values of the bounding edges of the clipping area, then clearly the above 'lambda's are not the ones to store. A suitable parameter for circles is the angle θ, so θ values will be stored for the circle-clipping algorithm rather than λ values. For the critical point (x', y') on the circumference of the circle, therefore, the next step is to calculate the angle θ from the horizontal about the centre of the circle (xc, yc) as follows:

$$\theta = \tan^{-1}\{(y' - yc) / (x' - xc)\}$$

Continuing in this manner with the remaining three sides of the viewport and a record is kept of the angles from the centre of the circle to the critical points. The angles may be stored in degrees corrected to lie in the range $0 \le \theta < 360$. These critical angles should be sorted into ascending order.

The clipped circle is the set of arcs drawn between alternate pairs of critical points. The next problem is select the right set of pairs. To determine if the arc from the first critical point to the second is to be drawn, compute the mid point on the arc between these two:

$$\theta_m = \{(\theta_1 + \theta_2) \bmod 360 \} / 2$$

(*Note* : the summed angle $\theta_1 + \theta_2$ must first be converted to the proper range 0 to 360 before division by 2.) The point on the circumference corresponding to θ_m is:

$$x_m = xc + r \; \cos \theta_m$$
$$y_m = yc + r \; \sin \theta_m$$

If this point is inside the viewport then the arc point pairs start from the first critical point otherwise they must start from the second critical point. The point (x_m, y_m) is inside the viewport if and only if the following inequalities hold:

$$xmin \le x_m \le xmax$$
$$ymin \le y_m \le ymax$$

Thus to draw clipped circles, an arc drawing routine must be called that needs the parameters 'xc', 'yx', 'r', 'θ1', and 'θ2'. If the hardware is only capable of drawing straight lines then this arc routine (and the unclipped circle routine) must be implemented in software. This has an advantage that the line drawing attributes carry over as attributes for arcs and circles. This is very nice. However software arc and circle drawing may be slow. If hardware arc drawing is available then that should be used to draw the arcs of a clipped circle. If furthermore the hardware provides a faster circle drawing function then the algorithm should first do a minmax test to see if the circle is wholly within the viewport and if so then the hardware circle drawing function is called. The circle is wholly within the viewport if the following conditions hold:

$$xmin \le xc - r$$
$$xmax \ge xc + r$$
$$ymin \le yc - r$$
$$ymax \ge yc + r$$

The program in Box 7-7 summarizes the main features of this algorithm.

Further generalizations

The clipping of ellipses and general quadric curves (conics) to rectangles can be done by the same method as for circles with the appropriate curve equation used in place of

Box 7-7 A circle clipping algorithm.

```
procedure circle_clip(rect : rectangle_type; xc,yc,r : real);
const
    eps = 1e-6;
    pi = 3.1415926;
var
    x1,y1,x2,y2,lam1,lam2,theta1,theta2,theta : real;
    angle_table : array[1..8] of real;
    nr_crossings,i : integer;
    finished : boolean;

procedure get_lambdas(var lam1,lam2 : real; var valid : boolean);
var
    a,b,c,d,discrim,deltax,deltay : real;
begin
    lam1 := -1; lam2 := -1; valid := false;
    deltax := x2 - x1; deltay := y2 - y1;
    a := deltax * (x1 - xc) + deltay * (y1 - yc);
    b := sqr(deltax) + sqr(deltay);
    c := sqr(x1 - xc) + sqr(y1 - yc) - sqr(r);
    discrim := sqr(a) - b * c;
    if discrim > 0 then
    begin
        d := sqrt(discrim);
        lam1 := (-a + d)/b;
        lam2 := (-a - d)/b;
        valid := true;
    end;
end;

procedure enter_theta(lam);
var
    theta : real;
begin
    if (lam >= 0) and (lam <= 1) then
    begin
        nr_crossings := nr_crossings + 1;
        x := x1*(1 - lam) + x2*lam;
        y := y1*(1 - lam) + y2*lam;
        theta := angle((y - yc) , (x - xc));
        angle_table[nr_lambdas] := theta;
    end;
end;

procedure make_table;
```

```
begin
    with  rect do
    begin
        x1 := xmin; y1 := ymin; x2 := xmax; y2 := ymin;
        get_lambdas(lam1,lam2,valid);
        if valid and (abs(lam2 - lam1) > eps) then
        begin
            enter_theta(lam1);
            enter_theta(lam2);
        end;
        x1 := xmax; y1 := ymin; x2 := xmax; y2 := ymax;
        get_lambdas(lam1,lam2,valid);
        if valid and (abs(lam2 - lam1) > eps) then
        begin
            enter_theta(lam1);
            enter_theta(lam2);
        end;
        x1 := xmax; y1 := ymax; x2 := xmin; y2 := ymax;
        get_lambdas(lam1,lam2,valid);
        if valid and (abs(lam2 - lam1) > eps) then
        begin
            enter_theta(lam1);
            enter_theta(lam2);
        end;
        x1 := xmin; y1 := ymax; x2 := xmin; y2 := ymin;
        get_lambdas(lam1,lam2,valid);
        if valid and (abs(lam2 - lam1) > eps) then
        begin
            enter_theta(lam1);
            enter_theta(lam2);
        end;
    end;
end;

procedure find_midpt(var x,y : real);
var
    midpt : real;
begin
    theta1 := angle_table[1]; theta2 := angle_table[2];
    theta := (theta1 + theta2);
    while theta > 360 do theta := theta - 360;
    while theta < 0 do theta := theta + 360;
    midpt := theta/2*pi/180;
    x := xc + r*cos(midpt);
    y := yc + r*sin(midpt);
end;
```

```
begin
    nr_angles := 0;
    make_table;
    if nr_angles >= 2 then
    begin
        find_midpt(x,y);
        if (xmin <= x) and (x <= xmax) and (ymin <= y) and (y <= ymax) then
            i := 0
        else
            i := 1;
        finished := false;
        while not finished do
        begin
            i := i + 1; if i > nr_angles then begin i := 1; finished := true; end;
            theta1 := angle_table[i];
            i := i + 1; if i > nr_angles then begin i := 1; finished := true; end;
            theta2 := angle_table[i];
            draw_arc(xc,yc,r,theta1,theta2);
        end;
    end;
end;
```

equation 7.3. For the general conic:

$$F(x, y) \equiv ax^2 + by^2 + 2hxy + 2gx + 2fy + c = 0$$

Joachimsthal's ratio equation is again a quadratic with two solutions for λ. This means that the conic can have 0, 1, or 2 points of intersection with a line segment. The same interpretations apply to these intersections as before: critical point(s) occur when there are two distinct λ values and at least one of these has λ in the range [0,1]. Arcs are drawn between alternate critical point pairs. This same algorithm can be used to clip any suitable curve. If it is not convenient to tabulate a curve parameter like λ which increases along the curve, the coordinates of the critical points can be tabulated. Duplicate points are easily detected but in this case it may be more difficult to sort the critical points in order along the curve.

The algorithm presented clips a given curve to a rectangle by finding critical points taking one side of the rectangle at a time. However as has been seen before for the application to line segment clipping, this algorithm does not depend on any geometrical properties of rectangles. The algorithm applies equally well to any polygonal clipping area and even general two-dimensional regions. All it needs to know to work is the list of line segments against which the curve will be clipped. The covering algorithms for circles and general conics being covered by rectangles, polygons, or two-dimensional regions are very similar to the corresponding clipping algorithms as seen for line segment covering. The fact that these routines do not depend on the geometrical layout of the clipping or covering areas but rather on the list of edges involved suggests that it would be better to pass the list of edges to these routines rather than the parameter of a particular geometrical shape, rectangle, polygon, or general region. A routine would still be needed to build up the edge list from the particular clipping or covering area type to be used in any given application. This routine could be called first and then pass the edge list on to the clipping or covering routine. If the object to be clipped or covered is also represented as an edge list on input to these general forms of the clipping and covering routines then clipping and covering can be happily intermixed. The clipping and covering routines would not draw actual lines in this case but return the line segments to be drawn in the same edge list parameters. The style of these general routines is as follows:

```
procedure general_clip(var clipping_object : edge_list_type;
                           clipping_area : edge_list_type);
procedure general_cover(var covering_object : edge_list_type;
                            covering_area : edge_list_type);
```

These can now be used to intermix the clipping and covering operations. For instance, suppose that lines are to be covered by three rectangular areas for text labels within a single clipping rectangle. Then the line or lines to be so covered are placed in a list and passed to the general clipping routine. The output list of edges is then fed in to the general covering routine. Another routine can be used to plot the final output list of edges. Of course the 'general_cover' covering routine if desired could be designed to do the drawing as well.

The 'general_clip' and 'general_cover' procedures above have very similar code. They both work on two lists of edges and output a third list of edges. They both find all intersection points (the critical points) along all edges in the first list with the edges of the second list. They both do ray tests to see if the end points of edges in the first list are contained in the area represented by the second list. The difference between the two procedures is in what pairs of points are taken for the output list of edges. For the 'general_clip' procedure, an end point of an edge in the first list will be an end point of an edge in the output list only if it is contained within the 'clipping_area' edge list. For the 'general_cover' procedure, an end point of an edge in the first list will be an end point of an edge in the output list only if it is not contained within the 'covering_area' edge list. It is therefore clear that the function of the 'general_cover' procedure can be done by the 'general_clip' procedure by simply taking the 'clipping_area' list as the 'covering_area' list and including in the 'clipping_area' edge list the four edges of the minmax box of the first edge list.

7.8 Hatching, pattern filling, and painting algorithms

Hatching involves drawing a family of curves close together clipped to and covered by any set of polygonal areas. In the simplest case the family of curves is a set of equidistant straight lines. These can be used to shade in particular areas of the display surface such as

Box 7-8 An algorithm to hatch in a general region with a family of parallel polylines.

```
procedure polyline_hatch(hline,delta,offset; F : region_type);
begin
    {determine the maximum and minimum x component of the endpoints of
    hline}
    hxmax := hline.pt1.x;
    hxmin := hline.pt2.x;
    if hline.pt2.x < hline.pt1.x then
    begin
        hxmax := hline.pt2.x;
        hxmin := hline.pt1.x;
    end;
    {translate hline by xmax-hxmax+offset in the x components of all its
    endpoints and likewise adjust hxmax and hxmin :}
    while hxmin < xmax do
    begin
        polyline_clip(hline,F);
        {translate hline by delta};
        hxmin := hxmin + delta.x;
    end;
end;
```

oceans in the case of maps. Another style of hatching is by concentric circles of uniformly increasing radii.

A straightforward method of implementing equidistant line hatching is to determine the leftmost line, clip it to the figure, add the increment to get the next hatch line, test that it is within the figure still, clip it to the figure, and so on. This is easily generalized to the hatching of polylines using the polyline clipping routine as shown in Box 7-8. As before 'xmin' and 'xmax' denote the minimum and maximum x components of all the vertexes of the polygon F. The quantity 'delta' is a vector which maps the points of one hatch line to those of the next hatch line: it contains two floating-point values 'delta.x' and 'delta.y' which are the relative displacements of the polyline vertexes between neighboring hatch lines. The only exception case is when the hatch line is parallel to the x axis and this can be catered for by replacing all references to x values in the above to y value references.

This algorithm involves many calls to 'segment_clip' and a large amount of processing. To reduce this load consider the case of hatching by lines rather than by polylines. The intersection information for one hatch line is very similar to that for the next hatch line. If the slopes of the intersecting edges of the polygon are stored, the next hatch line can rapidly be created from the current hatch line. Furthermore one can tell when new polygon edges intersect the hatch line by having the polygon vertex coordinates sorted in the direction perpendicular to the hatch lines. One way to do this is to transform all vertex coordinates to rotated axes (u, v) coordinates wherein the hatch lines are given by $u = $ constant. It is not necessary however to transform all points and work entirely in the (u, v) coordinate system. Only the u coordinates of all vertexes of the polygon F are needed and have to be sorted. The following pseudocode describes these ideas:

```
compute the u value of all vertexes of F
sort the vertex coordinates by u value
determine the least-u hatchline
while hatchline u is <= the maximum vertex u value do
      segment_clip(hline,F);
      record all slopes of the edges of intersection as well as the (x,y)
      intercept coordinates
      determine the u value of the next hatchline
      while hatchline u is < next biggest vertex u value do
            use the slopes to update the (x,y) intercept coordinates
            display the broken hatchline
            determine the next hatchline u value
```

By computing the new intersect coordinates using the stored slopes, it saves having to test for all intersections with every new hatch line. This algorithm can be improved again by testing for intersections with only the edges from the next encountered vertex given by the sorted array of u values. If the new vertex is the end point of a current edge of intersection, then that slope should be replaced by the slope of the joining edge, and the intersection coordinates recomputed.

This hatch algorithm allows us to fill regions with cross-hatching lines or solid dithered coloring using hatch lines which are at one pixel separation and that alternate between a pair of available screen colors. For raster graphics displays with low screen refresh rates (under 30 Hz) the solid filling should not be done with horizontal lines. Low refresh rates commonly occur when interlaced modes are used. If horizontal lines are used there will be glaring contrasts due to clashing with the horizontal raster of the screen. The use of vertical lines reduces this effect and also eliminates the requirement of computing the u coordinates of the polygon vertexes in a rotated coordinate system. The algorithm can also be immediately generalized to hatching of lines to regions as with the clipping routine. This results in solid area fill without the need for recursion and without the need for the area boundaries to be explicitly on the raster screen.

The scan conversion algorithm is a frequently used algorithm for area filling. It has some similarities to the hatching algorithm described above. The boundary of the area must first be drawn on the screen for this algorithm to work. In this case, parts of all scan lines on the screen that lie inside the minmax box for the area to be filled are considered in turn from the topmost to the bottommost scan line. The lines are drawn from left to right and a flag, which is initialized to false at the start of every scan line, is used to say whether or not to set the current pixel. Every time a boundary pixel is encountered the flag is negated corresponding to the scanning spot moving inside and outside of the area to be filled as it moves along a scan line.

A number of other algorithms for area filling on raster graphics equipment have been developed. These are called painting algorithms and they operate in image space, that is, by directly reading and writing to the pixels. Many of these other algorithms use recursion in order to paint out irregular pixel regions on the screen. A recursive paint algorithm (see Box 7-9) is given an initial pixel address to start painting from, the color (pixel value) to paint with, and the color of the boundary pixels. The algorithm reads the current pixel value and if this value is not a boundary color it sets the pixel to the desired

Box 7-9 A raster graphics area painting algorithm.

```
var
    pdraw, parea : integer;

procedure paint(dcx,dcy: integer);
var
    p : integer;
begin
    read_pixel(dcx,dcy,p);
    if (p <> pdraw) and (p <> parea) then
    begin
        write_pixel(dcx,dcy,parea);
        paint(dcx,dcy-1);
        paint(dcx,dcy+1);
        paint(dcx-1,dcy);
        paint(dcx+1,dcy);
    end;
end;
```

Box 7-10 A raster graphics pattern painting algorithm.

```
const
    Pattern_Width = 15;
    Pattern_Height = 15;

var
    pattern : array[0..Pattern_Width,0..Pattern_Height] of integer;
    pdraw : integer;

procedure pattern_paint(dcx,dcy : integer);
var
    p ,ppattern,i,j: integer;
begin
    i := dcx mod Pattern_Width; j := dcy mod Pattern_Height;
    ppattern := pattern[i,j];
    read_pixel(dcx,dcy,p);
    if (p <> pdraw) and (p <> ppattern) then
    begin
        write_pixel(dcx,dcy,ppattern);
```

```
            pattern_paint(dcx,dcy-1);
            pattern_paint(dcx,dcy+1);
            pattern_paint(dcx-1,dcy);
            pattern_paint(dcx+1,dcy);
      end;
   end;
```

painting color and then recursively calls itself to paint neighbouring pixels. The depth of recursive calls to the algorithm keeps increasing until a boundary pixels are encountered. Occasionally this sort of algorithm can be seen to hang a system. This occurs for highly irregular regions in systems where a set amount of memory is provided for this recursion. Evidently recursion stack space is exceeded. Other algorithms have been devised to fill regions with patterns rather than solid (uniform) colors. For example, one sort of algorithm can be used by cartographers to fill an area on a plotted map with the swamp or marsh symbol. Another sort of pattern filling algorithm works on raster graphics VDUs in image space: the pattern is stored in binary form and used as a mask for setting pixels in a painting algorithm. An algorithm of this sort is shown in Box 7-10.

Problems

7.1 How could the 'plot_line' procedure as described previously be modified to clip lines to the current viewport using the simple algorithm of Section 7.2?

7.2 Consider the line through points P and Q in the form $y = m\,x + c$. Show that if the product of the area code numbers of P is 1 then PQ does not intersect the rectangle 'rect' provided:

$$c > rect.ymax - m\ rect.xmin$$

and:

$$c < rect.ymin - m\ rect.xmax$$

What can be said of the other cases?

7.3 Implement the angle procedure described in Section 7.5. Use it to design a consistency test for non-self-intersecting polygons by the method mentioned in Section 7.4.

7.4 Write a procedure to test a region data structure for consistency as described in Section 7.4.

7.5   Write a minmax test routine that aids in clipping the general arc to viewports.

7.6   Write a routine to hatch a wedge shape with equidistant parallel hatch lines.

7.7   Write a procedure to clip circular arcs to any rectangular window.

7.8   Write a routine to hatch an arbitrary shaped polygon F with concentric circles which have equal increments in their radii.

7.9   Describe how to build a crosshatching procedure to fill any region.

7.10   Write a procedure to hatch a region in concentric circles of uniformly increasing radius. Use a circle clipping procedure.

7.11   Implement the algorithm given in Box 7-9 for area filling. Also implement a routine 'set_area_fill_color(pval : integer)' which simply sets the global variable 'parea' to 'pval', the pixel value selected by the user (after appropriate range checking). (An initialization procedure should set up default values for 'pdraw', the pixel value for drawing lines and curves, and 'parea' the pixel value for area fills.) Although this area fill algorithm is elegant, it is not efficient for it looks at every pixel to be painted more than once. Design a random small area to be filled entirely and bounded in pixel value 'pdraw'. Modify this painting algorithm to maintain a count of the number of times that 'read_pixel' is called for each pixel. Run the program and find out how many times boundary pixels are read, and how many times interior pixels are read. Suggest ways in which this algorithm could be made more efficient.

7.12   Implement the pattern painting algorithm given in Box 7-10. Also implement a procedure that sets up the 'pattern' global variable, and an initialization procedure that sets up the default pattern. The default pattern should have all elements of the 'pattern' array equal to the default area fill color 'parea'. Test the algorithm on a random two-dimensional area as in problem 7.11 and suggest ways that the algorithm can be made more efficient.

8

Graphics software packages

8.1 Historical perspective

Obviously, a graphics system is a collection of hardware and software: the hardware providing the graphics input and output functionality, and the software being designed to make this functionality easier to use. This system is closely analogous to a standard computer system consisting of a CPU, I/O devices, and a compiler or assembler to make the hardware easier to use. (See Figure 8-1.) In this analogy, the conventional character input/output devices of keyboard and VDU screen or printer (for instance) are analogous to the graphics input/output devices of digitizing tablet and raster graphics screen (for instance). The operational software in each system can also be compared: the compiler is analogous to the graphics software package (GSP). The compiler is the realization of a conventional computer language. In analogy the GSP effectively defines a graphics language. Just as compilers have evolved from their early beginnings in FORTRAN 2 and COBOL, so GSPs have likewise evolved to more powerful packages that are easier to use, control, and maintain.

In this section, the only concern will be with the software component of a graphics system as it appears to the user. It is important that the software be carefully designed to allow the full potential of the hardware to be exploited and that the system is easy to use from the user's point of view. This often results in a trade-off between portability on the one hand, where the GSP conforms to current graphics standards, and speed and functionality on the other where the GSP makes the best use of the hardware features. Graphics standards are discussed in Chapter 15. At this point of more concern is maximizing functionality by having the GSP match the hardware neatly rather than portability considerations via graphics standards.

There are currently three 'generations' of graphics software systems. The first generation graphics system is the graphics software package (GSP) of routines that link into a compiled applications program at link time. These were the first style of graphics system made and GSPs continue to be made after this style. Their disadvantages are that they tend to be language and hardware dependent. The second generation provides graphics as special statements available within a standard language. It was thought that this would increase the usefulness of the hardware. However the graphics extensions to the standard languages tended themselves to become nonstandard so that programs could not be as easily transported across to other hardware. The third generation provides access to any language via escape sequences or operating system intrinsics. This last method of implementing the graphics software has not been widely used yet. An example on professional microsystems is Digital Research's GSX which is covered in Chapter 15.

This chapter will only cover the first generation of graphics system software, the graphics package (the GSP). A graphics package is a library of subroutines that any application program can call. In practice these routines have typically been written in the FORTRAN language, and are FORTRAN callable subroutines. They can however be simply interfaced to other languages such as Pascal by declaring the subroutines to be external procedures. At program link time, the calls to the subroutines in the graphics package are satisfied.

The routines in the graphics package are used by the applications program to generate pictures on a plotter or VDU and to handle graphical interaction. A typical example of a graphics package is the Calcomp software package which is used to drive the Calcomp digital plotter. This was possibly the earliest GSP on the commercial market. The different computer graphics equipment manufacturers and suppliers provided GSPs together with the hardware to allow users to get the best use out of the equipment. As the capability and performance of computer graphics improved, so did the power and complexity of the GSP provided with the hardware. Today there are a large number of modern advanced GSPs available. The complexity is such that their usefulness and power are only fully understood by a relatively small number of programmers. These are the specialist graphics programmers. The next few sections describe graphics packages in general and discuss the useful design features.

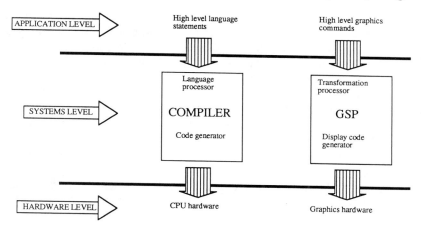

Figure 8-1 Analogy between graphics packages and compilers.

8.2 The user's view of a typical graphics software package

From the user's point of view, the typical graphics software package consists of a large number of routines which fall into a number of categories. These categories are:

1. Graphics setup procedures;
2. Data plotting procedures;
3. Graphics output procedures;
4. Attribute setting procedures;
5. Graphics input procedures;
6. Graphics segment manipulation procedures;
7. Debugging procedures.

These categories are listed in roughly the order in which the programmer must get to know them, the probable order of frequency of use, and the order in which they are best learned. Thus if a new GSP is provided by a company and if its routines are broken up into these categories and then the categories studied in this order, then the package should be learnt in the quickest most orderly fashion. After studying the GSP in this manner programming experimentation begins – this is the hands-on stage in the learning process for the new user of a GSP. Projects for experimentation in graphics programming are suggested later in this chapter, but first the general contents of each of these categories are discussed in the order given above.

Routines in the first category are nearly always needed to start up and close down the use of graphics. A start-up routine will initialize the internal parameters of the GSP, set all the default flags and attributes, and prepare the selected graphics devices for input and output. The shut-down routine(s) will flush all buffers, restore the hardware to its normal modes, and provide an orderly exit from the GSP (so as not to cause graphics junk to sporadically appear on the output, for instance). Simpler packages require the user to reset any conditions enabled in the system and allow the user to exit from graphics operations in any manner wished; and in these systems termination (and sometimes also initialization) routine(s) are not provided. Graphics set-up routines may be provided to allow the user to interactively specify the number and type of graphics workstations that the GSP must address. Enquiry functions may also be provided to tell the user the graphics characteristics of the device(s) being used, namely their addressable resolution in numbers of dot positions horizontally and vertically, the physical size of the output rectangle (the width and height in millimeters), the size (width and height in pixel counts) of its standard text characters, the number of text lines and columns, the workstation name and type, and so forth. Another function may tell the system user what version of the GSP is currently running.

An important pair of functions in the graphics set-up category are the window and viewport setting functions. The very important window setting concepts have been explained and made use of from the first chapter of this book and viewporting concepts were introduced in the previous chapter. Here these concepts are reviewed again. The viewport routines define areas of the display rectangle for specific graphics to appear in. These are usually rectangular subareas on the output rectangle. Many advanced GSPs today allow the user to set up many viewports at once. Each viewport being identified by a positive integer. A name (character string) suggestive of the purpose of the graphics viewport or indicative of the type of graphics it is to display would seem a better approach than the use of IDs (identifying numbers) but this style is frequently left to the programming skills of the user. A window, in contrast to a viewport, is a definition of user coordinate limits in two-dimensional space. It is a finite subset of abstract mathematical two-dimensional space. However one can equally well think of a 'window' as a recoordinatization of the viewport area of the screen in a coordinate system that happens to suit the user's purposes. From this point of view though it must be remembered that the window is not tied to the viewport for the viewport could be redefined to a different area and size of the output screen (say) without change in the user coordinate limits that map to it. Viewports and windows are really independent entities and separate routines are provided in advanced GSPs to use them. Note that many systems today are confusing the names 'window' with 'viewport'. Some systems also use the word 'graphport' to mean a viewport.

Other miscellaneous but important routines are also provided within this category. These are routines to prepare the graphics output display such as clearing the screen and drawing a border around the current graphics viewport to highlight the current active graphics area, and user alert functions such as setting console lights or beeping the terminal.

The second category consists of routines in the GSP to enable data plotting to be done quick and easily. These are basically all graphics output routines for producing standard graphs such as line charts, bar charts, and pie charts, and for labeling them. The category would provide facilities for the user to place labeled axes on the output and plot the points by bars, straight lines, or smoothed lines. This category of routines may be all that a particular company needs in graphics software commands for the foreseeable future. Labeled plots and charts are an end in themselves for many users of computer graphics. For those needing more subtle graphics outputs, the other categories would have to be studied.

The next category is that of graphics output primitives. These are the routines that enable the graphics programmer to place graphics elements wherever needed to build up an overall picture. These are the routines to draw points, line segments, arcs of circles, circles, graphics text in any font, and so on.

The fourth category is that of the attribute setting routines. These routines may not be needed by the programmer and indeed there could be attribute values that are never used. They are provided to modify the way in which the routines of the previous category produce graphics output on the screen. Each graphics element available to the user from the previous category would have at least one attribute to change its appearance in today's GSPs. For instance, lines can be altered with respect to thickness and appearance as in solid line, dotted line, dot dash style, and so forth. The GSP is initialized with default attribute values for all of the graphics output primitives but the user may wish to alter some of these.

The next category is rarely as well populated with routines as the last category. This category provides graphics input primitives for the user. There may be many input device kinds attached to a workstation, such as function keys, dials, light pen, digitizing tablet, and cross-hairs puck. Routines must be supplied to allow the user to get the full benefit of these various kinds of graphics input devices. This category also includes reading pixel values and copying rectangular blocks of pixels (sometimes called a cell) to an array in the user's program. If these latter functions are provided then the inverse functions of setting single pixel values or writing arrays to pixel blocks should be available in the graphics output category.

A graphics programmer may happily produce all graphics needed in particular commercial interest areas by using all of the above categories and with no need to recourse to the other categories of routines. For more advanced work, however, graphics picture structure and its storage becomes important. So in the sixth category are the routines that create graphics objects (or 'segments'), manipulate them, display or disable them, combine them, and store them to disk in some retrievable format. These types of graphics routines are of particular use in CAD systems. For example, an interior-design CAD system could allow a building to be put together containing various rooms, each with various items of furniture such as desks and chairs, and each of these items may have other items such as graphics workstations atop each desk. Such a graphics picture has a definite structure, and it is desirable to be able to rotate and reposition items (graphics objects) within the picture either singly or in groups. The routines in this category provide all these functions. Note that most practical graphics picture applications involve a *hierarchy* of graphics objects; that is, graphics objects may be constructed out of many simpler graphics objects some of which may have been constructed earlier out of other simpler graphics objects, and so on. Not all GSPs allow for this sophisticated hierarchical segmentation of the picture.

So it can be seen that GSPs today are a complex and large bundle of routines that address users at various levels. For some users the majority of the routines in the GSP may never be needed. Very few users would actually get around to making use of all routines in the GSP. Therefore it helps for the user to categorize the routines provided as above. After determining what categories of graphics will fulfill the present needs of the company, the user should become familiar with the routines found to be relevant and useful within the chosen set of categories.

8.3 **Requirements of a good graphics software package**

As previously mentioned, there is a structural analogy between a standard computer system and a computer graphics system. In this analogy, a GSP on a graphics system corresponds to a compiler for a standard language on a standard computer (though the GSP has usually been a lot simpler than a compiler). The compiler converts high-level language statements to binary codes that operate the CPU. In a similar fashion, a GSP can be thought of as converting high-level graphics commands (GSP routine calls) to the binary codes that drive the graphics equipment in its various modes. When a GSP is built, the software package must be able to generate these codes so as to build the graphics shapes desired by the user. Continuing with the analogy with compilers, languages have evolved to more powerful forms and so it is hoped that GSPs are likewise improving in areas of functionality and ease of use. The system must be user friendly in accordance with the following ground rules (see Newman & Sproull, 1979):

1. *Simplicity* — Features that are too complex for the application programmer to understand will not be used. These would be a waste of memory in the graphics package.
2. *Consistency* – A consistent graphics package is one that behaves in a generally predictable manner. Function and procedure names, calling sequences, error handling, and coordinate systems should all follow simple and consistent naming conventions or patterns without exception. This helps the applications programmer to quickly build up a conceptual model of how the graphics package operates.
3. *Completeness* – There should be no irritating omissions in the set of functions provided by the system as missing functions would have to be supplied by the user who may not have the necessary access to the computer's resources to be able to write them.
4. *Robustness* – Applications programmers are capable of misusing any graphics package. The system should accept such treatment with the minimum of complaint. When the user does something wrong, the system should report the error in the most helpful manner possible. Only under extreme circumstances should errors cause termination of execution (as this could cause the user to lose valuable data).
5. *Performance* – Graphics system performance is often limited by such factors as operating system response, the number of users currently logged in to the host computer, and terminal display characteristics. These delays may be unavoidable but the graphics system designer should not add to them with inefficient coding.
6. *Economy* – Graphics systems should be small and not expensive so that adding graphics to an existing applications program, without making it too big to run or expensive to use, can always be considered.

As far as what the package can do for the user, the following minimal requirements should be aimed at:

- Provide the ability to allow the user to define the coordinate system rather than being tied to the hardware device coordinates.
- Provide viewporting capability on the output medium.

- Provide basic graphical elements. At a minimum, several from the following should be provided: points, lines, rays, line segments, arrows, rectangles, circles, ellipses, arcs of circles and ellipses, sectors of circles, polygons, polynomial fits and splines, and text.
- Provide the capability of building named and identifiable graphics objects as groupings of output primitives.
- Provide the capability of manipulating graphics objects by instancing (copying) and transformations.
- Provide the ability to load and save graphics objects and whole pictures to and from secondary storage.
- Provide zoom capability for showing or adding small detail.
- Provide pan capability to build up and view large pictures.
- Aim at device independence.

8.4 Design philosophy for G2D

Now the overall design can be described of the simple graphics software package, for the input, manipulation, and display of two-dimensional graphics, that has been built up in the previous chapters. The package is called G2D which stands for Graphics for 2-Dimensions. The routine source listings given previously should be carefully studied again for a better understanding of G2D design philosophy, and for a better understanding of graphics software package design in general. A summary of G2D can be found in Appendix C, and Appendix B gives brief information on implementation and general usage of G2D.

One of the design philosophies is that of keeping track of only one graphics entity at a time. This saves the package itself from having to keep track of entities by identifying names or numbers and in this way memory requirements for the package are kept fairly low. For example the system works on the concept of a current graphics object. Similarly the system works with one window and one viewport at a time. A related simplifying design choice in G2D is that of keeping the details of transformations on the current graphics object away from the user. This is in contrast to many other popular GSPs that require the user to explicitly set up or at least handle (by way of data declaration and parameter passing) the transformation matrices. In Chapter 6, the routines for performing two-dimensional transformations were presented. These showed how the transformation matrices were constructed and how they changed point coordinates. In keeping with the concept of a current graphics object, most of this information is transparent to the user; that is, it is internal to the GSP software and not accessible by the user. All the user needs to know is by what angle the graphics object is being rotated, or by what displacement the graphics object is being translated, and so forth. These transformations incidentally are active transformations and only affect the current graphics object. They also take effect immediately when they are called.

Another choice in the design philosophy was to avoid as far as possible the need for package initialization and closing down routines. Many commercial graphics software packages have a number of routines for initializing various parts of the package and for various devices, and conversely for closing these all down. For the sake of ease of use these could be minimized. G2D provides a single initialization routine and a single termination routine. Even though some devices do not need special graphics termination code, the G2D termination procedure holds the graphics on the screen waiting for a user keypress before returning. However initialization routines for each of the compilation units in G2D are also provided. With UCSD Pascal the user need never know about the initialization routines because UCSD Pascal allows compilation units to have their own initialization and termination code which is invoked before and after use of the compilation unit. In this way G2D can be simplified by not requiring that the user call a special initializing or closing down routine. The user need not even set up a window because the G2D initialization procedure calls 'set_window(0, 0, 100, 100)' to create default user coordinates. The user can therefore call graphics output functions and immediately get the desired graphics. More generally though of course, the user would want to define his own user coordinate limits to the package and so then he must call the routine 'set_window' at least once. It should be noted that 'set_window' also creates a corresponding default viewport which is the whole screen. This saves the user from causing G2D to bomb by not having defined a viewport. Of course if the whole screen is not wanted as the viewport, then 'set_viewport' should be called after 'set_window'. Another routine called 'equalize_axes' is provided in G2D to make the aspect ratio of user coordinates square if this is desired.

G2D provides a large number of graphics output commands - eleven basic output functions and four higher level graphics output functions. This range of outputs provides broad scope for most applications. For example, G2D displays arcs, circles, and splines while a number of other packages require these routines to be provided by the user.

The G2D package also has a set of routines available from the 'g2d_data' compilation unit. These routines provide database maintenance for handling two-dimensional regions as discussed in the previous chapter. Points can be entered into the database and used to define polygon vertexes. The polygons are then grouped into regions. When a point is entered into the database it is allotted a unique integer identifier which is used to refer to the point. Points should not be deleted from the database if they are in use as vertexes in one or more polygons.

Graphical text with a number of attributes can be used in G2D. Details on how graphical text can be implemented in a graphics package are found in Section 8.6. Finally G2D provides metagraphics commands via the compilation unit 'g2d_object'. These routines allow G2D graphics commands, and their parameters to be stored away as they are called during execution of the application program. A G2D metagraphics command can cause this list of command calls (the current graphics object) to be rerun during execution of the same application program. Other metagraphics commands allow the coordinates in the current graphics object to be transformed by any of the usual two-dimensional transformations. Graphics objects can also be nested, merged, copied, and stored in disk files. This compilation unit therefore provides facilities similar to segments provided by some graphics VDU in hardware. The commands in 'g2d_data' can also be stored at execution time and in this way the G2D graphics database of points and regions can be stored at run-time.

8.5 Internal interaction of GSP commands

Many internal routines are needed to support the GSP user routines at the user interface. Consider for instance the processing that occurs when 'read_point' is called twice to digitize a line and 'plot_line' is called to display it. The 'read_point' routine waits for a key press and calls 'get_point' in the driver. The 'get_point' routine may be available from the hardware or may have to be implemented by simpler calls. For example, it may be implemented by a call to display cross hairs at a point and move them in accordance with numeric keypad controls, or it may have to actually implement the cross hairs itself using pixel writing in XOR mode. The hardware supplies device coordinates and these are converted to physical coordinate (millimeter) values by another routine in the driver so that 'get_point' returns physical coordinates. The 'read_point' procedure then converts the physical coordinates to user coordinates based on the current viewing transformation given the current window and viewport limits. The window and viewport data are stored inside the 'g2d_plot' compilation unit and a routine internal to that unit provides the transformation from physical to user coordinates. When 'plot_line' is called with the two end points in user coordinates, it first calls 'clip_line' to clip the user coordinates to the current window. If there is something left of the line then further processing is undertaken. Firstly both end points are converted to physical coordinates by a routine internal to 'g2d_plot'. After this the line drawing attributes, stored as a record of parameters in 'g2d_plot', are consulted to decide on which line style code to execute. For a solid line, this will simply be a call to 'line(px1,py1,px2,py2)' in the driver. This routine converts each end point from physical coordinates to device coordinates and then performs the appropriate move to and draw to hardware primitives. Thus the line finally appears on the output.

This overall process can be seen pictured in Figure 8-2. Input handlers receive graphics input and transmit this through various transformations to the output handlers. Much of the time however graphics data comes from file rather than from an input device. This data would have been digitized from an input device earlier or else typed in as a text metafile. This process is also displayed in Figure 8-2 which therefore shows the general construction of a GSP. It has been shown that a number of internal GSP routines are needed in this process of input to output. The clipping routine is an example of a routine internal to the package within the transformation processor part of this process. It is interesting to regard the process in Figure 8-2 as a pipeline taking input data through to output data. At various sites along this pipeline the graphics data is represented in different coordinate systems and parameters.

The clipping process is done in G2D in user coordinates. Other GSPs have the clipping at an earlier position along this pipeline. For instance, clipping could be done to the data when it is in physical coordinates within the 'plot_line' routine in 'g2d_plot', or in physical coordinates in the line routine in 'g2d_driver', or in device coordinates within the driver before the hardware move to and draw to primitives are called. There are advantages and disadvantages of doing the clipping at these various possible sites along the output pipeline and these should be weighed up before the total design of a GSP is finalized.

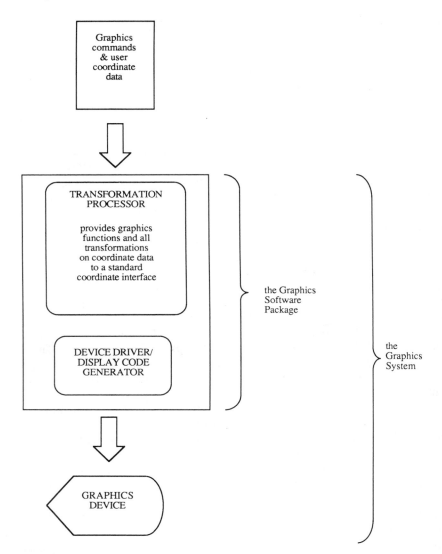

Figure 8-2 General construction of a GSP.

8.6 Adding software text

Text output, the printing of alphanumeric characters, has traditionally been a function provided by the hardware in computing equipment. Text generated by graphics software is now becoming more widespread. This software text offers flexibility but still not the speed (usually) of hardware text. The traditional hardware text for VDU screens has a number of limitations. For instance the character sizes are generally fixed. The characters can only be placed in given character cell locations on the screen. There is no variety of text fonts available. Hardware text usually cannot be written at any angle other than horizontally, vertically, or at 45 degrees. Hardware text cannot usually be drawn to any thickness either. All of these limitations can be overcome by using computer graphics to generate text in software. The general required formats for the text output can be programmed into the software. These formats are the text attributes such as text angle, size, slant, color, thickness, and what sort of justification might be used for text enclosed in a box.

One method for software text is to use pixel matrix templates. All printing characters are defined in a given-sized rectangular matrix of pixels. Then these pixel rectangles can be bit-mapped onto any graphics screen position. Writing the rectangles can be done by any bitwise logical operation on the pixel values of the background with the new template pixel values. In this way fonts of different pixel rectangle sizes may be mixed on the same screen and characters drawn on top of others need not wipe out the underlying graphics or software text. This method overcomes the problems of fixed character size, fixed cell positions, fixed font, and fixed thickness. There are restrictions or difficulties however with character sizing and rotations. Storing font character masks for all possible cases however takes too much memory and it is preferable if characters of different sizes and angles could be computed from one font definition file.

An easier method is use *vector generated* text rather than this *raster generated* text approach. In vector generated text, every character is simply a list of move to ('M' command) and draw to ('D' command) commands - the vector graphics primitives. Raster and vector definitions for the letter 'A' are shown in Figures 8-3 and 8-4. Vector graphics file data for the letter 'A' shown in these figures is:

```
* The letter 'A':
M   0,0
D   3,8
D   6,0
M   1,2
D   5,2
M   8,0
```

Note that every vector graphics character definition ends with a move to command that provides the intercharacter gap and the right position to start drawing the next character. The coordinates used in this file data for 'A' are *absolute user coordinates*. In contrast, *relative coordinates* specify a point by displacement values from the current position (CP). For example, if CP = (100,80) then relative coordinates of (30,20) actually refer to the point whose absolute coordinates are (130,100). Since edges in vector characters are usually very small, use of relative coordinate character definitions rather than absolute coordinate values can result in more compact storage of the character set. One strategy is to store the character set in absolute coordinates in a text file for easier editing, but when the text file is loaded by the package the coordinates are stored in memory more compactly using the relative coordinate form.

The coordinate values in the definitions of the characters should be regarded fom the conceptual point of view as relative coordinates since the absolute position of a particular string can vary. Equivalently the move to and draw to commands in its definition should

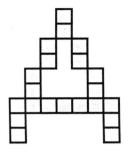 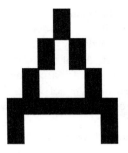

Figure 8-3 A raster graphics representation of the letter 'A'.

be considered as relative move to and relative draw to commands rather than absolute move to and absolute draw to commands. Denoting the relative move to command by 'm' and the relative draw to command by 'd', the above data for 'A' can be converted to relative commands as:

```
m   0,0
d   3,8
d   3,-8
m   -5,2
d   4,0
m   3,-2
```

Then to draw a character requires a procedure such as:

procedure draw_character(char_nr : integer)

which looks up the table of character definitions for character number 'char_nr' and then executes the list of relative commands for that character. A routine:

procedure draw_text(x,y : real; message : string_type)

then does an absolute move to the user coordinate point (x, y) and then calls 'draw_character' for each character in the input string message. Because each character stores relative move tos and draw tos the characters will be placed at the correct positions on the screen and also will be correctly spaced.

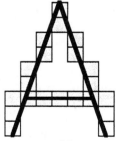 

Figure 8-4 A vector graphics representation of the letter 'A'.

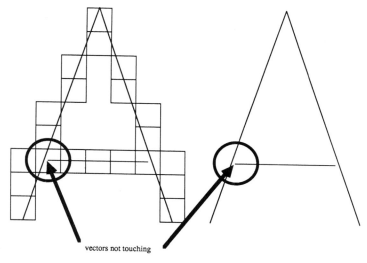

Figure 8-5 Errors observed on enlarging characters.

Since the vector graphics definition uses coordinate pairs (x, y) in defining each character, transformations such as translation, scaling, and rotation are easily done by the usual two-dimensional transformations mapping (x, y) to (x', y'). Real number values are used in these coordinate pairs, and care must be taken when defining the characters that the lines join up exactly. Otherwise errors will be apparent on scaling up the character. This can be seen in Figure 8-5. This also means that if many different transformations are required on the same text font, then the transformations should all start on the original untransformed data instead of transforming the transformed data. The latter method allows cumulative floating-point errors to creep into the data values. This suggests that the method of concatenating transformation matrices and then applying the concatenated transformation matrix to the original data each time is the appropriate method for character transformations.

Consider, for example, text scaling. This will be done by applying the normal two-dimensional scaling transformation with parameters sx and sy to all character coordinates. Note that in scaling up the character, the spacing between characters also scales up proportionally, and the text will still look right when displayed by 'draw_text'. The scaling matrix must be applied within 'draw_text' to all the coordinate pairs of each

Figure 8-6 Slanting characters with a shear transformation gives italics.

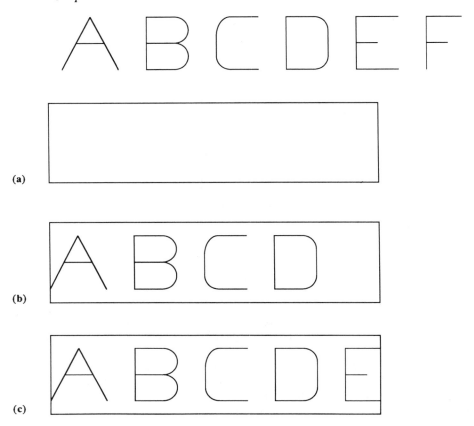

Figure 8-7 Three levels of text precision.

character before 'draw_character' is called. Scaling up text in this way however does not make the stroke proportionately thicker or thinner. Text thickness will be discussed later.

Consider now text rotations. Each character in the string must have its coordinate pair updated by matrix multiplication with the same rotation matrix. The proper character spacing is likewise preserved under text rotations. The slant transformations with positive parameter a produces italics mode:

$$x \rightarrow x' = x + a\ y$$
$$y \rightarrow y' = y$$

This can be seen in Figure 8-6. Finally, note that translations are not really required for drawing graphical text since the use of relative coordinates in character definitions and the starting point given by the (x, y) parameters in the call to procedure 'draw_text' provide suitable text positioning control.

Now what about mixtures of these transformations. Recall that each of the two-dimensional transformation groups – the translation group, the scaling group, the slant groups, and the rotation group are Abelian groups. However these transformations commute only among their own kind. Hence order is important when transformations of different kinds are mixed. When text is asked for at a certain angle and scaled to a certain size, this really means scale the characters first and rotate them second. In fact, there is an implicit ordering for text transformations and this implicit ordering is as follows:

1. Translate the characters. 3. Slant the characters.
2. Scale the characters. 4. Rotate the characters.

Hence it is necessary that the software implement the transformations in this order. The following procedures set the text attributes that determine the transformation of their coordinates:

procedure text_angle(degrees : real)
procedure text_scaling(scalex,scaley : real)
procedure text_slant(a : real)

Each of these provides the parameter(s) for building the corresponding 3 x 3 transformation matrices. The procedure 'draw_text' should start by taking the current text transformation attributes, forming the corresponding matrices and concatenating them in the order: scaling, slant, then rotation. This concatenated matrix is then applied to the coordinates in the definition of every character before 'draw_character' is called.

The term *text precision* is often used in computer graphics. Three levels of text precision are distinguished. These are called string precision, character precision, and stroke precision. They refer to how much of the text is affected by the clipping routine when the text goes over the edge of a viewport. String precision text is the lowest level of text precision. At this level, if part of a text string is outside of the viewport then the whole string is clipped or else all of it is displayed. Character precision text is medium quality with respect to clipping. At this level if part of a text string is outside of the viewport then only those characters that lie wholly or partly outside of the viewport will be clipped from the string. The highest precision text is stroke precision. At this level any parts of the text string lying outside of the viewport are neatly clipped at the viewport border by the normal line clipping algorithm. These three levels are illustrated in Figure 8-7. Vector generated text can provide stroke precision in user coordinates by using the high-level 'plot_line' procedure (which incorporates window clipping). Note that the 'draw_text' software needs to maintain a 'current position' parameter internal to the software text compilation unit in order to simulate the move to and draw to commands at the user coordinate level. This is the style of text and text precision level provided in the G2D package.

But how to implement the text thickness attribute has not yet been discussed. If a text character is drawn at (x, y) and then repeated at $(x+dx, y)$ where dx is the horizontal pixel spacing then the vertical and diagonal lines will be two pixels thick. Horizontal lines in the character will however still be only one pixel thick. If on the other hand the character were drawn starting at (x, y) and then again at $(x, y+dy)$ where dy is the vertical pixel spacing, then vertical lines would be only a single pixel wide. In order to make all lines, horizontal, vertical, and diagonal, two pixels wide alike the character must be drawn four times: once from (x, y), once from $(x+dx, y)$, once from $(x+dx, y+dy)$, and once from $(x, y+dy)$. These four starting points are the vertexes of a square. More generally, to produce text which is d pixels thick the character must be drawn $4d - 4$ times at each pixel increment position around the perimeter of a square with d pixels on each side. This

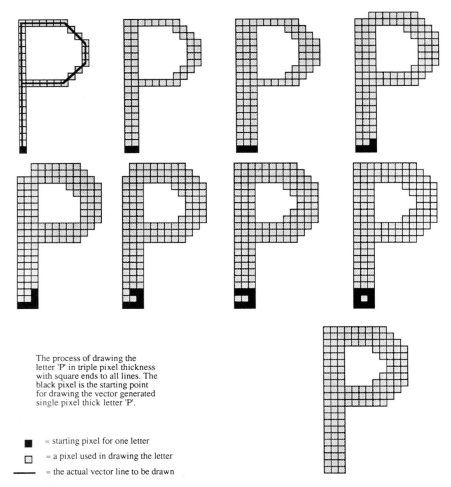

The process of drawing the letter 'P' in triple pixel thickness with square ends to all lines. The black pixel is the starting point for drawing the vector generated single pixel thick letter 'P'.

■ = starting pixel for one letter

▢ = a pixel used in drawing the letter

—— = the actual vector line to be drawn

Figure 8-8 Drawing a character in triple pixel thickness.

results in the ends of every line in the characters having squared off edges. Figure 8-8 shows this process for the case of triple pixel thickness on a letter having horizontal and vertical, and both forward and backward diagonal line segments. If rounded edges are desired then the character should be drawn from an even number of points around the circumference of a circle whose diameter is d pixels wide. The number of pixels around the circumference of a raster circle of diameter d pixels is not a straightforward function of d and is generally less than the integer part of πd. Examples of pixel circles for d equals 1 to 11 are shown in Figure 8-9. Repeating calls to the character drawing routine this many times slows down text message output by that factor. Optimization methods can be devised that save redrawing pixels in the thick character that have already been set. Alternatively, not drawing the character from every pixel on the perimeter may produce an acceptable (nonsolid filled) character pattern. Also for plotters with thick pens available it may not be necessary to draw the character from every pixel on the perimeter of a square

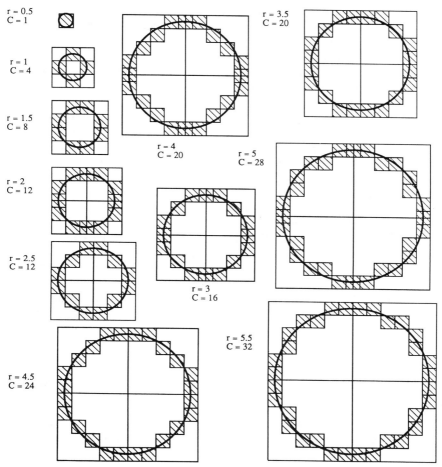

Figure 8-9 Digital circles of various integral and half-integral radii (integral diameters). Except for the case $r = 0.5$, the circumference C is always a multiple of four.

or circle but rather from every second pixel, for example.

The vector defined text on raster screens can also enable us to have more general fonts with colors. For instance, a character font could be defined that draws outlined (i.e. hollow) characters rather than stick figure characters. By adding another command in the text definition file, these closed areas can be colored in. Such a command would be 'Paint x,y' which the text software will interpret to mean that the point (x, y) is where coloring is to start (the *seed* point) and it ends on reaching the outline color of the hollow text. Other commands in the file can set the color for the outline and the color for the interior. Many interesting fonts can be built up in this way. For example, one font draws the characters as if they were made of three-dimensional blocks. By allowing another command to define the character code in the font, the character set can be extended to any special characters such as Greek alphabet, mathematical symbols, and icons. Figure 8-10 shows the Unifon font. A code number command means that the text font file character entries do not need to be in alphabetical (or ASCII) order. Font files defining characters by these commands in a text file tend to be very large data files. It is therefore useful to have a program that converts the data to compressed binary form. This saves room in secondary storage and means that font loading will be quicker.

A comparison can be made between the various kinds of text provided with graphics workstations. Firstly hardware generated text in the text screen is usually of fixed size, fixed cell positions, fixed slant, fast, and has automatic scrolling on reaching the last line of the screen. Another sort of text is that provided among the graphics hardware commands in ROM (read-only memory). This type of text will generally have a range of sizes, can be placed anywhere in the graphics output rectangle, may have a range of slants, is a bit slower than hardware text, and does not scroll. The ranges provided by this kind of text are often limited and the transformation parameters are limited to integer values only. In particular text rotations may be by integer degrees only because the hardware is fast at working with integers and floating-point processing is in these cases done in software. Integer rotations may not be desired since it can mean that end points of a text string may not join up exactly with other points. The final kind of text is that programmed in software as described above. This has full generality, but is slower than the others, and does not scroll. Hardware text has other attributes not often associated with the other graphical text methods such as whether the characters are underlined, whether they are displayed in inverse video, and whether the character flashes on and off (i.e. between the character and a blank). These extra attributes could also be simulated in software with some difficulty.

8.7 CAD user interfacing and design

With this being the final chapter on two-dimensional graphics, several application areas will be looked at for the graphics package called G2D built up over the previous chapters. There are far too many two-dimensional graphics applications than could be discussed here. Therefore more time will be spent discussing a small selection of applications as to their purpose, functionality provided, user interaction methods, typical outputs, and general software design approach, leaving many of the final coding details to the interested reader. This section will be concerned with the most widespread commercial use of computer graphics namely CAD (computer-aided design or drafting). While this section concerns generalities, the following section concentrates on two specific CAD application systems. Other applications of computer graphics apart from CAD will also be discussed in the next section.

CAD has been the earliest and biggest application area for computer graphics. Consequently many different approaches to the problem have been tried. The methods of constructing and describing geometrical shapes on a VDU to simulate real world objects have been well developed. The interfacing of this functionality to the user is of great importance to the success and viability of the CAD program. Typically CAD systems use graphics tablets with a menu area painted on the tablet surface. The user points to selected areas on the tablet menu to activate the various functions. For example, the user might point to a line segment menu choice, and then move the stylus to a digitizing area of the tablet to digitize the two end points of the line segment. As the stylus is moved over the

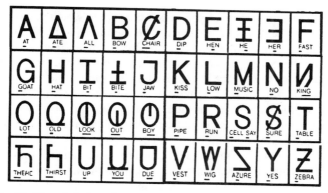

Figure 8-10 The Unifon alphabet shown here is based on the principle that the spelling of all words should correspond to their phonetic pronunciation.

digitizing area, a graphics cursor is seen to move correspondingly on the screen. When the two desired end points are finally entered, a line segment is drawn connecting them together on the screen. In the same sort of way the user can place circles, arcs, polylines, polymarkers, and spline curves – the simple graphics components of more complex objects wanted in CAD.

CAD applications need to be able to group these graphics elements into identifiable units that can be individually operated upon. The 'g2d_object' compilation module is for this purpose. As the user is putting together line segments and arcs on the screen, the application CAD program could be using the G2D metagraphics commands that inserts all graphics commands into an internal list. These objects can then be written to disk and read in again at some other time so that the development of graphics objects can be continued at a later time.

The user could put graphical elements in the wrong places or change an opinion about where some should go in the diagram. This calls for some editing capabilities for the graphics object command lists. The only editing functions provided by G2D are copying the object to another location, merging two graphics objects, transforming objects by translations, rotations and scalings, and deleting the whole of the current object. Once a 'plot_line' command is entered into the current graphics object for instance, G2D provides no command to remove it. Such command by command editing could be built into an enhanced version of G2D and the programming for this is straightforward. Alternatively, the CAD application program could remember graphics elements in its own area of memory where the user can do editing, and then write them to a graphics object metafile. For instance if a line segment is drawn then the CAD program can store its end points and draw the line segment in XOR mode. If the user decides later not to keep that line segment then the program erases it by redrawing the line with the stored end point coordinates again in XOR mode and this will erase the line segment from the screen. The program can then discard the end point coordinates.

Thus the CAD program allows the user to draw graphics elements on the screen by digitizing points with 'read_point' and calling the appropriate graphics element display routine selected by the user from a menu or by hit codes. The digitized point data could be stored by G2D in its 'g2d_data' points table database. If these are all drawn in XOR mode and the CAD program keeps track of which points apply to which graphics element then individual graphics elements could be deleted. The user needs to be able to 'pick' graphics elements for deleting. This can again be done by a call to 'read_point' and then the software looks for the closest point in its data base to this one. In finding the closest point it is not necessary to take the square root of the sum of the squares of coordinate differences. The point with the minimum distance squared is returned. Picking two points will pick a line segment for deletion and so forth for the other graphics elements. However the user may not want to just delete a graphics element but may wish to move it to a new location. This function can also be easily given to the user. One way of doing this is to delete the object and to redefine it elsewhere on the screen. Another way is to let the object be dragged across the screen to the desired location. This can be done by many deletions and redrawings of the line segment as the user moves a stylus across the screen. Another approach is to allow editing of graphics elements a point at a time. With the line segment example again, the user could pick one end point and digitize a new position for it. There upon the old line segment is deleted and the new one drawn. However dragging where the intermediate positions of graphics elements are seen in a change operation under the motion of a picking device is a highly intuitive and user friendly way of performing the operation. When this continuous motion approach is applied to changing a point at a time in the definition of the graphics element it is referred to as *rubber banding*. New line segments are drawn as if a moving rubber band were being used on the screen.

Once the user agrees that the graphics elements are in the right places, then they could all be drawn again in permanent write mode, that is, using pixel replace mode. At the same time graphics object appending command mode could be switched on so that the final shape can be stored and written to a disk file by G2D. The next time this shape is loaded in, it could be drawn in tempoary (i.e. XOR) mode if it needs to be edited, otherwise it could be drawn in permanent (i.e. replace) mode.

Another feature in two-dimensional CAD systems is the ability to *highlight* picked items. This could be a point, graphics element, a group of graphics elements, a graphics object, or several graphics objects. The purpose of highlighting is to let the user know which item the 'read_point' software has selected. Although the graphics cursor can be placed anywhere on the screen by the pointing device, CAD systems allow *grids* to be defined with the distance between adjacent grid points greater than one pixel. When a selection is made by the user, the graphics cursor must jump to the nearest grid point. This allows easier, quicker and more accurate creation and selection of graphics entities. The implementation of these concepts involves the 'read_point' procedure and and some additional code to compute the closest grid intersection to the current cross-hairs position. The point returned is then the grid site coordinates. (See problem 8.11.)

CAD systems have many other features than described here. The names of these features often reflect the area of application – they are terms drawn from the way object design is done in the real world in the different areas such as mechanical engineering, architecture, and carpentry. For example, chamfering is a way of adjusting sharp edges on a graphics object – the corners are cut off by a straight line. Another way of changing sharp corners is to fillet them. Filleting means to replace the sharp corner with a rounded one. These terms are illustrated in Figure 8-11. Many of these other features have to do with three-dimensional CAD systems and so will not be discussed here.

8.8 Graphics application projects

In this final section six application projects are listed that can be built using the G2D package. Sufficient description is provided with each project to enable students to build these programs for themselves.

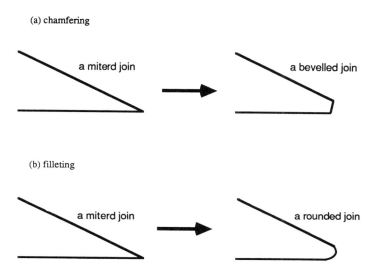

Figure 8-11 Chamfering (a) and filleting (b) are two ways of removing sharp corners in computer-designed parts in CAD/CAM software.

Project 1 - Electronic circuit CAD

In this application, the idea is to place electronic component symbols at certain places on the screen and connect them together with lines to represent wire connections. Each electronic symbol is a graphics object made of line segments, circles, and arcs. They will need to be in various positions on the output and at various angles. It is not likely that they would need to be drawn at different sizes so the scaling transformations are not needed. Each graphics object has one or more connection points where wires are to be joined onto the component. Diagonal connection lines from component to component are not allowed. If one connection point is at $(x1, y1)$ and the other at $(x2, y2)$, then at least two line segments are needed to join the components in the proper looking way for circuit diagrams. In this case the following calls would do:

```
plot_line(x1,y1,x2,y1);
plot_line(x2,y1,x2,y2);
```

The file of standard electronics symbols (see Box 5-4 and Figure 5-8) as graphics objects should be used by the program but not changed. The program reads in graphics objects such as resistors and transistors and makes instances of these symbols at various locations and angles under user control. Once the symbol instances are placed then the line connections can be added as above. These lines could go into a new graphics object. All of these graphics objects should be saved by the CAD program. The whole circuit diagram could be one graphics object. This means that the circuit component instances and wire connections graphics object are graphics objects nested inside the circuit graphics object (and called up when necessary by the 'display' procedure). After editing of circuit diagrams has been done by the methods suggested in the previous section all graphics objects associated with the final diagram can be saved in one output file.

Project 2 - Interior design CAD

This application places the plan view of various items of furniture around the plan of an office floor. The floor plan can include a number of rooms with doors opening in certain directions, fixed windows, and benches or desks. The user can move around other items such as chairs, desks, partition walls, computer terminals, cabinets, and pot plants. The object of the exercise is to come up with pleasing arrangements and to see what is possible in a given office space without becoming too cramped. Basically the same sort of programming as for the electronic CAD program is used here.

Project 3 - Business reports

Monthly sales reports can be displayed by vertical bar charts. These could be colored in and have stacked bars when more than one quantity is to be plotted on the same graph. The graph should be labeled on the axes and have a title. A simple program to draw these charts need only ask the user for the number of bars, and the y value for each bar. If stacked bars are to be used then the program should ask how may quantities are to be plotted, and input their y values per bar in the required stacking order. For graph labeling, the program can have a menu choice which allows the user to run 'read_point' to digitize the start point for a one line message, and then input the characters from the keyboard and then call 'draw_text'. This enables the user to place as many labels as desired wherever they are wanted. The labels however cannot go over more than one line and if they are too long for the screen then part of the message will be clipped. Another menu choice can allow the user to set the x and y scale factors for the text size.

Other kinds of plots should be options in another menu. Each kind of plot can show the same data but in its own format. Two obvious examples are pie charts and line graphs. The lines in line graphs for different quantities can be different styles or colors. For pie charts, several quantities can be simultaneously displayed by concentric pies of various radii. As another option, the user might select one of the quantities for display by itself.

Project 4 - Graphics artwork

Company logos and advertizing posters can be done by computer graphics with a package like G2D. Shapes must be built up on the screen by dots, lines, circles, arcs, and text. These would be written in temporary mode so that they can be shifted. The whole picture may be saved as a graphics object but no more than one graphics object would be needed. The program to produce this sort of sharp technological computer art would allow the user to select and place any available graphics element and finally get a screen dump.

General artwork on computer graphics equipment requires at least a freehand mode where curves are drawn through freehand motion of a digitizing device. The 'read_point' routine could be used for freehand work by digitizing close points and using a character for each to determine the brush type for the line connecting the points. However G2Ds 'read_point' is not so suitable for this type of graphics input operation because so many key presses are needed. Many digitizers have an input mode called *streaming* mode where the input device continually sends coordinate pairs to the host so long as consecutive coordinates are not the same. This is more suitable for freehand doodling. Another routine could be written to make use of this input mode. Color in the output is also an important aspect of artistic work and this is discussed later in Chapter 13. Street scenes, seaside scenes, and country scenes would require free form-lines, color, area fills, brush styles such as thickness, roundness, and air brush effects, and fast interactive hardware. This sort of artistic creation requires much more functionality than the G2D package as described to this point provides.

Project 5 - Transparency generator

Graphics artwork can also be output onto transparency sheets for use with overhead projectors. This sort of transparency usually needs only a limited number of graphics output functions. In particular boxes, circles, arrows, and text are the most commonly needed graphics. Freehand input is not required. The transparencies would be used in a lecture presentation and contain mainly text and flow chart type diagrams.

Project 6 - Word processing with graphics

Word processors in the past have been tied to alphanumeric data only. Yet people want diagrams within the printed text as well. Page-making and publishing software is now becoming available for relatively low-cost microcomputing graphics workstations. This project involves tacking graphics on to a standard word processor. This can be done by including within the text of a word processor file special commands that another program can recognize and use to insert graphics in the printed copy. This latter program reads a word processed file and prints it out. It checks for the special 'escape' commands that instruct it to send graphics data to the printer. It is assumed that the printer supports bit image graphics as with the hard-copy device discussed in Chapter 3. This simple system does not give you a 'What you see is what you get' (WYSIWYG) graphics word processor as on some modern microcomputers, but it does allow standard mainframe word processors or text editors used with standard alphanumeric (nongraphics) terminals to produce the same sort of results when the mainframe has advanced graphics equipment attached to it.

Problems

8.1   Implement the 'draw_text' procedure as described in the text. Create a text font file and test it with this routine.

8.2   Implement the text thickness attribute for the 'draw_text' procedure. Write a routine for square ends and another for round ends and have this as another attribute for text. How many pixel rewrites are there in Figure 8-8? How can these be avoided?

8.3   Extend the 'g2d_text' compilation routines to allow for outlined characters with area fill commands in the font definition file. Also allow character codes to be defined in the font file so that all codes do not have to be defined and the characters do not have to be entered into the font file in code order. Write a program that allows you to create vector defined font files interactively on the screen by moving the graphics cursor rather than entering coordinate numbers. Write a program to generate a font of outlined characters from a stick figure character font file.

8.4   Write a program to compress character font definition files to the smallest possible size. This will mean assigning meanings to bits within the data bytes. For example, high bit 0 means move to and 1 means draw to. Also the numbers are stored in binary form rather than as ASCII text strings. Modify 'draw_text' routines to interpret the compressed form of the text font.

8.5   Implement project 1.

8.6   Implement project 2.

8.7   Implement project 3. Ensure that your graphics package provides the following bar drawing routines:

    1. **procedure** draw_bar(height)
        - draws the next vertical bar in a bar chart at the default width, and updates the lower left corner from which the next bar will be drawn .
    2. **procedure** set_bar_start_point(x,y)
        - sets the lower left corner to start the next bar from.
    3. **procedure** set_bar_width(w)
        - sets the default bar width for all subsequent bars.
    4. **procedure** set_bar_stack(n,color_array)
        - sets the bar chart to stack 'n' bars in a column with the color of each. bar given in the array 'color_array'

Also ensure that the package provides the following procedures for drawing pie charts:

    5. **procedure** draw_wedge(radius,angle)
        - draws a color filled sector of a circle of given radius and angle

6. **procedure** set_wedge_center(x,y)
     - sets the center point for subsequent drawing of wedges
7. **procedure** set_wedge_start_angle(degrees)
     - sets the initial angle from which the next arc will be drawn.
     Subsequent wedges will draw from the angle where the previous
     wedge finished
8. **procedure** set_wedge_color(color)
     - sets the color to draw the next wedge
9. **procedure** set_wedge_pull_out_distance(d)
     - sets the displacement from the default origin for the next wedge
     only.

8.8   Implement project 4.

8.9   Implement project 5.

8.10   Implement project 6.

8.11   Implement the procedures:

```
procedure define_grid(x,y,dx,dy : integer);
procedure show_grid;
procedure hide_grid;
procedure read_grid_point(var k : char; var x,y : integer);
procedure show_cross_hairs;
procedure hide_cross_hairs;
procedure set_cross_hairs(x,y);
```

that would be useful in a CAD system. The first procedure defines a grid lattice
with a vertical grid line passing through the point ('x','y') in device coordinates and
parallel grid lines spaced by 'dx' pixels horizontally filling the display rectangle.
The grid contains a similar set of horizontal grid lines with one passing through
('x','y') and the others parallel and equally spaced by 'dy' pixels vertically. The grid
consisting of all horizontal and vertical parallel lines is not actually drawn until
'show_grid' is called, and the procedure 'hide_grid' can then be used to remove it
from the display. The procedure 'read_grid_point' allows the pointer device to move
the graphics cross-hairs freely around the screen by calling the 'read_point'
procedure. When a key is pressed, its value is returned in variable 'k' and the cross-
hairs snap to the nearest grid site. The device coordinates of this grid site are
returned in the variables 'x' and 'y'. Procedures 'show_cross_hairs' and
'hide_cross_hairs' allow the cross-hairs to be displayed or not displayed at any time.
The 'read_grid_point' procedure does not initialize the cross-hairs position on each
call, but allows the user to move the cross-hair on from where it was last left. The
procedure 'set_cross_hairs' allows the cross-hairs to be set at any desired device
coordinate position given by ('x','y').

9

Three-dimensional graphics objects

The next four chapters deal with three-dimensional graphics. There are four levels of sophistication in three-dimensional graphics:

1. Wire frame graphics – which uses only three-dimensional edges.
2. Solid geometry using flat faces – which uses edges and flat polygonal faces.
3. Smooth shaded surfaces – which allows curved surfaces with smooth changes in intensity or color.
4. Picture quality graphics – which includes curved surfaces with texturing.

This chapter and the next will only deal with the first two cases since the others involve the use of color fills which will be dealt with in Chapter 13.

9.1 Three-dimensional graphics elements

In three-dimensional graphics, some basic three-dimensional geometric concepts will need to be represented such as points, lines, circular arcs, circles, ellipses, polylines, splines, triangles, polygon faces, spheres, ellipsoids, polyhedrons, the general quadric surface, and spline surfaces. Some in this list are two-dimensional geometrical elements; that is, they lie wholly within a plane imbedded in three dimensions, while the remainder are true three-dimensional geometrical elements. The two-dimensional elements have been met before in Section 5.1. However, they must be looked at again because their mathematical definitions are in some cases more complex in three dimensions.

Points

In three dimensions, a point is represented by three coordinate values. Here a right-handed Cartesian coordinate system (see Figure 9-1) is used with the coordinates being x, y, and z.

A point can be represented in computer graphics by a pixel or other marker centred on the display rectangle location represented by (x, y). All the attributes of points discussed in Chapter 5 apply to three-dimensional points.

Lines

In three dimensions, a line is best represented by its two end points, $(x1, y1, z1)$ and $(x2, y2, z2)$. The length of the line is therefore:

$$l = \sqrt{[(x2\text{-}x1)^2 + (y2\text{-}y1)^2 + (z2\text{-}z1)^2]}$$

and the direction cosines of the line segment are given in the unit vector:

$$\mathbf{u} = (x2\text{-}x1, y2\text{-}y1, z2\text{-}z1) / l$$

Arcs

Any arc in three dimensions can be uniquely specified by three points $P1 = (x1, y1, z1)$, $P2 = (x2, y2, z2)$, and $P3 = (x3, y3, z3)$ through which it passes, just as in the two-dimensional case. The points $P1$ and $P3$ are the end points of the arc and $P2$ is any point on the arc between its end points. (*Note*: as in the two-dimensional case, while the three points required to define the arc are not unique amongst themselves, the arc that they define is unique.) It is an interesting mathematical exercise to determine the plane of the arc, its radius, and its arc angle from the parameters $x1$, $y1$, $z1$, $x2$, $y2$, $z2$, $x3$, $y3$, and $z3$. This is left as an exercise for the reader.

Circles

Circles in three-dimensional space can be defined in terms of three points: two on the extremities of a diameter of the circle, and a third on the circumference to define the plane of the circle. The center of the circle, its radius, and the equation of the plane that the circle lies in, can be easily calculated from the coordinates of these three points.

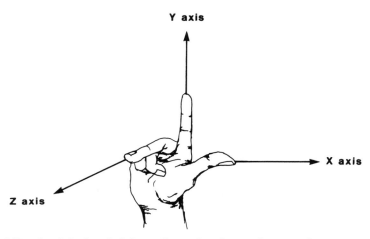

Figure 9-1 For the right-handed three-dimensional cartesian coordinate system the thumb of the right hand points along the x axis, the index finger along the y axis and the next finger along the z axis.

Ellipses

One way of defining an ellipse in three dimensions via three-dimensional points alone is based on the familiar fixed length string method for drawing an ellipse. Three points define the ellipse as follows: the first and last points are at the focuses of the ellipse and the second point lies somewhere on its circumference (such that the three points are not colinear). The three points define the plane of the ellipse, the 'string length', and hence the whole elliptic curve.

Polylines

Three-dimensional polylines are straightforward generalizations of their two-dimensional counterparts. They are defined by n vertexes (x_i, y_i, z_i) for $i = 1$ to $i = n$. Note however that the vertexes of three-dimensional polylines are not constricted to all lying within the same plane.

Splines

Three-dimensional splines are smooth curves in three-dimensional space and take the same point data input as for polylines, that is, real number triples (x_i, y_i, z_i) for $i = 1$ to $i =$

n. The formulas for two-dimensional splines easily generalize to three-dimensional spline curves. These will be presented in Section 9.2.

Triangles and polygonal faces

A facet or polygon face is the area enclosed by a polygon whose vertexes all lie within the same plane (i.e. are coplanar). Flat polygonal facets are easier to render in computer graphics since they usually have a uniform coloring. They are also mathematically convenient. The only polygon whose vertexes will always be coplanar is a triangle. For this reason, curved surfaces are often represented by many triangular facets joined together.

Spheres

The outline of a sphere is a perfect circle from whatever angle of view is taken. Therefore a sphere will be drawn the same as a circle. It can be defined by two points in three dimensions: its center point and a point on its surface, or alternatively two points on the outline great circle. In the former case, the circular outline will not generally pass through the second point but will enclose it on the screen. The second method is the same as defining and drawing circles.

Ellipsoids, spheroids, and quadric surfaces

An ellipsoid is a surface given by the equation:

$$[(x - x_c)/a]^2 + [(y - y_c)/b]^2 + [(z - z_c)/c]^2 = 1$$

where (x_c, y_c, z_c) is the center of the ellipsoid, and parameters a, b, and c are the x, y, and z semi-axis lengths. If any two of a, b, or c are equal, the ellipsoid is called a spheroid, and of course if all three are equal it is a sphere. The Earth, for instance, is sometimes approximated as an oblate spheroid. Quadric surfaces are generalizations of spheres and ellipsoids. They have equation:

$$a\,x^2 + b\,y^2 + c\,z^2 + d\,y\,z + e\,z\,x + f\,x\,y + g\,x + h\,y + k\,z + l = 0$$

Finding a suitable method for expressing these parameters via a minimal set of three-dimensional points is left as an exercise for the reader.

General surfaces

The general surface equations of three dimensions are:

$$x = f(u, v)$$
$$y = g(u, v)$$
$$z = h(u, v)$$

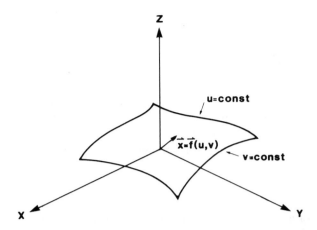

Figure 9-2 The general surface in three dimensions can be defined by a vector function of two parameters u and v which coordinatize a patch on the surface.

where u and v are curvilinear surface parameters. The parameters u and v can be considered as placing a coordinate system on the curved surface and curves of constant u or v can be drawn on the surface. (See Figure 9-2.) If the family of curves given by:

$$u = \text{constant}$$

on the above surface are spline curves, and the family of curves given by:

$$v = \text{constant}$$

on this surface are also spline curves, then the surface is called a *spline surface* (even though three-dimensional draughtsman's drawing splines were never invented). These are discussed in the following section.

9.2 Spline curves and surfaces

The value of two-dimensional spline curves has already been seen in Section 4.7. These curves can be readily extended to three-dimensional space where they are equally useful. Consider the generalized form of spline curves for three-dimensional space. Instead of using (x, y, z) for the coordinates of three-dimensional space, the notation (x_i) where $i = 1$ to $i = 3$ will be used. Recalling that a spline curve is a piecewise polynomial, it can be expressed generally as:

$$x \equiv x_1 = f_1(u) \equiv \sum a_{1Jk} \, s^k$$

$$y \equiv x_2 = f_2(u) \equiv \sum a_{2Jk} \, s^k$$

$$z \equiv x_3 = f_3(u) \equiv \sum a_{3Jk} \, s^k$$

In the functions f_1, f_2, and f_3, the parameter u is a global parameter along the whole of the spline curve with real values from 0 to u_{max} which should be a positive integer. For a given u value there are corresponding J and s values:

    J := trunc(u);
    s := u - J;

That is, J is the integer part of the global spline parameter u, and s is its fractional part. The parameter s thus ranges within the set $[0,1)$ and is the usual parameter along a polynomial section of a spline. The parameter $J = 0, 1, 2, \ldots$ is essentially the section number, and the quantities a_{1Jk}, a_{2Jk} and a_{3Jk} are the polynomial coefficients in each section. The sums are taken over $k = 0$ to $k = p$ where p is the degree of the polynomial pieces. For cubic splines, p equals three.

To evaluate (x, y, z) at any particular value of u by the equations above, the polynomial coefficients a_{iJk} must be known in each section. These are determined by control points and vectors and the dependence is linear so that the solution for the coefficients can be expressed in the form:

$$a_{1Jk} = \sum_l M_{kl} \, G_{1Jl}$$

$$a_{2Jk} = \sum_l M_{kl} \, G_{2Jl}$$

$$a_{3Jk} = \sum_l M_{kl} \, G_{3Jl}$$

where the sums are taken over $l = 1$ to $l = 3$. The matrix (M_{kl}) is the *spline matrix* of the particular kind of spline, and G_{iJk} is called the *geometry vector* .

The global spline function can therefore be expressed as:

$$x_i = \sum_{k=0,p} \sum_{l=1,3} M_{kl} \, G_{iJl} \, s^k \tag{9.1}$$

By swapping over the order of summation and bracketing terms this can be written as:

$$x_i = \sum_{l=1,3} \{ \sum_{k=0,p} M_{kl} \, s^k \} \, G_{iJl}$$

or:

$$x_i = \sum_{l=1,3} G_{iJl} \, B_l(s) \tag{9.2}$$

where:

$$B_l(s) = \Sigma_{k=0,p} \, M_{kl} \, s^k \qquad (9.3)$$

are the so called *blending functions* of the particular spline. For a given type of spline curve the M_{kl} are constant and so the blending functions are set. The actual shape of the curve is then determined by the control information in the geometry vector.

Typical examples of spline functions that are used in computer graphics are cubic splines (for which $p = 3$) such as Hermite splines, Bezier splines, and B-splines. These are summarized in Box 9-1. The geometry constants G_{iJl} used in equation 9.2 are expressed in the box in terms of surface quantities in order to disclose the meanings of these coefficients for the various splines. The cubic sections of Bezier splines can be extended to higher polynomials called Bezier curves using more than four control points per section. If $p+1$ control points with coordinates $(c_{1Jk}, c_{2Jk}, c_{3Jk})$, for $k = 0$ to $k = p$ are used in each section J, then the corresponding Bezier curve has blending functions which allow equation 9.1 to be rewritten as:

$$x_i(u) = \Sigma_{k=0,p} \, p \, ! \, / \, k \, ! \, / \, (p-k)! \, c_{iJk} \, s^k \, (1-s)^{p-k}$$

The equations above for spline curves in three dimensions can be readily generalized to spline surfaces where there are now two global spline parameters (u, v) rather than just u. Holding either u or v constant results in a spline curve in the other parameter. The formulas for three-dimensional spline surfaces are therefore:

$$x \equiv x_1 = f_1(u, v) \equiv \Sigma_k \, \Sigma_l \, a_{1Jl} \, b_{1Km} \, s^l \, t^m$$
$$y \equiv x_2 = f_2(u, v) \equiv \Sigma_k \, \Sigma_l \, a_{2Jl} \, b_{2Km} \, s^l \, t^m$$
$$z \equiv x_3 = f_3(u, v) \equiv \Sigma_k \, \Sigma_l \, a_{3Jl} \, b_{3Km} \, s^l \, t^m$$

or more compactly:

$$x_i = f_i(u, v) \equiv \Sigma_l \, \Sigma_m \, c_{iJKlm} \, s^l \, t^m \qquad (9.4)$$

In this formulation, c_{iJKlm} is the tensor product of the spline coefficients a_{iJl} and b_{iKm} for the u spline curves and v spline curves respectively. The parameters J and s are determined by u:

$$J = \mathrm{trunc}(u) \qquad (9.5a)$$
$$s = u - J \qquad (9.5b)$$
$$u = J + s \qquad (9.5c)$$

as before, and the parameters K and t are determined by v:

$$K = \text{trunc}(v) \qquad (9.6a)$$
$$t = v - K \qquad (9.6b)$$
$$v = K + t \qquad (9.6c)$$

The surface spline coefficients can also be expressed in terms of the geometry vectors G_{iJq} for the u splines and H_{iKr} for the v splines as:

$$c_{iJKlm} = \Sigma_q \, \Sigma_r \, M_{lq} \, G_{iJq} \, H_{iKr} \, M_{mr}$$

where q and r range from 0 to the powers of the u and v splines. Substituting this form of the surface coefficients into the general surface spline equation 9.4 gives a fourfold summation. By easy rearrangement of the order of summation, the surface blending functions can be defined as:

$$B_{qr}(s, t) = \Sigma_l \, \Sigma_m \, M_{lq} \, M_{mr} \, s^l \, t^m \qquad (9.7)$$

so that the spline surface is given by:

$$x_i(u, v) = \Sigma_q \, \Sigma_r \, B_{qr}(s, t) \, G_{iJq} \, H_{iKr} \qquad (9.8)$$

Box 9-1 Standard cubic spline ($p = 3$) data used in computer graphics.

Hermite splines
  Spline matrix :

$$M = \begin{pmatrix} 2 & -2 & 1 & 1 \\ -3 & 3 & -2 & -1 \\ 0 & 0 & 1 & 0 \\ 1 & 0 & 0 & 0 \end{pmatrix}$$

  Geometry vector :
$$G_{iJ0} = x_i(J)$$
$$G_{iJ1} = x_i(J+1)$$
$$G_{iJ2} = dx_i(J)/ds$$
$$G_{iJ3} = dx_i(J+1)/ds$$

Bezier splines
  Spline matrix :

$$M = \begin{pmatrix} -1 & 3 & -3 & 1 \\ 3 & -6 & 3 & 0 \\ -3 & 3 & 0 & 0 \\ 1 & 0 & 0 & 0 \end{pmatrix}$$

Geometry vector :

$$G_{iJ0} = x_i(J)$$

$$G_{iJ1} = x_i(J) + dx_i(J)/ds/3$$

$$G_{iJ2} = x_i(J+1) - dx_i(J+1)/ds/3$$

$$G_{iJ3} = x_i(J+1)$$

B-splines

Spline matrix :

$$M = \begin{pmatrix} -1 & 3 & -3 & 1 \\ 3 & -6 & 3 & 0 \\ -3 & 0 & 3 & 0 \\ 1 & 4 & 1 & 0 \end{pmatrix} / 6$$

Geometry vector :

$$G_{iJ0} = x_i(J-1)$$

$$G_{iJ1} = x_i(J)$$

$$G_{iJ2} = x_i(J+1)$$

$$G_{iJ3} = x_i(J+2)$$

Since the spline type determines the matrix M, the surface blending functions in equation 9.7 are a fixed set of functions for a given type of spline. Equation 9.8 coupled with equations 9.5a, b, and c, and 9.6a, b, and, c therefore show how to compute points on the spline surface for any values of the global surface parameters u and v. The exact shape of the surface depends on the control parameters in the geometry vectors G_i and H_i in equation 9.8. These vectors are usually subject to change by the user. For example, for B-spline bicubic surfaces the geometry vectors are grid points in space which the user may be at liberty to adjust. The B-spline surface does not pass through all of these control points: the surface passes near the points in a smooth curving manner. Of course with the general formulation of spline surfaces above, it is possible to have the u and v spline curves of different spline types or degrees. This is rarely done however. Styles for displaying surfaces on a flat graphics output rectangle will be considered in Section 12.3.

9.3 Graphics element display routines

For simple three-dimensional graphics, the user coordinate system (x, y, z) may be aligned such that the x axis is horizontal in the output display rectangle from left to right, the y axis is vertical running from the bottom of the display rectangle to the top and the z axis therefore (being a right-handed Cartesian coordinate system) is perpendicular to the display surface pointing directly out of the display surface. (See Figure 9-1.) In this way, a simple and natural way is defined for mapping from three-dimensional user coordinate space onto the display rectangle. The mapping is:

$$(x, y, z) \rightarrow (x, y)$$

that is, the z component is ignored and (x, y) is used in the manner of two-dimensional graphics for determining a position on the output display rectangle. Any mapping from a three-dimensional space to a two-dimensional space is called a *projection* and this particular projection is called the z or $(0,0,1)$ orthographic projection. Other more general kinds of projections will be presented in Chapter 10. A procedure 'project_point' will be used to map (x, y, z) to two-dimensional user coordinates. This procedure will be examined more generally in the next chapter. For current concerns, this procedure implements the z orthographic projection and therefore has the simple form:

```
procedure project_point(x,y,z : real; var u,v : real);
begin
    u := x;
    v := y;
end;
```

Using this method for converting three-dimensional coordinates (x, y, z) to two-dimensional user coordinates it is easy to implement the three-dimensional graphics element display routines in terms of the corresponding two-dimensional graphics element display routines. For example, to plot a three-dimensional line from $(x1, y1, z1)$ to $(x2, y2, z2)$, just call 'plot_line' the two-dimensional line plotting routine:

```
procedure plot_3D_line(x1,y1,z1,x2,y2,z2 : real);
var
    u1,v1,u2,v2 : real;
begin
    project_point(x1,y1,z1,u1,v1);
    project_point(x2,y2,z2,u2,v2);
    plot_line(u1,v1,u2,v2);
end;
```

Similar routines may be constructed for all the other graphics elements to be displayed. Note the naming convention being used here. Three-dimensional graphics element display routines have the generic name type:

plot_3D_element(defining 3D points list)

and the corresponding two-dimensional graphics element display routines have the generic name type:

plot_element(defining 2D points list)

All of these plotting procedures should be together in one compilation unit to construct a three-dimensional graphics package just as the two-dimensional plotting routines are kept in the compilation unit 'g2d_plot' for the G2D package. For the three-dimensional graphics package G3D, these plotting routines are kept in a compilation unit called 'g3d_plot'. A list of compilation units for G3D and the routines in them can be found in Appendixes D and E.

9.4 Three-dimensional graphics objects

Similarly to two-dimensional graphics objects, three-dimensional graphics objects are just collections of three-dimensional graphics display elements. Again a dynamic list structure is a useful data structure for holding graphics objects in the case of three dimensions. Graphics objects can be created as sequential text files where each line is a graphics command. The first line of the graphics object file data may have the form:

NAME <identifier>

which gives the graphics object an identifying alphanumeric name. This name can be used by the user program. After the 'NAME' command, any number of graphics element commands can be given, in any order, so long as they are implemented in the three-dimensional graphics package. Following the graphics element commands, there should be a line with 'END' only to signal the end of the graphics object definition. 'NAME' and 'END' commands allow many graphics objects to be stored within the one file. ('NAME' and 'END' for graphics objects are bracketing commands like 'procedure' or 'begin' and 'end' for program code segments.) A comment command, which is any line that starts with an asterisk, is a further aid to the user who must create or edit the data. Simple examples of three-dimensional graphics objects using this file structure are given in Box 9-2. Further examples will be discussed in Section 9.6.

As previously seen, the advantage of graphics objects being represented in text files in this way is that they can easily be corrected and changed by an ordinary text editor at an ordinary alphanumeric terminal. Another advantage is that the data can be easily transmitted and understood by another computer when it is in this textual form. A disadvantage is of course that files like these can consume considerable secondary storage space on a computer. This however is the nature of computer graphics – large amounts of data and data handling. A program can be provided to crunch the text data down to binary coded form for more compact filing. Direct access and indexed files may also be used for quicker input/output times within application programs.

9.5 Loading and saving three-dimensional graphics objects

Once a file of three-dimensional graphics objects has been created by a text editor, the graphics software then needs to be able to read and interpret the file. This calls for a graphics object loading procedure just as for two-dimensional graphics objects. The same sort of code can be used here. In fact the G2/3D package (the combined library of G2D and G3D) is made such that the same routine is used for loading two-dimensional graphics objects as for three-dimensional objects. After all, the loading routine is just reading in a file of executable graphics commands and three-dimensional commands are just an extra kind of command. The procedure 'load_object(var name : str_type)' returns the name of the next graphics object in the currently open graphics data input file in the parameter 'name'. (Alternatively, 'name' could be stored as a component of the global 'current_object' record and not passed as a variable as described for G2D.) The application program may want to use this 'name' parameter to search for a specific three-dimensional graphics object for display. Of course the file containing the three-dimensional graphics object must be first opened before being read by 'load_object', and this is done by the G2D 'open_input(file_name)' procedure.

To display a graphics object (list of graphics commands) a routine 'display_object' is required which parses each command and calls the appropriate procedure in G3D. This is the same function as performed by the 'display_object' procedure in the G2D compilation unit called 'g2d_object'. By extending the latter routine to parse and call the three-dimensional procedures as well, it can be used for both kinds of graphics objects.

While graphics objects may be created as text files by an ordinary editor and then read in to a program and displayed as discussed above, they can also be created or edited during execution of an application program. This kind of graphics object functionality is the same as offered in the compilation unit 'g2d_object' of the G2D package, and in fact can be invoked by reuse of the same routines. Thus, 'command_mode', can again be used to open the graphics object for appending with run-time graphics commands, and be used to close the current graphics object whenever needed. The procedure 'comment' can be used at run time to add comment lines to the current graphics object. The current graphics object can be copied to another area of main memory with the 'store_object' command of G2D, and any stored graphics object can be merged on to the current graphics object with the 'merge_object' command, or can replace the current graphics object with the 'restore_object' command. The current graphics object can also be deleted by the 'zero_object' command. The procedure 'display' can be used to display any stored graphics object, and 'print_object' can be used to see what is in the current graphics object. All these commands apply in G3D with a small amount of extension to the G2D module 'g2d_object'.

A problem may arise in using the 'command_mode' procedure to set the 'append' flag to true for those G3D routines that directly call G2D routines. The problem is that both the G3D routine and all calls of the G2D routines would be appended to the current graphics object in memory. This means that when the current object is subsequently displayed, the G2D procedures will be called twice. This problem may be overcome by not having those G3D routines directly call the G2D routines, but call instead code segments similar to the G2D routines. A simpler solution to the problem is for every time one of these G3D routines needs to call a G2D routine, it should first store the state of the 'append' flag, then set it to false, then call the required G2D routine, and finally restore the original boolean value to the 'append' flag. By manipulating the 'append' flag in this way, copying G3D procedures used at run-time will not also cause any G2D routines to be copied to the current graphics object.

Box 9-2 An example of two simple three-dimensional graphics objects.

```
NAME UNIT_CUBE
LINE 0 0 0 TO 1 0 0
LINE 1 0 0 TO 1 1 0
LINE 1 1 0 TO 0 1 0
LINE 0 1 0 TO 0 0 0
LINE 0 0 0 TO 0 0 1
LINE 1 0 0 TO 1 0 1
LINE 1 1 0 TO 1 1 1
LINE 0 1 0 TO 0 1 1
LINE 0 0 1 TO 1 0 1
LINE 1 0 1 TO 1 1 1
LINE 1 1 1 TO 0 1 1
LINE 0 1 1 TO 0 0 1
END
*
NAME PYRAMID
LINE 0 0 0 TO 1 0 0
LINE 1 0 0 TO 1 1 0
LINE 1 1 0 TO 0 1 0
LINE 0 1 0 TO 0 0 0
LINE 0 0 0 TO 0.5 0.5 0.7071
LINE 1 0 0 TO 0.5 0.5 0.7071
LINE 1 1 0 TO 0.5 0.5 0.7071
LINE 0 1 0 TO 0.5 0.5 0.7071
END
```

After an application program has created or modified one or more graphics objects it may then store them on secondary storage for later use. For this purpose a procedure must be provided for saving three-dimensional graphics objects. This needs the same sort of code as for saving two-dimensional objects, and in fact the G2D routines 'open_output(file_name)' and 'save_object(name)' can be used here. In this procedure, the parameter 'name' is an input parameter that is written into the current graphics data output file as the initial 'NAME' command. After the procedure writes all the graphics element commands to the current output file, it appends the 'END' command to signal the end of the graphics object. The output file itself is not closed by this procedure. A separate procedure 'close_output' would be used for this purpose and this also is provided by the G2D package.

9.6 Examples of three-dimensional graphics objects

Consider what procedure calls are required to display the graphics object of Box 9-2. First the file (say with file name 'eg1') must be opened for reading. Then the loading procedure

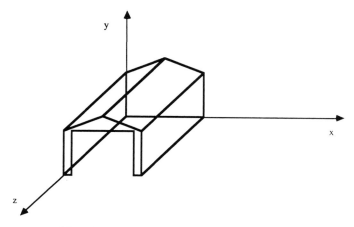

Figure 9-3 The garage graphics object of Box 9-3.

must be called. Lastly the three-dimensional graphics object display procedure must be called:

```
open_input('eg1');
load_3D_object(name);
display_3D_object;
```

This is the general programming code segment to display any three-dimensional graphics object. The program might however inspect the 'name' parameter to see that it has loaded the correct graphics object.

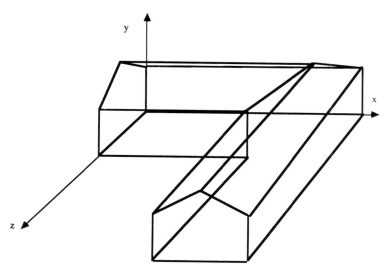

Figure 9-4 The house graphics object of Box 9-4.

Box 9-3 Three-dimensional graphics object data for a wire frame garage.

```
NAME Garage
* The back face of the garage:
POLYGON 5
(0,0,0) TO (6,0,0) TO (6,4,0) TO (3,6,0) TO (0,4,0)
* The front face of the garage with an open doorway:
POLYGON 9
(0,0,10) TO (1,0,10) TO (1,4,10) TO (5,4,10) TO (5,0,10) TO (6,0,10) TO
(6,4,10) TO (3,6,10) TO (0,4,10)
* Connection lines from the back face to the front face of the garage:
LINE (0,0,0) TO (0,0,10)
LINE (6,0,0) TO (6,0,10)
LINE (6,4,0) TO (6,4,10)
LINE (3,6,0) TO (3,6,10)
LINE (0,4,0) TO (0,4,10)
END
```

Box 9-4 Three-dimensional graphics object data for a wire frame L-shaped house.

```
NAME House
* The floor plan:
POLYGON 6
(0,0,0) TO (30,0,0) TO (30,0,30) TO (20,0,30) TO (20,0,10) TO (0,0,10)
* The ceiling:
POLYGON 6
(0,5,0) TO (30,5,0) TO (30,5,30) TO (20,5,30) TO (20,5,10) TO (0,5,10)
* The ridge of the roof:
LINE (0,8,5) TO (25,8,5)
LINE (25,8,5) TO (25,8,30)
* The roof joins:
LINE (0,5,0) TO (0,8,5)
LINE (0,8,5) TO (0,5,10)
LINE (30,5,0) TO (25,8,5)
LINE (25,8,5) TO (20,5,10)
LINE (30,5,30) TO (25,8,30)
LINE (25,8,30) TO (20,5,30)
* The wall joins:
LINE (0,0,0) TO (0,5,0)
LINE (30,0,0) TO (30,5,0)
LINE (30,0,30) TO (30,5,30)
LINE (20,0,30) TO (20,5,30)
LINE (20,0,10) TO (20,5,10)
LINE (0,0,10) TO (0,5,10)
END
```

A simple three-dimensional object given in Box 9-2 is a wire frame cube – it is made of line segments only. If a solid cube is wanted, then the facet graphics element should be used. Another wire-frame three-dimensional graphic object is given in Box 9-2, a pyramid. Box 9-3 shows a three-dimensional graphics object with more detail to represent a garage. This object contains the 'POLYGON' command which has parameters n, the number of vertexes, followed by the coordinates of the n vertexes. Notice the use of parentheses and commas as an alternative method for writing graphics object data. This style may be regarded as more readable to the user. Figure 9-3 shows the graphics object of Box 9-3, a garage. Similarly the graphics object of Box 9-4 which represents a house on the same scale as the garage is shown graphically in Figure 9-4. These more detailed examples show how useful it would be to have symbolic names for the points used within these graphics metafiles. This extension of the three-dimensional graphics object file structure is discussed further in problem 9.11.

In Chapter 11, the algorithms inside the G3D compilation unit 'g3d_data' are discussed. The latter compilation unit is analogous to the unit 'g2d_data' in the G2D package, and it allows the building, storage, and display of solids (as lists of polygonal facets) with hidden-line removal. These examples of graphics objects can be defined by 'g3d_data' commands (which can also be used in graphics object metafiles) so as to give the true three-dimensional appearance of solids rather than representations as mere wire frameworks.

9.7 The three-dimensional axes problem

Drawing axes onto the graphics output for the general user Cartesian coordinate system is the problem considered here. The two-dimensional case is not difficult. For two-dimensions, a procedure:

```
draw_axes(dxpdiv,dypdiv)
```

is needed to draw both the x and y axes so they fill the current viewport, where 'dxpdiv' and 'dypdiv' are the intervals between tick marks on the x and y axes respectively. If the window was set with:

```
set_window(xmin,ymin,xmax,ymax);
```

then the axes will be correctly drawn by the commands:

```
plot_line(xmin,0,xmax,0);
plot_line(0,ymin,0,ymax);
```

The G2D package keeps a memory of the window limits so it will be able to make these calls. The next job is adding on the tick marks. A simple way of doing this is to have four subprocedures to place ticks from the origin to the four extremities. On every fifth tick mark, the tick mark is drawn twice as long. The normal tick marks are 1 mm long. G2D may 'move_to' and 'draw_to' using physical coordinates to place these ticks. Ticks along the x axis are drawn upwards thus:

    move_to(x,0);
    draw_to(x,tick_size);

Ticks on the y axis are drawn horizontal to the right thus:

    move_to(0,y);
    draw_to(tick_size,y);

For three-dimensional axes, a routine is needed such as:

    draw_3D_axes(dxpdiv,dypdiv,dzpdiv)

The problem is filling the viewport correctly. To draw the axes lines, three calls to the three-dimensional line drawing procedure are necessary:

    plot_3D_line(xmin,0,0,xmax,0,0)
    plot_3D_line(0,ymin,0,0,ymax,0)
    plot_3D_line(0,0,zmin,0,0,zmax)

However, what the values of 'xmin', 'ymin', 'zmin', 'xmax', 'ymax', and 'zmax' are, such that they lie on the border of the viewport is not yet known. One approach could be to use very large positive and negative values for them and then let the clipping routine fit the lines neatly to the viewport. This has two problems though. Firstly, it's not general enough, for some window sizes the axes could be smaller than the viewport. Secondly, it consumes too much processor time especially in drawing too many ticks off the viewport when the viewport is much smaller than the actual axes size. The right course of action is obviously to determine the values 'xmin', 'ymin', 'zmin', 'xmax', 'ymax', and 'zmax' which when projected and transformed neatly fit the viewport. However, the inverse projection is not available (projection matrices have zero determinant and are not invertible). A trick way of solving this problem is to project some three-dimensional points on each axes such as $(10,0,0)$, $(0,10,0)$, and $(0,0,10)$. Suppose that $(10,0,0)$ projects to (u, v) on the viewing screen. Now extend the line $(0,0)$ to (u, v) on the viewing screen until it strikes the window on the viewing screen. The extrapolated points are then used for drawing the three-dimensional axes. In this way the three-dimensional axes line problem is reduced to the two-dimensional ray problem – draw the ray from $(0,0)$ through (u, v) clipped to the current window defined by ('umin','vmin') to ('umax','vmax'). To draw the ray, the line segment:

    plot_line(0,0,u*,v*)

is actually drawn where:

$$u^* = k\ u$$
$$v^* = k\ u$$

and the real constant k must be positive and such that:

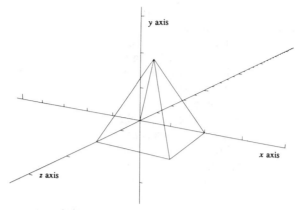

Figure 9-5 Three dimensional axes produced by the 'draw_3D_axes' procedure and a wire-frame pyramid. The x axis points to the right, the y axis upwards, and the z axis towards the viewer.

$$u^* = umax \text{ or } umin$$

or:

$$v^* = vmax \text{ or } vmin$$

whichever of the four possibilities is achieved with the smallest positive k value.

To place tick marks, the three-dimensional line plotting routine is kept looping until the projection of the three-dimensional base point is outside of the user window in the viewing plane. This means, for instance, that perspective projections will show the tick marks getting smaller as they recede into the distance, which is more realistic and suggestive of depth into the screen. (The procedure should also test when tick marks become less than a few pixels in size and then stop drawing them receding into the distance.) The direction that the tick marks are drawn can also allow the three axes to be readily distinguished even when they are not labeled. The tick marks for the x and y axes should be drawn in the same directions as for the two-dimensional axes drawing of G2D, that is, the tick marks are in the x-y plane pointing into the first quadrant of that plane. The tick marks on the z axis may be chosen as lying in the x-z plane pointing along the x axis direction. Figure 9-5 shows an example of using this three-dimensional axis drawing routine.

9.8 Three-dimensional graphics input

Hardware devices for three-dimensional graphics input are not widely available and are for the most part still in the experimental stage. One noteworthy three-dimensional input device allows the user to move a pen around an open box space. The pen emits electromagnetic radiation which is picked up by three detectors in corners of the box. The three-dimensional point is triangulated from the signal timing to these detectors in the same way that radar can position airplanes.

While other devices have been made, they are expensive and not generally available. This section will look at a simple way to digitize three-dimensional information by using a two-dimensional digitizing surface. In particular, what will be considered here is a software technique for digitizing three-dimensional shapes from a VDU screen that gives the viewer a feeling of three-dimensional depth.

When designing two-dimensional graphics shapes to be entered into a computer manually, a piece of graph paper with axes and horizontal and vertical lines lightly drawn is a most useful tool. For three-dimensional designs, it is common to use isometric graph paper. Isometric graph paper is different from ordinary graph paper in that the graph lines are not drawn horizontal and vertical but horizontal, and at +45 degrees to the horizontal and at -45 degrees to the horizontal. These lines help one to imagine a set of x, y, and z axes and the lines parallel to each of these axes. Isometric paper makes it very easy to visualize and draw three dimensional objects on a flat sheet of paper. Seeing the isometric shape of an object, it is easy to trace along the x, y, and z lines to determine the three-dimensional coordinates of each vertex.

The same idea can be applied to the VDU screen. First, the screen is blanked out and then a set of x, y, z isometric axes is drawn with the origin (0,0,0) at the center of the screen. Small tick marks may be drawn on the axes. It is helpful if the positive sides of each axis is drawn in bright white and the negative sides in a darker white or grey color. Initially a red dot is placed at the origin. The user can now give commands at the numeric keypad that will move the red three-dimensional cursor to define any point in three dimensions. The three-dimensional cursor in this method consists of two red lines which are parallel to any two of the x, y, or z axes parallels. (See Figure 9-6.) The default cursor shape has a red line from the z axis parallel to the x axis to the point P' of projection of the digitized point P onto the z-x plane. The second red line is from P to P' and hence is parallel to the y axis. In this shape the z axis is called the primary axis and the y axis the secondary axis. The z value at P can be read off immediately from where the primary line of the three-dimensional cursor strikes the z axis. The three-dimensional cursor can be thought of as two touching edges of a box having P and the origin at the extremities of a diagonal. The cursor always starts from one of the three axes and ends at P. It is clear therefore that there are six possible shapes for the cursor. The numeric keypad controls listed below allow the user to select any one of these six possible shapes. When a new primary line segment for the cursor is indicated, the old primary line segment becomes the new secondary line segment of the cursor.

Controls on the numeric key pad are as follows:

1   Moves the cursor one skip unit along an x axis parallel.
2   Selects the x axis as primary axis.
3   Moves the cursor back one skip unit along an x-axis parallel.
4   Moves the cursor one skip unit along an y-axis parallel.
5   Selects the y axis as primary axis.
6   Moves the cursor back one skip unit along a y-axis parallel.
7   Moves the cursor one skip unit along an z-axis parallel.

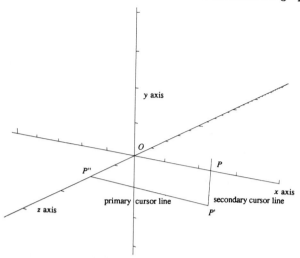

Figure 9-6 The three-dimensional graphics cursor produced by the 'read_3D_point' procedure. The axes are also shown as a reference.

8   Selects the *z* axis as primary axis.
9   Moves the cursor back one skip unit along an *z*-axis parallel.
+   Doubles the skip unit size (up to a maximum).
-    Halves the skip unit size (down to a minimum).
.   Resets the skip unit size to its default value (of 1).
*   Resets the three-dimensional cursor back to the origin.

These controls can be built into a three-dimensional input procedure called:

procedure read_3D_point(**var** ch : char; **var** x,y,z : real);

which is then analogous to the two-dimensional screen digitizing procedure 'read_point' discussed earlier. An alternative to having the '+' and '-' keys double and halve the coordinate increment (skip) size is to have them multiply it by 10 and 0.1 respectively, and this approach is called the *decimal gauge*. This enables the user to accurately locate any desired decimal coordinate location by careful use of the numeric keypad.

From Section 5.6 it was seen that two-dimensional graphics objects can be created from two-dimensional screen digitization with the procedure 'read_point'. This is because all graphics elements used in graphics objects were defined by parameters that are point coordinates. The procedure for doing this was called 'read_graphics_object'. Analogously for three dimensions, the procedure 'read_3D_point' can be used to create three-dimensional graphics objects by screen digitization and the procedure that does this may be called 'read_3D_graphics_object'. In the three-dimensional case, again all three-dimensional graphics elements used in three-dimensional graphics objects are defined by parameters that are three-dimensional point coordinates. For generalized graphics objects consisting of more than just the basic graphics elements of line segments, circles, arcs, ellipses, and so forth, the 'read_3D_graphics_object' procedure can be regarded as the procedure to create the graphics elements for the object. This is then saved to disk where other graphics commands such as attribute setting and screen set-up commands can be entered at the appropriate points in the file by using an ordinary text editor.

Problems

9.1   Prove that a circle in the general plane will be viewed (by the $z = 0$ orthographic projection) as an ellipse and derive its minor and major axes and their direction θ. In what way is the general ellipse transformed by this projection?

9.2   Determine the plane of an arc that passes through non-colinear points $P1$, $P2$, and $P3$ in three dimensions. Also determine its center, radius, and arc angle.

9.3   Use the results of problems 9.1 and 9.2 to implement the routines:

```
plot_3d_point(x,y,z)
plot_3d_line(x1,y1,z1,x2,y2,z2)
plot_3d_circle(x1,y1,z1,x2,y2,z2,x3,y3,z3)
plot_3d_arc(x1,y1,z1,x2,y2,z2,x3,y3,z3)
```

as suggested in Section 9.3.

9.4   Compute the center of an ellipse and its semimajor and semiminor axes lengths given three points in three-dimensional space (two focuses and a circumferential point). Implement the routine:

```
plot_ellipse(x1,y1,z1,x2,y2,z2,x3,y3,z3)
```

by computing these parameters and drawing a two-dimensional ellipse on the viewing plane.

9.5   Implement the procedure:

```
plot_sphere(x1,y1,z1,x2,y2,z2)
```

given its center $(x1, y1, z1)$ and a point on its surface $(x2, y2, z2)$. Determine a suitable manner for defining general ellipsoids by three-dimensional points and create a procedure for displaying them.

9.6   Write a procedure 'Bezier_curve(p,xarray,yarray,zarray)' to form a single Bezier curve section from $p+1$ points with components ('xarray[i]', 'yarray[i]', 'zarray[i]') for $i = 0$ to $i = p$. Write real functions:

```
B_spline_x(p,xarray,yarray,zarray,u)
B_spline_y(p,xarray,yarray,zarray,u)
B_spline_z(p,xarray,yarray,zarray,u)
```

which return the interpolated point $(x(u), y(u), z(u))$ for a B-spline defined by control points ('xarray[i]','yarray[i]','zarray[i]') for $i = 0$ to $i = p$. Write a procedure 'B_spline_curve(p, xarray, yarray, zarray)' that uses these functions to draw a continuous B-spline through the $p+1$ points.

9.7   Write real functions:

```
B_spline_x(p,xarray,yarray,zarray,u,v)
B_spline_y(p,xarray,yarray,zarray,u,v)
B_spline_z(p,xarray,yarray,zarray,u,v)
```

which return the interpolated point $(x(u, v), y(u, v), z(u, v))$ for a B-spline surface defined by control points ('xarray[i,j]','yarray[i,j]','zarray[i,j]') for $i, j = 0$ to p. Write a procedure 'B_spline_surface(p, xarray, yarray, zarray)' that uses these functions to draw a grid of continuous B-splines through the $p+1$ points for $u = 0$ to $u = p$ and $v = 0$ to $v = p$.

9.8   Implement the procedure 'read_3D_point' as described in Section 9.8.

9.9   Using the 'read_3D_point' procedure, write code that would allow users to create and save named three-dimensional objects by screen digitization. Use key codes 'P' for a point, 'L' for a line segment or polyline, 'A' for an arc, 'C' for a circle, and 'F' for a polygon.

9.10   Ensure that the 'display_object' procedure is extended to cater for bracketed coordinates as an optional form, and that it calls the three-dimensional routines including 'plot_3D_polygon'. Type in a graphics object file for the garage as in Box 9-4. Now write a program that loads in this graphics object, and displays and stores it in memory (via 'store_object'). The program should next call the procedure of problem 9.9 to create an additional object in the scene. Merge the two objects using 'merge_object' and then save the result to a new disk file.

9.11   It was observed in Section 9.6 that provision for symbolic point names within graphics metafiles would be very useful - making the file easier to read and less likely to contain errors. Extend the metafile structure to allow symbolic point definitions such as:

```
DEFINE A = (10,5,20)
DEFINE B = (15,5,30)
```

and allow the other commands to use these symbols, for example:

```
LINE A TO B
LINE A TO (10,5,0)
```

and so forth. The simplest way to provide for this feature is to modify the procedure 'load_3D_object' so that it builds and uses a symbol table - it is not necessary to make changes to 'save_3D_object'.

10

Three-dimensional transformations

10.1 General three-dimensional transformation groups

A transformation in three-dimensional space is a mapping from R^3 to R^3 usually depending on a set of parameters:

$$X' = F(X, A) \tag{10.1}$$

where $X' \equiv (x', y', z')$ and $X \equiv (x, y, z)$ are elements of R^3, points in three-dimensional space, and A stands for a set of parameters. By allowing the parameters in A to range over their valid domain of values, the functions in equation 10.1 form a set of transformations. This set of transformations forms a group in the mathematical sense if certain conditions are met. These conditions are:

1. There is an identity element $A = I$ such that $F(X, I) \equiv X$.
2. If $X' = F(X, A)$ and $X'' = F(X', B)$ then there are parameters $C = \phi(A, B)$, depending only on A and B, such that $X'' = F(X, C)$ for any X.
3. Every transformation has an inverse, that is, $\phi(A, B) = I$ can be solved for B in terms of A.

Since by the second condition A and B determine C, there must be a function ϕ such that $C = \phi(A, B)$. This function determines the 'multiplication table' for the group where the group multiplication operation is simply function composition. The three conditions are the sort of requirement computer graphics has for its transformations of objects in three dimensions. Three-dimensional transformations in computer graphics are therefore groups, and what follows here are the groups of particular interest.

The simplest group is the group of translational transformations:

$$X' = X + A$$

or in algebraic form:

$$x' = x + t_x$$
$$y' = y + t_y$$
$$z' = z + t_z$$

or in vector form:

$$\mathbf{x}' = \mathbf{x} + \mathbf{t}$$

where the group parameters are $A \equiv (t_x, t_y, t_z)$. Clearly the identity transformation occurs for $A = (0,0,0)$ and the group composition function is:

$$C \equiv \phi(A, B) = A + B$$

The set of all translations in three-dimensional space forms a three-parameter continuous (Lie) group.

The next simplest group is the group of dilatations:

$$X' = \alpha X$$

or in algebraic form:

$$x' = \alpha x$$
$$y' = \alpha y$$
$$z' = \alpha z$$

or in vector form:

$$\mathbf{x}' = \alpha \mathbf{x}$$

and the group parameter $A = (\alpha)$. In this case the identity transformation corresponds to $\alpha = 1$ and the group composition rule is:

$$\gamma = \alpha \beta$$

where $A = (\alpha)$, $B = (\beta)$ and $C = (\gamma)$. The set of dilatations in three-dimensional space clearly form a one-parameter Lie group.

Another useful group has the algebraic transformation equations:

$$x' = s_x \, x$$
$$y' = s_y \, y$$
$$z' = s_z \, z$$

The identity transformation occurs when the group parameters are $A \equiv (s_x, s_y, s_z) = I = (1,1,1)$ and the composition rule is:

$$C = \phi(A, B)$$
$$s_x'' = s_x \, s_x'$$
$$s_y'' = s_y \, s_y'$$
$$s_z'' = s_z \, s_z'$$

with:

$$A = (s_x, s_y, s_z)$$
$$B = (s_x', s_y', s_z')$$
$$C = (s_x'', s_y'', s_z'')$$

This set of transformations stretches or contracts objects by different amounts in the three directions and is obviously another group. It is a generalization of the group of dilatations, or to put it another way, the group of dilatations is a subgroup of the scaling group.

Another set of useful transformations is the set of stretch transformations. Using vector notation these are:

$$\mathbf{x}' = \mathbf{x} + (\alpha-1) \, x_u \, \mathbf{u}$$

where x_u is the component of $\mathbf{x}$ in the direction of the fixed unit vector $\mathbf{u}$, that is:

$$x_u = \mathbf{x} \cdot \mathbf{u}$$

The parameter in these transformations is $A = (\alpha)$. The identity transformation occurs for $\alpha = 1$ and the inverse transformation to that with parameter a has parameter $\beta = 1 / \alpha$.

Shear transformations are also useful in computer graphics. The vector equation of a shear transformation is:

$$\mathbf{x}' = \mathbf{x} + (\mathbf{b} \cdot \mathbf{x}) \, \mathbf{u} \qquad (10.2a)$$

where $\mathbf{u}$ is a constant unit vector and $\mathbf{b}$ holds the group parameters where:

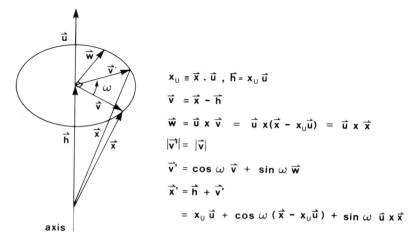

$x_U \equiv \vec{x} \cdot \vec{u} \;,\; \vec{h} = x_U\, \vec{u}$

$\vec{v} = \vec{x} - \vec{h}$

$\vec{w} = \vec{u} \times \vec{v} \;=\; \vec{u} \times (\vec{x} - x_U\vec{u}) \;=\; \vec{u} \times \vec{x}$

$|\vec{v}'| = |\vec{v}|$

$\vec{v}' = \cos \omega\, \vec{v} + \sin \omega\, \vec{w}$

$\vec{x}' = \vec{h} + \vec{v}'$

$\qquad = x_U\, \vec{u} + \cos \omega\, (\vec{x} - x_U\vec{u}) + \sin \omega\; \vec{u} \times \vec{x}$

Figure 10-1 The rotation of a vector **x** about an axis **u** through an angle of ω giving vector **x'**.

$$\mathbf{u} \cdot \mathbf{b} = 0 \qquad\qquad (10.2b)$$

In tensor form shears are:

$$x_i' = x_i + u_i\, b_j\, x_j$$
$$u_i\, b_i = 0$$

A final set of transformations is the set of rotations:

$$\mathbf{x}' = x_u\, \mathbf{u} + \cos(\omega)\,(\mathbf{x} - x_u\, \mathbf{u}) + \sin(\omega)\,\mathbf{u} \times \mathbf{x} \qquad (10.3)$$

where the unit vector direction **u** is constant and ω is the parameter. This formula can be seen by reference to Figure 10-1. When ω = 0, this is the identity transformation, and if equation 10.2a is solved for **x** in terms of **x'**, the inverse transformation to the one with parameter ω can be seen to be the transformation with parameter -ω. The composition rule can be proved to be:

$$\omega_3 = (\omega_1 + \omega_2)\ \text{modulo}\ 2\pi$$

It follows easily that three-dimensional rotations, as expressed in equation 10.3, form a one parameter Lie group. This vector formulation is better expressed in tensorial form:

$$x_i' = x_u\, u_i + \exp(e_{ijk}\, \omega_k)\,(x_j - x_u\, u_j)$$

where e_{ijk} is the alternating tensor in three dimensions,

$$\omega_i = \omega\, u_i$$

and the summation rule (that any repeated indexes in a term are shorthand for a summation over their entire range of values) is assumed. For $u = (1,0,0)$, the rotation is called a *pitch* ; for $u = (0,1,0)$, it is called a *yaw* ; and for $u = (0,0,1)$, it is called a *roll* . The reason why these special rotations are called pitch, yaw, and roll is that they are the motions of an airplane situated at the origin as shown in Figure 10-2.

Each of these groups is Abelian (i.e. commutative), but transformations from one group do not necessarily commute with transformations from another group. For example, a rotation by α about the x axis followed by a rotation by β about the y axis produces a different result to that obtained when first a rotation by β about the y axis is applied and then followed by a rotation by α about the x axis. This noncommuativity was also seen in the two-dimension groups, where for example rotation and translation transformations do not commute (see Section 6.8). Some transformations however do commute – such as the stretches from three groups based on orthonormal vectors $\{u, v, w\}$.

10.2 The 4 x 4 matrix formulation

The six kinds of groups mentioned in Section 10.1, translations, dilatations, scaling, stretching, shear, and rotations are all linear transformations in three-dimensional space. (If they were not then vector and tensor notation would not be applicable.) While the algebraic, vector, and tensor formulations of the transformation groups of the previous section are a convenient way of describing the various transformations mathematically, there are good reasons for implementing the transformations in software via the matrix formulation. The five groups are in fact all subgroups of the general linear group in four dimensions. Let us look at the 4 x 4 matrix representations of these transformation groups.

Using the homogeneous coordinate notations:

$$X = \begin{pmatrix} x \\ y \\ z \\ 1 \end{pmatrix} \qquad\qquad X' = \begin{pmatrix} x' \\ y' \\ z' \\ 1 \end{pmatrix}$$

The group transformations can be written in the form:

$$X' = A\,X$$

where A is a 4 x 4 matrix, the form of which is illustrated for each of the six groups.

1. *Translations* :

$$A = \begin{pmatrix} 1 & 0 & 0 & t_x \\ 0 & 1 & 0 & t_y \\ 0 & 0 & 1 & t_z \\ 0 & 0 & 0 & 1 \end{pmatrix}$$

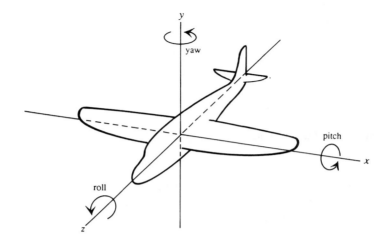

Figure 10-2 The pitch, yaw, and roll rotational motions of an airplane related to its intrinsic three-dimensional cartesian coordinate system.

2. *Dilatations* :

$$A = \begin{pmatrix} 1 & 0 & 0 & 0 \\ 0 & 1 & 0 & 0 \\ 0 & 0 & 1 & 0 \\ 0 & 0 & 0 & 1/\alpha \end{pmatrix}$$

3. *Scalings* :

$$A = \begin{pmatrix} sx & 0 & 0 & 0 \\ 0 & sy & 0 & 0 \\ 0 & 0 & sz & 0 \\ 0 & 0 & 0 & 1 \end{pmatrix}$$

4. *Stretchings* :

$$A_{ij} = \delta_{ij} + (\alpha-1) u_i u_j$$
$$A_{4i} = A_{i4} = 0$$
$$A_{44} = 1$$

5. *Shears* :

$$A_{ij} = \delta_{ij} + u_i b_j$$
$$A_{4i} = A_{i4} = 0$$
$$A_{44} = 1$$

6. *Rotations* :

$$A_{ij} = u_i \, u_j + \exp(e_{ijk} \, \omega_k) - \exp(e_{ilk} \, \omega_k) u_l \, u_j$$
$$A_{4i} = A_{i4} = 0$$
$$A_{44} = 1$$

10.3 Viewing three-dimensional graphics data

A three-dimensional graphics object is built from coordinate triplets (x, y, z). These have to be somehow mapped to the device coordinates (dcx, dcy) of the graphics output device. The natural way to do this is to select a plane in the three-dimensional space and project all vertexes down onto this plane. Points on this plane are then mapped to physical coordinates and thence to device coordinates for every output device. This plane is called the *viewing plane* and the mapping of three-dimensional points onto it is called the *viewing projection.*

A plane in space can be defined by a unit normal vector **n** and the distance of the plane from the origin p. The equation of the plane then has the form:

$$\mathbf{n} \cdot \mathbf{x} = p$$

(The normal **n** should be pointing away from the origin for p to be positive.) Alternatively, the unit normal **n** and any point **a** lying in the plane can be used. In this case the equation of the plane is:

$$\mathbf{n} \cdot (\mathbf{x} - \mathbf{a}) = 0$$

(because $p \equiv \mathbf{n} \cdot \mathbf{a}$). These two vectors **n** and **a** can be parameters to a procedure that defines the viewing plane.

Next the viewing plane must be *coordinatized* in some way; that is, a Cartesian coordinate system (x_{vp}, y_{vp}) must be defined on it in order for the projection function to be precisely specified. This can be done by providing two orthogonal unit vectors $\{e_x, e_y\}$ both lying in the plane which define the x axis and y axis directions within the plane. The vector e_x is the view right vector, and the vector e_y is the view up vector. These two vectors lie in the plane provided they are perpendicular to **n**:

$$e_x \cdot \mathbf{n} = 0$$

and:

$$e_y \cdot \mathbf{n} = 0$$

This means that $\{e_x, e_y, n\}$ form an orthonormal triad. Therefore, if e_x and n are known, for instance, e_y can be computed by a cross product:

$$e_y = n \times e_x$$

However, a point in the viewing plane must also be specified as the origin of this coordinate system. This is done by a three-dimensional position vector from the origin $(0,0,0)$ of the three-dimensional space coordinate system (x, y, z) to the origin of the viewing plane coordinate system (x_{vp}, y_{vp}). To save multiplicity of parameters, this vector may as well be the vector a used before to define the plane. Thus, in order to define a coordinatized viewing plane, four vectors, $\{a, e_x, e_y, n\}$, should be supplied. A procedure 'viewing_plane(ex,ey,n,a)' should be written to input these vectors and store the definition of the viewing plane.

Next, consider the various possible projections – the mappings from (x, y, z) to (x_{vp}, y_{vp}). These will be implemented as a procedure with the heading:

procedure project_point(x,y,z : real; **var** xvp,yvp : real);

By using this procedure, all of three-dimensional graphics can be reduced to two-dimensional graphics and all of the usual graphics routines that were studied in the package G2D for two-dimensional graphics are applicable. In particular, a call to 'set_window' will define a rectangular limit to the viewing plane coordinates and a call to 'set_viewport' will map this window on the viewing plane onto a physical viewport rectangle on the output display device. The next three sections cover the mathematics of three projections: the normal projection, the oblique projection, and the central projection.

10.4 Normal projections

In the normal projection every point P in three-dimensional space gets mapped to a point P' on the viewing plane such that PP' is normal (perpendicular) to that plane. The point P' is therefore also the closest point on the viewing plane to the point P in space. This definition will now be used to derive the mathematical equations of this projection. The reader should refer to Figure 10-3.

Let the vectors $x = OP$ and $x' = OP'$ represent the position vectors of the points P and P' where O is the origin of the three-dimensional coordinate system. Then $x' = x + PP'$ and since the vector PP' is normal to the viewing plane, there must be a real number λ such that $PP' = \lambda n$. The vector PP' is called a *projector* since it carries a point P, which is not on the plane, to a point P' which is on the plane. The value of λ can be determined since x' must lie in the viewing plane, that is:

$$p = n \cdot x' = n \cdot (x + \lambda n) \equiv n \cdot x + \lambda$$

so that:

$$\lambda = p - \mathbf{n} \cdot \mathbf{x}$$

Therefore the normal projection is given in vector form by the equation:

$$\mathbf{x}' = \mathbf{x} + (p - \mathbf{n} \cdot \mathbf{x})\,\mathbf{n}$$

and this can be written in tensor form as:

$$x_i{}' = P_{ij}\, x_j + P_i$$

where:

$$P_{ij} = \delta_{ij} - p^{-2} P_i\, P_j$$
$$P_i = p\, n_i$$

(and again $p \equiv n_i\, a_i$).

Having now found how to project a point P (generally) outside of the viewing plane onto the viewing plane as the point P', the final vector $\mathbf{x}'$ is however still expressed in terms of the three-dimensional coordinate system (x, y, z) and not yet in terms of the coordinate system on the viewing plane (x_{vp}, y_{vp}). To derive the viewing plane coordinates of P, it is necessary to take the inner product of the vector $\mathbf{x}'$ and the coordinate unit vectors on the viewing plane:

$$x_{vp} = \mathbf{e}_x \cdot (\mathbf{x}' - \mathbf{a})$$
$$y_{vp} = \mathbf{e}_y \cdot (\mathbf{x}' - \mathbf{a})$$

or using tensor notation:

$$x_{vp} = e_{xi}\, P_{ij}\, x_j + e_{xi}\, (p_i - a_i)$$
$$y_{vp} = e_{yi}\, P_{ij}\, x_j + e_{yi}\, (p_i - a_i)$$

It is clear from these equations that the normal projection is a set of linear equations. This means that matrix methods can be used in implementing the equations in software. The matrix formulation will be given in Section 10.7.

Normal projections are also called *orthographic* or *axonometric* projections. They are used predominantly in engineering drawings. In the special case when $n_x = n_y = n_z$ (each equal to $1/\sqrt{3}$ since $\mathbf{n}$ is a unit vector) the projection is called the *isometric* projection of an object whose principal edges are lined up with the x, y, and z axes. If any two only of the components of $\mathbf{n}$ are equal the projection is called a *dimetric* projection, and if none are equal it is called a *trimetric* projection for such an object. If $\mathbf{n} = (1,0,0)$ the projection is the *x-orthographic* projection or *side* view. If $\mathbf{n} = (0,1,0)$ then the projection is the *y-orthographic* projection or *plan* view. If $\mathbf{n} = (0,0,1)$ then the projection is the *z-orthographic* projection or *elevation*.

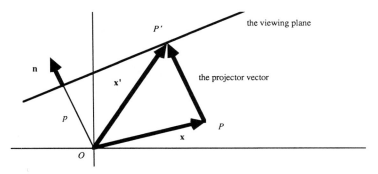

Figure 10-3 The normal projection from P to P' in the viewing plane. This figure shows a side on view of the viewing plane which has unit normal vector $\mathbf{n}$ and distance p from the origin O of the three-dimensional coordinates. For the normal projection the projector vector PP' of the position vector $\mathbf{x} = \mathbf{OP}$ of any point P in three-dimensional space is parallel (or antiparallel) to $\mathbf{n}$.

10.5 Oblique projections

For an oblique projection, every point P in three-dimensional space is mapped to a point P' on the viewing plane, such that PP' is at a certain fixed angle (not necessarily normal) to that plane. The normal projection is therefore a special case of the oblique projection. The oblique projection is also called the cylindrical projection. Note that the oblique projection requires an additional a vector, say $\mathbf{d}$, be specified to indicate the direction that points will be projected toward the viewing plane. The magnitude d of the direction vector $\mathbf{d}$ is irrelevant in this projection. This definition of the oblique projection is sufficient to derive its mathematical formulation. The reader should refer to Figure 10-4.

Let the vectors $\mathbf{x} = \mathbf{OP}$ and $\mathbf{x}' = \mathbf{OP}'$ again represent the position vectors of the points P. and P' where O is the origin of the three-dimensional coordinate system. Then $\mathbf{x}' = \mathbf{x} + PP'$ and since the projector PP' is in the direction of $\mathbf{d}$, there must be a real number λ such that $PP' = \lambda \mathbf{d}$. The value of λ can, as before, be determined since $\mathbf{x}'$ must lie in the viewing plane, that is:

$$p = \mathbf{n} \cdot \mathbf{x}' = \mathbf{n} \cdot (\mathbf{x} + \lambda \mathbf{d}) \equiv \mathbf{n} \cdot \mathbf{x} + \lambda (\mathbf{n} \cdot \mathbf{d})$$

so that:

$$\lambda = (p - \mathbf{n} \cdot \mathbf{x}) / (\mathbf{n} \cdot \mathbf{d})$$

Therefore the oblique projection is given in vector form by the equation:

$$\mathbf{x}' = \mathbf{x} + (p - \mathbf{n} \cdot \mathbf{x}) \mathbf{d} / (\mathbf{n} \cdot \mathbf{d})$$

This can be written in tensor form as:

$$x_i' = Q_{ij} x_j + q_i$$

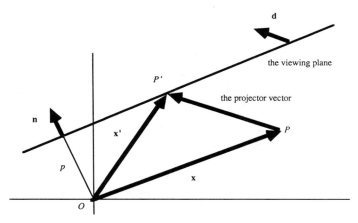

Figure 10-4 The oblique projection from P to P' in the viewing plane. This figure shows a side on view of the viewing plane which has unit normal vector **n** and distance p from the origin O of the three-dimensional coordinates. For the oblique projection the projector vector PP' of the position vector $\mathbf{x} = \mathbf{OP}$ of any point P in three-dimensional space is parallel to a given vector **d**.

where:

$$Q_{ij} = \delta_{ij} - d_i\, n_j\ /\ (d_k\, n_k)$$
$$q_i = p\, d_i\ /\ (d_k\, n_k)$$

(and again $p \equiv n_i\, a_i$). Note that the magnitude of **d** is irrelevant to the tensor Q_{ij} and vector q_i: scaling **d** up or down does not change these quantities.

Finally to derive the viewing plane coordinates:

$$x_{vp} = \mathbf{e}_x \bullet (\mathbf{x}' - \mathbf{a})$$
$$y_{vp} = \mathbf{e}_y \bullet (\mathbf{x}' - \mathbf{a})$$

or using tensor notation:

$$x_{vp} = e_{xi}\, Q_{ij}\, x_j + e_{xi}\, (q_i - a_i)$$
$$y_{vp} = e_{yi}\, Q_{ij}\, x_j + e_{yi}\, (q_i - a_i)$$

It is clear from these equations that the oblique projection is also a set of linear equations. This means that matrix methods can be used in implementing the equations in software. Note also that:

$$Q_{ij} \rightarrow P_{ij} \quad \text{and} \quad q_i \rightarrow p_i$$

in the special case when **d** and **n** are parallel or antiparallel, that is:

$$d_i = d\, n_i$$

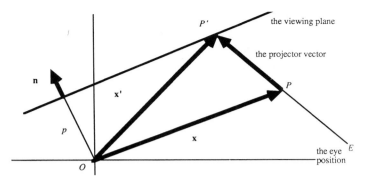

Figure 10-5 The central projection from P to P' in the viewing plane. This figure shows a side on view of the viewing plane which has unit normal vector **n** and distance p from the origin O of the three-dimensional coordinates. For the central projection the projector vector PP' of the position vector $\mathbf{x} = \mathbf{OP}$ of any point P in three-dimensional space is parallel to the vector EP emanating from the central point E which is the viewing (eye) position.

where d is a constant. This shows that the normal projections are a special case of the oblique projections. The normal and oblique projections are together called parallel projections since the projectors are always parallel lines.

Oblique projections are often used in engineering drawings. Two special cases of the oblique projection most frequently used are called the cavalier and cabinet projections. If $n_x = n_y = 0$, then $n_z = 1$ because **n** is a unit vector. If also $p = 0$, then the viewing plane coincides with the plane of the x and y axes, $z = 0$. The equations of the oblique projection then reduce to:

$$x' = x - z\, d_x / d_z$$
$$y' = y - z\, d_y / d_z$$

The components of **d** can have any values. The case where $\mathbf{d} = d\,(\cos\alpha,\ \sin\alpha,\ 1)$ is known as the *cavalier* projection, and the case where $\mathbf{d} = d\,(\cos\alpha,\ \sin\alpha,\ 2)$ is known as the *cabinet* projection.

10.6 Central projections

The central projection requires that a point (the central point) E, say, be specified first. The central point E must be outside of the viewing plane. The projected point P' for any point P in space is that point on the viewing line EP which intersects the viewing plane. The central point E is also called the *eye position* because the point P in space is projected onto the point P' on the viewing plane as if it were viewed by an eye at E. The eye position is also occasionally referred to as the view reference point. From this definition, the mathematical equations of the central projection will now be derived. The reader should refer to Figure 10-5.

Let the vector $\mathbf{e} = \mathbf{OE}$ be the eye position vector, and $\mathbf{x} = \mathbf{OP}$ and $\mathbf{x}' = \mathbf{OP}'$ again represent the position vectors of the points P and P' where O is the origin of the three-dimensional coordinate system. Then $\mathbf{x}' = \mathbf{x} + \mathbf{PP}'$ and this time the projector $\mathbf{PP}'$ is a fraction λ of the vector from P to E. Therefore:

$$\mathbf{PP}' = \lambda\ \mathbf{EP}\ = \lambda\ (\mathbf{x} - \mathbf{e})$$

so that:

$$\mathbf{x}' = \mathbf{x} + \lambda\ (\mathbf{x} - \mathbf{e})$$

Again the value of λ can be found from the requirement that $\mathbf{x}'$ must lie in the viewing plane, that is:

$$p\ = \mathbf{n} \bullet \mathbf{x}' = \mathbf{n} \bullet \mathbf{x} + \lambda\ \mathbf{n} \bullet (\mathbf{x} - \mathbf{e})$$

which gives:

$$\lambda = (p - \mathbf{n} \bullet \mathbf{x})\ /\ \mathbf{n} \bullet (\mathbf{x} - \mathbf{e})$$

Therefore, the central projection is given in vector form by the equation:

$$\mathbf{x}' = \mathbf{x} + (p - \mathbf{n} \bullet \mathbf{x})\ (\mathbf{x} - \mathbf{e})\ /\ \mathbf{n} \bullet (\mathbf{x} - \mathbf{e})$$

The central projection can be expressed in tensor form as follows:

$$x_i{}' = x_i\ + (p - n_j x_j)\ (x_i - e_i)\ /\ (n_k x_k - n_k e_k)$$

It is clear that this equation is nonlinear in x_i and so does not have a three-dimensional matrix formulation. However it can be expressed as a linear equation in homogeneous coordinates (because it is a lineo-linear relation, that is, a ratio of linear polynomials) and so it does have a four-dimensional matrix formulation. This can be seen by introducing homogeneous coordinates X for P and X' for P' where:

$$X_i\ = x_i$$
$$X_4 = 1$$

Now reexpressing the central projection equation as a rational polynomial equation gives:

$$x_i{}' = \{(p\ - n_j e_j)\ x_i\ - p\ e_i\ + n_k x_k\ e_i\}\ /\ (n_k x_k\ - n_k e_k)$$

so the transformation in homogeneous coordinates is:

$$X_i{}' = (p - n_j e_j)\ X_i\ - p\ e_i\ + n_k X_k\ e_i \equiv A_{ij}\ X_j\ + A_{i4}\ X_4$$

$$X_4{}' = n_k X_k\ - n_k e_k \equiv A_{4j}\ X_j\ + A_{44}\ X_4$$

After this *linear* transformation from X to X', it is possible to determine the components of the transformed point by:

$$x_i' = X_i' / X_4'$$

Note that this is the first case of a 4 x 4 transformation affecting the fourth component of the homogeneous coordinates: if X_4 is equal to one, after being transformed by A the fourth component X_4' is no longer unity. Four-dimensional homogeneous coordinates always correspond to three-dimensional coordinates by scaling the first three components down by the fourth component.

Finally to derive the viewing plane coordinates again use:

$$x_{vp} = e_x \cdot (x' - a)$$
$$y_{vp} = e_y \cdot (x' - a)$$

The vectors e, e_x, e_y, and a essentially represent a *synthetic camera*, which forms the two-dimensional images from the objects in three-dimensional space. Effectively, there is a camera placed at the eye position e which points in the direction $a - e$. The up direction for the synthetic camera is e_y, and the pan right direction is e_x. See Figure 10-6 and problem 10.7.

The viewing plane is oblique to the viewer if $e - a$ is not parallel to n. It may however be regarded as normal to the viewer by a change of origin of the viewing plane by setting a to the point of the normal projection of E (the eye position) onto the viewing plane. If E goes off to infinity, then we can replace $x - e$ by a constant vector (after suitable rescaling) d, and this shows that the oblique projection is a special case of the central projection.

The central projection is also known as the *perspective projection*. Three special cases are important. They are distinguished by the way they project axial lines, that is, lines that are parallel to the x, y, or z axes. If any two of the components n_x, n_y, and n_z of n are zero then the projection is called a *one-point perspective* projection. For this choice of n, two axial directions are parallel to the viewing plane, and one is normal to the viewing plane. The projections of axial lines that are parallel to the viewing plane are parallel lines that do not meet. However the projection of lines parallel to the axis that is normal to the viewing plane all intersect at a common point called the *vanishing point* (and hence the name one-point perspective projection). This point is in fact the normal projection of the eye position onto the viewing plane. If on the other hand only one of the components of n is zero then the projection is called a *two-point perspective* projection. In the projection of the axial lines for this case only lines parallel to the axis corresponding to the zero component in n are projected as parallel lines on the viewing plane. The other projected axial lines (extended to infinity) meet at two different finite vanishing points. Finally, if none of the components of n are zero then the projection is called a *three-point perspective* projection because the projected axial lines intersect in three distinct vanishing points, one on each of the three axes. (See problem 10.12.)

10.7 Concatenated graphics object transformations

The advantage of using 4 x 4 matrices for the transformations rather than using the algebraic formulations is that concatenation of transformations is much simpler. If a graphics object is to be transformed first by a transformation represented by the 4 x 4 matrix A, and then by a transformation represented by the 4 x 4 matrix B, then the concatenated (i.e. resultant) transformation is equivalent to using the 4 x 4 matrix C where $C = B A$ where matrix multiplication is used. If C is applied to the graphics object, then each point X (in homogeneous coordinates as a column vector) is transformed to X' by matrix multiplication: $X' = C X$. It is clearly a lot less computational work to compute $B A$ and then $C X$ for every point in the graphics object than to transform every point in the graphics object by the algebraic formula corresponding to matrix A and then transform every point again by the algebraic formula corresponding to matrix B.

Furthermore, all of the projections from three dimensions to the viewing plane presented above can also be represented by 4 x 4 matrices. Thus, let A be the 4 x 4 matrix of the projection, and let i and j range from 1 to 3 then the components of A in each projection are given by:

1. *Normal projection* :

$$A_{ij} = P_{ij}$$
$$A_{i4} = P_i$$
$$A_{4i} = 0$$
$$A_{44} = 1$$

2. *Oblique projection* :

$$A_{ij} = Q_{ij}$$
$$A_{i4} = q_i$$
$$A_{4i} = 0$$
$$A_{44} = 1$$

3. *Central projection* :

$$A_{ij} = (p - n_k e_k) \delta_{ij} - e_i n_j$$
$$A_{i4} = -p\, e_i$$
$$A_{4j} = n_j$$
$$A_{44} = -n_k e_k$$

Furthermore, the final transformation from three-dimensional spatial coordinates on the viewing plane to the two-dimensional viewing plane coordinates is also a linear transformation and can be represented by a 4 x 4 matrix, say B, where:

$$B_{1j} = e_{xj}$$
$$B_{2j} = e_{yj}$$

$$B_{44} = 1$$

$$B_{14} = -e_{xk}\, a_k$$
$$B_{24} = -e_{yk}\, a_k$$

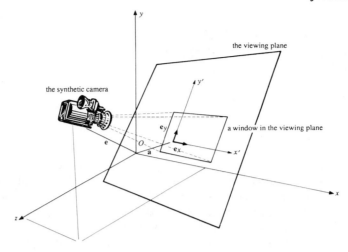

Figure 10-6 The synthetic camera projects three-dimensional graphics data to two-dimensional graphics data on the viewing plane.

and all other components are zero. Hence if M is the concatenated 4 x 4 graphics object manipulation transformation, and A is the 4 x 4 projection matrix to be used, then $B\ A\ M$ is the compound transformation giving the viewing plane coordinates of the manipulated, projected, and recoordinatized three-dimensional object:

$$X' = B\ A\ M\ X$$

and the viewing plane coordinates are interpreted from the first two components of X':

$$x_{vp} = X_1' / X_4'$$
$$y_{vp} = X_2' / X_4'$$

It therefore proves to be useful to have 4 x 4 matrix operations set up as procedures and built in to the three-dimensional graphics package.

10.8 Examples of graphics object transformations

A summary of the Pascal coding required to perform all of these transformations in three dimensions can now be made. The routines described here form part of the three-dimensional graphics package G3D. Firstly, three global types are needed, namely a type to store the 4 x 4 matrices, a type to store homogeneous coordinates, and a type to represent three-dimensional vectors, thus:

```
type
    matrix = array[1..4,1..4] of real;
    homogeneous_point = array[1..4] of real;
    vector_type = array[1..3] of real;
```

Three global matrices are stored by G3D:

```
var
    ctm,pm,rm : matrix;
```

The first is 'ctm', the current transformation matrix, which is a concatenation of all graphics object manipulation transformations issued to date. The second is the projection matrix, 'pm', which corresponds to a normal, oblique, or central projection. The third is the recoordinatization matrix, 'rm', the 4 x 4 matrix *B* described in the previous section, which converts points on the viewing plane to viewing plane coordinates.

Any viewing of three-dimensional graphics data first requires that the viewing plane be defined. Defining the viewing plane requires four vectors 'vp_x', 'vp_y', 'vp_normal', and 'vp_origin' (an orthonormal triad and a position vector) to be set values. These vectors are global (within the G3D compilation unit) and are set to default values by the G3D initialization procedure 'init_G3D'. The default values would be:

$$vp\_x = (1,0,0)$$
$$vp\_y = (0,1,0)$$
$$vp\_normal = (0,0,1)$$
$$vp\_origin = (0,0,0)$$

A user procedure may be provided to allow the user to set the vectors:

```
procedure viewing_plane(vp_x,vp_y,vp_normal,vp_origin : vector_type);
```

Now for the routines that create the various types of 4 x 4 matrices that will be needed. Firstly, the 'viewing_plane' procedure above should not only check and store the four vectors but it can also set up the recoodinatization matrix 'rm'. The procedure 'init_G3D' will call 'viewing_plane' using the default vector values above. Secondly, there is a need for procedures to set up the 4 x 4 matrices to represent the various projections and transformation to viewing plane coordinates:

```
procedure normal_projection;
procedure oblique_projection(dx,dy,dz : real);
procedure central_projection(ex,ey,ez : real);
```

These three procedures construct a global matrix called 'pm' (the 4 x 4 projection matrix). The procedure 'init_G3D' should call one of these to initialize a projection matrix for G3D. Thirdly procedures are needed to maintain the current transformation matrix 'ctm'. Many more procedures are required in this category as described below.

It is useful to have a procedure that makes the 4 x 4 identity matrix:

```
procedure identity_matrix(var a : matrix);
```

The procedure 'init_G3D' should call 'identity_matrix(ctm)' to initialize the current transformation matrix to no transformation. To set up the various graphics object manipulation transformations, procedures are needed to make the appropriate matrices:

procedure make_translation(tx,ty,tz : real; **var** a : matrix);
procedure make_scaling(sx,sy,sz : real; **var** a : matrix);
procedure make_rotation(angle,dx,dy,dz : real; **var** a : matrix);

In the 'make_rotation' procedure, the parameters 'dx', 'dy', and 'dz', are the components of the axial direction vector **d** for the rotation. The unit vector **u** used for the axial direction previously is therefore the normalization of **d**, that is, $\mathbf{u} = \mathbf{d} / |\mathbf{d}|$.

The package also needs a four-dimensional matrix multiplication procedure, say:

procedure multiply_matrix(a,b : matrix; **var** c : matrix);

a procedure for transforming points in homogeneous coordinate form given a 4 x 4 matrix:

procedure transform_point(x : homogeneous_point; a : matrix;
        var xprime : homogeneous_point);

and procedures for setting up and reading homogeneous coordinates:

procedure make_homogeneous(x,y,z : real;
        var xho : homogeneous_point);
procedure read_homogeneous(xho : homogeneous_point;
        var x,y,z : real);

If the fourth component of 'xho' is close to zero then an error may be flagged by the latter routine and the outputs set to a standard point such as the origin. Using these internal G3D procedures, it is easy to see how the procedure 'project_point' used in Chapter 9 for a special case would work in general. The procedure is shown in Box 10-1.

Box 10-1 A procedure to project a point into two-dimensions.

```
procedure project_point(x,y,z : real; var xvp,yvp : real);
var
    xho : homogeneous_point;
    compound : matrix;
    zvp : real;
begin
    make_homogeneous(x,y,z,xho);
    matrix_multiply(pm,ctm,compound);
    matrix_multiply(rm,compound,compound);
    transform_point(xho,compound,xho);
    read_homogeneous(xho,xvp,yvp,zvp);
end;
```

Now consider what high-level routines should be provided to the user for transforming and viewing three-dimensional graphics objects. Obviously the following are mandatory user routines:

```
init_G3D
normal_projection
oblique_projection
central_projection
viewing_plane
```

which initialize G3D and allow objects to be viewed. A simple but helpful user friendly routine to add in here is:

procedure set_vector(**var** a : vector_type; vx,vy,vz : real);

which helps users set up three-dimensional vectors in a readable way. High-level routines should also be provided to automatically create object manipulation matrices and concatenate them with 'ctm'. These would be:

procedure rotate_object(angle,dx,dy,dz : real);
procedure scale_object(sx,sy,sz : real);
procedure translate_object(tx,ty,tz : real);.

Users generally prefer to work in degrees, so the angle parameter in the 'rotate_object' procedure is input in degrees and the procedure converts it to radians before calling 'make_rotation' to make the 4 x 4 rotation matrix. After making the matrices, each of these routines calls 'multiply_matrix(a, ctm, ctm)' to concatenate the new transformation with previous transformations. The user will also need to be able to reset 'ctm' to the identity matrix occasionally, so as to forget old transformations and build a new one. Since 'ctm' is internal to the G3D and not available to the user a special routine may be provided:

procedure new_transform;

which simply calls 'identity_matrix(ctm)'. Finally the user can call 'display_object' to see the results of the transformations. Two approaches are used here. In the first approach, a procedure 'update_object' is provided to the user. This procedure simply applies 'ctm' to every vertex of the current graphics object. The stored data values are therefore changed at the time 'update_object' is called. A second approach is to have 'display_object' itself multiply 'ctm' into each vertex and then display each graphics element. In this second way, the transformed graphics object is seen but unless 'display_object' is called the graphics object data is not changed. The latter approach eases the burden on the user: there is no need to keep remembering to update the object. The latter approach can also be extended so that whenever the user issues a 'save_object' or 'store_object' command, the data is updated. Note that after the update 'ctm' should be reinitialized to the identity matrix so that multiple saves, stores, or displays do not keep applying the 'ctm' over and over (unless this is what is wanted in the package).

Consider the garage graphics object of Box 9-3 and suppose that it lies on a block of land with vertices (0,0,0), (60,0,0), (60,0,50) and (0,0,50). (See Figure 10-7.) In the middle of this block is a hill of height 5 units (in the y direction). The problem is to form the perspective view of the garage from 15 units above the top of the hill. The projection plane is the *x-y* plane. The following procedure calls will achieve the required view:

```
init_G3D;
open_input(garage_file);
load_3D_object(name);
central_projection(30,20,25);
display_3D_object;
```

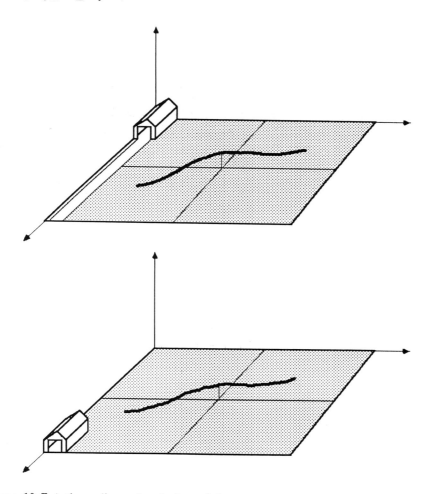

Figure 10-7 A three-dimensional view of the garage of Box 9-3 on a block of land, (a) with a long driveway, and (b) with the garage abutting the front boundary of the land.

Supposing now that the garage is to be placed abutting the main road rather than at the back of the block, and that it should be 50 percent longer than the standard garage. The following G3D calls will produce this picture:

```
init_G3D;
set_vector(ex,0,0,-1);
set_vector(ey,0,1,0);
set_vector(ez,1,0,0)
set_vector(a,0,0,0);
viewing_plane(ex,ey,ez,a);
open_input(garage_file);
load_3D_object(name);
scale_3D_object(1,1,2);
translate_3D_object(0,0,40);
central_projection(30,20,25);
display_3D_object;
```

where 'ex','ey','ez', and 'e' are declared as type 'vector_type' in the user program. The user must be careful to enter values of one for those directions not being scaled in the 'scale_object' call, and should also note the effect of scaling on the displacement value t_z = 40 for the 'translate_object' call. What, for example, is the effect of interchanging the 'scale_object' and 'translate_object' calls? An example of combining two graphics objects in one picture is shown in Figure 10-8. (See problem 10.3.)

Problems

10.1   Implement the procedures:

```
make_translation
make_scaling
make_rotation
identity_matrix
matrix_multiply
make_homogeneous
read_homogeneous
transform_point
```

Test these out on the second example given in Section 10.8 by hardcoding transformation parameters and printing out the final vertex coordinates for the graphics object.

10.2   Implement the procedures:

```
viewing_plane
normal_projection
```

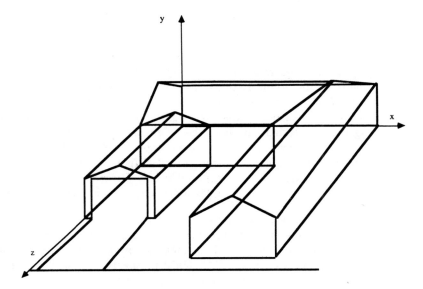

Figure 10-8 A three-dimensional view of a scene constructed from the graphics objects defined in Boxes 9-3 and 9-4. The garage has been translated by 10 units in the *z* direction.

```
oblique_projection
central_projection
set_vector
project_point
```

Test these out on the example given in Section 10.8 by hardcoding projection and viewing plane parameters and printing out the final vertex viewing plane coordinates for the graphics object.

10.3 Write code using G3D calls to produce the picture in Figure 10-8. Assume that the file 'buildings_file' contains first the graphics object called 'garage' as in Box 9-3, followed by the graphics object called 'house' as in Box 9-4. Note that path lines are to be added in the picture.

10.4 Prove mathematically that two rotation matrices with different axial directions **u** do not commute.

10.5 Prove that the formula $X' = B\,A\,M\,X$ for the compound transformation of a point as discussed in Section 10.7 does yield the correct viewing plane components (x_{vp}, y_{vp}) for the general viewing matrix B, projection matrix A, and model manipulation matrix M. Note especially the case where A is a perspective transformation that alters the fourth component in homogeneous coordinates.

10.6   The dilatation, scaling, stretching, shearing, and rotation transformations in Section 10.1 are all relative to the origin. These are in a sense, absolute transformations. Generalize each of these transformations to act about a central point **c** other than the origin. Express the transformations in vector form, tensor form, and define 4 x 4 matrices for each. Show how procedures for each of these transformations can be made by making a translation to the origin (by parameter - **c**), making the transformation about the origin, and then translating back by parameter **c**. Finally, construct globals and a user procedure called 'centre_point(c : vector_type)', and change the user routines like 'rotate(angle,dx,dy,dz)', 'scale(sx,sy,sz)', and 'translate(tx,ty,tz)' so that they perform their transformations with respect to the center **c**. Make sure that the center is initialized by 'init_G3D'.

10.7   Construct a three-dimensional turtle graphics style compilation unit for defining the viewing. Procedures should be provided to move and place a synthetic camera in the same way that a turtle robot is manipulated in three dimensions. Build it from the routines discussed for G3D. Only perspective views are used. The compilation unit should provide the following routines:

        set_tripod(x,y,z)
        pan(angle : real)
        dip(angle : real)
        tilt(angle : real)
        set_focus(f : real)
        zoom(distance : real)
        init_camera

Refer to Figure 10-6.

10.8   Build a three-dimensional multi-airship graphics system generalizing turtle graphics. The following routines should be provided:

        select_airship(n : integer);
        forward(distance : real);
        pitch(angle : real);
        yaw(angle : real);
        roll(angle : real);
        sky_writing(on_or_off : boolean);
        init_airships;

This package should be used in conjunction with the turtle graphics style viewing package of problem 10.7.

10.9   In photography, the fish-eye lens is used to obtain some unusual visual results. This lens can also be simulated with computer graphics (see Figures 10-9 and 10-10). The projection of the point P can be described geometrically (independent of

perspective projection   fisheye lens projection

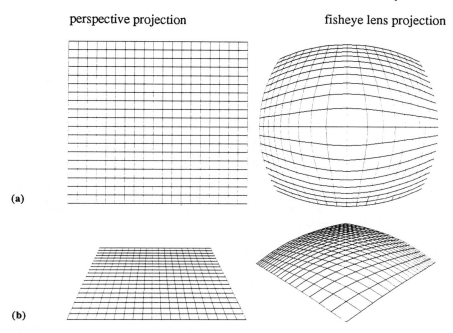

(a)

(b)

Figure 10-9 Perspective and fisheye camera lens projections of (a) a plan view and (b) an oblique view of a square grid.

coordinate systems) as follows (see Figure 10-11). Join the line from P to E, the viewing position, and find that point P' on PE which intersects a sphere of radius r centered on E. The point P' is then projected horizontally to the point P'' on the viewing plane which is tangential to the sphere. Using the vector notation of Section 10.6:

$$\mathbf{x}' = \mathbf{x} + \lambda \, (\mathbf{e} - \mathbf{x})$$
$$\mathbf{x}'' = \mathbf{x}' + \mu \, \mathbf{n}$$

The parameter μ is determined from the fact that P'' is on the viewing plane:

$$\mu = p - \mathbf{n} \cdot \mathbf{x}$$

and λ is determined by the fact that P' is on a sphere, that is $|\mathbf{x}' - \mathbf{e}| = r$ which leads to:

$$\lambda = 1 - r \, / \, |\mathbf{x} - \mathbf{e}|$$

Combining these formulas gives the projection transformation equations:

$$x'' = [r \, \mathbf{x} + (D - r)(\mathbf{e} - \mathbf{n} \, (\mathbf{n} \cdot \mathbf{e})) + (p \, D - r \, (\mathbf{n} \cdot \mathbf{x})) \, \mathbf{n}] \, / \, D$$

where:

$$D = |\mathbf{x} - \mathbf{e}|$$

Show that for the special case where $O \equiv P$ (so that $p = 0$), $\mathbf{n} = (0,0,1)$ and $\mathbf{e} = (0,0,-r)$ that the transformation simplifies to:

$$x'' = r\,x\,/\,D$$
$$y'' = r\,y\,/\,D$$
$$D = \sqrt{[x^2 + y^2 + (z + r)^2]}$$

and use these equations to draw fish-eye lens views of a grid as in Figure 10-9. Also prove (mathematically) that for large values of z compared with x and y, the fish-eye lens projection reduces to the central projection.

10.10 Show that the z orthographic projection used in Section 9.3 is a special case of the general equation for normal projections given in Section 10.4 where $p = 0$ and $\mathbf{n} = (0,0,1)$. Similarly derive the equations for the x and y orthographic projections using $p = 0$, $\mathbf{n} = (1,0,0)$ and $p = 0$, $\mathbf{n} = (0,1,0)$ respectively.

Figure 10-12 shows a typical drawing of three-dimensional cartesian coordinates on a flat two-dimensional page. From the drawing derive its inherent projection equations:

$$x' = x - z \cos \alpha$$
$$y' = y - z \sin \alpha$$

Show that this is a special case of the vector equation for oblique transformations as given in Section 10.5 with $\mathbf{d} = (\cos \alpha, \sin \alpha, 1)$, the special case being the Cavalier projection as mentioned in that section.

Derive the simplest case of the perspective projection equations from the general vector equation for central projections given in Section 10.6, namely:

$$x' = x\,/\,(1 - z\,/\,f)$$
$$y' = y\,/\,(1 - z\,/\,f)$$

by setting $p = 0$, $\mathbf{n} = (0,0,1)$, $\mathbf{e} = (0,0,f)$, $\mathbf{e}_x = (1,0,0)$ and $\mathbf{e}_y = (0,1,0)$.

10.11 The spherical eye projection (see Figure 10-13) maps a line PQ of length y to the arc RP' of length y' on the retina. Derive the equations:

$$x' = d \tan^{-1}(x\,/\,z)$$
$$y' = d \tan^{-1}(y\,/\,z)$$

and show that for large values of z compared with x and y, this approximates to the fisheye lens projection (which in turn approximates to the central projection).

10.12 Prove that if any two components of **n** are zero in the general central projection then the projections of lines in the direction of the axis corresponding to the non-zero component of **n** onto the viewing plane always intersect at one point. Show that this point, the vanishing point, is the normal projection of the eye position onto the viewing plane.

Consider the case when only one component of **n** is zero, and show that lines parallel to one axis are projected as parallel lines on the viewing plane. Show that lines parallel to the other two axes always intersect at two vanishing points, and determine the viewing plane coordinates of these points. (See Figure 10.14.) Determine the coordinates of the three vanishing points that occur when no component of **n** is zero. (See Figure 10.15.)

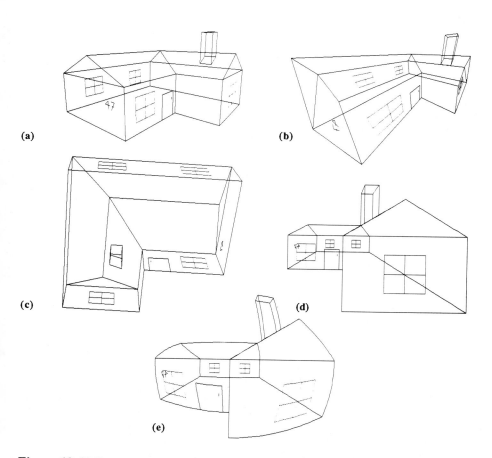

(a)

(b)

(c)

(d)

(e)

Figure 10-10 Four perspective views of a wireframe house ((a) to (d)), and a fisheye lens view (e) of the same house. The house number, 47, is used to tell whether the viewing point (*E*) is in front of the house or behind it.

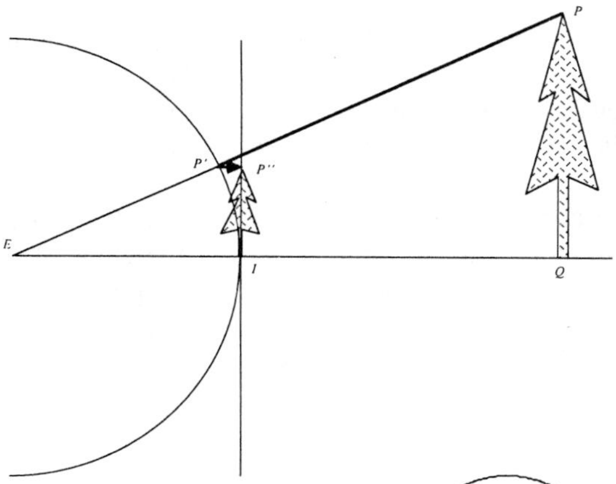

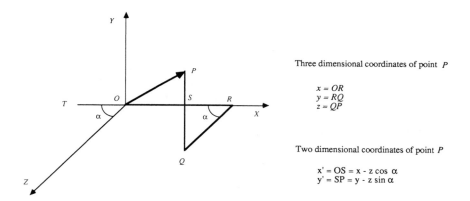

Figure 10-11 The geometrical construction of the fisheye lens projection.

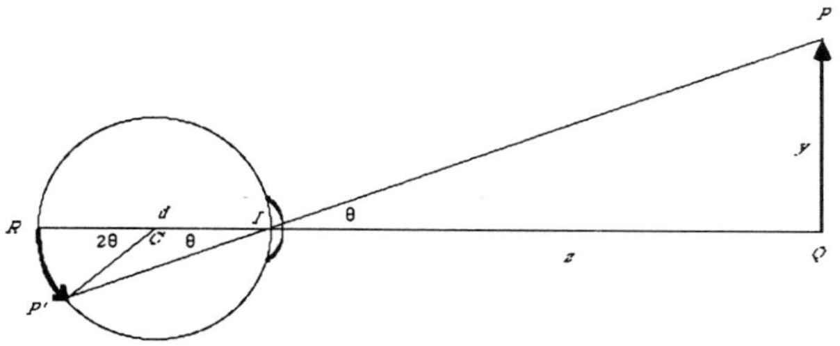

Figure 10-13 Rays from an object PQ of height y pass through the iris I and strike the retina at the back of the eye forming an inverted image. Assuming that the eye is spherical of diameter $d = RI$, the arc length of the image is $RP' = d\,\theta = d\,\tan^{-1}(y\,/\,z)$.

Three dimensional coordinates of point P

$$x = OR$$
$$y = RQ$$
$$z = QP$$

Two dimensional coordinates of point P

$$x' = OS = x - z\cos\alpha$$
$$y' = SP = y - z\sin\alpha$$

Figure 10-12 The usual representation of the three-dimensional cartesian coordinate system in mathematics when drawn on paper is a special case of the oblique projection. Visualizing this diagram as a three-dimensional picture and as a two-dimensional picture simultaneously provides a quick way of obtaining the relationship between the three-dimensional coordinates (x,y,z) and the two-dimensional viewing-plane coordinates (x',y'). In the three-dimensional interpretation of this picture $\alpha = \pi/2$ but in the two-dimensional interpretation $\alpha < \pi/2$. In the two-dimensional interpretation S is the point of intersection of the two lines PQ and OX in the plane. In the three-dimensional interpretation S is two distinct points in the same line of sight.

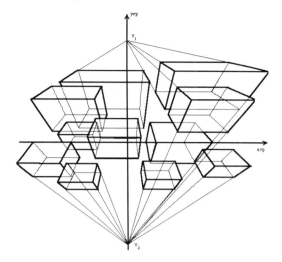

Figure 10-14 Unit cubes displayed with the central projection illustrate two-point perspective projections. The parameters used are $p = 0$, $\mathbf{n} = (0,1,1) / \sqrt{2}$, $\mathbf{e} = (0,5,4)$, $\mathbf{e}_x = (1,0,0)$, $\mathbf{e}_y = (0,1,-1) / \sqrt{2}$ with a two-dimensional window $(-4, -4, 5, 5)$. The cubes illustrate that y and z axial lines converge to the vanishing points V_1 and V_2.

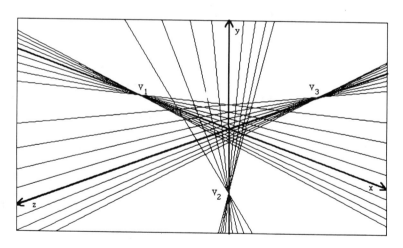

Figure 10-15 Axial lines generated with the central projection with $p = 0$, $\mathbf{n} = (1,1,1) / \sqrt{3}$, $\mathbf{e} = (5,5,5)$, $\mathbf{e}_x = (1,0,1) / \sqrt{2}$, and $\mathbf{e}_y = (-1,2,1) / \sqrt{6}$, in a window $(-25, -25, 20, 20)$. This is a three-point perspective projection since lines parallel to the x axis intersect at V_1, lines parallel to the y axis intersect at V_2, and lines parallel to the z axis intersect at V_3 on the viewing plane.

11

Three-dimensional graphics algorithms

11.1 Types of algorithms required

In order to turn three-dimensional geometric data into a graphics picture on a flat two-dimensional screen, many unique algorithms must be called upon. Clearly a projection algorithm, which converts three-dimensional points (x, y, z) to two-dimensional coordinate (xs, ys) that can then be mapped to device coordinates by the usual viewing transformation, is a fundamental requirement. The projection transformation can come in many varieties as seen in Chapter 10. Also, there is a need to clip three-dimensional lines and surfaces to a rectangular region of the viewing plane space so that the output graphics has a tidy viewported appearance. When lines, curves, or surfaces are partially or totally blocked by nearer surfaces, hidden-line and hidden-surface algorithms are required. The true color rendition of each point on a curved surface in three dimensions can only properly be determined by a technique called ray tracing that will be presented in more detail in Chapter 13.

A number of 'behind the scenes' algorithms are also used in three-dimensional graphics. Some of these are the list processing operations and the three-dimensional vector operations. These are discussed in Sections 11.3 and 11.4 respectively. Many intuitive geometric operations such as moving an object until it first touches any point of another object, or giving the high-level command to 'place one object neatly on top of another' also require considerable intelligence to be programmed into the software.

The attribute programming for three-dimensional graphics is much the same as for two-dimensional graphics. Three-dimensional text requires more attributes than two-dimensional text (discussed in Section 11.7). The three-dimensional graphics package developed in this book, G3D, does allow three-dimensional lines to be dashed lines but does not attempt to ensure that the dashes are also drawn in perspective so that they get shorter the further they are away from the eye. This problem in attribute programming is not a difficult change, and is left as an exercise for the reader.

11.2 Use of two-dimensional algorithms

The traditional way to clip three-dimensional line segments as produced by a routine like 'plot_3d_line' is to construct the three-dimensional equivalent of the two-dimensional window and clip the line to its boundary in analogy with the clipping of two-dimensional lines to the window boundary. The three-dimensional equivalent to the window is called the *viewing volume* . The standard viewing projection is the perspective projection and the viewing volume for this projection is also called the *viewing pyramid* or *frustum*. The simplest case to consider is when the viewing plane coincides with the plane of the x and y axes. These volumes are illustrated for this case in Figure 11-1 for the normal, oblique and central projections. Sometimes 'fore' (or 'near' or 'hither') and 'yon' (or 'far' or 'thither') bounding planes are also used. These are planes parallel to the viewing plane - and so for this choice of viewing plane, the fore and yon planes are simply defined by $z = zmax$ and $z = zmin$ respectively, and result in the viewing volume having finite rather than infinite size as illustrated in Figure 11-2. Any graphical objects that lie outside of this volume will not be displayed on the graphics output device. Since the boundaries of the window on the viewing plane are given by $xmin, ymin, xmax,$ and $ymax$, the viewing volume is defined by the inequalities:

$$xmin \leq x \leq xmax$$
$$ymin \leq y \leq ymax$$
$$zmin \leq z \leq zmax$$

for normal projections,

$$xmin + d_x z \leq x \leq xmax + d_x z$$
$$ymin + d_y z \leq y \leq ymax + d_y z$$
$$zmin \leq z \leq zmax$$

for oblique projections, and

$$f(z) \, xmin \leq x \leq f(z) \, xmax$$
$$f(z) \, ymin \leq y \leq f(z) \, ymax$$
$$zmin \leq z \leq zmax$$

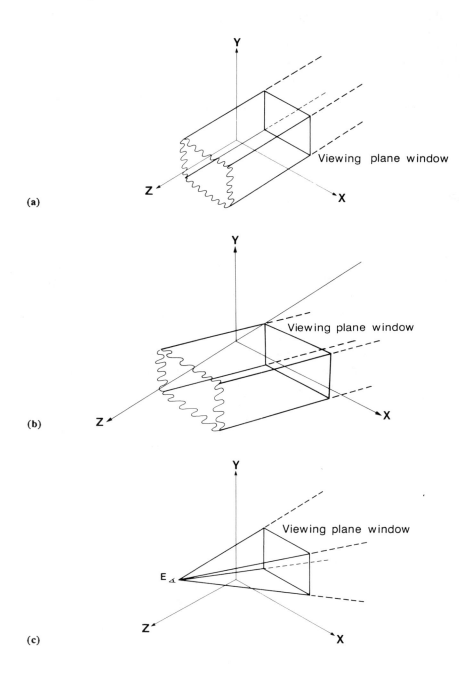

Figure 11-1 The infinite viewing volumes for (a) normal, (b) oblique, and (c) central projections where the viewing plane is the plane of the $x\,y$ axes.

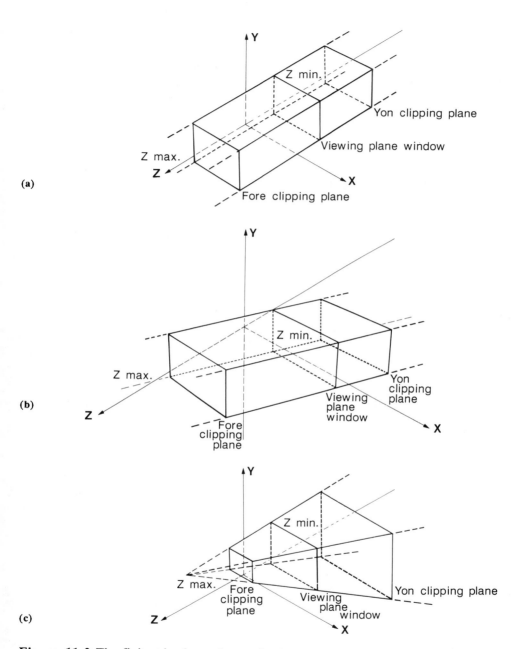

Figure 11-2 The finite viewing volumes for (a) normal, (b) oblique, and (c) central projections where the viewing plane is the plane of the *x y* axes showing fore and yon clipping planes.

for the central projection where:

$$f(z) = 1 - z \ / f$$

where (x, y, z) are coordinates of the eye system with the eye placed at $(0, 0, f)$. (These inequalities are easily obtained for the viewing volumes of any general projection transformation by inverting the projection transformation equations.)

The process of rendering three-dimensional graphics can now be described as follows. Three-dimensional world points are first clipped to the view volume. If the view volume is infinite this means checking all points against only four planes. If the view volume is finite (i.e. fore and yon planes are also defined) then this means checking all points in the three-dimensional scene against six planes. The points are then projected onto the intersection of the viewing volume and the viewing plane. This intersection is a two-dimensional window that is mapped to a viewport in two-dimensional normalized device coordinates. The NDC values are finally transformed to particular device coordinates on the graphics output device. In another method, the three-dimensional world (user) coordinates inside the view volume are mapped in a one for one correspondence onto three-dimensional NDCs. Three-dimensional NDCs are points inside the unit cube $[0,1]^3$. The third NDC coordinate is ignored and the first two map to device coordinates for the particular graphics output device in use. Similar mappings occur if physical coordinates are used rather than NDCs.

Rather than create new algorithms, such as clipping (see problems 11.1, 11.2, and 11.3), specifically for three-dimensional graphics, the plan in this book is to build on the routines that have been made so far for two-dimensional graphics. A simple alternative to the three-dimensional viewing problem described above, is to project the three-dimensional objects to become two-dimensional objects on the viewing plane, and then use the straightforward two-dimensional algorithms described earlier to give the generated graphics picture the feeling of realism. The clipping is easily done in two dimensions, and hidden-line and surface elimination can be accomplished by applying the two-dimensional clipping and covering algorithms. Thus the viewing process of this book is to project the three-dimensional coordinates (x, y, z) onto the viewing plane, then clip them to the two-dimensional window on the viewing plane (in viewing plane user coordinates relative to the eye), then transform to a viewport in physical coordinates, and finally conversion to device coordinates.

The viewing volume for the normal projections will therefore be an infinitely long rectanguloid and for oblique projections this is slanted away from the normal to the viewing plane. For the central projections, the viewing pyramid is used. Points behind the camera position obviously should be rejected. If a point to be projected coincides (to within 'epsilon') with the camera position then it should be projected to the center of the two-dimensional window on the viewing plane. This point is a singular point in the central projection equations and therefore must be carefully handled.

Through the reuse of the two-dimensional algorithms, the routines in 'g3d_plot' such as 'plot_3d_line' and 'plot_3d_arc' will simply transform the three-dimensional coordinates to two dimensions by calling the 'project_point' procedure (Section 10.4), and then calling the appropriate 'g2d_plot' routines. This has already been done in Section 9.2.

11.3 Computer representation of solids

Any polyhedron can be represented by a list of facets where each facet is stored as a list of vertexes. Other properties such as color, pattern, and surface texture may be associated with each facet, and likewise properties such as part number and weight may be associated with the polyhedrons. The facets may be any generalized region, as discussed in Section 7.4, allowed in the 'g2d_data' compilation unit. Clearly another compilation unit is needed to provide list processing functions in three dimensions in analogy with the unit 'g2d_data', and this unit will be called 'g3d_data'. The basic objects in 'g3d_data' are:

• the three-dimensional points table;
• polygons (each being a list of coplanar three-dimensional points in the table);
• facets (each being a list of coplanar polygons in three dimensions);
• polyhedra (each being a closed list of facets in three dimensions);

and each will need the nine list processing functions given in Box 7-4. Additionally there should be the 'draw_polygon', 'draw_facet', and 'draw_solid' procedures in the 'g3d_data' unit.

The points table may be a static array or have a dynamic structure. A static array of fixed size is the simplest arrangement. The following declarations set up this sort of structure:

```
const
    max_nr_points = 1000;
type
    point_type = record
        x,y,z : real;
        end;
var
    nr_points : integer;
    points_table : array[1..max_nr_points] of point_type;
```

If it is likely that the system will have points frequently added or deleted from it during the use of the graphics, then a dynamic list structure is more appropriate. This can be set up by the following Pascal declarations:

```
type
    point_type = record
        name : string;
        x,y,z : real;
        ptr : ^point_type;
        end;
var
    points_table : ^point_type;
    nr_points : integer;
```

Note : no header record is used for simplicity since there is to be only one list of points in 'g3d_data'. Care should be taken over deleting points since the other structures all depend on the points table. For this reason, it could be considered safer to have the points stored in a table rather than a dynamic list, and not provide the user with a point deletion routine. The user can then delete all other objects, polygons, facets, and solids, but to delete points would mean to delete the entire points table and all objects.

On the other hand for polygons, facets, and solids, there can be many of each of these kinds of lists so list headers are appropriate for them. Since an industry-extended Pascal like UCSD Pascal does not fully support the software engineering concept of *data abstraction*, the list processing functions must be implemented over again for every new base type. Consider a simple case where facets are not lists of polygons, but simply a single plane polygon. Then the routines in Box 11-1 would suit such a version of 'g3d_data'. The list structures are similar to those introduced in Chapter 7, namely:

```
type
    vertex_node = record
        ipt : integer;
        next, prev : ^vertex_node;
    end;
    polygon_header = record
        nr_vertices : integer;
        first, last : ^vertex_node;
    end;
    polygon_type = ^polygon_header;
    polygon_node = record
        polygon : polygon_type;
        next, prev : ^polygon_node;
    end;
    region_header = record
        nr_polygons : integer;
        first, last : ^polygon_node;
    end;
    region_type = ^region_header;
```

The points table inside 'g3d_data' can be used by more than just the polygon, facet, and solid structures of 'g3d_data'. Since all three-dimensional graphics elements, such as line segments, circles, arcs, spline curves, and spline surfaces, are defined by points alone they could also use the points in the 'g3d_data' points table. A routine in Box 11-1 ('get_3d_point') returns the coordinates of a particular point number in the table. The returned coordinates are then given to the specific graphics element drawing routine. The advantage of extending the use of this points table in this way is that other elements can be accurately tied in with the 'g3d_data' objects. At all magnification scales, the graphics elements will pass through the right points. This accuracy would not be provided if the defining points were approximated by using a graphics input routine for example.

Consistency checks on these objects must be made. For polygons:

1. The vertexes must all be coplanar.

Box 11-1 Routines for a simple version of the 'g3d_data' compilation unit.

```
function     get_nr_3d_points : integer;
procedure    enter_3d_point(x,y,z : real);
function     get_3d_point_id(x,y,z : real) : integer;
procedure    delete_3d_point(x,y,z : real);
procedure    change_3d_point(ipt : integer; x,y,z : real);
procedure    get_3d_point(ipt : integer; var x,y,z : real);


{The 9 List Functions for Polygons :} {A polygon is a list of vertices}
procedure    new_3d_polygon(var f : polygon_type);
procedure    append_3d_vertex(ipt : integer; f : polygon_type);
function     get_3d_polygon_size(f : polygon_type) : integer;
function     get_3d_vertex_nr(ipt : integer; f : polygon_type) : integer;
procedure    insert_3d_vertex(ipt,ivert : integer; f : polygon_type);
procedure    delete_3d_vertex_nr(ivert : integer; f : polygon_type);
procedure    delete_last_3d_vertex(f : polygon_type);
procedure    delete_3d_polygon(f : polygon_type);
function     get_3d_vertex(ivert : integer; f : polygon_type) : integer;


{The 9 List Functions for Solids :} {A solid is a list of 3D polygons}
procedure    new_solid(var s : solid_type);
procedure    append_3d_polygon(f : polygon_type; s : solid_type);
function     solid_size(s : solid_type) : integer;
function     get_3d_polygon_nr(poly : polygon_type; s : solid_type) :
             integer;
procedure    insert_3d_polygon(poly : polygon_type;ipoly : integer; s :
             solid_type);
procedure    delete_3d_polygon_nr(ipoly : integer; s : solid_type);
procedure    delete_last_3d_polygon(s : solid_type);
function     get_3d_polygon(ipoly : integer; s : solid_type) :
             polygon_type;
procedure    delete_solid(s : solid_type);


{Miscellaneous routines :}
procedure    init_g3d_data;
procedure    display_solid(s : solid_type);
procedure    hidden_line_style(style : integer);
procedure    load_solid(s : solid_type);
procedure    save_solid(s : solid_type);
```

2. There must be no self crossings in the edges of the polygon.

For facets:

1. There should be at least one polygon.

2. All polygons should be coplanar.

3. None of the polygons should intersect any of the others.

As shown in Chapter 7, some algorithms, such as clipping and covering, do not need to have the polygon edges in a region in any particular order – the list of actual edges being sufficient on its own. The three-dimensional algorithms in 'g3d_data', in particular hidden-line removal, will also not require the edges to be in any particular order. Therefore the following two extra check criteria for facets are not strictly necessary:

4. Nested polygons should be labeled in alternating senses.

5. The outermost polygon should be labeled in the anticlockwise sense.

In constructing a three-dimensional graphics package these two criteria may still be enforced so that greater assurance over the validity of facets in three dimensions is maintained. Criterion 4 concerns the *relative* orientation sense of polygons and criterion 5 concerns the *absolute* orientation sense of polygons. Of course, with regard to criterion 5, a polygon in a plane in three dimensions has no absolute clockwise or anticlockwise sense unless one side of the plane is selected as the top side. Specifying the 'top side' can be done by providing a normal vector to the plane, or else by asserting that the outermost polygon is anticlockwise.

In addition, a check must be made on 'solids'. As a random collection of facets in space does not constitute a polyhedron, a closure condition is required. The Euler formula:

$$v - e + f = 2$$

where:

$$v = \text{the number of vertexes}$$
$$e = \text{the number of edges}$$
$$f = \text{the number of faces}$$

applies to all polyhedral shapes whether they are convex or concave. However a set of facets that fulfills Euler's formula is not necessarily a closed surface. That is, Euler's formula is not a suitable criterion as to whether a set of facets form a polyhedron. A useful criterion for when a set of facets forms one or more closed surfaces is that every edge forms part of exactly two facets. (The analogy in two dimensions is that a set of line segments forms one or more closed polygons provided that every vertex is the end point of exactly two edges in the set.) It is not a difficult matter for a utility routine to check the data for a polyhedral solid to see if this criterion is met and that therefore the data does indeed represent a three-dimensional solid.

11.4 Three-dimensional support routines

Support routines are obviously needed for all the data consistency checks mentioned in the previous section. (See the problems.) Other support routines are also needed for other compilation units. In particular, 'g3d_view' needs a lot of three-dimensional vector routines. The vector type is defined as:

Box 11-2 Support routines for vector operations.

---

procedure set_vector(**var** v : vector_type; x,y,z : real);
    sets the components of vector v to x, y, and z
procedure scalar_product(s : real; a : vector_type; **var** b : vector_type);
    returns the vector b as the scalar s times the input vector a
procedure vector_sum(a,b : vector_type; **var** c : vector_type);
    returns the vector c as the sum of input vectors a and b
procedure vector_diff(a,b : vector_type; **var** c : vector_type);
    returns the vector c as the input vector a minus the input vector b
function dot_product(a,b : vector_type) : real;
    returns the scalar inner (dot) product of input vectors a and b
procedure cross_product(a,b : vector_type; **var** c : vector_type);
    returns the vector c as the vector (cross) product of input vector a times
    input vector b
function triple_product(a,b,c : vector_type) : real;
    returns the scalar which is the vector triple product of the input vectors a, b,
    and c
function norm(a : vector_type) : real;
    returns the norm (or length) of the input vector a
procedure normalize(**var** a : vector_type);
    returns the vector a normalized (that is converted into a unit vector)

```
type
    vector_type = record
        x,y,z : real;
        end;
```

Note that this is the same structure as for 'point_type', and in many versions of Pascal, variables of either type may be used interchangeably. Useful vector routines are those that assign components to a vector, form the scalar product, add vectors, subtract vectors, form the dot product of two vectors, form the cross product of two vectors, form the triple product of three vectors, return the norm of a vector, and normalize a vector. Pascal headers for such routines are shown in Box 11-2.

Two other useful vector operations can be included in this list. The first is a routine to rotate a vector about a given axis by a specified angle. This routine can be used in rotating the camera triad for instance. Figure 10-1 shows the relationships between vectors in a rotation and the derivation of the equation of rotation, equation 10.3, as discussed in Section 10.1. This equation can be used to write a procedure to perform the three-dimensional rotation and the result is presented in Box 11-3. The mathematical variable names have been preserved in the Pascal code. The inputs to the procedure are 'x', the vector to be rotated, 'axis' the vector that specifies the axial direction about which the rotation is to take place, and 'angle' the number of degrees for the rotation. Since it is possible that a program that calls this procedure may not pass a unit vector as the axial vector, the input vector 'axis' is first normalized to give the unit vector 'u' that is used in

Box 11-3 An implementation of the procedure to rotate a vector about an axis in three dimensions. The notations used are the same as those in Figure 10-1.

```
procedure rotate_vector(x,axis : vector_type; angle : real;
              var xprime : vector_type);
{Rotates vector x about the axis vector 'axis' through 'angle'
 degrees to become output vector xprime.}
const
    pi = 3.1415926;
var
    xu,cos_theta,sin_theta : real;
    u,xparallel,temp1,temp2,v,w,vdash : vector_type;
begin
    u := axis; normalize(u);
    xu := dot_product(x,u);
    scalar_product(xu,u,xparallel);
    vector_diff(x,xparallel,v);
    cross_product(u,v,w);
    cos_theta := cos(angle*pi/180); sin_theta := sin(angle*pi/180);
    scalar_product(cos_theta,v,temp1);
    scalar_product(sin_theta,w,temp2);
    vector_sum(temp1,temp2,vdash);
    vector_sum(xparallel,rdash,xprime);
end;
```

equation 10.3. Note that the procedure does not change the vector 'axis', and the program that calls this procedure may well expect the 'axis' vector not to be changed. The 'angle' parameter is not the ω of equation 10.3 because it is in degrees rather than radians. (Higher level users prefer to work in degrees.) Note that in the rotation, the component of the initial vector **x** in the direction of the axis vector υ does not change in the rotation. This component of **x** is called $\mathbf{h} = (\mathbf{x} \cdot \upsilon) \upsilon$ in the mathematical formula, but is called 'xparallel' in the procedure for clarity. The component of **x** orthogonal to the axis is given by $\mathbf{v} = \mathbf{x} - \mathbf{h}$. The procedure uses the vector support routine 'vector_diff' to obtain the vector 'v'. The vector 'w' perpendicular to 'u' and 'v' is next obtained by the vector support routine 'cross_product'. At this point in the code 'u', 'v', and 'w' form an orthonomal triad of vectors, and all the terms in the right hand side of equation 10.3 are known. By using the scalar product and vector sum routines, the terms on the right hand side of equation 10.3 are added together resulting in the rotated vector 'xprime' In this way the procedure in Box 11-3 implements the formula using the more basic vector support routines listed in Box 11-2. It can readily be seen how easily and cleanly the algorithm can be implemented once the support routines of Box 11-2 are provided. In passing, note that the magnitude of the axial vector 'axis' is not significant in this operation: the axial vector may equally well be a unit vector. It is however common to take the rotation angle as the magnitude of the axial vector and then the procedure for this operation only requires two input parameters rather than three.

The other useful vector operation is 'orthonormalize(a,b,c)' which inputs three vectors 'a', 'b', and 'c' and orthonormalizes them if possible by the Schmidt orthonormalization process. The three vectors are then returned as outputs together with the functional value of 'orthonormalize' which is a boolean saying whether the orthonormalization process was successful or not. The orthonormalization will be unsuccessful if the three input vectors are coplanar. This can be determined by seeing if their triple product is too close to zero.

A triplet of vectors defines a parallelepiped with one vertex at the origin. A fourth vector can be used to define the displacement of a parallelepiped away from the origin. There are a number of three-dimensional support routines that apply to parallelepipeds defined by four vectors. For example, routines are needed to determine whether a given point is inside a parallelepiped or not, to clip lines and curves to parallelepipeds, and to say whether two parallelepipeds intersect or not. The volume of the parallelepiped is given by the triple product of its three edge vectors.

11.5 Hidden-line and hidden-surface removal

Three-dimensional wire frame graphics becomes extremely difficult to interpret when the number of line segments involved grows large. There is ambiguity with even a small number of line segments as for instance in determining which panels of a wire frame cube are at the front of the cube and which are at the back side of it. Also when thousands of line segments are needed on top of each other the result is an uninterpretable blob of white (or whatever drawing color is being used). Solid geometry can be produced in computer graphics by the process of hidden-line removal. Figure 11-3 shows the difference between the wire frame display of a cube and the solid geometry view using a hidden-line algorithm.

How does a hidden-line algorithm work? In the example in Figure 11-3, there are 12 line segments in the displayed object and no more than 9 of these should be displayed at any time. Three lines must be 'hidden', that is, not draw in the graphics rendition. This example of a cube has a particularly simple solution to the hidden line problem. It will be

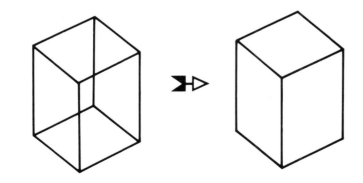

Figure 11-3 A wireframe cube versus a solid panel cube.

noted that the three lines to be removed all emanate from one vertex of the cube: the most distant vertex from the viewer. The algorithm has therefore only to determine which of the eight vertexes is most distant from the eye position, that is, for which:

$$(x\text{-}eye.x)^2 + (y\text{-}eye.y)^2 + (z\text{-}eye.z)^2$$

has maximum value, and then not draw those lines that have this vertex as one of their end points.

This method can be generalized to many convex volumes. The algorithm first determines which points are hidden and then line segment connections to these points are not drawn. For some convex polyhedrons, however, the number of hidden vertexes will depend on the orientation of the object for viewing. In this case the simple criterion for whether a point is hidden, that is, a search for the n most distant points (n being the number of points always hidden) is not applicable.

There are many other hidden-line removal algorithms that work only for special cases. An example of this sort of algorithm is the backside elimination algorithm which only draws the facet if the facet's normal is not pointing away from the camera. This method in general does not work if the polyhedron is concave, or if there is more than one polyhedron in the scene to be displayed. Another method is called the depth array surface elimination algorithm (or the painter's algorithm). This algorithm finds the centroid of each facet and sorts the facets by the distance of the centroid from the viewing position. The surfaces are then drawn with area fill from the back surface to the front. A problem with this algorithm is that one facet can be partly in front of another facet and also partly behind it so that complicated solid shapes are rendered wrongly. Furthermore area filling may not be desired or available on the equipment being used so that this algorithm would be inappropriate. Scenes of polyhedrons can be drawn by just lines, or by area fills (i.e. colored in polygon areas on the display rectangle). The algorithms that eliminate the hidden parts for the line drawings are called hidden-line removal algorithms, and the algorithms that eliminate the hidden parts for area-filled scenes are generally referred to as hidden-surface removal algorithms. Hidden-surface removal algorithms can produce the effects of hidden-line removal algorithms when they are restricted to monochrome graphics (i.e. one foreground color and one background color), and are therefore more general. Further discussion on hidden-surface removal and the correct rendering of three-dimensional scenes to be more realistic than scenes of polyhedrons alone, can be found in Chapter 13.

Consider now a more general approach to hidden-line removal. The concave polyhedron solid shown in Figure 11-4 consists of ten facets, twenty four edges, and sixteen vertexes. (It is readily checked that these conform to Euler's formula.) The hidden-line removal technique described here works on the two-dimensional projection of all the vertexes of the solid onto the viewing plane. The procedure to draw the polyhedron draws every edge of the solid in turn. To draw an edge L, the software looks for all intersections of the projected edge L' with every other projected edge of the solid. Intersection points on L' with line parameter λ strictly between 0 and 1 (i.e. in the open set $(0,1)$) are collected and sorted. These points are called here *critical points* on the edge L'. The edge L' is now considered as broken down into smaller pieces between the end points and critical points, and each piece is drawn one after the other. If a line segment L' has n critical points on it,

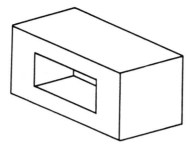

Figure 11-4 A concave polyhedron with hidden lines removed.

then the line segment is broken up into $n+1$ pieces for separate drawing. To remove the hidden lines, pieces are not drawn if they are invisible. To determine the visibility of a piece of a line segment, consider the midpoint M along that piece, and construct a line of sight from the eye (camera) position E to that midpoint. The midpoint is visible if EM does not intersect any facets of the solid. To determine this visibility of M, a loop must be made through all facets F of the solid finding those whose two-dimensional projection F' contain M' and then determine whether M is in front of facet F or not. This unique approach to hidden-line removal makes considerable use of the two-dimensional support routines (particularly containment and intersection of lines) that were described in Chapter 7. It is applicable to complex concave polyhedrons and multiple polyhedrons as in Figures 11-5 and 11-6. The algorithm is implemented in the procedure 'display_solid' indicated in Box 11-1. The routine 'hidden_line_style' also in that box allows the user to set the line attribute for the hidden lines to be no line, solid line, or broken line. (These are the standard attributes for lines as discussed for 'plot_line'.) Thus for hidden-line removal the 'hidden_line_style' parameter will be no line, but for the more general hidden-line processing the visible-line style and hidden-line style may independently be any available line style attribute.

Hidden line and surface algorithms can be categorized as predominantly object space or predominantly image space algorithms. In the former case the algorithm decides visibilities by geometric constructions in three dimensions as in the geometric hidden line processing algorithm above, and in the latter case visible portions are decided through operations on the pixels as in the painter's algorithm.

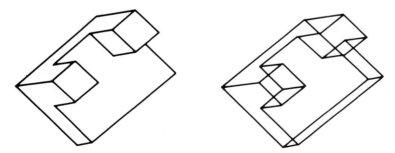

Figure 11-5 A more complex concave polyhedron typical of engineering drawings with hidden lines removed.

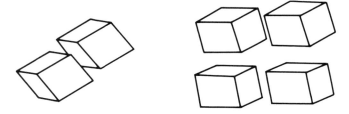

Figure 11-6 Multiple convex polyhedrons also require hidden line removal.

11.6 Intuitive three-dimensional construction operators

Three-dimensional geometry is a lot more difficult an area of study than two-dimensional geometry where one can easily experiment with pen, paper, ruler, and compass. Many problems in three-dimensional geometrical manipulations are difficult to visualize. A simple example of the three-dimensional visualization problems people often have, is to present a fancy looking regular polyhedron and then ask what shape the cross section is for a given plane passing through the polyhedron. Another difficult type of visualization problem is to be given a polyhedral solid and be told to rotate it by so many degrees about one axis, followed by so many degrees about another axis in space. Picture the new orientation of the solid and compare it with taking the original orientation and performing the rotations in reverse order. Unlike the simple two-dimensional rotation group, the three-dimensional rotation group is non-Abelian and this added complexity makes visualizing the effects of rotations on a solid much more difficult than visualization of two-dimensional rotation effects on two-dimensional objects. A final example of three-dimensional operational difficulties is provided in the famous Rubik's cube.

The construction of three-dimensional objects for graphical display is often referred to as *solid modeling*. One way of constructing three-dimensional objects for graphical display is to create a metafile such as Box 9-4 through use of a text editor. It is very difficult however to make sure that complex three-dimensional solids are correctly defined. As already shown, a simple three-dimensional solid can be defined by a list of vertexes, and a list of facets each of which is a list of vertex indexes. In this arrangement, it is difficult to make sure that the data is right. Displaying the metafile data can show glaring errors in the data but these can be hard and tedious to track down in the data file itself. For instance, without the facility of symbolic point names within the metafile, repeatedly used vertexes could easily be mistyped in several places. It is also too easy to forget a facet or two which will also cause errors but only in some views of the object. Such a data structure is very tedious to create in the first place anyway for even simple solids have many vertexes and facets. Working out the coordinates of every vertex can be very difficult (even for mathematically regular polyhedral shapes – see problem 11.10), and then making sure that every facet is accounted for is also difficult because the object has to be accurately visualized. The textual definition method for constructing solids leaves little opportunity for experimenting and creating new complex shapes. Graphics programs for solids modeling with simple intuitive constructional and editing functions are therefore most valuable tools.

Because three dimensions gives greater conceptual difficulties, it is important to give a lot of thought to the user interface in three-dimensional graphics application programs. The interface should at least be *user-friendly*. A user-friendly interface is one that provides a menu of commands in terms meaningful to the general public, and that reports on misuse of the system in messages equally meaningful. But the interface must be more than just user-friendly, it must be *intuitive*. An intuitive interface (coined here) is one that simulates the way a person would perform a corresponding operation on real objects. Rather than have the menu commands do things that suit the way computers operate, the operations available should mimic the things that people working with real three-dimensional objects would do. This is not the place to dwell upon the design of the physical side of the user interfacing – that is, whether it be by arrow keys, selected alphanumeric keys, or mouse with one or more buttons, coupled with pull-down (or pop-up) menus, or by digitizing pad command selection, and so forth – instead, the underlying procedures that allow an intuitive interface will be dealt with. These procedures will be called the intuitive procedures for three-dimensional graphics. They require fast interactive graphics.

Three-dimensional vertexes can easily be created visually using the 'read_3d_point' routine. To make three-dimensional wireframe structures the solids modeling program must allow pairs of vertexes to be selected so that an edge can be formed between them. This process is illustrated in Figure 11-7. Likewise selecting vertexes is useful for modifying polyhedral structures where it is desired to move a vertex to a new location as illustrated in Figure 11-8. Picking or selecting an existing vertex is thus a commonly needed function. It can be implemented using the 'read_3d_point' procedure by allowing the user to use 'read_3d_point' to place the three-dimensional graphics cursor near to the vertex of the polyhedron that is required. When an appropriate key is pressed to indicate

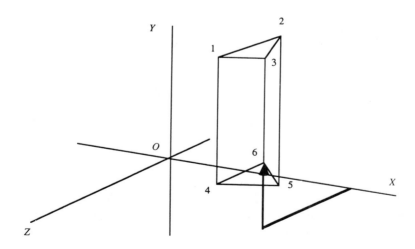

Figure 11-7 The use of the procedure 'read_3d_point' is sufficient for the interactive construction of wireframe graphics objects. It is first used to create the vertexes in three dimensions and then used (within 'select_vertex') to select pairs of vertexes to define the edges of the object.

that the selection has been made, the procedure should return with the coordinates of the nearest vertex in the 'g3d_data' data base. A procedure of the form:

procedure select_vertex(**var** x,y,z : real)

is therefore required for this intuitive operation. Note that the three-dimensional point returned by 'read_3d_point' is not ('x','y','z') but a point close by. The software looks up the vertex table for the polyhedron to find the nearest *visible* vertex to the point given by 'read_3d_point', and the coordinates of this vertex are then looked up and returned. A subsequent call to 'plot_3d_point(x,y,z)' in a different color, size, or point style, may be used to highlight the selected vertex. The point read in appears to *snap to* the nearest vertex.

A second basic intuitive operation is to select an edge on a polyhedron. This can work by calling 'read_3d_point' twice and the edge is selected whose end-point vertexes are nearest to the two points read in. Alternatively 'read_3d_point' might be used only once and the procedure returns that edge closest to the point digitized by 'read_3d_point'. A procedure for this would have the form:

procedure select_edge(**var** x1,y1,z1,x2,y2,z2 : real)

A third basic intuitive operation is to select a facet on a polyhedron by pointing to three vertexes. This routine might call 'read_3d_point' three times and find the facet in the list of facets for the polyhedron that has three vertexes nearest to the three points read in. A form for such a procedure could be:

procedure select_facet(**var** x1,y1,z1,x2,y2,z2,x3,y3,z3 : real)

These three select routines will be useful for manipulating polyhedrons. For example, it would be possible to translate a polyhedron by selecting a vertex, calling 'read_3d_point', and using the difference in coordinate values as the parameters for the translation. This parallel translates the polyhedron so that the selected vertex finally resides at the three-dimensional point read in. Another operation for intuitively implementing a three-dimensional transformation is to select an edge of a polyhedron as above and use this as an axis for rotating the polyhedron. By selecting any other vertex on the polyhedron and then using 'read_3d_point' to define a new point P in space, the selected vertex rotates into the plane of the selected edge and P and the rest of the polyhedron follows it. (To avoid an ambiguity, the selected vertex after rotation should lie on the same side of the selected edge as P does.) A polyhedron may also be rotated by selecting any three vertexes $P1$, $P2$, and $P3$ and digitizing a fourth point $P4$ in space by use of 'read_3d_point'. In this case the axis of rotation is the line $P1P2$ and the point $P3$ is moved into the plane defined by the three points $P1$, $P2$ and $P4$. Scaling transformations can also be done intuitively on a polyhedron by showing the minmax box of the polyhedron and allowing its corner points to be moved.

Another kind of intuitive operation on polyhedrons (but one not using selection of a vertex, edge, or facet of the polyhedron itself) is to define a line in space, specify an angle, and then rotate the polyhedron about the line as axis by that angle. The axis is

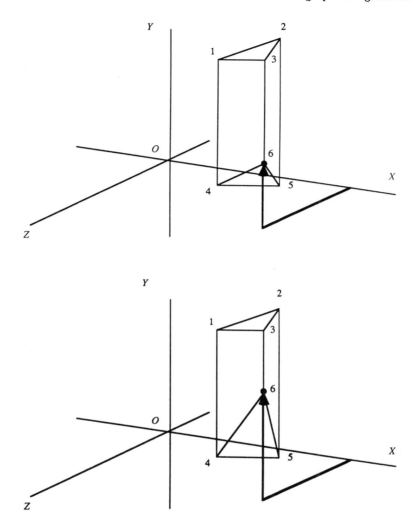

Figure 11-8 Any polyhedral vertex may be selected by using 'select_vertex' and then moved to a new position given by a call to the 'read_3d_point' procedure.

defined by two calls to 'read_3d_point'. Another operation would be to slice a polyhedron into two polyhedrons by defining a plane to pass through it. A plane in three dimensions is defined by three calls to 'read_3d_point'. If a vertex on the polyhedron is first selected (as above) and then a plane through the polyhedron is defined, then the selected vertex can serve to indicate which part of the polyhedron is saved and which part is thrown away (discarded from the data structure in 'g3d_data'). This leads to other general editing and constructional functions for polyhedrons.

Construction can be aided by providing some primitive three-dimensional solids for the user to build with. As an example:

procedure block(x,y,z,dx,dy,dz)

produces a rectanguloid (right parallelepiped) with one vertex at ('x','y','z') and the diagonally opposite vertex at ('x+dx','y+dy','z+dz'). The sides are parallel to the x, y, and z axes and have lengths 'dx', 'dy', and 'dz' respectively. More general solids to use are right pyramids and prisms based on any shaped polygon as base and with specified height. Slanted pyramids and prisms (the latter class including the general parallelepipeds) are also of use. Other primitives (involving curved edges) are spheres, cones, and cylinders. The user needs to be able to dynamically create these solids, saw them up into smaller pieces, and glue pieces together. An intuitive way of constructing new shapes from these supplied primitives is not only to allow arbitrary sizes, positions, and orientations of them, but to also allow set operations to be performed amongst the objects. When set operations are allow on objects which are themselves the result of set operations then arbitrarily complex shapes can result. The objects are treated as being sets containing an infinite number of points in space, and the typical set operations used in this way are union, intersection, and set difference of the objects. Figure 11-9 shows an example of performing these operations. These operations however tend to be computationally difficult with increasing difficulty the more they get applied (making the objects more complex shapes). This is because it is time consuming determining the exact surface of intersection of two or more complex three-dimensional shapes when objects are represented inside the computer by their bounding surface definitions. Another way of representing objects in the computer that reduces the amount of computational effort in these sort of operations is the use of octrees which store information about the internal space of a solid rather than its surface. The octree representation is the generalization to three dimensions of the quadtree technique for two dimensions. The sides of the bounding minmax volume of a solid are bisected yielding eight rectanguloids. Each of these rectanguloids are likewise subdivided if the rectanguloid is not totally inside or outside of the solid. The leaves of the octree are rectanguloids totally contained within the solid and the solid is the union of all the leaves. The leaves are usually small volumes and they are called *voxels*. Octrees however can consume considerable memory space, and will not be pursued further here.

As established above, it is necessary to be able to select points, lines, and planes in space to facilitate editing three-dimensional objects. These operations can use one, two, and three calls to 'read_3d_point' respectively. However, sometimes points are to be obtained in a different way such as by specifying a distance or a proportion. The former method needs a routine called, say, 'get_point_by_distance' with two points, $P1$ and $P2$, and a distance, d, as input parameters. This routine uses the two points $P1$ and $P2$ to define a line, and then the distance parameter d specifies the distance to the desired point, $P3$, from $P1$ along this line (in the direction of $P2$, if d is positive). The computed point $P3$ is then returned by the routine. In the latter method, a routine could be used called 'get_point_by_proportion' with input parameters $P1$, $P2$, and λ. The points $P1$ and $P2$ may be obtained by two calls to 'read_3d_point', and the parameter λ is the line parameter that specifies where the output point $P3$ is located on the line $P1P2$. A user interface that requires the user to type in distances, angles, and proportions, is of the earlier nonintuitive kind: it is a nongraphical interface, and slows down graphics editing. Therefore two other useful routines, 'get_distance' and 'get_angle', should be implemented.

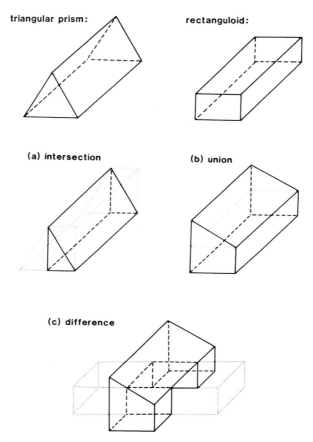

triangular prism:

rectanguloid:

(a) intersection

(b) union

(c) difference

Figure 11-9 An example of using set operations on two primitive three-dimensional objects - a triangular prism and a rectanguloid. (a) results from intersection of the triangular prism and the translated and rotated rectanguloid. The union of this and a new rectanguloid results in (b). A third rectanguloid is rotated and subtracted from the result of (b) to give the object in (c).

The former inputs two points $P1$ and $P2$ and returns the distance between these two points. The latter inputs three points, $P1$, $P2$, and $P3$, and returns the angle, $\angle P1P2P3$, that they form. This angle may subsequently be used in another procedure that uses an angle to determine a point in space. Note that routines that have points as input parameters, may receive these points not only from 'read_3d_point' but from any routine (such as 'get_point_by_proportion') that outputs a point. These methods show that some points, lines, and planes used in the construction of a solid may not finally reside in the data for that solid : they are merely temporary construction points, lines, and planes.

Suppose, for example, that the simple shape shown in Figure 11-10 is to be created. Start by selecting two points in space, say P and Q. These define a rectanguloid as opposite vertexes of a diagonal, and a call to the 'block' procedure will display it. Then

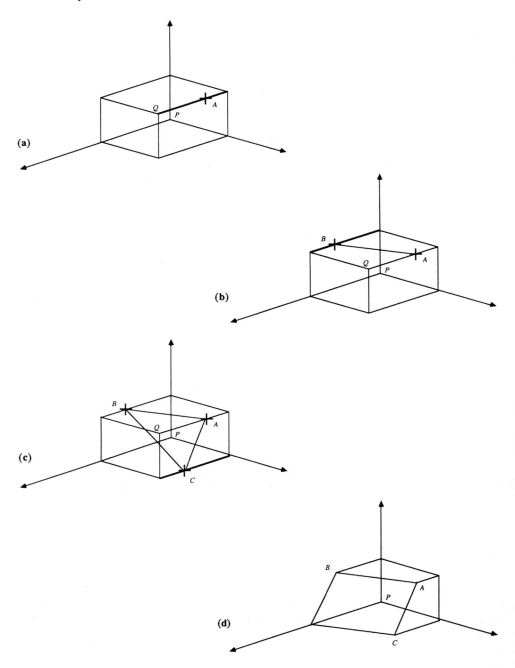

Figure 11-10 A simple example of editing a block in four steps (a) to (d). The procedures used are 'select_edge', 'get_point_by_proportion', and 'slice_solid'.

select a top edge on the rectanguloid and from its end points select a point A one third of the way from the first end point. Using a similar operation on a parallel edge of the rectanguloid gives a line AB on the top face of the rectanguloid. Repeating this on a third edge provides three points A, B, and C which define a plane that slices through the rectanguloid. By now selecting a vertex of the rectanguloid (say Q) and passing it plus the points A, B, and C to procedure 'slice_solid' (which is an intuitive operation) the edge is cut off leaving the desired shape. All the facets will be correctly defined and this shape can be saved to disk for reuse later. Clearly many construction points which are not recorded in the vertex table in the file were used in creating this object.

A similar intuitive operation is needed to cut prismatic holes out of solids. First a plane is defined by selecting three points in space (by any of the above point selection methods). From then on a routine similar to 'read_3d_point' is needed to allow the user to define a polygon in the plane, but unlike 'read_3d_point' the routine should restrict the three-dimensional cursor movement to remain within the plane previously defined. An alternative way of defining a base polygon for the prism is to clear the screen and use the two-dimensional routine 'read_point' as in Figure 11-11. At the end of the polygon definition process, the two-dimensional polygon is mapped onto the selected plane. This can be done by selecting three vertexes in the two-dimensional polygon and asserting that the first must map to some selected point A in the plane and that the second vertex must lie on the line AB where B is a second selected point in the plane. The third vertex has to lie on the same side of the line AB as a third selected point C in the plane. (This overcomes the ambiguity for just two points where the polygon may be flipped over the wrong way.) The process is illustrated in Figure 11-12. Having created the polygon base usually on a facet of the solid, another point in space must be selected to define the height of the prism. The height is the perpendicular distance of the latter point above the plane of the base polygon. This defines a prism that may cut a hole out of the solid, go right through the solid, or add a prismatic bump to the solid.

Two objects may be 'glued together' in the following manner. First three points, say, A, B, and C must be selected on a facet of the first solid. Next three points, say, A', B', and C', are selected on a facet of the second solid. To glue the solids into one, the second solid is (parallel) translated towards the first so that points A' and A coincide. The second solid is then rotated so that point B' lies along the line AB. Finally the second solid is rotated about the axis AB so that point C' is in the plane ABC. Again there is ambiguity in the final configuration. This can be removed by selecting a fourth point D and D' for both solids and specifying that in the final configuration D' must lie on the same side of the plane ABC as D does.

By using these sorts of intuitive commands, complicated three-dimensional solids can be constructed and modified. The software has to be able to maintain the data base of facets and vertexes. It is also desirable for the software to be able to merge adjoining coplanar facets. That is, if two coplanar facets have one or more edges in common then these should be removed in the list describing the facet so that the join lines do not appear when the object is displayed. This can mean that facets may merge into more than one polygon. As an interactive editing system, these methods assume that very fast interactive graphics and graphics computation (especially with hidden lines) is available. With fast interactive graphics, the user can turn the object as it is being edited and look at it from different positions and angles.

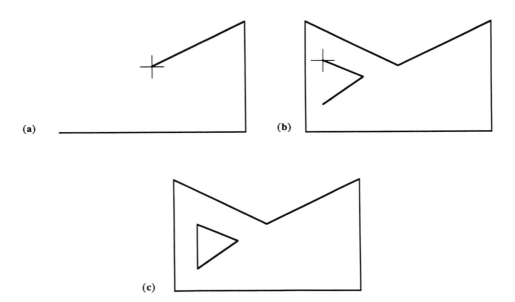

Figure 11-11 Facets can be created interactively by removing the three-dimensional scene temporarily, and digitizing two-dimensional polygons in the viewing plane using the two-dimensional 'read_point' procedure.

11.7 Three-dimensional text

The graphics text supplied in 'g2d_text' is two-dimensional only. This means that it will be drawn on the viewport via the viewing plane (two-dimensional user) coordinates and without regard to the three-dimensional user coordinates. In many cases this may be all that is needed. However it may be desired to add text to graphics that blends into the three-dimensional depth feeling of three-dimensional graphics. This means, for instance, that the text could be written on a plane other than the viewing plane and then it would be drawn smaller the further away the letters become in a message string under perspective projections. To achieve this, it may be thought that all that is needed is to replace the way the routines in 'g2d_text' call 'plot_line', the two-dimensional line plotting procedure, with similar calls to 'plot_3d_line' to obtain the appearance of three-dimensional lines. However this is not a simple change in the unit.

When text is drawn as graphics in three dimensions, more attributes are required to define how the text is placed and appears. Again among the requirements is a point from which the text starts. This could be specified by a three-dimensional vector, **a** say. Next a direction vector, say **b**, to show the base line direction that the text would be drawn in. A third vector, **c** say, is the 'up-vector' which shows which way is up for the text characters. The vector **c** should be orthogonal to **b** and both vectors may just as well be unit vectors. The three vectors **a**, **b**, and **c** then define a plane in three-dimensional space – it is the

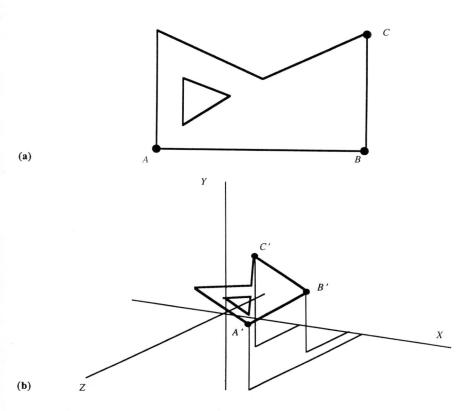

(a)

(b)

Figure 11-12 A facet can be positioned in three-dimensions by picking three of its vertexes such as A, B, and C as in (a). This step can be done during the two-dimensional design of the facet in Figure 11-10. The facet can then be placed anywhere in three dimensions by digitizing three points A', B', and C' through the use of 'read_3d_point'. Then the facet is translated so that A coincides with A' and rotated so that $\overline{AB}$ is in the line $A'B'$ and C lies in the plane $A'B'C'$ and on the same side of $A'B'$ as C' is.

plane through **a** and spanned by the orthonormal basis set {**b**, **c**}. A procedure such as:

procedure text_plane(a,b,c : vector_type)

could be set up to define the plane for text to be drawn.

    The procedure for building the routines of 'g3d_text' can now be visualized. This compilation unit can use the same graphics text definition files as 'g2d_text' for simplicity. This means that 'g3d_text' will produce the same stick figure characters, though now in three dimensions. The initial drawing point for each character is the lower left corner of the character as before, and 'g3d_text' must maintain this variable as an internal parameter. The current drawing point to be denoted by the three-dimensional vector **d** should be initialized to the origin in the text plane, that is:

$$\mathbf{d} = \mathbf{a}$$

The text definition files, it should be recalled, consist of commands of the form:

move u ,v

and

draw u ,v

with u and v being in user units relative to the current drawing point. These data are purely two-dimensional, and the conversion of them to real three-dimensional points is done as follows:

$$\mathbf{d'} = \mathbf{d} + u\ \mathbf{b} + v\ \mathbf{c}$$

A line from **d** to **d'** is then drawn by the 'g3d_plot' command:

plot_3d_line(x,y,z,x',y',z')

where:

$$
\begin{array}{lll}
x = d_x, & y = d_y, & z = d_z \\
x' = d_x', & y' = d_y', & z' = d_z'
\end{array}
$$

are the components of the vectors **d** and **d'**. For a 'move (u,v)' command the current drawing point components (x, y, z) are simply updated to the values (x', y', z') without graphics output.

The other routines inside 'g2d_text' can also be implemented in 'g3d_text' by carrying them over into the text plane. For example, text rotation, scaling, and slant transformations transform the (u, v) values in the viewing plane coordinate system to new values (u', v') in the same way as in two dimensions. The routines can have the same names as their two-dimensional counterparts but their implementations will be different as discussed above. Obviously the two compilation units 'g2d_text' and 'g3d_text' should not be declared as in use simultaneously because of this name clash. (Alternatively, the names in 'g3d_text' could be made different.) The unit 'g3d_text', therefore, consists of six routines analogous to the six 'g2d_text' routines plus the one above for setting the text plane. They are listed in Box 11-4.

Another kind of text for three-dimensional graphics is solid text. Each character is a polyhedron and hidden lines may or may not be removed for different effect. Solid text is particularly appealing in color as discussed in Chapter 13.

Box 11-4 Three-dimensional text routines in the 'g3d_text' compilation unit.

```
procedure load_font(filnam : string)
    loads a graphics text font from the specified file
procedure text_plane(a,b,c : vector_type)
    sets the plane for drawing text in three dimensions
procedure text_angle(degrees : real)
    defines the angle of the text line relative to vector b
procedure text_scaling(sx,sy : real)
    scales the text characters by sx,sy in b & c directions
procedure text_box(w,h,m : real)
    sets the box for text to fit in (width, height & margin)
procedure text_justification(justn : justification_type)
    sets the attribute of text justification within its box
procedure draw_text(u,v : real;message : string)
    draws the text from (u,v) relative to the origin a.
```

11.8 Three-dimensional metagraphics

Metagraphics commands are useful in three-dimensional graphics just as in two-dimensional graphics. They can be used to group three-dimensional commands into three-dimensional graphics objects that can be transformed by rotations, scalings, and translations, copied to multiple instances, nested into other graphics objects, written to disk, and read from disk. The transformation commands apply to the point data in the graphics object, and naturally have no effect on graphics setup, control, and viewing commands. As far as possible use has been made of the two-dimensional routines in three-dimensional graphics, and it can be seen that three-dimensional metagraphics can also be done with many of the two-dimensional metagraphics commands as contained in the compilation unit 'g2d_object'. Such functions as opening a disk file and loading a three-dimensional graphics object from it are obviously the same as for two-dimensional metagraphics. A list of commands in the 'g2d_object' two-dimensional metagraphics compilation unit that can be used equally for three-dimensional objects is shown in Box 11-5. The parameters used in these routines are the same as discussed earlier for 'g2d_object'.

Some metagraphics commands are unique to three dimensions however. Obviously the transformations of rotations, scalings, and translations apply to three-dimensional data only. These require an extra compilation unit which will be called 'g3d_object'. When three-dimensional plotting routines are called, it is undesirable for all the two-dimensional routines that are called from within the three-dimensional routines, to also be recorded in the graphics object metafile: only the three-dimensional plot command names should be recorded. One way this can be achieved is by having a new command, say 'meta_graphics(dim)' that says whether the two-dimensional or the three-dimensional graphics commands are stored. However, this means that the value of 'dim' should influence 'g2d_plot' as well as the 'g3d_plot' routines where they write into the current

Box 11-5 'g2d_object' routines useful in three dimensions.

procedure command_mode(execute,append:boolean)
    determines if graphics commands are executed or appended or both
procedure comment(str : string)
    insert a comment line into the current graphics object
procedure input_file(filename : string)
    open a disk file for reading a graphics object from
procedure close_input
    close the current input file
procedure output_file(filename : string)
    open an output file for writing a graphics object to
procedure close_output
    close the current output file
procedure load_object(**var** name : string)
    load the next graphics object into memory from the input file
procedure save_object(name : string)
    append the current graphics object to the current output file
procedure store_object(obj : object_pointer)
    take a local memory copy of the current graphics object
procedure restore_object(obj : object_pointer)
    copy the specified graphics object to be the current graphics object
procedure merge_object(obj : object_pointer)
    append the specified graphics object to the current graphics object
procedure display_object
    display the current graphics object
procedure display(obj : object_pointer)
    display the specified graphics object
procedure zero_object
    empty the current graphics object
procedure print_object
    print out the commands in the current graphics object

Box 11-6 Routines in the compilation unit 'g3d_object'.

procedure meta_graphics(dim)
    sets the metagraphics dimension to 2 or 3
procedure rotate_3d_object(axis : line_segment_type; theta : real)
    rotates the current graphics object about the specified axis
procedure scale_3d_object(axis : line_segment_type; scale : real)
    scales the current graphics object by the scale factor along the specified
    axis
procedure translate_3d_object(displ : vector_type)
    translates the current graphics object by the given displacement

graphics object metafile: the G2D routines would have to be recoded for the sake of G3D metagraphics. In a better approach, the procedure 'meta_graphics(dim)' is not required and G3D routines are treated like any other routine for recording into the current graphics object: any G3D routines that are called will not cause any G2D routines called from within the G3D routines to also be recorded because the 'append' flag is modified (saved and set to 'false' then later restored) within the G3D routines when necessary. In this approach, two-dimensional and three-dimensional transformations can be applied to the graphics objects without confusion since two-dimensional transformations will only affect the coordinate parameters of G2D routines and three-dimensional transformations will only affect the coordinate parameters of G3D routines. Box 11-6 shows the procedures to be put into 'g3d_object'.

Problems

11.1 Generalize the simple two-dimensional line clipping algorithm of Section 7.2 to the clipping of three-dimensional line segments defined by end-point coordinates (x_1,y_1,z_1) and (x_2,y_2,z_2) to the rectanguloid viewing volume of the normal projection.

11.2 Rewrite the algorithm in problem 11.1 along the lines of the improved clipping method using parametrized lines as given in Chapter 7. That is, consider the line to be clipped as given by:

$$x = (1-\lambda)\, x_1 + \lambda\, x_2$$
$$y = (1-\lambda)\, y_1 + \lambda\, y_2$$
$$z = (1-\lambda)\, z_1 + \lambda\, z_2$$

Next obtain the λ values for intersection of this line with the six planes that bound the view volume. The best way is to use the inequations that define the view volume rather than the exact equations that define each plane. The inequations below yield six inequalities for λ:

$$x \geq f(z)\ xmin \qquad x \leq f(z)\ xmax$$
$$y \geq f(z)\ ymin \qquad y \leq f(z)\ ymax$$
$$z \geq zmin \qquad z \leq zmax$$

If there are any values of λ that simultaneously satisfy these six inequalities and also lie in [0,1] then the line will be plotted for values of λ in the solution set.

11.3 Write a general procedure for clipping a three-dimensional line segment to any convex hull. The convex hull is a polyhedron defined by n surfaces and the volume that they carve out of space, that is:

$$a_{1j}\, x + a_{2j}\, y + a_{3j}\, z \le b_j$$

for $j = 1$ to $j = n$. The algorithm used should be a straightforward generalization of the algorithm of problem 11.2.

11.4   Generalize Euler's formula to n -dimensions as:

$$N_n = \Sigma_{i\,=\,0\;\text{to}\;n}\; (-1)^n\; N_i$$

showing how this conforms to the usual Euler formula in three dimensions and how it applies to two-dimensional regions. Note how the generalized formula applies to connected and disconnected regions for dimension $n = 2$ and $n = 3$. Find two-dimensional cases and three-dimensional cases that if a set of lines segments in the former case, and facets in the latter apply the generalized rule in the respective dimension, then this does not guarantee that the sets are closed in two and three dimensions.

11.5   Prove that if given any set of line segments from which are extracted the set of end points of these line segments, and if every end point is an end point of exactly two line segments in the set, then the line segments form a set of closed polygons which may be convex or concave. Similarly prove that if given any set of planar regions (lists of plane polygons as in Chapter 7), called facets, and the set of edges bounding these facets are extracted, then if every edge is common to exactly two facets in the set, the facets form a set of closed polyhedrons which may be convex or concave.

11.6   Implement the vector procedures listed in Box 11-2 as an independent compilation unit called 'g3d_support'. Implement the procedure 'rotate_vector' as presented in Box 11-3 and include it in 'g3d_support' as well. Implement the 'orthonormalize(a,b,c)' procedure described in Section 11.4 and include it in the unit 'g3d_support'.

11.7   Implement the compilation unit 'g3d_data' where facets are single polygons, setting up the routines shown in Box 11-1 as the user interface to the unit. Implement the hidden-line removal algorithm as given at the end of Section 11.5 together with the routine 'hidden_line_style' to set the appearance of the hidden lines.

11.8   Generalize the 'g3d_data' compilation unit of problem 11.7 to allow facets to be lists of polygons rather than just a single polygon. Write routines to perform the consistency checks detailed in Section 11.3 for polygons, facets, and solids.

11.9   Implement the intuitive operators discussed in Section 11.6 with the following procedure names:

```
select_vertex
select_edge
select_facet
translate_solid
turn_solid (such that a selected edge P1P2 is in the line P1P3)
rotate_solid (by a given angle about a given axis)
slice_solid
```

Also implement the useful routines:

```
get_point_by_distance        (or a more abbreviated name)
get_point_by_proportion      (or a more abbreviated name)
get_distance
get_angle
```

11.10 Work out algebraically the exact coordinates of the vertexes of the five Platonic solids. This problem requires considerable thought to even think of a method of attack for the more difficult shapes such as the dodecahedron and icosahedron. One method suggested here is to first work out the vertexes of the regular polygon in the plane that is used for the facets. Now use algebraic *folding_operators* that rotate a polygon (or any points) out of the plane by any angle. Determine the angle by the requirement that when two polygon faces are folded separately up out of the flat plane two edges of these polygons will become coincident.

12

Three-dimensional graphics packages

12.1 Extending two-dimensional packages with three-dimensional routines

There are a variety of ways of constructing a three-dimensional graphics package. One method is to construct the graphics package as three-dimensional from the beginning. The user would then normally be doing three-dimensional graphics. If only two-dimensional graphics was wanted then essentially all the three-dimensional routines can be used but with z set to zero throughout. The two-dimensional graphics output primitives are then considered to be just a special case of the three-dimensional graphics output primitives – the case when the the third coordinate is always zero. In other three-dimensional GSPs of this kind, a special routine is called by the user to assert whether two- or three-dimensional graphics will be done with the default being three-dimensional graphics again. If two-dimensional graphics is set then the system essentially sets all z coordinate values to zero saving the user from doing that chore. In both of these methods, the three-dimensional routines and the two-dimensional routines are all embedded within the one large compilation unit.

There is another approach to three-dimensional GSP construction. In this approach, the three-dimensional graphics package is based upon an underlying two-dimensional graphics package, rather than being constructed independently. This aids in development and provides a simpler and consistent package for the user. The reason that this is possible is that the three-dimensional data must eventually be transformed to two-dimensional representation for viewing on standard (two-dimensional) graphics output devices. One way of producing three-dimensional graphics would be to make the user first define a plane in the three-dimensional space, and then the user would call the two-dimensional package routines to place graphics entities on that plane. The viewing algorithms of the three-dimensional package would then ensure that the two-dimensional graphics produced would have the correct three-dimensional appearance. In this scheme, no three-dimensional graphics primitives would actually be provided – the user instead selects planes in three-dimensions and writes on these planes using the two-dimensional output primitives.

An alternative approach to three-dimensional graphics, and one that also implements graphics output only via an underlying two-dimensional graphics package, is to supply three-dimensional graphics primitives to the user but have the three-dimensional graphics elements immediately projected onto the two-dimensional viewing plane and then implemented as two-dimensional graphics elements by the two-dimensional graphics package. This means that all three-dimensional graphics output primitives are actually implemented as calls to the two-dimensional graphics output primitives. This is the case with the G3D package described in this book. The modules in the G3D package depend on and make use of the routines in the modules in the G2D package. The combined set of modules and routines can be referred to as the G2/3D package. A closer look is now taken at the relationship between the modules in the G2D and G3D packages.

In Figure 12-1 is shown the relationship between the six modules of the G2D two-dimensional graphics package, the application program using G2D, and the hardware that this software runs on. This diagram is arranged so that the highest level routines are at the top of the diagram and the lowest level routines are at the bottom. The application program may either access a higher level module or alternatively bypass it to the lower level module(s) underneath that module. Thus the application program will call the routines in the 'g2d_object' module if it wants to use any metagraphics commands. If the application does not need to produce two-dimensional text in graphics, or draw polygons and regions but wants to draw lines, arcs and circles then it only needs to access the 'g2d_plot' module. If text is wanted then the application program will have to declare that it is going to use the 'g2d_text' module. Similarly, if polygons and regions are to be used then the application program must declare that it will use the 'g2d_data' compilation unit. For more direct and simpler graphics needs, the application program could use the driver module 'g2d_driver' alone. The driver module of course does not have any grouping of commands: the 'g2d_object' metagraphics commands only apply to routines in the 'g2d_text', 'g2d_data', and 'g2d_plot' modules. The next step is to look at how the three-dimensional package G3D can make use of the G2D routines.

Figure 12-2 shows that G3D consists of six modules that depend on two modules 'g2d_plot' and 'g2d_driver' from the G2D package. The application program that uses G3D

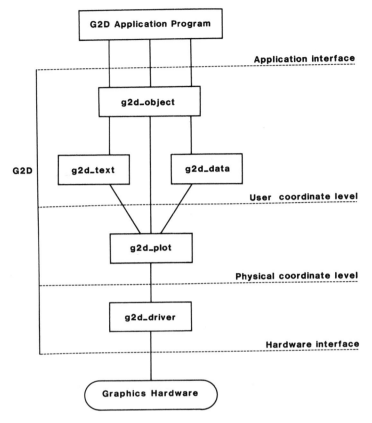

Figure 12-1 The relationship between the G2D modules, a two-dimensional graphics application program and the graphics hardware.

must declare that it will access the 'g3d_view' module. The view module defines how the three-dimensional graphics is to be viewed, that is, the position and orientation of the synthetic camera that takes a 'photograph' or 'movie' of a three-dimensional model or scene. This module then defines how the three-dimensional coordinate data is converted into two-dimensional data on the viewing plane. At that point the 'g2d_plot' module takes over and converts the graphics on the viewing plane in two-dimensional user coordinates into physical coordinates which the driver unit, 'g2d_driver', then outputs to the graphics hardware. If the user only wants three-dimensional line segments, arcs, and circles, then the program should declare that it will use 'g3d_plot'. If three-dimensional text is wanted then the program should also declare that it will use 'g3d_text'. If only three-dimensional text is to be used then it is not necessary to declare the 'g3d_plot' module. Likewise, if the user wishes to display multifaceted solids then the program should declare that it will use the 'g3d_data' module. Again it is not necessary that the program declare 'g3d_plot' if no actual 'g3d_plot' routines such as three-dimensional arc drawing will be called. Finally, the application program must declare 'g3d_object' if it wants to group aggregate or manipulate three-dimensional graphics objects.

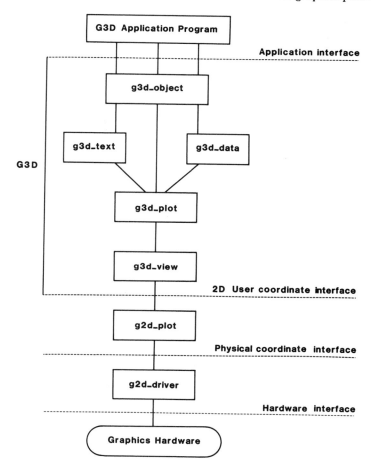

Figure 12-2 The relationship between the G3D modules, a three-dimensional application program and the G2D graphics package.

12.2 Summary of the G3D package

In this section the essential routines in the modules of G3D are listed and described. More details of the routines exported from the G3D modules can be found in Appendix E. Only an essential subset of the G3D routines is listed here.

Intitialization routines

init_g3d_plot
    Initializes system variables in the 'g3d_plot' module.
init_3d_data
    Initializes system variables in the 'g3d_data' module.

init_camera

    Initializes the camera state variables in the 'g3d_view' module.

init_jet

    Initializes the status of the jet for three-dimensional turtle graphics.

Three-dimensional world-view setup routines

normal_projection

    Declares that normal projection will be used.

oblique_projection(dx,dy,dz)

    Declares that the oblique projection in the specified direction will be used.

central_projection

    Declares that the central projection with the default eye position will be used.

dip(angle)

    Dips the synthetic camera that views the three-dimensional world scene.

pan(angle)

    Pans the synthetic camera that views the three-dimensional world scene.

tilt(angle)

    Tilts the synthetic camera that views the three-dimensional world scene.

focal_length(f)

    Sets the distance from the synthetic camera to the viewing plane.

set_tripod(x,y,z)

    Sets the position of the synthetic camera (the eye position).

aim_for(x,y,z)

    Aims the camera at the point (x, y, z) by rotating the camera.

Graphics output routines

draw_3d_axes(dxpdiv,dypdiv,dzpdiv)

    Draws the axes according to the current three-dimensional world view.

plot_3d_line(x1,y1,z1,x2,y2,z2)

    Draws a three-dimensional line segment.

plot_3d_arc(x1,y1,z1,x2,y2,z2,x3,y3,z3)

    Draws a three-dimensional arc of a circle. This will generally appear as an elliptic arc.

plot_3d_circle (x1,y1,z1,x2,y2,z2,x3,y3,z3)

    Draws a three-dimensional circle. In general the current three-dimensional world view will cause this to appear to be an ellipse on the screen.

Graphics input routine

read_3d_point(ch,x,y,z)

    Returns the three-dimensional coordinates of a point digitized from the screen and the character typed to indicate the end of digitization.

Graphics object routines

load_3d_object(name)
Loads the current G3D graphics object from a nominated disk file.
save_3d_object(name)
Saves the current G3D graphics object to a nominated disk file.
store_3d_object(object)
Makes a memory copy of the current graphics object with the specified name.
restore_3d_object(object)
Restores the nominated memory resident graphics object as the current graphics object.
rotate_3d_object(angle,dx,dy,dz)
Rotates the current G3D graphics object by the specified angle (in degrees) about the direction given.
translate_3d_object(tx,ty,tz)
Translates the current G3D graphics object by the specified displacement values.
scale_3d_object(factor,dx,dy,dz)
Scales the current G3D graphics object in the direction specified by the nominated factor.
display_3d_object
Displays the current G3D graphics object according to the current three-dimensional world view set up.

In addition to the G3D routines above, some routines from G2D are required. In particular the following setup and control routines are needed:

clear_screen
set_window(xscreen_min,yscreen_min,xscreen_max,yscreen_max)
set_viewport(pxmin,pymin,pxmax,pymax)
draw_border
beep

which have the same function as described before for G2D. They apply within the two-dimensional viewing plane. In fact, the user could call any G2D routine and the graphics will occur within the viewing plane and apply all over the current viewport on the graphics output device. However it would be preferrable in most cases not to mix two-dimensional and three-dimensional graphics input and output primitives. Therefore when doing three-dimensional graphics, only the five routines listed above from G2D need be used. It should also be noted that some Pascal systems (such as UCSD Pascal) allow compilation units themselves to execute the initiation and termination codes upon being loaded into memory. With such a system it is no longer necessary for the user to explicitly intitialize the graphics package modules. However, sometimes initialization routines are needed apart from at the start of a program. For example, the user may often want to reinitialize the camera after a long sequence of camera dipping, panning, and tilting rather than remembering the sequence so that it could be undone.

The following sections discuss various applications for the G3D package of routines.

12.3 **Three-dimensional mathematical plots and topography**

Mathematics often uses various functions without ever having pictured what the shapes that they define actually look like. Computer graphics provides the valuable opportunity to quickly generate pictures of mathematical functions and this plotting permits a deeper understanding of whatever function is being used. In Chapter 4, the value was shown in being able to visualize a mathematical function of one variable. This function may take the form:

$$y = f(x)$$

or more generally:

$$x = fx(t)$$
$$y = fy(t)$$
$$z = fz(t)$$

and is suitable for plotting with a two-dimensional graphics package such as G2D. A three-dimensional graphics package such as G3D now gives an opportunity to plot a function of two variables, say of the form:

$$z = f(x, y)$$

Whereas a function of one variable defines a curve, a function of two variables defines a surface in three-dimensional space. However, this form of the equation of a surface is not the most appropriate form for the arrangement of axes in G3D. Figure 12-3 shows that a single-valued function $z = f(x, y)$, viewed from above from the default camera position, would fill the entire window and give the viewer little detail or clue to its actual shape. If however the surface is specified by a functional form $y = f(x, z)$ then the default view would be edge on or oblique and this view would be more informative. Of course, the synthetic camera could always be moved around to a more useful position, but instead a start will be made by looking at a simple algorithm for displaying surfaces viewed from along the z axis for which the surface equation:

$$y = f(x, z)$$

will be appropriate. Usually only a finite segment of the surface will be wanted and this can be defined by specifying limits on the variables as follows:

$$xmin \leq x \leq xmax$$
$$zmin \leq z \leq zmax$$

There are several ways of conveying the idea of a surface on monochrome two-dimensional graphics output devices. These all consist of drawing extra lines on the surface so that the viewer can visualize where it curves. First of all the boundary of the surface patch at least should be drawn. The boundary consists of the following four curves (refer to Figure 12-3b.):

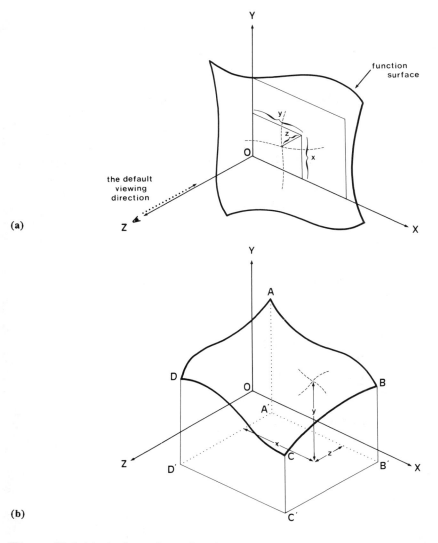

Figure 12-3 (a) A view of a surface in three dimensions given by $z = f(x,y)$. (b). A view of a surface in three dimensions given by $y = f(x,z)$. The area enclosed within *ABCD* is the function surface, with supports *AA'*, *BB'*, *CC'*, and *DD'*, and with base *A'B'*, *B'C'*, *C'D'*, and *D'A'*.

1. *Curve AB*

$$y = f(x, zmin) \text{ for } x = xmin \text{ to } x = xmax$$

2. *Curve BC*

$$y = f(xmax, z) \text{ for } z = zmin \text{ to } z = zmax$$

3. *Curve CD*

$$y = f(x, zmax) \text{ for } x = xmin \text{ to } x = xmax$$

4. *Curve DA*

$$y = f(xmin, z) \text{ for } z = zmax \text{ to } z = zmin$$

These curves could be drawn as a sequence of small three-dimensional line segments by calls to 'plot_3d_line'. The line segments may be of equal increments in the curve parameter (*x* for curve *AB* and so forth) or may be varied to adjust to the changing radius of curvature of the true curve as discussed in Chapter 4.

A better feeling for the position of the surface patch in three-dimensional space can be gained by adding the supports and the base. The supports of the surface are the lines *AA'*, *BB'*, *CC'*, and *DD'* where *A'*, *B'*, *C'*, and *D'* are the vertical projections of the corner points *A* , *B* , *C* , and *D* down onto the *x-z* plane. Hence code to draw the supports is:

```
ay := f(xmin,zmin);
plot_3d_line(xmin,ay,zmin,xmin,0,zmin);
by := f(xmax,zmin);
plot_3d_line(xmax,by,zmin,xmax,0,zmin);
cy := f(xmax,zmax);
plot_3d_line(xmax,cy,zmax,xmax,0,zmax);
dy := f(xmin,zmax);
plot_3d_line(xmin,dy,zmax,xmin,0,zmax);
```

The base consists of the four line segments *A'B'*, *B'C'*, *C'D'*, and *D'A'*. A similar Pascal code segment will draw the base.

Some methods for conveying the nature of the surface curvature within its four boundaries are:

1.   extra supports at significant points on the surface (such as peaks and troughs);
2.   parallel horizon lines;
3.   a grid of equally spaced *x* and *z* lines (i.e. lines parallel to the *x* and *z* axes respectively) projected up onto the surface as curves on the surface;
4.   contour lines, that is, curves on the surface of constant *y* values at equal heights up the *y* axis.

These various techniques are illustrated in Figure 12-4. The same curve drawing routine should be used for drawing the surface curves interior to the boundary as was used for drawing the boundary itself.

In the simplest surface plotting routines all parts of all grid lines are fully visible and no attempt is made at not drawing the curves over surface folds where parts of the surface become hidden from the camera. When the number of grid lines is large and the surface has a wavy curvature the grid lines actually detract from rather than contribute to our understanding of the nature of the surface. This problem can be seen in Figure 12-5.

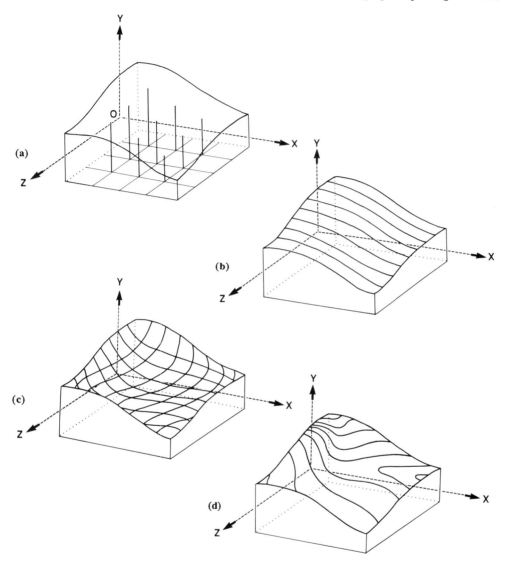

Figure 12-4 (a),(b),(c) and (d). Different ways of rendering a surface for a vector graphics or monochrome graphics output device.

Using specially adapted hidden-line techniques these algorithms can be improved so that invisible parts of the surface are not drawn. This is a form of a hidden-surface routine.

A simple technique for ensuring that hidden parts of the surface are not drawn is to draw a family of surface curves whose projections onto the x-z plane are parallel to the x axis and these curves are drawn from the front to the back, that is, from $z = zmax$ to $z = zmin$. At each x interval the maximum and minimum screen y value is recorded and points on the surface that dip between the current maximum and minimum y at a given x

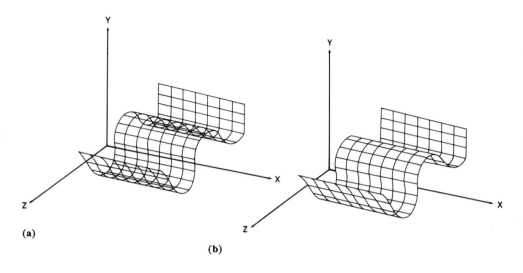

(a)

(b)

Figure 12-5 A gridded surface (a) without and (b) with hidden surfaces removed.

are not drawn. A simple procedure that implements this idea is shown in Box 12-1 and a sample result is shown in Figure 12-6. It calls on two other routines 'maximum(a,b)' and 'minimum(a,b)' which (naturally enough) return the maximum and minimum of the real numbers 'a' and 'b'. It will also be noted from the code that it calls the two-dimensional line drawing procedure rather than 'plot_3d_line'.

This procedure is limited to viewing surfaces of the form $y = f(x, z)$ from along the z axis. Notice that the first statement 'init_camera' overrides any three-dimensional view that the user may have already set up. The projection transformation is essentially the orthographic projection:

$$xscreen = x$$
$$yscreen = y$$

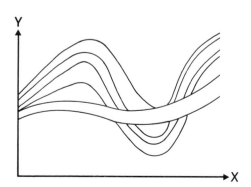

Figure 12-6 A surface in three dimensions with surface hiding.

Box 12-1 A procedure to plot the surface $y = f(x,z)$.

```
procedure plot_surface(function f(x,z : real) : real;
              xmin,xmax,zmin,zmax : real; nx,nz : integer);
{Draws lines on the screen to represent the surface :
              y = f(x,z)
in three dimensions where
              xmin <= x <= xmax
and           zmin <= z <= zmax
using nx points in the x direction and nz points in the z direction.}
const
    max_dim = 100;
var
    deltax,deltaz,x,y,z,xscreen,yscreen,xold,yold : real;
    ix,iz : integer;
    max,min : array[1 .. max_dim] of real;
begin
    init_camera;
    if nx > max_dim then nx := max_dim;
    deltax := (xmax - xmin)/(nx - 1); deltaz := (zmax - zmin)/(nz - 1);
    x := xmin; z := zmax; y := f(x,z); project_point(x,y,z,xold,yold);
    for ix := 2 to nx do {plot the front horizon line}
    begin
        x := xmin + (ix - 1)*deltax;
        y := f(x,z);
        project_point(x,y,z,xscreen,yscreen);
        max[ix] := yscreen; min[ix] := yscreen;
        plot_line(xold,yold,xscreen,yscreen);
        xold := xscreen; yold := yscreen;
    end;

    for iz := 2 to nz do {plot successive horizon lines back to the furthest one}
    begin
        x := xmin;
        z := zmax - (iz - 1)*deltaz; y := f(x,z);
        project_point(x,y,z,xold,yold);
        if yscreen > max[1] then max[1] := yscreen;
        if yscreen < min[1] then min[1] := yscreen;
        for ix := 2 to nx do
        begin
            x := xmin + (ix - 1)*deltax;
            y := f(x,z);
            project_point(x,y,z,xscreen,yscreen);
            if yscreen > max[ix] then
```

```
      begin
          plot_line(xold,maximum(yold,max[ix-1]),xscreen,yscreen);
          max[ix] := yscreen;
      end
      else if yscreen < min[ix] then
      begin
          plot_line(xold,minimum(yold,min[ix-1]),xscreen,yscreen);
          min[ix] := yscreen;
      end;
      xold := xscreen; yold := yscreen;
    end;
  end;
end;
```

but it would be more convenient to generalize the algorithm to allow any view of the surface. Note also that the resulting plot is not perfectly accurate at points where the surface curve dips below the maximum and reemerges on the other side. This problem is illustrated in Figure 12-7 where the point ('xscreen','yscreen') lies between 'max[ix]' and 'min[ix]' and the previous point (at 'ix-1') was above the maximum. Instead of drawing the line *AC* where *C* is the point of intersection of lines *AE* and *DB*, the algorithm draws the line *AB*. The same approximation is done for the line below the minimum. The error does decrease however as 'nx' increases. Increasing 'nx' is often not desirable, for example, when the grid method (3 above) is to be used – too many lines close together result in blacking out the plot. Another method which increases the dimension of the 'max' and 'min' arrays and interpolates values for the arrays between 'ix' intervals will be described below.

The procedure in Box 12-1 can be easily extended to plot surfaces from oblique angles as shown in Figure 12-8. From that figure, it can be seen that the projection transformation is:

$$xscreen = x - z \cos(\alpha)$$
$$yscreen = y - z \sin(\alpha)$$
$$0 < \alpha < \pi/2$$

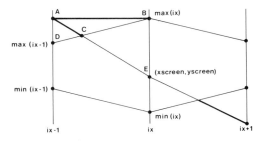

Figure 12-7 Line segment approximation for the procedure in Box 12-1.

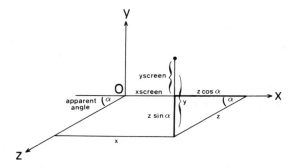

Figure 12-8 The oblique view of the *xyz* coordinate system.

A little calculation shows that this transformation is indeed the oblique projection of Section 10.5 with:

$$\mathbf{n} = (0,0,1)$$
$$\mathbf{d} = (\cos(\alpha),\sin(\alpha),1) \, / \, \sqrt{2}$$

The modification of the algorithm in Box 12-1 requires more than just changing the projection transformation from the oblique view, for the width of the plot is now bigger:

$$xscreen\_range \equiv xscreen\_max - xscreen\_min$$
$$= (xmax - xmin) + (zmax - zmin) \cos(\alpha)$$

The 'max' and 'min' arrays need to be dimensioned to greater than 'nx' on account of this. This new dimension size is computed by dividing the 'xscreen' range by the change in 'xscreen' values:

$$dim = \text{round}(\text{abs}(xscreen\_range \, / \, (deltax - deltaz \, \cos(\alpha))))$$

A larger value for 'dim' than this could be used to dimension 'max' and 'min' to get more accurate and smooth curves without increasing the number of grid lines.

The algorithm in Box 12-1 initialized the 'max' and 'min' arrays from the values of 'yscreen' on the front line. In the modified algorithm, this will not work since it will not initialize all values of 'max' and 'min' now that 'dim' > 'nx'. A solution to this problem is to have another array, called 'valid' say, that takes boolean values that say whether the corresponding values of 'max' and 'min' are initialized or not. The new algorithm must start by setting all components of 'valid[]' to false. Another problem that arises in the oblique view case is that the increments along the x axis of successive polylines do not fall at the same values of 'xscreen'. In fact when 'max' and 'min' are dimensioned to size 'dim' given above, successive x values of the knot points on one polyline do not correspond to consecutive components of the 'max' and 'min' arrays – this should be fixed by interpolating values for 'max' and 'min' from ('xold','yold') the previous point to ('xscreen','yscreen') the current point. In this interpolation, care should be taken to replace the 'max[ ]' values with the *maximum* of its previous value and the interpolated value, and likewise each 'min[ ]' value should be replaced with the *minimum* of the previous value in 'min' and the calculated interpolation value. In this way the inaccuracy depicted in Figure 12-7 is properly overcome. Some oblique views using the modified algorithm can be seen in Figure 12-9.

The oblique views are still restricted to using the *x-y* plane as the viewing plane; that is, the viewing plane has normal $\mathbf{n} = (0,0,1)$ and passes through the origin of coordinates. It would be preferable to have the procedure 'plot_surface' expect the user to have set up a projection transformation which it uses rather than have the procedure enforce a restricted view on the surface. The ideas of the previous version of the algorithm can be retained for this more general case, but now a preliminary calculation must be done to determine which polyline is the 'front' one, that is, closest to the synthetic camera. A routine called 'field_depth' in 'g3d_view' is provided for this purpose. It simply returns the dot product of $\mathbf{c}_z$, the *z* direction of the synthetic camera, and the relative position vector of the point. This routine is therefore applied to the four corners of the surface, and the ordering of the double for-loops is then based on the two closest corners to the camera. At this level of generality it would be sensible to input the function as three functions:

$$x = fx(u, v)$$
$$y = fy(u, v)$$
$$z = fz(u, v)$$

with:

$$umin \le u \le umax$$
$$vmin \le v \le vmax$$

The methods described in this section are also suitable for plotting spline surfaces since these can also provide a height parameter *y* for every coordinate pair (x, z) in the base plane. The difference is that the former surfaces are determined by an explicit function, whereas splines patch functions together and the surface coordinates come out from algorithms rather than explicit functions. These algorithms can be written as Pascal functions also and then the same 'plot_surface' procedure can be used to plot spline surfaces as for other mathematical surfaces.

On graphics output devices with a large number of colors or intensities, surfaces can be rendered more realistically by smooth shading with light reflections and so forth. These methods are introduced in the next chapter. Even if these methods are available on graphics equipment there are still some reasons why line curves might be used to render surfaces. One reason is that representing a surface by a patchwork of polygons or by horizon polylines is much faster than smooth shading that attempts full realism. The application may not need surfaces to be rendered realistically and of course one hundred percent realism is never achieved anyway. Finally when considering mathematical surface plots as covered in this section there is often a need to be able to read values from the plot (to some level of accuracy). Having visible grid lines on the surface gives us this capability in the same way that curves in two dimensions can be used to estimate function values by sight.

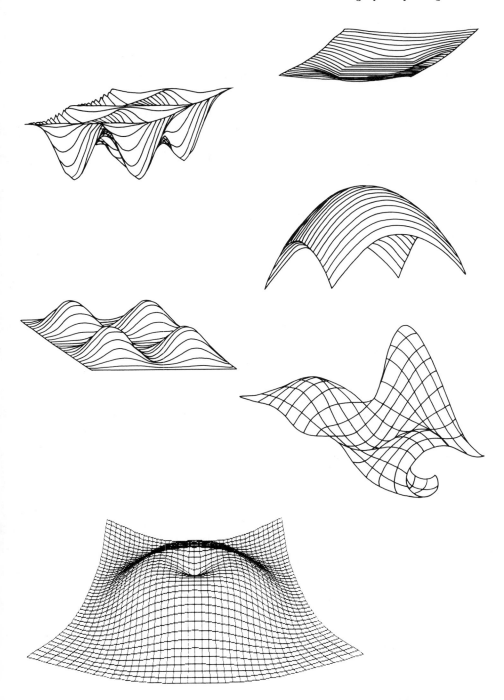

Figure 12-9 Oblique views of surfaces with hidden lines.

12.4 Building design

Computer graphics has been used in the building industry in a number of ways. In housing construction, graphics programs have been written to enable a client to see what a house would look like based on sketchy plans supplied by the client. (See Figure 12-10a.) The builder can show the house on a graphics screen from different angles. The program can also tell the builder the quantity of materials required and the total cost based on current or projected prices. There is little difficulty in altering the house plan – rearranging rooms, their sizes, positioning of doors, cupboards, windows – and then recomputing the three-dimensional picture of the house and analyzing the new costing. Once a house design is settled on, the program can draft the architectural house plan outputting it to a plotter.

A similar sort of program, useful to builders, is one that sites predesigned houses on blocks of land using computer graphics. In this program, the builder has a number of set house plans which are stored in the computer. Only slight variations on these plans are catered for by the builder. The builder also has surveying information on all the blocks of land that are planned to be built on, and this information is also entered into the computer. When a customer comes in to the office, the builder can ask what block of land the client would like to buy and which house design the client would be interested in owning. The program will then draw the house on the block of land in three-dimensional perspective for the customer to approve. The advantage of this program is that a client is able to see what will be constructed before its actually made. This can even be seen in relation to the shape and slope of the block of land that is wanted. The program allows the customer to place the house at various angles and positions within the block of land. With each setting of the house, a garage, driveway, and footpaths can be added and the landscape gardening can be considered on the block for the lawn and garden.

An application for three-dimensional computer graphics, which was in use for some time before the housing programs as described above were made, is the design and construction of city office blocks. (See Figure 12-10b.) A graphics program will show on the VDU screen a set of big buildings as they currently exist. The user can then add the proposed new building at various sites to see how it will blend into its surroundings. The program can be used to see whether a new taller building would cause serious blocking out of smaller buildings. Some programs are capable of plotting the shadow cast by the new building onto surrounding buildings for any hour of the day. As a result of using this program, the building design may be approved or changed, or it may be built on a different site.

12.5 Mechanical engineering CAD

In mechanical engineering, accurate designs are needed for metal blocks that form parts of mechanical engines and so forth. A surprising number of different parts are necessary. Traditionally, these designs have been created by hand and stored as paper drawings.

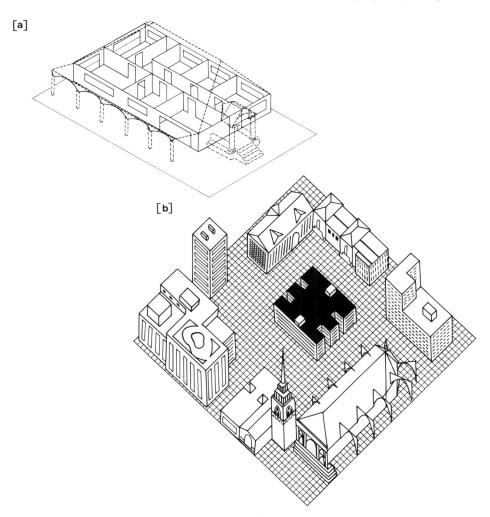

Figure 12-10 (a) House and (b) office block displays.

Computer-aided design has replaced much of the manual design work for mechanical parts. Now designs are created on computer graphics screens and stored on magnetic disks and tapes. Designs created with the aid of the computer can be much more accurate than hand-drawn designs. Paper copies can be readily produced if needed by sending the computer graphics design to a plotter. Graphics designs kept on disk can be easily modified when necessary and this saves a lot of effort over redrawing the whole design.

The parts are often cut by a mechanical lathe controlled by a computer. This equipment is called an NC (numerically controlled) machine and the computer that controls the lathe is typically programmed by instructions on paper tape. CAD systems and NC machinery can be linked together. In the simplest form, the CAD computer creates a paper tape suitable for use by the NC machine, punched in accordance with the graphical information relevant to the CAD part to be milled. In more advanced systems no paper tape is used, and there is a direct electrical link from the CAD computer to the NC machine. In these ways the computer not only aids design of mechanical parts, but also aids in their manufacture. Such systems are called CAD/CAM (computer-aided design/ computer-aided manufacturing) systems.

12.6 Instructional solid geometry

Fast interactive three-dimensional computer graphics can be used as a tool to improve the ability to visualize solids. An example of this sort of application is found in the typical exercises set for first year engineering students. In these exercises the students are given the isometric view of a three-dimensional solid. Examples of such views are shown in Figure 12-11. From each of these isometric drawings, students are expected to produce the three orthographic views: side, plan, and elevation views. The orthographic views for the isometrically drawn object in Figure 12-11a can be seen in Figure 12-12. Note that dashed lines are drawn for the hidden lines in the orthographic views, and that the hidden lines are invisible for the isometric views. In another set of exercises, the engineering student is given two orthographic views of a solid as in Figure 12-13a and from these alone must be able to visualize the object being described and draw its isometric view as in Figure 12-13b.

A computer graphics program can be made to do these jobs on a graphics screen as a computer-aided learning tool. The program can be described simply via a menu-driven programming format. When the program is started the following menu appears:

```
Choose one of :
0    exit this program
1    load an object
2    display the isometric view of the object
3    display the first isometric view of the object
4    display the second isometric view of the object
5    display the third isometric view of the object
6    display the general axonometric view of the object
7    set the hidden-line style

Your choice = ?
```

If choices 2, 3, 4, 5, or 6 are requested before any object is loaded from file then a warning message appears as follows:

```
No object loaded yet! Use option 1.
```

The lecturer must supply the objects on a file for the students, and they can be loaded by name. They would be stored in a sequential text file (for simplicity) and in increasing order of difficulty. The student practices three-dimensional visualization skills by loading an object and then calling for its isometric view. The computer then draws the isometric view of the object on the screen. The student's task is to then sketch the three isometric views of the object on paper. After trying to solve the problem, the student then asks the computer to display the correct answers by selecting menu options 2, 3, and 4. After running through a series of tests like this, the student can try the other type of exercise on a different file of objects. This time after loading an object the student will call menu

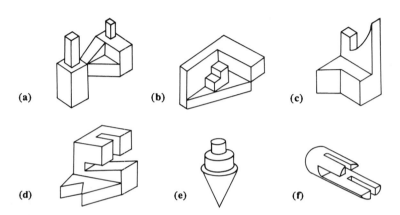

(a) (b) (c)

(d) (e) (f)

Figure 12-11 Typical isometric engineering drawings. Note that hidden lines are invisible.

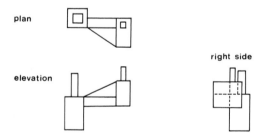

plan

right side

elevation

Figure 12-12 The three orthographic views are determined from the isometrically drawn object in Figure 12-11a.

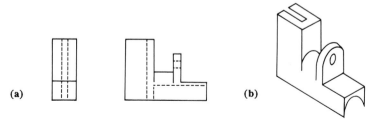

(a) (b)

Figure 12-13 Given two orthographic views (a), the third orthographic view and the isometric view (b) may be determined.

choice 2, memorize it (or sketch it on paper) and then call menu item 3. A better method is of course to have a split screen with two images viewable at once. Given this information, the student has to attempt to sketch the isometric view on paper. Having done this the answer can be checked by selecting menu item 1. If after struggling with the visualization of any object, the student still cannot understand the answer then by calling upon options 6 and 7 further clarification can be had about the object. Option 6 asks for a general viewing angle (pitch, yaw, and roll) for the solid and then displays the object from this alternative view. Option 7 allows the switching on or off of the hidden lines as dashed lines as these can further assist in the visualization in axonometric displays.

This program is easily implemented using the G3D package. Note that all three-dimensional projections used are just special cases of the normal projection, and so 'normal_projection' should be called from the module 'g3d_view'. This software provides the student with a self-paced, self-help learning aid for visualizing engineering drawings. (See problem 12.9.)

12.7 Molecular structures

The study of the interaction and reactions between complex molecular compounds in chemistry is complicated by the need to visualize the stoichiometry or three-dimensional interaction of the molecules in the reaction. Computer graphics offers a feasible way of watching the slowed down simulation of a chemical reaction. The molecules are represented by different-sized spheres (the atoms) connected by rods (the molecular bonds). Atoms of different elements are differentiated by their color (and possibly size). In this way, computer graphics can be an aid to understanding chemistry.

A demonstration program to represent hydrocarbons can be easily implemented using the G3D package. First assume that all bonds are single bonds. Then every carbon atom can be considered to be at the center of a regular tetrahedron. To draw a hydrocarbon, this program first clears the screen and then draws a small sphere (a circle on the screen colored appropriately, say green or black). The sphere is then surrounded by four bonds (solid white lines, say) in the directions that form a tetrahedron and at the end of each bond is a small sphere (yellow say) representing a hydrogen atom. Figure 12-14 shows a representation of the ethane molecule. The user can now select any of the hydrogen atoms (using 'read_3D_point') which will then be converted into a carbon atom and be given three bonds connecting to three new hydrogen atoms in such a way as to form a tetrahedral shape around this new carbon atom. The program allows the user to continue in this fashion converting hydrogen atoms into carbon atoms and making the whole hydrocarbon molecule bigger every time. Strictly speaking, the program should orient the bonds so that hydrogen atoms are as far apart as possible. If the program also gives the user the ability to view the molecule that is being constructed from any angle then this will provide a valuable tool in understanding complex hydrocarbon molecules. Perspective views add to this realism and can be easily implemented by decreasing the radius of the atomic spheres in proportion to the distance of the atom from the eye position. The program can also print out the molecular formula and the current molecular weight.

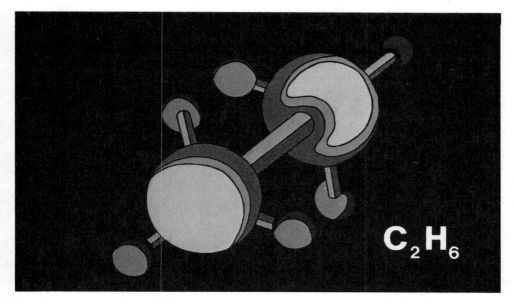

Figure 12-14 (Color Figure 1) Molecular construction: the ethane molecule.

12.8 Computer sculpture

The computer sculpture program is a program to imitate the artistic activities of a sculptor. (See Figure 12-15.) The screen shows initially a large rectangular block representing the block of stone that the sculptor starts with. The block is in a fixed position, but controls are provided so that it can be viewed from any position above ground level. The user is provided with chisels of different sizes. Any chisel can be selected at any time. A point on the surface of the stone gives the point of striking; and the angle of striking and the strike force are specified by a second point off the stone's surface. The distance between the points is a measure of the strike force applied to the chisel at that point on the surface of the stone. After these choices, a chip is taken out of the stone. The depth of the chip equals the distance between the two points that define the strike force. The shape of the chip is tetrahedral with one triangular facet corresponding to the V-shaped point of the chisel. The height of this triangle is the depth of the chip. The object of the program is to chip the stone into a recognizable statue. Final products can be saved to disk and later restored for viewing.

The difficult part of implementing this program is keeping a store of the current shape of the stone. This can be done by recognizing that the surface is always a set of convex polygonal facets. It starts off as six rectangular facets. Every chip introduces three new triangular facets. The vertexes may be stored in a table, and the facets should be kept in dynamic list structure.

A similar sort of program starts with a spherical blob, covered with a network of lines. The user is allowed to select any point at the intersection of the lines, and move it

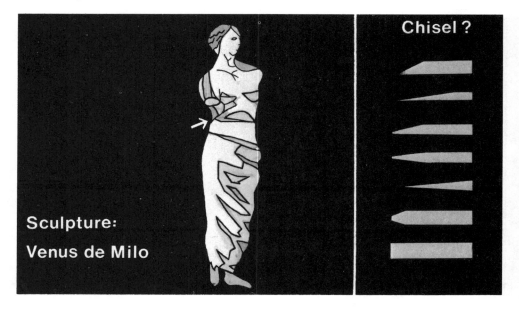

Figure 12-15 (Color Figure 2) Simulating the activity of a sculptor in computer graphics.

inwards or outwards any reasonable amount. The surface then reforms itself to the new points position – it becomes a two-dimensional spline surface that can be moulded into any shape by the user. This program simulates an artist shaping clay.

Problems

12.1   Implement the mathematical function plotting program given in Box 12-1. Test it on the following functions:

1. $y = S \cos(2 \pi x / \lambda_x + \pi) \cos(2 \pi z / \lambda_z + \pi) / 4$
2. $y = S \sin(2 \pi x / \lambda_x) \sin(2 \pi z / \lambda_z)$
3. $y = S (a - b / r)$
4. $y = S \sin(2 \pi / r)$
5. $y = S r \sin(2 \pi / r)$
6. $y = S / r \sin(2 \pi r)$
7. $y = S \sin(2 \pi r)$
8. $y = S (a x^2 + b z^2)$
9. $y = S (a x + b z) / r^2$

where a, b, λ_x, and λ_z are parameters, S is the function scale factor, and:

$$r = \sqrt{(x^2 + z^2)}$$

Your test program should run a repeat loop that clears the screen and asks for a function number, and the value of the parameters before plotting. Include the support lines and base lines in each surface plot. A function number less than one or greater than nine causes program termination.

12.2   Modify the 'plot_surface' procedure as described in Section 12.3 to allow oblique views of the surface. Test your procedure on the nine functions of problem 12.1. Again include the four support lines and four base lines in each surface plot, but only show those parts of these lines that are not obscured by the surface.

12.3   What is required to form a grid surface of lines (like a fish net) which has line hiding? Implement such a procedure based on the procedure of problem 12.2.

12.4   Modify the 'plot_surface' procedure of problem 12.2 to allow general views of a surface which is given in the form:

$$x = fx(u, v)$$
$$y = fy(u, v)$$
$$z = fz(u, v)$$

12.5   Write a procedure to plot a surface defined by a set of grid points:

$$(x_{ij}, y_{ij}, z_{ij}) \text{ for } i = 1 \text{ to } nx, j = 1 \text{ to } nz$$

where:

$$x_{ij} > x_{kj} \text{ for } k < i, x_{ij} < x_{kj} \text{ for } i < k$$
$$z_{ij} > z_{ik} \text{ for } k < j, z_{ij} < z_{ik} \text{ for } j < k$$

Use straight line segments between neighboring points and do not display hidden parts of the surface.

12.6   Write a procedure to input the points as in problem 12.5, but this time to plot a smooth Hermite spline surface through the points rather than using straight line segments. Write a similar procedure that plots Bezier splines – remember that these do not pass through the intermediate lattice points which are control points for the surface. Using this procedure, write a program to simulate clay modelling in a simplistic manner by displaying a Bezier spline surface and allowing the user to pick and move control points by a limited amount.

12.7   Write a program using G3D to load a selected three-dimensional graphics object representing a house and draw it positioned on a block of ground represented by a surface as given in problem 12.5. The base of the house should be parallel to the x-z plane and with a y value corresponding to the minimum y value on the area selected for the house.

12.8   Write a program using G3D to draw a scene of realistic-looking office buildings. Use the 'g3d_data' unit to make the buildings as solids based on lists of facets. Assume that the ground is perfectly flat and the *x-z* plane. Display the buildings with hidden lines removed and from any selected view point. Produce hard copies of a sequence of such scenes from slightly above street level to represent a guided tour around the city's central business district.

12.9   Use 'g3d_data' and other G3D routines to implement the engineering drawing computer-aided learning tool for students of engineering as described in Section 12.6.

12.10   Write a program to represent hydrocarbon molecules as discussed in Section 12.7.

13

Computer graphics realism

13.1 Color theory

Color is a property of light revealed by it striking the back of the eyes, either directly from a light source, through a transparent filter, reflected from objects, or a combination of methods. Light has itself been studied scientifically for many centuries. Under some circumstances light behaves as if it were many small particles, called photons. Photons have no mass and carry energy at the constant speed c in straight lines, where $c = 3 \times 10^8$ m/sec. This is the speed of light in a vacuum, and it is a constant of nature. The speed of light v when it passes through transparent or semitransparent (transluscent) medium is less than the value c above. The refractive index, n, of the medium is defined by the ratio $n = c / v$ and is greater than unity. In other circumstances, light refracts and bends around corners like traveling waves. In this point of view, light is a wave of electromagnetic

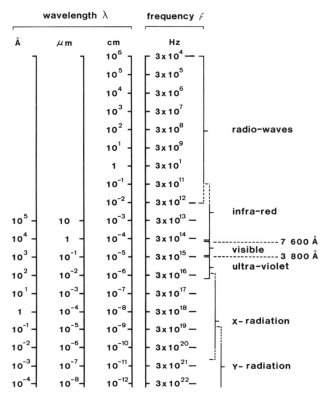

Table 13-1 The electromagnetic spectrum.
1 micron (μm) = 10^{-6}m; 1 Ångstrom (Å) = 10^{-10}m
1 hertz (Hz) = 1 cycle per second (cps)

radiation. The simple plane wave has frequency f, and wavelength λ where $\lambda f = c$. The energy carried by each photon in the equivalent corpuscular point of view is $E = hf$ where h is Plank's constant (h = 6.63 x 10^{-34} joule-sec). The human eye only responds to a small range of wavelengths (or equivalently frequencies), namely 3800 to 7600 angstroms, and this is called the visible spectrum. The detected color of the light is determined by the frequency (or wavelength) of the light waves. See Table 13-1.

Sir Isaac Newton's famous experiment showed that a prism separates white light into a band of colors – the visible colors of the spectrum. This is because the refractive index of a transparent substance such as glass is a function of the frequency of the light and so by Snell's law, the amount of bending (angle of refraction) caused by the transparent medium of glass depends on the frequency. Since white light is a chaotic mixture of all visible frequencies, a glass prism will separate the frequencies out of white light. Another prism can be used to recombine the separated frequencies back into white light. The spectrum of colors produced in this way is a natural one-dimensional arrangement of colors – see Figure 13-1. The spectrum however does not show every color that could be wished for as spectral colors are pure colors, also called *hues*. A pure color is made of

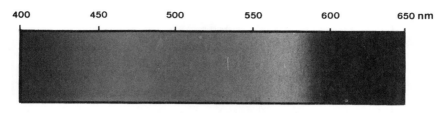

Figure 13-1 (Color Figure 3.) The one-dimensional spectrum of colors.

monochromatic light (i.e. light of a single frequency only). Also of interest is the selection and definition of shades and mixtures of these hues, such as pinks and browns, but these cannot be shown on a one-dimensional color map like Figure 13-1 – more than one dimension is needed to display all visible colors.

When white light shines onto a colored filter, only the frequencies corresponding to the color of the filter pass through it – the other frequencies in the white light are absorbed. If a beam of white light strikes an object of a particular color, then the object will reflect the frequencies of its color and absorb all the others. When these reflected rays enter the eyes, the object is seen to have the color given by the visible frequencies of those light rays. If the white light first passes through a filter before being reflected by the object and if the filter has already removed some of the frequencies normally reflected by the object, then the object will not appear to be its normal color and rather more darkened. If the filter removes all frequencies that the object reflects then the object appears black which means that no rays reflected from it enter the eyes. These are examples of what is known as color subtraction. If the object is colored white, then it reflects equally all frequencies that impinge upon it. If two beams of light pass through two differently colored filters and then strike a white object at the same place, then the object reflects the combined frequencies from both beams. This process is called color addition.

Figure 13-2 shows color addition. In this figure, three beams of circular cross section are shone onto a white matte screen in a darkened room in such a way that the beams

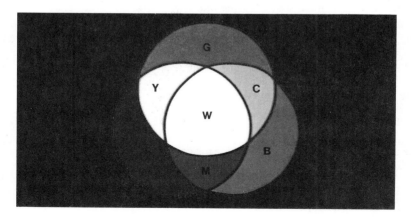

Figure 13-2 (Color Figure 4.) Color addition of three circles within a square.

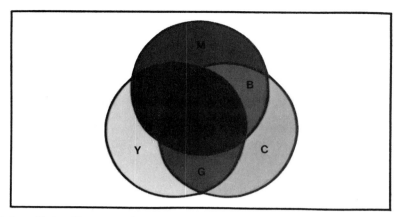

Figure 13-3   (Color Figure 5.) Color subtraction of three circles within a square.

slightly overlap each other. The three beams are colored red, green, and blue respectively. Where two beams overlap on the screen, a different color is seen; and where all three colors overlap, the screen appears white. Figure 13-3 illustrates the concept of color subtraction. In this case white light floods an artist's white canvas. The artist has spread three paints in three overlapping circles on the canvas as shown. Although the artist only uses three different paint colors, sky-blue (cyan), deep pink (magenta), and yellow, in those overlapping areas where the paint colors mix, different colors are seen reflected.

Thus colors can be 'added' by shining two or more different colored beams of light onto the same area of a viewing screen – the screen reflects the combined wavelengths. And colors can be 'subtracted' by mixing paints of different colors – each pigment removes wavelengths from the incident white light leaving the color resulting from whatever wavelengths are left. A form of arithmetic or algebra may be useful here. The following is a description of such an algebra, and its applicability and usefulness will be demonstrated.

Consider three standard light sources, red of intensity R, green of intensity G, and blue of intensity B. These are called the *additive primaries*. Reference to Figure 13-2 shows that other colors called secondaries are obtained by addition of the primaries. For example, the red and green beam combine to form yellow. This could be expressed as:

$$Y = R + G \tag{13.1}$$

Likewise green and blue form cyan (sky-blue):

$$C = G + B \tag{13.2}$$

and blue and red beams combine to produce the color magenta (purple):

$$M = B + R \tag{13.3}$$

Adding all beams gives white light:

$$W = R + G + B \tag{13.4}$$

Using equations 13.1 to 13.4 which derive from color addition experiments, the following results for color subtraction can be postulated:

$$Y = W - B \qquad (13.5)$$
$$C = W - R \qquad (13.6)$$
$$M = W - G \qquad (13.7)$$

Furthermore:

$$Y + C + M = 2 W \qquad (13.8)$$

which can be interpreted to mean that color addition of the secondaries C, M, and Y gives white of twice the brightness as obtained by combining the original R, G, and B lights.

Equations 13.1 to 13.3 express the secondaries in terms of the primaries alone. The secondaries can also be expressed in terms of the primaries alone by using equations 13.5 to 13.8 as follows. From equation 13.6:

$$R = W - C$$

and by substituting for W from equation 13.8:

$$R = (-C + M + Y) / 2$$

and similarly:

$$G = (C - M + Y) / 2$$
$$B = (C + M - Y) / 2$$

The complementary color to a color c is that color c' which added to c gives white:

$$c + c' = W$$

so that the complementary of a color c can be obtained by:

$$c' = W - c$$

It is clear that the complement of the complement of a color c is the original color c again:

$$(c')' \equiv c$$

Thus it is obvious that the complement of red is cyan, of green is magenta, and of blue is yellow, that is:

$$R' = C$$
$$G' = M$$
$$B' = Y$$

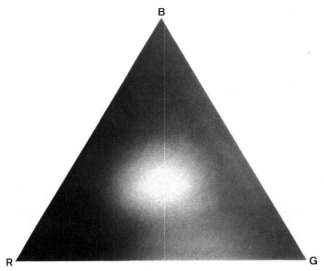

Figure 13-4   (Color Figure 6.) Maxwell's color triangle.

Through color addition experiments (varying the choice of primaries) as described for Figure 13-2 it was found that just three *primary additive hues,* namely red, green, and blue, were needed to form virtually any visible color. The different visible colors could be distinguished by the different proportions of red, green, and blue required to form each color by color addition. This led James Clerk Maxwell in 1855 to construct his famous color triangle as shown in Figure 13-4. The vertexes of the triangle represent the maximum intensity of a primary color with no other color added in. Colors along the edge represent various combinations of the primary colors at the two ends of that edge, and colors inside the triangle are additive interpolations of all three primary colors. To quantify colors, Maxwell's triangle is drawn as an equilateral triangle whose bisectors RX, GY, and BZ are each scaled to be 100 units long. The assumption is that the intensities

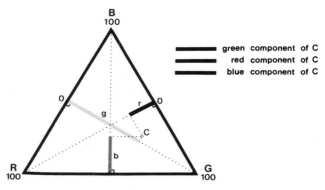

Figure 13-5   (Color Figure 7.) This diagram shows the construction lines used to measure colors on Maxwell's triangle.

in the corners are equal, otherwise a scalene triangle would be used. In this system then, any color **c** can be represented as a triplet (see Figure 13-5):

$$\mathbf{c} = (r, g, b)$$

where r is distance from X along XR of a line parallel to GB that passes through the desired color **c**, g is distance from Y along YG of a line parallel to BR that passes through the desired color **c**, and b is distance from Z along ZB of a line parallel to RG that passes through the desired color **c**. It can be proved geometrically that:

$$r + g + b = 100 \tag{13.9}$$

so it is open to interpret r as the percentage of red primary (0 to 100), g as the percentage of green, and b as the percentage of blue that make up the color by color addition. The three vertexes are obviously (100,0,0), (0,100,0), and (0,0,100). In consequence of this equation, the intensities of all colors in Maxwell's triangle are the same. This represents a limitation in the selection in colors since for instance color mixtures of red, green, and blue on color graphics VDUs present a range of intensities. Consider a line on Maxwell's triangle from the red corner R to the midpoint of the opposite side. Along this line g and b values are equal and range from 0 to 50 as can be seen by using the grid diagram Figure 13-6. The point on this line where g and b both equal 33.3 is the centroid, O, of the triangle and the color at that point is white. At the G-B edge g and b both equal 50 and the color is cyan. Intermediate colors are pale cyan colors increasing in paleness from X

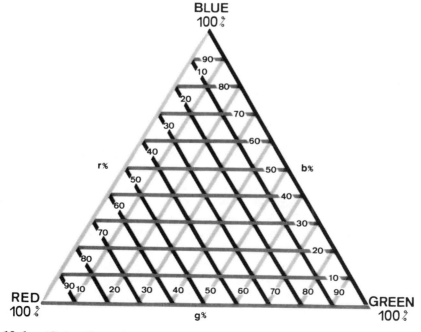

Figure 13-6   (Color Figure 8.) The (r,g,b) coordinate grid for Maxwell's triangle.

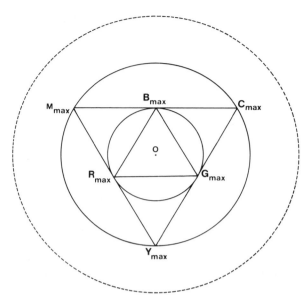

Figure 13-7   Maxwell's triangle altered to show color intensity as proportional to the distance from O to the color. Thus the maximum intensity of cyan, C_{max}, is double the maximum intensity of either green (G_{max}) or blue (B_{max}). By adding red intensity, pale cyan approaches the limiting intensity shown by the dashed circle.

to O. At the centroid, O, the color is white. Colors between R and O are the complementary colors to those from X to O, namely, shades of pink increasing to red at R. If this line is extended outside of the triangle to the point where g and b both equal 100 (intensity levels that are provided on a color graphics VDU) then the point C_{max} is reached (see Figure 13-7).

   While Maxwell's triangle displays a smoothly changing selection of colors it does not show all possible hues that the eye can detect. The human eye is capable of detecting about 180 hues. Clearly the range of colors can be increased by increasing or decreasing the R, G, or B maximum intensities at the vertexes of Maxwell's triangle. This still does not allow the description all the visible colors within the triangle. If however subtraction of the R, G, and B primaries is allowed as well as addition, then all color hues can be reached. This implies the possibility of negative coordinate values for r, g, or b and that means that some hues are displayed at a position outside of Maxwell's equilateral triangle. When all visible hues are thus added to Maxwell's triangle, a horseshoe shape emerges. The science of colorimetry (color measurement) has quantified these results into the CIE chromaticity diagram shown in Figure 13-8. CIE (from the French Commision Internationalle de l'Eclairage) is the International Commission of Illumination that has defined color standards. Colors around the edge of the chromaticity tongue represent pure colors (monochromatic or single-frequency light). A line joining two such points shows all intermediate colors between the two pure colors as extremes. The point W inside the tongue represents white. A line from W to a point P on the edge of the tongue shows all pasteis of a given color from zero saturation at W to 100 percent saturation at P. The curve can therefore be used to determine the dominant frequency in a color, say C in Figure 13-9. By joining a line from W to C and then extending this to the edge of the tongue, the dominant frequency can be read (i.e. that for 100 percent saturation). The complementary color to a color C can be found from the diagram by joining a line from C to W and then extending the line further to C' such that:

$$WC \, / \, WP = WC' \, / \, WP'$$

where P and P' are the points of intersection of the line CC' with the tongue edge. The pure colors at P and P' are also complementary.

Colors can be defined by intensity values for their standard red, green, and blue light components. Therefore, a two-dimensional arrangement of colors is not really adequate and a three-dimensional solid must be used. The two-dimensional color charts can be regarded as plane slices through a three-dimensional color solid. An example of a color solid is the RGB cube which can show all possible colors for given maximum intensities on the red, green, and blue components. The idea is shown in Figure 13-10.

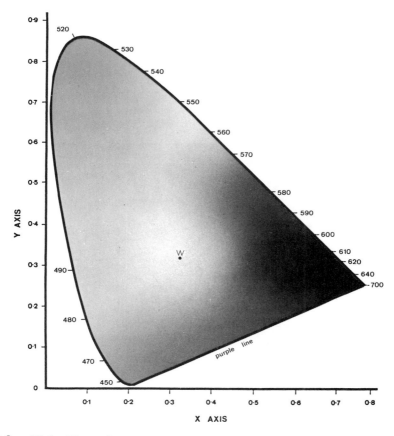

Figure 13-8   (Color Figure 9.) The colored CIE chromaticity diagram.

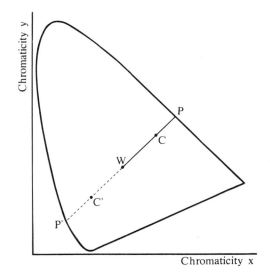

Figure 13-9   Color measurements using the CIE chromaticity chart. Color P' is the complement to color P. Color C' is the complement to color C where C' divides the line WP' in the same ratio that C divides the line WP. The percentage distance of C from W relative to P is the saturation of color C.

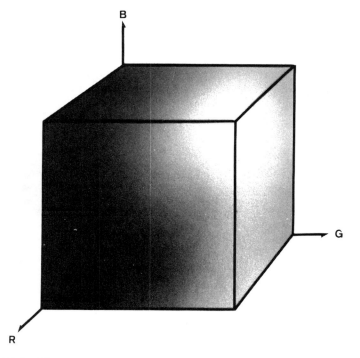

Figure 13-10   (Color Figure 10.) The RGB color cube.

By a change of coordinates from the color space of Figure 13-10, more useful parameters can be chosen for defining colors. In the ink, dye, and painting industry it is standard to define colors by the subtractive primary components C (cyan), M (magenta), and Y (yellow). The transformation between RGB and CMY definitions of a color is:

$$C = W - R$$
$$M = W - G$$
$$Y = W - B$$

For example, the color defined by 100 percent red (i.e. maximum red), 50 percent green (i.e. half maximum in green), and 50 percent blue (half maximum in blue color) can equally well be defined as 0 percent cyan (use no cyan ink), 50 percent magenta ink, and 50 percent yellow ink.

Another alternative set of parameters for defining colors is the HLS system. H stands for hue and is the pure color corresponding to the dominant frequency in the color. In the HLS system, hue is an angle from 0 to 360 measured around the color wheel (the largest circle inside Maxwell's triangle centered on the centroid) starting from pure red (or pure blue in some systems). L stands for luminance or lightness by which is actually meant the brightness or total intensity of the light of that color. S stands for color strength or saturation which means the extent to which the hue frequency dominates over other components. Saturation is also called the purity of the color. It is defined as the percentage of nonwhite content in the color, and can be measured from the CIE chromaticity chart by locating the color C on the chart and extending a line from W through C to P on the tongue of the chart. The proportion of lengths along this line gives the saturation as shown in Figure 13-9:

$$S = WC \,/\, WP \quad 100$$

The lower the saturation or purity of a color, the more it is diluted with white, that is, the paler the colour is. The higher the saturation or purity of a color, the less white it has and the deeper or stronger the color. The HLS system is a good system for categorizing and selecting colors because it uses parameters that match people's perception of light and corresponds to how colors are described in everyday language. It is very easy in this system to intuitively define or modify colors. On the other hand, specifying the amount of red, green, and blue to give the desired color by color addition is much harder and less intuitive – it is more suited to the hardware than to humans.

But what is the relation between the HLS parameters and the RGB parameters for defining colors. Suppose that the red, green, and blue intensities are given that define a color as R, G, and B. Then the L parameter is the total intensity of the light:

$$L = I_{red} + I_{green} + I_{blue} \equiv R + G + B$$

Suppose, for example, that the minimum intensity of R, G, and B corresponded to blue (B) as in Figure 13-11. Then the intensity of white light in the color is $I_{white} = 3\,B$. The intensity of pure color in the given color is therefore:

$$I_{col} = L - 3\,B$$

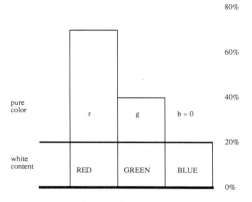

Figure 13-11 RGB percentage bars for a mixed color.

and so the saturation is given by:

$$S = I_{col} / L \ 100$$

The color can be thought of as being composed of the amount I_{white} of white light plus $r = R - B$ of red and $g = G - B$ of green. (Note that $I_{col} = r + g$.) The ratio of the extra amounts of green and red determines the hue:

$$H = g / I_{col} \ 120$$

The algorithm for generating $H, L,$ and S given $R, G,$ and B values, in the general case, is shown in a procedure in Box 13-1. This algorithm is founded on the physical notions in the theory of optics and consequently is not the same as presented by other authors. For example, another formulation defines hue in the above simple case as g / r 120. That definition causes hue angles to bunch unevenly rather than spread evenly around the color wheel for equal intensity changes at constant L and S.

Stippling is a method used to render grey shades between black and white by uniformly spaced black dots on paper. The greater the density of the dots, or the bigger their diameter, the blacker the shading effect produced. From the normal viewing or reading distance the dots are not noticed. Stippling is used, for instance, in printing black and white photographs in newspapers. This technique can also be used on monochrome graphics output devices to achieve grey scales, though with computer graphics equipment only a discrete range of dot diameters and spacings are available. The dots on such equipment would be clusters of pixels.

When applied to color computer graphics output devices, the technique is known as *halftoning*. A typical application of halftoning on a graphics VDU uses 'superpixels' which are 4 × 4 square arrays of screen pixels. Each pixel in the superpixel can be set to any of the s available screen colors for the VDU giving s^{16} combinations for the superpixel. If the superpixel is of significant physical size (near one millimeter say) then care should be taken to arrange the pixel colors as homogeneously as possible within the

Box 13-1 Conversions between RGB and HLS color definition systems.

```
procedure RGB_to_HLS (R, G, B : real;
                var H, L, S : real);
{Converts Red, Green, and Blue intensities R,G,B to Hue, Luminance and
Strength H,L,S.
Hue is an angle 0 to 360 around the color wheel counterclockwise from red.
Luminance is brightness, the total luminous intensity of the color (same units
as R,G,B).
Strength S is the purity percentage, that is, percentage of pure hue relative to
white content.}
var
    white, red_excess, green_excess, blue_excess, total_color : real;
begin
    L := R + G + B;
    white := minimum(R, G, B);
    red_excess := R - white;
    green_excess := G - white;
    blue_excess := B - white;
    total_color := L - 3 * white;
    S := total_color / L * 100;
    if blue_excess = 0 then
        H := 120 * green_excess / total_color
    else if red_excess = 0 then
        H := 120 * (1 + blue_excess / total_color)
    else if green_excess = 0 then
        H := 120 * (2 + red_excess / total_color);
end;


procedure HLS_to_RGB (H, L, S : real;
            var R, G, B : real);
{Converts color parameters H, Hue, L Luminance, and S Strength to
R red, G green, and B blue intensity values.}
var
    white, red_excess, green_excess, blue_excess, total_color : real;
    hue_factor : real;
    hue_sector : integer;
begin
    white := L * (1 - S / 100) / 3;
    total_color := L - 3 * white;
    hue_sector := trunc(H / 120) mod 3;
    hue_factor := (H - hue_sector * 120) / 120;
    if hue_sector = 0 then
    begin
        blue_excess := 0;
        green_excess := hue_factor * total_color;
```

```
        red_excess := total_color - green_excess;
    end
    else if hue_sector = 1 then
    begin
        red_excess := 0;
        blue_excess := hue_factor * total_color;
        green_excess := total_color - blue_excess;
    end
    else if hue_sector = 2 then
    begin
        green_excess := 0;
        red_excess := hue_factor * total_color;
        blue_excess := total_color - red_excess;
    end;
    R := white + red_excess;
    G := white + green_excess;
    B := white + blue_excess;
end;
```

superpixel. The color combinations within the superpixel will then mix in the eye to give the impression of a new previously unavailable color on the VDU. Since each pixel is actually a triad of red, green, and blue phosphors at various available intensities, each halftone (a superpixel) can be categorized by its total intensities of red, green, and blue, and the superpixel supplies the user with a much greater range of red, green, and blue intensities. Superpixels can be chosen as 2 x 2, 3 x 3, or 4 x 4 squares of pixels, but larger sizes are usually too chunky. Superpixels of the 4 x 4 size effectively reduce the available screen resolution by a factor of a quarter in the x and y directions. Thus halftoning is a trade off between resolution and the number of simultaneous on-screen colors. If the algorithm for painting with halftones snips off parts of superpixels that go over the boundaries of the paint area then there is no practical loss of graphics resolution. It is easy to modify the painting algorithm to do this. (See Box 7-10.) The result is a *pattern painting algorithm* based on a rectangular pixel pattern: instead of setting interior pixels to the same pixel value (and hence color), the algorithm selects a pixel value from the pattern based on the screen address coordinates modulo the width and height of the pattern rectangle.

Dithering is much the same idea as halftoning except that black pixels are not allowed. In order to get the smoothest arrangement, an area to be filled with a dithered color is often filled with vertical lines alternating between two pure nonblack colors. By having the lines vertical there is no clash of contrasting colors with the screen refresh rate that could otherwise cause annoying flickering especially if the screen refresh is interlaced at a low speed (25 to 30 Hz). By using only two pure colors a smooth effect is produced and the eye does not detect the individual pure colors involved. Dithering by this method will produce $s(s-1)/2$ new smooth colors on a screen that provides s pure colors. Area filling with this technique has similarities with but is distinct from the commonly used scan conversion method whereby horizontal scan lines are drawn where they are inside the area in raster sequence.

13.2 **Programs to experiment with color**

In order to produce color in the graphics output, it is necessary to introduce some color commands:

1. 'set_color(color_nr : integer)' – causes all subsequent graphics output to be in the logical color given by 'color_nr', an index into the color look-up table (CLUT).
2. 'paint(x,y : real; color_nr,nb : integer; ba : int_array)' – flood-fills the screen in the logical color 'color_nr' starting from the user coordinate point (x, y) up to the boundaries specified in the 'ba' array. The parameter 'nb' is the number of boundary colors. For example, if 'nb = 3', 'ba[1] = 20', 'ba[2] = 16', and 'ba[3] = 210' then the painting area does not cross any lines with logical color 20, 16, or 210.
3. 'fill_area(n : integer; xa,ya : real_array; col : integer)' – flood-fills the polygon whose vertexes are $(xa[1], ya[1])$ to $(xa[n], ya[n])$ with the logical color 'col'.
4. 'define_color(col,r_value,g_value,b_value : integer)' – defines a logical color 'col' (index into the color look-up table) by its red, green, and blue components.
5. 'read_color(col : integer; var r_value,g_value,b_value : integer)' – reads the contents of the color look-up table at index (logical color) 'col'. The returned red, green, and blue values are the RGB intensity values in the corresponding physical color.

These five procedures are usually available in one form or another on modern color graphics raster VDUs. They can be used to make the following color graphics programs.

Spectrum program
This program simply shows a horizontal band of colors across the screen in the form of the spectrum of the rainbow. The band is bounded above and below by a white line, and a frequency axis is marked out below the band with labels and tick marks.

Maxwell's triangle program
Whereas the previous program shows a limited number of colors (the pure colors only) one-dimensionally, this program shows colors in a two-dimensional spread. An equilateral triangle is drawn in the center of the screen and the r, g, b axes are divided up into the n steps to make 2^n small equilateral triangles that are color-filled according to their (r, g, b) coordinates. The number n is chosen so that the number of triangles does not exceed the number of displayable colours. (If halftoned painting is not used, then n is usually the number of bit planes.)

The mixture program
The purpose of this program is to allow the user to select the exact color combination that is wanted. It is useful to designers from all areas who need to select aesthetic color combinations. The text screen shows the main menu of the program:

    0   exit this program
    1   set default colors
    2   load a file of colors
    3   edit a color
    4   save colors to a file
    5   swap over colors

When the program is started a set of, say, 16 color boxes is drawn and this menu appears. The color boxes have white borders, are across the bottom of the screen, as in Figure 13-12, (or stacked one on top of each other at the right-hand side of the screen) and are numbered below (or on their left-hand sides). The colors inside the boxes are the default colors set by the program (such as all black). If menu choice 3 is selected (by entering '3', or through the use of arrow keys or mouse until the required option is highlighted, and then a button or return is pressed), then the user is asked for a color box to edit (1 to 16 here). After selecting an on-screen color, that box is highlighted by having its border changed to red, the number to the left of the box changes from white to red, and the larger current-color box is filled with the color selected. In place of the menu, another box appears which contains three horizontal bars partially filled with red, green, and blue to indicate the percentages of the additive primaries that make up the current color. (See Figure 13-12.) The top bar is labeled with the letter 'R' in red and to the right of each bar is the percentage value (0 to 100) of that component of the current color. If the user presses the '+' key then the red bar fills up by an increment and pressing the '-' key it decrements the red bar in steps. (Repeated presses of the '-' key eventually empties the bar to zero). At any time the user may stop pressing the '+' or '-' key, causing the movement in the red bar to stop, when the desired color is reached. At the same time that the red bar is changing, so is the percentage figure at the right hand end of the red bar and the current color is continually adjusted to the changing percentage of red. The user may now adjust green, blue, or red at any time by first selecting the primary by typing 'R', 'G,' or 'B' (without pressing return). The currently selected bar is indicated by a letter 'R', 'G', or 'B' in red, green, or blue respectively at the left hand end of the selected primary color bar. An alternative system is to move the mouse cross hairs into the desired color-bar area and clicking a button to indicate the selection. The mouse can also be used to replace the use of the '+' and '-' keys by moving it either above or below the current level of primary color within the selected color bar. To exit from this color editing mode, a button may be pressed (such as the escape key) or else a submenu item selected by the mouse. The user is then faced with the option of replacing the selected on-screen color with the current edited color both of which should be still visible on the screen or not. (The on-screen colors should be visible at all times throughout the run of the program.)

Another useful feature to have during the edit mode is to allow the CMY and HLS color systems to be used in place of the RGB system. This feature can be incorporated by allowing the user to type any of the letters 'C', 'M', or 'Y' to get CMY bars and percentages replacing the RGB bars and percentages, and pressing any of the letters 'H', 'L', or 'S' to alternatively get the HLS bars and percentages of the current edit color. The CMY and HLS bars would then operate in a similar fashion to the operation of the RGB bars. For editing HLS values, a color wheel and two bars would be more appropriate than three bars. The color wheel can have a small arrow which moves around the circumference and points to the current hue. The intensity bar would be colored in the selected hue and the saturation bar drawn in white. (See Figure 13-13.)

Main menu choice 5 is useful for rearranging the on-screen colors to suit the user so that they show a gradation of color change from color 1 to color number 16. The colors could, for instance, be in a particular order for coloring a terrain relief map by height contours.

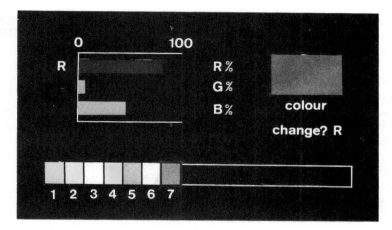

Figure 13-12 (Color Figure 11.) The screen layout for the 'mixture' program while editing the RGB values of a color. The color currently being edited is highlighted with a red border at the bottom of the screen.

Dither program

The purpose of this program is to display a screen of boxes colored in by dithers. The white border around the top left dither box flashes (for instance, by repeatedly drawing the border in white and then black) to indicate the currently selected dither. The color codes of the two pure colors that go to make the dither are displayed in a dialog box at the bottom right-hand corner of the screen. By using the left, right, up, and down arrow keys or else the mouse, the user can select any dither box on the screen and find out its codes. By pressing some other key, the program can proceed to the next screen load of dither colors.

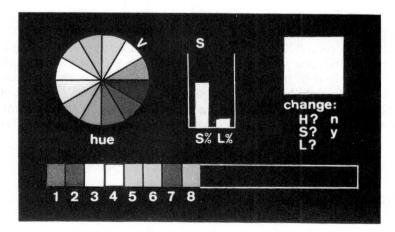

Figure 13-13 (Color Figure 12.) The screen for the 'mixture' program while editing HLS color values. The color currently being edited is highlighted with a red border at the bottom of the screen.

Pressing the escape key terminates the program. It is interesting to note the variety of colors that come up in this program. The pattern is generated by essentially by the following code segment:

```
clear_screen;
more := true; color1 := 1; color2 := color1 + 1;
row := 1; column := 1;
while more do
begin
    draw_dither_box(row,column,color1,color2);
    color2 := color2 + 1;
    if color2 > max_nr_colors then
    begin
        color1 := color1 + 1; color2 := color1 + 1;
        if color1 > max_nr_colors then more := false;
    end;
    column := column + 1;
    if column > max_column_nr then
    begin
        column := 1; row := row + 1;
        if row > max_row_nr then more := false;
    end;
end;
```

The above code is self-explanatory.

Picasso program

This program paints two-dimensional on-screen drawings by using any available colors on the VDU. The colors could be pure colors specified by a number 0 to s-1 (s being the number of available pure colors), a halftone specified by R, G, and B values, or a dither specified by 'color1', and 'color2' values (as in the code segment above). The user would run the mixture or dither program above to determine the codes of the sort of colors wanted. The areas to be painted are identified by a cross hairs under numeric keypad control or mouse control. An option in the program allows the sequence of painting commands to be saved in a file to disk in a format that allows quick repainting of the scene. Two examples of scenes produced with this program are illustrated in Figure 13-14.

13.3 Surface rendering

It has been shown that an easy way to represent three-dimensional solid objects is to define a number of polygonal facets so that they cover the surface of the object. Each facet may be associated with a color and then the object can be displayed colored, with hidden surfaces removed. However this rendering of the object assumes that there are no point

Figure 13-14 (Color Figure 13.) Two pictures produced by the 'picasso' program.

sources of light so that the object is illuminated by ambient white light only. That is, so far the assumption is that all objects are flooded with a uniform homogeneous distribution of white light. This ambient light originates from a finite light source (often the sun) but due to scattering by particles in the atmosphere, multiple reflections from everyday objects, filtering through pulled shades, and so forth the light loses its organized directional nature (as in light beams) and rays of light travel in every direction at every point. The intensity (light flux per unit cross-sectional area and per unit time) of this ambient light will be denoted as I_a. A further assumption is that the ambient light is white light; that is, the intensity of each frequency of visible light is the same. When this ambient light strikes a solid object, the object will reflect some of the light, absorb some (which may heat up the object), and perhaps transmit some through the object. As previously seen for the refractive index, the amount of refraction, absorption, and transmission due to a medium generally depends on the frequency of light striking the medium. The proportion of light energy of a given frequency reflected by the surface is called the reflectance coefficient or the *reflectivity* of the surface and in general it is a function of the frequency of the incident light. The total proportion of light intensity reflected averaged over all frequencies is called the *albedo* of the object's surface. An albedo can have a value between 0 and 1. Optically smooth surfaces reflect light specularly according to the law of relection; that is, the incident light ray and reflected light ray are in the same plane as the surface normal and make the same angle with the normal vector. A diffuse surface reflects light uniformly in all directions (of a hemisphere) irrespective of the direction of the incident light ray. Up to this stage, the light has been assumed to be ambient only, so that these surface reflection properties are not relevant and light will be reflected in all directions.

To render solid objects more realistically however, many conditions must be taken into account, such as the lighting of the object, the orientation of the facets, the reflection properties of each surface, the distances of each facet and light sources, the refractive indexes, and the absorption coefficients. To include some of these features in rendering three-dimensional scenes, consider the simple set up shown in Figure 13-15. The point E is the viewing position, P is the point of reflection on a facet, and S is the position of a point light source. Assume that the ambient light intensity is I_a and that the point source emits light of intensity I_S at unit distance from S. Denote the position vector of E as x_E, of P as x, and of S as x_S. Assume that the reflection coefficients for the facet at P under red, green, and blue lights are k_R, k_G, and k_B. The distance from S to P is r where:

$$r = SP = \text{norm}(x - x_S)$$

and a unit vector in that direction is therefore $(x - x_S) / r$. The distance from P to E is d where:

$$d = PE = \text{norm}(x_E - x)$$

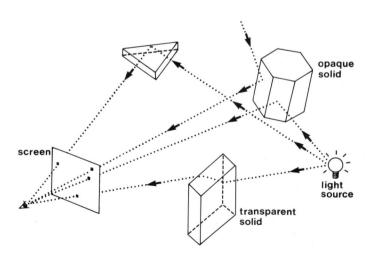

Figure 13-15 The diagrammatic relationship between the eye, a VDU screen, a light source, and various objects which either reflect, refract, or total-internally reflect the light rays.

and a unit vector from P to E is $(x_E - x) / d$. Let the unit normal vector to the facet at P be n.

The simple case is where the source emits no light, that is, $I_S = 0$. Then using only ambient light and taking into account the distance of the reflecting surface d from the eye position E, the intensity received at E from the direction EP is:

$$I_R = I_a + k_R I_a / d^2$$
$$I_G = I_a + k_G I_a / d^2$$
$$I_B = I_a + k_B I_a / d^2$$

These equations show that the ambient light tends to make more distant objects paler; that is, color strength (saturation) diminishes to zero as distance d increases. This is what would be expected: objects become hazy with distance into the atmosphere. On the other hand, for very small distances the second term in the equations dominates and the color strength is then very high.

Now consider a light source of intensity I_S at position x_S and assume that the facet has perfectly diffuse reflection. The source emits light omnidirectionally and so by Lambert's law of illumination the incident intensity of light radiated from the source directly to the point x is given by:

$$I_{inc} = I_S / r^2$$

This equation says that the light intensity falls off as the inverse square of the distance from the source. If the light source modeled is the sun then the distance from the sun is very large in relation to the distance between the objects in a scene and so light from the sun can be regarded as parallel rays of constant intensity. For rendering a scene with street lights fading into the distance however, this formula can be used to add realism.

Facets that are turned away from the eye appear dimmer than when they are in full view and illuminated by a light source. Lambert's cosine law of lighting can be applied in this case:

$$I_P = I_{inc} \cos(i)$$

where i is the angle of incidence (in radians). This states that the actual amount of light energy received per unit area per unit time on a surface at P is the intensity of the light beam times the cosine of the angle of incidence of the light beam. This cosine is the dot product of the surface normal and the direction of the light beam. Lambert's law can be understood by reference to Figure 13-16. The beam has energy E spread over cross-sectional area A and hence the intensity of the incident beam is $I_{inc} = E / A$. The energy E is then spread over the mat surface of area $A' = A / \cos(i)$ so that the intensity of light across the surface element at P is $I_P = E / A' = E / A \cos(i) = I_{inc} \cos(i)$ as above. This means that the intensity of light from a source reflected from a facet of an object will be dimmer by a factor of $\cos(i)$. The incident energy on the facet at P is therefore $I_S A \cos(i) / r^2$. This energy is then reflected equally in all directions over the hemisphere (of radius

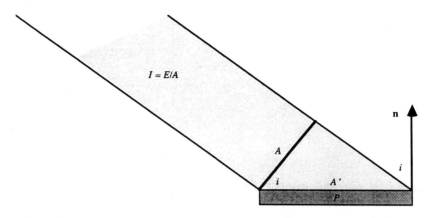

Figure 13-16 A light beam of intensity I and cross-sectional area A strikes a mat surface of area A' at point P at an angle of incidence i to the surface normal vector $\mathbf{n}$. As a result, the light intensity on the surface is I_P which is reduced by a factor of $\cos i$ from I.

d, say, to reach point E) around P as shown in Figure 13-17. Therefore the light intensities reaching E will be:

$$I_R = I_a + k_R \{I_a / d^2 + I_S A [\mathbf{n} \cdot (\mathbf{x}_S - \mathbf{x})] / (2 \pi d^2 r^3)\}$$
$$I_G = I_a + k_G \{I_a / d^2 + I_S A [\mathbf{n} \cdot (\mathbf{x}_S - \mathbf{x})] / (2 \pi d^2 r^3)\}$$
$$I_B = I_a + k_B \{I_a / d^2 + I_S A [\mathbf{n} \cdot (\mathbf{x}_S - \mathbf{x})] / (2 \pi d^2 r^3)\}$$

If the nonambient light is from one or more local point sources (rather than being a beam of light from a distant source such as the sun), then a sum must be formed over the local point sources:

$$I_f = I_a + k_f \{I_a + A / (2 \pi) \sum I_{S_i} \mathbf{n} \cdot (\mathbf{x}_{S_i} - \mathbf{x}) / r_i^3\} / d^2$$

for $f = R$, G, and B. For remote light sources (such as the sun) the source rays are parallel

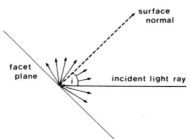

Figure 13-17 A ray of light strikes a mat surface area at an angle giving diffuse reflection.

and the following form is appropriate:

$$I_f = I_a + k_f \{I_a - A / (2 \pi) I_{beam} \; \mathbf{n} \cdot \mathbf{d}_{beam}\} / d^2$$

where I_{beam} is the intensity of the beam, and $\mathbf{d}_{beam}$ is its direction (a unit vector). Combinations of local and remote light sources may similarly be modeled by these equations. The effect of these various light sources on diffuse facets then is to increase the facet's brightness to a lesser or greater extent depending on the angles of incidence, the distances, and the surface area of the facet.

To generalize to nondiffuse facets is more difficult since the reflected light energy is then no longer spread evenly over the hemisphere about P as shown in Figure 13-18. Formulas have been postulated for the nondiffuse reflection, such as:

$$I_{refl} = W(i) (\cos(\theta)^n) I_{inc}$$

where $W(i)$ replaces $k_f \cos(i)$, θ is the angle between the normal at P, $\mathbf{n}$, and the direction PE (so that $\cos(\theta) = \mathbf{n} \cdot (\mathbf{x}_E - \mathbf{x}) / d$), and the power n specifies how close to diffuse ($n = 0$) the surface is. Another approach to this problem is to break the facet down into smaller

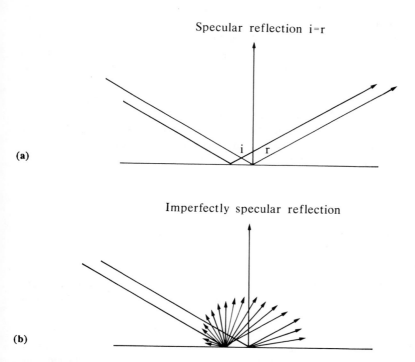

(a)

Specular reflection i=r

(b)

Imperfectly specular reflection

Figure 13-18 Non-diffuse reflection of a light ray from an imperfectly specular surface (i.e. a realistic surface that is not perfectly shiny).

facets and use the diffuse equation over them. This should be done in particular if the facet is so large that parameters such as r and i vary significantly.

Absorption of light in the atmosphere can also be included in the model by including factors of exp($-\mu$ r) and exp($-\mu$ d) over light paths where μ is the atmospheric absorption coefficient. This coefficient is very small in the case of the atmosphere, but for transparent substances like glass it can be significant. It is therefore more applicable to use Lambert's absorption law (see next section) when the transmission of light through various media is included.

Two special shading techniques are frequently used in computer graphics to make flat facets appear to have smooth curvature in the graphics output. The first of these is called Gouraud shading. This method assigns to each vertex of a solid the average of the normal vectors of the adjoining facets and then computes the light intensities at each vertex using (usually) a simplified approximation to a shading formula above that incorporates Lambert's cosine law. The R, G, and B intensities for every spot on a facet are then obtained by interpolating from the R, G, and B intensities computed at the vertexes. Linear interpolation is used, and in this way Gouraud shading makes the surfaces of objects appear to be round, but the silhouetted edges are still the straight edges of polygonal facets. If the surfaces were really curved then surface highlights due to near specular reflection of point sources would be small and round. Gouraud shading does not render such surface highlights well – they tend to appear spread out too much and be less intense. The second shading technique, called Phong shading, renders highlighting better: facets again appear curved, and highlighted spots due to the reflections of bright light sources from the imaginery curved surface appear more realistically. In Phong shading, instead of interpolating R, G, and B intensities to every spot on a facet, the averaged normal vectors at the vertexes are interpolated to every spot on the facet. The R, G, and B light intensities at every spot on a facet are then computed, and the spot shaded using a normal vector for that spot which is interpolated from these averaged normals. The facets are divided into spots at which the computations are made. These may correspond to screen pixels, or be subpixels (grid sites using integer and half integer device coordinate address values) which are averaged to provide truer pixel values. This process obviously takes a lot more computation time than the simpler Gouraud shading technique, but the resulting graphics output is more pleasing.

13.4 Ray tracing

Ray tracing is a technique that uses the laws of geometrical optics to determine the nature of the light reaching the eye from all points in a picture and thus produce a very accurate and realistic rendition of the scene. According to geometrical optics, light rays are sent in straight lines in all directions from a point source of light. A ray continues in a straight line until it hits a surface; at which point it splits into two rays, one reflected from the surface and the other transmitted through the medium. The Law of Reflection states that the angle of incidence equals the angle of reflection and that the incident and reflected rays and the surface normal are coplanar. Snell's Law governs the direction of the refracted (transmitted) ray.

Geometrical optics does not take into account the losses of light energy that occur in the real world. When a light ray is reflected at a surface, not all of the light energy is reflected – some is absorbed into the reflecting object. When light is transmitted through a transparent medium, the light energy that comes out of the medium is less than what went in due to absorption by the medium: the further the transmitted light travels through the medium the weaker it gets, in accordance with Lambert's law of absorption:

$$I = I_0 \exp(-\mu\, d\,)$$

where I_0 is the intensity of light entering the medium, I is the intensity at distance d into the medium, and μ is the absorption coefficient. The *opacity* of the medium is defined as:

$$\kappa = \mu\,/\,(3\,\rho)$$

where ρ is the density of the medium. If the medium is opaque (i.e. κ is very large) then there is no transmitted ray. Geometrical optics is only concerned with the cases $\kappa = 0$ (perfectly transparent) and $\kappa = \infty$ (perfectly opaque). Under these conditions all light paths in geometrical optics are reversible; that is, if geometrical optics predicts that a ray of light will travel from point A to point B via various intermediate points, then a ray of light would also travel from B to A via the same intermediate points.

Of all the light rays emitted from the light sources for a scene, very few actually reach the eye. It would be far too costly to construct a scene by following every possible light ray from every source and recording those that strike the eye. Therefore in the ray tracing algorithm imaginary light rays are projected back from the eye to points in the scene using the laws of geometrical optics until they hopefully meet a light source. Rather than having to trace an infinite number of rays then the algorithm need only trace one ray per screen pixel.

This backward ray tracing produces a treelike series of forked paths: each node of the ray path tree corresponds to a surface in the three-dimesional scene. There is one tree per pixel. The leaves of this tree are either a light source or else correspond to a ray that does not terminate. In practice a limiting sphere in the background color is placed around the scene so that those rays that do not terminate on a light source strike this sphere and adopt its color. After constructing a tree, the light values at the leaves are noted and then the tree is processed to compute the light values at the nodes going backwards to the root of the tree. The light value at the root is then the value that the pixel should be set to. If all leaves of a tree strike the limiting sphere then the pixel forms part of a shadow in the scene. More accuracy can be achieved by computing the light value at the corners of each pixel rather than at the center and then averaging these values to give the pixel value. This latter technique is an anti-aliasing method.

Ray tracing is a very slow process because one tree must be generated and processed per pixel on the screen. However if sufficient tree depth is allowed in the program, ray tracing creates very realistic renderings of three-dimensional scenes. It correctly accounts for any collection of objects with hidden surfaces, any number of light sources, reflections, transparency, and shadows. Obviously diffraction and other wave effects of light are not correctly modeled and extinction of light due to absorption is ignored.

13.5 Graphics animation techniques

Computer graphics animation is the use of computer graphics equipment where the graphics output presentation dynamically changes in real time. This is often also called *real-time animation* because of the prevalence of non-real-time or pseudoanimation (to be discussed later). Computer graphics animation by this definition is obviously not possible on hard-copy and DVST output equipment since these do not have selective erasure. For true graphics animation to occur, part of the graphics being displayed must be erased and redrawn in a slightly modified position without destroying the rest of the picture. The following loop of pseudocode illustrates the method of real-time animation:

1. Draw the scene.
2. Store the background that will be overwritten by the object at (x, y).
3. Draw the animation object centered at point (x, y).
4. Compute the new position $(xnew, ynew)$, angle, shape, and so forth for the next frame.
5. Restore the background at (x, y).
6. Update the object coordinates: $x \leftarrow xnew$, $y \leftarrow ynew$.
7. Goto step 2.

Care must be taken, in the animation code, that these steps appear in the right order.

Let t_i denote the time taken for step i in the above loop. The total time of the loop body is therefore:

$$T = t_2 + t_3 + t_4 + t_5 + t_6$$

The animation object is visible only during steps 3 and 4, that is, for the time interval:

$$t_{vis} = t_3 + t_4$$

and in steps 2, 5, and 6 the object is not on the screen. To attain the appearance of animation without flicker, the requirement is that the time the object is invisible be relatively short, that is:

$$t_2 + t_5 + t_6 < t_{vis}$$

Another way of saying this is that t_{vis} / T should be as close to unity as possible. This can always be achieved by adding a suitably long delay into step 4, that is, by increasing t_4. However for real-time animation, a further requirement is that the frame display time T be short enough for the eye to merge sequential frames into continuous motion by persistence of vision. This effectively means that:

$$T < 1/25 \text{ sec}$$

Now T is a function of the number N of pixels in the animation object. If N is reduced then T will be reduced. What must be found is the largest value of N for which this criterion is met.

There are four useful benchmark programs that can be made to determine the suitability of various graphics VDUs for animation, and in particular help to find the number N. These four programs measure the pixel reading and writing times. They use the hardware primitive commands in device coordinates. In the first benchmark program, a large rectangle of $n \times m$ pixels is painted by setting one pixel at a time. The time taken is measured. Then the program is rerun, but with the pixel write statement commented out in the compiled code. The time for executing the second program is the overhead and this is subtracted from the first time. The difference is divided by $n \times m$ to yield the individual pixel writing time in pixels per second. The program is repeated with various values of n and m, and then the average pixel writing time w_p is noted. The second benchmark program measures the line drawing time. Instead of drawing an $n \times m$ rectangle a pixel at a time, the rectangle is drawn by n lines each m pixels long. This benchmark yields the pixel writing time in line drawing, and the averaged result can be recorded as w_l pixels per second and so many millimeters per second. The third benchmark program fills an $n \times m$ rectangle by the hardware area fill primitive and also yields an averaged pixel writing time. The result of this benchmark is recorded as w_a pixels per second and as so many square millimeters per second. The last benchmark program reads the pixel value of every pixel in an $n \times m$ rectangle (throwing away the values read). The result is the averaged pixel reading time, recorded as r_p pixels per second. If the time measurement in any of these benchmark programs is too small for stopwatch or real-time clock (RTC hardware in the host) measurement, then the graphics function is repeated p times over the same $n \times m$ rectangle so that an accurate time can be measured. It is worthwhile doing this benchmarking for all graphics VDUs available. Generally the reading time is slower than the individual pixel writing time which is slower than the line writing time, and the area filling time is the fastest. It is interesting to see how different devices differ between themselves in speeds for the four different operations. If the animation object consists of N_p pixels individually written, N_l pixels written by line drawing, and N_a pixels written by the area filling primitive, then the minimum time to draw the animation object will be:

$$t_{min} = N_p / w_p + N_l / w_l + N_a / w_a$$

and the total number of pixels in the object is:

$$N = N_p + N_l + N_a$$

Using only the fastest pixel writing scheme ($N_p = N_l = 0$) gives the maximum number of pixels that can be used for real-time animation on the particular graphics VDU as:

$$N_{max} = w_a / 25$$

This number is usually much less than the total number of pixels available on the screen. The ratio $\eta = N_{max} / ndh / ndv$ provides a dimensionless measure for comparing the variety of computer graphics raster VDU equipment for their real-time animation capabilities. (See problem 13.7.)

A process called *tweening* is often used in step 4 of the animation loop. It is applicable to animation objects defined by a sequence of points, and that change shape from frame to frame. For example, suppose that an animation object contains a polygon given by n vertexes (x_i, y_i) for $i = 1$ to $i = n$. The change in each of these coordinates from frame to frame will in general be independent and different for each i: x_i and y_i can be thought of as independent functions of time:

$$x_i = x_i(t), \quad y_i = y_i(t)$$

for each i. The frame time t is an integer multiple of T, the animation loop period, say $t = k\ T$. The shape of such a polygon is known initially ($t = 0$) and for a small number of other frames called *key frames*. The shape of the polygon in between these key frames is derived by linear interpolation of the coordinates at the nearest previous and next key frames. If the nearest key frames are at frame time $t1 = k1\ T$ and $t2 = k2\ T$ with $k1 < k2$ then the tweening algorithm says that vertex i at frame time $t = k\ T$ has coordinates:

$$x_i = \{x_i\ (k1\ T)\ (k2 - k) + x_i\ (k2\ T)\ (k - k1)\} / (k2 - k1)$$
$$y_i = \{y_i\ (k1\ T)\ (k2 - k) + y_i\ (k2\ T)\ (k - k1)\} / (k2 - k1)$$

These values are easy to compute and allow arbitrary digitized animation objects to be easily animated from just a few key frames. When digitizing key frames, it is very important to ensure that the vertexes from one key frame to the next keep in correct correspondence. Special effects, such as objects appearing to turn inside out, are obtained when vertex ordering is changed between key frames. (See problem 13.8.)

Pseudoanimation is creating a sequence of stills (hard copy or soft copy), photographing or videotaping (i.e. storing directly to a video recorder) each still as one *frame*, and then later playing back the frames at a faster speed. Visual animation requires a playback of at least 25 frames per second. Thus if the animation loop time $T > 1/25$ sec for an animation frame on a particular computer graphics VDU, then only pseudoanimation is possible for that frame sequence on that device. Now consider the computing power and cost of making a feature film using computer graphics pseudoanimation throughout.

A normal television set has typically of the order of 500 scan lines and this would be too low a resolution for cinematic films because they are projected onto large screens and then the scan lines would be very obvious. About 1500 scan lines would be sufficient resolution for film making. Since the aspect ratio for CRT screens is 3/4 this implies a VDU screen resolution of 2000 x 1500. However cinematography uses a wide screen, the aspect ratio of which is actually 1/2. This means getting a nonstandard-shaped CRT and using a resolution of 3000 x 1500. The total number of pixels is therefore 4.5 million per frame in the film. Now since the eye can detect about thirty thousand different colors (including all shades and intensities of all hues), a large number of bit planes are required. Eight bits per electron gun gives 24 bits per pixel and this provides 2^{24} (or over 16 million) simultaneous screen colors. This is certainly satisfactory and will ensure that no sharp differences are seen in the shading of curved surfaces. Since there are 3 bytes per pixel and 4.5 million pixels this requires that the device have 13.5 megabytes (MB) of pixel RAM. The film will also require 13.5 megabytes of storage per frame. A feature film would go for 90 minutes, so at 24 frames per second (the standard rate for films) the total storage required for the film is 1.75 TB. A terabyte (TB) is 10^{12} bytes. This is an enormous amount of secondary storage! An estimate can also be made of the computer CPU needed time to create the data. Using the most sophisticated graphics rendering algorithms (including ray tracing) would require 1000 to 10000 machine code operations (ops) per pixel. Taking the value to be 6 Kops/pixel, then with 3 bytes/pixel and 1.75 Terrabytes altogether, the film requires 3.5 Pops of CPU power. A peta-operation (Pop) is 10^{15} (or more strictly 2^{50}) operations. For a VAX 11/780 which is rated as a 1 Mips (one million instructions per second) machine this would take 3.5 Gsec. One gigasecond (Gsec) is 10^9 (more strictly 2^{30}) seconds which is 11.6 Kdays or 31.7 years. In other words it would take a VAX over 100 years to make the 90 minute feature film assuming no errors were made and there was no downtime! A supercomputer such as a CDC Cyber 205 or Cray XMP can operate much faster than a VAX midicomputer. (A midicomputer is midway between a minicomputer and a mainframe computer in CPU power.) Supercomputers are capable of 50 Mflops. A megaflop is a million floating-point operations per second. Thus a supercomputer is easily 50 times faster than a VAX and would take about 2.2 years. The new range of supercomputers expected to run at 30 Gflops (about 3×10^{10} floating point operations per second) would reduce this time down to about a month.

True full-screen (all pixels) high-resolution realistic animation is not achievable on present computer graphics hardware as the movie example above shows. However, animation can be done in a limited way on todays graphics equipment by a number of hardware and software tricks:

1. CLUT manipulation;
2. Bit-plane manipulation;
3. Use of UDCs;
4. Special drawing modes;
5. Sprites;
6. Bit blitting.

Some of these techniques will now be looked at more closely.

CLUT manipulation

Pixel values in pixel RAM are indexes to color values in the color look-up table (CLUT), not the color values themselves. The color of a pixel on the screen is found by first looking up pixel RAM to find its pixel value (logical color), and then using this value as an index into the CLUT. This returns the actual value (physical color) to be sent to the RGB electron guns and hence the actual color displayed by that pixel. This method therefore makes use of the 'set_color' and 'define_color' procedures mentioned before.

A simple example of this method will be to show how to display the sun rising and setting over the ocean. The sun will be bright yellow (color value = 'sun_color'); the ocean, dark blue (color value = 'sea_color'); and the sky, cyan (color value = 'sky_color').

The following procedure calls will draw the background:

```
init_G2D;
set_window(0,0,100,100);
draw_border;
define_color(sea_color,sea_red,sea_green,sea_blue);
set_color(sea_color);
plot_line(0,30,100,30);
bc[1] := white;
paint(10,10,sea_color,1,bc);
define_color(sky_color,sky_red,sky_green,sky_blue);
set_color(sky_color);
bc[2] := sea_color;
paint(10,90,sky_color,2,bc);
define_color(sun_color,sun_red,sun_green,sun_blue);
```

This sets up the graphics screen as shown in Figure 13-19. The above code assumes that constants 'sea_color', 'sea_red', 'sea_green', 'sea_blue', and so forth have been declared with suitable values, and that the boundary color array 'bc' has been declared. Now the various suns must be drawn. These will initially be invisible, but then revealed one by one to simulate the sun rising in the east (right-hand side of the screen) and setting in the west (the left-hand side of the screen). The final picture will only display three colors, viz 'sun_color', 'sea_color', and 'sky_color' which leaves s-3 other logical colors (also called *palettes*) to be manipulated in the CLUT (where s is the number of screen colors as

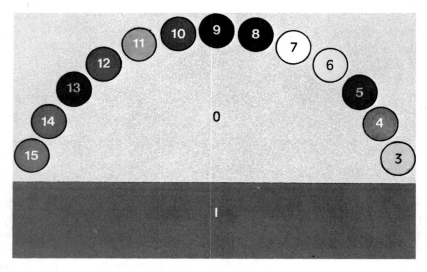

Figure 13-19 (Color Figure 14.) The CLUT manipulation animation programming technique sets pixel values 3 to 15 to color 0 (light blue) initially and then alternately sets each to color 2 (yellow say) and then back to color 0. This gives the effect of the sun rising in the east and setting in the west.

before, that is, the length of the CLUT). So s-3 invisible suns can be drawn using palettes (i.e. CLUT indexes or equivalently logical-color numbers) set up in the array 'col[i]' for $i = 1$ to $i = s$-3. The general code for this is:

```
for i := 1 to s-3 do
begin
    define_color(col[i],sky_red,sky_green,sky_blue);
    set_color(col[i]);
    plot_circle(x[i]-r,y[i],x[i]+r,y[i]);
    bc[1] := col[i];
    paint(x[i],y[i],1,bc);
end;
```

The body of this loop is repeated for $i = 1$ to $i = s$-3 where $(x[i], y[i])$ is the position of the ith sun and r is its radius. (The x and y arrays are assumed to have been previously set up in sequence along the circular arc of the sun's path across the sky from the right-hand side of the screen to the left-hand side.)

Having set up the graphics, animation is achieved by the following loop:

```
for i := 1 to s-3 do
begin
    define_color(col[i],sun_red,sun_green,sun_blue);
    <insert suitable timing delay here>
    define_color(col[i],sky_red,sky_green,sky_blue);
end;
```

This simply makes each predrawn sun appear in yellow and then switch back to invisible (i.e. sky-blue) in turn giving the effect that the orb actually moves across the screen. This method of animation can be very fast.

Bit-plane manipulation

There are two distinct bit-plane manipulation techniques for animation. The first is:

The double frame buffer method – Suppose that the hardware has eight bit planes, numbered 0 through to 7 (Figure 13-20). Let these be grouped into two buffers:

Frame buffer 0 ≡ bit planes 0 to 3
Frame buffer 1 ≡ bit planes 4 to 7

The idea here is to display one frame of the animation sequence in one buffer while the next frame is being drawn and prepared in the other buffer. When the second frame is ready it is displayed and the contents of the first buffer are cleared to begin drawing the next frame, and so on. For this sort of technique to work, the hardware has to be able to only display any selected combination of bit planes and disable the others. A hardware primitive, usually supplied, has the following general form from Pascal:

procedure display_planes(bit_map : integer);

where 'bit_map' is a binary number with one bit representing each bit plane. If a bit in the parameter 'bit_map' is set then the corresponding bit plane is enabled for graphics display, otherwise it is disabled.

This animation technique is best illustrated by the following pseudocode loop:

0.   Initialize the frame counter to 0.
1.   Increment the frame counter.
2.   Clear buffer 0.
3.   Draw the current frame in buffer 0.
4.   Display buffer 0 on the graphics screen.
5.   Increment the frame counter.
6.   Clear buffer 1.
7.   Draw the next frame in buffer 1.
8.   Display buffer 1.
9.   Increment the frame counter.
10. If not the last frame then goto step 2.

In this example with eight bit planes, the 'bit_map' parameter is an eight-bit byte so that its valid values are 0 to 255 only. Buffer 0 corresponds to 'bit_map' value 15, and buffer 1 to 16*15 = 240. These can be set up as constants in the Pascal code:

```
const
    buffer0 = 15;
    buffer1 = 240;
```

Then step 4 in the pseudocode above is:

```
display_planes(buffer0);
```

and step 8 is:

```
display_planes(buffer1);
```

It is also helpful if the hardware has a primitive like:

procedure erase_planes(bit_map : integer);

to clear the bit planes selected in the 'bit_map' parameter. Such a command would be used in step 2 (erase_planes(buffer0)) and step 6 (erase_planes(buffer1)). To draw in buffer 0, only the pixel values from 0 to 15 should be used. In order to draw only into buffer 1, the pixel values are limited to 16 times the corresponding pixel values for buffer 0. The 16 physical colors that these 16 logical-color numbers (or palettes) correspond to in each buffer could be (and should be) the same. The pixel writing mode has to be set to OR mode for drawing so that no change occurs to the other buffer when drawing into a buffer.

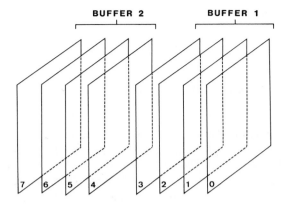

Figure 13-20 Double buffering.

This mode bitwise ORs the new pixel value with the old pixel value. Clearly in this method any animation frame can contain no more than $2^{(p/2)}$ different pure colors out of the selection of $s \equiv 2^p$ pure colors available on the graphics VDU (p being the pixel depth), though by halftoning many thousands of other colors are possible. Suppose that the 16 physical colors to be used are defined in the structures:

```
type
    colour_type = record
        red,green,blue : integer;
        end;
var
    pcol : array[1..16] of colour_type;
```

Then these colors would have to be matched against the logical colors as follows:

```
for i = 1 to 16 do
begin
    logical_color := i-1;
    define_color(logical_color,pcol[i].red,pcol[i].green,pcol[i].blue);
    logical_color := 16*logical_color;
    define_color(logical_color,pcol[i].red,pcol[i].green,pcol[i].blue);
end;
```

Step 3 would then consist of using code like:

```
for i = 0 to 15 do
begin
    set_color(i)
    {graphics drawing commands for color i}
end;
```

and step 7 would be similar:

```
for i = 0 to 15
begin
    set_color(i*16)
    {graphics drawing commands for color i}
end;
```

Note: The double buffering method allows faster and more realistic animation than using all available bit planes as a single frame buffer even though it results in the loss of numbers of displayable pure colors. Thus if t_1 is the time to draw one frame, and t_2 is the time needed to display it for viewing ($t_2=1/25$), then the animation rate in single frame buffering is $1 / T$ where $T=t_1+t_2$. However in double frame buffering, the animation rate is $1 / T$ where $T = \max\{t_1, t_2\}$. If t_1 and t_2 are of the same order of magnitude, then the double frame buffering method will produce animation at twice the speed of the single frame method. For a slow graphics VDU however, $t_1 \gg t_2$ and so the two animation methods give the same animation rate and then there is no advantage in the double buffering method, but rather a disadvantage since fewer pure colors are available per frame. Again as stated above, t_1 is a function increasing linearly with the number of pixels in the frame that the computer must draw – so the fewer the number of pixels to be animated the faster it will run. The following alternative bit plane manipulation technique has significant advantages over both the single and the double frame buffering techniques in the case $t_1 \gg t_2$.

Triple buffer method – This method is suitable where the animation occurs over a background scene which is static for most of the time. A number of bit planes are allocated to the static scene and are displayed continuously, while the remaining bit planes are split into two groups for double buffering as before. For a VDU with eight bit planes, use bit planes 4 to 7 for the static background scene, and double buffer using bit planes 0 and 1 (buffer 0), and 2 and 3 (buffer 1) as in Figure 13-21. First the next scene is written into planes 4 to 7, and then their visibility is switched on. Meanwhile the first frame of the animation object(s) is written into buffer 0 and then displayed while the next frame is written into buffer 1. The flicking between buffers 0 and 1 continues until the next background scene is needed and the process repeats. This process is summarized in the following pseudocode:

1. Disable all bit planes: 'display_planes(0)'.
2. Draw the scene into buffer 2 (bit planes 4 to 7).
3. Display the background scene: 'display_planes(240)'.
4. Draw the first frame of the animation object into buffer 0.
5. Repeat:
    5.1 Display scene (buffer 2) and buffer 0: 'display_planes(243)'.
    5.2 Clear buffer 1: 'erase_planes(12)'.
    5.3 Draw the next frame of the object into buffer 1.
    5.4 Display the scene and buffer 1: 'display_planes(252)'.
    5.5 Clear buffer 0: 'erase_planes(3)'.

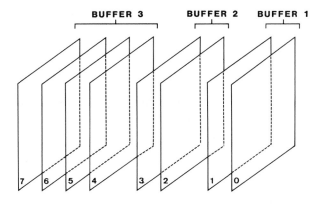

Figure 13-21   Triple buffering.

5.6 Draw the next frame of the object into buffer 0.
Until finished with this scene.

Finally, note the following points about this triple buffering example. In the above arrangement of bit planes, the scene can show up to 16 pure colors out of the available screen colors $s = 2^8 = 256$. This is a significant reduction in available colors. However, halftoning will allow many more so long as care is taken that the primaries are selected among the 16 visible pure colors. The animation object(s) themselves can only be in four colors, but halftoning can again be used to allow various shades. The real advantage of triple buffering is that the background scene does not have to be redrawn for each frame. This saves a lot of time, and makes real-time animation more accessible. Again, the fewer the number of pixels per animation object, the lower t_1 will be, and hence the faster the animation can be done.

The UDC technique

UDC stands for user-defined character set. Many of the early microcomputers produced graphics by special graphics characters. Some characters could be defined by the user. Typically each character is 16 rows of 8 pixels and is defined by an array of 16 eight-bit bytes. The bytes are bit maps saying which pixel in the row is on (bit value 1) or off (bit value 0). This type of graphics operates only on the text screen. The text screen is very fast because it has much less memory to access. For example, if the text screen has 25 rows with 80 characters per row, only 2 Kbytes are needed to represent the screen. Because memory is much cheaper these days, more than one byte is often allocated to each character cell on the text screen. The purpose of extra bytes is to store text attributes, such as foreground and background colors, and whether the character is blinking, underlined, in inverse video, or protected (so that the cursor cannot move onto that cell). UDCs take advantage of this fast screen and also all the text attributes for special graphics effects. UDC graphics is also called *indirect* graphics because pixels are set indirectly – by defining a pixel in a character and then by writing the character at the appropriate screen text cell position. Only a limited amount of graphics can be done this way because the number of UDCs available is always small. The user no longer has control over each pixel on the screen independently. However the technique is very fast. When the graphics VDU provides a text screen and graphics screen as separate areas of memory then these two screens can usually be displayed simultaneously as well as one at a time. In this case a high-resolution full-color detailed background scene could be drawn by using the full capabilities of the independent graphics screen and at the same time using UDCs on the text screen for high-speed animations.

Other techniques

A brief summary follows of the three other animation programming techniques. Method four is the use of special drawing modes. One approach is to use the OR pixel writing mode for drawing the animation object and then the AND NOT pixel writing mode to erase the object. Let p_{back} be the pixel value of a background pixel about to be written over by the animation object, and p_{object} a pixel value of the animation object. Then in drawing the animation object in OR mode the new pixel value is:

$$p_1 = p_{back} \text{ OR } p_{object}$$

using a bitwise logical OR operation on the two binary numbers. The resulting logical color p_1 could be paletted to a suitable physical color. On erasing the animation object in preparation for the next frame the new pixel value is:

$$p_2 = p_1 \text{ AND NOT } p_{object}.$$

To leave the background undisturbed p_2 must equal p_{back}. This can only be so if the background and the animation object do not share common pixel value bits. An alternative pixel writing mode used for animation is the XOR mode because of the identity in Boolean algebra:

$$a \equiv ((a \text{ XOR } b) \text{ XOR } b)$$

The first time the object is drawn in XOR mode it appears, but not in logical color b unless a is zero. When the object is drawn a second time in XOR mode on the same position the object vanishes and the background is fully restored. This mode therefore makes animation programming very easy. It is often used for graphics cursors and rubber-banding. (See problem 13.13.)

The last two animation methods mentioned usually work with specialized hardware for animation. A sprite is a graphics shape used in animation and games programs. Each sprite provided in the system has its own memory area similar to but smaller than pixel RAM and which will be mapped onto a rectangle on the graphics screen. For example, a sprite may be defined as a pixel rectangle 24 pixels wide by 21 high. Effectively Pascal routines to create the sprite would be:

```
procedure write_sprite_pixel(sprite_nr,dcx,dcy,col : integer);
```

which sets the pixel at device coordinates (*dcx*, *dcy*) in the sprite RAM for sprite number 'sprite_nr' to the logical-color number 'col'. The sprite RAM could also be read by a similar routine:

procedure read_sprite_pixel(sprite_nr,dcx,dcy : integer;
    var pval : integer);

which returns the pixel value (logical color) at coordinates (*dcx*, *dcy*) in sprite RAM 'sprite_nr'. (An integer function returning 'pval' might be used instead of such a procedure.)

To animate the sprite, only one procedure is needed:

procedure place_sprite(sprite_nr,dcx,dcy,mode : integer);

which shows sprite RAM number 'sprite_nr' at device coordinates (*dcx*, *dcy*) on the full graphics screen according to the mode specified. A mode value of zero disables display of the sprite, and of one shows it. Other modes may be supplied to set its precedence so that it can be displayed in front of some colored objects, behind others, and so on. Because sprite memory is implemented as an independent memory in hardware, sprite graphics is very fast and does not destroy the graphics data in the regular pixel RAM. Sprite graphics can be simulated in software by screen rectangle 'get' and 'put' commands such as:

procedure read_rectangle(dcx1,dcy1,dcx2,dcy2 : integer;
    var pixel_data : int_array);

This routine reads the pixel values in the rectangle defined by device coordinates (*dcx*1 , *dcy*1) to (*dcx*2, *dcy*2) as opposite corners, and stores the data in a user array called 'pixel_data'. The opposite routine is:

procedure write_rectangle(dcx1,dcy1 : integer;
    pixel_data : int_array; mode : integer);

which writes the pixel data stored in the user array 'pixel_data' back into pixel RAM at the rectangle whose lower left corner is (*dcx*, *dcy*) in device coordinates. In animation applications this second rectangle is probably a different screen rectangle but of course it is the same size as the original. The mode parameter can tell the hardware what pixel writing mode to use, such as XOR, when the pixels in 'pixel_data' overwrite the current pixel values at that area of the screen. Because this 'sprite simulation' is in software rather than hardware, it is slower and also changes graphics pixel RAM.

The final technique is called bit blitting which comes from the words bit block transfers. A block or rectangle of pixels is defined, a new lower left corner is specified, and then the bits are copied to the new rectangle location according to a specified pixel writing mode. This is very similar to the 'get pixel rectangle' and 'put pixel rectangle' described in the previous paragraph. The differences are firstly that the pixel data is not returned to the user, for example, into an array parameter. Instead the transfer occurs only from pixel RAM to pixel RAM. This in itself tends to make blitting a faster process than software 'get rectangle' and 'put rectangle' commands. Secondly, bit blitting is normally implemented in the hardware as a single machine-code instruction. Consequently the process is extremely fast and amazing real-time animations of multiple objects is possible. Real-time animation programming involving more than one animation object are ideally programmed in a language that allows concurrent processes such as Concurrent Pascal. The coprocesses can send semaphore signals to each other such as when they collide or other events occur. Apart from translations, other transformations, such as rescaling, rotation, inversion, and change of colors, can be applied to pixel rectangles (also called bit map images or bit blocks). This sort of graphics programming is called graphics image oriented programming in contradistinction to graphics object oriented programming. Further study of this very interesting topic is left to the reader.

13.6 Fractals

In many applications it is enough to use smoothed approximations to objects in the real world. However some objects would look more realistic if they had some controlled irregularity in their rendition. Consider, for instance, the map of an island. The coast is never actually a smooth curve. The length of the coast of an island depends on the scale of measurement - the length of the measuring stick, that is, the resolution of the measuring equipment. The higher the resolution, the greater the perimeter works out to be. In some applications in computer graphics, such as inventing realistic looking maps of islands, a method is needed for building in this controlled irregularity and the use of random 'fractals' provides a way of doing this.

A *fractal* is an object whose shape is irregular at all scales, that is, no matter at what scale it is scrutinized, irregular detail (i.e. nonsmoothness) is observed. A fractal therefore contains infinite detail. This is unlike the standard shapes of Euclidean Geometry such as straight lines, polygons, conics, quadric surfaces, and polyhedra, which are characterized by having integer dimensionality. Thus finite and infinite curves are one-dimensional objects, finite and infinite surfaces are two-dimensional, and volumes are three-dimensional objects. Fractals on the other hand have fractional dimension. A fractal imbedded in n-dimensional space could have any fractional dimension between 0 and n.

Several ways of defining the dimensionality of point sets have been devised. One straightforward way is to use boxes of decreasing side length to measure the size of the point set. Suppose that the minimum number of cells (squares in two dimensions, cubes in three dimensions, etc.) of side length s that totally enclose (or approximately enclose with improving approximation as s tends to zero) the point set is $N(s)$. As the size s of the cells decreases they will contain less empty space and be a truer measure of the size of the point set. For curves, N is found to be proportional to $1/s$ and the dimensionality is $D = 1$; for surfaces N is proportional to $(1/s)^2$ and $D = 2$; and for volumes, $N(s)$ is proportional to $(1/s)^3$ and $D = 3$. For fractal point sets none of these proportionalities apply. In general, the dimensionality D of a point set can be found from the following formula:

$$D = \lim_{s \to 0} \ln(N(s)) / \ln(1/s) \qquad (13.9)$$

The actual size of the point set is then given by:

$$S = \lim_{s \to 0} N(s)\, s^D \qquad\qquad (13.10)$$

For curves, S is the length of the curve; for surfaces, S is the surface area; and for volumes, S is the volume measure.

Fractal geometry, the study of fractals in space – in contrast to Euclidean geometry – was developed by Benoit Mandelbrot in the 1950s. He coined the term *fractal* in 1975. Many fractals have been discovered and investigated since that time. One method of making fractals is to consider the limit of a sequence of polylines or polygons. Another method is by considering the limit of repeated application of mathematical functions to generate the coordinates of points. These examples of fractals have lead to the classification of fractals into two kinds: the *geometric fractal* and the *random fractal*. A geometric fractal is a fractal that repeats self-similar patterns over all scales. A random fractal may be like a geometric fractal but the patterns are no longer perfect and have random defects at every scale. Many objects in the real world such as coastlines, the shape of a bush or tree, and blood vessels are more accurately described by random fractals than by smooth approximations, and for these shapes fractal geometry rather than the normal Euclidean geometry should be employed. Consider now a simple example of a geometric fractal.

The triadic Koch curve (see Figure 13-22) was discovered by H. von Koch in the early 1900s. It is the limit K of a series of plane curves K_n:

$$K = \lim_{n \to \infty} K_n$$

where:

$$K_n = \text{triadic Koch curve of level } n$$

K_0 is a straight horizontal line segment of length *smax*. K_1 has a triangular kink in the middle and is of length $(4/3)$ *smax*. K_2 is shown in the diagram and has length $(16/9)$ *smax*. In general K_n has length:

$$l_n = (4/3)^n \ smax$$

Therefore the length of K is $l_\infty = \infty$: the fractal is infinitely long even though it occupies a finite area. The definition of dimensionality of a point set, equation 13.9, can be used to determine the dimensionality of K, and the curves K_n can be used as approximations to K at the various scales. Using squares of side $s = (1/3)^n$, the curve K_n requires $N = 4^n$ squares. Substituting these into equation 13.9 and using the limit, n tends to infinity, it is seen that the Koch fractal has dimensionality $D = \ln 4\, /\, \ln 3 \approx 1.2619$. The size measure in equation 13.10, like the length calculation, gives infinity for S. While K (or any other fractal) cannot truly be represented in computer graphics because of its infinite detail, it can be approximated by any of K_n; remembering that K_n is itself not a fractal but only an approximation to one at scale n.

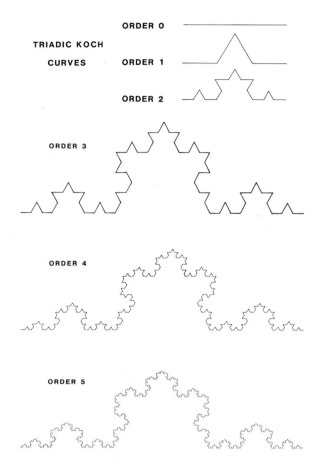

Figure 13-22 Triadic Koch curves.

The triadic Koch curve fractal can be seen to be based on a simple replacement rule. In order to create K_{n+1} from K_n, the K_0 type pattern is replaced by a K_1 type pattern wherever the K_0 type pattern is detected. This is the simple rule for generating the triadic Koch curve.

Additionally it should be noted that patterns appear at various positions, angles, and scales. This calls for the use of *relative graphics programming*. That is, a procedure should be written to draw the basic replicating pattern. This procedure should use only relative graphics primitives and no absolute graphics primitives. Recall that relative graphics primitives do not use absolute coordinates in referring to points and so forth but rather relative coordinates which are in fact displacement vectors from the current graphics cursor position. (After the primitive is called, the graphics cursor is also updated by the displacement.) Once this procedure is written, it can be called numerous times within the program, and the one procedure can readily produce all desired positions, orientations, and scalings of the particular pattern.

Because geometric fractal patterns are built on similar subpatterns and so on *ad infinitum*, they are recursive; that is, a fractal pattern is defined in terms of itself. Fractal programming will therefore rely on the use of recursive programming together with the use of relative graphics output primitives.

The student should take careful note that a lot of effort can be wasted trying to code fractals by not using the right approach. Several cases (low *n* values) may be solved and come out right, but the program will go haywire for larger *n*. Incorrect design can easily lead to incorrect patterns in the higher orders usually with the line being drawn right off the screen. Correct fractal programming requires care to be taken over three vital ingredients of the program:

1. the correct pattern replacement rule;
2. use of relative graphics primitives only (and not absolute graphics primitives) in one pattern generation procedure;
3. correct usage of recursion (and not iteration).

The correct approach can be likened to maintaing a 'turtle' – a robot that can move around in two dimensions that has a pencil for drawing with. The turtle is defined by accompanying global parameters:

1. position of the turtle: (x, y);
2. heading of the turtle: θ the angle from the x axis.

These three real numbers define the turtle's state at any time. Being absolute parameters, they should not be directly accessible to the turtle graphics programmer. They should only be modified by three commands:

1. 'init_g2d_turtle' – resets the turtle to the center of the screen and pointing to the right.
2. 'forward(s)' – moves the turtle forward a distance of *s* units in the direction that it is pointing.
3. 'turn(a)' – turns the turtle anticlockwise through an angle of *a* degrees.

Turtle graphics with just these three turtle commands is vey easily built on top of a two-dimensional graphics package such as G2D. Box 13-2 shows how this can be done. Figure 13-23 shows the idea of a simulated turtle robot on a graphics screen.

For the triadic Koch curve, the basic pattern is simply:

$$K_1 \equiv forward(s)$$

and the replacement rule is:

$$K_n = K_{n-1}; turn(60); K_{n-1}; turn(-120); K_{n-1}; turn(60); K_{n-1}$$

as can be seen in Figure 13-25a.

Note that in any system of global coordinates, the effect of a graphics command does not depend on the sequence of commands that went before. In relative graphics (also called 'turtle geometry' and 'turtle graphics') on the other hand they do.

Box 13-2 Procedures that implement a simple version of turtle graphics.

```
{Include the G2D graphics package:}
{$I 'g2d_plot'}

var
    xold, yold, x, y : real;

procedure init_turtle;
begin
    init_G2D;
    set_window(-100,-100,100,100);
    xold := 0; yold := 0;
    x := 0; y := 0;
    angle := 0;
end;

procedure turn (degrees : real);
begin
    angle := angle + degrees;
    while angle > 360 do
    angle := angle - 360;
    while angle < 0 do
    angle := angle + 360;
end;

procedure forward (s : integer);
begin
    x := x + round(s * cos(angle * pi / 180));
    y := y + round(s * sin(angle * pi / 180));
    plot_line(xold, yold, x, y);
    xold := x; yold:= y;
end;
```

Each of the turtle graphics commands should be implemented as a separate procedure. The Pascal programs 'Triadic_Koch_Curve' (shown in Box 13-3) and 'Quadric_Koch_Curve' (Box 13-4) show examples of turtle graphics programming to produce fractal (approximations). The quadric Koch curve is illustrated in Figure 13-24. It would be useful to add more commands and another two turtle state parameters to this list. The extra state parameters are:

pen_is_down, turtle_visible : boolean

and (absolute) commands to set these parameters:

1. 'pen_up' – subsequent calls to 'forward' will not draw lines on the screen.

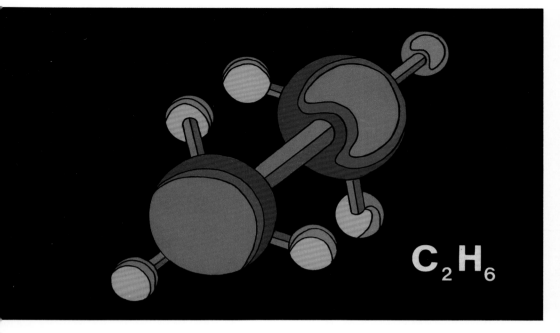

Color Figure 1 (Figure 12.14 in text.) Molecular construction: the ethane molecule.

Color Figure 2 (Figure 12.15 in text.) Simulating the activity of a sculptor with computer graphics.

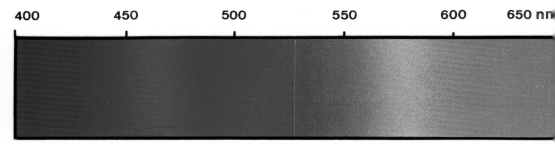

Color Figure 3 (Figure 13.1 in text.) The one-dimensional spectrum of colors.

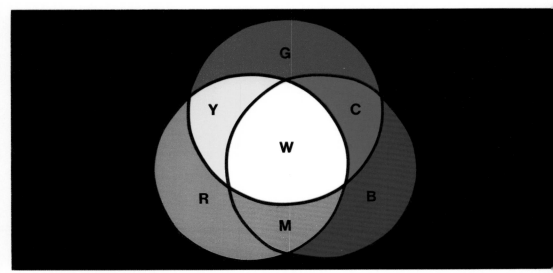

Color Figure 4 (Figure 13.2 in text.) Color addition of the additive primaries red (*R*), green (*G*), and blue (*B*).

Color Figure 5 (Figure 13.3 in text.) Color subtraction of the secondaries (the subtractive primaries) cyan (*C*), magenta (*M*), and yellow (*Y*).

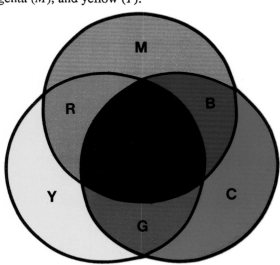

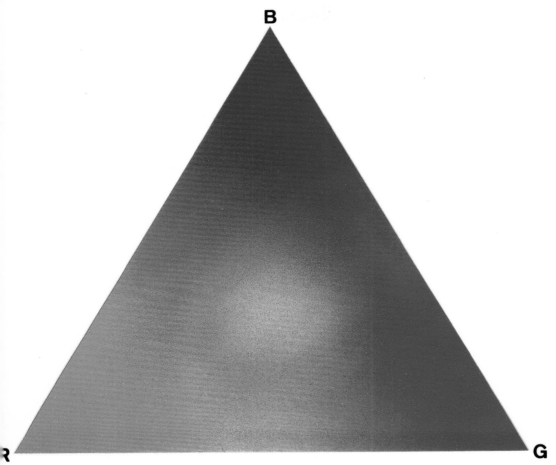

Color Figure 6 (Figure 13.4 in text.) Maxwell's color triangle.

13.5

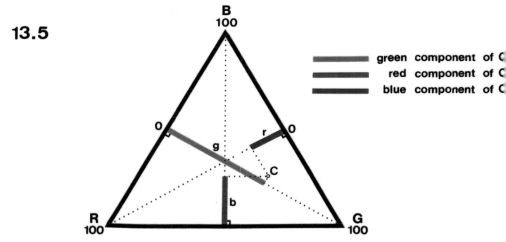

green component of C
red component of C
blue component of C

Color Figure 7 (Figure 13.5 in text.) A diagram showing the constructs that determine the red (R), green (G), and blue (B) components of a color c in Maxwell's triangle.

Color Figure 8 (Figure 13.6 in text.) The (r, g, b) coordinate grid for Maxwell's triangle.

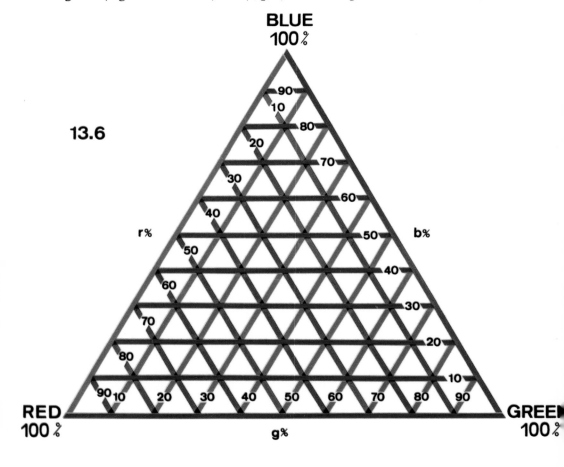

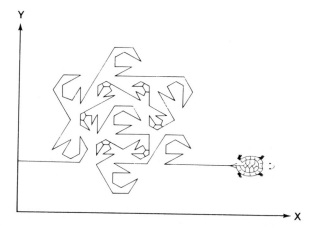

Figure 13-23 Turtle graphics – two-dimensional relative graphics – is the trail left by a programmable turtle robot.

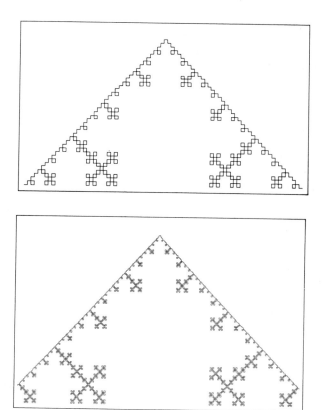

Figure 13-24 Quadric Koch curves.

(a)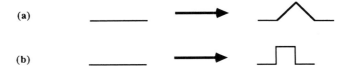

(b)

Figure 13-25   Replacement rules for (a) the triadic and (b) the quadric Koch curves.

2. 'pen_down' – subsequent calls to 'forward' will draw lines on the screen.
3. 'show_turtle' – a triangle appears on the screen to represent the turtle and it moves corresponding to the turtle's position with every 'forward' command.
4. 'hide_turtle' – the turtle symbol does not appear on the screen.

Consider some more geometrical fractals along the same lines as the triadic Kock curve. The quadric Koch curve is similar to the triadic Koch curve. Its replacement rule is shown in Figure 13-25b.

Box 13-3 A turtle program to draw the triadic Koch curve.

```pascal
program Triadic_Koch_Curve(input,output);
{This program produces the triadic Koch fractal curve.}
{Include the turtle graphics commands:}
{$I 'g2d_turtle'}

const
    smax = 512;
var
    order, s : integer;

function compute_size (order : integer) : integer;
var
    i : integer;
    l : real;
begin
    l := smax;
    for i := 1 to order do
        l := l / 3;
    compute_size := round(l);
end;

procedure triadic (i : integer);
begin
    if i > 1 then
    begin
        triadic(i - 1);
        turn(-60);
```

```
            triadic(i - 1);
            turn(120);
            triadic(i - 1);
            turn(-60);
            triadic(i - 1);
        end
        else
            forward(s);
    end;

    begin {main routine}
        init_turtle;
        write('Order of triadic Koch curve? (eg 5)');
        readln(order);
        s := compute_size(order);
        if s > 0 then
            triadic(order)
        else
            writeln('Order too big!');
    end.
```

Box 13-4 A turtle program to draw the quadric Koch curve.

```
program Quadric_Koch_Curve(input,output);
{This program produces the quadric Koch fractal curve.}
{Include turtle graphics:}
{$I 'g2d_turtle'}

const
    smax = 512;
var
    order, s : integer;

function compute_size (order : integer) : integer;
var
    i : integer;
    l : real;
begin
    l := smax;
    for i := 1 to order do
        l := l / 3;
    compute_size := round(l);
end;

procedure quadric (i : integer);
```

```
begin
    if i > 1 then
    begin
        quadric(i - 1);
        turn(-90);
        quadric(i - 1);
        turn(90);
        quadric(i - 1);
        turn(90);
        quadric(i - 1);
        turn(-90);
        quadric(i - 1);
    end
    else
        forward(s);
end;

begin
    init_turtle;
    write('Order of Quadric Koch curve? (eg 4)');
    readln(order);
    s := compute_size(order);
    if s > 0 then
        quadric(order)
    else
        writeln('Order too big!');
end.
```

Clearly many variations on this theme are possible. Examples of other replacement rules are shown in Figure 13-26. Another technique is to close fractals by joining fractal pieces together. Thus the triangular triadic Koch curve is shown in Figure 13-27 and the square quadric Koch curve is shown in Figure 13-28. Many fascinating patterns can be developed in this way. Patterns can be designed that resemble magnified views of snowflakes, no two of which are ever the same.

One can also show that the length of the limiting quadric Koch curve is infinite though it occupies a finite area of the plane, and according to the definition of dimensionality, the dimensionality of the quadric Koch curve is $\ln(5) / \ln(3)$ or about 1.465. Clearly a wide range of fractals can be created by minor variations along these lines. Although all of these fractals were created as lines in a plane, they should not be regarded as one-dimensional objects: each member of the sequence of polylines is one-dimensional but the limit itself is not one-dimensional as seen for the triadic Koch fractal.

When randomness is introduced in the fractal drawing process, the resulting fractal is much more like realistic objects in nature. Randomness can be added by the use of a PRNG (pseudo-random number generator) which affects the parameters of the turtle commands as follows:

$$s = s1 + s2 \, prng$$
$$a = a1 + a2 \, prng$$

where:

$s1$ = the expected distance parameter as generated by the fractal pattern algorithm (assuming no randomness)

$s2 \, prng$ = the distance disturbance term

$a1$ = the expected angle parameter as generated by the fractal pattern algorithm (assuming no randomness)

$a2 \, prng$ = the angle disturbance term

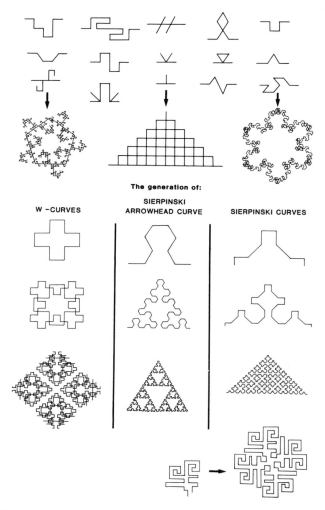

Figure 13-26 Examples of replacement rules.

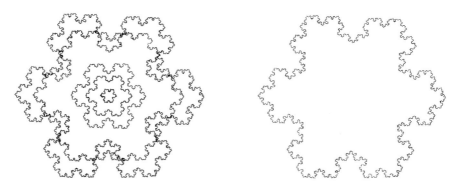

Figure 13-27 The closed triadic Koch curve.

> *prng* = the pseudo-random number (between 0 and 1) returned by the psuedo-random number generator, and is different for every call.

Total randomness (*s1* and *a1* small compared with *s2* and *a2* respectively) would destroy any vestige of a pattern in the fractal. Usually, there is a need to limit or control the amount of randomness that is introduced. This means that *a2* and *s2* should be small compared with *a1* and *s1*, that is:

Figure 13-28 The closed quadric Koch curve.

$$a1 \neq 0 \neq s1$$

and:

$$|a2| << |a1|, |s2| << |s1|$$

The programs 'Tree_fractal' and 'Tree_fractal2' given in Boxes 13-5 and 13-6 respectively, show turtle graphics programming of random fractals. The output of these programs is shown in Figure 13-29. Random fractal programming is also used to make realistic looking mountain ranges. One way this is done is to create and store three vertexes, say A, B, and C, and use them to draw a triangle on the screen. This is the lowest level approximation to the mountain. To form the next approximation to the mountain a point is selected on each edge of the triangle and then displaced by a random amount. Suppose A' is selected on AB, B' on BC, and C' on CA and then A' is moved to A'', B' to B'', and C' to C''. The six vertexes A, B, C, A'', B'', and C'', are stored and four triangles are drawn based on them. The four triangles are $AA''C''$, $BB''A''$, $CC''B'$, and $A''B''C''$. The next approximation applies the same method to each of the four triangles. If each triangle is area filled with a random shade, then successive approximations look more and more like a mountain. Another method of making fractal mountains is to work in three dimensions rather than two. Start with a horizontal quadrilateral say, $ABCD$. The next approximation selects four points along the four edges, say A' on AB, B' on BC, C' on CD, and D' on DA, and randomly displaces them in three dimensions giving points A' $\rightarrow A''$, $B' \rightarrow B''$, $C' \rightarrow C''$, and $D' \rightarrow D''$. A point inside the quadrilateral, E say, is also selected and randomly displaced in three dimensions to E'. The second approximation now has four quadrilaterals $AA''E'D''$, $BB''E'A''$, $CC''E'B''$, and $DD''E'C''$. For the third approximation the same method is applied to these four quadrilaterals. An advantage of the three-dimensional method is that normals can be computed for each quadrilateral and then the quadrilateral can be realistically shaded and hidden surfaces removed.

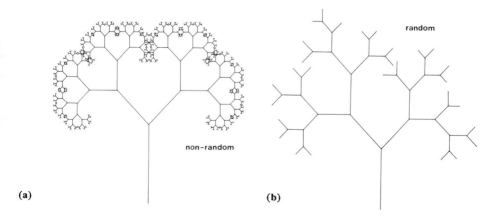

random

non-random

(a)   **(b)**

Figure 13-29   Tree fractals: (a) non-random, and (b) random.

Box 13-5 A turtle graphics program to draw a symmetrical tree.

```
program Tree_fractal(input,output);
{This program produces the plane tree fractal curve.}
{Include turtle graphics:}
{$I 'g2d_turtle'}

const
    smax = 64.0;
    fraction = 0.61803;
var
    s : real;

procedure branch (s : real);
begin
    if s > 1 then
    begin
        s := s * fraction;
        turn(-45);
        forward(s);
        branch(s);
        forward(-s);
        turn(90);
        forward(s);
        branch(s);
        forward(-s);
        turn(-45);
    end;
end;

begin
    init_turtle;
    s := smax;
    turn(-90);
    forward(s);
    branch(s);
end.
```

Box 13-6 A turtle graphics program to draw a realistic tree.

```
program Tree_fractal2;
{This program produces the plane tree fractal curve}
{including random branch generation.}
{Include turtle graphics:}
{$I 'g2d_turtle'}
```

```
const
    smax = 64.0;
    fraction = 0.61803;
var
    s : real;

procedure branch (s : real);
var
    s1, s2 : real;
begin
    s := s * fraction;
    if s > 5 then
    begin
        turn(-45);
        s1 := s + 0.2 * s * prng;
        forward(s1);
        branch(s1);
        forward(-s1);
        turn(90);
        s2 := s + 0.15 * s * prng;
        forward(s2);
        branch(s2);
        forward(-s2);
        turn(-45);
    end;
end;

begin
    init_turtle;
    s := smax;
    turn(-90);
    forward(s);
    branch(s);
end.
```

The examples of fractals described so far result from the limiting cases of line drawing sequences. As mentioned earlier, other examples of fractals have been investigated that result from plotting points rather than lines. Typically, a seed point (x, y) is provided and this generates a second point (x', y') through a pair of equations:

$$x' = fx(x, y)$$
$$y' = fy(x, y)$$

By applying the functions fx and fy to (x', y') and repeating the process an infinite sequence of points is obtained. For most choices of functions fx and fy the points rapidly move off to infinity and so do not produce anything interesting. There are some functions which generate sequences of points which remain finite. An example is $z' = f(z) = z^2$, where $z = x + i y$ and $z' = x' + i y'$ are complex numbers and $i = \sqrt{-1}$. A seed point (x, y) for which $|z| < 1$ will tend to the origin after an infinite number of applications of the squaring function f. If the seed point has $|z| > 1$ then it will move off to infinity. However seed points with $|z| = 1$ remain on the circle $|z| = 1$ in the complex plane (i.e. $x^2 + y^2 = 1$). The interesting points do not form a fractal but an ordinary circle in the case $f(z) = z^2$. Other complex quadratic functions do however yield fascinating fractals. The functions $f(z) = \lambda z(1-z)$ produce the circle fractal, the dragon fractal, and the puffy cloud fractal for $\lambda = 3$, i, and 1 respectively. For real λ greater than 4 nothing interesting is produced as the points lie on a straight line. For small real λ (e.g. $\lambda = 0.1$) a circle (or ellipse) is produced. The functions $f(z) = z^2 + c$ produce the famous Mandelbrot set when the starting z seed value is zero, and the Julia sets for other seed values.

While the square function repels most points away from the unit circle, the inverse function $\sqrt{z}$, the square root function, attracts them (all points except the origin) to the circle. So likewise with the inverse to the general complex quadratic function, it can be expected that arbitrary points will be eventually attracted to the particular fractal. Therefore the program to draw these sorts of fractals asks for any seed point z and for any coefficients needed in the quadratic and then repeatedly applies the inverse of the quadratic to the function and plots the resultant points. Usually the first dozen or so points are not near the fractal, but after about a dozen applications of the inverse quadratic function the point is attracted close enough to the fractal to be sufficient for plotting the fractal at the finite resolution of the graphics screen. The quadratic function gives two roots both of which tend to the fractal point set. For example, the inverse of the function:

$$z = \lambda w (1 - w)$$

is:

$$w = (1 \pm \sqrt{(1 - 4 z / \lambda)})/2$$

The program therefore randomly selects one or other of these roots at each iteration. In implementing this program it is good software engineering practice to make a library of complex number operations that the main program calls as seen in Box 13-7. The program listing can be found in Box 13-8 and sample fractal output in Figure 13-30.

Turtle graphics can also be used to generate self-similar space-filling patterns. Figure 13-31a shows a triangular spiral which is easily generated by the program in Box 13-9. Similarly the square spiral of Figure 13-31b was generated through the simple program in Box 13-10. Other more complex self-similar patterns are seen in Figure 13-32. (See problem 13.11)

Figure 13-30 Fractals produced by an iterated function system (IFS). The program is shown in Box 13-8.

Figure 13-31 Space filling curves: (a) triangular and (b) square spirals.

HILBERT CURVES

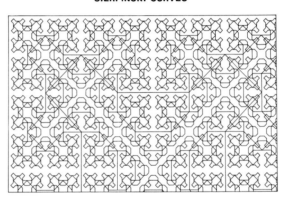

(a)

SIERPINSKI CURVES

(b)

SIMPLE

COMPLEX

(c)   **(d)**

(e)

Figure 13-32   Space filling fractal patterns: (a) Hilbert curves, (b) Sierpinski curves, (c) simple W-curve, (d) complex W-curve, and (e) a complex pattern.

Box 13-7 Procedures for the use of complex numbers.

```
{This compilation unit 'complex_functions' provides complex number
arithmetic}
{operator procedures and functions.}

type
    complex = record
        r, i : real;
    end;

var
    a1, a2, a3, a4 : real;
    x1, x2, x3, x4 : complex;
    cr_factor : integer;
    valid : boolean;

function correct (x : real) : real;
const
    epsilon = 1e-2;
begin
    correct := epsilon * round(x / epsilon);
end;

function real_cuberoot (x : real) : real;
var
    l, sign : real;
begin
    if x = 0 then
        real_cuberoot := 0.0
    else
    begin
        sign := 1;
        if x < 0 then
            sign := -1;
        l := ln(sign * x) / 3.0;
        real_cuberoot := sign * exp(l);
    end;
end;

{Complex Functions follow :}

procedure correct_complex (x : complex; var answer : complex);
begin
    answer.r := correct(x.r);
    answer.i := correct(x.i);
end;
```

```
procedure complex_number (rl, im : real; var answer : complex);
begin
    answer.r := rl;
    answer.i := im;
end;

procedure write_complex (x : complex);
begin
    x.r := correct(x.r);
    x.i := correct(x.i);
    if (x.r <> 0.0) or (x.i = 0.0) then
        write(x.r : 6 : 2);
    if x.i <> 0.0 then
    begin
        if x.i > 0.0 then
            write(' + ')
        else
        begin
            write(' - ');
            x.i := -x.i;
        end;
        write(x.i : 6 : 2, ' * i');
    end;
    write(' ' : 2);
end;

procedure add (x, y : complex; var answer : complex);
begin
    answer.r := x.r + y.r;
    answer.i := x.i + y.i;
end;

procedure subtract (x, y : complex; var answer : complex);
begin
    answer.r := x.r - y.r;
    answer.i := x.i - y.i;
end;

procedure multiply (x, y : complex; var answer : complex);
begin
    answer.r := x.r * y.r - x.i * y.i;
    answer.i := x.r * y.i + x.i * y.r;
end;

procedure divide (x, y : complex; var answer : complex);
```

```pascal
var
    d : real;
begin
    d := sqr(y.r) + sqr(y.i);
    if d > 0 then
    begin
        answer.r := (x.r * y.r + x.i * y.i) / d;
        answer.i := (x.i * y.r - x.r * y.i) / d;
    end
    else
    begin
        write('** divide by zero error **');
        answer.r := 0;
        answer.i := 0;
    end;
end;

function angle (dx, dy : real) : real;
const
    pi = 3.1415926;
begin
    if (dx = 0) then
        if dy >= 0 then
            angle := pi
        else
            angle := -pi
    else if (dx > 0) and (dy >= 0) then
        angle := arctan(dy / dx)
    else if (dx < 0) and (dy >= 0) then
        angle := pi - arctan(-dy / dx)
    else if (dx < 0) and (dy < 0) then
        angle := pi + arctan(dy / dx)
    else if (dx > 0) and (dy < 0) then
        angle := 2 * pi - arctan(-dy / dx);
end;

procedure square_root (x : complex; var answer : complex);
var
    r, theta, r2, theta2 : real;
begin
    r := sqrt(sqr(x.r) + sqr(x.i));
    theta := angle(x.r, x.i);
    r2 := sqrt(r);
    theta2 := theta / 2;
    answer.r := r2 * cos(theta2);
    answer.i := r2 * sin(theta2);
```

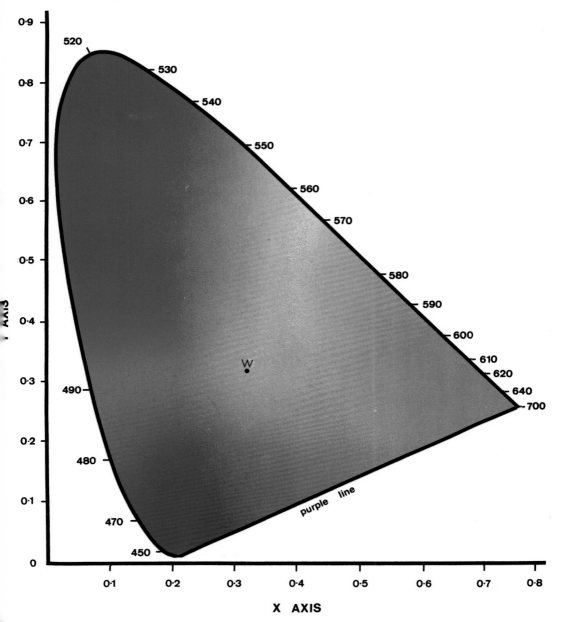

Color Figure 9 (Figure 13.8 in text.) The CIE chromaticity chart that generalizes Maxwell's triangle.

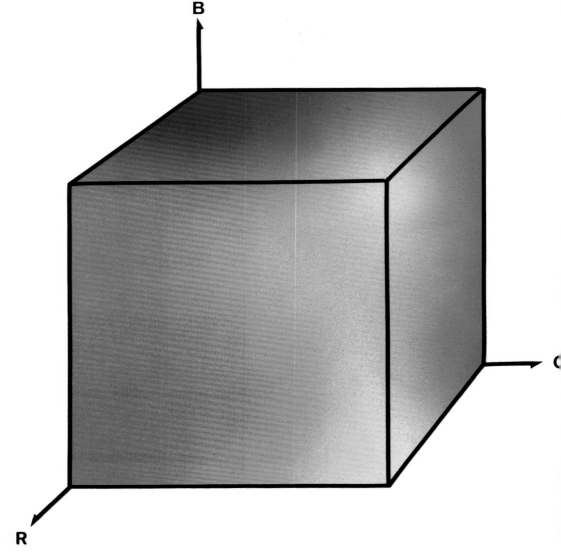

Color Figure 10 (Figure 13.10 in text.) The RGB color cube.

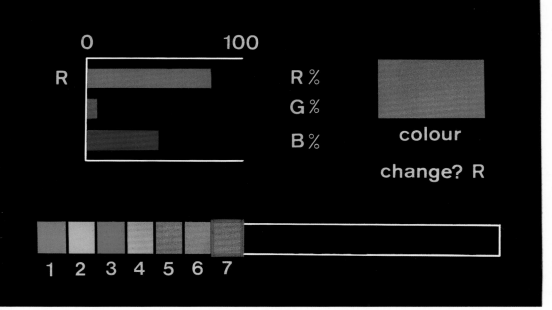

Color Figure 11 (Figure 13.12 in text.) The screen layout used by the MIXTURE program whilst editing the RGB values of a color. The color currently being edited is highlighted with a red border at the bottom of the screen.

Color Figure 12 (Figure 13.13 in text.) The screen layout used by the MIXTURE program whilst editing the HLS color values. The color currently being edited is highlighted with a red border at the bottom of the screen.

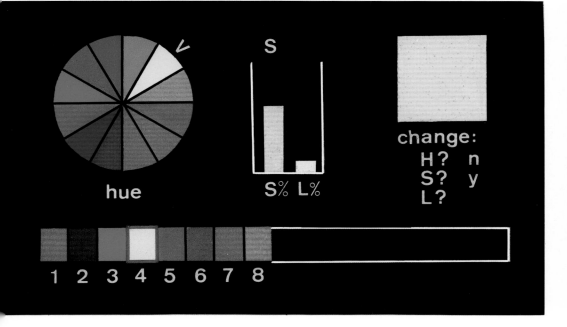

Color Figure 13 (Figure 13.14 in text.) Two pictures produced by the PICASSO program.

Color Figure 14 (Figure 13.19 in text.) The CLUT manipulation programming technique initially sets pixel values 3 to 15 to color 0 (which is assigned to light blue) and then alternately sets each to color 2 (assigned to yellow) and then back to color 0. This gives the effect of the sun rising in the east and setting in the west.

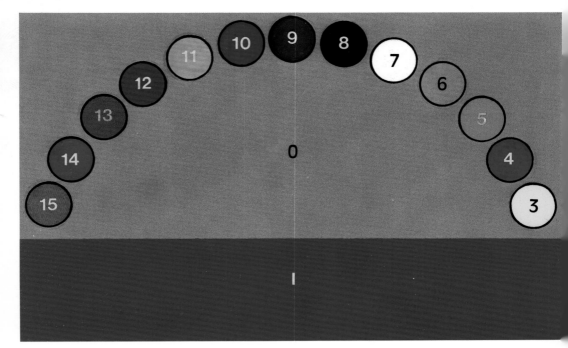

```
end;

procedure cube_root (x : complex; var answer : complex);
const
    pi = 3.1415926;
var
    r, theta, r2, theta2 : real;
begin
    r := sqrt(sqr(x.r) + sqr(x.i));
    theta := angle(x.r, x.i);
    r2 := real_cuberoot(r);
    theta2 := (theta + 2 * pi * cr_factor) / 3;
    answer.r := r2 * cos(theta2);
    answer.i := r2 * sin(theta2);
end;

procedure negate (var z : complex);
begin
    z.r := -z.r;
    z.i := -z.i;
end;
```

Box 13-8 A program to produce fractals by complex function iteration.

```
program iterated_function;
{The idea of this program is to produce a fractal shape
by plotting the results of iterated function calls.}

{Libraries to include:}
{$I 'complex_functions'}
{$I 'g2d_plot'}

var
    z,lambda : complex;
    key,count : integer;
    x,y,scale : real;

procedure phi(z : complex; var w : complex);
{This procedure provides the roots w of the equation:
    z = lambda*w*(1-w)
where lambda is a given complex constant}
var
    temp,c1,c2,c3 : complex;
begin
    divide(z,lambda,temp);
```

```
        complex_number(-4,0,c1);
        multiply(c1,temp,temp);
        complex_number(1,0,c2);
        add(temp,c2,temp);
        square_root(temp,temp);
        if prn < 0.5 then negate(temp);
        add(c2,temp,temp);
        complex_number(0.5,0,c3);
        multiply(c3,temp,w);
end;

procedure setup_phi;
var
        rl,im : real;
        i : integer;
begin
        writeln('PLOT OF AN ITERATED COMPLEX FUNCTION');
        write('Enter real and imaginery parts of lambda :');
        readln(rl,im);
        complex_number(rl,im,lambda);
        write('Initial point x,y (eg 0 0):');
        readln(x,y);
        complex_number(x,y,z);
        write('scale = ?'); readln(scale);
        scale := output_width/scale;
        {Throw away the first few inaccurate points:}
        for i := 1 to 10 do
                phi(z,z);
end;

begin
        init_G2D;
        set_window(-50,-50,50,50);
        setup_phi;
        clear_screen;
        count := 0;
        repeat
                phi(z,z);
                x := scale*z.r ;
                y := scale*z.i;
                plot_point(x,y);
                count := count + 1;
                sample_key(key);
        until chr(key) = 'x';
        writeln(count,' points plotted.');
end.
```

Box 13-9 A turtle program to draw a space filling triangular spiral.

```
program spiral1;
{This program produces the triangular spiral curve.}
{Include turtle graphics:}
{$I 'g2d_turtle'}

var
    i, j, h : integer;

begin
    init_turtle;
    write('i = ? (eg 50)');
    readln(i);
    write('h = ? (eg 50)');
    readln(h);
    for j := 1 to i do
    begin
        forward(h);
        h := h + 4;
        turn(120);
    end;
end.
```

Box 13-10 A turtle program to draw a space filling square spiral.

```
program spiral2;
{This program produces the square spiral curve.}
{Include turtle graphics:}
{$I 'g2d_turtle'}

var
    i, j, h : integer;

begin
    init_turtle;
    write('i = ? (eg 50)');
    readln(i);
    write('h = ? (eg 50)');
    readln(h);
    for j := 1 to i do
    begin
        forward(h);
        h := h + 4;
        turn(90);
    end;
end.
```

13.7 Graftals and particle systems

Fractal programming techniques provide a way of generating an enormous amount of graphics data based on a few simple rules. This is an example of a graphics data-base amplifier. Other techniques within the class of graphics data-base amplifiers have also be developed and they find application in the realistic representation of many other objects in nature. One of these techniques is to use *graftals*, a name coined by Alvy Ray Smith, and another technique is called *particle systems* pioneered by Bill Reeves.

Graftals are applicable to realistic rendering of plants, shrubs, and trees. Typically, a tree is represented by a string of symbols 0, 1, [, and]. For example, 0 may mean a brown segment of a branch and 1 mean a green segment of a branch. The left bracket [represents a branching point in a tree and the right square bracket] indicates the termination of a branch. A procedure 'display_graftal' can take as input a syntactically acceptable string based on these four symbols and draw the tree it corresponds to on the screen. The angle of branching is fixed and [is alternately interpreted as branching left and right. Another procedure called 'transform_graftal' takes as input a graftal string and outputs a new graftal string based on some simple replacement rules. To transform the input string, it is scanned from start to end. Brackets are ignored. Each bit in the string generates a new string of bits (a subtree) which are written to the output string. An example of a context-free set of replacement rules is:

$$0 \rightarrow 1[0]1[0]0$$
$$1 \rightarrow 11$$

If the initial string is 0 then these rules generate a realistic-looking ferntree after about 12 generations.

As an example of a set of context-sensitive replacement rules, the subtree generated from the current bit in the input string can depend on the bit before and the bit after the current bit in the input string. This clearly means that there must be eight different production rules in this scheme rather than two as in the context-free example above. If there is no bit preceding the current bit (as for the first bit in the graftal string) then, for the purposes of generating a subtree the bit value 1 is added to its left. When the end of a branch is reached or there are no more bits to the right then for the purposes of generating a subtree the bit value 1 is appended to the right. An example of a useful set of context-sensitive graftal production rules is:

$$000 \rightarrow 0$$
$$001 \rightarrow 1$$
$$010 \rightarrow 0$$
$$011 \rightarrow 1$$
$$100 \rightarrow 0$$
$$101 \rightarrow 00[01]$$
$$110 \rightarrow 0$$
$$111 \rightarrow 0$$

These simple replacement (production) rules when applied to an initial graftal string consisting of 0 only, surprisingly results in a very realistic-looking bush.

Other types of plants can be modeled by using other replacement rules. The 'display_graftal' procedure could be enhanced so that it adds leaves and flowers to the ends of the branches for added realism. Variations in the branching angles drawn also result in different-looking plants. Typically only about 10 generations are needed to make realistic-looking pictures.

Graftals have a close relationship to fractals. While they are not fractals because fractals contain infinite detail, they are often called subfractals. Parallel string transformations can be applied to turtle graphics as well as graftal strings. A sequence of turtle graphics commands can be represented by a compact string with 'F' standing for forward, 'T' standing for turn, and commands separated by semicolons. Thus, for example, the string '3(F27;T120)' means repeat 3 times, moving forward by 27 units and then turning anticlockwise through 120 degrees. The result is an equilateral triangle. A procedure 'interpret_turtle_commands(str)' could be written to input such strings and convert them to appropriate calls to 'forward' and 'turn' thus displaying the string. Another procedure called 'transform_turtle_commands' could be written to input a turtle command string, such as the example above; and replace commands with new commands, by a set of replacement rules, and output the new turtle command string. An example of a replacement rule would be:

Fa;   →   Fa / 3;T60;Fa / 3;T-120;Fa / 3;T60;Fa / 3;

If the 'transform_turtle_commands' procedure used this replacement rule then repeated application of the procedure would generate the sequence of closed triadic Koch curves. After each transformation the screen may be cleared and then 'interpret_turtle_commands' called to display the next generation of the curve. Each generation is a closer approximation to the fractal that results from an infinite number of transformations.

Particle systems are suitable for realistic rendering of fuzzy objects in motion such as fire, clouds, smoke, sea waves, and grass. To repesent a fuzzy object, many thousands of particles are created by the computer and moved about in space according to the laws of physics. The computer keeps a record of a number of properties of each particle such as position, velocity, acceleration, color, and transparency. Particles also exist for a limited period of time and then become extinct. New particles are being created continually with random properties. Particles are created randomly within a 'generation shape' which could be a rectangular plate, circular plate, or sphere for example, much like an air brush spraying dots of paint into an area. Each particle is displayed as a single pixel in each frame or else as a line (a streak) representing motion blur in fast animations. A particularly nice application of particle systems is in displaying a rotating galaxy where each particle represents a star. Although a galaxy contains 10^{11} stars, only of the order of 10^4 particles are required to make a realistic rendition on a computer graphics terminal.

13.8 Three-dimensional turtle graphics

The concept of two-dimensional turtle graphics can be extended to three dimensions by allowing the turtle to move in three dimensions. It is more meaningful to refer to this three-dimensional robot as a jet airplane rather than a 'turtle', and therefore the term 'jet graphics' will be used for three dimensions and 'turtle graphics' for two dimensions. Also here, right-handed Cartesian coordinates are used. For viewing purposes, the user x and y axes are aligned as before along the horizontal and vertical axes of the screen. This therefore means that the z axis is pointing out of the screen at the user.

The state of the jet plane can again be represented by:

1. position (x, y, z);
2. heading and orientation of the jet.

To specify the exact orientation of the airplane at any time, a triad of unit vectors are set up at the center of the plane. These are shown in Figure 13-33. The vectors are e_x, e_y, and e_z. Note that e_z points in the same direction that the airplane is pointing. This is the unit vector:

$$e_z = u = (\cos \alpha, \cos \beta, \cos \gamma)$$

where the three direction cosines obey:

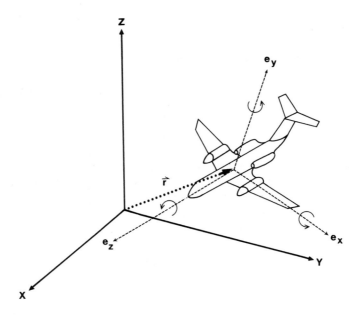

Figure 13-33 A jet airplane with triad of orthonormal orientation vectors used for three-dimensional relative graphics.

$$(\cos \alpha)^2 + (\cos \beta)^2 + (\cos \gamma)^2 = 1$$

The jet responds now to an extended set of commands for relative graphics in three dimensions. Seven of these are listed below.

1.   'init_jet' – initializes the jet state to:

$$\mathbf{r} \equiv (x, y, z) = (0,0,0)$$
$$\mathbf{e}_x = (1,0,0) \equiv \mathbf{i}$$
$$\mathbf{e}_y = (0,1,0) \equiv \mathbf{j}$$
$$\mathbf{e}_z = (0,0,1) \equiv \mathbf{k}$$

2.   'fly(s)' – the direction cosines are used to determine the next absolute position of the jet plane in the 'fly' command as follows:

$$x' = x + s \cos \alpha$$
$$y' = y + s \cos \beta$$
$$z' = z + s \cos \gamma$$

that is:

$$\mathbf{r}' = \mathbf{r} + s \, \mathbf{u}$$

The next two commands 'trail_on' and 'trail_off' simply set on or off the 'jet_trail' boolean variable which must be included in the jet's state:

3.   'trail_on' – causes the jet to emit a trail of white smoke that can be seen in the sky. On the graphics screen, a solid line is seen representing the smoke trail.
4.   'trail_off' – switches off the smoke trail. This means that the jet moves through three-dimensional space without leaving its path indicated.

For changing the orientation of the jet there are three commands, one to rotate it about each of its axial directions $\mathbf{e}_x$, $\mathbf{e}_y$, and $\mathbf{e}_z$. Using traditional terminology in airplane turns these are:

5.   'pitch(a)' – rotates the jet about its $\mathbf{e}_x$ axis which is horizontal through the left wing. This causes the nose of the jet to rise and the tail to dip.

$$\mathbf{e}_z' = \cos(a) \, \mathbf{e}_z - \sin(a) \, \mathbf{e}_y$$
$$\mathbf{e}_y' = \sin(a) \, \mathbf{e}_z + \cos(a) \, \mathbf{e}_y$$

6.   'yaw(a)' – rotates the jet about its vertical axis $\mathbf{e}_y$. This causes the jet's nose to veer right.

$$\mathbf{e}_x' = \cos(a) \, \mathbf{e}_x - \sin(a) \, \mathbf{e}_z$$
$$\mathbf{e}_z' = \sin(a) \, \mathbf{e}_x + \cos(a) \, \mathbf{e}_z$$

7.   'roll(a)' – rotates the jet about its e_z axis which is the axial direction of heading of the jet. This rotation cause the right wing to dip and the left wing to rise.

$$e_y' = \cos(a)\, e_y - \sin(a)\, e_x$$
$$e_x' = \sin(a)\, e_y + \cos(a)\, e_x$$

Another boolean to include in the jet state is 'jet_visible' and this can be switched by the jet commands :

8.   'show_jet' – a visible representation of the jet is seen moving across the screen with every 'fly' command.
9.   'hide_jet' – makes the jet invisible.

To visualize the orientation of the airplane on the screen, a set of commands to control a synthetic camera should be implemented. The camera needs an orientation and position just as an airplane 'turtle' does – see Figure 13-34. These commands are:

```
init_g3d_view;
set_tripod(x,y,z : real);
pan(angle : real);
dip(angle : real);
```

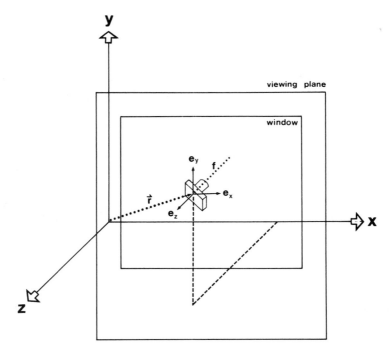

Figure 13-34 The synthetic camera as a three-dimensional turtle.

```
tilt(angle : real);
focus(focal_distance : real);
zoom(distance : real);
```

The commands for controlling the camera are also just like the commands for controlling the airplane. This leads to the idea of building a three-dimensional multiturtle graphics package where each turtle is both a viewing camera and a skywriting (line drawing) airplane. Using concurrent animation programming all turtles could be moving simultaneously and the current view of their artwork can be swapped from turtle to turtle. Some fascinating formation flying has been achieved with software based on these ideas as well as the drawing of three-dimensional fractals and graphtals.

Problems

13.1   Prove that equation 13.9 holds for Maxwell's triangle. Also prove that if the r, g, and b axes in Maxwell's triangle are each divided up into n equal parts (from 0 to 100) then the number of triangular cells so defined inside Maxwell's triangle will be 2^n. Write a program to draw and paint Maxwell's triangle with 2^n cells where n is a number suited to the range of colors available on the color graphics VDU that you work on.

13.2   Implement the procedures:

```
RGB_to_HLS
HLS_to_RGB
set_color
fill_area
paint
define_color
read_color
```

as described in Sections13.1 and 13.2. Use these to make the 'Spectrum' program of Section 13.2.

13.3   Use the procedures of problem 13.2 to make the 'Maxwell_triangle' program described in Section 13.2. Allow the user to increase or decrease the vertex primary color intensities to produce different shades of the colors inside Maxwell's triangle.

13.4   Implement the 'Mixture' program as described in Section 13.2 on a color graphics VDU.

13.5   Implement the 'Dithers' program as described in Section 13.2 on a color graphics VDU.

13.6   Implement the 'Picasso' program as described in Section 13.2 on a color graphics VDU.

13.7   Implement the four graphics animation benchmark programs for a graphics VDU that is available to you, and tabulate its animation speed characteristics. Using the pixel reading and writing times only, how many pixels N could be used in real-time animation? Determine the dimensionless characteristic number η for the graphics device as defined in Section 13.5.

13.8   Write a program to do tweening of filled polygons and polylines. Assume that the key frame data is available from a file. (Design a suitable format for this file.)

13.9   Write a program using CLUT manipulation to display rotating wheels where each wheel has six spokes and a rim. Around the border of the screen have the 'circulating lights' used in advertising. These are a series of small circles which are yellow when on and black when off. How do you make the lights appear to go round? Make the program circulate the wheels and lights clockwise, and then anticlockwise, over and over.

13.10   In generalizing the tree fractal programs of Section 13.6, what programming algorithm should be used to make a three–fork tree? How can you make it randomly mix two– and three–fork branches? How can you allow randomized branch angles as well as lengths? Write the graftal program to draw shrubs. How does it compare with the fractal method?

13.11   Write the following fractal programs:

(a)   A program to draw the C fractal. (Refer to Figure 13-35.)
(b)   A program to represent a random walk.
(c)   A program to draw a jagged mountain skyline.
(d)   A program to draw jagged circles useful as tree outlines in architectural building plans.
(e)   A program to draw concentric Hilbert curves as in Figure 13-32a.
(f)   A program to draw Sierpinski curves as shown in Figure 13-32b.
(g)   A program to draw W-curves as shown in Figure 13-32d.

13.12   Implement the pixel rectangle 'get' and 'put' procedures with the names 'read_rectangle' and 'write_rectangle' as in Section 13.5 in terms of the raster graphics primitives:

```
procedure read_pixel(dcx,dcy : integer; var pixel_value : integer);
procedure write_pixel(dcx,dcy,pixel_value : integer);
```

Figure 13-35 The C fractal curve showing some low order approximations.

Use the 'read_rectangle' and 'write_rectangle' procedures to implement the bit blitting function in software:

procedure BITBLT(dcx1,dcy1,dcx2,dcy2,dcx3,dcy3 : integer);

which reads the pixel rectangle defined by device coordinates ('dcx1','dcy1') and ('dcx2','dcy2') as opposite corners (the *source* rectangle), and copies the data to a rectangle of the same size with corner corresponding to ('dcx1','dcy1') located at ('dcx3','dcy3') (the *destination* rectangle). Note that care must be taken when the source and destination rectangles overlap, that source pixels are not changed before being read: use of 'read_rectangle' and 'write_rectangle' with a temporary intermediate storage area overcomes this problem but slows down the 'BITBLT' function. Fast graphics workstations have the 'BITBLT' function provided in the hardware.

13.13   *Rubber-banding* is a graphics line drawing technique where the line to be drawn moves with the current pointer position. Typically 'read_point' is used to select the first end point of a line, and then the line is drawn from that point to the current position of the pointer device which the user moves until a button or keypress indicates a final position for the second end point. The line appears to stretch and shrink like a rubber band. A suitable animation technique for implementing rubber-banding is use of the XOR pixel write mode. Write a program to draw a polyline using rubber-banding. Use 'read_point' to get the first point and assume that the procedure:

procedure pointer_position(**var** dcx,dcy : integer);

returns the current position of the pointer device (mouse, light pen, cross-hairs etc.) in device coordinates as ('dcx','dcy'). Also use a procedure to sample the keyboard or mouse buttons. After a keypress or button-press the current line segment is fixed on the screen and the next one in the polyline moves like a rubber band. The polyline is finished when the user presses 'X' at the keyboard.

This idea of tentative line segments can be applied to other shapes as well. Implement a procedure that uses 'read_point' to select a corner of a rectangle and uses 'pointer_position' above to define and draw a rectangle in XOR mode. Use this procedure to define rectangles for the 'BITBLT' function of problem 13.12. This program allows repeated bit blitting until the key 'Q' is pressed to indicate the end of the program.

14

Graphics languages

14.1 Analysis of graphics languages

Over the next four sections, a review and analysis of four different categories of graphics languages for a variety of graphics equipment will be undertaken. The purpose here is not so much to teach how to use these languages, as to see how they can be compared and analyzed for graphics functionality. Each of these sections will start with simple languages and then follow with progessively more complex languages in their category. For each example, an answer to the following questions is sought:

- How many graphics statements are provided?
- Identify the graphics setup commands.
- What coordinate system(s) are used and does the language have windowing?
- Does the language have viewporting, clipping, and covering?
- What graphics output (drawing elements) commands are available?
- What graphics attributes can be set for the output commands?
- What graphics input and inquiry commands are provided?
- Does the language allow for graphics objects (the grouping of elements into more complex shapes)?
- Are transformations available for the graphics objects?
- Are there special commands to aid animation?
- Are three-dimensional commands available or only two-dimensional commands?

It should be noted that graphics input commands return information to the user's program through parameters. For graphical input, this information is strictly coordinate data for graphics elements. Nevertheless other kinds of input such as graphics object (segment) selection, function key input, mouse and puck button input, analog real-number input, and string input found in many systems can also loosely be counted under graphics input commands. A related type of input command is the graphics enquiry command that returns to the program information about the current setup parameters and attributes set in the graphics system for output parameters. These graphics enquiry commands are sometimes also loosely called graphics input commands, and both graphics input and graphics system enquiry commands are sometimes lumped into the same category.

Answering all of these questions for each graphics language or system provides a very comprehensive overview that stamps each system like a fingerprint, and is useful in comparing one graphics language with another. Thus this analysis might show, for instance, that one language is strong on output primitives (i.e. the language has many graphics output commands such as line segments, circles, arcs, markers, polymarkers, polylines, and splines) but short on attributes for them, viewporting capability and metagraphics commands, while for another language the reverse situation might well hold. Analysis of graphics languages and packages in this way, improves the ability to make decisions on questions such as, for particular areas of applications of computer graphics, which languages are the most appropriate, provide the optimum value for the purchase price, and assure the least amount of programmer effort.

Sufficient details are provided of the graphics languages mentioned in this book, for the reader to persue this analysis process to the full. Although this analysis may not be persued to completion for every language mentioned, a fingerprint summary of each language or system will be formed by simply stating the number of graphics commands provided by the language and the number of commands within up to eight categories: control, output, attribute, input, enquiry, metagraphics, debugging, and setup. The bounding line between one category and another is not always clear cut and as a result our GSP and graphics language fingerprint summaries are not exact, but they will do for the purposes of cross comparisons.

Commands in the *control* category are those that perform some general hardware control function such as initializing and closing down the graphics hardware, clearing the screen, and beeping the terminal. The *output* category consists of all those commands that produce a graphics element for the output image. The *attribute* setting commands are those that set the value of an attribute, that is, a parameter which directly effects the output style or nature of one or more graphics output drawing elements. These commands are usually named as 'set_something' and are easy to detect. The *input* commands consist of those that return graphics coordinate data, key and button press data, and analog signal values to the program. The *enquiry* category return to the program the present values of output attribute parameters and other graphics system internal parameters such as window and viewport dimensions, and current output device and its resolution. The *metagraphics* commands are those used for collecting the graphics commands into graphics objects (i.e. segments), storing them on disk as metafiles, reading them from disk, and otherwise manipulating the graphics objects. Sometimes *debugging* commands are provided to the programmer. These help the user to know the internal state of the graphics system by printout of user graphics data information. They also provide for error trapping and logging. The final category of graphics command is the graphics *setup* category which sets up the graphics software (in contrast to the control category that sets up the hardware) for the desired graphics input and output format. This category includes windowing and viewporting commands, and all others not categorized by the previous seven categories.

The first exercise should be to perform the analysis described above for the G2D and G3D instructional graphics packages built up throughout this book. The G2D package as described has about 88 different routines. These are made up of 3 control functions, 21 output functions, 15 attribute setting functions, 1 graphics input function, 15 metagraphics functions, 4 debugging functions, and 33 software setup functions. There are no GSP status enquiry functions. These are of course trivial to implement and the package could readily be expanded with copious enquiry functions. On the other hand, the actual users of G2D (or similar package) who have constructed the package for themselves would probably access the data structures internal to the package directly rather than invent further routines for doing this. The extra routines can cause excess memory usage and processing overhead that might unacceptably slow down the software or make the program too large to run. The designer of the GSP might also feel that the user program should keep track of what attributes and controls it has set at any time where necessary thus doing away with the need for enquiry commands. It can be seen that G2D has a plentiful supply of output primitives and attributes to go with them. The G3D package adds a further 61 routines to those of G2D. These extra routines consist of 8 three-dimensional output functions with 6 attribute functions, and 47 setup routines. The abundant supply of three-dimensional setup routines is mainly to supply the high-level intuitive camera positioning and aiming commands.

With each language it should be born in mind the resolution, and the number of available and on-screen colors for the particular device(s) for which the language is designed. It should also be born in mind that the graphics statements listed below are in many cases a subset of all the statements available in a full programming language.

14.2 Plotter languages

In this section are the details of how some typical plotters are programmed. The specific examples are intended to convey the general knowledge of what functions are involved in plotter languages and what part graphics programmers must play in building sophisticated graphics software based on them.

Calcomp (California Computer Products) is one of the oldest companies involved in making plotters. Graphics commands to their plotters are provided through a FORTRAN package called the CALCOMP package. The package provides a rather small selection of commands for producing graphics output. A short list and functional summary of CALCOMP commands is shown in Box 14-1. These commands are the names of FORTRAN subroutines that are called with parameters to interface to the hardware. Although designed for FORTRAN application programs, the CALCOMP package is compatible with other languages such as Pascal. Note the level of these commands. It can be seen immediately that the package is two-dimensional only. There are no metagraphics commands for defining graphics objects or transforming them. There are no commands for setting up user coordinates or windows. Only physical coordinates are used but the origin of the physical coordinates may be anywhere on the plot paper. From these observations an assessment the level of the graphics commands provided can be made and as expected, the CALCOMP commands are low-level graphics commands in physical coordinates as are suitable for driving the Calcomp plotters. As such they are directly useful to those who want to use computer graphics to produce graphs of data plots with axes and simple two-dimensional line drawings. The CALCOMP commands can be used as a basis for building the higher levels of graphics for more sophisticated applications as described in this book.

The list of CALCOMP commands in Box 14-1 shows three setup commands (LIMITS, TEK40X, and ENDPL), four output commands (AXIS, CIRCL, PLOT, and SYMBOL) and one attribute setting command (PENC). The graphics elements displayable are thus line segments, circles, arcs of circles, spirals, and text. Other graphics elements must be implemented in software by the user of this plotter. The device works on physical coordinates with no windowing, viewporting, graphics objects, transformations, or three-dimensional commands. Of course, there are no possibilities of animation on a plotter.

The next plotter command language is that for the Roland plotters. Box 14-2 summarizes these commands. These commands are not FORTRAN subroutine names. Each command is a string consisting of a letter followed by literal parameters, separated by commas and spaces, and terminated by a carriage return. The commands are executed by printing them to the plotter (as if it were a printer). Again note that only the two-dimensional physical coordinate level is provided. All parameters are integers with physical coordinates being in tenths of a millimeter. The graphics functions supported are line segments, arcs of circles, circles, sectors of circles, a text font, and rectangles (empty or hatched). Of the 19 commands, 12 are output commands, 6 set attributes, and 1 provides hardware control. Graphics output commands are thus naturally enough well catered for.

The final example of a plotter language is HP-GL, the graphics language for the Hewlett Packard plotters such as the HP 7475 plotter. From Box 14-3, it is immediately obvious that there are many more instructions in this language than in the previous two

Box 14-1 A list of most commonly used CALCOMP package routines.

AXIS	Draws a single labeled axis with tick marks at any angle.
CIRCL	Draws arcs, spirals, and complete circles.
ENDPL	Closes the plot file and queues it for the Calcomp plotter.
LIMITS	Sets the user's physical plot size limits in centimeters and plotter usage time in seconds.
PENC	Changes the current drawing pen to one of four available colors.
PLOT	Multifunction line drawing command.
SYMBOL	Plots text at any angle and size.
TEK40X	Redirects Calcomp calls to a Tektronix 40xx VDU rather than the plotter.

Box 14-2 Brief summary of Roland plotter commands.

Ax,y	Sets the center (for G and K commands) as (x, y).
Bl	Sets length of dashes and their spacing as $l/10$ mm for dashed lines. See the L command.
Cx,y,r,t1,t2	Draws an arc of center (x, y), radius r and from angle $t1$ to $t2$ in degrees 0 to 360.
Dx,y...	Draws a line from the current pen position to (x, y) or optionally a polyline.
Er,t1,t2	Draws an arc from the current position, with radius r from $t1$ to $t2$ degrees (0 to 360).
Gr,t1,t2	Draws an arc of radius r from $t1$ to $t2$ (0 to 360) about center set by the 'A' command.
H	Returns the pen carriage to home position – lower left corner coordinates (0,0).
Ix,y...	Draws a line by increments (x, y), that is, relative coordinates and optionally a polyline.
Jn	Selects pen number n (1 to 8) from the pen holder.
Kn,r1,r2	Draws pie chart segments using grads n = 1 to 100, inner and outer radii $r1$ and $r2$.
Lp	Sets the line style to solid (p = 0) or dashed (p = 1). See also the 'B' command.
Mx,y	Moves the pen to (x, y) with pen up off the paper.
Nn	Draws a special marker at the current pen position. n = 1 to 10 for different markers.
Pccccc	Draws the text string *ccccc* from the current pen position.
Qn	Sets the direction of drawing the text where n = 0 to 3 only.
Rx,y...	Moves the pen by increments (x, y), that is, relative coordinates and optionally a polyline.
Sn	Sets the text size where n = 0 to 15.
Tn,x,y,d,t	Draws hatched rectangles of width x, height y, at separation d, and angle t (four angles available only).
Xp,q,r	Draws a horizontal (p = 1) or vertical (p = 0) axis with $r+1$ tick marks at separation q.

examples. The instructions in HP-GL are more comprehensive and powerful than in the previous languages. Many instructions are interlinked and must be used in conjunction and in a certain order. Some instructions allow real numbers rather than just integers. As with the Roland plotter language, commands are character strings that are sent to the plotter as if it were a printer. Output graphics functions are line segments, arcs, circles, circle sectors, text, polylines, and polymarkers. User coordinates can be set up as well as viewports in the output rectangle. A limited form of graphics object can be defined via the 'UC' instruction. This particular instruction is used to set up special symbols not available in the plotter's character set. It can be used to make small logos, or CAD symbols such as resistor and capacitor, or to define a new character font. The command itself consists of the letters 'UC' followed by pairs of (*x,y*) relative displacements with each pair optionally preceded with a pen-up or pen-down code and terminated by a special terminating character (the semicolon). In summary, this language has 56 commands made up of 16 output functions, 18 attribute setting functions, 2 graphics input functions, 8 software enquiry functions, 3 control functions, 2 debugging functions, and 7 software setup functions.

These three examples of plotter languages demonstrate the need for graphics software packages to be built around these devices along the lines taught throughout this book. In particular, note that while some languages allow some attributes for the graphics output functions the usual variety is not available and this must be added in software. Software is needed to provide real user coordinates, viewporting, grouping of primitives, transformations, and three-dimensional graphics.

14.3 Graphics extensions to BASIC

Applesoft BASIC running on Apple microcomputers is an extension of the BASIC language with graphics statements. Applesoft BASIC graphics statements are found in Box 14-4. The only graphics output elements provided are line segments and 'shapes'. In addition to these statements, programmers must use a number of PEEK and POKE statements to read and write directly to memory registers. Applesoft BASIC does not provide for user coordinates, viewports, or three-dimensional graphics. No clipping is

Box 14-3 List of HP-GL instructions and their meanings.

AA	Draws an arc in absolute coordinates.
AR	Draws an arc using relative coordinates.
CA	Defines an alternative character set by number for use with the 'SA' instruction.
CI	Draws a circle.
CP	Moves the pen carriage.
CS	Selects the standard character set.
DC	Exits from digitize mode.
DF	Returns plotter to default conditions.
DI	Defines the direction for drawing text.
DP	Puts the plotter into digitize mode waiting for a point to be set by arrow keys.
DR	Sets the direction for drawing text relative to its current direction.
DT	Defines the terminating character in the 'LB' instruction.
EA	Draws a rectangle.
ER	Draws a rectangle using relative coordinates.
EW	Draws the outline of a circle sector (a 'wedge').
FT	Sets a fill style for the 'RA', 'RR', and 'WG' instructions.

IM	Sets a bit mask to determine which errors will be reported by the error indicator LED.
IN	Initializes the plotter.
IP	Sets the scaling points.
IW	Defines a viewport for plotting.
LB	Draws the specified character string.
LT	Sets the line style to one of seven possibilities.
OA	Outputs the current pen position to the host computer in physical coordinates.
OC	Outputs the current pen position to the host computer in user coordinates.
OD	Outputs the last digitized pen position to the host computer in physical coordinates.
OE	Outputs the error code from the plotter to the host.
OF	Outputs the number of plotter device units per millimeter to the host.
OH	Returns the current viewport limits to the host.
OI	Outputs the plotter's identification (type name) to the host.
OO	Outputs to the host a bitmap showing what options the plotter has.
OP	Outputs the current device coordinate limits in plotter units to the host.
OS	Outputs to the host a bitmap showing the plotter's status.
OW	Outputs the current viewport limits to the host in device coordinates.
PA	Draws a polyline if the pen is down else moves to the last point.
PD	Puts the pen down.
PR	Draws a polyline using relative coordinates (displacements) if pen is down.
PS	Tells the plotter what standard paper size to plot to.
PT	Determines the spacing between lines drawn in a solid area fill.
PU	Raises the pen off the paper.
RA	Defines and shades a rectangle using absolute coordinates.
RO	Defines whether the *x* axis is along the paper or across the paper.
RR	Defines and shades a rectangle using relative coordinates.
SA	Selects the alternative character set for use with the 'LB' instruction.
SC	Scales the *x* and *y* coordinate units to user coordinates.
SI	Sets the character width and height.
SL	Sets the character slant as a slope value.
SM	Designates a character to be plotted in a polypoint.
SP	Selects a pen from the pen holder by number.
SR	Sets the character width and height relative to the paper size.
SS	Selects the standard character set for the 'LB' instruction.
TL	Sets the tick length for drawing on axes.
UC	Draws user-defined characters.
VS	Sets the pen velocity.
WG	Draws and solid fills a circle sector.
XT	Draws one *x* axis type tick at the current pen position.
YT	Draws one *y* axis type tick at the current pen position.

Box 14-4 Graphics statements in Applesoft BASIC.

DRAW n AT x,y	Draws shape number *n* starting from (*x, y*) (in replace mode).
HCOLOR= c	Sets the current color for all graphics output.
HGR, HGR2	Puts the computer into 'high-resolution' mode.
HOME	Clears the graphics screen.
HPLOT x,y	Turns on a dot at device coordinates (*x, y*).
HPLOT a,b TO c,d	Draws a line from (*a, b*) to (*c, d*). Also allows polylines to be drawn.
HPLOT TO x,y	Draws a line from the last point referenced to (*x, y*).
ROT= n	Rotates the current shape through 360*n* / 64 degrees.
SCALE= n	Scales up or down a shape uniformly.
SHLOAD	Loads a shape table (of up to 255 shapes) from disk.
XDRAW n AT x,y	Draws shape number *n* starting from (*x, y*) in XOR mode for animations.

Box 14-5 Graphics statements in Microsoft BASIC.

CIRCLE (X,Y),R	Draws a circle centered at (*X, Y*) with radius *R* with arc options.
CLS	Clears the screen.
COLOR	Sets the current color for drawing graphics.
DRAW	Draws a string of graphics commands using relative device coordinates.
GET(x1,Y1)-(X2,Y2),a	Reads a rectangle from pixel memory into a user array variable.
LINE(X1,Y1)-(X2,Y2)	Draws a line from (*X1, Y1*) to (*X2, Y2*) or a box with options.
PAINT (X,Y),C	Paints an area starting from (*X, Y*).
PMAP(X,code)	Returns a device coordinate given a world coordinate.
POINT(code)	Returns *x* or *y* device or user coordinates of the last referenced point.
PSET(X,Y)	Set the pixel at device coordinates (*X, Y*) on.
PRESET(X,Y)	Set the pixel at device coordinates (*X, Y*) off.
PUT(X,Y),a	Writes binary data in an array to a rectangular area of pixel memory.
SCREEN	Sets the current screen number, resolution, and mode.
VIEW(X1,Y1)-(X2,Y2)	Defines a viewport on the screen in device coordinates.
WINDOW	Defines user coordinates for the display.

provided in the language. It does not allow general metagraphics commands, but limited metagraphics is provided by the shape-table concept which allows outlines of arbitrary shapes to be drawn and animated. Use of color is extremely limited and the resolution is low (280 x 192). In summary, there are 11 graphics commands of which three are output primitives, one sets attributes, one is a control routine, one is for software setup, and there are five metagraphics commands.

Microsoft BASIC is another example of a graphics language in the category of graphics extensions to a standard language. This means that the standard language has built into it special statements to facilitate the use of the graphics hardware it is to run on. In the case of Microsoft BASIC, there is considerable enhancement from the original Dartmouth BASIC. As well there are a number of special statements as tabled in Box 14-5 especially included in the language for graphics. The precise number of parameters, their ranges and functions vary from machine to machine on which the Microsoft company have installed their version of BASIC.

The fifteen functions in Box 14-5 can be divided into one control and four setup functions, seven output functions, two input functions, and one attribute setting function. The output primitives are lines and circles (and often arcs of circles by means of more parameters on the CIRCLE command). The GET and PUT functions provide block pixel reads and writes and therefore can be useful for animation programming. The DRAW command allows for a collection of moveto and drawto type subcommands to implement a form of graphics object. Scaling and rotation subcommands are also provided within DRAW and the objects can be used in animation programming. In summary then, Microsoft BASIC provides a small but useful set of graphics statements to perform most two-dimensional graphics functions within the limitations of the hardware.

Graphics extensions to BASIC provide easy access to graphics for novice programmers because of the interpretive nature of BASIC. Although BASIC is a useful language for testing small programs, it does not have the power of higher level programming languages such as industry-extended Pascal which incorporate many software engineering principles. The BASIC statements cannot be accessed from other languages such as Pascal either. These two examples also show that graphics extensions to BASIC are by no means standardized. This means that graphics programs often lack portability if written in BASIC for microcomputers. Even with Microsoft BASIC, the differences in implementations of the statements in Box 14-5 as to their number of parameters and the meaning of each parameter causes some difficulty in the transportation of graphics programs written in BASIC between even similar computers.

14.4 Versions of LOGO

LOGO is a language based on turtle graphics and was invented by Seymour Papert. Its original purpose was to train young children in the use and programming of a computer. It is a full language that includes graphics statements in an easy to use form via turtle graphics commands. Its ease of use and capability for producing many pleasant graphics patterns with minimal effort has been an attraction to many other users especially in the

Box 14-6 Apple LOGO graphics commands.

BACK n	Moves the turtle backwards *n* units.
BACKGROUND	Outputs the background color number (0 to 6).
CLEAN	Clears the graphics screen without changing the turtle's status.
CLEARSCREEN	Clears the graphics screen, homes the turtle, and shows it.
DOT [x y]	Places a dot at device coordinate position (*x, y*).
FENCE	Causes LOGO to print an error message if the turtle goes off the screen.
FORWARD n	Moves the turtle forward *n* units.
FULLSCREEN	Sets the whole screen for turtle graphics.
HEADING	Outputs the turtle's heading as a number from 0 to 360.
HIDETURTLE	Makes the turtle invisible.
HOME	Sets the turtle to the center of the screen pointing upwards.
LEFT a	Turns the turtle anticlockwise by *a* degrees.
PEN	Outputs the pen status (up, down, erase, or reverse) and color.
PENCOLOR	Outputs the pen color, a number from 0 to 5.
PENDOWN	Sets the turtle's imaginary pen down so it can draw lines.
PENERASE	Replaces the pen with an eraser (the turtle now draws in the background color).
PENREVERSE	Reverses any colors that the pen passes over (XOR mode).
PENUP	Lifts the turtle's pen so that no lines will be drawn.
POS	Outputs the turtle's position.
RIGHT a	Rotates the turtle *a* degrees clockwise.
SETBG c	Sets the background color to *c* (0 to 6).
SETHEADING a	Makes the turtle point in direction *a* degress clockwise from north.
SETPC c	Sets the color that the turtle's pen draws with to *c* (0 to 5).
SETPEN [s c]	Sets the turtle's pen to status *s* (up,down,erase, and reverse) and color *c* (0 to 5).
SETPOS [x y]	Moves the turtle to the absolute position (*x, y*) in device coordinates.
SETX x	Sets the turtle's absolute *x* coordinate position as *x*.
SETY y	Sets the turtle's absolute *y* coordinate position as *y*.
SHOWNP	Outputs true or false depending on whether the turtle is visible or not.
SHOWTURTLE	Makes the turtle visible on the screen.
SPLITSCREEN	Uses only half of the screen for turtle graphics and the other half for text.
TEXTSCREEN	Disables graphics output and uses the entire screen for text messages.

TOWARDS [x y]	Outputs the required heading for the turtle to move towards (x, y).
WINDOW	Clears the screen and allows the turtle to disappear right off the edges.
WRAP	Causes the turtle to reappear and continue moving on the opposite side if it goes off the screen.
XCOR	Outputs the x coordinate of the current position of the turtle.
YCOR	Outputs the y coordinate of the current position of the turtle.

microcomputer area. Versions of the language appear on virtually all of the popular microcomputers. In this section, two different implementations of LOGO are reviewed, and again they are viewed in the light of their graphics capability only – what graphics setup commands are needed, what output primitives are provided, what attributes these can have, are there graphics input functions, capabilities for grouping primitives, user coordinates, viewporting, clipping, covering, and so forth.

First, a look at Apple LOGO. A summary of Apple LOGO graphics statements is given in Box 14-6. This list of 36 graphics commands has 11 graphics control and setup commands, 4 graphics output commands, 13 attribute setting commands, and 8 inquiry commands. The relatively large number of attribute setting commands relate to the turtle's internal state (position, heading, pen state, visibility, and color). These also account for the inquiry commands which return the state parameters to the program. There are no graphics input type commands. From this list, it can be seen that Apple LOGO as a graphics language provides only for line drawing and placing dots, with attributes being color and pixel writing mode. No graphics metacommands for grouping of output primitives are provided: this is expected to be done by the user through program modules.

The second example is Atari LOGO. A summary of Atari LOGO graphics statements is given in Box 14-7. This is a more advanced LOGO implementation with more graphics commands (44) and multiturtle operation. There are 10 graphics control and setup commands, 4 graphics output commands, 17 attribute setting commands, and 13 enquiry commands. Its structure is rather similar to Apple LOGO and other versions of LOGO. Atari LOGO has a feature for grouping turtle commands into a list *l* which can be executed by the 'ASK' and 'EACH' commands. This allows for a form of graphics object through the language statements.

From these two examples, it is seen that LOGO provides two-dimensional graphics commands and the output primitives are usually only line segments. The attributes that effect the appearance of the output primitives are color and pixel writing mode only. Pixel reading, user-defined coordinate systems, full viewporting, and graphics objects and their transformations are usually not provided. The essential nature of turtle graphics is, of course that only relative graphics commands are provided to the user. To maintain the turtle LOGO stores parameters for the turtle status such as position and heading which the output primitives alter without direct access by the user.

Box 14-7 Atari LOGO graphics statements.

ASK t l	Asks turtle *t* to perform the list of instructions *l*.
BACK n	Moves the turtle backwards *n* units.
BG	Outputs the background color number.
CLEAN	Clears the graphics without changing the turtle's status.
COLOR	Outputs the turtle's current color.
CS	Clears the graphics screen and initializes the turtle.
EACH l	Makes each active turtle run the instruction list *l* in turn.
EDSH s	Allows turtle shape *s* to be edited (s = 1 to 15).
FORWARD n	Moves the turtle forward by *n* units.
GETSH n	Outputs the bitmap pattern of shape *n* as sixteen 8-bit bytes.
HEADING	Outputs the turtle's heading as an integer 0 to 360 degrees (North = 0 degrees).
HOME	Moves the turtle to the center of the screen pointing north.
HT	Makes the turtle invisible.
LEFT n	Turns the turtle to the left through *n* degrees.
PC p	Outputs the color number of pen *p* (three pens available p = 0, 1, or 2).
PE	The turtle erases any lines it passes over.
PEN	Outputs the turtle's current pen status – up, down, erase, or XOR mode.
PD	Places the turtle's (imaginery) pen down so that it will draw.
PU	Lifts up the turtle's pen so no lines will be drawn.
PN	Outputs the current pen number in use (allows three pens 0, 1 or 2).
POS	Outputs the coordinates of the turtle.
PUTSH s d	Gives shape number *s* the bitmap byte list pattern *d*.
PX	Puts the turtle drawing into XOR mode.
RIGHT n	Turns the turtle right through *n* degrees.
SETBG c	Sets the background color to *c* (c = 0 to 127).
SETC c	Sets the current turtle drawing color to *c* (c = 0 to 127).
SETH n	Sets the direction of motion of the turtle to *n* degrees (0 to 360).
SETPC p c	Sets the color of pen number *p* (= 0, 1, or 2) to color c = 0 to 127.
SETPN p	Sets the pen that the turtle is currently using to *p* (p = 0, 1, or 2).
SETPOS [x y]	Sets the turtle position to device coordinates (*x*, *y*).
SETSH s	Sets the shape of the current turtle to shape *s* (s = 0 to 15).
SETSP s	Sets the speed of the current turtle to *s* where $-200 < s < 200$.
SETX x	Sets the *x* component of the turtle's position to *x*.
SETY y	Sets the *y* component of the turtle's position to *y*.
SHAPE	Outputs the current shape number (0 to 15) of the turtle.
SHOWNP	Outputs true or false depending whether the turtle is set to visible or not.

SPEED	Outputs the current turtle's speed.
ST	Makes the turtle visible on the screen.
TELL t	Tells LOGO which turtle(s) *t* to use out of 0, 1, 2, or 3.
WHO	Outputs the currently selected turtles in use.
WINDOW	Clears the screen and allows turtles to disappear off the edges.
WRAP	Causes the turtle to reappear and continue moving on the opposite side if it goes off the screen.
XCOR	Outputs the *x* coordinate of the current position of the turtle.
YCOR	Outputs the *y* coordinate of the current position of the turtle.

14.5 Third-generation graphics systems

'Third-generation' graphics systems provide a language of high-level graphics statements independent of the programming language being used on the system. In many cases, the graphics language software is provided in ROM chips in the hardware, and in other cases it is resident in main memory having been either loaded at boot-up time with the operating system or by running a special program.

The first of these systems to look at is SGL, the Sord Graphics Language, provided on the Japanese Mitsui Sord graphics computers. The particular instance of the language selected is the Sord M68 graphics machine which has a resolution of 640 x 400 in 16 on-screen colors. The graphics statements provided are listed in Box 14-8. To execute any SGL statement from any language, the statement need only be written to the screen, as a normal output statement terminated by a carriage return, after the machine is put in to graphics mode. Graphics mode is entered by a certain escape sequence. (*Note* : no carriage returns should be used on escape sequences, that is, Pascal 'write' statements rather than 'writeln's should be used.) In graphics mode, any number of SGL commands can be given via say Pascal 'writeln' statements. To return from graphics mode to alpha mode another escape sequence must be issued.

From Box 14-8 it can be seen that SGL provides 40 graphics functions to programmers: 15 setup and control functions, 15 output functions, and 10 attribute setting functions. There are no graphics input or SGL inquiry functions. Pixels could only be 'read' by maintaining a sparse list (i.e. a table of the nonzero pixel values coupled with an indexing table that gives the pixel addresses of entries in the first list). This sparse list structure must be maintained by the user who must note that most SGL commands will require the structure to be updated. It is obviously simpler if the hardware provides pixel reading capability. Again as there are no SGL attribute and internal parameter inquiry functions, the user's software must record any values set if it needs them later. Unlike the previous languages, this language does provide a large number of output primitives: marker symbols, polymarkers, line segments, polylines, polygons, rectangles (bars), circles, arcs, pie segments, area fills, axes, and text. It is also possible to draw ellipses and elliptic arcs by the combination of WINDOW and CIRCLE commands. Both absolute and relative coordinates are allowed in many of these output commands.

A second example of a third generation graphics system is the Quickdraw ROM package inside the Apple Macintosh computer. There are too many routines in Quickdraw to list in this chapter and so interested readers are referred to the Macintosh manuals.

A third example of a third generation graphics system is the GSX extensions to CP/M or MS-DOS operating systems for microcomputers. These routines are not ROM resident but are loaded into main memory and are called in a similar way to other operating system intrinsics. GSX will be discussed in more detail in Chapter 15.

Box 14-8 SGL graphics commands for the Sord M68.

CP stands for the Current Position, a (usually) invisible graphics cursor which is moved by various commands including MOVE.

ARC x y a i
> Draws the arc of a circle starting at the CP with center (*x*, *y*) and given arc angle *a* by line segments at every increment of *i* degrees. *Note*: this draws close to true circles by assuming the pixels are square. Ellipses and elliptical arcs are obtained by using the WINDOW command (see below).

AXIS [xm], [ym], [xM], [yM], [div_length]
> Draws the *x* and *y* axes with minor and major divisions along the *x* axis at 'xm' and 'xM' increments and along the *y* axis at 'ym' and 'yM' increments where the major divisions are tick marks of length 'div_length' and the minor divisions are half this length.

BACKCOLOR col_nr
> Sets the background color of the screen.

BAR x, y, width, height
> Draws a box with lower left corner at (*x*, *y*), and given width and height.

CIRCLE r, [theta_start], [theta_end], [theta_increment]
> Draws the arc of a circle of radius *r*, center at the CP, from the start to the end angle with straight line segments at every 'theta_increment'.

COLOR col_nr [,edge_col]
> Sets the current drawing color and optionally the edge color for POLYGON, PIE, and BAR commands.

CONNECT x1, y1, x2, y2
> Draws a line from (*x*1, *y*1) to (*x*2, *y*2).

CSIZE width, height
> Sets the dot width and height for graphics text characters. Initially the width is 8 and the height 16 pixels.

CURSOR col_nr
> Sets the cursor to the specified color. Initially it is black.

DEGREE
> Sets the unit of angular measure to degrees. (See GRAD.)

DIRECTION theta
> Sets the direction for drawing text. This is initially zero, that is, horizontal.

DISPLAY bit_plane

Allows selective display of the four bit planes by the 'bit_plane' mask. If 'bit_plane' is zero then the screen blanks. If it is 15 then all bit planes are simultaneously visible on the screen.

DRAW x1, y1 [,x2,y2 ...]

Draws a polyline, that is, line segments from the CP to (*x*1, *y*1) then to (*x*2, *y*2), and so forth if specified. After each line segment the CP is updated to the last point.

EDGE edge_type

Sets the style for edges on use of the BAR command. 'Edge_type' has four possible values:

0   Draw the edge with the currently set line type.
1   Draw the edge with solid line segments.
2   Do not draw the edge; hatching will include the edge.
3   Do not draw the edge; hatching will not include the edge.

ERASE [bit_plane1], [bit_plane2]

Both parameters are bit plane masks (i.e. have allowed values 0 to 15). The bits set in the 'bit_plane1' mask indicate which planes are erased and the bits set in the 'bit_plane2' mask specify which planes are displayed.

FIELD pattern_nr

Sets the pattern for hatching in the BAR, POLYGON, PIE, and PAINT commands. Valid pattern numbers are 0 to 29, 100, and 101. The latter two are for allowing the pattern to be set by the HALFTONE and PATTERN commands respectively.

FRAME

Draws a border around the current viewport on the screen.

GINIT

Initializes the graphics display system, restoring all defaults, and clears the screen.

GRAD

Sets the current unit of angular measure to grads which are percentages of a full turn. (Thus 100 grads = 360 degrees.)

HALFTONE redpc, greenpc, bluepc

Sets the halftone color pattern. Halftoning is a technique for obtaining more colors from a graphics VDU. It uses 4 x 4 cells of (16) pixels each one of which can be set to any of the 16 available colors on the M68. The color combinations mix in the eye thus giving about 4000 different 'colors' on the screen. Note that with this method though, the resolution becomes 1/4 coarser. The parameters 'redpc', 'greenpc', and 'bluepc' are the percentages (0 to 100) of the 16 pixels per cell that are set to red, green, and blue respectively. To use a halftone pattern the command FIELD 101 must be given.

LINETYPE [lin_type][, vis_length][, invis_length]

Sets the current line type for drawing all lines. The parameter 'lin_type' may be:

0   Solid line;
1   Broken line;
2   Dot-and-dash line;
3   Double-dot-and-dash line.

The optional parameters 'vis_length' and 'invis_length' specify the lengths of the visible and invisible segments for nonsolid lines. The dots for line types 2 and 3 are half the length of the invisible segments in the line.

MARKER marker_nr
    Sets the current marker type. Values of 'marker_nr' are:

0   No mark;
1-15   Special M68 marker symbols;
32-127   ASCII characters;
161-223   Katakana symbols.

MODE pix_w_mode
    Sets the pixel writing mode. Valid 'pix_w_mode' values are:

0   Replace mode (ignores the previous colour of a pixel):

$$p2 := p$$

1   OR mode adds the selected color to the current pixel color value:

$$p2 := p \text{ OR } p1$$

2   Erase mode subtracts the selected color (p) from the current pixel color value:

$$p2 := p1 \text{ AND NOT } p.$$

MOVE x, y
    Sets the CP to the specified point (x, y).

ORIGIN h, v
    Sets the origin for character symbols within the 8 x 16 character cell. Allowed values are 0 to 7 for h and 0 to 15 for v. When the text is drawn, this origin is placed at the CP.

PAINT x, y [,bcol1] [,bcol2] ...
    Colors a bounded area starting from the point (x, y). The parameters 'bcol1' and so forth specify the different colors of the boundary of the paint region.

PALETTE pallette_nr, color_code
    Sets the palette number (logical color) to the specified color_code

(physical color). Since colors are drawn by setting pixel values to the palette number rather than the physical color number and the hardware has a color look-up table to translate pixel values to physical colors for display on the screen, these colors displayed on the screen can be instantaneously changed. This is done by changing entries in the 16 x 4 bit color look-up table which is achieved by this PALETTE command.

PATTERN 101 [,pallete_nr, byte1, byte2, ... byte16]

Creates a pattern for the BAR command. The pattern is 8 pixels wide and up to 16 pixels high. The parameters byte1, byte2, and so forth specify the pixels in each row of the pattern. If a bit is set in the byte the corresponding pixel is set to the logical pallete color. Bit 0 is the leftmost pixel and byte1 is the top row of 8 pixels. Use several PATTERN commands to set different colors in the pattern cell. The command FIELD 101 must be issued in order to use this user defined pattern.

PIE r, [theta_start, theta_end, theta_increment]

Draws a sector of a circle using the same parameters as for CIRCLE. Thus in order to draw a complete pie several calls to PIE should be made.

PLOT x1, y1, x2,y2, ...

Sets the pixels at $(x1, y1)$, $(x2, y2)$, and so forth.

POLYGON x1, y1, x2, y2, x3, y3, ... xn, yn

Draws a polygon between the knot points $(x1, y1)$, $(x2, y2)$, to (xn, yn) where $n \leq 63$.

RDRAW dx1, dy1, dx2, dy2, dx3, dy3, ... dxn, dyn

Draws a polyline by the displacements specified from point to point starting from the CP. (It is a relative draw since $(dx2, dy2)$ is the displacement vector relative to point 1 which is displaced by $(dx1, dy1)$ from the CP, and so forth.)

RMOVE dx, dy

Moves the CP by the displacement vector (dx, dy).

ROTATE [theta]

Rotates the coordinate system about the CP by the specified angle. If theta is omitted then the coordinate system is realigned to the initial horizontal and vertical coordinate system.

RPLOT dx1, dy1, dx2, dy2, dx3, dy3, ... dxn, dyn

Plots *n* points by displacements starting from the CP.

SLANT theta

Initially characters drawn by TEXT are upright. This command slants the characters relative to the vertical.

SPEED code

Sets the graphics drawing speed. The parameter 'code' is:

0   For normal drawing speed;
1   For high-speed graphics drawing (causes screen flicker during drawing).

TEXT string

> Draws the characters in the specified string starting from the CP. Note that there must be a space character between TEXT and the first character of the string and that the string should not be quoted. It is terminated by a carriage-return character. For example:
>
> TEXT Hello There.
>
> VIEWPORT [xmin, xmax, ymin, ymax]
>   Defines a rectangle on the M68 screen in which subsequent graphics will be displayed. Omitting all parameters causes the whole screen to be the viewport. This is the initial condition.
> WINDOW uxmin, uxmax, uymin, uymax
>   Sets up user coordinates within the currently defined viewport on the M68 screen. Valid user coordinates range from -32767 to 32767.

14.6 The learning-curve problem

Having analyzed a number of graphics languages by the method described in Section 14.1, the results can now be tabulated as shown in Table 14-1. The table enables languages to be compared under the different categories at a glance. Of course bar charts would have more visual appeal. From the table, for instance, it can be seen that the demonstration package G2/3D has the most number of total commands, output commands, and attribute setting commands followed in each of these categories by HP-GL. The only languages listed that do not have digitizing graphics input commands are Applesoft BASIC and SGL. This omission can herald programming difficulties for some applications.

There is a vast number of other graphics languages available on other graphics systems – too many to consider here. However, the examples given in the preceding sections are simple case studies that show typical graphics language design styles and how these can be analyzed. In view of this plethora of graphics languages, it is now time to turn to a uniform approach to training in the use of graphics languages – especially in the professional area where compiled languages and GSPs are used.

The learning of computer graphics systems has often been slowed down by the need (in some cases) to learn a different programming language, construct a syntactically correct program, and have it compiled, linked, and loaded. The amount of time spent in this development cycle decreases the learning rate for any graphics package. The fact that graphics programmers have to learn a large graphics software package and develop bug-free compiled programs using GSP routines that they are not totally familiar with has often meant that graphics projects take considerably longer development time than other projects. This learning-curve problem occurs in the commercial world when expensive graphics equipment and software have been installed, and time and money must further be spent on familiarizing the programmers and users of the new equipment.

A solution to this problem is the use of interpretive graphics languages. This means that for every GSP to be used, a GSP interpreter is written. The remainder of this chapter

Table 14-1 Comparison of graphics languages by command categories.

Name	N	O	A	I	E	C	D	M	S
G2D	88	21	15	1	0	3	4	15	33
G3D	61	8	6	0	0	0	0	0	47
G2/3D	149	29	21	1	0	3	4	15	80
CALCOMP	8	4	1	0	0	0	0	0	3
Roland	19	12	6	0	0	1	0	0	0
HP-GL	56	16	18	2	8	3	2	0	7
AppleSoft	11	3	1	0	0	1	0	5	1
Microsoft	15	7	1	2	0	1	0	0	4
Apple LOGO	36	5	13	3	5	1	1	0	8
Atari LOGO	44	8	11	3	10	1	0	2	9
SGL	40	16	14	0	0	2	0	0	8

Note: N = total number of graphics commands
O = number of output commands
A = number of attribute setting commands
 I = number of graphics input commands
E = number of graphics attribute enquiry commands
C = number of hardware control languages
D = number of debugging commands
M = number of metagraphics commands
S = number of graphics set-up commands.

will be spent looking at how software package interpreters can be automatically constructed. Once the system manager has generated an interpreter, the student/user/programmer has far quicker and direct access to the graphics package than the traditional compiled program approach. Interactive calls can be made to the package routines via the corresponding interpreter and the immediate response seen of each routine. By the use of interpreters it is possible for graphics users to become thoroughly familiar with several different graphics packages quickly and at the same time.

Similarly most computer graphics hardware has its own native graphics language or associated graphics package, a few simple examples of which were seen in the previous sections. Consequently there is a plethora of graphics packages available on the market today. Unfortunately these do not all conform to a standard philosophy for graphics and with respect to graphics standards there are several to choose from. (Computer graphics standards will be discussed in more detail in the next chapter.) In education there are also several graphics packages which one would want to teach so that students would become more aware of the different approaches to graphics available in the market place. For example, any of the following list may be taught: CALCOMP, TIGS, SGL, RGL, HGL, ReGIS, PLOT10, PLOT 50, QUICKDRAW, GSX, GKS, Core, DI-3000, IGL, and so forth. Most of these packages consist of well over 50 modules for user access. In traditional programming environments only part of one of these packages can be adequately taught in a one-semester introductory graphics course. This problem is exacerbated by a high student-to-graphics-terminal ratio that seems to be the norm.

Since the introductory graphics course is to teach graphics package design principles it should not be slowed down by program language difficulties. The problem can be overcome by the invention of graphics package interpreters. Essentially the interpreter waits for the user to type the name of a package routine and then the values for input parameters. It then calls the specified routine to perform the required graphics function and also prints out any variables returned from the call. The interpreter essentially converts the package into an easy to learn interactive language neatly hiding programming language implementation difficulties. The interpreter can also set up defaults such as calling package initialization routines to help the novice and prevent system crashes. The interpreter can contain many other features such as on-line information about the package routine and error messages.

With this concept applied to several packages the students/users/programmers can become acquainted very quickly with more than one package. It is however desirable to have a uniformity among these interpreters as regards their user interface and special interpreter intrinsic commands. Therefore an interpreter generator program should be created first. This is a program that creates interpreters for any package given the names and parameter interfacing of each of its routines. The next section discusses GSP interpreter design and GSP interpreter generator design.

14.7 Graphics package interpreter design

At its simplest, a package interpreter waits for a user command which consists of a name of a callable routine within the package followed by the required input parameters for that call as literals. The parameters are passed as literals. For array and record parameters, all components are to be typed in the command line in the order of the components. The totality of input parameters may span several input lines. The interpreter parses this input command string extracting the routine name and converting the parameters to internal format in internal interpreter variables, and then calls the appropriate package routine with these values. After returning from the package routine, any output parameters from the routine are displayed (printed on the screen) in order, and the interpreter loop begins again, waiting for the next user command. Pseudocode for the design of an interpreter is as follows:

```
print the sign on message
initialize exit := false
repeat
    read in a command line from the keyboard
    if left substring of the command line = first routine name then
        extract each parameter from the command line for routine #1
        (placing them in variables within the interpreter program)
        call routine #1
```

```
        print any output parameter values from routine #1
    else if left substring of the command line = routine #2's name then
        extract each parameter from the command line for routine #2
        call routine #2
        print output variables
    else ....
        etc.
    else if left 3 characters of the command line are 'END' then
        exit := true
    else
        report an invalid command line      ·
until exit = true
print sign off.
```

In looking for valid package commands to interpret, comparison is done with the left n characters of the command line, where the routine name is n characters long. It is handy to have the names of the routines in the package sorted in alphabetical order and implemented in this order within the interpreter source code of nested-if statements, for the purposes of debugging and extending the interpreter (at some later time).

After identifying the routine name to be called, the interpreter must set up the input parameters to call this routine. These are read from the command line in the same order as they appear in the routine's header. In general, the interpreter program needs to declare a small number of variables for every possible different type of input parameter used in the package. The interpreter also needs one procedure to scan every possible different type of literal parameter used in the package. Usually, and especially so with FORTRAN packages, only the data types real, integer, and character string (and possibly logical) variables are needed. Logical values are the easiest to detect – the program looks for either a T (or TRUE) or F (or FALSE) and sets a variable accordingly. For strings, the spaces are skipped until a single quote is found, and then the characters are gathered until a second single quote is detected in the command line. Pseudocode for detecting strings is therefore:

```
module get_string
inputs : command_line and pointer
outputs : a_string, pointer
code :
    initialize a_string to the null string
    while the current character pointed to by pointer is a space
        increment the command_line buffer pointer
    if next character ≠ single quote then report a command line error
    else
        repeat
            get the next command_line character
            if not a single quote then concatenate it onto the right hand
            end of a_string
        until the second single quote or end of command line is detected
```

> **if** no single quote is detected **then** report a command line error
> **return** a_string

The routine for extracting real numbers from the command line is slightly more complicated than this. To extract integer values, simply call the 'get_real' routine and truncate the real number so obtained to an integer. All parameters of the correct types are then, assuming no errors in the command line were detected, passed to the package routine in question along with uninitialized variables for the output parameters. After the call, the values of the output parameters are returned to the user by printing them on the screen.

The following Pascal code segment illustrates these ideas for three simple routines in the G2/3D package developed in this book. The routines chosen are:

1. 'clear_screen' – to clear the graphics screen. It takes no arguments.
2. 'plot_line(x1,y1,x2,y2)' – to draw a line in the current color between the user coordinates ('x1','y1') and ('x2','y2'). This takes four real inputs.
3. 'read_point(ch,x,y)' – to read a graphics point from the screen by manipulation of a cross-hairs graphics cursor. The user coordinates ('x','y') of the selected point are returned when the user stikes the hit key code 'ch' at the alphanumeric keyboard. The character 'ch' is also returned.

```
if copy(command,1,12) = 'clear_screen' then
    clear_screen
else if copy(command,1,9) = 'plot_line' then
begin
    pointer := 10;
    x1 := get_real(command,pointer);
    y1 := get_real(command,pointer);
    x2 := get_real(command,pointer);
    y2 := get_real(command,pointer);
    plot_line(x1,y1,x2,y2);
end
else if copy(command,1,10) = 'read_point' then
begin
    read_point(ch,x,y);
    writeln(ch:2,x:8:2,' ',y:8:2);
end
else ...
```

The interpreter can also help beginner students by making any graphics initialization calls to the package that are necessary to its proper usage. Then if the student forgets the opening and closing protocol with any package, the interpreter neatly makes up for his mistakes. The interpreter can also check routines that should only be called once, or that should be called in pairs, by means of internal flags. These are typical errors for novices that slow them down from learning the real functionality of a package. By using an interpreter that automatically does this, and allows interactive package calls, the student accelerates the learning of the package. Finally, consider the software design for an automatic interpreter generator.

An interpreter along the lines described above can be automatically generated for any graphics package. This ensures a uniformity among the interpreters for the various packages that are to be used or taught. The generator is driven by one or two text files. The first of these is an interpreter skeleton program; that is, an initial piece of code that is always the same for all interpreters. This is copied straight into the new interpreter. The rest of the new interpreter is developed depending on the routine names and the structures of the parameters to be passed in the routines in the package to be interpreted. This information can be supplied to the generator either interactively (from keyboard prompting) or from a file. The format of this file is as follows:

```
number of routines in the package
the name of routine #1
the number of parameters passed for routine #1
parameter #1 I/O flag (I = input parameter, O = output parameter)
parameter #1 type (I = integer, R = real, S = string, L = logical)
parameter #2 I/O flag (I = input parameter, O = output parameter)
parameter #2 type (I = integer, R = real, S = string, L = logical)
etc.
name of routine #2
etc.
```

This file must be typed in once for any given package. Then with any new interpreter enhancements, the generator may be updated and the latest version of the interpreter can be quickly developed.

14.8 Interpreter enhancements

The interpreters described so far have no intrinsic ('interpreter-only') commands beyond the 'END' command to terminate the session with the interpreter. There are several ways of enhancing the versatility of these interpreters with extra interpreter-only commands. For example, the 'HISTORY' and 'NO HISTORY' commands are very useful for recording the sequence of interpreter commands that a user wants to have recorded. Every time the 'HISTORY' command is given, all subsequent command lines will not only be interpreted in the normal manner, but also be stored in a standard history file until a 'NO HISTORY' or 'END' command is received by the interpreter. To store the sequence of interpreter commands in a file other than the default history file, a file name is given after the HISTORY keyword. The history recording feature can be enabled and disabled as many times as desired by the user in any one session. On the next session with the interpreter, the user can reenact all the commands that were stored by use of the history feature in two ways. The first way is to use indirect input on invoking the interpreter. Indirect input in command lines to operating systems is a feature of many modern operating systems. Typically the operating system command would look like the following:

```
prompt>interpreter < history
```

In this method the user loses control of the interpreter to the history file which of course must end with the 'END' command to exit the interpreter and return control back to the user at the operating system level. This enables the session to be demonstrated by the student. The second method is via an extra interpreter intrinsic command 'RERUN <history file name>'. The interpreter then executes every command line in the specified file until end of file is encountered whereupon control is returned to the user within the one interpreter session. Clearly several different history files may be rerun in the one session in this manner. It is also possible for the history feature to be enabled to record part of a history file and be switched off by a 'NO HISTORY' command edited into a history file.

A parallel concept to recording the history of interpreter commands is generating an actual program that implements each of the package calls made by the interpreter. Any suitable target language can be catered for here. The interpreter intrinsic commands for this are 'PROGRAM' and 'NO PROGRAM' which work similarly to the 'HISTORY' and 'NO HISTORY' commands. Note that the resulting program is monolithic and consists essentially of a fixed set of suitable declarations and a sequence of package routine calls without loops and decisions. Nevertheless the program can be compiled and will generate the same graphics results that rerunning the history command file would give via the intereter. The compiled program version is faster and more flexible. The interpreter approach to generating a compilable graphics program has the advantages of immediate response and easy testing of all package routines and then provides seed code for more general software incorporating graphics calls. The programs generated by the 'PROGRAM' command can become modules in the final graphics program.

Other minor utility enhancements that can be implemented in interpreters are prompts and comments. The 'PROMPT' and 'NO PROMPT' commands allow and disable prompts appearing on every command line input to the interpreter. The 'PROMPT' command can optionally take one or more string arguments which become user defined prompts to replace the interpreters default prompts. (The initial default prompt may change to other special prompts for continuation lines where a command stretches over more than one input line.) Many novice users do not like being faced with an empty screen, and prefer to have prompts to indicate when the interpreter is ready for the next line of GSP command input, and allowing them to set their own prompts is a pleasant feature. Another minor enhancement is allowing comment inputs to the interpreter. Comment lines can be distinguished by a special character (such as '*' or '#') as the first character in the command line. These are of little importance during the running of an interpreter session, but are of much more use when the HISTORY command is used. The comments are then written into the history file which will be viewed later as an ordinary text file. The comments help the user remember what was being done, and also serve as guides in dividing up a long file of graphics commands into meaningful sections. The extra commands 'ECHO ON', 'ECHO OFF', and 'ECHO COMMENTS' can be used especially during the replay of history files. The first echoes all command lines being interpreted onto the screen. The second command echoes none of the command lines so that only the developing graphics is seen. The third command only echoes the comments in the history file. This is helpful for the user to know where the interpreter is up to in replaying the history file.

More difficult enhancements to the interpreter allow the user to declare parameters, assign values to them, and pass them to the package routines. Additionally, loop and decision control structures could be added to the interpreter, and then later the ability to call command modules with parameter passing. None of these concepts have been seriously implemented at this stage. They really mean building a new language based around the routines of the package as basic statements.

It has been found that the use of graphics package interpreters greatly increases the learning rate for any package. In the teaching area, this means that provided there are adequate ratios between the number of students of graphics and graphics terminals and terminal access hours, the use of interpreters as described in this chapter enables more than one distinct graphics package to be mastered satisfactorily by students at the introductory graphics teaching level. Such a course, designed for third year computing science students, in practice is called upon to cater for students from other faculties and even other tertiary teaching institutions who will in general not have the same level of programming competence. For some of these students, the interpreters can be an end in themselves, enabling various packages to be used to produce repeatable graphics output. For the students with competent programming skills, the interpreters serve to introduce various packages for functionality and utility comparisons, and to provide seed graphics code around which user friendly applications programs are built. History files are a way of making graphics programming highly readable. From a teachers point of view this means that graphics projects are easier to mark. For the general user, they represent a convenient, portable, readable format for storing graphics.

The reader may by now have noticed the strong similarity between GSP interpreter history files and the graphics object metafiles for GSPs such as G2/3D. By carefully enforcing uniformity between these two sorts of files, they can be used interchangeably for either purpose. Thus the interpreter can be used as a tool for creating graphics object files (metafiles) for a GSP and conversely, GSP metafiles created by compiled application programs using the GSP can be viewed and examined easily under the interpreter for that GSP. This means that the GSP interpreter is a very useful tool in the development of computer graphics output and software.

Problems

14.1   Design a sparse list structure for storing pixel data as described in Section 14.5.

14.2   Write procedures to extract literal integers, reals, chars, strings, and booleans from a given command line string. The inputs to each function are the command line string called 'command', and 'pointer' an integer pointing to the first character in the command string from which analysis will start. This latter parameter must be updated and returned by the 'get' function for further use by the calling procedure.

14.3   Implement an interpreter for G2D with intrinsic commands PROGRAM, NO PROGRAM, HISTORY, NO HISTORY, and REPLAY to rerun the history file.

14.4   Extend the interpreter of problem 14.3 to the full G2/3D system.

14.5   Create the interpreter generator as described in Section 14.7. Make sure that it
will accurately create the interpreters of problems 14.3 and 14.4.

14.6   Apply the interpreter generator of problem 14.5 to some other sort of graphics
system such as the third-generation style in SGL as presented in Section 14.5.

14.7   How could the interpreter of problem 14.2 be extended to allow the user to
declare and use parameters? Allow the user to give the follwing sorts of
commands in the interpreter:

DECLARE REAL P
ASSIGN P := 3.14159

and then use the declared parameter(s) in GSP procedure calls in place of the
literals. The use of parameters in this manner can save the user retyping long
numbers, a common source of errors. Now extend the interpreter to allow
assignments to arithmetic expressions rather than to just literals as in the above
ASSIGN command.

14.8   Extend the interpreter of problem 14.7 to include FOR-loops and IF-statements
on compound interpreter commands surrounded by BEGIN and END commands.
Allow the interpreter to ignore blanks and tabulations from the start of command
lines. In the case of FOR-loops, if the next command after the FOR command is
'BEGIN' then the body of the FOR-loop is a compound statement. In this case
the loop body is not executed as it is typed in but only after the terminating
END command is given.

14.9   Design an interpreter enhancement that allows histories to be sent to specified
files by extending the 'HISTORY' command to accept a string parameter
indicating the file name:

HISTORY file-name

The RERUN (or REPLAY) command should then optionally accept a string
indicating which file to replay. Allow REPLAY commands to be nested inside
history files. This should be done by having the 'interpret(command)' procedure
of the interpreter, open the nominated file, read every line of the file recursively
calling itself on each, and on reaching end of file to close the nominated history
file.

14.10   Incorporate the GSP interpreter extensions described in problems 14.7, 14.8, and
14.9 into the interpreter generator of problem 14.5. Some other extensions to
interpreters that could be included are:

• TRACE ON and TRACE OFF commands which single step replays through history files asking the user whether to call the particular GSP routine or not for each command line of the history file.

- Allow for macros in the interpreter. The user may define a macro to save retyping a long sequence of GSP calls. The macros may be passed parameters.
- Include a HELP command that can interactively give the user information on how to call any nominated interpreter command: whether a GSP routine call or an interpreter intrinsic command.

It is clear that such interpreters can be extended almost *ad infinitum* so that in the end they become fully new programming languages based around the GSP!

15

Computer graphics standards

15.1 **The history of standards**

Some examples of computer graphics standards are:

CORE – the Core graphics standard;
GKS – the Graphics Kernal System;
PHIGS – the Programmer's Hierarchical Interactive Graphics System;
GSX – the Graphics System eXtension;
NAPLPS – the North American presentation-level-protocol syntax.

Each of these graphics standards will be discussed in more detail in the next few sections.

During the 50s, 60s, and even the 70s, computer graphics equipment manufacturers went their own ways in graphics equipment design. Generally, the functions available on early graphics equipment was very limited, for instance, hardware text plus 'move_to' and 'draw_to'. The equipment was programmed at the low level of direct hardware control. Although similar technologies were used (as developed in universities and publicly available), this resulted in a variety of programming methodologies for graphics, and a variety in functionality and capabilities of computer graphics equipment. This diversification has its advantages in that a free market is good for the development of quality products and the determination of what features are desired by the customers.

However in some cases, the graphics hardware was only suited to one make of host mainframe. This meant that companies using computer graphics equipment tended to be locked in to one supplier (e.g. HP, IBM, Calcomp, Tektronix, etc.) and even one model of graphics equipment.

A small set of software routines were developed by the hardware manufacturers to help their customers get the best use of the equipment and promote sales. These were the beginnings of hardware-centered GSPs. However there was little similarity between packages and no agreement between manufacturers on GSP design. Since the GSP development was done mostly by hardware experts, the resulting software was not the most desirable form that suits software specialists, and this did not help in the development of large graphics applications programs.

As more complex software was developed in-house for the computer graphics equipment, the cost of moving the software to other (newer and better) computer graphics equipment became prohibitive. Companies would have to stick it out as far as possible with the aging equipment that they had. This problem is symptomatic of the general *software crisis*, the general problem addressed by the new discipline of Software Engineering, wherein old company software has been extended, updated, modified, managed, changed, improved, and 'maintained' to the limit that any further slight alterations are bound to cause a catastrophic software crash.

This is not just a problem for the user companies, but also for the computer manufacturers since they must continue to sell their latest offerings. Manufacturers saw this problem and provided the following solutions to their customers:

1. Compatibility with old equipment. The manufacturers made sure that their product line maintained 'upwards compatibility', that is, that any new products could do everything that the previous generation of products could do, but in addition had new improved functions. Importantly, the old hardware codes were retained in the newer models to access the functions of the older equipment. In many cases, to maintain company competitiveness, manufacturers also supplied cross-company compatibilty – manufacturers supplied terminal emulation facilities for terminals made by other manufacturers. The most notable example here is Tektronix 4010 compatibility. Many graphics workstations claim compatability with the old Tek 4010 graphics terminals so that a customer's software investment in graphics software that drives Tek 4010 terminals does not have to be discarded. IBM PC graphics compatibility is another example (in more recent times).

2. The manufacturers began supplying higher level language packages for driving their graphics equipment. These were virtually all libraries of FORTRAN callable subroutines, that is, GSPs to make the full use of the graphics equipment easier for the programmer. These high-level language libraries removed the low-level programming burden from the customer so that graphics software development could proceed much faster than it had in the past. This step is comparable to the introduction of high-level language compilers in place of low-level assembly language programming. Probably the first such library was the CALCOMP package provided by the Calcomp Company for its line of high-quality plotters. Tektronix released a package called PLOT 10. PLOT 10 is a library of 145 FORTRAN subroutines for driving Tektronix terminals.

Hardware graphics functionality improved and communications standardized. Manufacturers supported a range of similar graphics equipment all operating under the same GSP, but these were totally dissimilar between manufacturers.

However, the GSPs supplied by such companies as Calcomp, Tektronix, HP, and IBM grew with time and became less and less alike. There was no direct correspondence of subroutine for subroutine in numbers, functionality, or parameter passing mechanisms, and GSPs differed with respect to their design philosophies. Over time a programmer could expect to become familiar with only one GSP at a time due to the learning curve involved. This difference among the various GSPs supplied by the manufacturers, and the difficulty in becoming familiar with any one package quickly due to its size, meant that there was again considerable expense in moving company software to new computer graphics equipment from another supplier. Again standardization was seen to be necessary. The solution to the original graphics software compatability problem was to provide higher level access to graphics. Now it is seen to be necessary to standardize the high-level libraries. As such a computer graphics standard today means a package of standard routines for graphics functions – a standard GSP – usually available in several languages.

The earliest attempt at standardizing graphics in the US was the ACM (Association for Computing Machinery) Workshop on Machine Independent Graphics held in April 1974 at the National Bureau of Standards near Washington. The goal of that conference was to define a single method for describing computer graphics pictures that could be used for every possible graphics output device. In 1977, the Graphics Standards Planning Committee (GSPC) of the ACM produced the CORE system. The GSPC consisted of a large number of industry representatives and academics from universities in the US. This version of CORE incorporated input and output capabilities for many types of graphics peripheral devices. However it did not address the raster graphics equipment which was starting to become popular at that time. A revised version of CORE incorporating functions suitable to the raster graphics technology was produced by the same committee in 1979. Subsequently the Graphical Kernal System (GKS) was developed in Europe by Deutsches Institut fur Normung (DIN), the German standardization institute, and it was accepted as an international standard. The CORE System never reached the level of an international standard, but it formed a working basis for international standards such as GKS.

The next few sections will look at these standards in some detail. Summaries of some of the standards can be found in Appendixes F, G, and H. Each standard can be analyzed by the same criterion used in the previous chapter for analyzing the graphics functionality of GSPs and graphics languages.

15.2 The CORE system

The GSPC formulated CORE after considering many current hardware-centered GSPs as used in the industry at that time. Ideas and terminologies were selected as 'best' from this variety. Academic generalizations and ideals were also added to make the final version of the CORE system. CORE is a large GSP consisting of around 237 routines. Of these, 86 are control functions, 21 are output functions, 29 are attribute setting functions, and 101 are classified as input functions. Eight of the control functions govern segments. Segments are essentially the same as graphics objects as discussed for G2D and G3D. In CORE, segments are identified by a number rather than an identifying name as in G2D and G3D. Many of the other control functions concern defining various specifications for a multiworkstation setup where each workstation can have a variety of graphics input peripheral devices. The workstations are identified by a workstation (WS) number (WSid). Each graphics input peripheral is identified by its class and ID number. There are six classes of input device with the following names:

1. button device – returns an integer to the program. Typically function keys and mouse buttons are button devices. They are used to indicate menu choices.
2. pick device – returns a segment number picked from a VDU screen. Typically a lightpen for a CRT screen or a mouse are used as pick devices.
3. keyboard device – returns a character string to the program. Typically the keyboard attached to a VDU is used for this device.
4. valuator device – returns a real number to the program. Typically a dial giving analog values to the processor via an ADC (analog-to-digital convertor) is used for this type of device.
5. locator device – returns graphics point coordinates (x, y). Typically a digitizing tablet is used for this.
6. stroke device – returns a sequence of n point coordinates in one series. Typically this type of device is a digitizing stylus in streaming mode for two dimensions or a joystick for three dimensions.

The output functions provided are 'move_to', 'draw_to', 'marker', 'polymarker', 'polyline', and 'text' in graphics. The first five have versions with absolute user coordinates and relative user coordinates, both in two and three dimensions. The text function is only two-dimensional, but has a large number of attributes to specify the text drawing plane and direction of the text. Note that no provision is made for arcs, circles, ellipses, splines, or other curves. These are assumed to be implemented by the user in software, though today several of these are already in hardware on most graphics workstations.

Segments may be 'temporary' or 'retained'. Temporary segments are essentially the same as using G2D or G3D graphics output routines without storing them in graphics objects, while retained segments are like storing the G2D or G3D commands in the current graphics object. If the screen is redrawn the temporary segment primitives do not reappear – only those that have been saved in the retained segments. In CORE, only one segment can be open at a time so that hierarchical picture segmentation is not possible in CORE.

Attributes in CORE can refer to individual output primitives or to retained segments as a whole. Temporary segments do not have assigned attributes. Output primitive attributes are 'static'; that is, once the primitive is drawn its attributes can not be changed. Segment attributes on the other hand are 'dynamic', that is, they can be changed by CORE calls, and the next time that segment is drawn it will show the new attributes. Attributes for lines and polylines are color, intensity, linestyle, linewidth, and pen (in the case of plotters); for markers and polymarkers, symbol number; and for text, font, charwidth, charheight, dx_plane, dy_plane, dz_plane, dx_charup, dy_charup, dz_charup, charpath, charjust (the justification style), and charprecision.

The output primitives also have an attribute called 'pick_id' which can be used by the input functions to tell the program which primitive is being pointed to. Retained segments have a different set of attributes to those for output primitives. There is only one static attribute for retained segments, namely the image transformation type which could be none, two-dimensional translations, three-dimensional translations, general two-dimensional transformations, or general three-dimensional transformations. Retained segments have four dynamic attributes which are visibility, highlighting, detectability, and image_transformation. Visibility is a boolean flag saying whether or not the segment is shown on the output. Highlighting causes the segment to stand out, such as by blinking or increased intensity. Detectability refers to whether or not the pick device can select the segment, and image transformation is the list of translation, scale, and rotation parameters for transforming all primitives of the segment.

Some other features of CORE are that it stores graphics data internally in NDCs, it uses the CP (current position) concept (and therefore provides the 'moveto' and 'drawto' functions, in user coordinates, for the user as seen above), and its transformations are passive ones using a CTM (current transformation matrix). It contains routines for two and three dimensions that are compatible, that is, can be mixed together within the one application program. Typical implementations also provide commands to write and read metafiles (files to store segments, i.e., graphics objects, on secondary storage).

At this time software houses were seeing the potential market in a standardized GSP and strove to be first on the market with a CORE package. Companies using computer graphics also saw the benefits of this standardization and decided to take the plunge, spend the effort in software changeover, and buy into CORE graphics. Examples of CORE graphics implementations are DI-3000 (supplied by Precision Visuals), TIGS, and SunCore. The following examples from SunCore in Pascal show the flavour of CORE graphics programming.

```
begin
    setupsurf(dsurf);
    e := initializecore(BASIC,NOINPUT,TWOD);
    e := initializevwsurf(dsurf,FALSE);
    e := setviewport2(0.125,0.875,0.125,0.75);
    {set up a user coordinate window:}
    e := setwindow(-50.0,50.0,-50.0,50.0);
    e := moveabs2(-10.0,-10.0);
    e := lineabs2(10.0,10.0); {implements the 2D drawto function};
    e := closetempseg;
    e := deselectvsurf(dsurf);
    e := terminatecore;
end.
```

In this code fragment, BASIC, NOINPUT, TWOD, and FALSE are globally defined integer constants, and 'dsurf' is a record variable of a predefined SunCore type 'vwsurf' to describe the characteristics of the display surface to be used by the program. The parameter 'dsurf' must have its record components set up by the user, and in the above piece of code this is done in a user routine called 'setupsurf'. Note that all SunCore Pascal CORE routines are functions that return an integer result ('e' above). This is because SunCore is actually implemented in C (whose routines are always functions) but access is possible from Pascal. The program simply draws a line in two dimensions in a temporary segment. A full list of SunCore Pascal routines can be found in Appendix F.

Although many major companies in the US moved their graphics software over to CORE, CORE graphics did not become the universal graphics standard everyone hoped for: it never became an international standard. However it did define graphics terminology and guide future developments in computer graphics, forming the basis of the newer graphics standards.

15.3 The GKS international standard

After CORE, GKS was developed in Germany. It was initiated by the ISO (International Standards Organization) rather than the ACM and so was assured of reaching international acceptance unlike CORE. GKS is now fully defined and documented. It was finally released in language bindings for FORTRAN, Pascal, and C toward the end of 1985. Unlike CORE however, GKS provides two-dimensional graphics only. In fact GKS uses many of the CORE two-dimensional concepts though it is simpler than CORE. For instance, like CORE, it is based on NDCs. It would have been much better if GKS was based on physical coordinates (millimeters, say) so that the preservation of aspect ratios would be guaranteed. Unlike CORE however, GKS does allow for *bundled* attributes (explained below). There are many books available now that explain GKS. GKS consists of 112 routines, 50 of which may be classified as control functions, 7 output functions, 35 attribute setting functions, and 20 input functions. Like CORE, it supports multiple workstation environments with the same six classes of graphics input peripherals. It also supports segments, but not hierarchical segments. The output primitives are pixel blocks (cell arrays), text, polygonal filled areas, polymarkers, and polylines. GKS also allows for access to any extra hardware-implemented graphics output primitives via a general routine called the Generalized Drawing Primitive (GDP). Thus although GKS also does not support arcs, circles, and so forth, they are supposed to be accessed through this very device-dependent routine (if the functions exist in the hardware). Unlike CORE, GKS is not filled out with inquiry functions that return to the program GKS parameters and primitive and segment attributes that have been set. The application program is itself expected to remember what parameters and attributes it has set if it needs them. GKS input is also via request mode, sample mode, or event mode. Request mode is the usual device read method where the program waits for the answer. Sample mode is where the device is scanned to see what current value it has (if it has one) and this is returned to the program – there is no waiting to hold up program execution. For event mode, inputs are placed in a queue and the program can look at the event queues at any time and either read a value and act on it, or do so later. The input functions in GKS are mostly one of each

10.   text color index;
11.   area interior style;
12.   area filling style;
13.   area color index.

The 13 element boolean array LASF sets the so called Aspect Source Flag for each of these attributes to INDIVIDUAL (i.e. unbundled and therefore global) or BUNDLED.

While GKS has gained a lot of popularity, it is not certain that GKS will be the 'final' graphics standard, or that it will be universally accepted or used, even though it has been declared as an international standard. One obvious disadvantage of GKS is that its implementations tend to produce slow graphics. Many graphics applications need graphics at the fastest speed possible. Another disadvantage is that while GKS programs can be ported from one device to another (providing they both have the GKS standard, and in the same language) aspect ratios will in general not be preserved in the output graphics. Also attribute indexes beyond those defined in the standard would produce unpredictable results in the graphics. Furthermore the standard is not language independent in that to use another programming language, the GKS binding in the new language must be purchased.

15.4 GSX – a standard for microcomputers

GSX is an attempt at making a graphics standard which is language and device independent. It is essentially an extension of the operating system and lies resident in main memory. It is accessed in a similar way to the usual operating system intrinsic functions. GSX is a two-dimensional graphics system with many analogies with GKS. It is written by Digital Research and runs on microcomputer-based graphics workstations with the popular CP/M or MS-DOS operating systems. Current implementations of this package, however, seem to be limited to these operating systems and as yet it is not widely used. Extensive details on the GSX system can be found in Appendix H. This appendix also shows how Pascal programs can interface to the memory resident GSX functions by means of a procedure called GSXINT and associated parameter block data structure. The 60 functions of GSX have been dressed up as Pascal procedures in Appendix H for easier access from Pascal. Inside each of these procedures the interfacing procedure GSXINT is called with the appropriate parameter block data values set up to perform the nominated function. After GSXINT is called, any output values from GSX are read from the parameter block record and converted to the appropriate output variables of the Pascal procedure. It is clear from the explanation of this 'Pascalizing' process of GSX that GSX could equally well be dressed up for any other language the user wanted it in. In this way GSX is an operating system and language-independent graphics system, that is, it is a third-generation graphics system. (See Section 14.5 for further discussion on third-generation graphics systems.)

Appendix H can be used to do a fingerprint count analysis of GSX just as was done for graphics language examples in the previous chapter. This information can then be tabulated together with fingerprint information for other standards, such as CORE and

Table 15-1 Comparison of some graphics standards by command categories.

Name	N	O	A	I	E	C	D	M	S
SunCore	207	27	36	9	69	6	2	11	47
GKS	112	7	44	18	0	16	2	12	13
GSX	60	10	15	9	4	19	0	0	3

GKS, similar to the tabulation of graphics languages done in Table 14-1. The results of such an analysis are presented in Table 15-1. (The column headings have the same meaning as explained under Table 14-1.) From Table 15-1 it can be observed that of the three standards, CORE, GKS, and GSX, CORE has the most and GSX the least number of routines. GKS has the least number of output commands but the greatest number of attribute setting routines for the output commands. All three provide polyline, polymarker, and text as output primitives. CORE adds movetos, drawtos, and markers to this list while GKS adds only cells and area fills. However GSX adds five more graphics output element types beyond those supplied by GKS. These are bars, arcs, circles, wedges, and graphics characters. Thus GSX is richest in output primitive types (having ten distinct types) while CORE has six distinct types and GKS has only five distinct types provided as standard (others can of course be added by the user). The table also shows that only GSX does not intrinsically provide metagraphics (segmentation) routines. When the standards tabulated in Table 15-1 are compared with the languages tabulated in Table 14-1, what immediately springs to notice is that the standards have many more graphics routines provided in them than any of the languages. (G2/3D is not a 'graphics language' but a graphics software package – a graphics adjunct to a language.)

15.5 Other graphics standards

PHIGS is another standard created in the US which like CORE has not received the international stamp of approval. It is so 'high-level' in its graphics standardization, that the choice of data structuring is not available to the user. Such high-level standardization results in inflexibility from the point of view of the user, and verges on turnkey graphics systems.

NAPLPS (pronounced 'nap-lips') is a set of rules and conventions for describing how data bytes of information should be formatted and interpreted for communication of two-dimensional graphics. It grew out of the need for mass distribution of graphical information by videotext and teletext systems to low-cost user-friendly home microcomputer graphics terminals. NAPLPS was created through a joint effort by the American National Standards Institute (ANSI) and the Canadian Standards Institute (CSA) around 1982. It is very similar to the Canadian Telidon system for videotext. Basically it provides an immense extension to the ASCII character set (see Appendix A). Certain of these modes for each of the possible input peripherals. For a full list of GKS routines, parameters, and their meanings refer to Appendix G. Samples of GKS routines are described below.

To draw a polyline of n points, the two-dimensional world coordinates of the points are placed into two real arrays, say 'xpts' and 'ypts' and then the GKS procedure called as follows:

    polyline(n,xpts,ypts);

For instance, drawing three line segments will require $n = 4$ points to be set up. To fill in a triangular area on the other hand only needs $n = 3$, and the arrays 'xpts' and 'ypts' to store the vertexes of the triangle.

Attributes for polylines can be bundled into a group indicated by a single index. The routine:

    set_polyline_rep(id,i,ltyp,wid,col)

defines bundle number 'i' for polylines on workstation number 'id'. The parameters 'ltyp', 'wid', and 'col' are the attributes line type, line width factor, and line color. Line types can be solid ($ltyp = 1$), dashed ($ltyp = 2$), dotted ($ltyp = 3$), and dash-dotted ($ltyp = 4$). Higher values for 'ltyp' are implementation dependent. Whenever polyline index number 'i' is invoked, as in:

    set_polyline_index(i)

the other attributes are automatically applied. The attributes for bundle 'i' can be different for every workstation. After setting the polyline index (bundle number) as above, the different attributes will be used on the different workstations whenever a polyline call is made.

Attributes for polymarkers can similarly be bundled into a group indicated by a single index. The routine:

    set_polym_rep(id,i,mtyp,mscale,col)

defines bundle number 'i' for polylines on workstation number 'id'. The parameters 'mtyp', 'mscale', and 'col' are the attributes marker type, marker size factor, and marker color. Marker types can be set with:

    set_polym_index(mtyp)

where:

$$\text{'mtyp'} \quad \begin{aligned} &= 1 \text{ for a dot '.'} \\ &= 2 \text{ for a small cross '+'} \\ &= 3 \text{ for an asterisk '*'} \\ &= 4 \text{ for a small circle 'o'} \\ &= 5 \text{ for a cross 'X'} \end{aligned}$$

Higher values for 'mtyp' are implementation dependent. Whenever polymarker index number 'i' is invoked, as in:

set_polym_rep(i)

the other attributes are automatically applied. The polymarker can then be drawn with these attributes by the command:

polymarker(n,xpts,ypts);

Attributes for area fills can similarly be bundled into a group indicated by a single index. The routine:

set_fill_area_rep(id,i,is,s,col)

defines bundle number 'i' for area fills on workstation number 'id'. The parameters 'is', 's', and 'col' are the attributes of interior style, pattern scale, and color. Interior styles can be hollow (i.e. no filling), solid, pattern, and hatch. Whenever area fill index number 'i' is invoked, as in:

set_fill_area_index(i)

the other attributes are automatically applied. The area can then be filled according to these attributes by the command:

fill_area(n,xpts,ypts);

The output primitive attributes for all primitives can be set in bundles like this or they can be set individually. If not set in workstation bundles then the attributes set are global to all workstations and so are approximated to the desired output on every different workstation. GKS provides a routine:

set_aspect_source_flags(LASF)

to indicate whether an attribute is globally set or comes from a workstation bundle. GKS has 13 output primitive attributes that can be dealt with in this way:

1. line type;
2. line width scale factor;
3. line color index;
4. marker type;
5. marker size scale factor;
6. marker color index;
7. text font and precision;
8. character size factor;
9. character spacing;

control bytes change the meaning of subsequent bytes from being ASCII text characters to many other alternatives. Among these alternatives are mosaic (block graphical) character sets, UDCs (user-definable characters), and a set of primitive commands with their parameters called the PDI (picture description instruction) set. The graphics primitives covered in PDI are text, points, lines, arcs, rectangles, and polygons. These may be expressed in relative or absolute coordinates (using NDCs), and filled in or hollow. The data format for the parameters allows for any resolution on the receiving VDU. This standard is likely to become much more widespread in the future.

GKS is continuing to develop. Work is in progress on defining a three-dimensional extension to GKS. This can be expected to again be similar to the three-dimensional side of CORE. The three-dimensional version of GKS may well attempt to include hierarchical segmentation.

While the various standards vie against one another for prominance, the de facto standards like PLOT 10 persist in the workplace.

15.6 Strategies for device independence

Many graphics software packages have been surveyed in this book, and the reader should now be in a good position to construct a GSP similar to any of the ones described. All GSPs must interface to graphics hardware devices in some manner. Making a GSP as portable as possible across a broad range of computer graphics hardware is a problem requiring careful attention. For each graphics device there should be a code unit incorporating all the chosen graphics primitives of 'moveto', 'drawto', 'clear', and 'getpoint', and the device characteristics 'ndh', 'ndv', 'width', and 'height', as global constants. This code unit is called a *device driver* . Ordinarily, the device driver is linked into the package at package (not application) link time. In this approach, the GSP has a single integrated device driver. GSPs are usually marketed in linkable object-code form, rather than in source-code form, to safeguard the designer's intellectual property rights. This means that for a bought package, the buyer is dependent on the supplier for the built-in device driver. If the supplied device driver does not exactly match the user's hardware, then all of the powerful functionality built into the GSP may well be useless. (This has often been the case for running graphics software on microcomputers which are claimed to be hardware compatible.) Likewise, when graphics hardware is upgraded, or new graphics hardware installed, the GSP with integrated device driver may fail to execute.

One way of overcoming this problem is for the designer to supply the GSP and device driver as separate object modules. If the GSP and device driver are not integrated, then the buyer can select and buy new device drivers as the need arises. Device drivers are cheaper than the GSP, and are often given away free. The user might buy several or all available drivers, and link in the driver appropriate to the graphics hardware for which the application program, based on the GSP, is intended.

In a third method the package is specifically built to handle up to a set number of devices simultaneously. There are 'ndev' devices and the characteristics 'ndh', 'ndv', 'width', and 'height' are arrays dimensioned from 1 to 'maxdev'. The GSP contains routines to initialize and address devices, and the application programmer must always call these routines with the correct parameters for the graphics hardware to be used. A disadvantage of this approach is that the unused device drivers consume valuable host main memory. Also remembering the correct initialization and termination codes may be irksome to the programmer, and detract from the readability of the application program source code. Such a system is valuable in a multiple workstation environment. Nevertheless, the same problem arises, of needing new device drivers when graphics hardware is upgraded.

A fourth approach to device independence is to have the GSP produce an output file of graphics commands in a standard format. This file is then passed through another program that converts the standard low-level graphics commands to machine code for a particular graphics device. The two steps can be combined by using directed output: at the command line the ouput of an application can be directed ('piped') to the desired driver. This method does not allow interactive graphics, for there is no control as to where the input comes from or where it goes to from within the program.

In choosing any of these approaches, two design decisions must be answered. Firstly, is the GSP designed for a single graphics device or a multiple workstation environment? Secondly, is the device driver to be integrated in the object code or separate. Of course, if the designer released details of the device-driver interface expected by the GSP, then application programmers could implement their own drivers when necessary. This may take the form of a description of the required routine names, their parameters and parameter types, and any global constants required, or else the high-level source code of one or more drivers may be provided.

15.7 Future trends with standards

When the short history of computer graphics standards is surveyed, no indication is seen of universal acceptance of any particular one. It does not appear that any one standard is suitable for the variety of application areas in computer graphics. It may well be that current computer graphics standards are attempting to standardize computer graphics systems at a very high software level, too high a level, rather than at the hardware level as with other standards. In general, the hardware technology seems to lead the software programming style. A new breakthrough in hardware may render current computer graphics standards seriously lacking. (This happened to CORE when raster graphics hardware gained prominence.)

Is it likely then that GKS, say, would be implemented at chip level? This could be so for the basic graphics input/output, and attribute functions. Many of the control functions apply to supporting multiple workstations and the perceived totality of possible attached graphics input devices. These would be unnecessary inside a single workstation. If the workstation provides for particular kinds of graphics input devices then separate chips would be used to interface to them.

Perhaps computer graphics standardization should consist of specifying *escape sequences* for a specific set of graphics functions for every graphics device. The graphics functions should consist of a specific set of output and input primitives and a standard set of attributes for the output primitives. This standardization would then be analogous to the ANSI standardization of VT100 escape sequences and control codes. This style of standardization then would be *language, device,* and *operating system independent* Whereas, not everybody would be prepared to accept a standardized high-level GSP, they would be prepared to accept standardized graphics terminals in this sense. Just as a standard set of escape sequences that control the text screen (such as cursor rendition; cursor positioning; character, line, and block text deletion, and character, line, and block text insertion escape sequence commands) allow screen editors and similar text-only programs to be ported from terminal to terminal, so standardized escape sequences for graphics functions would result in portable graphics software no matter what the source language was.

A suggested list of graphics functions for low-level standardization is as follows:

1. *Input primitives*
   (a) return the pixel value of a specific pixel address;
   (b) return the physical color value of a specific logical palette;
   (c) return the current graphics position CP coordinates;
   (d) return the current text screen cursor position;
   (e) return the current attribute for every output primitive attribute;
   (f) return the device's resolution (e.g. 639,399);
   (g) block read of pixels.

Note: input primitives are initiated by an escape sequence which causes the hardware to respond with an escape or output sequence to the program in which the requested information can be found. A simple style would be to have the program send the escape sequence:

ESC I <input primitive ID code> <param1> <param2>

to which the hardware responds by returning the escape sequence:

ESC I <param1> <param2>

to the program. The former escape sequence is placed in a write statement in any language and the latter is received in the program by a read statement. The parameters <param1> and <param2> are appended as relevant to the appropriate input primitive.

2. *Output primitives* – (to generate visible graphics when called)
   (a) draw a line segment;
   (b) draw an arc;
   (c) place a marker;
   (d) fill an area;
   (e) draw text (in graphics);
   (f) block write of pixel values;
   (g) block copy of pixel values (blitting).

3. *Attribute setting functions* – (alter the way output primitives will appear. The following list is a minimal set.)
   (a) move to (modify CP coordinates);
   (b) set drawing color;
   (c) set line style;
   (d) set a palette to a physical color;
   (e) set the marker style;
   (f) set the text font;
   (g) set the text direction;
   (h) set the text size;
   (i) set the pixel writing mode (replace, OR, AND, NOT, NAND, XOR etc);
   (j) set the halftoning pattern for area fills.

A disadvantage of the use of escape sequences is that the hardware requires an escape sequence processor, which is an interpreter in **firmware**. Interpreters slow down graphics because time is required to parse escape sequences, extract parameters, and convert them to machine form before the commands can be performed. To obtain the fastest performance in graphics, direct control of the hardware is necessary.

15.8 The future of computer graphics

The increasing use of silicon chips by society has brought down their price, and demand is by far strongest for memory chips. Every processor whatever its make or peculiarities needs basically the same kind of RAM chips for its main memory. Furthermore processor chips have been becoming more powerful with regard to their memory addressing range. This has meant that either more RAM chips would be used and this would consume more physical space or else higher density memory chips had to be made. The march of technological progress has brought us cheaper and higher memory-sized RAM chips. An immediate consequence of greater memory is the dedication of more of this memory to graphics. This has resulted in higher screen resolutions and more on-screen and available colors for the user to select from. Undoubtably this trend will continue, and compact high-resolution full-television-style colored graphics terminals will become commonplace.

But high resolution is not so desirable if the graphics drawing speed is going to be slow. Another observable trend in computer graphics equipment development has been the increase in speed of writing pixels. This has been primarily dependent on memory chip access cycle times which have been steadily improving over the years. It is anticipated therefore that in the future, RAM chips will not only be more compact and hold more memory bits at lower cost, but that will also perform faster. Speed improvements in the chips however does appear to be reaching a ceiling limit. Alternative architectures for addressing memory (such as parallel access in interleaved RAM) are providing new approaches to the speed problem with dramatic results. Another approach to the speed problem has been the 'put it in hardware' syndrome. What was previously done in software is now done in firmware (ROM, that is, read-only memory): what was previously done in firmware is now done in hardware. As software is more and more relegated to hardware so in general the speed of the functions is increased. Graphics processors are doing this now: implementing the graphics functions previously implemented in software, via a high-level language, in much more efficient machine code ROM or direct hardware functions.

There is a trend towards allowing standard television video signals to be shown on color graphics VDUs as well as the usual graphics. Systems will allow video frames to be captured in graphics frame RAM and saved on disk for later image processing or enhancement and reproduction. Likewise graphics images on the screen can be downloaded as a video signal to video recorders and other standard television equipment. In the future, mixed video and graphics will probably be commonplace. One or more (movable) viewports on the screen could show a video tape or television signal and other viewport areas could show computer-generated graphics. Graphics may also be superimposed on a television image. These systems will probably be used frequently in teleconferencing and replace the telephone with audio and visual communications.

The future could well see many more smaller, more powerful, and cheaper graphics personal computer systems in widespread usage. At the physical level it can be expected that all these graphics devices will meet the same standard to various grades within the level. Thus all standard graphics functions and attributes may not be provided on a particular unit but the graphics commands that are provided are the same from a programming point of view. Operating systems of the future are likely to be based on interactive graphics rather than the traditional character string computer/human communication style. Many user-interface-managers (UIMs) are now being made. These are graphics interfaces on top of standard character-oriented operating systems. They control windows and icons and provide immediate user feedback with the mouse control.

Finally, we can expect that huge graphics databanks will emerge. Sales of computer graphics data will become as important and perhaps even more profitable than sales of computer programs. This will be especially so of three-dimensional graphics data which is as a rule generally harder to digitize than two-dimensional graphics information. A lot of improved, easy to use three-dimensional graphics software packages will be readily available for all graphics VDUs in the future. It is conceivable that in the future, television sets will display three-dimensional holographic images. Computer graphics systems will surely take advantage of this technology for displaying realistic three-dimensional graphics.

Problems

15.1   The MDP system is a way of storing low-level graphics in a readable and editable form. A picture in MDP format is a text file with one graphics command per line. The first character on the line specifies the kind of command. The command letters are I, M, D, P, and C, which stand for initialize, move, draw, paint and color. The 'I' command does not take any parameters. It clears the screen. The M command takes two parameters, 'px' and 'py', the physical coordinates to which the current drawing point is moved. The 'D' command also takes two coordinates, 'px' and 'py', which are the physical coordinates that a line is drawn to from the CP. The 'P' command takes three parameters, 'rpc', 'gpc', and 'bpc', which are the percentages of red, green, and blue for the area painting color. Painting is done by the flood fill algorithm up to the boundaries in the current drawing color. The 'C' command has three parameters also, 'rpc', 'gpc', and 'bpc', which are the red, green, and blue percentages for the drawing color. A line starting with any other character is ignored, that is, treated as a comment by the MDP system. Write a program called 'ShowMDP' that accepts an MDP file or direct MDP commands from the keyboard, and produces the corresponding graphics output for an available color graphics VDU. Box 15-1 contains a simple MDP file. Use this data in your 'ShowMDP' program, and compare the result with Figure 15-1.

Box 15-1 The contents of the file 'mountains.mdp', a simple example of an MDP file.

```
* Data file for a simple house-mountain scene
* using the MDP device-independent graphics picture storage format.
*
* Frame the picture:
M       0       0
D       120     0
D       120     90
D       0       90
D       0       0
* Ground level:
M       0       20
D       120     20
* Paint the grass green:
M       60      10
P       0       100     0
* Draw the house wall:
M       25      20
D       25      45
D       95      45
D       95      20
* Draw the window:
M       30      30
D       50      30        .
D       50      40
D       30      40
D       30      30
* Paint the window yellow:
M       40      35
P       100     100     0
```

```
* Draw the door:
M       80      20
D       80      40
D       90      40
D       90      20
* Paint the door yellow:
M       85      30
P       100     100     0
* Paint the front of the house white:
M       60      30
P       100     100     100
* Draw the roof:
M       25      45
D       20      45
D       60      60
D       100     45
D       95      45
* Paint the roof red:
M       60      50
P       100     0       0
* Draw the mountain tops:
M       0       65
D       20      80
D       40      65
D       55      75
D       75      60
D       90      70
D       120     55
* Paint the mountains mauve:
M       10      50
P       100     0       100
* Paint the sky:
M       75      80
P       0       100     100
* End of scene.
```

15.2   The MDP system described in problem 15.1 is useful for storing digitized pictures (stills). Write a program called 'CreateMDP' that creates an MDP file using a digitizing device, such as a digitizer tablet and puck, or a mouse coupled to a color graphics VDU.

15.3   Write a program called 'EditMDP', which opens an MDP file and steps through the MDP commands, displaying each one graphically, allowing the user to make changes. The program must pause after executing every line of the MDP file, waiting for a key press from the user to indicate what editing action is to take

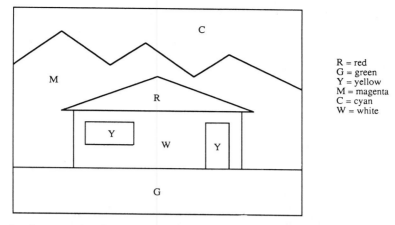

Figure 15-1 A simple example of the output from the program 'ShowMDP' using the MDP data file of Box 15-1. (See problem 15.1.)

place. Use carriage return to step on to the next MDP command, 'B' to step backwards, 'I' to insert a new command, 'F' to move faster, 'S' to single step, and the delete key to delete the current MDP command. When 'F' is pressed, the program no longer waits after each MDP command line is executed, but it does sample the key board. When 'S' is pressed, the program returns to the single-step mode where it waits after every MDP command line for an editing command from the keyboard. The program should produce an output file which is the edited version of the input file. The 'Q' key will quit editing, copying the remainder of the edited file to the new file and displaying the graphics at the same time. The 'X' key will exit immediately from the program without copying the rest of the edit file.

15.4   Implement a multi-workstation driver suitable for GKS in the following way. Write procedures:

'InitWS(wid : integer)' – clears the display rectangle of workstation number 'wid'.
'MoveWS(wid : integer; ndcx,ndcy : real)' – sets the CP for workstation number 'wid'.
'DrawWS(wid : integer; ndcx,ndcy : real)' – draws a line in the current drawing color from the CP to the point ('ndcx','ndcy') in NDCs and updates the CP for workstation number 'wid'.
'PaintWS(wid : integer; rpc,gpc,bpc : real)' – paints from the CP in the color with red, green, and blue percentages as 'rpc', 'gpc', and 'bpc' for workstation number 'wid'. The painting stops at boundaries drawn in the current drawing color for that workstation.
'ColorWS(wid : integer; rpc,gpc,bpc : real)' – sets the current drawing color

with red, green, and blue percentages as 'rpc', 'gpc', and 'bpc' for workstation number 'wid'.

Use 'wid' = 0 as the debug workstation which simply prints the name of the primitive being called and the value of its parameters. Implement this driver for 'MaxNrWS = 2' workstations. If 'wid' is greater than 'MaxNrWS' then no error is to be reported and no action taken.

15.5   Using the driver of problem 15.4, implement the following GKS routines (see Appendix G):

polyline	set_polyline_color_index
polymarker	set_polym_color_index
fill_area	set_fill_area_color_index
draw_text	set_text_color_index
set_window	set_viewport
select_normalization_transf	
open_GKS	close_GKS
open_WS	close_WS
activate_WS	deactivate_WS

To implement the 'fill_area' routine using 'PaintWS' (from problem 15.4) involves drawing the polygon outline in the current drawing color, then finding an interior point of the polygon, and painting from that point as seed point. Finding an interior point is a problem full of pitfalls. However, the following special method is suitable. To find an assured interior point of a polygon with vertexes (x_i, y_i) for $i = 1$ to $i = n$, find a vertex k with the minimum y coordinate, and vertex m with the second minimum y coordinate:

$$y_k <= y_m <= y_i$$

for all $i = 1$ to $i = n$. Then the interior point is (x,y) where:

$$x = x_k , y = (y_k + y_m) / 2$$

15.6   Extend the GKS implementation described in problem 15.5 to the following GKS routines:

create_segment	close_segment
rename_segment	delete_segment
evaluate_transf	
set_visibility	set_segment_priority
set_highlighting	set_segment_transf

associate_seg_with_WS   copy_seg_to_WS
insert_segment   delete_seg_from_WS

The parameters for 'evaluate_transf' are:

'evaluate_transf(cx,cy,tx,ty,theta,sx,sy : real;
   switch : SwitchType; **var** m : MatrixType)

where ('cx','cy') is the center for rotations and scalings, 'tx', 'ty' are the translation displacements, 'theta' is the angle of rotation in radians and 'sx' and 'sy' are the scale transformation parameters. 'SwitchType' is an enumerated type so that 'switch' is either 'WC' (world coordinates) or 'NDC' (normalized device coordinates). The matrix generated is 'm' which may be implemented as a 3 x 3 matrix or the reduced 2 x 3 form. Use the data declarations given in Box 15-2 and illustrated in Figure 15-2 for implementing segment storage for each workstation.

Box 15-2 Data structure definitions for workstation independent segment storage and simulated workstation dependent storage when the workstations do not have local memory. The definitions are illustrated in Figure 15-2.

```
const
        POLYMAX = 100;
        MaxWorkStationNr = 6;
type
        { The following code segment defines the types NTnode and NTptr.
        NTnode is for storing normalization transformations. Every time the
        user calls
                SetWindow(tid, xmin, xmax, ymin, ymax)
        or      SetViwport(tid,ndcxmin,ndcxmax,ndcymin,ndcymax)
        with a new 'tid' (transformation ID number), a new NTnode is
        created with the supplied or default values entered into it. All NTnodes
        are linked together in a single list started from globals called FirstNT
        and LastNT of type NTptr. This list is doubly linked with next and
        previous pointers of type NTptr.}
        NTptr   = ^NTnode;
        NTnode = record
                tid                             : integer;
                xmin,xmax,ymin,ymax             : real;
                next, prev                      : NTptr;
        end;

        {The following code segment defines the types:
                SegStorage
                DListPtr
```

```
         DListNode
         SegPtr
         SegHeader
         PrimPtr
         PrimNode
```

and the DispList array. The DispList is dimensioned to the number of workstations available. DispList[wid] is of type SegStorage which contains two pointers, 'first' and 'last', that define what segments are currently associated with workstation number 'wid'. Each DListNode points on to the next and back to the previous node (if any) in the display list for that workstation and also points to a segment header. A segment header record (of type SegHeader) contains global attribute data for the segment, plus pointers to the primitive nodes in the segment. Each primitive node (of type PrimNode) contains the defining data for a GKS output primitive plus next and previous pointers to other primitive nodes in the chain for the segment.

This structuring allows segments to be stored once only in the host's main memory, no matter how many workstations have copies of them in their own segment storage areas. They don't really have copies - they all point to the same segment data in main memory!}

{Enumerated type of the four GKS primitives:}

```
PrimTypes = (pline, pmark, farea, txtat);
RealArray = array[1 .. POLYMAX] of real;
string255 = packed array[0..255] of char;
```

{A primitive node is a variant record containing the parameters for the corresponding GKS output primitive - polyline, polymarker, fill area or text at:}

```
PrimPtr = ^PrimNode;
PrimNode = record
       case p : PrimTypes of
           pline, pmark, farea    : (n : integer; xa, ya : RealArray);
           txtat                  : (x, y : real; s : string255);
end;
```

{A segment header points to a list of primitive nodes and contains information for the segment as a whole - segment identity number, visibility etc.:}

```
SegPtr = ^SegHeader;
SegHeader = record
       sid                                 : integer;
       visible, highlighted, detectable    : boolean;
       matrix                              : array[1..2,1..3] of real;
       first, last                         : PrimPtr;
end;
```

{The segment storage display list for a workstation is a list of segments. Each node in this list is of type DListNode which points to one segment.}

```
DListPtr = ^DListNode;
DListNode = record
        s                 : SegPtr;
        next, prev        : DListPtr;
end;
SegStorage = record
        first, last       : DListPtr;
end;
{Each of the workstations has this segment storage structure:}
DispList = array[0 .. MaxWorkStationNr] of SegStorage;
```

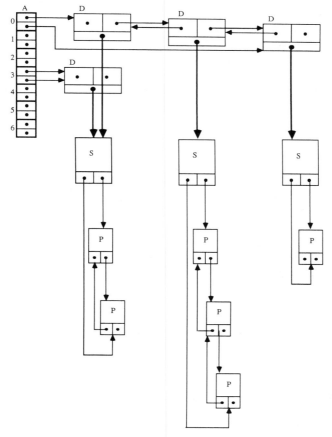

Figure 15-2 A suggested dynamic data structure for maintaining workstation-dependent and workstation-independent segment storage in an implementation of GKS. The array labeled A contains pointers to display lists for each workstation. In this example there are 7 workstations. The nodes labeled D are of type 'DListNode' (as in Box 15-2) and have pointers to segment header nodes labeled S. Each segment header points to a list of primitive nodes labeled P.

15.7   Use pixel rectangle primitives, 'get_rectangle' and 'put_rectangle', and the procedure 'get_point(var k : char; var dcx,dcy : integer)' which returns the pointer device's coordinates when a key 'k' is pressed to implement the icon manager for a UIM. The icon manager is a library of routines that allows icons to be created, displayed, moved and selected on a raster graphics VDU. Assume that an icon is a 32 x 32 pixel rectangle. Implement the routines:

'function CreateIcon' : integer – which clears the screen, shows a large 32 x 32 grid in which the user may turn on or off the squares using the pointer device, and on pressing the escape key it returns the icon sequence number for this new icon.

'procedure PutIcon(IconNr,dcx,dcy : integer)' – which places the nominated icon at the nominated device coordinate position. ('dcx,dcy') is the lower left corner for placing the icon.

'function SelectIcon : integer' – waits for the pointer device's button or a key press, and uses the pointer device's current coordinates to select one of the displayed icons. Use the 'InsideRectangle' procedure from Chapter 7. If the pointer is not inside the minmax rectangle for any icon then zero is to be returned.

'procedure SaveIcons(filename : string)' – writes the pixel array data for all icons created into the nominated file.

'procedure LoadIcons(filename : string)' – loads the pixel array data from the nominated file. The icons will be assigned icon ID numbers in the sequence in which they were read from the file (continuing on from the sequence number of any currently loaded or created icons).

'procedure HideIcon(IconNr : integer)' – removes the nominated icon from the screen, but does not delete it from memory. 'PutIcon' can be used to redisplay it later on.

'procedure InvertIcon(IconNr : integer)' – inverts the nominated icon to complementary colors. If the icon is not displayed, then the next time it is displayed it will be in inverted form. By calling this procedure twice, the icon reverts to its normal appearance.

'procedure EditIcon(IconNr : integer)' – clears the screen, displays the same large 32 x 32 grid used in 'CreateIcon', with the nominated icon displayed on the grid (in large colored squares instead of pixels). The user may then use the pointer device to select squares to cycle their color through the available colors and hence edit the icon. Editing is terminated by pressing the escape key.

15.8   Use GKS, the pixel rectangle primitives (see problem 15.6) and the pointer primitive 'get_point' (see problem 15.6) to implement the window manager for a UIM. The window manager is a library of routines that allows windows to be created, selected, and written to on a raster graphics VDU. Implement the routines:

'function CreateWindow(xll,yll,xur,yur : integer) : integer' – which draws a rectangle on the screen with lower left corner at ('xll','yll') and upper right corner at ('xur','yur') in device coordinates and returns the sequence number of the window. This is to become the current GKS viewport. Any calls to GKS graphics primitive will appear clipped in this area of the screen until another call to 'CreateWindow' is made.

'function SelectWindow : integer' – calls 'get_point', determines which window rectangle the pointer device is pointing to, and then redisplays that window. That window consequently becomes the 'front' window.

'procedure WriteToWindow(str : string)' – places the character string 'str' inside the current front window at the current cursor position using the GKS 'TextAt' primitive. Text must wrap around corners rather than be clipped, and the window contents must scroll after the bottom line is full. When this function is used to draw text into a window (rather than a direct call to 'TextAt'), the text attributes must be such that text is drawn horizontally from left to right.

'procedure HideWindow(WindowNr : integer)' – erases the specified window from the screen and redraws any others that were overlapping. Once hidden, a window cannot be selected by 'SelectWindow'.

'procedure DeleteWindow(WindowNr : integer)' – erases the nominated window from the screen and releases system memory allocated to it. Any windows overlapping this window are redrawn.

The window manager must maintain an ordered list of the windows so that it keeps track of which one is in front. For each window it must store the rectangle limits, the 'WriteToWindow' cursor position, the background pixel rectangle before it was created, and its contents area. The contents are only recorded when a new window is created.

15.9 Use GKS, the pixel rectangle primitives (see problem 15.6) and the pointer primitive 'get_point' (see problem 15.6) to implement the menu manager for a UIM. The menu manager is a library of routines that allows menus to be created, displayed, selected from, and hidden to on a raster graphics VDU. Implement the routines:

'function CreateMenu(str : string) : integer' – allocates space for a new menu record, storing the menu title as 'str' and returning the sequence number for the menu as its ID. (No graphics is drawn.)

'function AppendToMenu(MenuNr : integer; str : string) : integer' – appends the item named 'str' to the menu, returning the item sequence number.

'procedure PutMenu(MenuNr, dcx,dcy : integer)' – displays the menu header (title only) at the point ('dcx','dcy') as lower left corner in device coordinates.

'function SelectMenu : integer' – uses 'get_point' and the 'InsideRectangle' procedure to find what menu heading the pointer device is pointing to, and then returns its menu number (or zero if no menu title is pointed to).

'procedure ShowMenu(MenuNr : integer)' – displays the full list of items underneath the menu heading if the menu heading is already displayed.

'function SelectMenuItem(MenuNr : integer) : integer' – uses 'get_point' to select a menu item from the nominated menu if it is displayed.

'procedure HideMenu(MenuNr : integer)' – erases the nominated menu from the screen.

'procedure HideMenuHeading(MenuNr : integer)' – removes the entire menu information from the screen for the nominated menu.

'procedure InvertMenu(MenuNr : integer)' – inverts all pixels in the menu heading rectangle for the nominated menu.

'procedure InvertItem(MenuNr,ItemNr : integer)' – inverts only the rectangle containing the nominated item in the nominated menu if it is currently displayed.

'procedure SaveMenus(filename : string)' – stores all currently defined menus into the nominated external disk file.

'procedure LoadMenus(filename : string)' – opens the nominated file and loads in all menu data from the file.

15.10   Implement an encoder for a reduced version of NAPLPS that only uses ASCII codes and PDI codes. This is a program that accepts graphics commands as text strings and converts them to binary data according to the NAPLPS code scheme. Assume all bytes are 7 bits of data with no parity bit. By default all bytes are interpreted as ASCII codes but the control character SO (ASCII code 14 decimal) causes byte values from 32 and up to be interpreted as PDI codes. In this mode bytes 32 to 63 are graphics commands and byte values greater than 63 are data values (operands for the graphics commands). The control character SI (ASCII code 15 decimal) reverts all byte interpretations to the normal ASCII codes as in Appendix A. Allow the user to type control-N (SO) and control-O (SI) into the program to switch modes. The program should respond to these control codes by announcing which mode it is in. In graphics command mode input lines should be checked to see if they are valid PDI graphics names (select suitable strings). The output from the program should go to a nominated file on disk. (The detailed definition of NAPLPS can be obtained from the American National Standards Institute.)

15.11   Implement a decoder for the reduced version of NAPLPS described in problem 15.10. This is a program that accepts binary codes, interprets them according to the NAPLPS code scheme, and produces the corresponding graphics on a color raster VDU. The program ignores modes other than ASCII and PDI.

Appendix A

ASCII character codes and related routines

Control			Special			Upper case			Lower case		
Dec	Hex	Char	Dec	Hex	Char	Dec	Hex	Char	Dec	Hex	Char
000	00	NUL	032	20	SPACE	064	40	@	096	60	'
001	01	SOH	033	21	!	065	41	A	097	61	a
002	02	STX	034	22	"	066	42	B	098	62	b
003	03	ETX	035	23	#	067	43	C	099	63	c
004	04	EOT	036	24	$	068	44	D	100	64	d
005	05	ENQ	037	25	%	069	45	E	101	65	e
006	06	ACK	038	26	&	070	46	F	102	66	f
007	07	BEL	039	27	'	071	47	G	103	67	g
008	08	BS	040	28	(	072	48	H	104	68	h
009	09	HT	041	29	)	073	49	I	105	69	i
010	0A	LF	042	2A	*	074	4A	J	106	6A	j
011	0B	VT	043	2B	+	075	4B	K	107	6B	k
012	0C	FF	044	2C	,	076	4C	L	108	6C	l
013	0D	CR	045	2D	-	077	4D	M	109	6D	m
014	0E	SO	046	2E	.	078	4E	N	110	6E	n
015	0F	SI	047	2F	/	079	4F	O	111	6F	o
016	10	DLE	048	30	0	080	50	P	112	70	p
017	11	DC1	049	31	1	081	51	Q	113	71	q
018	12	DC2	050	32	2	082	52	R	114	72	r
019	13	DC3	051	33	3	083	53	S	115	73	s
020	14	DC4	052	34	4	084	54	T	116	74	t
021	15	NAK	053	35	5	085	55	U	117	75	u
022	16	SYN	054	36	6	086	56	V	118	76	v
023	17	ETB	055	37	7	087	57	W	119	77	w
024	18	CAN	056	38	8	088	58	X	120	78	x
025	19	EM	057	39	9	089	59	Y	121	79	y
026	1A	SUB	058	3A	:	090	5A	Z	122	7A	z
027	1B	ESC	059	3B	;	091	5B	[	123	7B	{
028	1C	FS	060	3C	<	092	5C	\	124	7C		
029	1D	GS	061	3D	=	093	5D	]	125	7D	}
030	1E	RS	062	3E	>	094	5E	^	126	7E	~
031	1F	US	063	3F	?	095	5F	_	127	7F	DEL

Standard abbreviations for ASCII control characters

ACK	= Acknowledge	≡ CTRL/F	
BEL	= Bell	≡ CTRL/G	
BS	= Backspace	≡ CTRL/H	
CAN	= Cancel	≡ CTRL/X	
CR	= Carriage return	≡ CTRL/M	
DC1	= Device control 1	≡ CTRL/Q	≡ XON
DC2	= Device control 2	≡ CTRL/R	
DC3	= Device control 3	≡ CTRL/S	≡ XOFF
DC4	= Device control 4	≡ CTRL/T	
DEL	= Delete		
DLE	= Data link escape	≡ CTRL/P	
EM	= End of medium	≡ CTRL/Y	
ENQ	= Enquiry	≡ CTRL/E	
EOT	= End of transmission	≡ CTRL/D	
ESC	= Escape	≡ CTRL/[	
ETB	= End of transmission block	≡ CTRL/W	
ETX	= End of text	≡ CTRL/C	
FF	= Form feed	≡ CTRL/L	
FS	= Form separator	≡ CTRL/\	
GS	= Group separator	≡ CTRL/]	
HT	= Horizontal tab	≡ CTRL/I	
LF	= Line feed	≡ CTRL/J	
NAK	= Negative acknowledge	≡ CTRL/U	
NUL	= Null	≡ CTRL/@	
RS	= Record separator	≡ CTRL/^	
SI	= Shift in	≡ CTRL/O	
SO	= Shift out	≡ CTRL/N	
SOH	= Start of heading	≡ CTRL/A	
STX	= Start of text	≡ CTRL/B	
SUB	= Substitute	≡ CTRL/Z	
SYN	= Synchronous idle	≡ CTRL/V	
US	= Unit separator	≡ CTRL/_	
VT	= Vertical tab	≡ CTRL/K	
XOFF	= Transmission off	≡ CTRL/S	
XON	= Transmission on	≡ CTRL/Q	

Throughout the text it has been assumed that the collation sequence (i.e. the order of the characters) is as in the ASCII code above, that is, 'ord(ch)' gives the ASCII code for the character 'ch', and 'chr(byte)' gives the character corresponding to the ASCII code in the eight-bit value 'byte'. If this is not the case on a specific computer then it is not difficult to create Pascal functions, say, 'ascii_ord(ch)' and 'ascii_chr(byte)' that translate between variables of type 'char' and integers of the subrange type 0..255. For instance, these functions can at least be implemented by table look-up.

Another function relating to ASCII character codes has been of use to us in the text.

This is the function 'char_type' which takes as input a byte value (i.e. an integer 0..255) and returns an answer which is an element of the set type:

```
type
    char_types = (control, special,digit, upper_case, lower_case, udc);
    byte_type = 0 .. 255;
```

Note that 'udc' stands for user-defined character commonly used on many modern microcomputers to allow the user to implement new character symbols such as mathematical symbols, Japanese characters, or graphics characters. The 'udc's are often the bytes from 196 to 255 inclusive. The following code implements the required function:

```
function char_type(byte : byte_type) : char_types;
begin
    if byte < 32 or byte = 127 then char_type := control
    else if (byte >= 48 and byte <= 57) then char_type := digit
    else if (byte < 65) or (byte >= 91 and byte <= 96) or (byte >= 123)
        then char_type := special
    else if byte <= 90 then char_type := upper_case
    else if byte <= 122 then char_type := lower_case
    else char_type := udc;
end;
```

The following simple program demonstrates the usage of this function:

```
program ascii_codes;
var
    byte : 0 .. 255;
{include the char_type function code above}
begin
    repeat
    write('Enter a byte value :');
    readln(byte);
    case char_type(byte) of
        control :
            writeln('Control character : ^',chr(byte+64):1);
        special :
            writeln('Special character : ',chr(byte):1);
        digit :
            writeln('A digit : ',chr(byte):1);
        upper_case :
            writeln('An upper case letter : ',chr(byte):1);
        lower_case :
            writeln('A lower case letter : ',chr(byte):1);
        udc :
            writeln('A User Definable Character #',(byte-127):3);
```

```
      end;
   until byte = 4;
   writeln('<< END OF PROGRAM >>');
end.
```

The following function uses 'char_type' to convert letters to upper case:

```
function fold_up(in_string : string) : string;
var
    out_string : string;
    i,ichar : integer;
begin
    for i:= 1 to length(in_string) do
    begin
        ichar := ord(in_string[i]);
        if char_type(ichar) = lower_case then ichar := ichar-32;
        out_string[i] := chr(ichar);
    end;
    fold_up := out_string;
end;
```

Appendix B

User manual for G2D

This appendix presents a summary of how to use G2D, the set of two-dimensional computer graphics routines described in this book.

G2D is a library of routines, written in Pascal and available to Pascal programs for producing two-dimensional graphics easily. It is not designed primarily for efficiency or applicability, but as an educational tool. It is a simple GSP to teach how graphics software packages can be constructed. It consists essentially of the Pascal graphics routines that were built up progressively from Chapter 1 through to Chapter 8.

It is useful when constructing a graphics software package like G2D, to have a version of Pascal that can build libraries of Pascal procedures as independent compilation units. (UCSD Pascal and SVS Pascal are examples that do.). Such a Pascal compiles 'units' as well as programs. A unit begins with the keyword 'unit' and then a unit name similar to the standard Pascal keyword 'program' and program name combination. An 'interface' section in the unit declares what constants, types, variables, procedures, and functions are exported from the compilation unit and available to Pascal programs (or other units). These exported procedures do not then have to be redeclared in a user program as external procedures – the program simply declares that it *uses* the compilation unit. Working versions of G2D have been implemented in various versions of Pascal which have these sorts of facilities. At least six compilation units are used. These are called:

1. 'g2d_driver' – provides hardware primitive functions in physical coordinates for use by G2D.
2. 'g2d_plot' – provides basic two-dimensional user graphics functions in user coordinates.
3. 'g2d_data' – provides list processing and data storage functions for two-dimensional shapes.
4. 'g2d_text' – provides graphical text functions by graphics calls.
5. 'g2d_turtle' - provides turtle graphics functions
6. 'g2d_object' – provides grouping, transformation, internal storage, and metafiling of graphics commands.

The contents of each of these units, and descriptions of all the user routines in G2D are listed in Appendix C.

The user program needs to declare which of these units it will use. The simplest graphics application would declare only that it uses the unit 'g2d_plot'. All G2D application programs must start by initializing G2D and then declaring user coordinates. The former is done by a call to 'initialize_G2D' and the latter by a call to 'set_window'. The procedure 'initialize_G2D' also sets a default window (which is (0,0,100,100)) and viewport (which is the whole output display rectangle) so that it is not actually necessary to call 'set_window'. Every call to 'set_window' also changes the current viewport to be the whole of the output display rectangle. Therefore 'set_window' should be followed by a call to 'set_viewport' if a different viewport is desired. Since these routines are part of the 'g2d_plot' unit, it follows that every G2D program must declare that it at least uses 'g2d_plot'. More generally an application program would declare that it uses 'g2d_plot', 'g2d_data', 'g2d_text', 'g2d_turtle' and 'g2d_object'.

After these initializations, the program can call 'plot_line' to draw line segments, 'plot_arc' for drawing arcs, and so forth. (See Appendix C for the other G2D plotting routines provided.) The termination routine 'terminate_G2D' should always be called last since some graphics hardware requires special graphics close-down operations to be performed (such as returning dynamically allocated pixel RAM). Note however that UCSD Pascal has the nice feature (at the expense of a slow and bulky run-time system) of allowing initialization routines to be automatically called on beginning an application program. It similarly allows for termination routines to be called automatically when the application program finishes. In this case, the user need not call 'initialize_G2D' and 'terminate_G2D', and these might not then be supplied as external routines available to Pascal programs.

In a Pascal programming environment other than this, where independent compilation units cannot be made, the application programs may have to have one or more pseudocomment statements to include the required G2D Pascal source code from these files. In this case G2D will be recompiled every time a new application program is made or modified.

Appendix C

Summary of G2D routines

This appendix gives a summary of the routines in the graphics package G2D, which were described progressively in Chapters 1 through to 8. A guide to using these routines is given in Appendix B.

Commands in the compilation unit 'g2d_plot'
Graphics setup routines
initialize_G2D

This routine must be called first. It sets all attributes to their default values, enables the default software text font, sets default input and output devices, sets the default window to the graphics output screen size in physical coordinates, sets the current transformation matrix to unity, and clears all flags (to, say, no active object, no I/O files, trace off, and no errors).

select_input_device(device : device_names)

Selects the current device from which graphics input will be read.

select_output_device(device : device_names)

Selects the current graphics output device.

clear_output

Clears the current graphics output device. For a VDU the screen is cleared. For a plotter, pens are returned to their holder and the arm taken home.

set_window(xmin,ymin,xmax,ymax : real)

Defines the limits of user coordinates and creates a default viewport which is the entire output rectangle to which these coordinates are mapped.

set_viewport(pxmin,pymin,pxmax,pymax : real)

Sets a viewport in the output rectangle in physical coordinates (mm from the bottom left of the display rectangle). G2D clips all graphics output to the display rectangle or the current viewport whichever is smaller.

beep

Causes the graphics terminal to beep once.

locate_cursor(row,col : integer)

Moves the text cursor in the text screen to the given text line number and character column number.

wait_for_key(**var** key : char)

Suspends processing until the user types a key. The character typed is not echoed to the screen, and is output from this routine in the parameter 'key'.

equalize_axes

Expands the user coordinate ranges in the minimal way so that the user coordinate window is geometrically similar to the selected viewport.

set_rectangle(x1,y1,x2,y2 : real;**var** rect:rectangle_type)

Sets up the output parameter 'rect' which is of type 'rectangle_type' to correspond to the rectangle with opposite vertexes having coordinates $(x1,y1)$ and $(x2,y2)$.

clip_line(rect:rectangle_type; x1,y1,x2,y2 : real;
                var x1clipped,y1clipped,x2clipped,y2clipped : real) : boolean

A boolean function that takes as inputs a rectangle and the end points of a line segment, and then returns the end points of the clipped line segment. If the line segment is outside of the rectangle, then the clipped end points are not valid and the function returns the boolean value of false, otherwise it returns the value of true.

cover_line(rect:rectangle_type; x1,y1,x2,y2 : real)

Inputs a rectangle parameter and the end points of a line segment and then draws the line as covered by the given rectangle.

draw_border

Draws a rectangle around the current viewport edge.

terminate_G2D

Properly closes down the graphics system.

Data plotting routines

draw_axes(dxpdiv,dypdiv : real)

Draws vertical and horizontal axes with tick marks spaced every 'dxpdiv' x units along the x axis and similarly for the y axis.

plot_polypoint(nr_pts : integer; xarray, yarray : real_array)

Draws a polymarker of 'nr_pts' points given by ('xarray[i]','yarray[i]') for 'i' = 1 to 'i' = 'nr_pts' using the currently set marker symbol.

plot_polyline(nr_pts : integer; xarray, yarray : real_array)

Draws a polyline through 'nr_pts points' given by ('xarray[i]', 'yarray[i]') for 'i' = 1 to 'i' = 'nr_pts'.

plot_polygon(nr_pts : integer; xarray, yarray : real_array)

Draws a closed polygon through 'nr_pts' points given by ('xarray[i]', 'yarray[i]') for 'i' = 1 to 'i' = 'nr_pts'.

plot_Bezier_curve(nr_pts : integer; xarray, yarray : real_array)

Draws a two-dimensional Bezier curve using the 'nr_pts' control points given by ('xarray[i]', 'yarray[i]') for 'i' = 1 to 'i' = 'nr_pts'.

plot_B_spline(nr_pts : integer; xarray, yarray : real_array)

Draws a B-spline curve using 'nr_pts' points given by ('xarray[i]', 'yarray[i]') for 'i' = 1 to 'i' = 'nr_pts'.

plot_spline(nr_pts : integer; xarray, yarray : real_array)

Draws a natural cubic spline through 'nr_pts' points given by ('xarray[i]','yarray[i]') for 'i' = 1 to 'i' = 'nr_pts'.

draw_curve(function xf,yf : real; lambda1,lambda2 : real)

Draws a mathematical curve given by:
$$x = xf(\lambda), y = yf(\lambda) \text{ for } \lambda = \text{lambda1 to } \lambda = \text{lambda2}.$$

draw_bar(height : real)

Draws one bar of a bar chart at the specified height and aligns ready for the next bar.

draw_wedge(radius, angle : real)

Draws one wedge of a pie chart of the given radius and angle and aligns ready for the next wedge of the pie chart.

Drawing graphics elements
plot_point(x,y : real)

Draws the current marker symbol (default is a dot only) at the point (x, y).

plot_line(x1,y1,x2,y2 : real)

Draws a line segment from $(x1, y1)$ to $(x2, y2)$.

plot_arc(x1,y1,x2,y2,x3,y3 : real)

Draws the arc of a circle going anticlockwise from $(x1, y1)$ through the point $(x2, y2)$ to the final point $(x3, y3)$.

plot_circle(x1,y1,x2,y2 : real)

Draws a circle where $(x1, y1)$ and $(x2, y2)$ are the end points of a diameter.

Graphics input
read_point(**var** code : char; **var** x,y : real)

Reads a point in user coordinates from the current graphics input device after the character given by 'code' has been pressed.

Setting output primitive attributes
set_point_style(index : integer)

Sets the marker (dot, cross, square etc.) for representing points.

set_point_size(size : real)

Sets the diameter of the point marker symbol in millimeters.

set_point_color(color : colors)

Sets the color that points are drawn in.

set_line_style(index : integer)

Sets the line type: solid, dotted, dot-dash, and so forth.

set_line_width(width : integer)

Sets the line thickness in number of pixels across.

set_line_color(color : colors)

Sets the color that lines are drawn with.

set_clipping(on_or_off : boolean)

Allows software clipping of lines to be turned off for faster execution of graphics output.

set_axes_tick_size(size : real)

Sets the size of tick marks in millimeters if 'size' > 0 otherwise sets the default tick size.

set_bar_width(width : real)

Sets the width for drawing bars in a bar chart as width in user coordinates (*x* component).

set_bar_start_point(x,y : real)

Defines the lower left corner of the next bar to be drawn. This call is only needed for the leftmost bar of a simple bar chart since the 'draw_bar' routine automatically updates the position ready for the next bar to be drawn.

set_bar_stack_size(n : integer)

Defines how many bars will be stacked vertically in a multiple (i.e. stacked) bar chart. When 'draw_bar' is called it will align for each bar in the stack, bottom to top, before moving right for the next column of bars.

set_bar_color(ibar : integer; color : colors)

Defines the color to fill each bar 'ibar' in a stacked multibar chart.

set_bar_hollow

Sets all bars to no area filling.

set_wedge_center(x,y : real)

Sets the center of a circle for a pie chart drawing.

set_wedge_start_angle(degrees : real)

Sets the angle (anticlockwise from the *x* axis in degrees) of the first wedge in a pie chart. The default initial angle is zero.

set_wedge_color(color : colors)

Sets the color for filling in subsequent pie segments (wedges).

set_wedge_pullout_distance(distance : real)

Sets the distance that the next wedge to be drawn in a pie chart will be pulled out from the pie chart away from the center of the pie chart circle as 'distance' in user coordinate units. Initially this distance is zero so that no pie pieces are pulled out.

set_wedge_hollow

All subsequent calls to 'draw_wedge' will produce hollow wedge pie pieces, outlined in the current wedge color.

set_curve_nr_segments(n : integer)

Sets the number of line segments with which a curve will be drawn in 'draw_curve' over unit intervals of the curve parameter λ.

set_polygon_color(color : colors)

Sets the color with which hollow and solid polygons are drawn.

set_polygon_fill(on_or_off : boolean)

If the 'on_or_off' parameter is true then polygons will be area-filled otherwise they will be hollow.

set_Bezier_nr_segments(n : integer)

Sets the number of line segments with which a Bezier curve will be drawn.

set_B_spline_nr_segments(n : integer)

Sets the number of line segments with which B_spline curves will be drawn.

Commands in the compilation unit 'g2d_text'
init_g2d_text

Initializes the internal parameters and default attributes for the 'g2d_text' unit.

load_font(file_name : string_type)

Loads a text font from a font file to be the font in which text will be drawn.

set_text_scaling(sx,sy : real)

Sets the *x* and *y* scaling for all characters to be drawn.

set_text_angle(theta : real)

Sets the angle of the line along which characters are to be drawn.

set_text_xslant(sx : real)

Produces italic characters by a slant transformation with parameter 'sx'.

set_text_justification(just : justification_type)

Sets the justification of text in the text box to 'none', 'left', 'center' or 'right'.

set_text_box(width,height,margin : real)

Defines the box size in which the text will be drawn.

set_text_color(col : colors)

Sets the color in which the graphical text characters will be drawn.

set_box_color(edge,interior : colors; boxon : boolean)

Sets the edge and interior colors for the box enclosing the text and flags whether or not the box is to be drawn.

draw_text(x,y : real; message : string_type)

Draws a text message starting from the point (x, y).

Commands in the compilation unit 'g2d_data'
Graphics data base
init_g2d_data

Initializes the G2D internal two-dimensional graphics data base.

get_nr_points : integer

An integer function to return the number of points stored in the G2D data base.

enter_point(x,y : real)

Stores a two-dimensional point into the G2D data base (unless the point is already in the data base).

get_point_id(x,y : real) : integer

An integer function to return the identity number for the given point in the internal data base points table in G2D.

delete_point(x,y : real)

Deletes the specified point from the G2D data base – use with caution!

change_point(ipt : integer; x,y : real)

Changes the coordinates of point with ID number 'ipt' to those given.

new_polygon(**var** f : polygon_type)

Creates an empty polygon list header node pointed to by 'f'.

append_vertex(ipt : integer; f : polygon_type)

Appends the point with ID 'ipt' in the data base as the last vertex in 'f'.

polygon_size(f : polygon_type) : integer

A function to return the number of vertexes in the given polygon.

get_vert_nr(ipt : integer; f : polygon_type) : integer

An integer function to return the vertex number (e.g. third) for the point 'ipt' in polygon 'f'. If point identity number 'ipt' in the G2D data base is not a vertex of 'f' then zero is returned.

insert_vertex(ipt,ivert : integer; f : polygon_type)

Inserts point number 'ipt' after vertex number 'ivert' in polygon 'f'. If 'ivert' is zero then 'ipt' is inserted as the first vertex of 'f'.

delete_vertex_nr(ivert : integer; f : polygon_type)

Deletes vertex number 'ivert' from the list of vertexes for polygon 'f'.

delete_last_vertex(f : polygon_type)

Deletes the last vertex in the list of vertexes for polygon 'f'. This is the opposite of the 'append_vertex' procedure.

delete_polygon(f : polygon_type)

Deletes the whole polygon structure 'f'. (Vertex points are not deleted from the G2D data base points table.)

get_vertex(ivert : integer; f : polygon_type) : integer

Returns the point ID number for vertex number 'ivert' in polygon 'f'.

display_polygon(f : polygon_type)

Displays the specified polygon in the graphics output rectangle.

polygon_fill(color : colors; f : polygon_type)

Paints the interior of the polygon 'f' in the color specified.

new_region(**var** r : region_type)

Creates an empty two-dimensional region list header node pointed to by 'r'.

append_polygon(f : polygon_type; r : region_type)

Appends the specified polygon to the list of polygons pointed to by 'r'.

region_size(r : region_type) : integer

Returns the number of polygons in the region 'r'.

get_poly_nr(f : polygon_type; r : region_type) : integer

Returns the positional number of polygon 'f' in the region (list of polygons) 'r'. If 'f' is not in 'r' then zero is returned.

insert_polygon(f : polygon_type; ipoly : integer; r : region_type)

Inserts polygon 'f' into the list 'r' after polygon number 'ipoly'. If 'ipoly' is zero then 'f' becomes the first polygon in the list structure 'r'.

delete_poly_nr(ipoly : integer; r : region_type)

Deletes polygon number 'ipoly' from the polygon list 'r'.

delete_last_polygon(r : region_type)

Deletes the last polygon from the list 'r'. This is the opposite to the procedure 'append_polygon'.

get_polygon(ipoly : integer; r : region_type) : polygon_type

Returns a pointer to polygon number 'ipoly' in region 'r'.

delete_region(r : region_type)

Deletes the list of polygons defining the region 'r'. The polygons themselves are not deleted.

display_region(r : region_type)

Displays the list of polygons in 'r'.

region_fill(color : colors; r : region_type)

Paints the interior area of the specified region in the specified color.

Commands in the compilation unit 'g2d_turtle'
init_g2d_turtle

Initializes the status (position, orientation, and visibility) of the turtle for turtle graphics.

crawl(distance : real)

Causes the turtle to move forward by the specified distance.

turn(degrees : real)

Changes the orientation of the turtle by the specified number of degrees anticlockwise.

Setting turtle attributes
pen_up

The turtle's imaginery pen is lifted from the screen so that further movements do not cause a line to be drawn.

pen_down

The turtle's imaginery pen is lowered so that further movements of the turtle will cause lines to be drawn on the screen.

show_turtle

The turtle is made visible on the screen. (It is a small triangular-shaped icon.)

hide_turtle

The turtle becomes invisible so that it is not seen on the graphics screen.

Commands in the compilation unit 'g2d_object'

Graphics object manipulations
command_mode(exflag,apflag : boolean)

Sets the execute and append flags for graphics commands. When the execute flag is set G2D graphics commands will be executed. When the append flag is set G2D graphics commands called by a program will be appended to a list called the current graphics object internal to G2D. The default condition is 'exflag' = true, 'apflag' = false.

comment(message : str_type)

Writes the message string as a comment into the current graphics object. Comments are lines starting with an asterisk so this routine simply writes an asterisk, space then the message to the current graphics object command list.

select_input_file(filename : string_type)

Specifies and opens the metafile from which the graphics objects will be read.

close_input_file

Closes the G2D graphics object input metafile.

select_output_file(filename : string_type)

Specifies a metafile to which graphics object commands will be written.

close_output_file

Closes the G2D graphics object output metafile.

load_graphics_object(**var** name : string_type)

Loads the next graphics object as the current active object from the input file most recently openned, and returns the name of the object explicitly in the 'name' parameter or else a string indicating end of file or disk error.

save_graphics_object(name : string_type)

Writes the current graphics object to the output file replacing the old name with the name specified in the input parameter, 'name'.

store_graphics_object(**var** obj : object_type)

Copies the current graphics object (list of G2D commands) to a list structure pointed to by the user variable 'obj'.

restore_graphics_object(obj : object_type)

Copies the G2D command list structure pointed to by user parameter 'obj' to the current graphics object internal G2D list structure. This replaces the old current graphics object list with that given by 'obj'.

merge_graphics_object(obj : object_type)

Appends the G2D command list pointed to by 'obj' to the end of the current graphics object in G2D.

delete_graphics_object

Deletes the current graphics object inside G2D.

set_origin(x,y : real)

Sets the pivot point for rotations and scalings of the current graphics object in G2D.

rotate_graphics_object(theta : real)

Rotates the current graphics object by 'theta' degrees. All commands in the list with coordinate pairs (x, y) have the coordinates updated to (x', y') by this rotation transformation.

scale_graphics_object(sx,sy : real)

Scales the current graphics object by scale factors 'sx' in the x direction and 'sy' in the y direction. All commands in the list with coordinate pairs (x, y) have the coordinates updated to (x', y') by this scaling transformation.

translate_graphics_object(tx,ty : real)

Translates the current graphics object by the displacements 'tx' in the x direction and 'ty' in the y direction. All commands in the list with coordinate pairs (x, y) have the coordinates updated to (x', y') by this translation.

display_graphics_object

Reruns the list of G2D commands in the current graphics object.

display_object(obj : object_type)

Reruns the list of G2D commands in the graphics object pointed to by 'obj'. Since 'display_object' is a G2D command that may be in a graphics object, displaying an object may call for the displaying of other objects in a nested fashion. This allows hierarchical graphics objects in G2D.

Debugging
error_level(n : integer)

Sets the severity level for misuse of the G2D system.

trace_graphics(on_or_off : boolean)

Switches on or off the G2D trace mode which is a step by step printout of what graphics commands G2D processes in program execution. Each graphics command is done after the user presses a key.

print_graphics_object

Prints out the commands stored in the current graphics object in G2D.

print_object(obj : object_type)

Prints out the list of G2D commands stored in the graphics object pointed to by 'obj'.

A minimal implementation of G2D consists of the following selection of routines:

initialize_g2d	clear_output	set_window
set_viewport	beep	draw_axes
draw_border	plot_point	plot_line
plot_arc	plot_circle	set_point_style
point_size	set_line_style	read_point

Routines in the compilation unit 'g2d_driver'
This is the graphics device driver interface. Application programs are not expected to call these routines. They are called by the above G2D routines.

Graphics setup and control
drawing_mode(mode : mode_type)

Sets the drawing mode to temporary (XOR mode) or permanent (replace mode).

sample_key(**var** key_code : integer)

Samples the keyboard for a key without waiting or echoing a key. If no key was pressed then -1 is returned in the 'key_code' otherwise the ASCII code is returned.

home

Sends all cursors (graphics and text) to home positions.

clear

Clears the current output device's display rectangle.

Graphics output functions
move_to(px,py : real)

Moves the graphics cursor to ('px','py') in physical coordinates.

draw_to(px,py : real)

Draws a line from the current graphics cursor position to ('px','py') and updates the graphics cursor to ('px','py') in physical coordinates.

line(px1,py1,px2,py2)

Draws a line from ('px1','py1') to ('px2','py2') in physical coordinates on the output.

circle(px1,py1,px2,py2)

Draws a circle with ('px1','py1') and ('px2','py2') as end points of a diameter (in physical coordinates).

arc(px1,py1,px2,py2,px3,py3)

Draws the arc of a circle on the output device starting from point ('px1','py1'), passing through point ('px2','py2') and ending at point ('px3','py3') in physical coordinates.

Graphics input function
show_xhairs

Displays the two-dimensional graphics cursor on the output device.

hide_xhairs

Disables the display of the two-dimensional graphics cursor on the output device.

get_point(**var** px,py : real)

Returns the coordinates of the current position of the graphics cursor in physical coordinates.

Appendix D

User manual for G3D

This appendix presents a user manual for the G3D package which is built up progressively in Chapters 9 to 12 of the text. G3D is an extension of G2D. It consists of six extra compilation units of Pascal routines which make calls to the six compilation units of G2D as described in Appendexes B and C. These compilation units are called:

1. g3d_view – provides three-dimensional vector operators, the normal, oblique, and central projection functions and camera control.
2. g3d_plot – provides the basic three-dimensional user graphics functions in user coordinates similar to the two-dimensional versions in the compilation unit 'g2d_plot'.
3. g3d_data – provides list processing, data storage, and display functions for three-dimensional scenes. Hidden-line removal is provided for in general three-dimensional scenes.
4. g3d_text – allows the same text fonts as in 'g2d_text' to be viewed on planes in three-dimensional space.
5. g3d_jet – provides three-dimensional turtle graphics (i.e. jet graphics) commands.
6. g3d_object – provides nested grouping, transformation, internal storage, and metafiling of three-dimensional graphics commands.

The routines in each of these units are described in Appendix E. That appendix also lists those G2D routines that may validly be used while doing three-dimensional graphics with G3D. It should be noted that the user may use *any* of the G2D functions simultaneously with G3D functions. For example, two-dimensional and three-dimensional lines may be drawn in the same graphics plot by calls to 'plot_line' and 'plot_3d_line'. No conflicts are generated by mixing two-dimensional and three-dimensional calls. When used in this way the total graphics package is referred to as G2/3D.

For three-dimensional graphics applications, the user must again initialize the system by a call to 'initialize_G3D'. This also initializes G2D (i.e. it calls 'initialize_G2D') which sets up a default user window and viewport. However it also initializes the projection type to central, that is, perspective projection, and initializes the position and orientation of the synthetic camera. This is an imaginery camera in the three-dimensional world that projects three-dimensional points onto a plane in front of it, called the *viewing plane*. The viewing plane has a window in it set by the two-dimensional procedure 'set_window'. This window, the rectangle on a plane in front of the viewing camera, can be imagined to be like the projection screen for a movie projector. By setting this window to different sizes, more or less of the projected three-dimensional world can be seen – it acts somewhat like an aperture setting for the synthetic camera.

The compilation unit 'g3d_plot' makes calls to the routines in 'g2d_plot' which in turn makes calls to routines in the unit 'g2d_driver'. However to use routines in 'g3d_plot' the user program need only declare that it uses the unit 'g3d_plot'. To do three-dimensional text 'g3d_text' and 'g2d_text' should be declared in the application program. The former allows the user to define a plane in three dimensions and then draw text onto this plane. The latter unit allows the user to change the attributes of the text being displayed. Note that if 'draw_text' is called then flat two-dimensional text will appear on the viewing plane. This is an example of mixing two-dimensional and three-dimensional graphics outputs, that is, using the combined system G2/3D. Also to do three-dimensional metagraphics, both 'g3d_object' and 'g2d_object' should be declared as used by the program because many of the basic metagraphics commands in G2D are applicable in G3D as well.

After all other graphics calls are done, 'terminate_G3D' should be called to close down the graphics system properly. This routine also calls 'terminate_G2D' so that the latter should not be called when using G3D or G2/3D. In UCSD Pascal versions 'terminate_G3D' is not explicitly provided as a user routine and is called automatically by the system at the end of a program.

Appendix E

Summary of G3D routines

This appendix presents a summary of the three-dimensional graphics routines taught in this book which form the G3D graphics package. Appendix D briefly describes how to use G3D. This package uses many of the G2D routines which are described in Appendix C. Those G2D routines needed for G3D are listed below:

initialize_G2D	terminate_G2D	select_input_device
select_output_device	clear_output	set_window
set_viewport	beep	locate_cursor
wait_for_key	draw_border	set_point_style
set_point_size	set_point_color	set_line_style
set_line_width	set_line_color	load_font
set_text_scaling	set_text_angle	set_text_xslant
set_text_justification	set_text_box	set_text_color
set_box_color	comment	select_input_file
close_input_file	select_output_file	close_output_file
load_graphics_object	save_graphics_object	store_graphics_object
restore_graphics_object	merge_graphics_object	delete_graphics_object
display_graphics_object	display_object	error_level
trace_graphics	print_graphics_object	print_object

The extra routines needed for G3D follow:

Commands in the compilation unit 'g3d_view'
Special view control commands
init_g3d_view

Initializes the synthetic camera to location (0,0,100) in three-dimensional space, with camera vectors parallel to the axes and focal length of 100. The projection kind is set to central projection.

normal_projection

Sets subsequent three-dimensional graphics output to be done by a normal projection.

oblique_projection(dx,dy,dz : real)

Sets subsequent three-dimensional graphics output to be done by the oblique projection where the direction of viewing the objects is given by (dx, dy, dz).

central_projection

Sets subsequent three-dimensional graphics output to be done by the central projection.

project(x,y,z : real; **var** xvp,yvp : real)

Projects the three-dimensional point (x, y, z) in user coordinates to a point in the viewing plane with viewing plane coordinates (xvp, yvp).

Camera setup commands
set_camera(cx,cy,cz : vector_type)

Sets the camera vectors directly. (This must be used with caution.)

set_tripod(x,y,z : real)

Sets the camera location to (x, y, z) in three-dimensional user coordinates.

set_aperture(width, height : real)

Resets the window on the viewing plane to have the specified width and height in user coordinates with its origin (the center of the window rectangle) being directly in front of the camera.

focal_length(f : real)

Sets the distance of the viewing plane from the camera to f.

aim_for(x,y,z : real)

Very useful to get the camera to look in a desired direction. The camera will point towards the given point and reorient itself in the minimal way. It does not however alter the camera focal length, that is, the distance from the camera to the viewing plane. The next function does.

focus_on(x,y,z : real)

Performs the 'aim_for' function but also adjusts the camera focal length so that the new camera focus becomes the point (x, y, z) in user coordinates.

field_depth(v : vector_type) : real

A real function to return the viewing distance of a point with three-dimensional position vector v from the camera in the camera view direction.

viewing_plane(vx,vy,n,a : vector_type)

Defines the viewing plane. The vector 'n' is the normal to the viewing plane, and vector 'a' is the position vector of the origin of viewing plane coordinates in the viewing plane. The vectors 'vx' and 'vy' are the unit vectors along the x and y axes of the viewing plane coordinate system.

Camera movement commands
dip(degrees : real)

Dips the camera down by the given number of degrees.

pan(degrees : real)

Pans the camera around by the given number of degrees.

tilt(degrees : real)

Tilts the camera by the given number of degrees.

camera_right(distance : real)

Moves the camera to its right by the specified distance in user units.

camera_up(distance : real)

Moves the camera upwards by the specified distance in user units.

camera_out(distance : real)

Moves the camera backwards away from the subject by the specified distance in user units.

swivel_right(degrees : real)

The camera is swiveled around its subject to the right while still aiming at the subject.

swivel_up(degrees : real)

The camera is swiveled in its upward direction around the point of focus (the subject) while continuing to aim at the subject.

zoom(factor : real)

The camera distance to the subject is adjusted by the specified zoom factor.

Commands in the compilation unit 'g3d_plot'
plot_3d_point(x,y,z : real)

Plots a marker at the projection of (*x*, *y*, *z*) according to 'point_style'.

```
plot_3d_line(x1,y1,z1,x2,y2,z2 : real)
```

Plots a line segment between the two points in three dimensions. G2D attributes apply.

```
plot_3d_arc(x1,y1,z1,x2,y2,z2,x3,y3,z3 : real)
```

Plots a three-dimensional arc starting from (*x*1, *y*1, *z*1) passing through (*x*2, *y*2, *z*2) and ending at (*x*3, *y*3, *z*3). The arc forms part of a circle but its projection is not circular in general.

```
plot_3d_circle(x1,y1,z1,x2,y2,z2,x3,y3,z3 : real)
```

Plots a three-dimensional circle which has the points (*x*1, *y*1, *z*1), (*x*2, *y*2, *z*2), and (*x*3, *y*3, *z*3) on its circumference. The result may not appear circular due to the three-dimensional projection being used.

```
plot_3d_polypoint(n : integer; xa,ya,za : real_array)
plot_3d_polyline(n : integer; xa,ya,za : real_array)
plot_3d_polygon(n : integer; xa,ya,za : real_array)
plot_3d_Bezier_curve(n : integer; xa,ya,za : real_array)
plot_3d_B_spline(n : integer; xa,ya,za : real_array)
```

Plot three-dimensional curves based on the array of *n* three-dimensional points (*xa*[*i*], *ya*[*i*], *za*[*i*]) for *i* =1 to *i* = *n* analogous to the two-dimensional versions of these routines. (See Appendix C.)

```
draw_3d_axes(dxpdiv,dypdiv,dzpdiv : real)
```

Draws the three-dimensional axes with tick marks at every 'dxpdiv', 'dypdiv', and 'dzpdiv' units along the *x*, *y*, and *z* axes.

```
read_3d_point(var key : char; var x,y,z : real)
```

Draws three-dimensional axes and a two-line-segment three-dimensional graphics cursor from the axes to the currently selected point in three dimensions. The current point can be moved by using the numeric keypad: keys 9, 6, and 3 increase the *x*, *y*, and *z* coordinates, and 7, 4, and 1 decrease them. The + key doubles the coordinate increment size and the - key halves it with minimum allowed increment of one (in user coordinate units). The '.' key reduces *x*, *y*, and *z* increments to unity, and the * key sends the cursor home to (0,0,0). The 8, 5, and 2 keys set the primary segment of the cursor to the *x*, *y*, or *z* axis.

Commands in the compilation unit 'g3d_data'
init_g3d_data

This empties the three-dimensional data base held by G3D.

get_nr_3d_points : integer

This function returns the number of three-dimensional points currently stored in the G3D graphics data base.

enter_3d_point(x,y,z : real)

Stores the given point in the G3D data base (if it's not already there).

get_3d_point_id(x,y,z : real) : integer

This returns the point ID number for a given point. If the point is not in the G3D data base then the ID returned is zero.

delete_3d_point(x,y,z : real)

Deletes the point (x, y, z) from the G3D data base if it was there.

change_3d_point(ipt : integer; x,y,z : real)

Changes the point with ID 'ipt' in the G3D data base to have the specified coordinates.

get_3d_point(ipt : integer; **var** x,y,z : real) : boolean

Returns the coordinates of the point with ID 'ipt' in the G3D data base. If a point with this ID is not found in the data base then 'get_point' will be false, otherwise true.

new_3d_polygon(**var** p : polygon_type)

Creates an empty polygon list header node pointed to by 'p'.

append_3d_vertex(ipt : integer; p : polygon_type)

Appends the point with ID 'ipt' in the G3D data base as the last vertex in 'p' (if such a point is in the data base).

polygon_size_3d(p : polygon_type) : integer

Returns the number of vertexes in the polygon 'p'.

get_3d_vertex_nr(ipt : integer; p : polygon_type) : integer

Returns the ordinal vertex number of the point with ID 'ipt' in the polygon 'p' if 'ipt' exits in the data base and is in the polygon 'p'.

insert_3d_vertex(ipt,ivert : integer; p : polygon_type)

Inserts the point with ID 'ipt' (if it exists) into the vertex list for polygon 'p' after vertex number 'ivert'.

delete_3d_vertex_nr(ivert : integer; p : polygon_type)

Removes vertex number 'ivert' from the polygon 'p' (provided 'p' has at least 'ivert' number of vertexes).

delete_last_3d_vertex(p : polygon_type)

Deletes the last vertex from polygon 'p'.

delete_3d_polygon(p : polygon_type)

Deletes the entire polygon data structure 'p'. (Note that the vertex points will still be in the G3D points table data base.)

get_3d_vertex(ivert : integer; p : polygon_type) : integer

Returns the point ID for vertex number 'ivert' in polygon 'p'.

new_facet(**var** f : facet_type)

Creates an empty three-dimensional facet list header node pointed to by 'f'.

append_3d_polygon(p : polygon_type; f : facet_type)

Appends the specified polygon to the list of polygons pointed to by 'f'.

facet_size(f : facet_type) : integer

Returns the number of polygons that constitute the facet 'f'.

get_3d_poly_nr(p : polygon_type; f : facet_type) : integer

Returns the positional number of polygon 'p' in the facet (list of polygons) 'f'. If 'p' is not in 'f' then zero is returned.

insert_3d_polygon(p : polygon_type; ipoly : integer; f : facet_type)

Inserts polygon 'p' into the list 'f' after polygon number 'ipoly'. If 'ipoly' is zero then 'p' becomes the first polygon in the list structure 'f'.

delete_3d_poly_nr(ipoly : integer; f : facet_type)

Deletes polygon number 'ipoly' from the list 'f'.

delete_last_3d_polygon(f : facet_type)

Deletes the last polygon in the list 'f'.

get_3d_polygon(ipoly : integer; f : facet_type) : polygon_type

Returns a pointer to the polygon number 'ipoly' in the list 'f'.

delete_facet(f : facet_type)

Deletes the entire list structure for facet 'f'. The polygons that make up the items in the list 'f' are not however deleted.

display_facet(f : facet_type)

Displays the facet 'f'.

new_solid(**var** s : solid_type)

Creates an empty three-dimensional solid list header node pointed to by 's'.

append_facet(f : facet_type; s : solid_type)

Appends the specified facet to the list of polygons pointed to by 's'.

solid_size(s : solid_type) : integer

Returns the number of polygons that constitute the solid 's'.

get_facet_nr(f : facet_type; s : solid_type) : integer

Returns the positional number of facet 'f' in the solid (list of facets) 's'. If 'f' is not in 's' then zero is returned.

insert_facet(f : facet_type; ifacet : integer; s : solid_type)

Inserts facet 'f' into the list 's' after facet number 'ifacet'. If 'ifacet' is zero then 'f' becomes the first facet in the list structure 's'.

delete_facet_nr(ifacet : integer; s : solid_type)

Deletes facet number 'ifacet' from the list 's'.

delete_last_facet(s : solid_type)

Deletes the last facet in the list 's'.

get_facet(ifacet : integer; s : solid_type) : facet_type

Returns a pointer to the facet number 'ifacet' in the list 's'.

delete_solid(s : solid_type)

Deletes the entire list structure for solid 's'. The facets (and their substructures) that make up the items in the list 's' are not however deleted.

display_solid(s : solid_type)

Displays the solid 's'.

hidden_line_style(style : integer)

Sets the line style for the hidden lines in using 'display_solid'. These can be any of the line styles provided for ordinary lines, that is, no line, solid line, dashed line and so forth.

Commands in the compilation unit 'g3d_text'
text_plane(a,b,c : vector_type)

Defines the plane in three-dimensional space in which the graphics text will be drawn. The three points with position vectors **a**, **b**, and **c** define the plane and its normal is given by the cross product of (**b** - **a**) with (**c** - **a**). The direction of text writing is given by the vector (**b** - **a**) and character upwards vector is (**c** - **a**).

draw_3d_text(u,v : real; message : string_type)

Draws text by calls to 'plot_3d_line' using the current projection kind. The text is drawn on the text plane starting at displacement (u, v) from the origin (point **a** on the text plane) where u and v are text plane coordinates.

Commands in the compilation unit 'g3d_object'
rotate_3d_object(axis : vector_type; degrees : real)

Rotates all three-dimensional point coordinates in the current graphics object by the number of degrees about the specified axial direction.

scale_3d_object(sx,sy,sz : real)

Scales all three-dimensional point coordinates in the current graphics object by the factors 'sx', 'sy', and 'sz' in the x, y, and z directions respectively.

translate_3d_object(tx,ty,tz : real)

Translates all three-dimensional point coordinates in the current graphics object by the given displacements in the x, y, and z directions.

initialize_G3D

Calls all initialization routines mentioned above as well as 'initialize_G2D'.

terminate_G3D

Completes the usage of G3D in the normal manner.

Appendix F

CORE graphics routines

The following list is the list of all CORE graphics routines provided in the SunCORE implementation of CORE for the Pascal language. Altogether there are 183 routines provided in this implementation of the CORE standard, Sun Computers have added another 24 routines (marked with an asterisk below) to keep CORE relevant on modern graphics equipment making a total of 207 routines. A list of 54 further CORE functions not implemented by Sun Computers is included at the end of this appendix.

Routine name	Routine function
* allocateraster	Creates a new raster record in user memory (on the heap).
awaitanybutton	Waits for the user to press a button until a timeout and returns which button was pressed.
awtbuttongetloc2	Waits for user to press a button and then returns the locator coordinates.
awtbuttongetval	Waits for the user to press a button and then returns the valuator value.
awaitkeyboard	Waits for the user to type a string of characters.
awaitpick	Waits for the user to press a button and the returns the nearest segment.
awaitstroke2	Waits for user to draw a line with stroke device (e.g. mouse) until timeout.
beginbatchupdate	Indicates start of a batch of segment updates to be done when 'endbatch' found.
closeretainseg	Closes the currently open retained segment.
closetempseg	Closes the currently open temporary segment.
createretainseg	Creates a new empty and open retained segment by number.
createtempseg	Creates a new empty and open temporary segment (no ID number).
defcolorindices	Defines entries in the color look-up table of a view surface.
delallretainsegs	Deletes all retained segments. If one was opened, it is closed and then deleted.
delretainsegment	Deletes a retained segment given its ID number.
delselectvwsurf	Deselect a specified view surface.
endbatchupdate	Indicates the end of a batch list of updates and so it performs the updates.

* filetoraster	Reads a disk file to a screen raster.
* freeraster	Frees the memory set aside for a raster.
* getmousestate	Returns the current mouse position and up/down state of its buttons.
* getraster	Reads the raster (a rectangle of pixel RAM) into allocated user memory.
initializecore	Initializes the CORE graphics system.
initializedevice	Initializes a specified input device (pick/keyboard/stroke/locator/etc.).
initializevwsurf	Initializes a CORE for the specified output device.
inqcharjust	Returns the current justification attribute for text strings.
inqcharpath2	Returns the 2D 'charpath' attribute for text strings.
inqcharpath3	Returns the 3D 'charpath' attribute for text strings.
inqcharprecision	Returns the 'charprecision' attribute for text strings.
inqcharsize	Returns the 'charsize' attribute for text strings.
inqcharspace	Returns the 'charspace' attribute for text strings.
inqcharup2	Returns the 2D 'charup' attribute for text strings.
inqcharup3	Returns the 3D 'charup' attribute for text strings.
inqcolorindices	Returns the RGB values in the color look-up table.
inqcurrpos2	Returns the 2D world coordinates of the CP (current position).
inqcurrpos3	Returns the 3D world coordinates of the CP.
inqdetectability	Returns the current detectability attribute (an integer).
inqecho	Returns the echo type for the specified device.
inqechoposition	Returns the NDC position of the echo reference point for a device.
inqechosurface	Returns the viewing surface for echoing for a specified device.
inqfillindex	Returns the current color number for filling areas.
inqfont	Returns the current font attribute for text (Roman, Greek, OldEnglish, etc.).
inqhighlighting	Returns the current highlighting attribute for segments.
inqimgtransform2	Returns the current segment 2D transformation parameters.
inqimgtransform3	Returns the current segment 3D transformation parameters.
inqimgxformtype	Returns the current segment transformation type (none, 2D translates, etc.).
inqimgtranslate2	Returns the current segment 2D translation parameters tx,ty.
inqimgtranslate3	Returns the current segment 3D translation parameters tx,ty,tz.
* inqinvcompmatrix	Returns the inverse of the composite transformation and viewing matrix.
inqkeyboard	Returns size of keyboard character buffer, initial string and cursor.
inqlineindex	Returns the current color number for drawing lines and polylines.
inqlinestyle	Returns the current line style (solid, dotted, dashed, dotdashed).
inqlinewidth	Returns the current line width as a percentage of NDC space, that is, the screen.
inqlocator2	Returns the 2D position of the specified locator device in NDCs.
inqmarkersymbol	Returns the current marker symbol number.
inqndcspace2	Returns the dimensions of 2D NDC space.

inqndcspace3	Returns the dimensions of 3D NDC space.
inqopenretainseg	Returns the number of the currently open retained segment.
inqopentempseg	Returns true if a temporary segment is currently open else returns false.
inqpen	Returns the currently used pen number.
inqpickid	Returns the pick ID attribute for output primitives.
inqpolyedgestyle	Returns the current polygon edge style attribute (draw edge or not).
inqpolyintrstyle	Returns the current polygon interior style (plane or smooth shaded).
inqprimattribs	Returns the list of all attributes for all output primitives.
inqprojection	Returns the projection type (perspective or parallel) and center/direction.
* inqrasterop	Returns the current setting of the 'raster op' attribute.
inqretainsegname	Returns the list of all current retained segment ID numbers.
inqretainsegsurf	Returns the number of surfaces and their ID numbers a segment is drawn on.
inqsegdetectable	Returns the detectability attribute for the specified retained segment.
inqseghighlight	Returns the highlight attribute (T or F) for the specified retained segment.
inqsegimgxform2	Returns the 2D transformation parameters for all segments.
inqsegimgxform3	Returns the 3D transformation parameters for all segments.
inqsegimgxfrmtyp	Returns current image transformation type (none, 2/3D translate, etc.).
inqsegimgxlate2	Returns current 2D translation parameters for segments.
inqsegimgxlate3	Returns current 3D translation parameters for segments.
inqsegvisibility	Returns whether the specified segment has visibility on or off.
inqstroke	Returns the buffer size, distance, and time parameters for a stroke device.
inqtextextent2	Returns WC (World Coordinates) width and height of a 2D character string.
inqtextextent3	Returns WC width, height, and depth of a 3D character string.
inqtextindex	Returns the current color number for drawing text and markers.
inqvaluator	Returns the current value of a valuator device and its minimum and maximum values.
inqviewdepth	Returns the front and back clipping distances from the view reference point.
inqviewplanedist	Returns the distance of the view plane from the view reference point.
inqviewplanenorm	Returns the components of the view plane normal vector.
inqviewrefpoint	Returns the coordinates of the view reference point.
inqviewup2	Returns the 2D view up direction vector.
inqviewup3	Returns the 3D view up direction vector.
inqvwcntrlparms	Returns if window, front and back plane clippings and if RH or LH WCs.

inqviewingparams	Returns view reference point, plane normal and distance, front and back distances, and so forth.
inqviewport2	Returns the coordinates of the 2D viewport.
inqviewport3	Returns the coordinates of the 3D viewport.
inqvisibility	Returns the current visibility attribute for segments.
inqwindow	Returns the limits of the viewing window.
inqworldmatrix2	Returns the 3 x 3 current transformation matrix for 2D WCs.
inqworldmatrix3	Returns the 4 x 4 current transformation matrix for 3D WCs.
lineabs2	Draws a line from the CP to the 2D WC point specified.
lineabs3	Draws a line from the CP to the 3D WC point specified.
linerel2	Draws a line from the CP to a 2D WC point by the displacement specified.
linerel3	Draws a line from the CP to a 3D WC point by the displacement specified.
mapndctoworld2	Converts 2D NDCs to WCs
mapndctoworld3	Converts 3D NDCs to WCs
mapworldtondc2	Converts 2D WCs to NDCs
mapworldtondc3	Converts 3D WCs to NDCs
markerabs2	Plots a marker symbol at the specified 2D WC point.
markerabs3	Plots a marker symbol at the specified 3D WC point.
markerrel2	Plots a marker symbol at the specified 2D WC displacement from the CP.
markerrel3	Plots a marker symbol at the specified 3D WC displacement from the CP.
moveabs2	Moves the CP to the specified 2D WC point.
moveabs3	Moves the CP to the specified 3D WC point.
moverel2	Moves the CP by the specified 2D WC displacement.
moverel3	Moves the CP by the specified 3D WC displacement.
newframe	Clears the view surface and all visible retained segments are redrawn.
* polygonabs2	Draws a polygon in 2D WCs given 'xarray', and 'yarray', and n the number of points.
* polygonabs3	Draws a polygon in 3D WCs given x, y, and z arrays and the number of points.
* polygonrel2	Draws a polygon in 2D WCs given x and y displacements, and the 'nr' of points.
* polygonrel3	Draws a polygon in 3D WCs given x, y, and z displacements, and the 'nr' of points.
polylineabs2	Draws a polyline in 2D WCs given x and y arrays, and the 'nr' of points.
polylineabs3	Draws a polyline in 3D WCs given x, y, and z arrays, and the 'nr' of points.
polylinerel2	Draws a polyline in 2D WCs given x and y displacements, and the 'nr' of points.
polylinerel3	Draws a polyline in 3D WCs given x, y, and z displacements,

	and the 'nr' of points.
polymarkerabs2	Draws a polymarker in 2D WCs given x, and y arrays, and the 'nr' of points.
polymarkerabs3	Draws a polymarker in 3D WCs given x, y, and z arrays, and the 'nr' of points.
polymarkerrel2	Draws a polymarker in 2D WCs given x, and y displacements, and the 'nr' of points.
polymarkerrel3	Draws a polymarker in 3D WCs given x, y, and z displacements, and the 'nr' of points.
printerror	Prints a user string then a standard error message for the specified 'err nr'.
* putraster	Writes bit data from a user record (a 'raster') to rectangle in pixel RAM.
puttext	Draws the specified text string at the CP.
* rastertofile	Writes bit data from a user record (a 'raster') to a file.
renameretainseg	Changes the ID number of a retained segment to a new number.
reportrecenterr	Returns the error number of the most recent error in usage of CORE.
* restoresegment	Loads a retained segment from a specified file and closes the file.
* savesegment	Saves a retained segment to a given file with all attributes and using NDCs.
selectvwsurf	Adds a specified view surface to the list of selected view surfaces for output.
setbackclip	Enable or disable 3D clipping to the back plane of the viewing pyramid.
setcharjust	Specifies how text strings should be justified.
setcharpath2	Sets the 'charpath' attribute for the text output primitive in 2D WCs.
setcharpath3	Sets the 'charpath' attribute for the text output primitive in 3D WCs.
setcharprecision	Sets the precision for drawing text (string character or stroke precision).
setcharsize	Sets the 'charsize' attribute for the text output primitive in WCs.
setcharspace	Sets the 'space' attribute for the text output primitive in WCs.
setcharup2	Sets the 'charup' attribute for the text output primitive in 2D WCs.
setcharup3	Sets the 'charup' attribute for the text output primitive in 3D WCs.
setcoordsystype	Selects the left-handed or right-handed world coordinate system.
setdetectability	Sets the default detectability attribute for subsequently created segments.
* setdrag	Sets segment drawing mode to XOR (so segments can be dragged) else by 'raster op'.
setecho	Sets the type of echo for a specified device of a given device class (pick, etc.).
setechogroup	Sets the type of echo for a given group of devices of a given

	device class.
setechoposition	Sets the echo reference point in NDCs (e.g. for rubber band locator echo).
setechosurface	Specifies the viewing surface on which echoing will be done for a device.
setfillindex	Sets the color number for area fills.
setfont	Sets the font number for the text output attribute.
setfrontclip	Enables or disables 3D clipping to the front plane of the viewing pyramid.
sethighlighting	Sets the default highlighting attribute for subsequent segments.
setimgtransform2	Sets the default 2D image transformation for subsequent segments.
setimgtransform3	Sets the default 3D image transformation for subsequent segments.
setimgxformtype	Sets the default image transformation type for subsequent segments.
setimgtranslate2	Sets the default 2D image translation tx, ty for subsequent segments.
setimgtranslate3	Sets the default 3D image translation tx, ty, tz for subsequent segments.
setkeyboard	Sets the character buffer size, initial string, and cursor for the keyboard.
* setlightdirect	Sets the position of a light source in 3D NDCs for Gouraud and Phong shading.
setlineindex	Sets the color number for drawing lines.
setlinestyle	Sets the line style for drawing lines (solid, dotted, dashed, or dotdashed).
setlinewidth	Sets the line width attribute for drawing lines in percentage of NDC space.
setlocator2	Sets the initial locator position in 2D NDCs for the specified locator device.
setmarkersymbol	Sets which marker symbol to draw.
setndcspace2	Sets the 2D NDC space width and height (usually 1.0, 0.75).
setndcspace3	Sets the 3D NDC space width, height, and depth (usually 1.0, 0.75, 1.0).
* setoutputclip	Enables/disables output clipping in NDCs before conversion to DCs.
setpen	Sets a pen for plotter devices.
setpick	Sets the aperture (selection sensitivity square) of a specified pick device.
setpickid	Sets the pick ID attribute for the 'await pick' input function.
setpolyedgestyle	Specifies the method for drawing (or not) the edges of a polygon.
setpolyintrstyle	Selects the method for filling polygons – plain or smooth shaded (for 3D).
setprimattribs	Sets all output primitive attributes in one call (*bundled attributes*).

setprojection	Selects parallel or perspective projection with a direction/center.
* setrasterop	Selects drawing mode for all output primitives: replace, OR, or XOR.
setsegdetectable	Sets the detectability attribute (a 'nr' meaning not, low to high) for segment.
setseghighlight	Sets the highlighting attribute (true or false) for the named segment.
setsegimgxform2	Sets the default 2D image transformation for subsequently created segments.
setsegimgxform3	Sets the default 3D image transformation for subsequently created segments.
setsegimgxlate2	Sets the default 2D image translation for subsequently created segments.
setsegimgxlate3	Sets the default 3D image translation for subsequently created segments.
setsegvisibility	Sets the visibility attribute for the current named segment.
* setshadingparams	Sets shading parameters for rendering 3D polygons – ambient percent, and so forth.
setstroke	Initializes the specified stroke device – x, y, buffer size, and minimum separation.
settextindex	Sets the logical color number for drawing text and markers.
setvaluator	Initializes a specified valuator with an initial value and its minimum and maximum.
* setvertexindices	Sets the color indexes for 3D polygon vertexes for Gouraud smooth shading.
* setvertexnormals	Sets the normal vectors for 3D polygon vertexes for Phong smooth shading.
setviewdepth	Sets the front and back distances in the viewing pyramid.
setviewplanedist	Sets the distance to the view plane from the view reference point – in WC units.
setviewplanenorm	Sets the view plane normal vector in WCs (relative to view 'ref' point).
setviewrefpoint	Sets the view reference point in WC.
setviewup2	Sets the view up direction in 2D graphics on the view plane.
setviewup3	Sets the view up direction in 3D graphics on the view plane.
setviewingparams	Sets all viewing parameters in a single procedure call.
setviewport2	Sets the limits for the current viewport in 2D NDC units.
setviewport3	Sets the limits for the current viewport in 3D NDC units.
setvisibilty	Sets the default visibility for subsequently created segments.
setwindow	Sets the window on the view plane in (u, v) coordinates.
setwindowclip	Enables or diables clipping against the (u, v) window in the view plane.
setworldmatrix2	Sets the 2D WC 3 x 3 transformation matrix for all 2D output primitives.
setworldmatrix3	Sets the 3D WC 4 x 4 transformation matrix for all 3D output primitives.

* setzbuffercut	Sets the piece-wise linear cutaway depth values z for each x in NDC units.
* sizeraster	Computes the size (w, h, d) of a raster in DCs for a given surface rectangle.
terminatecore	Closes down the CORE graphics package properly.
terminatedevice	Disables a specified device to CORE by device class and number.
terminatevwsurf	Close down a specified view surface to CORE.

An additional 54 CORE Graphics routines have not been implemented in Sun CORE. These are listed below by functional name.

Synchronous input functions

initialize group	terminate group	await stroke 3
set echo segment	set button	set all buttons
set 3D locator	set 2D locator port	set 3D locator port
inquire input capabilities	inquire input device characteristics	
inquire stroke dimension (2D or 3D)	inquire locator dimension (2D or 3D)	
inquire pick	inquire button	inquire 3D locator
inquire 2D locator port	inquire 3D locator port	
inquire echo segments		

Asynchronous input functions

enable device	disable device	enable group
disable group	disable all	read 2D locator
read 3D locator	read valuator	await event
flush device events	flush group events	flush all events
associate	disassociate	disassociate device
disassociate group	disassociate all	get pick data
get keyboard data	get 2D stroke data	get 3D stroke data
get 2D locator data	get 3D locator data	get valuator data
inquire device associations	inquire device status	

Control functions

inquire output capabilities	inquire selected surfaces
set immediate visibility	make picture current
inquire control status	set visibilities
log error	

Escape functions

escape	inquire escape

Appendix G

GKS routines

GKS is the current two-dimensional graphics standard. It is bought as a software package of graphics routines callable from a specific language. The 112 GKS routines are listed below with brief explanations of the parameters used and the purpose of each routine. In the routine names, a number of abbreviations have been used:

ASF	an aspect source flag
char	character
col	color
def	deferral
defmode	deferral mode parameter
GDP	generalized drawing primitive
GKS	the graphical kernal system
GKSM	a GKS metafile
h/w	hardware
LASF	the 13 element array list of ASFs
NDC	normalized device coordinates
polym	a polymarker
polyl	a polyline
regmode	the regeneration mode parameter
rep	representation
transf	transformation
WC	world coordinates
WS	workstation
WSid	a WS identification number

The use of GKS is briefly described in Chapter 15.

accumulate_transf(m1,p,m2)	Applies transf matrix of parameters 'p' to 'm1' giving matrix 'm2'.
activate_WS(WSid)	Selects graphics output to go to the specified WS.
associate_seg_with_WS(id,n)	Associates segment number 'n' with workstation number 'id'.
await_event(t0,id,c,dev)	Waits until t0 timeout for an input event and returns device info.
cell_array(x1,y1,x2,y2,nrows,ncols,pixel_array)	Writes the 'pixel_array' cell data to a rectangle on the display.

clear_WS(WSid,control_flag)	Clears the specified WS's output display.
close_GKS	Terminates GKS properly.
close_segment	Closes the currently open segment.
close_WS(WSid)	Closes WS number WSid to GKS.
copy_segment_to_WS(id,n)	Copies the primitives of segment 'n' from GKS storage to WS 'id'.
create_segment(n)	Creates a new open segments with the ID number 'n'.
deactivate_WS(WSid)	Disables graphics output from going to the specified WS.
delete_segment(n)	Deletes segment number 'n'.
delete_seg_from_WS(id,n)	Deletes segment number 'n' from workstation number 'id'.
draw_text(x,y,a_string)	Draws a text string starting from ('x','y') in WCs.
emergency_close_GKS	Closes GKS saving as much data as it can – used in case of an error.
error_handling(e,f,err_file)	Local installation error routine which calls 'error_logging'.
error_logging(e,f,err_file)	Records error number 'e' on the error file when doing GKS function 'f'.
escape(fnid,elen,eseq)	Invokes a nonstandard h/w function,escape 'eseq' of length 'elen'.
evaluate_transf(pars,matrix)	Makes the transformation matrix from rotation and so forth parameters.
fill_area(n,xa,ya)	Draws a filled polygon with vertexes ('xa[i]','ya[i]') 'i'=1 to 'i' = 'n'.
flush_device_events(id,c,dev)	Deletes all queued events for device 'dev' of class 'c' on WS 'id'.
GDP(n xa,ya,gdp_id,l,dat)	Invokes a specified GDP with n points and 'data_len' other values.
get_choice(n)	Reads the choice event integer 'n'.
get_GKSM_item_typ(id,t,l)	Returns current item type 't' and length 'l' from GKSM WS 'id'.
get_locator(t,x,y)	Reads locator event coordinates ('x','y') using NDC to WC transf 't'.
get_pick(s,n,pid)	Returns segment number 'n' from pick event and pick status 's' and ID.
get_string(l,a_string)	Reads the message 'a_string' of length 'l' from a string event.
get_stroke(m,t,n,xa,ya)	Reads up to 'm' stroke event points ('xa[i]','ya[i]') 'i'=1,'n' by transf 't'.
get_valuator(val)	Reads the valuator event value 'val'.
init_choice(id,cid,t,params)	Initializes choice device 'cid' on WS 'id' to the parameters specified.
init_locator(id,lid,t,params)	Initializes locator number 'lid' on WS 'id' to the parameters specified.
init_pick(id,pid,t,params)	Initializes pick device 'pid' on WS 'id' to the

init_string(id,sid,t,params)	parameters specified. Initializes string device 'sid' on WS 'id' to the parameters specified.
init_stroke(id,did,t,params)	Initializes stroke device 'did' on WS 'id' to the parameters specified.
init_valuator(id,vid,t,params)	Initializes valuator number 'vid' on WS 'id' to the parameters specified.
insert_segment(n,matrix)	Insert segment 'n' transformed by 'matrix' into the current open seg.
interpret_item(t,l,dat)	Performs the GKS graphics command 'dat' read in of length 'l', type 't'.
message(WSid, mess_string)	Sends the character string to the specified WS.
open_GKS(error_file)	Initializes GKS for use and sets the error message file.
open_WS(WSid,conid,WStype)	Connects WS number WSid to GKS by connection 'conid'.
pack_data_record(f,p,l,dat)	Packs the parameters of GSK function 'f' into data 'dat' of length 'l'.
polyline(n,xa,ya)	Draws a polyline through ('xa[i]','ya[i]') for 'i' = 1 to 'i' = 'n'.
polymarker (n,xa,ya)	Draws markers at points ('xa[i]','ya[i]') for 'i' = 1 to 'i' = 'n'.
read_GKSM_item(id,m,n,dat)	Reads up to 'm' records from GSKM WS 'id' as 'n' records in 'dat'.
redraw_all_segs(WSid)	All visible segments stored for the WS are redrawn.
rename_segment(n1,n2)	Renumbers segment number 'n1' as having ID number 'n2'.
request_choice(id,cid,data)	Reads the current data from choice device 'cid' on WS number 'id'.
request_locator(id,lid,data)	Reads the current data from locator 'lid' on WS number 'id'.
request_pick(id,pid,data)	Reads the current data from pick device 'pid' on WS number 'id'.
request_string(id,kid,data)	Reads the current data from string device 'kid' on WS number 'id'.
request_stroke(id,sid,data)	Reads the current data from stroke device 'sid' on WS number 'id'.
request_valuator(id,vid,data)	Reads the current data from valuator 'vid' on WS number 'id'.
sample_choice(id,cid,data)	Samples the current data from choice device 'cid' on WS number 'id'.
sample_locator(id,lid,data)	Samples the current data from locator 'lid' on WS number 'id'.
sample_pick(id,pid,data)	Samples the current data from pick device 'pid' on WS number 'id'.
sample_string(id,kid,data)	Samples the current data from keyboard 'kid' on WS

	number 'id'.
sample_stroke(id,sid,data)	Samples the current data from stroke device 'sid' on WS number 'id'.
sample_valuator(id,vid,data)	Samples the current data from valuator 'vid' on WS number 'id'.
select_normalization_transf(t)	Selects a normalization transf for output (see 'set_window').
set_aspect_source_flags(LASF)	Sets each of the 13 ASFs to INDIVIDUAL or BUNDLED.
set_char_expansion_factor(f)	Sets the character expansion factor for ASF = INDIVIDUAL.
set_char_height(h)	Sets the character height when the ASF is INDIVIDUAL.
set_char_spacing(s)	Sets the character spacing for ASF = INDIVIDUAL (unbundled).
set_char_up_vector(dx,dy)	Sets the character up vector ('dx','dy') in WCs.
set_choice_mode(id,cid,m,e)	Sets choice device 'cid' on WS 'id' to mode 'm' and echo status 'e'.
set_clipping_indicator(c)	Sets the clipping indicator for the current normalization transf.
set_color_rep(id,c,r,g,b)	Defines the color c by red, green, and blue intensity levels.
set_def_state(WSid,d,r)	Sets the deferral state of WS number 'WSid' to deferral 'd' and regeneration 'r'.
set_detectability(n,det)	Set the detectability attribute of segment number 'n' to 'det'.
set_fill_area_color_index(c)	Sets the fill area color index when the ASF is INDIVIDUAL.
set_fill_area_index(index)	Selects a bundle index for filling areas.
set_fill_area_int_style(s)	Sets the fill area interior style when the ASF is INDIVIDUAL.
set_fill_area_rep(id,i,is,s,c)	Sets the fill area index,interior style,style, and color on WS 'id'.
set_fill_area_style_index(i)	Sets the fill area style index when its ASF=INDIVIDUAL.
set_highlighting(n,hil)	Set the highlighting attribute of segment number 'n' to 'hil'.
set_line_type(linetype)	Sets the global line type when the ASF is INDIVIDUAL (unbundled).
set_linewidth_scale_factor(w)	Sets the global line width when the ASF is INDIVIDUAL.
set_locator_mode(id,lid,m,e)	Sets locator 'lid' on WS 'id' to mode 'm' and echo status 'e'.
set_marker_scale_factor(s)	Sets the marker size scale factor when the ASF is INDIVIDUAL.
set_marker_type(m)	Sets the global marker type when the ASF is

	INDIVIDUAL.
set_pattern_ref_point(x,y)	Sets the fill area pattern reference point ('x','y') in WCs.
set_pattern_rep(id,p,c,r,pat)	Defines pattern number 'p' by the 'pat' array with 'r' rows and 'c' columns.
set_pattern_size(sx,sy)	Sets the fill area pattern size in WCs.
set_pick_identifier(id)	Selects the current pick device by its number 'id'.
set_pick_mode(id,pid,m,e)	Sets pick device 'pid' on WS 'id' to mode 'm' and echo status 'e'.
set_polyline_color_index(c)	Sets the global polyline color when the ASF is INDIVIDUAL.
set_polyline_index(index)	Selects the bundle index for subsequent polylines.
set_polyline_rep(id,p,l,w,c)	Sets polyline index, linetype, width, and color for WS number 'id'.
set_polym_color_index(c)	Sets the polymarker color index when the ASF is INDIVIDUAL.
set_polym_index(index)	Selects a bundle index for subsequent polymarkers.
set_polym_rep(id,p,m,s,c)	Sets polymarker index, type, size, and color for WS number 'id'.
set_segment_priority(n,pri)	Set the segment priority attribute of segment number 'n' to 'pri'.
set_segment_transf(n,matrix)	Set the transformation matrix for segment number 'n'.
set_string_mode(id,kid,m,e)	Set string dev (keyboard) 'kid' on WS 'id' to mode 'm' and echo 'e'.
set_stroke_mode(id,sid,m,e)	Sets stroke device 'sid' on WS 'id' to mode 'm' and echo status 'e'.
set_text_alignment(ha,va)	Sets the horizontal and vertical alignment for text.
set_text_color_index(col)	Sets the text color when the ASF is INDIVIDUAL (unbundled).
set_text_font_and_prec(f,p)	Sets the text font 'f' and precision 'p' when the ASF is INDIVIDUAL.
set_text_index(index)	Selects a bundle index for drawing text (with ASF=BUNDLED).
set_text_path(dirn)	Sets the path direction for drawing text.
set_text_rep(id,i,f,p,x,s,c)	Sets text index, font, precision, expansion, spacing, and col on WS 'id'.
set_valuator_mode(id,vid,m,e)	Sets valuator 'vid' on WS 'id' to mode 'm' and echo status 'e'.
set_viewport(t,x1,x2,y1,y2)	Defines the viewport for window number 't' using NDCs.
set_viewport_inp_pr(t1,t2,r)	Sets relative priority 'r' of overlapping viewports 't1','t2' for input.
set_visibility(n,vis)	Set the visibility attribute of segment number 'n' to 'vis'.
set_window(t,x1,x2,y1,y2)	Defines window 't' using minimum and maximum x and y values in WCs.

set_WS_vpt(id,x1,x2,y1,y2)	Sets the WS 'id's viewport in device coordinates.
set_WS_wind(id,x1,x2,y1,y2)	Sets WS 'id's window in NDCs.
unpack_data_record(f,l,dat,p)	Unpacks a packed GKS function 'f' from 'dat' of length 'l' to params 'p'.
update_WS(WSid,regen_flag)	Updates the specified WS's output performing all deferred actions.
write_item_to_GKSM(id,t,dat)	Write non-graphical (descriptive) data 'dat' to the GKS metafile.

Appendix H

GSX routines

GSX, the Graphics System eXtension, is an extension of the popular microcomputer operating systems CP/M and MSDOS to provide standardized graphics functions. The graphics functions are memory resident intrinsics of the extended operating system and are called from any programming language in a similar way to the usual operating system intrinsic functions. It is the product and trade mark of Digital Research.

One way of calling the GSX functions is via an assembly language interface routine called say GSXINT. The parameter for passing to GSXINT is a parameter block pointer. The parameter block consists of five integer arrays which store the input and output integer values that GSX works with. The following declarations show how Pascal can interface to GSX.

```
type param_block_type = record
    control :        array[1..5] of integer; {the GSX Control array}
    intin   :        array[1..100] of integer; {the GSX integer input array}
    ptsin   :        array[1..100] of integer; {the GSX points input array}
    intout  :        array[1..50] of integer; {the GSX integer output array}
    ptsout  :        array[1..20] of integer; {the GSX points output array}
    end;
    param_block_ptr = ^param_block_type;
var
    pblock : param_block_ptr;

procedure GSXINT(pblock : param_block_ptr); external;
```

The global parameter 'pblock' must be initialized by the Pascal new function and the appropriate values placed in the integer arrays and then GSXINT(pblock) called to get the appropriate GSX function. The meanings of the five elements of the control array are:

'control[1]' = the GSX function number (1 to 33)
'control[2]' = the number of elements in the 'input_points' array
'control[3]' = the number of points in the 'output_points' array
'control[4]' = the number of parameters in the 'input_params' array
'control[5]' = the number of parameters in the 'output_params' array.

The GSXINT assembly language code basically calls a memory location in the operating system which is the start of a jump table based on the value of control[1]. Control is thus passed to the GSX code for the appropriate GSX function. This operation can easily be visualized as a Pascal case structure with control[1] as the determining expression and for each possible value 1 to 33 there is a routine called for the required function.

```
case control[1] of
    1 : open_device(...  )
    2 : close_device(... );
    3 : initialize_device(...  );
    4 : update_device(...  );
{etc.}
```

Although GSX recognizes 33 different values for control[1] (1 to 33), some of these GSX functions have distinct subfunctions (identified by a second control element value). As a result, GSX has effectively 60 distinct functions. In order for the GSX concepts to be more readily understandable to the general reader the function names, variable names, and terminology employed by Digital Research in their GSX manuals are not always adhered to here. What has been done is to make a separate Pascal procedure for each of the 60 GSX functions. Each procedure sets up the parameter block with appropriate integer values in the arrays worked out from the inputs to the procedure. Then it calls GSXINT(pblock) and translates the outputs in the parameter block from GSX to the appropriate output parameters of the procedure. This involves a considerable amount of code (which is not included here).

Graphics setup and control functions

open_workstation(ws_id,defaults,characteristics);

Causes the graphics device specified by the workstation identifier 'ws_nr', to become the current device for graphics I/O from the application program via the I/O functions of GSX. The integer 'defaults' array of 9 elements must be supplied, and the routine returns the characteristics of the workstation in the 51 element integer array called 'characteristics'.

close_workstation;

Terminates the current workstation correctly, and disables it for further I/O.

clear_workstation;

Clears the output rectangle of the current workstation. For example, if the workstation is a VDU screen, it clears the screen; if it is a graphics printer, it form feeds the paper; and if it is a single sheet digital plotter, it prompts the user to insert a new sheet of paper into the plotter.

update_workstation;

Causes all graphics commands queued up for the device to be executed.

get_text_screen_size(nr_rows,nr_columns);

Returns the number of rows and columns where the alphanumeric mode cursor can be placed on the output device.

enter_graphics_mode;

Causes the graphics workstation to enter graphics mode.

exit_graphics_mode;

Causes the graphics workstation to exit from graphics mode into alpha mode (if it has these separate modes of operation).

get_tablet_status(available);

Returns a Boolean variable 'available' which says whether a graphics tablet is connected to the workstation or not.

do_hard_copy;

Causes the device to generate a hard copy of the current output display surface on the workstation if it has an associated hard-copy unit.

Alphanumeric control functions (not strictly graphics!)

move_cursor_up;

Moves the alpha cursor up one row if possible (i.e. on the top row no action is taken).

move_cursor_down;

Moves the alpha cursor down one row if possible (i.e. on the bottom row no action is taken).

move_cursor_right;

Moves the alpha cursor right one column position if possible (i.e. when the cursor is at the extreme right-hand position no action is taken).

move_cursor_left;

Moves the alpha cursor left one column position if possible (i.e. when the cursor is at the extreme left-hand position no action is taken).

move_cursor_home;

Moves the alpha cursor to its home (i.e. initial) position which is normally the upper left-hand corner: row number = column number = 1.

erase_to_end_of_screen;

Erases the alpha display surface from its present position to the bottom right-hand corner.

erase_to_end_of_line;

Erases the alpha display surface from the current alpha cursor position to the end of the current row.

set_cursor_location(row_nr,column_nr);

Places the alpha cursor at the specified row and column numbers on the alpha display surface of the current workstation.

display_text_string(a_string);

Outputs the specified string from the current alpha cursor position on the alpha display surface of the current workstation.

set_reverse_video_on;

Causes all subsequent text to be displayed in reverse video on the alpha display surface.

set_reverse_video_off;

Causes all subsequent text to be displayed in normal video format on the alpha display surface.

get_cursor_location(row_nr,column_nr);

Returns the current row and column numbers of the alpha cursor on the alpha display surface of the currently opened graphics workstation.

place_text_cursor_at_graphics_coordinates(ncx,ncy);

Places the alpha cursor at any position on the output display surface specified by the GSX normalized device coordinates ('ncx','ncy').

disable_cursor;

Makes the alpha cursor invisible on the output display surface.

Graphics output (drawing) functions

draw_a_polyline(nr_pts,x_array,y_array);

Displays a polyline on the graphics device. The arrays 'x_array' and 'y_array' hold the GSX normalized device coordinates of the 'nr_pts' points.

draw_a_polymarker(nr_pts,x_array,y_array);

Displays a marker at each of the points in the arrays.

write_text_at_graphics_coordinates(x,y,a_string);

Outputs the string specified at the point ('x', 'y') in GSX normalized device coordinates.

fill_polygon_area(nr_pts,x_array,y_array);

Fills in the polygon defined by the points specified with the current fill color and style.

write_graphics_cell(xll, yll, xur, yur, len, nr_row, nr_used, nr_col, method, pixel_array);

Writes the 'pixel_array' data into the pixels in the output device surface within the rectangle whose lower left-hand point is ('xll','yll') and upper right point is ('xur','yur') in GSX normalized device coordinates. The 'pixel_array' is an integer array dimensioned to 'nr_row' times 'nr_col'. 'len' should be 'nr_row' times 'nr_col'. 'nr_used' is the number of elements of 'pixel_array' that are to be used from each row. 'method' = 1,2,3, or 4 for replace, overstrike, complement and erase pixel writing methods.
GDPs are generalized drawing primitives that are built into the hardware of the graphics output devices. GSX recognizes five different kinds of GDPs and allows the user to implement a further three GDPs that the hardware may supply. The five GDPs recognized by GSX are:

draw_bar(xll,yll,xur,yur);

Draws a bar defined by the points input.

draw_arc(start_angle,end_angle,x_cent,y_cent,radius);

Draws the arc of a circle. Start and end angles are specified in tenths of a degree counterclockwise from the horizontal. The center and radius are specified in GSX normalized device coordinates.

draw_pie_slice(start_angle,end_angle,x_cent,y_cent,radius);

Draws the arc of a circle with two radii to form a closed area. Start and end angles are specified in tenths of a degree counterclockwise from the horizontal. The center and radius are specified in GSX normalized device coordinates.

draw_circle(x_cent,y_cent,radius);

Draws a circle where the center and radius are specified in GSX normalized device coordinates.

print_graphics_character(x,y,graphics_char_string);

Prints the string of graphics characters at the specified location ('x','y') in GSX normalized device coordinates on printers that have graphics characters.

Set graphics attribute functions

set_character_height(r_height,a_height,cell_width,cell_height);

Selects the available character height nearest to the requested value 'r_height' and returns the actual height set in 'a_height'. It also returns the width and height of the character cell into which subsequent characters will be placed on the output display surface. All parameters here are integer pixel counts.

set_character_up_vector(r_angle,a_angle);

Selects the available text angle nearest the request angle 'r_angle' and returns it in 'a_angle'. Angles are in tenths of a degree counterclockwise from the horizontal.

set_color(color_index,red_intensity,green_intensity,blue_intensity);

Creates a palette, that is, associates a color index with a specific mix of red, green, and blue pigments. The intensities are in units of tenths of a percent. All parameters are inputs to this routine. Color indexes (i.e. palettes) range from 0 to a device dependent maximum.

set_polyline_line_style(r_style,a_style);

Selects the available line style returned in 'a_style', closest to that requested in the input parameter 'r_style'. These parameters are integers greater than zero with 1 meaning a solid line.

set_polyline_line_width(r_width,a_width);

Selects the available line width closest to that requested in 'r_width' by the user and returns this actual width in 'a_width'. Both parameters are integers, the number of pixels wide the lines are to be drawn.

set_polyline_color(r_color_index,a_color_index);

Selects the closest color index 'a_color_index' to the one requested in 'r_color_index' according to the indexes that have been set by 'set_color'.

set_polymarker_type(r_type,a_type);

Sets the marker type closest to that requested by 'r_type' and returns the actual type code in 'a_type'. These are integers from 1 to a device dependent maximum greater than or equal to 5. The first five markers are set by GSX to be:

```
1   .
2   +
3   *
4   O
5   X
```

set_polymarker_scale(r_height,a_height);

Select the marker height closest to that available. 'r_height' is the input requested height in pixels and the output parameter 'a_height' is the actual height selected.

set_polymarker_color(r_palette,a_palette);

Selects a color index for drawing polymarkers. 'r_palette' (input) is the requested color index and 'a_palette' (output) is the closest available palette selected by GSX.

set_text_font(r_font,a_font);

Sets the text font for subsequent text operations. 'r_font' (input) is the requested font number and 'a_font' (output) is the one selected by GSX. Font numbers are integers from 1 to a device dependent number.

set_text_color(r_palette,a_palette);

Sets the color index for text output. 'r_palette' is the (input) requested color index and 'a_palette' is the (output) color index selected by GSX.

set_fill_style(r_style,a_style);

Sets the fill interior style to be used in subsequent polygon fill operations. 'r_style' is the (input) requested fill style number and 'a_style' (output) is the style number selected by GSX. Available style numbers are:

```
0   hollow    2   pattern
1   solid     3   hatch
```

set_hatch_type(r_type,a_type);

Sets the polygon fill hatch type index. This type has no effect unless hatch style was selected by 'select_fill_style'. The type is an integer from 1 to a device dependent limit greater than 3. The first four indexes are:

1	vertical hatch lines	3	hatch lines at 45°
2	horizontal hatch lines	4	hatch lines at -45°

'r_type' (input) is the requested type and 'a_type' (output) is the hatch type actually selected by GSX.

set_fill_color(r_pallete,a_pallete);

Sets the color index for painting in polygons. 'r_palette' is the (input) requested color index and 'a_palette' is the (output) color index selected by GSX.

set_writing_mode(r_mode,a_mode);

Sets the way pixels are written. 'r_mode' is the (input) requested mode and 'a_mode' is the output actual mode set by GSX. The GSX writing mode numbers are:

1. replace
2. overstrike
3. complement (i.e. use the XOR function)
4. erase

set_input_mode(device,wait);

Sets the input mode for a specified logical input device:

1. locator
2. valuator
3. choice
4. string

The input mode can be either request, that is, read, or sample. In the former, GSX waits for a result, and in the latter, the driver returns the status of the input device (i.e. whether or not a value is available from it) without waiting. The user should first set the appropriate device number and then set the Boolean parameter 'wait' to either true or false. After setting the input mode, GSX returns it in the parameter 'wait'. Note, for example no sample input mode may be available for a particular input device, and then GSX will return 'wait' as true no matter with what value this routine was called.

Graphics input functions

get_requested_color(palette,red,green,blue);

Returns the red, green, and blue intensities as tenths of a percent for a given color index palette as requested by usage of the 'set_color' routine.

get_actual_color(palette,red,green,blue);

Returns the actual red, green, and blue intensities as tenths of a percent for a given color index palette which were actually set on the workstation by calls to 'set_color'.

read_graphics_cell(xll,yll,xur,yur, nr_row, nr_col, color_array, nr_rows_used, nr_cols_used);

Reads the pixel values in the rectangle whose lower left-hand coordinate is ('xll','yll') and upper right-hand coordinate is ('xur','yur') in GSX normalized device coordinates.

read_locator(locator_nr,x1,y1,successful,key,x2,y2);

Set the specified locator device to the point ('x1','y1') and wait for a response within a given timeout. The locator numbers are:

1   default locator device for the current workstation
2   cross hairs
3   graphics tablet
4   joystick
5   lightpen
6   plotter
7   mouse
8   trackball
>8   workstation dependent

If the read was successful then this is indicated by the Boolean flag 'successful' and the locator terminating character (e.g. the hit code in the case of moving cross hairs on the screen) is returned in 'key' and the final position of the locator in ('x2','y2'). All coordinates are in GSX normalized device coordinates.

sample_locator(locator_nr,successful,x,y);

Sample the specified locator device. If a point is available from the locator then 'successful' is set to true and the coordinates of the point are available in 'x' and 'y'.

read_valuator(valuator_nr,val1,successful,val2);

Initializes the specified valuator to value 'val1' (an integer) and waits for a change within a timeout. If a new value is available then the Boolean flag 'successful' is set to true and the value is returned in 'val2'.

sample_valuator(valuator_nr,successful,val);

Samples the specified valuator for a value. If a value is available then the Boolean flag 'successful' is set to true and the value is returned in 'val'.

read_choice(choice_dev_nr,choice1,successful,choice2);

Sets the initial choice value on the specified choice device to 'choice1' and then waits for a new value within a timeout. If a new value is available then the Boolean 'successful' will be true and the new choice value will be in 'choice2'. Choice device numbers in GSX are:

  1   default choice device for the current workstation
  2   the function keys
  >2 workstation dependent

sample_choice(choice_dev_nr,successful,choice);

Samples the specified choice device. If a value is available then the Boolean 'successful' will be true and the choice value will be in 'choice'. Choice device numbers in GSX are:

  1   default choice device for the current workstation
  2   the function keys
  >2 workstation dependent

read_input_string(string_dev_nr,maxlength,echo,out_string);

Waits for a character string from a specified string device within a timeout. The maximum string length to read is also input and the Boolean 'echo' says whether to echo the input characters on the current output device or not. The string device numbers are:

  1   the keyboard
  >1 device dependent

sample_input_string(string_dev_nr,maxlength,echo,out_string);

Samples for a character string from a specified string device. The maximum string length to read is also input and the Boolean 'echo' says whether to echo the input characters on the current output device or not. The string device numbers are:

  1   the keyboard
  >1 device dependent

Appendix I

Bibliography

The books listed below constitute useful further reading for the interested student. Further references can be found within the books cited below.

Abelson, H. and diSessa, A. *Turtle Geometry*, MIT Press, 1980.

Angell, I. O. *A Practical Introduction to Computer Graphics*, MacMillan, 1982.

Arens, H. *Colour Measurement*, Focal Press, 1967.

Artwick, B. A. *Applied Concepts in Microcomputer Graphics*, Prentice Hall, 1984.

Baxendale, S. *The First Computer Design Coloring Book*, Harmony Books NY, 1979.

Bell, D. *Microcomputer Colour Graphics Systems*, Pitman, 1982.

Besant, C. B. and Lui, C. W. K. *Computer-Aided Design And Manufacture*, Ellis Horwood Series in Engineering Science, John Wiley & Sons, 1986.

Bowyer,.A. and Woodwark, J. *A Programmer's Geometry*, Butterworths, 1983.

Chamberlin, G. J. and Chamberlin, D. G. *COLOUR, Its Measurement, Computation and Application*, Heyden, 1980.

Chasen, S. H. *Geometric Principles and Procedures for Computer Graphic Applications*, Prentice Hall, 1978.

Clulow, F. W. *COLOUR, Its Principles and Their Applications*, Fountain Press, 1972.

Demel, J. T. and Miller, M. J. *Introduction to Computer Graphics*, Brooks/Cole, 1984.

Edwards, R. *Microcomputer Art*, Prentice Hall, 1985.

Foley, J. D. and Van Dam, A. *Fundamentals of Interactive Computer Graphics*, Addison Wesley, 1982.

Glassner, A. S. *Computer Graphics User's Guide*, Sams & Co, 1984.

Gardan, Y. and Lucas, M. *Interactive Graphics In CAD*, Kogan Page, 1984.

Gasson, P. C. *Geometry of Spatial Forms*, Ellis Horwood Series Mathematics and its Applications, John Wiley & Sons, 1983.

Giloi, W. K. *Interactive Computer Graphics*, Prentice Hall,1978.

Greenberg, D,.Marcus, A,. Schmidt, A. H., and Gorter, V. *The Computer Image : Applications of Computer Graphics*, Addison-Wesley, 1982.

Guest, J. *New Shapes, A Collection Of Computer-Generated Designs*, R A Vowels, Melbourne, Australia, 1979.

Harrington, S. *Computer Graphics A programming Approach*, McGraw-Hill, 1983.

Harris, D. *Computer Graphics and Applications*, Chapman & Hall, 1984.

Hearn, D. and Baker, M. P. *Microcomputer Graphics Techniques & Applications*, Prentice Hall, 1983.

Hopgood, F. R. A., Duce, D. A., Gallop, J. R., and Sutcliffe, D. C. *Introduction to the Graphical Kernal System GKS*, Academic Press, 1983.

Martin, G. E. *Transformation Geometry, An Introduction To Symmetry,* Springer-Verlac, 1982.

Marx, E. *Optical Color and Simultaneity,* Van Nostrand Reinhold, 1983.

Mufti, A. A. *Elementary Computer Graphics,* Prentice_Hall, 1983.

Myers, R. E. *Microcomputer Graphics With Apple II Examples,* Addison-Wesley, 1982.

Myers, R. E. *Microcomputer Graphics For The IBM PC,* Addison-Wesley, 1984.

Newman, W. M. and Sproull, R. F. *Principles of Interactive Computer Graphics,* McGraw-Hill, 1979.

Park, C. S. *Interactive Microcomputer Graphics,* Addison Wesley, 1985.

Pedoe, D. *Circles, A Mathematical View,* Dover, 1979.

Pedoe, D. *Geometry And The Visual Arts,* Dover, 1976.

Peitgen, H.-O. and Richter, P. H. *The Beauty of Fractals,* Springer-Verlag, 1986.

Plastock, R. A. and Kalley, G. *Computer Graphics,* Schaum Outline Series, McGraw-Hill, 1986.

Pugh, A. *Polyhedra – A Visual Approach,* University of California Press, 1976.

Read, R. C. *Tangrams – 330 Puzzles,* Dover, 1965.

Resnick, R. and Halliday, D. *Physics,* John Wiley and Sons, 1966.

Rogers, D. F. and Adams, J. A. *Mathematical Elements For Computer Graphics,* McGraw-Hill, 1976.

Rossottii, H. *Colour, Why the World Isn't Grey,* Pelican, 1983.

Schachter, B J (ed.).*Computer Image Generation,* Wiley & Sons, 1983.

Scott, J. E. *Introduction to Interactive Computer Graphics,* Wiley & Sons, 1982.

Sommerville, D. M. Y. *Analytical Conics,* G Bell & Sons, London, 1956.

Stockton, J. *Designer's Guide To Color,* and, *Designer's Guide To Color 2,* Angus & Robertson, 1984, 1985.

Thornburg, D. D. *Discovering Apple Logo,* Addison-Wesley, 1983.

Waite, M. *Computer Graphics Primer,* Howard Sams & Co, 1979.

Walker, B. S., Gurd, J. R., and Drawneek, E. A. *Interactive Computer Graphics,* Crane, Russak & Co, 1975.

Wenninger, M. J. *Polyhedron Models, Dual Models,* and *Spherical Models,* Cambridge University Press, 1985, 1983, and 1979 respectively.

Index